April 2010

To Pat & John —

You won't find anything quite as wonderful as Huckleberry Island in here, but hopefully other things will catch your fancy.

Love,
Lu

Buildings of Pennsylvania

PITTSBURGH AND WESTERN PENNSYLVANIA

The Society of Architectural Historians gratefully acknowledges the support of the following, whose generosity helped bring *Buildings of Pennsylvania: Pittsburgh and Western Pennsylvania* to publication:

    Anonymous

    Heinz Architectural Center, Carnegie Museum of Art

    National Park Service, Heritage Documentation Programs,
       HABS/HAER/HALS Division

    National Endowment for the Humanities, an independent federal agency

    Vira I. Heinz Endowment

Initial and ongoing support for the Buildings of the United States series has come from:

    National Endowment for the Humanities, an independent federal agency

    Graham Foundation for Advanced Studies in the Fine Arts

    Pew Charitable Trusts

    University of Delaware

    Ford Foundation

    Samuel I. Newhouse Foundation

    Samuel H. Kress Foundation

    David Geffen Foundation

    Furthermore, a program of the J. M. Kaplan Fund

    University of Missouri

    Richard H. Driehaus Foundation

BUILDINGS OF

Pennsylvania

PITTSBURGH AND WESTERN PENNSYLVANIA

Lu Donnelly

H. David Brumble IV

Franklin Toker

WITH CONTRIBUTIONS BY
Clinton Piper, Sally McMurry, and Laura Ricketts

University of Virginia Press
CHARLOTTESVILLE AND LONDON

University of Virginia Press
© 2010 by the Society of Architectural Historians
All rights reserved
Printed in the United States of America on acid-free paper

First published 2010

9 8 7 6 5 4 3 2 1

LIBRARY OF CONGRESS CATALOGING-IN-PUBLICATION DATA

Donnelly, Lu.
   Buildings of Pennsylvania. Pittsburgh and western Pennsylvania / Lu Donnelly,
H. David Brumble, IV, Franklin Toker ; with contributions by Clinton Piper, Sally
McMurry, and Laura Ricketts.
      p.   cm. — (Buildings of the United States)
   Includes bibliographical references and index.
   ISBN 978-0-8139-2823-4 (cloth : alk. paper)
   1. Architecture—Pennsylvania—Pittsburgh. 2. Architecture—Pennsylvania.
3. Pittsburgh (Pa.)—Buildings, structures, etc. I. Brumble, H. David, 1977–
II. Toker, Franklin. III. Title. IV. Title: Pittsburgh and western Pennsylvania.
NA735.P53D66   2010
720.9748′8—dc22

                                                                    2009008036

Frontispiece: David L. Lawrence Convention Center (AL15). (Historic American Buildings Survey. Prints and Photographs Division, Library of Congress, Nicholas Traub, photographer)

CONTENTS

HOW TO USE THIS BOOK

Buildings of Pennsylvania: Pittsburgh and Western Pennsylvania is the first of two volumes documenting the range of architecture in the Commonwealth of Pennsylvania. The second volume, *Buildings of Pennsylvania: Philadelphia and Eastern Pennsylvania,* will cover the eastern part of the commonwealth. Since there is no universally accepted division between western and eastern Pennsylvania, geographical formations and settlement patterns have determined the division for the volumes.

This book covers thirty-one western counties organized into five regions spiraling counterclockwise from the urban area surrounding Pittsburgh. Each region has a short introduction describing the terrain and the history of the counties within it. The first region, Pittsburgh and Allegheny County, and the second region, the counties surrounding Pittsburgh, are part of the Allegheny Plateau. The third region, the south-central portion of western Pennsylvania, covers the ridge and valley system that arcs from the southwest to the northeast. The north-central, fourth, region includes the great forest, a stream-etched plateau similar, but higher than, the geography of the first and second regions. The stepped river plain adjacent to Lake Erie comprises the fifth region.

Within the regions, the towns and buildings in each county are arranged in a drivable pattern. The territory of western Pennsylvania, never easy to navigate, requires detailed county maps. The maps included in this volume are meant to be supplemented by an electronic GPS system or the #10 highway maps produced by the commonwealth, which can be viewed as pdfs at http://www.dot.state.pa.us/Internet/Bureaus/pdPlanRes.nsf/infoBPRCarto MapsinPDFandDJVU?OpenForm or ordered from the Pennsylvania Department of Transportation.

In Pennsylvania, one lives in a county and either a city, a borough, or a township within that county. These are the municipal governments that provide services to the citizenry. These designations are complicated, since the three forms of local government are not defined by size, but by form of government. Western Pennsylvania has thirty-six of the state's fifty-seven cities (populations under 80,000, nearly twice as many as eastern Pennsylvania). A borough can be smaller or larger than a city, and is defined by the fact that its citizens have chosen a council form of government. Townships are often found in rural and less densely populated areas, and their often irregular boundaries are based on the old metes and bounds survey system. As an example of the complexity, Allegheny County, with Pittsburgh at its center, has 128 additional municipalities in it: four more cities, eighty-two boroughs, and forty-two townships.

In this book, each county's entries begin at the county seat and spiral out from there. Each entry is assigned a two-letter county code—derived from the county's name—and a number. Following the number is the name of the property, with a historic or common name in parentheses. The building's beginning and completion dates of construction are given when both are known; if only one date is given, it is the building's completion date. The dates are followed by the name of the architect or engineer, followed by the dates of any additions and their designers. Finally, the address of each entry is listed.

Due to space restrictions, many properties of interest are not included in this volume. Those that are here will hopefully serve as an introduction to the region and an impetus for further study of the commonwealth's architecture and landscape design. This volume also introduces the many architects active in the five regions, the first time these Pennsylvania architects have been drawn together in a single book. We hope this will inspire further studies of those whose bodies of work merit in-depth research.

Almost all the buildings and sites described in this book are visible from a public right-of-way. We assume that our readers will respect the privacy and property rights of individual property owners. While all properties were extant in 2008, some may be vulnerable to decay, alteration, and demolition while the editing and production of this book have been in progress.

FOREWORD

The primary objective of the Buildings of the United States (BUS) series is to identify and celebrate the rich cultural, economic, and geographic diversity of the United States of America as it is reflected in the architecture of each state. The series was founded by the Society of Architectural Historians (SAH), a nonprofit organization dedicated to the study, interpretation, and preservation of the built environment throughout the world.

The Buildings of the United States series will eventually comprise more than sixty volumes documenting the built environment of every state of the United States of America, including both high-style and vernacular structures. The idea for such a series was in the minds of the founders of the SAH in the early 1940s, but it was not brought to fruition until Nikolaus Pevsner—the eminent British architectural historian who had conceived and carried out Buildings of England, originally published between 1951 and 1974—challenged the SAH to do for the United States what he had done for his country.

The authors of each BUS volume are trained architectural historians who are thoroughly informed in the local aspects of their subjects. In each volume, special conditions that shaped the state, together with the building types necessary to meet those conditions, are identified and discussed: barns and other agricultural buildings, factories and industrial structures, bridges and transportation buildings, and parks take their places alongside the familiar building types conventional to the nation as a whole—courthouses, city halls, libraries, religious buildings, commercial structures, and the infinite variety of domestic architecture, from workers' houses to mansions. Although the great national and international architects of American buildings receive proper attention, outstanding local architects, as well as the buildings of skilled but often anonymous carpenter-builders, are also brought prominently into the picture. Each book in the series deals with the very fabric of American architecture, with the context in time and in place of each specific building, and with the entirety of urban, suburban, and rural America. Naturally, the series cannot cover every building of merit; practical considerations dictate difficult choices in the buildings that are represented in this and other volumes. Furthermore, only buildings in existence at the time of publication are included.

The BUS series has received generous and ongoing support from the National Endowment for the Humanities; the Graham Foundation for Advanced Studies in the Fine Arts; the Pew Charitable Trusts; the Ford Foundation; the Samuel H. Kress Foundation; the University of Delaware; and the National Park Service, HABS/HAER/HALS Division. For this volume, the SAH is also enormously indebted to the donors listed earlier in this volume and to the many individual members of the SAH who have made unrestricted contributions to BUS.

We thank the authors, the University of Virginia Press, and the SAH board. We would also like to express our appreciation to the current members of our Editorial Advisory Committee, listed earlier in this volume, and to the committee's former members.

Karen Kingsley
EDITOR IN CHIEF
BUILDINGS OF THE UNITED STATES

ACKNOWLEDGMENTS

A book of this scale covering such a large territory is the work of many hands. When Franklin Toker stopped me on the sidewalk behind the Carnegie Library in the spring of 1992 and proposed that we work on this book together, we could not know that seventeen years would pass before publication. A dozen of those years were spent in an office at Heinz Architectural Center of the Carnegie Museum of Art due to the hospitality of Richard Armstrong, former Henry J. Heinz II director, and present and former staff. Among those who helped immeasurably by providing collegiality and many insightful suggestions are Dennis McFadden, Rebecca Sciullo, Tracy Myers, Joseph Rosa, Bethany Mummert Hopman, Divya Rao, Raymund Ryan, and Mattie Schloetzer.

There are hardly words to express my thanks to Al Tannler of the Pittsburgh History and Landmarks Foundation and Martin Aurand of the Architectural Archives at Carnegie Mellon University. They read through stacks of manuscript pages and answered innumerable questions with unfailing good humor and serious purpose. This book would not have happened without their support.

The invaluable contributors to the book include Laura Ricketts, who helped establish much of our earliest methodology and returned to work on the introduction; Dr. Sally McMurry of the Pennsylvania State University, who corralled graduate students to work on the Centre County portion of the book and edited their pieces, and who shot photos and wrote many of the entries in that section; Clinton Piper, Museum Programs Assistant at Fallingwater, who did all the fieldwork and drafted the entries for Westmoreland and most of Fayette County and continued to be supportive and engaged through all the years of research and writing; and, finally, coauthor David Brumble, who began as an intern and ultimately devoted several years to the completion of all of the fieldwork and the writing of four counties.

Many interns helped with everything from filing to fieldwork. They include Peter Moore, Michael Danzuso, Amy DeCamp, Seth Gall, Abby Gould, Sun Joo Kim, Amber King, Sara Lemond, Bill McGovern, Eroica Poulakos, Henry Wyatt, Kelly Curran, James A. Jacobs, Sarah Rossbach, and Katherine Reilly.

Staffs of the libraries and archives in all thirty-one counties of western Pennsylvania provided contacts, information, and resources, especially those in Allegheny, Beaver, Erie, and Huntingdon counties. Several staff members of the Carnegie Museum of Natural History helped with the Native American section of the introduction, especially Verna Cowin and Dick George. Special thanks also to several devoted volunteers, including Pauline and Jim Parker, Frank Kurtik, Christopher Marston at HAER, Mark Brown for his insights into bridge construction, and photographers Monica Murphy and Paula Mohr. Barry Bergdoll contributed the entry on the Cecilia and Robert Frank House in Allegheny County and Terry Necciai supplied information on all things rural or located in Washington County.

Thank you to Pauline Saliga, executive director of the Society of Architectural Historians, and her excellent staff, especially Bill Tyre and intern Julie Knorr. SAH editors refined the manuscript: assistant editors Samuel Albert and Gabrielle Esperdy and, of course, the tireless Karen Kingsley, editor in chief. And many thanks to Mark Mones, project editor; Toni Mortimer, copy editor; and Marilyn Bliss, indexer, at the University of Virginia Press.

My family has participated in many ways in the writing of this book, from proofreading by my sister, Barbara Schleck; to office and fieldwork by my children, Ned and Helen Donnelly; to general support from my husband, who never questioned me taking the family car on over 50,000 miles of field trips.

We have tried our best to keep errors out of this book by sending drafts to readers in many of the counties. Of course, any errors are strictly my responsibility.

Lu Donnelly
PITTSBURGH, DECEMBER 2008

Introduction

This book is an orderly framework placed over the jumble of reality—and what a luxuriant jumble surrounds us in western Pennsylvania. The rolling hills change colors with the seasons, from delicate greens in the spring to brilliant golds and auburns in the fall. The swirling fog, sudden spurts of snow, and intense sunshine—sometimes in the same day—characterize our lives. Driving through the thirty-one counties of western Pennsylvania, the human struggle to settle the landscape and provide spaces to live and work is revealed in the towns and buildings in this book, each of which speaks to the aspirations of those who built them.[1]

The buildings included in this volume range from the mid-eighteenth century to those recently completed. Some were designed by famous architects, others by architects whose work is locally known, and some by unknown architects or carpenters. Some buildings perform their functions with grace and beauty or clever utility, while others respond so well to their setting and evoke such vivid images of the lives of their builders that they demanded inclusion.

Western Pennsylvania is physically and culturally different from eastern Pennsylvania. It has more in common with its close neighbors—northwestern West Virginia, eastern Ohio, and southwestern New York State—than with the Piedmont region surrounding Philadelphia. Twenty-seven of the thirty-one counties included in this volume are considered rural. Allegheny, Beaver, Erie, and Westmoreland counties are the only four defined as urban.[2] While western Pennsylvania has an ever-growing suburban presence, farms and rural buildings survive in great numbers and several are represented in this volume. Industrial buildings are also an integral part of western Pennsylvania's landscape, and where possible, typical industrial sites, which are accessible and have some architectural integrity, have been included.

Although there are significant differences between western and eastern Pennsylvania, there is no universally accepted division between the two. Geographical barriers and settlement patterns have determined the division between this and the forthcoming companion volume, *Buildings of Pennsylvania: Philadelphia and Eastern Pennsylvania*. The ridge and valley system running through Centre, Huntingdon, and Fulton counties created a transportation

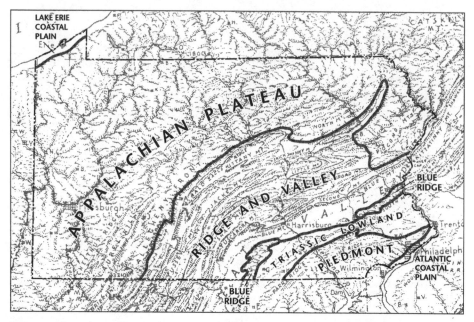

Topographic regions of Pennsylvania. Landforms played a major role in the period of settlement and the city plans for each region. The first, second, and fourth regions (The Western Capital, Rolling Hills and Rolling Mills, and Great Forest) are part of the Appalachian Plateau; the third region (Ridge and Valley) is part of the Ridge and Valley system; and the fifth region (Oil and Water) includes the Lake Erie Coastal Plain and extends into the Appalachian Plateau.

barrier that delayed the settlement of these counties until the late 1760s. Blue Mountain in Franklin County was a similar obstacle to westward migration. Also, while the north-central counties of Potter and Tioga share a comparable geography and culture, the inclusion of Potter County in this volume and Tioga in the other is based on the former's settlement generally twenty years later than Tioga County's.[3]

Navigating the region by river is complicated by the presence of five different watersheds; two of these riverine systems were the first major highways for European settlers. The Susquehanna River on the eastern boundary and its tributaries—the West Branch and the Juniata River—penetrate to the central core of the Commonwealth of Pennsylvania[4] and empty into Chesapeake Bay, in Maryland, and, ultimately, into the Atlantic Ocean. The Monongahela and Allegheny rivers join to create the Ohio River, which flows to the Mississippi River, and, in due course, to the Gulf of Mexico. This river basin ties western Pennsylvania to the rest of the upper Midwest and the South. A third watershed empties several short streams into Lake Erie, and is named for the lake. The fourth flows into the Potomac River and Chesapeake Bay from southern Somerset, Bedford, and Fulton counties. A fifth minor watershed is located in north-central Potter County and surrounds the Genesee River, which flows north through south-central New York State and empties into Lake Ontario near Rochester, New York.[5]

NATIVE AMERICAN HABITATION

Archaeologists divide early human habitation of western Pennsylvania into three eras: Paleo-Indian from approximately 10,000 to 8000 BCE; Archaic from approximately 8000 to 1000 BCE; and Woodland from approximately 1000 BCE to European contact c. 1610. Remains from a rock shelter at Meadowcroft (ws16), in Washington County, thirty miles southwest of Pittsburgh, establish a human presence in the area as early as the end of the last Ice Age, c. 14,000 to 12,000 BCE.

The Adena people of the Early Woodland period were among the first to make pottery and experiment with the cultivation of plants. Although they have been assigned a name by archaeologists, they are not a tribe like the eighteenth- and nineteenth-century Native Americans, but a people who performed a number of similar activities such as hunting, gathering, and mound building.[6] The Hopewell from the Middle Woodland era succeeded the Adena, appearing in the area around 100 CE. The Hopewell participated in a national trading system, importing from the west such resources as copper and mica. Their earthen burial mounds with enclosed stone structures have been excavated near the Meadowcroft site as well as at more northern locations along the Allegheny River.[7]

Around 1000 BCE, an agricultural revolution introduced maize into a diet that previously had consisted primarily of squash and beans. This increased the nutritional content of the crops available to Native Americans in the area, and they gradually formed an economy based on farming rather than foraging. The Monongahela people built hundreds of villages during their seven-hundred-year occupancy of western Pennsylvania. After 900 CE, their culture spread as far east as Somerset County and as far north as Butler and Armstrong counties. Each village was made up of round huts built of bent saplings tied with vegetable fibers, covered with bark, and open at the top to vent the smoke. These house types, nearly ubiquitous in the Northeast and upper Midwest, were typically arranged one or two deep in a circle around a central plaza and surrounded by a wooden palisade. Villages varied in population from 50 to 300 people and were occupied as long as the environment could sustain them. The Monongahela suffered through two crippling droughts in the late sixteenth and early seventeenth centuries that devastated their maize crops and left them vulnerable to attack by the Iroquois. One theory suggests that they moved east and south out of what is now Pennsylvania or were absorbed by other tribes. They essentially vacated the area by approximately 1635.[8]

The Erie tribe settled around present-day Erie between 900 CE and 1300 CE. They coexisted with the Susquehannocks, who, during the same period, settled in north-central Pennsylvania along the North and West branches of the Susquehanna River. Both spoke a version of the Iroquoian language and built large villages of up to 2,000 people who lived in longhouses. The buildings

Model of Monongahela hut, built by Fred Crissman and donated to the Carnegie Museum of Natural History.

Model of Proto-Iroquois longhouse, built by Fred Crissman and donated to the Carnegie Museum of Natural History.

of these proto-Iroquois groups in northern Pennsylvania and southern New York ranged from 40 to 200 feet long and were generally 17 feet wide, with rounded ends and arched roofs. They were constructed of bent saplings tied in place with fibrous thongs to create the frame, which was covered with elm bark. The interior provided shelter for a group of extended families related through the female line. Archaeological remains indicate that the earlier central hearths later evolved into a series of hearths shared by families across the central aisle from one another.[9]

By the 1500s, tribes, growing in population, fought over expanding territorial needs. Trade and intertribal adoptions kept Native American cultural traits fluid, but there were tribal differences, which were exacerbated and manipulated by Europeans in the 1600s, whose encounters with the Native Americans increased steadily through a complex series of broken treaties. These encounters also brought epidemics, which decimated tribes and caused further migrations.

The Lenni Lenape or Delaware tribe was ravaged by decades of battling not only white settlers and their European allies but other tribes as well. Each time the Delaware moved west they incurred the wrath of another tribe and were forced to vie for food in areas that were rapidly being depleted. They sold their lands along the Delaware River to the Dutch and, later, to William Penn, and moved to central Pennsylvania and the Susquehanna River area. In 1720, the Delaware were conquered by the Iroquois and resettled in western Pennsylvania and eastern Ohio. Here they allied themselves with the losing side in a series of mid- to late-eighteenth-century battles—with the French in the French and Indian War, with Pontiac in the eponymous 1763 rebellion, and with the British during the American Revolution. Finally, in the

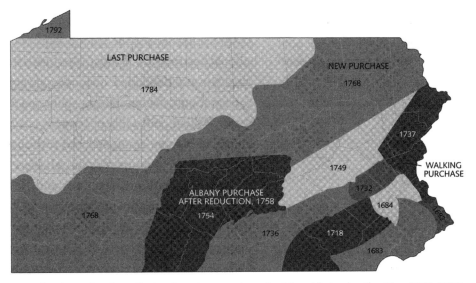

Major land transfers from Native Americans to the colonial and federal authorities, 1682–1792. In nearly every case European settlement preceded the transfer dates.

late 1790s, they began a series of migrations to the continent's interior, where they ultimately were so completely absorbed by the Cherokee tribe that their separate tribal designation had to be reissued by the federal government in 1996.

Several town names in western Pennsylvania memorialize the struggle between the native population and the settlers. Burnt Cabins in Fulton County, for example, recalls the attempts by William Penn's men to keep settlers from squatting on lands still technically held by the tribes. Kittanning in Armstrong County was a Delaware village before Colonel John Armstrong destroyed it in 1756. In Huntingdon County, Kishacoquillas Valley, named for a Seneca chief, now hosts Amish farms.

The German, Scots-Irish,[10] Welsh, and Dutch settlers who came into Pennsylvania set up owner-occupied farms and small towns for their mills and supply centers. Native tribes, who needed hunting lands and room to move their villages when the surrounding countryside could no longer support them, found individual ownership alien to them. The two cultures never coexisted easily. Consequently, remnants of once large tribes such as the Delaware, Mingo, and Shawnee migrated across the lands of western Pennsylvania, constantly moving away from stronger tribes and European settlers.

PROPERTY RIGHTS AND EUROPEAN SETTLEMENT

Land ownership throughout the commonwealth has had a long and contentious history. William Penn's dream was a state tolerant of all religions and prosperous through the work of many farmers. Problems began even before the land could be held officially. Penn stipulated that all land transferred to European ownership must be purchased from the native tribes. He began the process in 1682 with the purchase of land along the Delaware River from the Delaware tribe. Over a century later, in 1784, his sons completed the purchases by buying the northwestern section of the commonwealth from the Six Nations. Throughout this long process, settlers continually began to farm lands that had not yet been officially purchased.

Unfortunately, loose bookkeeping by the colonial government led to the practice of squatting. In most western Pennsylvania cases, while official ownership may have rested in the hands of wealthy Philadelphians or large speculative land companies, those actually farming and living on the land declared ownership. Claiming "tomahawk rights," they marked their territory by notches on bordering trees; they believed that building a cabin and planting fields determined ownership. In general, the custom was to grant those who built a barn and a house and tilled the fields the first right of refusal when land was to be sold. But with poor records and an understaffed land office, the courts spent years trying to sort out who owned what.

The difficulty of determining land ownership in the region was exacerbated by the confusion over which state held jurisdiction over a given area.

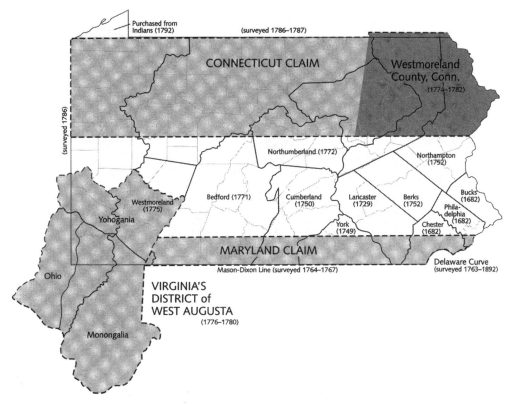

Purchased from Indians (1792)

(surveyed 1786–1787)

CONNECTICUT CLAIM

Westmoreland County, Conn. (1774–1782)

(surveyed 1786)

Northumberland (1772)

Northampton (1752)

Westmoreland (1775)

Bedford (1771)

Cumberland (1750)

Lancaster (1729)

Berks (1752)

Bucks (1682)

Yohogania

Phila-delphia (1682)

York (1749)

Chester (1682)

MARYLAND CLAIM

Delaware Curve (surveyed 1763–1892)

Mason-Dixon Line (surveyed 1764–1767)

Ohio

VIRGINIA'S DISTRICT of WEST AUGUSTA (1776–1780)

Monongalia

Evolution of Pennsylvania's boundaries, 1682–1892.

Pennsylvanians fought to protect their boundaries from a host of territorial neighbors' counterclaims. Maryland claimed land in eastern Pennsylvania as far north as Philadelphia until, after prolonged litigation, the Mason-Dixon Line was surveyed in 1763 and established the southern boundary to within twenty-four miles of the present western boundary. Virginians, traveling up the Monongahela River valley, claimed all of the present counties of Allegheny, Beaver, Fayette, Greene, Washington, and Westmoreland until 1786. These settlers brought their slaves and sought to extend the plantation system. Virginia encouraged settlement by offering larger land patents for lower prices than Pennsylvania. Virginia also arranged for local militia to fend off attacks by Native Americans, and advance its interests. Many settlers in the southwestern counties were only familiar with Virginia colonial representatives. During the American Revolution, Pennsylvanians and Virginians were encouraged to resolve their border dispute, and by 1786, the Mason-Dixon Line and its extension across the final twenty-four miles of Greene County was accepted by both states as the southern boundary of Pennsylvania; the western boundary was established in 1785–1786. The Virginia deeds were grandfathered into Pennsylvania's land warrants after the borders were defined. When the area was officially declared a part of Pennsylvania, where a 1780 law limited slavery, many families from Virginia and Maryland moved to Kentucky, a state that did not prohibit slave owning.

Connecticut's claim of nearly the entire northern tier of counties state-wide was the most contentious. For nearly fifty years, between 1753 and 1800, settlers from both colonies were killed in a lethal struggle for land ownership and for access to the western territories that in turn enraged the Iroquois, land-starved Connecticut Yankees, the British, and citizens of the commonwealth.

Early Pennsylvanians were a mix of ethnicities that were consciously recruited from Europe by William Penn. Skilled craftsmen and farmers came from three major areas: England, Germany, and northern Ireland. Generally, the English settled around Philadelphia and in those areas of southwestern Pennsylvania to which Virginia lay claim. German farmers sought out the limestone valleys in central Pennsylvania that reminded them of their homeland. Over 200,000 Scots-Irish Presbyterians immigrated to the American colonies between 1717 and 1788. Those who chose to live in Pennsylvania initially settled in the river valley of the Susquehanna in clusters separate from but adjacent to the earlier German settlements. Many of these first Scots-Irish settlers moved rather quickly into the southwestern border territories. Here they found the "Gateway to the West," a name initially ascribed to Cumberland, Maryland, and moved continually westward throughout the first half of the nineteenth century. From the 1780s to the early 1800s, the designation aptly applied to the southwestern corner of Pennsylvania, where the Ohio River originated and carried thousands of immigrants to their western destinations.

TOWN BUILDING

Between 1783 and 1795, the commonwealth surveyed seven sites on the western border to stimulate frontier settlement and secure its boundaries. It laid out the towns of Pittsburgh, Beaver, Allegheny (now a part of Pittsburgh), Erie, Franklin, Waterford, and Warren, and sold lots to those who were willing to come and settle within two years.[11] Slowly these towns, roughly modeled after Philadelphia with a grid plan and central green square surrounded by a courthouse and commercial buildings, became the models for many towns in western Pennsylvania, such as Meadville and Waynesburg.

The dispute over interstate boundaries influenced building types in particular ways. Bolstered by the opening of the Erie Canal in 1825, the Connecticut Yankees of New England settled along an east–west swath stretching one hundred miles south of the New York border. Only these northern counties formerly claimed by Connecticut have frame Greek Revival houses similar to those found in New England. The type is rarely seen farther south than northern Lawrence County.

In the southwestern corner of Pennsylvania, Virginian Isaac Meason hired English architect-builder Adam Wilson to design his house, Mount Braddock

(FA27). It is the only dressed-stone, seven-part Palladian plan house in the nation and among the most sophisticated houses in western Pennsylvania. It shares design elements with substantial houses in Maryland and Virginia. With interior fittings commensurate with the refinement of the design, there is no comparable house from this early period in the state. Mount Braddock is "a unique expression of the English Palladian villa in America"[12] and could only have been built in the area once thought part of Virginia.

In the central counties of the Ridge and Valley region, farmers of German descent built their two-story houses with distinctive inset porches under a single pitched roof for extra stability under frequent heavy snows. When they migrated westward, their building techniques and customs adapted to changing circumstances, making western Pennsylvania a stylistic crossroads. While German settlers who remained in the central counties were more likely to retain particular porches or siding techniques associated with German builders, as they progressed farther west they encountered the Scots-Irish and English settlers from Virginia and Maryland, who brought with them their own building traditions.[13] Free from the stylistic conformity of the eastern seacoast, and in the relative isolation of the frontier, these building patterns blended and shifted so that the predominant style of architecture in this region is most accurately labeled "eclectic."

Early buildings in western Pennsylvania also reflect the difficulty of obtaining skilled workers. The vision of the owner might dictate how a building should look, but the craftsman's training and skill dictated how the building *did* look, and not always with felicitous results. Albert Gallatin, Thomas Jefferson's treasury secretary, complained that his Scots-Irish contractor Hugh Graham made his Fayette County house look like an "Irish Barracks" on the outside and a "Dutch Tavern" inside (FA9).[14]

The relatively small settlements and sprawling farmsteads of western Pennsylvania required that settlers master the use of the axe for road and field clearing and use the most available material to build defensive forts and domestic shelters. The tradition of logging and building with logs permeated the region. As settlements grew, the raising of oversized buildings like barns

MAIN BLOCK OF HOUSE & SIDE PAVILIONS

CELLI DRAWING, W. PA. ARCHITECTURAL SURVEY, 1936

Facade of the Isaac Meason House, "Mount Braddock" (FA27), and its dependencies.

and churches required communal efforts and provided opportunities for socializing.

LOG BUILDINGS

Though log structures were prevalent in western Pennsylvania before the Civil War, few have lasted intact into this century. Log buildings with a single pen (or room) that could be expanded with a loft or second room were the norm. As the area progressed from trapping and hunting to farming, the buildings evolved from temporary shelters and occasional trading posts to cabins and barns, springhouses and sheds.

The first major log structures were the French and English forts. The French claimed interior territory stretching from the Gulf of St. Lawrence through the Great Lakes into Pennsylvania at Erie, then south along the Allegheny and Ohio rivers to New Orleans. While France's forces in the New World were better trained than the British militias, English colonists, who most often established farms, vastly outnumbered them. To protect their exposed frontier in western Pennsylvania, the French built four forts between 1753 and 1755: Fort Presque Isle at Erie and Fort Le Boeuf at Waterford in Erie County; Fort Machault at Franklin in Venango County; and Fort Duquesne at Pittsburgh's Point. While highly trained military engineers designed these frontier forts, essentially they were wood squares with bastions at the corners. The forts could withstand light artillery, but generally depended on earthworks and moats for additional protection for their stores of powder and supplies. The French network of trappers, traders, professional military men, and Native American allies could not retain mastery of this vast territory. By 1759, when the English captured Fort Niagara, at the mouth of the Niagara River in northwest New York, the French had burned or abandoned their four western Pennsylvania forts, ending French claims to the territory.

Between 1750 and 1765, the British built over fifty forts in the region to defend the interests of English colonists. They ranged from simple fortified stone or log houses to elaborate defense compounds like Fort Pitt (1759–1761), built on the ruins of Fort Duquesne at Pittsburgh's Point during the French and Indian War. Little trace remains today of these forts. Reconstructions at Fort Ligonier in Westmoreland County, Fort Necessity in Fayette County, and Fort Roberdeau in Blair County (BL25) attempt to explain what was essentially a temporary building type.

Most of the English forts were constructed by professional engineers. The settlements surrounding the forts, which consisted of gardens, housing for officers, and Native American encampments, eventually evolved into villages and towns, such as Pittsburgh in Allegheny County and Ligonier in Westmoreland County. While these sites were initially strategic military strong-

Drawing of Fort de la Presque Isle, by Charles M. Stotz, 1976. One of five French forts in the Allegheny Valley (all of which were square with corner bastions), Fort de la Presque Isle, built in 1753 and destroyed by the French in 1759, was constructed of squared logs, laid horizontally under the direction of engineer Captain Chevalier Francois Le Mercier.

holds, as soon as the need for the fort diminished, logs from the structure were pilfered and used for other purposes. The logging, construction, and carpentry skills of the soldiers who built the eighteenth-century forts were later used to build farmhouses, sawmills, and barns.[15]

One of the most surprising survivors of the log era is the 1797 courthouse in Waynesburg, Greene County (GR6). While most existing log structures are reconstructions or were relocated to a new site, this is an authentic public building of the late eighteenth century, which was uncovered and restored between 2000 and 2002.

Though more refined building practices were common in much of western Pennsylvania by the early nineteenth century, log structures remained an expedient option in areas without ready access to prefinished parts and skilled labor. Difficult roads and remote locations help to explain the chronological disparity between two small Roman Catholic chapels, St. Patrick's of 1806 in Armstrong County (AR6) and St. Severin's of 1851 in Clearfield County (CF7). Both are single-room, rectangular log structures whose building dates are separated by forty-five years. The choice of log construction for St. Severin's was dictated both by the expedience of building with materials at hand in the great forest, as well as a desire on the part of its Benedictine builders for a simple form to reflect the ideal of a life close to nature.

STONE BUILDINGS

By the late eighteenth century, settlers of means occasionally built houses or inns of locally quarried sandstone. The Jean Bonnet Tavern of c. 1762 in Bedford County (BD20) stylistically reflects the buildings of Maryland or eastern Pennsylvania. The Colonel Edward Cook House (1774–1776) in Fayette County (FA17) also employs the building techniques of Cumberland Valley and Philadelphia in a less refined manner. It is built of random-laid limestone quarried on the site, instead of the usual sandstone. Cook's house typically served many purposes: as manor house to his 3,000-acre holdings; as headquarters for his saw- and gristmills run by twenty slaves; as a retail outlet for the region; and as a resting place for travelers, George Washington and Albert Gallatin among them.[16]

The plans of many early stone houses in western Pennsylvania fall into three general categories: a two-room-deep, five-bay central-hall plan; a cubical three-bay side-hall plan; and a one-room-deep plan with both three- and five-bay variations.[17] The Cook house is of the first type, but with four bays instead of the standard five. The squarish configuration of the Dorsey house of 1787 in Washington County matched the second of the three categories—the cubical mass. Measuring nearly thirty-five feet on each side, the imposing house had exquisite Adamesque carvings around its entrance and on the mantels and cabinets. The two-over-two side-hall plan constructed with

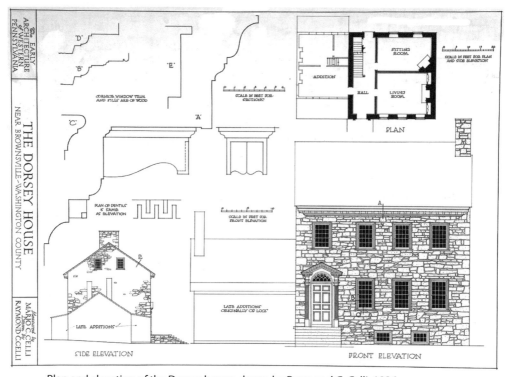

Plan and elevation of the Dorsey house, drawn by Raymond C. Celli, 1936.

both dressed and random-laid fieldstone overlooked the Monongahela River north of Brownsville. Without proper stewardship, it burned in 1993. The John Frew House (see AL129; c. 1790, c. 1840; 105 Sterret Street), near Pittsburgh's suburb of Crafton in Allegheny County, is a fine example of the third type of stone building plan. The one-room-deep original portion of the random rubble fieldstone house has large, cut-stone quoins at the corners. When a one-and-one-half-story brick extension was added later, the two structures were incorporated under a single roof.

The ethnicity of the owners and masons of the region's many stone houses is not always identifiable by either their choice of building technique or style.[18] During the mid- to late-eighteenth century, settlers coming to western Pennsylvania often belonged to a second generation that was born in the colonies. Their ties to Europe were more nostalgic than real.

Stone was typically the preferred building material for important or institutional buildings such as the Greersburg Academy of 1802 at Darlington in Beaver County (BE33). While it is of roughly dressed stones, the small square building housed a Presbyterian theological seminary. It represents the early appearance and sustained presence of sites of higher learning in western Pennsylvania. A series of twenty academies, many initially constructed of stone, were founded in the region before 1816 to train men for the ministry and the law. Several of them later became colleges and universities.

BRICK BUILDINGS

Stone and brick buildings in eighteenth-century western Pennsylvania were built using the material close at hand. Brick was used in the construction of Fort Pitt as early as 1759, but it was not used regularly in the region until the 1790s. Although many houses in Pittsburgh and Washington were made of brick by the late eighteenth century, the material was just beginning to be used in rural areas. Bricks were too heavy a commodity to transport over rudimentary roads; only in early turnpike and canal towns with local clay deposits were most houses constructed of brick. Hookstown in Beaver County, built between 1806 and 1840, is characterized by red brick five-bay houses in a vernacular interpretation of the popular Greek Revival style. West Overton in Westmoreland County hosts a distinguished collection of brick buildings built over the course of the nineteenth century. From its founding in 1803, the Overholt farm grew into a major whiskey distillery, with a wide variety of pre–Civil War brick structures on its forty-five-acre site, now preserved as a museum.

Refractory bricks—those burned to special hardness and used to line furnaces and kilns in the iron and glass industries—were produced as early as the 1830s in Clinton County at Queen's Run.[19] As steel mills proliferated in the mid-nineteenth century, the production of refractory brick boomed.

Engraving of Thomas Ross farm in Greene County (GR19), from *Caldwell's Illustrated Historical Centennial Atlas of Greene County, Pennsylvania* (1876).

By the 1920s, half-a-dozen counties in western Pennsylvania produced two-thirds of all the refractory brick in the United States.[20]

FARMS AND RURAL BUILDINGS

Western Pennsylvania farmers grow a wide assortment of crops including hay, oats, and mushrooms, as well as operating dairy farms. Special conditions also allow for the raising of grapes in Erie County, potatoes in Cambria County, sheep in Greene County, and Christmas trees in Indiana County.[21] Farmers often turned to rural publications and journals for the latest trends. The octagonal DeElmer Kelly barn of 1900 in Crawford County (CR22) and the Calvin Neff round barn of 1910 in Centre County (CE12) are examples of this. Today, nineteenth-century wood, stone, and brick barns are being replaced by pole barns, the prefabricated metal-clad buildings that are suitable for large equipment and require less maintenance than wooden barns.

The vast majority of western Pennsylvania farms have been in operation for generations, which is reflected in the assortment of structures from different eras dotting the farmstead. For example, an elegant, four-bay stone house of 1787 is the centerpiece of a 500-acre farm held by the Ulery family near Zollarsville in Washington County (WS20) for nearly two hundred years.[22] Nearby are buildings dating from the early to mid-nineteenth century, including two houses, a school, a gristmill, and the Zollarsville Methodist Church. Stahl Farm, "Dairy of Distinction," in Somerset County (S06), has been in that family since 1782, although the barn with Gothic-arched louvers dates from 1876, and the house, built with upright planks sheathed in siding, from 1886. Here the barn acts as a billboard to exhort Pennsylvania Turnpike travelers to "Drink Milk." The Blough farmhouse of c. 1830 in Somerset County (S08), with its traditionally German inset porch and upright

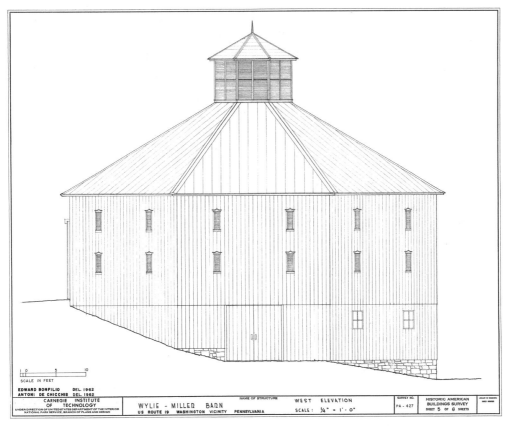

EDWARD BONFILIO   DEL. 1962
ANTONI DE CHICCHIS   DEL. 1962

| CARNEGIE INSTITUTE OF TECHNOLOGY
UNDER DIRECTION OF UNITED STATES DEPARTMENT OF THE INTERIOR
NATIONAL PARK SERVICE, BRANCH OF PLANS AND DESIGN | WYLIE - MILLER BARN
US ROUTE 19 WASHINGTON VICINITY PENNSYLVANIA | NAME OF STRUCTURE
WEST ELEVATION
SCALE : ¼" = 1'- 0" | SURVEY NO.
PA - 427 | HISTORIC AMERICAN BUILDINGS SURVEY
SHEET 5 OF 6 SHEETS | LIBRARY OF CONGRESS
INDEX NUMBER |

West Elevation, Wylie-Miller barn (demolished), 1962. Robert Wylie was inspired to build this 1888 octagonal barn by Elliott W. Stewart, a lecturer on agriculture at Cornell University, well-known western New York farmer, editor of the Buffalo *Live-Stock Journal,* and author of *Feeding Animals,* which was reprinted four times. By 1888, Stewart's design for his own sixty-foot octagonal barn south of Buffalo had already been published in several popular agricultural journals. This barn was credited to master builders John Vester and the McPeak brothers. Stewart asserted that octagonal barns were a superior design for several reasons: they required less expensive lumber because fewer large beams were used in the construction; the compact shape shortened the distances between the farmers' chores; and with a self-supporting roof there were no interior beams in the hay mow, increasing storage space and helping the structure withstand strong winds better than rectangular barns.

plank construction, is complemented by the barn decorated with barn stars and built in 1902 using funds from the sale of the farm's mineral rights to a nearby coal company.

Farmers showed pride in their accomplishments and celebrated the 1876 centennial of the United States by paying to have their farm sketched, and specifying which prize bull, horse or sheep, carriage or orchard would be included. Only six of western Pennsylvania's thirty-one counties do *not* have centennial atlases that pictured farms and whole towns from a bird's-eye view. The atlases portrayed an idealized, Arcadian landscape of peace, order, and harmony, celebrating neatly cultivated fields and prize-winning livestock. They are in stark contrast to the rampant industrialization occurring at the time.[23]

Today, many counties in Pennsylvania have state-funded Agricultural Land Preservation Boards overseen by the Department of Agriculture to help farmers preserve their family farms through scenic and conservation easements and other alternatives to sale and development.

INDUSTRY

Some farms were developed specifically to support local industries. For example, as imported European iron became too costly, the earliest colonists began manufacturing iron in America. Iron production required acres of trees to produce its charcoal fuel. By 1810, the center of the industry had moved away from the depleted forests of the eastern seaboard and into the Juniata River valley where the trees remained plentiful. Production centered around a large stone furnace with housing nearby for the workers and the owner. Every iron plantation in western Pennsylvania needed a supporting farm to supply food, raw materials, and animal labor. The Huntingdon Furnace complex, established in 1805, now a family farm, best illustrates this phenomenon (HU17). By the 1830s, iron plantations dotted the central counties.

The Cambria Iron Company of Johnstown (CA16) learned to exploit the means, methods, and manpower of iron and steel production from their founding in 1852. As the company's promotional literature boasted, within a mile of their headquarters they could find all the coal, ore, lime, stone, and

Bird's-eye-view lithograph of Cambria Iron Company's Johnstown mill (CA16), in Cambria County, drawn by G. M. Greene, 1888, a year before the Johnstown flood.

Shoe and Leather Petroleum Company, Pioneer Run, Venango County, Pennsylvania, 1865. During the oil boom, hillsides were shorn of trees that were used as raw material for derricks, barrels, and shantytowns in the northwestern counties.

brick that they needed to become the largest rail producer in America by the 1870s.[24] The lessons learned at Cambria were picked up and rapidly expanded by others, especially Andrew Carnegie at his Edgar Thomson Works (1873) in Braddock (AL57).

Extractive industries, from stone quarries to lime pits, swept through western Pennsylvania with little regard for environmental consequences. The region surrounding Pittsburgh was rapidly degraded by coal mining, coke burning, and glassmaking. In the northern counties, logging interests clear-cut the primeval forests and left thousands of acres littered with tree stumps that occasionally blazed themselves into wastelands. In Venango County and, later, McKean County, oil discoveries fostered boomtowns that went bust when the oil wells proved shallower than expected.

The physical remnants of these exploitive industries are everywhere in western Pennsylvania. Not only patch towns but less isolated single-industry towns often outlive their major employers. Steel towns, such as Duquesne and Aliquippa, and glassmaking towns like Charleroi and Glassport grew almost overnight on the shores of the Monongahela and Ohio rivers. Ford City, a small town with a ghostly glass manufacturing building sprawled along its riverfront, retains a full complement of owner-occupied housing along its residential streets. The discovery of oil contributed to the growth of towns like Oil City, Titusville, Bradford, and Franklin, and they now rely on tourism and service industries since little oil business remains. While their mills and factories have shut down, the remaining worker housing, commercial districts, and industrial hulks clearly reveal the social history of the recent past.

During the massive industrialization of the nineteenth century, the population of western Pennsylvania shifted from a Protestant majority to a Roman Catholic majority as immigrants from southern Ireland, eastern Europe, and the Mediterranean countries streamed in to work the factories and forges. Roman Catholic churches proliferated, particularly in densely populated areas where different nationalities built separate churches distinguished by language and customs. The Cambria City neighborhood (see CA25, CA26, and CA27) in Johnstown, with ten different ethnic churches in thirty blocks, is the most striking example of this phenomenon.

EARLY TRANSPORTATION: ROADS AND CANALS

As settlements took root and farming changed from a subsistence to a commercial level, the importance of the river system increased. Settlements along navigable creeks or near the Susquehanna and Ohio river systems shipped their produce after the 1760s in canoes, then on flatboats and arks. The first flatboat went from Pittsburgh to New Orleans in 1782.[25] By 1815, steamboats plied the waters and made return trips upstream possible.[26] No boat-related architecture remains since boatyards consisted primarily of open sheds and scaffolding.

Overland travel, often tortuous but vital, followed the natural contours of the land. The route from the Potomac River to the Ohio River across southwestern Pennsylvania had a typical evolution. First it was a buffalo road; next it was an Indian trail, named for Chief Nemacolin of the Delaware tribe; then it was widened to a horse trail by the military under General Edward Braddock; after 1817 it became the National Road; and today, with some alterations, it is U.S. 40.

Packhorse trails peaked in the 1790s, followed by the era of turnpikes from 1800 to 1840. Conestoga wagons (first built in Lancaster, Pennsylvania) made larger shipments possible, but the hauling was arduous and unpredictable

Engraving showing loaded canal boats being transferred to an inclined plane, from *History of the Pennsylvania Railroad Company* by William Bender Wilson (Philadelphia: H. T. Coates & Company, 1899).

as mud made the going very slow. Towns grew at major intersections, sometimes around an inn, and often at sites where mills operated; Perryopolis in Fayette County is an excellent example.

The industrial growth of western Pennsylvania was partly fueled by the continuing technological changes in transportation. When the Erie Canal opened in southern New York State in 1825, the commercial interests in Philadelphia were threatened by competition from the merchants of New York City and Baltimore. To ensure western trade, Pennsylvania needed a competitive statewide transportation system. The commonwealth began construction of a canal system in 1825, and in 1835, the Pennsylvania Canal opened from Philadelphia to Pittsburgh. But while the use of the canal decreased the cost of transporting farm produce from $120 to $30 a ton, its building and maintenance expenses nearly bankrupted the commonwealth.[27] One of the unanticipated benefits of the canal was the experience that a cadre of engineers garnered from the incredible structural feats required to traverse the state's mountains. They included the nine-mile-long Staple Bend Tunnel of Cambria County (CA11), the country's first railroad tunnel, and the Allegheny Portage Railroad (see CA8), designed to pull loaded canal boats on wheeled platforms over the mountains in a series of ten inclined planes. Engineer John A. Roebling was inspired by the heavy hemp cables of the Portage Railroad to invent twisted-wire rope, which he manufactured in Saxonburg,

Engraving of Logan House, Altoona, Blair County, Pennsylvania, from *Philadelphia and Its Environs* (Philadelphia: J. B. Lippincott & Co., 1875).

Butler County, in 1842.[28] All this activity, often in remote parts of western Pennsylvania, led to the growth of small villages along the canal's path such as Saltsburg, in Westmoreland County.

By the time the Pennsylvania Canal opened, it already had two major disadvantages: first, the Erie Canal in New York was well established, and second, cargo needed to be transferred several times during shipping across Pennsylvania (an unnecessary step along the Erie). Already Philadelphia had lost the title of commercial port capital to New York City. In just two decades the canal was overwhelmed by a competing technology—the railroads— leaving many canal towns stalled in the 1850s.

RAILROADS

All the major industries of western Pennsylvania benefited from rail service. The success of the Pennsylvania Railroad's main line spurred the growth of a series of narrow-gauge short lines to serve out-of-the-way lumbering sites, coal mines, coke ovens, and steel furnaces after the 1870s.

The city of Altoona was created out of farmland to serve the needs of the Pennsylvania Railroad, and several substantial red brick buildings remain to recall the railroad's dominance. Altoona's Logan House, built by Pennsylvania Railroad carpenters in 1852 and closed in 1927, became a model of the luxury railroad hotel designed as a layover for through passengers. The railroads also popularized destination resorts for passengers seeking cooler climates in the summer months. Wooden hotels in the mountains, like those at Bedford

Springs (BD16) in Bedford County and Cambridge Springs (CR21) in Crawford County, remain nearly intact. Although Andrew Carnegie's favorite hotel at Cresson, Cambria County, was demolished, many of the large Queen Anne summerhouses stand nearby.

Roundhouses, repair shops, and switching and signaling towers also remain as artifacts of the railroads. One of the most complete assemblages of buildings relating to a feeder line railroad is at Orbisonia in Huntingdon County (HU13), where the Broad Top railway system ran tourist trains for many years. At Conway in Beaver County (BE44) an enormous rail classification yard, begun in the 1880s, continues to sort freight cars bound for destinations from St. Louis to Montreal.

Heavy railcars and engines required nearly level surfaces to traverse the hills and valleys of western Pennsylvania. This could only be accomplished by the ingenuity of railroad engineers, who designed a network first of sturdy stone and timber and, later, metal bridges and viaducts that allowed trains to ascend and descend precipitous hills at a gradual rate. The Horseshoe Curve of 1854 in Blair County (BL24) remains as an extraordinary symbol of the Pennsylvania Railroad, the world's largest railroad for most of its existence and known internationally for its engineering prowess.[29]

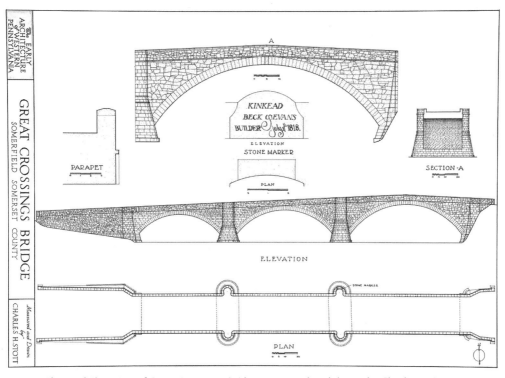

Plan and Elevation of Great Crossings Bridge measured and drawn by Charles H. Stott, c. 1936. This stone bridge, which once carried the National Road (U.S. 40) across the Youghiogheny River between Fayette and Somerset counties, is now submerged beneath Youghiogheny Lake.

BRIDGES

One of the earliest surviving bridges in western Pennsylvania is the "S" Bridge built in 1817 east of Claysville along the path of the National Road in Washington County. This stone bridge is a rarity, due to its curved approaches and early masonry. Its larger cousin, the Great Crossings Bridge, lies beneath the waters of Youghiogheny Lake to the east in Fayette County. Built between 1815 and 1818, the magnificent sandstone structure carried the National Road from the village of Somerfield to the eastern bank of the Youghiogheny River. Today, the triple-span, segmental-arched bridge is visible only during a severe drought. The U.S. Army Corps of Engineers consigned it to this on-again, off-again fate in 1944 when the river was dammed to control flooding.

As a leader in the production of iron and steel, western Pennsylvania is dotted with surviving metal bridges. The Dunlap's Creek Bridge in Brownsville (FA14; 1836–1839) is the oldest cast-iron bridge still in use. It was designed by the U.S. Army Corps of Engineers and fed onto a 630-foot-long wooden covered bridge that spanned the Monongahela River from 1833 to 1910.[30] Covered bridges were popular in Pennsylvania, which boasts more than any state in the Union, with 27 percent of them located in four western Pennsylvania counties: Bedford, Greene, Somerset, and Washington.

THE AUTOMOBILE AND ITS IMPACT

Road improvements were spurred on by the proliferation of the automobile. The number of registered automobiles in the United States grew rapidly from eight thousand in 1900 to over a million in 1913 and fifteen million in 1923.[31] This increase necessitated dramatic changes in roads, support services, and city planning. Both Pittsburgh and Johnstown sought planning advice for autoways from Frederick Law Olmsted Jr., a leader in the newly emerging profession of city planning, after his famous father had retired.[32] The population's explosive growth and auto-aided mobility melded suburbs and cities into new semi-urban typologies in the second half of the twentieth century.

Two generations of cross-state highways built specifically to accommodate automobile traffic cross the southern half of Pennsylvania. The Lincoln Highway (U.S. 30), established in 1913, was part of a paved connection between New York City and San Francisco. Two survivors of the unique buildings along the road are Dunkle's Art Deco–style Gulf Service Station of 1933 (BD9) and the tourist cabins at the Lincoln Motor Court of 1945 (BD19), both in Bedford County. The second generation of cross-state highways, the Pennsylvania Turnpike (I-76), was conceived in 1934 and opened six years later as the first modern limited-access highway in the United States. The turnpike stimulated such obvious building types as tollbooths and rest stops (BD14) in addition to the crossroad town of Breezewood in Bedford County, a conglomeration of fast-food and hotel chains. Marketing these highways as linear historic districts and cultural conduits has highlighted the importance of their unique inns, restaurants, and service buildings.

POST–WORLD WAR II

During World War II, military needs built the local steel industry and other heavy industries into a juggernaut. Following a postwar boom, these industries began to decline in the 1960s. By the late 1970s, many closed, depressing small towns along the major rivers. In the wake of this dramatic loss, the region has turned from brawn to brains. Research activities have generated high-tech companies and industrial parks such as Armstrong County's Parks Bend Farm and Industrial Park established in 1990 (AR17), reusing both the land and imagery of a former dairy farm in a semirural area. The Pittsburgh Technology Center constructed from 1990 on the site of a former Jones and Laughlin steel mill (AL44) consists of several new metal and glass buildings designed by Pittsburgh architects.

Colleges and universities have always been important in the region, and the forty-five campuses of western Pennsylvania experienced an unprecedented building boom in the second half of the twentieth century. Since the 1960s, dozens of contemporary buildings have been added to these campuses with their earlier Georgian-styled and Collegiate Gothic buildings. Today these colleges and universities are among the largest employers in western Pennsylvania.

TOURISM

Tourism is another growing industry that relies on service rather than manufacturing, and it is now a major economic engine in western Pennsylvania. Amusement parks such as the National Historic Landmark Kennywood Park in Allegheny County (AL54), Idlewild Park in Westmoreland County (WE28), and Lakemont Park in Blair County (BL22) opened in the late nineteenth century as picnic groves accessed via rail or trolley lines from nearby urban areas. These three parks, adapting to changing tastes over time, have safeguarded the best of their natural plantings and traditional rides while expanding into new areas such as roller coasters, thrill rides, and children's theme parks.

Contrasting with the fantasy of the planned parks, the region also profits from the story of its industrial past. A railroad museum in Altoona (BL7), a lumber museum in Potter County (PO7), a maritime museum in Erie (ER8), and a coal mining museum in Windber, Somerset County, all document the varied history of major local industries. Two of these museums have reused substantial nineteenth-century buildings to house their exhibitions, offices, and archives. Johnstown has museums dedicated to the historic flood of 1889 (CA14) and to the immigrant experience of the various ethnic groups imported to work in its mills.

The west side of Main Street (PA 44), Coudersport, Potter County, in northern Pennsylvania, surrounded by forested hills, is one of the many late-nineteenth-century commercial districts in Pennsylvania worth preserving.

The National Park Service has refurbished the Albert Gallatin house in Fayette County (FA9), and the commonwealth maintains the Harmonists' town of Economy, built between 1825 and 1830 in Beaver County. Living-history museums such as Old Bedford Village in Bedford County (BD13) and Meadowcroft in Washington County (WS16) interpret rural life with reconstructed buildings from the early nineteenth century. The region's historical societies and historic homes, particularly the Baker house in Blair County (BL19) and Clayton, in Allegheny County (AL107), use architecture to help an audience understand life in another era.

Western Pennsylvania's state parks are popular destinations for picnics, hiking, and camping. These forested areas are the result of conservation measures taken in the early twentieth century. In 1895, the commonwealth created a Department of Forestry in response to the devastation wrought by the lumber industry, especially in western Pennsylvania's north-central counties. The department founded tree nurseries that supplied close to one billion seedlings to replant Pennsylvania's forests between 1902 and 1993.[33] In the 1930s, the federal government sped the reclamation process by creating the Civilian Conservation Corps (CCC) to rebuild roads and dams and to provide cabins for overnight camping in the state parks. The Western Pennsylvania Conservancy has protected 204,000 acres since 1932.[34] The group contributes significantly to natural tourism by defending wetlands, planting urban gardens, and preserving and offering public tours of Frank Lloyd Wright's Fallingwater in Fayette County (FA28).

Many former rail lines abandoned after the decline of heavy industry have become forested trails. Since the late 1980s, volunteers have worked to join two former rail beds to create 150 continuous miles of the Great Allegheny Passage, the longest rail-to-trail in the eastern United States, linking McKeesport in Allegheny County with Meyersdale in Somerset County and, ultimately, Cumberland, Maryland. At Cumberland, the trail joins with the Chesapeake and Ohio (C&O) canal towpath to Washington, D.C.[35]

HISTORIC PRESERVATION

Residents of western Pennsylvania care deeply about their towns and cities and, over the years, have fought to save various buildings when time and funding permitted. In 1964, the Pittsburgh History and Landmarks Foundation (PHLF) organized campaigns to preserve and reuse serviceable buildings to rejuvenate neighborhoods, extend and improve the life of small business districts, save energy, and generate tax dollars. The foundation's first project was the successful rehabilitation of Victorian row houses in the Manchester neighborhood of Pittsburgh's North Side. The work of the PHLF was enhanced by the federal government's tax incentives in 1976 for the preservation of historically designated commercial buildings and the Economic Recovery Tax Act of 1981, which prompted over $2 billion of private investment nationwide.[36] In the 1980s, the PHLF was joined by Preservation Pennsylvania and smaller, local preservation organizations, which track and publicize the buildings needing attention in their communities.

Since 1980, the region's small towns have been well served by the Main Street program of the National Trust for Historic Preservation and the commonwealth's Department of Community and Economic Development. As Main Street managers preach, towns that showcase their individuality and understand what distinguishes them from others flourish. In western Pennsylvania several have capitalized on their individuality with quirky celebrations including Rain Day in Waynesburg, Greene County, and Groundhog Day in Punxsutawney, Jefferson County. Brookville, Hollidaysburg, and Franklin have excelled at retaining the best buildings along their main commercial streets and attracting appropriate new building. Franklin has taken this success further by joining with nearby Oil City in marketing both areas and telling the story of the oil boom.

ARCHITECTS

The impetus for historic preservation comes from a desire to save the best buildings, which are often designed by architects. Residents of western Pennsylvania usually looked toward the closest urban area for professional architects. The citizens of Erie hired architects from Buffalo and Cleveland; those

The town square or "diamond" of Meadville, Crawford County, with the William Strickland–designed courthouse of 1824–1828 (*left,* demolished); the Greek Revival Meadville Unitarian-Universalist Church (CR4; 1835–1836) designed by George W. Cullum (*center rear*); and a c. 1830 version of Christ Episcopal Church (CR3) designed by John Henry Hopkins, author of *Essay on Gothic Architecture,* published in 1836 (*right,* replaced).

along the Ohio border turned to Youngstown and Akron; and those in the central southern regions looked to Baltimore and Philadelphia. Pittsburgh also drew architects from far away.

The earliest trained architects in the region came originally from England. Benjamin Henry Latrobe (1764–1820) came to Pittsburgh to design a steamboat in 1813, and while there designed house alterations and drew preliminary plans for the United States Arsenal in Pittsburgh's Lawrenceville neighborhood (after 1830 called the Allegheny Arsenal; AL93) before he returned to Washington, D.C., in 1814.[37] John Chislett (1800–1869) trained in Bath, England, before he immigrated to Pittsburgh, where he lived from 1833 until his death. Among his designs are the Burke Building (AL25), several school buildings, and the second Allegheny County Courthouse of 1842, which burned in 1882. Chislett's final years were spent as the superintendent and landscape designer of the Allegheny Cemetery (AL95).

New Jersey born, but known as a Philadelphian, William Strickland (1788–1854) designed the former Crawford County Courthouse in Meadville between 1824 and 1828 (demolished c. 1866). Its Greek Revival style was emulated nearby on the town square by George Washington Cullum (1809–1892) in his Meadville Unitarian Church of 1836, originally the Independent Congregational Church.[38]

The prolific firm of Barr and Moser, composed of John Upton Barr (1815–c. 1900) and his partner Henry Moser (1821–1908), was active in western Pennsylvania during the 1860s and 1870s. A remarkable number of their brick buildings are extant, including the Italianate-styled Old Main buildings at California University of Pennsylvania (ws23) and Washington and Jefferson College in Washington County (ws4).

Besides Henry Moser, in the era between 1850 and World War I, numerous architects of German ancestry or training were at work in the region. Charles F. Bartberger (1823–1896), Frederick C. Sauer (1860–1942), and Richard Kiehnel (1870–1944) collectively designed hundreds of buildings from churches and schools to residences and small commercial buildings. Add to this partial list of professional architects the Harmonists' designer Frederick Reichert Rapp (1775–1834) and the vernacular Mennonite and Amish builders, and one begins to understand the pervasiveness of the Germanic influence.

After Henry Hobson Richardson (1838–1886) built his Allegheny County Courthouse and Jail (AL1), many local architects grafted his characteristically lithic forms onto their courthouses, churches, residences, and commercial buildings of the 1880s and 1890s.[39] The architects building on Richardson's foundation in the era between 1886 and 1920 included the firm of Longfellow, Alden and Harlow, who started offices in Pittsburgh and Boston, opening the door to several other firms from the latter city. Rutan and Russell, Peabody and Stearns, and MacClure and Spahr all had offices in Pittsburgh.[40] Another Bostonian, Ralph Adams Cram (1863–1942), designed half-a-dozen churches in the region.[41]

Frederick John Osterling (1865–1934) graduated from a technical school in Pittsburgh and apprenticed with a local architect. After touring Europe, he opened his own architectural office in Pittsburgh in 1888.[42] Two works in particular show the range of his design talents, the Polk Center, an institution for the mentally challenged in Venango County (VE11), and the Washington County Courthouse (ws1). At Polk, Osterling designed an entire brick campus between 1893 and 1897 in a hybrid style with architectural elements from barns, classicism, and the Shingle Style. His Washington County Courthouse is a Classical Revival "palace" with a grand central stair and dome influenced by his admiration for the architecture of the Ecole des Beaux-Arts.

Henry Hornbostel (1867–1961), a New Yorker, won the competition to design the Carnegie Technical Schools for patron Andrew Carnegie (AL43). Hornbostel designed the majority of the buildings on that campus and founded the architectural school, as well. He moved the city beyond academic revival styles by lending them a fresh interpretation and creating exquisite details. Hornbostel, educated at the Ecole des Beaux-Arts in Paris, designed the majority of his buildings for Pittsburgh. His works showed that using Beaux-Arts elements in a progressive way could raise a design above the purely antiquarian.[43]

By the turn of the twentieth century, the region's architects were well publicized in the national architectural journals and held biannual and then annual exhibitions of their works. These latter were organized between 1898 and 1916 by the Pittsburgh Architectural Club and the Pittsburgh Chapter of

Pennsylvania Railroad, Allegheny Station, Federal Street (demolished), North Side of Pittsburgh, designed by Price and McLanahan, built in 1905–1906.

the American Institute of Architects. In the early twentieth century, local industrialists began hiring architects with national reputations to design highrise offices and buildings. This loosely allied group, inspired by the World's Columbian Exposition of 1893 in Chicago and the City Beautiful movement, advocated for progressive governments, urban park systems, and classical buildings in cities large and small. Daniel H. Burnham (1846–1912) of Chicago, the exposition's director of works, designed twelve office buildings in western Pennsylvania, including the First National Bank in Uniontown for a coal baron in Fayette County (FA3).[44] Burnham's widespread influence was felt even in Clearfield, a small town in central Pennsylvania, in the Clearfield County National Bank and Dimeling Hotel of 1904 (CF2) designed by the firm of Beezer Brothers of Pittsburgh, twins who began their careers in Altoona. The era was also characterized by commercial buildings and manor houses (AL20, AL88) in a variety of historic styles designed by Pittsburgh-based Benno Janssen (1874–1964), who was known for his sophisticated designs and unerring eye for detail.

Andrew Carnegie's steel wealth produced libraries worldwide. Especially handsome ones survive in Erie (ER16) and Pittsburgh (AL41), designed by Longfellow, Alden and Harlow (later Alden and Harlow). Small, exquisite libraries, such as the Benjamin Franklin Jones Memorial Library in Aliquippa of 1929 (BE41) designed by Brandon Smith (1889–1962), acted as a democratizing influence for generations of new Americans.

One of the most talented architects of Roman Catholic churches based in

Pittsburgh was John Theodore Comes (1873–1922), who designed hundreds of churches nationwide. He brilliantly incorporated color and texture into his designs (BU8, WE24) and was influenced by the works of Ralph Adams Cram and English architect A. W. N. Pugin, as well as books on the churches of Germany, England, and Italy.[45]

Railway stations and movie theaters offer an array of architects' talents as their designers freely sampled various historical periods and building traditions. A prime example is Washington County's Waynesburg and Washington Railroad station of 1906 (WS8.2), designed by the Philadelphia firm of Price and McLanahan. This firm's larger commission, the enormous North Side station with Flemish echoes stood in Pittsburgh for over fifty years before it was demolished in 1955.[46] The following year, Pittsburgh demolished the Baltimore and Ohio Railroad station designed by Philadelphian Frank Furness (1839–1912) that had a tower like "a huge freight locomotive advancing from the train shed, thrusting itself forward into the city."[47] Erie has preserved and reused its Warner Theater of 1931 (ER18) designed by Rapp and Rapp, which epitomizes the exotic movie palaces of the era with its gilded lobby and giant marquee.

The region was also home to several prolific architects who purposely chose to focus their practices outside of Allegheny County. William George Eckles (1866–1932) of New Castle, in Lawrence County, and John Charles Fulton (1856–1924) and Harry W. Altman (1884–1966), both of Uniontown, Fayette County, designed hundreds of schools, houses, churches, and public buildings throughout western Pennsylvania. Although their work has generally been overlooked by architectural historians, it serves as an architectural context for the region.

Frederick Gustavus Scheibler Jr. (1872–1958) designed in a progressive mode based on European precedents, especially the turn-of-the-twentieth-century Viennese Secessionists. His commissions were uniformly modest and not well publicized, except for the Old Heidelberg Apartments of 1905 in Pittsburgh (AL105).[48]

The first modern building in western Pennsylvania to capture the national imagination was Frank Lloyd Wright's Fallingwater of 1936 (FA28). Much has been written about the house on the waterfall, and it has attracted generations of architecture enthusiasts to western Pennsylvania. There followed a succession of houses in the region designed by famous modernists such as Walter Gropius and Marcel Breuer's Frank House in Pittsburgh in 1938 (AL111) and their war housing in New Kensington the following decade (WE23). Wright designed a second house in Fayette County, Kentuck Knob, in 1954–1956 (FA29). Peter Berndtson's (1909–1972) and Cornelia Brierly's (1913–) houses spanning the 1930s and the 1950s (WE4, CE22, and at Meadow Circles on Lutz Lane in Allegheny County) reflect their time at Wright's Taliesin studio. And the work of Raymond Viner Hall (1908–1981) brings organic principles to school buildings as well as residences (CM5 and MK16).[49]

552 Neville Street, Pittsburgh, designed by Tasso Katselas.

Church designs broke out of the Gothic Revival mode in the 1960s. Roman Catholic church design responded to new liturgical requirements after Vatican II (1962–1965), and other denominations rethought the character and the interior spaces needed for worship. The St. Vitus Roman Catholic Church of 1963 (LA15) in New Castle designed by P. Arthur D'Orazio (1909–2000), an architect from Youngstown, Ohio, took the shape of a nautilus. Its irregularly organized, brightly colored, punched-out windows are similar to those used by Le Corbusier at the Chapel of Notre Dame du Haut, Ronchamp, France, in 1955. Harrold Zion Evangelical Lutheran Church of 1964 in Westmoreland County (WE10) was designed by the Greensburg firm Roach Walfish and Lettrich in the shape of a triumphantly curved sail. Non-Western building traditions were imported to western Pennsylvania by Pittsburgh-based Shashi D. Patel (1942–) and eleven master masons at the Hindu-Jain Temple of 1981–1990 (AL127). Here they built seven separate towers in the Nagradi style typical of north and central India.

A vibrant residential design scene spawned several later generations of modernists including A. James Speyer (1913–1986), Ludwig Mies van der Rohe's first American graduate student at the Armour Institute in Chicago, who designed two of his five houses in Pittsburgh in the 1960s (AL110). Tasso Katselas (1927–) designed some of the earliest Brutalist buildings in Pittsburgh and often used brick in combination with exposed reinforced concrete, as seen at 552 Neville Street (1958). He used pilotis to support the bulk of this building as Le Corbusier often did to open the space at street level. An imaginative house in Ligonier Valley (WE31) designed in the mid-1980s by Roger Cesare Ferri (1949–1991) elaborated traditional themes with a whimsically modern interpretation. In Pittsburgh, Arthur Lubetz (1940–) and his innovative firm designed the Lynn Williams Place apartments for the elderly in 2003 at 3710 Brighton Road in Pittsburgh's Brighton Heights neighborhood. Its corner detailing looks like two puzzle pieces about to mesh.

Pittsburgh garnered national attention in the 1950s when a public/private partnership cleared the historic Point and such nationally known architects as Eggers and Higgins with Irwin Clavan designed three of the chrome-alloyed steel Gateway Center buildings (AL7). Harrison and Abramovitz designed eight buildings in the city between 1951 and 1974. The Pittsburgh firm of Mitchell and Ritchey played their part by adding Mellon Square park in 1955 with landscape architects Simonds and Simonds (AL28.1). The lead designers of the park, architect James A. Mitchell (1907–1999) and his partner Dahlen Ritchey (1910–2002), also taught generations of students at their alma mater, Carnegie Technical Institute (now Carnegie Mellon University). Michael Graves resurrected a sense of monumentality in Johnstown, Cambria County (CA20), with his postmodern design for the Crown American Building in 1989. The firm of Bohlin Cywinski Jackson (BCJ) in a joint venture with Burt Hill Kosar Rittelmann brought the region away from its industrial base and firmly into the research-led economy with their Software Engineering Institute of 1984–1987 at 4500 5th Avenue in Pittsburgh.

Western Pennsylvania, once a region of belching smokestacks and fiery blast furnaces, where Pittsburgh inspired the description "Hell with the lid off," today has become a leading center of the green architecture movement by supporting the design of sustainable and energy efficient buildings using recycled products. Rafael Viñoly's dramatic design for Pittsburgh's David L. Lawrence Convention Center of 2003 with its sweeping roofline is the best-known example (AL15). The building provides abundant natural light from glass curtain walls, cross ventilation, and an environmental cooling system drawing from an underground reservoir. Green buildings like this symbolize a better future for both architecture and the environment of western Pennsylvania.

NOTES

1. Most guidebooks to western Pennsylvania include one-third of the counties from Somerset to the western border. Since the Society of Architectural Historians has assigned two volumes to the commonwealth, the state has been split into two portions, and central Pennsylvania has been divided in two.

2. Center for Rural Pennsylvania, "Rural/Urban PA," www.ruralpa.org/rural_urban.html (accessed July 18, 2003). The four urban counties each have a population density greater than 274 people per square mile.

3. Trappers and traders penetrated these areas earlier, but towns and permanent settlements did not develop in the southern counties until after the 1760s and in the north-central counties until 1820. See E. Willard Miller, ed., *A Geography of Pennsylvania* (University Park: Pennsylvania State University Press, 1995), 89.

4. The term "commonwealth," from the Old English referring to the common "weal" or well-being of the citizens, has no legal distinction from the word "state." In the commonwealth's five constitutions since 1776, the two terms have been used interchangeably. Four states chose to be commonwealths: Pennsylvania, Massachusetts, Virginia, and Kentucky. Jere Martin, *Pennsylvania Almanac* (Mechanicsburg: Stackpole Books, 1997), 32.

5. Linda L. Steiner, "Six Ways to the Sea," undated bulletin from the Pennsylvania Fish and Boat Commission.

6. Daniel K. Richter, "The First Pennsylvanians," in *Pennsylvania: A History of the Commonwealth*, ed. Randal M. Miller and William Pencak (University Park: Pennsylvania State University Press, and Harrisburg: Pennsylvania Historical and Museum Commission, 2002), 19.

7. Verna L. Cowin, "Western Pennsylvania Stone Mounds: Looking for Patterns," in *Foragers and Farmers of the Early and Middle Woodland Periods in Pennsylvania*, ed. Paul A. Raber and Verna L. Cowin (Harrisburg: Pennsylvania Historical and Museum Commission, 2003), 85–100. Another Adena site, the Grave Creek Mound, has been identified at Moundsville, West Virginia.

8. "Drought Ended Monongahela Indian Culture," *Pittsburgh Post-Gazette*, Monday, November 11, 2002. Archaeologists at the Carnegie Museum of Natural History studied tree-ring records from West Virginia that showed droughts from 1587 to 1589 and 1607 to 1612; whether this motivated the migration is unclear.

9. Richter, "First Pennsylvanians," 23.

10. While editorial policies dictate using the term "Scots-Irish," western Pennsylvanians normally refer to this group as "Scotch-Irish." Either way, the term is unknown in Ulster and admittedly problematic but accurate here for a variety of reasons. By the time the Lowland Scots who migrated to northern Ireland came to western Pennsylvania, many had been in Ireland for four generations. Their Presbyterian faith and Scottish ancestry distinguished them from the Irish around them and to the south, and in their own minds they were "Irish of the North." The fact that the names, such as Derry, Tyrone, and Donegal, they brought to western Pennsylvania reflected their time in Ireland rather than Scotland testifies to the length of their stay there and their thorough enculturation. The term "Scots-Irish" is used here since "it expresses a historical reality: the Scots who lived in Ulster before they came to America simply were not, in background, religion, and many other aspects of culture, identical with the Irish of the southern provinces of Leinster, Munster, and Connaught; neither were they, after many decades, any longer identical with the people of Scotland." James G. Leyburn, *The Scotch-Irish: A Social History* (Chapel Hill: University of North Carolina Press, 1962), 333.

11. Philip Shriver Klein and Ari Hoogenboom, *A History of Pennsylvania* (University Park: Pennsylvania State University Press, 1980), 186.

12. Dan Deibler and George E. Thomas, "National Historic Landmark Nomination" (Washington, D.C.: U.S. Department of the Interior, National Park Service, December 1, 1990). Statement of Significance, Section 8, 2.

13. "Excluding the small number of exceptional German farmers in Somerset and Westmoreland, it is impossible to predict the ethnicity of a settler based on the size, building material, or value of his home or outbuildings." Jennifer Lee Ford, "Landscape and Material Life in Rural Southwestern Pennsylvania, 1798–1838" (Ph.D. diss., University of Pittsburgh, 2001), 104.

14. Letter dated September 17, 1823, from Albert Gallatin to his daughter Frances Gallatin, as quoted in *The Life of Albert Gallatin* by Henry Adams (Philadelphia: L. B. Lippincott, 1879), 589–90. He called the style "hiberno-teutonic."

15. Charles Morse Stotz, *Outposts of the War for Empire: The French and English in Western Pennsylvania: Their Armies, Their Forts, Their People, 1749–1764* (Pittsburgh: University of Pittsburgh Press, 1985), 60–66. Nearly a million bricks were also used at Fort Pitt to face the western embankment. Charles Morse Stotz, *The Early Architecture of Western Pennsylvania* (Pittsburgh: University of Pittsburgh Press, 1995), 254–55.

16. Historic American Buildings Survey, PA 412, Lamont H. Button and Charles Morse Stotz, 1936 report.

17. Karen Koegler, "Building in Stone in Southwestern Pennsylvania: Patterns and Process," in *Perspectives in Vernacular Architecture, V: Gender, Class, and Shelter,* ed. Elizabeth Collins Cromley and Carter L. Hudgins (Knoxville: University of Tennessee Press, 1995), 202.

18. Ibid.

19. Kim E. Wallace, *Brickyard Towns: A History of Refractories Industry Communities in South-Central Pennsylvania* (Washington, D.C.: America's Industrial Heritage Project, HABS/ HAER, 1993), xx.

20. Corinne A. Krause, *Refractories, the Hidden Industry: A History of Refractories in the United States, 1860–1985* (Pittsburgh: American Ceramic Society Incorporated, 1987), 7.

21. Pennsylvania Farm Bureau, 2003. www.pfb.com/counties/.

22. It was sold out of the family in the early 1970s.

23. Joseph A. Caldwell, *Caldwell's Illustrated Combination Centennial Atlas of Greene County, Pennsylvania* (1876; Windmill Publications, Inc., 1995), 37.

24. Cambria Iron Company Pamphlet, 1853, as quoted in Kim E. Wallace, ed., *The Character of a Steel Mill City: Four Historic Neighborhoods of Johnstown, Pennsylvania* (Washington, D.C.: HABS/HAER, 1989), 10; Sharon A. Brown, *Cambria Iron Company: America's Industrial Heritage Project, Pennsylvania* (Washington, D.C.: United States Department of the Interior, National Park Service, 1989), ix.

25. Stevenson Whitcomb Fletcher, *Pennsylvania Agriculture and Country Life, 1640–1840* (Harrisburg: Pennsylvania Historical and Museum Commission, 1971), 1:242.

26. Ibid., 1:243. The *New Orleans* was the first stern-wheeler to make the trip from Pittsburgh to New Orleans, in 1811, but the *Enterprise* was the first steamboat to make the trip downriver and back, in 1815.

27. Ibid., 268.

28. Staff of the *Butler Eagle* newspaper, *Butler County, Pennsylvania, Celebrates Its Bicentennial* (Pittsburgh: The Local History Company, 2001), 35.

29. Randall M. Miller and William A. Pencak, eds., *Pennsylvania: A History of the Commonwealth* (University Park: Pennsylvania State University Press, 2002), xii; Timothy Jacobs, *The History of the Pennsylvania Railroad* (New York: Smithmark Publishers, 1995), 8.

30. The Monongahela Covered Bridge was built by contractors LeBaron and DuMond in the fall of 1831, and the first toll was collected on it October 14, 1833.

31. Karl B. Raitz, ed., *The National Road* (Baltimore: Johns Hopkins University Press, 1996), 426; Stephen Mark, "Save the Auto Camps!" National Park Service, www.nps.gov/ crla/mark5.

32. John F. Bauman and Edward K. Muller, "The Olmsteds in Pittsburgh: Part I, Landscaping the Private City," and "Part II, Shaping the Progressive City," *Pittsburgh History* 76,

nos. 3 and 4 (1993/1994): 195, 200. The firm Olmsted, Olmsted and Eliot laid out the industrial village of Vandergrift in 1895 in Westmoreland County. Frederick Law Olmsted Jr. produced *Pittsburgh, Main Thoroughfares and the Down Town District,* etc., in February 1911 for Pittsburgh's Committee on City Planning.

33. Paul T. Fagley, comp., Genevieve T. Volgstadt, ed., "A Teacher's Guide to Greenwood Furnace" (Greenwood Furnace State Park, Department of Conservation and Natural Resources, 2001), 6–1, 6–2.

34. Western Pennsylvania Conservancy, www.wpconline.org/aboutwpchome.htm.

35. Bill Metzger, *The Great Allegheny Passage Companion: Guide to History and Heritage along the Trail* (Pittsburgh, Pa: The Local History Company, 2003), xii. The abandoned lines served the Pittsburgh and Lake Erie Railroad's Youghiogheny Branch to Connellsville and the Western Maryland Railway's Connellsville Extension.

36. Richard Longstreth, *The Buildings of Main Street: A Guide to American Commercial Architecture, Updated Edition* (New York: AltaMira Press, 2000), 1–2.

37. Charles Morse Stotz, *The Early Architecture of Western Pennsylvania* (Pittsburgh: University of Pittsburgh Press, 1995), 20–23, 255–56, 264–66. The dates of Latrobe's stay in Pittsburgh vary, sometimes within a single source; for instance, Stotz lists 1813–1815 on p. 20, and 1812–1814 on p. 255. Lawrenceville historian James Wudarczyk found in his research that Latrobe lived in Pittsburgh from 1813 to late 1814. See http://www.lhs15201 .org/articles_b.asp?ID=24. Little remains of the arsenal buildings.

38. George Cullum was born in New York City, moved to Meadville as a child, and graduated third in his class from West Point. He achieved the rank of major general in the Civil War, and near the end of the war became superintendent of West Point. His sister was married to a member of one of the church's founding families, the Huidekopers.

39. "The Best Ten Buildings in the United States," *American Architect & Building News* 17 (June 12, 1885): 282; James F. O'Gorman, *Three American Architects: Richardson, Sullivan, and Wright, 1865–1915* (Chicago: University of Chicago Press, 1991), 26, 30, 32.

40. Margaret Henderson Floyd, *Architecture after Richardson: Regionalism before Modernism—Longfellow, Alden and Harlow in Boston and Pittsburgh* (Chicago: University of Chicago Press, 1994), 242.

41. Roman Catholic, Episcopal, Presbyterian, and United Church of Christ. Ralph Adams Cram, *American Church Building of Today* (New York: Architectural Book Publishing Co., 1929); Ann Miner Daniel, "The Early Architecture of Ralph Adams Cram, 1889–1902" (Ph.D. diss., University of North Carolina, Chapel Hill, 1978).

42. Frederick Osterling's oeuvre cries out for full documentation. His works are known in a dozen counties of Pennsylvania, as well as West Virginia and New Jersey. His father owned a lumberyard and planing mill on Pittsburgh's North Side, then Allegheny City. Osterling apprenticed with local architect Joseph Stillberg.

43. Walter C. Kidney, *Henry Hornbostel: An Architect's Master Touch* (Lanham, Md.: Roberts Rinehart Publishers, 2002), xvii, xix. See Charles L. Rosenblum's excellent preface.

44. Franklin Toker, *Pittsburgh: An Urban Portrait* (University Park: Pennsylvania State University Press, 1986), 40.

45. John Theodore Comes, "Catholic Art and Architecture: A Lecture to Seminarians" (Privately printed, 1918), 5, 17.

46. James D. Van Trump, *Life and Architecture in Pittsburgh* (Pittsburgh: Pittsburgh History and Landmarks Foundation, 1983), 228. Known as the Pittsburgh, Fort Wayne and Chicago Railroad Station, it was ultimately purchased by the Pennsylvania Railroad.

George E. Thomas, *William L. Price: Arts and Crafts to Modern Design* (New York: Princeton Architectural Press, 2000), 125. Architect Will Price's brother-in-law was put in charge of the railroad's western division.

47. Van Trump, *Life and Architecture in Pittsburgh,* 224.

48. Martin Aurand, *The Progressive Architecture of Frederick G. Scheibler Jr.* (Pittsburgh: University of Pittsburgh Press, 1994), 5, 8.

49. Charles Rosenblum, "Precedent and Principle: The Pennsylvania Architecture of Peter Berndtson and Cornelia Brierly," *Frank Lloyd Wright Quarterly* (Spring 1999): 10.

The Western Capital—Pittsburgh and Allegheny County

It took four tries to establish Pittsburgh. The Point—the place at which the Monongahela and Allegheny rivers meet to form the Ohio—was fortified both by a party of Virginians and by the French in 1754, then by the British in 1759–1761. But these military settlements were not in city form, even if a 1760 census counted some 200 squatters living in houses around the British fort. Pittsburgh was laid out as a city in 1784 by surveyor George Woods for the heirs of William Penn, but it was unclear to which county it belonged, and even to which state, since it was claimed both by Pennsylvania and Virginia. Logically, when Pennsylvania carved out Allegheny County in 1788, it should have designated it Pittsburgh County, as a western counterpart to Philadelphia County in the east. That would have integrated the state's concern for the administration of justice with the city's concern for its own power base. But Allegheny County was created not to exalt Pittsburgh but to curtail it: the rival city of Allegheny was laid out (by David Redick) on the opposite bank of the Allegheny River in 1788. Pittsburgh stole the dignity of being county seat from Allegheny City almost at once, and in 1907, it gobbled up the rival settlement to become its North Side. Merely looking at the layouts of Allegheny City and Pittsburgh shows a striking difference in character: Allegheny City was broad, elegant, even utopian in its mix of buildings and green pastures in a perfect square, whereas Pittsburgh was cramped, overbuilt, and somewhat crooked in a jumbled street plan that shoehorned commercial enterprises along the richly profitable Monongahela and Allegheny riverbanks.

As it rose in its industrial wealth, Pittsburgh appeared uncultured and brash to the rest of the nation. What was not obvious then, and remains too little studied now, is that as a trade and distribution center, Pittsburgh and the whole of western Pennsylvania had roots both old and deep. When Europeans came here, they found only modest Native American settlements of the Delaware in modern-day Lawrenceville and McKees Rocks and smaller transient groupings of the Seneca and Shawnee. Probably gone by then was a Late Prehistoric village that had flourished at McKees Rocks from about 900 BCE. Still visible today is the natural base for what was once McKees Rocks mound—the largest in Pennsylvania—which had been occupied by Native Americans during the Early and Middle Woodland Periods, possibly as early as 1000 BCE. What these remains show is an extensive trade network along the riverine systems of the midcontinent; in those remote pre-European days, it was not the Ohio River valley but the East Coast that was hinterland. The rise of industrial Pittsburgh as a global center of exchange thus followed an ancient template.

The role of Pittsburgh in western Pennsylvania would always be one of dominance, but the metropolis had to be interdependent with the small towns surrounding it. They were literal feeders during agricultural days, then allegorically so, when immense amounts of industrial production—often carefully and precisely orchestrated from one mill to the next—came from those same sites that were now turned into industrial satellites. Consequently, Pittsburgh's growth pattern was organic rather than orthogonal, expanding seven times from the Point over the next 250 years.

The first of these seven expansions was the creation of the rivals, Pittsburgh and Allegheny City, in the 1780s. Architecture in those two preindustrial towns overwhelmingly followed the sober Federal and Greek Revival styles from the 1790s to the middle of the nineteenth century. The city had two professional architects early on, both British born, in visiting Benjamin Henry Latrobe and resident John Chislett. The most impressive of the city's buildings from this era are mainly lost, as one would expect, but a few reconstructed walls and the Blockhouse remain from Fort Pitt (AL6); the Neill Log House of c. 1787 still stands in Schenley Park on E. Circuit Road; and south of the city, Woodville Plantation (AL132) survives as a surprisingly high-style exemplar of domestic architecture on the fringes of the frontier settlement. Otherwise, we have to depend on lithographs to acclaim Latrobe's Allegheny Arsenal (AL93), Chislett's second Allegheny County Courthouse (1835–1841, burned 1882), and the massive "Homewood" house (1835, demolished 1924) that gave its name and social cachet to the city's eastern suburbs. Bedford Square (see AL48) on the South Side survives to give the general massing if not the specific structures of that part of the city around 1815, and the nearby Bedford School (see AL48) of 1850 and the contemporary Mexican War Streets district (AL76) on the North Side are good representatives of Greek Revival in Pittsburgh.

Around 1800, there was a second expansion from the core, resulting in the creation of a half-dozen detached settlements along Pittsburgh's riverbanks. Along the Allegheny River, Bayardsville (now the Strip) was platted around 1800, and William Foster's Lawrenceville followed in 1812. On the south bank of the Monongahela, Birmingham was platted by Dr. Nathaniel Bedford on land owned by his father-in-law, John Ormsby, in 1811, while on the Ohio River, the settlements of Manchester and Sewickley were founded between the 1820s and the mid-nineteenth century.

Like so many overcrowded and poorly built American cities, Pittsburgh suffered a calamitous fire (recorded locally as the "Great Fire" or "Big Fire") on April 10, 1845. It burned through fifty-six acres in twenty-six blocks, about a third of the Golden Triangle, as well as one-quarter of a mile along the Monongahela shore. About one thousand buildings were lost (thankfully only two deaths were recorded). As one would expect, new wooden buildings became extremely rare in Pittsburgh after midcentury, though it was generally held that this was more a consequence of the power of the brick trusts than of farsighted city planning.

A third expansion, from midcentury to around 1875, was sparked by the arrival of the Pennsylvania Railroad in Pittsburgh in 1852. This led almost immediately to the formation of a string of railroad suburbs east of downtown, in Shadyside, Homewood, Point Breeze, Wilkinsburg, Edgewood, and Swissvale. Some aesthetes preferred to live at even greater remove from Pittsburgh, at Evergreen Hamlet and Sewickley in the Allegheny and Ohio river valleys, respectively. These near and far suburbs showcased the Gothic Revival, which had earlier manifested itself in Pittsburgh in such works as John Haviland's Western Penitentiary of 1828 (demolished).

This post–Civil War era saw the predictable importation of new styles in the Romantic tradition: Italianate and Renaissance Revival, Second Empire, and the beginnings of the Romanesque Revival. Topographically, the period marked the integration of the building and landscape architectural traditions, as in Allegheny Cemetery (AL95). Some downtown relics from this era are Dollar Savings Bank (AL27), the cast-iron facades on Liberty and Penn avenues, and the Italianate storefronts around Market Square. Even richer are three long, crowded streets that testify to post–Civil War prosperity and that have recently sprung vigorously back to life: E. Carson Street on the South Side, E. Ohio Street on the North Side, and Butler Street in Lawrenceville. While Philadelphia designers such as John Notman and Isaac Hobbs had much influence on the midcentury city, Joseph W. Kerr, Charles F. Bartberger, and other local architects led the outsiders in terms of volume.

The stage was now set for a fourth expansion from the core, in the industrial satellite communities in the Allegheny, Ohio, and Monongahela river valleys. From 1875 to 1910, industrial Pittsburgh reached its apogee, both in its factories and the huge institutional buildings created from its new wealth. Virtually all the early mills were later cannibalized or razed, but certain archaeological survivals still stand in the Strip and Lawrenceville. Just two mills keep some of their original functions on their original sites today: Andrew Carnegie's United States Steel Edgar Thomson Works in Braddock (AL57) and H. J. Heinz's food-processing plant on the North Side (AL81), but the whole Pittsburgh district resonates with hundreds of factories and thousands of worker houses that survive in mill towns such as Natrona, Homestead, Turtle Creek, and Wilmerding, and a little later in McKees Rocks, Duquesne, and Clairton.

The tremendous wealth from industry flowing into the city from the 1890s until World War I refurbished Pittsburgh's downtown, where the Triangle was truly made golden. After the creation of the industrial plants, the spending by the robber barons of their vast wealth is the second most characteristic moment in the architecture of Pittsburgh. The new governmental and commercial architecture featured both medieval-based styles, such as the train station by Frank Furness (AL125), and the Beaux-Arts idiom. The latter was the style of choice for Carnegie's partners Henry Phipps, Henry Oliver, and Henry Clay Frick for the skyscrapers they commissioned from New York City's George B. Post and Chicago's Daniel H. Burnham and others. The masterpiece of the era remains H. H. Richardson's Allegheny County Courthouse and Jail (AL1), which combined elements of both stylistic camps. The Courthouse and the sumptuous corporate buildings gave Pittsburgh national and international prominence in architecture.

The same years preceding World War I saw a fifth major expansion from the downtown, setting an elegant ring around the old urban core through the application of City Beautiful ideas to the middle- and upper-management neighborhoods of Oakland, Shadyside, Squirrel Hill, Highland Park, Point Breeze, and the North Side. A score of mansions survive on 5th, Penn, and Ridge avenues from the years in which those streets held the highest concentration of millionaires in the United States.

What best survives from City Beautiful Pittsburgh are three new parks and their linked thoroughfares, all laid out by city planner Edward Manning Bigelow between 1890 and 1925. The parks are Schenley, Frick, and Highland; the thoroughfares are Bigelow Boulevard, Boulevard of the Allies (conceived around 1910 but delayed until the 1920s), Beechwood Boulevard, and Highland Avenue. These four carriage roads—probably originally planned as five—would have formed a twenty-mile ring around that portion of Pittsburgh lying between the Monongahela and Allegheny rivers. The best of Bigelow's roads today bears his name, though it was initially called Grant Boulevard. This stylish roadway was opened in 1901 to lead motorists from Grant Street in the Golden Triangle to Schenley Plaza in Oakland, and beyond into Schenley Park. The road still branches off at Grant Street at 7th Avenue (today marked by the USX Tower [AL17] instead of the Beaux-Arts pylon once proposed) and snakes for about six miles along a cyclopean retaining wall cut into an escarpment some one hundred feet above the Strip. This is the best part of Bigelow, aestheticizing the industrial districts of the Allegheny River valley and Polish Hill.

After Polish Hill and a picturesque swerve over Bloomfield, Bigelow Boulevard awkwardly picks its way through the then new development of Oakland—whose growth it had spurred enormously—into Schenley Plaza. The boulevard then snakes its way from west to east through Schenley Park (under the new name of Schenley Drive), then changes name again for a third serpentine run across Squirrel Hill as Beechwood Boulevard. The fourth element is Washington Boulevard, picking up from Beechwood in Point Breeze at the intersection of 5th and Penn avenues, whence it took pioneer motorists down a wooded ravine to the Allegheny River shoreline. The fifth element would presumably have been a return boulevard along the Allegheny to downtown: Butler Street does this functionally but without Bigelow's characteristic aesthetic touch.

Egged on by Bigelow, Pittsburgh's industrial elite began to endow the East End with a string of monuments that would end only with World War II. Andrew Carnegie took the lead with the creation of his Library, Institute (AL41), and Technical School (today Carnegie Mellon University, AL43). Entrepreneur Franklin Nicola doggedly pursued the concept of the City Beautiful until the Oakland district yielded a baseball park, society hotel, fashionable clubs, model homes of the Schenley Farms district, and a Beaux-Arts Acropolis-style campus for the University of Pittsburgh. The Mellon family contributed heavily to Oakland's medical complex, then took the lead in three monuments of still eye-catching scale: Mellon Institute (AL37), the Cathedral of Learning (AL38), and East Liberty Presbyterian Church (AL98).

From roughly 1910 to 1940, there was a sixth expansion from the downtown core, this one also to accommodate the motorcar. A set of ambitious roads and public works projects turned a set of discrete urban sites into a loose web of suburbs. First came the Liberty Tubes, tunneling under Mount Washington to reach Mount Lebanon and the nearer South Hills. Two picturesque expressways followed: Allegheny River Boulevard, leading to the wealthy suburb of Oakmont, and Ohio River Boulevard to the even more glamorous Sewickley. These were the years that left Art Deco buildings in almost every corner of the city: the Allegheny County Airport (AL60), Allegheny General Hospital (AL78), the Art Deco storefronts on E. Carson Street, New Granada Theater on the Hill (AL120), and a sort of institutional Art Deco in Buhl Planetarium (AL74). Modernism came to the fore in the 1930s with Frank Lloyd Wright's office in the Kaufmann Department Store (moved in 1974 to the Victoria and Albert Museum in London), and the world-famous Fallingwater for the same Kaufmann family in nearby Fayette County (FA28).

The seventh expansion from Pittsburgh's core paralleled post–World War II growth across the nation and gave the city a whole new chain of suburbs in South Hills, North Hills, and suburban corridors branching off the Pennsylvania Turnpike and Parkways East and West. But the Pittsburgh Renaissance from 1945 through 1969 (known as Renaissance I) had even greater impact in the rebuilding of the Golden Triangle, in what was one of the most massive reconstructions of a city core in the nation. "Renaissance" is an important term in Pittsburgh history, but its local meaning is a postwar movement that was crucial to the survival of the city. Pittsburgh reached its highest rates of industrial production in World War II, but even by 1944, when the local politicians, academics, and business leaders formed the Allegheny Conference on Community Development (ACCD), it was clear that without massive redevelopment Pittsburgh would be bypassed in the postwar economy. The main thrust of Pittsburgh's Renaissance I involved federally mandated flood control on the three rivers, stringent air pollution controls, and the creation of the nation's first Urban Redevelopment Authority with the power to flatten sizeable portions of the city. The flood and pollution controls reversed the worst environmental effects of Pittsburgh's two centuries of industrial production. For the built environment, the most visible and positive achievements of the Pittsburgh Renaissance were Point State Park (Gateway Center; AL7) and Mellon Square (AL28.1), all downtown, and their attendant skyscrapers; the worst excesses of urban renewal took place outside the Golden Triangle, on the North Side, in East Liberty, and the Hill.

Renaissance II, from the late 1970s to around 1990, operated differently than Renaissance I. The goals and priorities of the first were set by the Allegheny Conference and professional groups, and implemented by the public sector; in the second, the public sector did more of the planning and agenda setting, with a more diverse power base in the private corporate and neighborhood groups. This Renaissance spawned completion of the light rail system in 1983, rebuilding of Grant Street, an agreement for a new Midfield Terminal Complex at the Pittsburgh International Airport (1992, Tasso Katselas Associates; bordering PA 60), and several downtown skyscrapers, including PPG (AL24), Dominion (AL10), Fifth Avenue Place (AL8), Oxford Centre (AL3), and One Mellon Bank Center (AL19).

Renaissance II also expanded into the neighborhoods, where Main Street and preservation programs worked to encourage contextualism and infill rather than urban expansion—much of which was sprawl by that point. Suddenly Pittsburgh found itself with revitalized neighborhoods, a host of recycled buildings: Heinz Hall (AL11), Benedum Center (AL31), The Pennsylvanian (AL16), the Mattress Factory (AL77), Andy Warhol Museum (AL67), a new wave of downtown skyscrapers, two sports stadiums (Heinz Field for the Steelers and PNC Park for the Pirates), and a convention center (AL15). Pittsburgh's city government remains committed to the integration of its new developments in Squirrel Hill, South Side, and the Hill, with their preexisting old neighborhoods nearby; citizens groups try their best to keep city government to its promise. There have been some notable failures (the Waterfront mall in Homestead being the most prominent), but for the most part the new buildings blend well into old contexts. Prominent examples since the 1980s are Crawford Square (AL121) on the Hill, the South Side Works on E. Carson Street, and the Village of Shadyside.

It was only in the 1980s that small communities such as Monroeville, Southpointe, and Cranberry (the latter two in adjoining counties south and north of Pittsburgh) emerged with a character decisively detached—culturally and physically—from the old urban core.

Pittsburgh continues to be an important place for innovative architecture. Since 1993, when several local environmentally conscious nonprofit organizations united to open a branch of the Green Building Alliance in Pittsburgh, the city has embraced the ideals and philosophy of environmentally friendly building. As a place degraded by its industrial boom, Pittsburgh learned early and well that cleaning the environment deterred urban decay. With the help of local foundations and the enthusiastic cooperation of local cultural entities, green building techniques are becoming the norm in new building, as in the new David L. Lawrence Convention Center (AL15), and in additions to older buildings. Pittsburgh is consistently among the top three American cities for buildings with the Leadership in Energy and Environmental Design (LEED) rating. This city that was famous for embracing its smoky atmosphere, because it indicated that the citizenry was working, is now preaching the gospel of green building and clean air.

GOLDEN TRIANGLE

The 255-acre Golden Triangle is roughly comparable in shape to Lower Manhattan from its tip to Greenwich Village, and Pittsburgh's skyline creates an equally strong image. Although it has fewer skyscraper towers and their scale is less dramatic, the urban matrix is a good deal tighter, since the Golden Triangle is entirely isolated from the rest of the city by the sharp rise of the Bluff and the Hill and by the intrusive Crosstown Expressway (I-579)—an unsung legacy to Pittsburgh from New York City's Robert Moses.

Nature carved out this triangle where the Allegheny and Monongahela join the Ohio River, but geopolitics early on shaped it into a miniature city.

Bird's-eye-view lithograph of the Golden Triangle, Pittsburgh, by Otto Krebs, 1874.

In 1784, Pennsylvania obliged the descendents of William Penn to sell off their last holdings in the commonwealth, the so-called Manor of Pittsburgh among them. The rudimentary and illegal settlement around Fort Pitt lacked a coherent street plan, and was never platted into saleable lots, so the Penns asked George Woods and his teenage assistant Thomas Vickroy to lay out this triangular town in the spring of 1784. The Woods-Vickroy double-grid plan was more expedient than elegant, but it endures today as the sacred cow of Pittsburgh urbanism. Actually, only three projects have dared modify it: Gateway Center (AL7) from 1950 to 1968, PPG Place in 1979–1984 (AL24), and Oliver/PNC Plaza bounded by 5th, Liberty, and 6th avenues and Wood Street in 1968. Pittsburgh's downtown is so small and so walkable that the entire district functions as a well-preserved and cohesive mercantile exchange.

The nickname "Golden Triangle" was bestowed in the years of feverish industrial expansion following the Civil War. The Triangle's wealth is diminished now, but it still serves as headquarters for a significant grouping of Fortune 500 companies, and there are few American districts that can match its architectural riches. The Burke Building (AL25) is a learned essay in Greek Revival, Dollar Savings Bank (AL27) in Italianate, H. H. Richardson's Allegheny Courthouse and Jail (AL1) the unparalleled exemplar in Romanesque Revival, a clutch of churches sings the rhapsody of Gothic Revival, and whole blocks of Grant Street and 4th Avenue shout the excesses of Beaux-Arts. There are varieties of modernism, too: superb Art Deco interiors in the Koppers Building (AL18) and the William Penn Hotel (AL20); the post–World War II classics of Gateway Center (AL7); and worthy contemporary designs in the new ALCOA (AL66), the David L. Lawrence Convention Center (AL15), and the CAPA school (AL14). The two strongest impulses in the current Golden Triangle are a reemphasis on the rivers, which gave the city birth, and a push to convert unneeded commercial and industrial space to housing. Downtown Pittsburgh is finally getting what it has most lacked in the past half century: permanent residents.

AL1 Allegheny County Courthouse and Jail

1883–1888, Henry Hobson Richardson. 436 Grant St.

Along with Trinity Church in Boston, this complex must be accounted as the masterpiece of Richardson's standing works; it is also the second most frequently imitated building in the United States after Independence Hall. The building was pivotal for Pittsburgh. Before the courthouse, Pittsburgh had not a single monumental building, nor did it have a proper downtown, since its main streets were given over to industry. With the construction of the courthouse, everything changed. Grant Street was edged with palatial skyscrapers, industry cleared out of the downtown, and Pittsburgh's citizens had, at last, a model of great architecture on a grand scale that private patrons like Carnegie, Frick, Heinz, and Westinghouse could emulate when they considered designs for their offices, factories, and charitable benefactions. Judge Thomas Mellon was alone in protesting the extravagance of the new courthouse.

After the Greek Revival Courthouse—a decent but provincial building—burned in 1882, the Allegheny County commissioners planned for the most modern of government buildings. They selected their architect with equal care. The short list included two prominent westerners (William W. Boyington of

AL1 ALLEGHENY COUNTY COURTHOUSE AND JAIL, east towers and courtyard

Chicago and Elijah E. Myers of Detroit), two prominent easterners (John Ord of Philadelphia and George Post of New York City, who ceded his place to Richardson at the last moment), and Pittsburgh architect Andrew Peebles, who failed to exhibit his drawings by the deadline of December 1883.

Richardson took the lead from the first, with elaborate photolithographs showing the proposed building in the smoky setting of downtown Pittsburgh. The design appropriated medieval sources on the outside: Salamanca Cathedral's detailing for the front tower; Venice's campanile for those at the rear; cornice from Notre-Dame in Paris; the Bridge of Sighs from Venice; basic hollow-rectangle massing from the Palazzo Farnese in Rome; and the four miniature towers a copy of his own work for Sever Hall at Harvard University. Inside, the building showed the best of the early Beaux-Arts methodology of French architects J.-N.-L. Durand and Henri Labrouste: superb circulation; inventive and economical use of space; natural illumination flooding in from the courtyard and the street; maximum efficiency for judges, juries, lawyers, and police; and even decent accommodation for the accused. The "newer" Beaux-Arts thinking was present as well, evident in the dramatic main staircase that recalls the one at Charles Garnier's Opera in Paris, and in the courtrooms that originally were

of operatic sumptuousness. Courtroom 321 was stunningly restored by UDA Architects in 1987, spurred on by architectural historian Lu Donnelly and financed by the lawyers of Allegheny County. The jail was converted to courtrooms and offices for the county's family courts by IKM Architects in 2000.

Richardson's strength as a designer is also evident in the courtyard. Here he dropped all allusion to history and worked in the pure rhythmic abstraction of his walls of Massachusetts granite. It was perhaps the first design for a public building in the nation that did not draw from any one specific historical source. When this courtyard facade design was turned to street facade for his Marshall Field Wholesale Store (1885–1887) in Chicago, it had an impact on American design for decades.

Richardson also considered the relationship between the courthouse and jail with Pittsburgh's downtown. The front tower acts like a compass, with the sun lighting up first its east face (toward the Hill and Oakland), then its south face (toward South Side), and, finally, its west face (Grant Street, but darkened now by the Frick Building), as though it were a sort of civic cathedral for the citizenry. The configuration of the long sides, with their brooding arches flanked by tiny towers, almost surely comes from Roman city gates: to enter the Courthouse is to enter the city in microcosm.

Though critical reaction has always fixated on the more dramatic jail, which now houses supplementary courtrooms, it is in the courthouse that one sees best Richardson's genius for providing not only the required functions but also fulfilling the client's longing for an image.

AL2 City-County Building

1915–1917, Edward B. Lee and Palmer, Hornbostel and Jones. 414 Grant St.

The building serves as Pittsburgh's city hall and accommodates additional courtrooms for the county. The detailing appears to be by Edward Lee, who won the competition for the City-County Building in 1914, and here used a modern interpretation of classicism, while the parti almost certainly came from Henry Hornbostel. He turned away from the most obvious elements of Richardson's court-

AL2 CITY-COUNTY BUILDING

house—the elaborate towers, projecting and receding pavilions, and extravagant pointed roof—to craft a simple hollow-rectangle plan and nine-story granite elevation that speaks as much the language of business as the rhetoric of government. Decorative touches at the City-County Building are limited to the high triple-arched portico, the Doric colonnade above it, and the barrel-vaulted interior galleria. This leads from an entrance loggia with Guastavino tiled vaults and cuts axially through the light-court. It is one of the most joyous spaces of the whole downtown: fifty-feet high and four times as long, flooded with light from all four sides and glistening with bronze columns.

AL3 Oxford Centre

1983, Hellmuth, Obata, Kassabaum (HOK).
301 Grant St.

This mixed-use development accommodates a retail atrium at street level, with an adjoining parking garage, social club, and athletic center. Over this base sit four interlocking octagons paneled in silver-painted aluminum and glass, reaching a height of forty-six stories. The stylistic flair of Oxford Centre finds no specific counterpart among the staid older buildings of Grant Street, but the geometric clarity of the octagonal towers is analogous to the more sober buildings, and the generous outlay of public space at the base makes Oxford the best stylistic "good neighbor" among all the post–World War II buildings downtown.

AL4 Smithfield Street Bridge

1880–1883, Gustav Lindenthal. Smithfield St.
and the Monongahela River

This, the oldest of Pittsburgh's extant bridges, is the third at this site. The first on this site and in Pittsburgh was the covered wooden Monongahela Bridge of 1818 built by Lewis Wernwag to replace a ferry crossing, four years after he had completed an unparalleled 340-foot single-span timber bridge in Philadelphia. Destroyed in the Great Fire of 1845, it was replaced by John A. Roebling's Monongahela Suspension Bridge. When traffic loads reduced its stability a generation later, this second bridge was torn down.

Construction of the present bridge began in 1880 under Charles Davis. Only the sandstone piers of his design were erected when he was replaced by Gustav Lindenthal, who used the piers to carry a combination of an arch and a suspension bridge. This lenticular truss, which resembles a double convex lens seen on edge, is typical of design and engineering of the era, using small pieces that were easily manufactured, assembled, and transported to the site. There are two 360-foot spans, for a total length of 1,185 feet with approach spans. As one of the first primarily steel highway bridges in the United States, Smithfield fittingly marked both the transition of bridge materials from wrought iron to steel and the coming of age of Pittsburgh's steel industry.

In 1889, two trusses were added parallel to the original ones to accommodate horsecars. These were moved to widen the bridge for electric streetcars in 1911, which required replacing Lindenthal's original portals with the Gothic Revival entranceways of 1915 by Stanley Roush that stand today. The current aluminum railings were installed in 1933 in conjunction with an aluminum deck—the first use of structural aluminum in a bridge. Over the years, the piers have been reinforced with concrete, and decorative lighting was added to the upper arches of the trusses, to make the bridge equally distinctive at night.

AL5 United Steelworkers Building (IBM Building)

1961–1963, Curtis and Davis. 60 Blvd. of the
Allies

This was one of the more closely watched construction projects of the 1960s, as it was a landmark in the return of the bearing wall that had done only intermittent structural service since the early steel-skeleton Chicago skyscrapers of the 1880s. The welded stainless steel web of these thirteen-story truss walls is constructed of three different strengths of steel, which progressively lighten as the building rises and the load lessens. This web is dual purpose, being both the structure and a sunscreen for the interior. With its floor, wall, and elevator loads all carried on a central core, the open interior, with spans up to fifty-four feet, enjoys the highest possible internal flexibility. Though the fussiness of the honeycomb exterior marks it as a postwar period piece, the structural innovation articulated here has become a standard alternative to the nonbearing curtain wall.

AL6 Fort Pitt and the Blockhouse

1759–1761, Captain Harry Gordon, engineer; 1953 rebuilt, Charles M. Stotz; 1764 Blockhouse. Point State Park

These remnants are the physical core of Pittsburgh and the metaphorical core of western Pennsylvania. In 1753, a twenty-one-year-old George Washington urged Virginia's Governor Robert Dinwiddie to erect a fort at the Forks of the Ohio. The next year, Virginia constructed Fort Prince George at the Point, but it was replaced almost immediately by the French Fort Duquesne, a four-bastioned

AL5 UNITED STEELWORKERS BUILDING (IBM BUILDING)

fort of which nothing remains today but a few artifacts and a modern stone outline showing the location. When the British dislodged the French in 1758, they put up a hasty replacement, but also began construction of an elaborate five-bastioned pentagonal fortress with earthen breastworks, thirteen-foot-high brick revetment walls, and stone quoins. The total perimeter of the fort and its escarpments was about half a mile; it was protected on the landward side by extra earthworks and a moat.

The fort barely withstood a siege during Pontiac's Rebellion of 1763, spurring Colonel Henry Bouquet to add two redoubts for sharpshooters; one survives as the pentagonal Blockhouse. While the Blockhouse—probably the oldest building in western Pennsylvania—survives, though almost totally rebuilt, the Fort itself was demolished in 1797, and its million bricks went into the town's new homes and warehouses. The fort site was overrun in 1852 by the tracks of the Pennsylvania Railroad, which, for a century, used the Point as a freight depot. When archeologists from the Carnegie Museum of Natural History ascertained in 1941 that the fort's foundations were still intact about ten feet below the industrial detritus, Charles Stotz undertook a meticulous, though partial, reconstruction of its primary walls and two bastions.

Access to Point State Park from Gateway Center is cut off by eight lanes of highway traffic. The park's main entrance has such a low clearance that architect Gordon Bunshaft of Skidmore, Owings and Merrill suggested a flattened arch portal to Charles Morse Stotz (1898–1985), who used post-tensioned concrete for its three ribbed arches. The inventor of that concrete technique, eminent French engineer Eugène Freyssinet came to Pittsburgh to personally supervise its construction. A wide pedestrian bridge at its center funnels visitors away from the low edges and carries them over a cobblestoned reflecting pool into the park.

AL7 Gateway Center

1950–1968. Bounded by Fort Duquesne Blvd., Stanwix St., Blvd. of the Allies, and Commonwealth Pl.

This development saved Pittsburgh as a post–World War II city. Together with the green

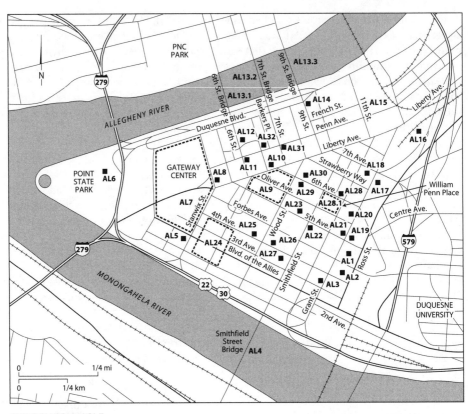

GOLDEN TRIANGLE

acreage of Point State Park, the office buildings of Gateway Center radically transformed the sooty downtown into an approximation of Le Corbusier's towers-in-a-park unbuilt scheme of the 1920s for Paris. The developer, the Equitable Life Assurance Society, had earlier financed Irwin Clavan's cruciform-tower housing estates in Manhattan. Here, modernist designer Clavan worked with traditionalists Otto Eggers and Daniel Higgins, who had completed John Russell Pope's National Gallery and the Jefferson Memorial in Washington, D.C. The towers of One, Two, and Three Gateway (Eggers and Higgins with Clavan) were drawn up in 1947 as the beginning of what was intended to be a forest of a dozen or more blocks for leading Pittsburgh corporations such as Jones and Laughlin Steel, PPG Industries, People's Gas, and Westinghouse. Only three of the chrome-alloyed steel uniform designs were realized, but these have proved surprisingly versatile and durable. Their maintenance has been impeccable, and the outdoor plazas function as the lunchtime

breathing space they were always intended to be. Interestingly, the more traditional Beaux-Arts-style planning of the walkways and fountain of Gateway Plaza are more appealing today than the informal gazebos and planters of Equitable Plaza on the opposite side of Liberty Avenue.

After this experiment in coordinated design, Gateway Plaza (1950–1953, Clarke and Rapuano, landscape architects) was filled out with independent designs for a hotel, apartment block, and problematic high-rise of professional offices atop a parking garage. The three-block Equitable Plaza (1955–1968, Simonds and Simonds, landscape architects) attempted no design uniformity, though there is a loose volumetric linkage between the Post-Gazette Building (a rehabilitation of a prewar structure), the Verizon Building (former Bell Telephone Building, 1958, Press C. Dowler and William C. Dowler), the former IBM Building (AL5), and the Pennsylvania State Office Building (1957, Altenhof and Bown). The distinguished International Style firm of

Harrison and Abramovitz took a conventional approach to the design of their Westinghouse Building of 1968. On a podium overlooking the Monongahela River, but still striking is the same firm's Four Gateway of 1960, with almost column-free floors served by an extruded—and still glistening—stainless steel service core.

AL8 Fifth Avenue Place

1985–1987, The Stubbins Associates, with Williams Trebilcock Whitehead. 120 5th Ave.

Fifth Avenue Place is surprisingly unsubtle for a design by much-respected postwar modernist Hugh Stubbins. Its overscaled windows, arbitrary jumps between glass- and granite-paneled outer skin, and uninspired crowning pinnacle are unavoidable blemishes in the first view any Pittsburgh visitor gets coming in from the airport. The adjacent old Joseph Horne department store at the northeast corner of Stanwix Street and Liberty Avenue (1892, 1900, W. S. Fraser; 1922, Peabody and Stearns of Boston) was remodeled as an office block in the mid-1990s and renamed Penn Avenue Place. The configuration left the Beaux-Arts exterior of the old store intact as a dignified visual anchor to the downtown, but much compromised by neighboring Fifth Avenue Place.

AL8 FIFTH AVENUE PLACE

AL9 PNC Plaza and 210 6th Avenue

1968–2008. Bounded by Wood St. and 5th, Liberty, and 6th aves.

There are four skyscrapers shoehorned onto this block that has been reconfigured to accommodate the latest: 3 PNC Plaza (2007–2009, Gensler, with Astorino Architects), a green design with two interlocking structures of differing height and surface treatment that contains a hotel, condominiums, and retail and office space in its twenty-three stories. Luckily Skidmore, Owings and Merrill (SOM) minimized the bulk of its 2 PNC Plaza (1974, Natalie DeBlois for SOM) by creating two skewed thirty-four-story, octagonal towers of reflective glass, which nicely complement the squared orientation of the adjacent thirty-story 1 PNC Plaza tower (1972, Welton Becket and Associates). DeBlois's participation made 2 PNC Plaza (formerly the Equibank Building) the world's largest designed by a woman at that time. The fourth skyscraper at 210 6th Avenue is the tallest (at thirty-nine stories) and was built first (1968, William Lescaze and Associates). While it has had a variety of owners over the years, the rectangular, wine-red high-rise has retained two colorful ceramic murals (neither of which is now visible), one by Pierre Soulages in the north lobby and the other by Virgil D. Cantini in the south lobby.

AL10 Dominion Tower (Consolidated Natural Gas Tower)

1987, William Pedersen for Kohn Pedersen Fox Associates. 625 Liberty Ave.

Dominion Tower is an example of the corporate lavishness of the 1980s by a favored architectural firm of that decade. Like their Cincinnati headquarters for Procter and Gamble, Dominion is a richly detailed skyscraper carefully tailored to the shapes and sizes of neighboring buildings. An inviting plaza and pedestrian arcade outside and opulent use of traditional luxury materials inside give Dominion both distinctive character and human scale. These qualities make Dominion superior to Pittsburgh's other 1980s skyscrapers, particularly the unyielding coldness of PPG Place (AL24) a few blocks away.

Clad in panels of brown and pink granite, this thirty-two-story tower is meant to be seen as much from a distance as close-up. At

AL10 DOMINION TOWER (CONSOLIDATED NATURAL GAS TOWER)

AL12 RENAISSANCE PITTSBURGH HOTEL (FULTON BUILDING)

a distance, its most obvious feature is a barrel-vaulted roof framed by arched steel trusses that mimic the nearby Sixteenth Street Bridge (AL80) over the Allegheny River. Closer, Dominion's complex massing and adroitly placed stone cornices align its bulk with the twenty-story Midtown Towers (former Keenan Build-

ing, 1907, Thomas Hannah) to the north. On its south side, the tower scales down to a four-story segment that keeps it from overwhelming Heinz Hall (AL11) and an adjacent small park. The visual deference to Heinz Hall is appropriate, since Dominion stands on land owned by a Heinz foundation; its land rent supports the Pittsburgh Cultural Trust as the current overseer of the neighborhood.

AL11 Heinz Hall (Penn Theater)

1927, C. W. Rapp and George Rapp; 1971 restored, Stotz, Hess, MacLachlan and Fosner. 600 Penn Ave.

Marcus Loew's Penn Theater, which opened as the "Temple of the Cinema," has the mixture of French Baroque and Rococo features that were a hallmark of movie-theater specialists Rapp and Rapp of Chicago. The Penn was one of the first old cinema palaces in the nation to find new life as a concert hall. H. J. Heinz II personally financed its revival, using his own favorite hall, the Vienna Opera, as guide. Of particular note is the massive four-story arched window with decorative cartouche. The Heinz endowments added the garden plaza next door as an intermission space in summer.

AL12 Renaissance Pittsburgh Hotel (Fulton Building)

1906, Grosvenor Atterbury; 2000–2001, J. G. Johnson Architects, with CelliFlynnBrennan Architects and Planners. 107 6th St.

This is the sole survivor of a set of downtown skyscrapers erected by Henry Phipps, the most socially minded of Carnegie's partners, for both profit and social betterment. Grosvenor Atterbury, creator of innovative housing designs in Forest Hills, New York, was as progressive as his patron, although in Pittsburgh only this commercial tower (now a 300-room hotel) survives, and not his Pittsburgh bath houses, swimming pools, or subsidized housing. The Fulton's trademark was its seven-story-high arch fronting the Allegheny, which twenty years later also became the leitmotif for the neighboring Roberto Clemente Bridge (AL13.1). That visual homage to the riverfront—all too rare in Pittsburgh—was made complete around 1990, when trompe l'oeil painter Richard Haas added a bold mural about steelmaking on the bare riverfront facade of the Byham (formerly Gayety) Theater (101 6th Street) of 1903.

AL13 Three Sisters Bridges

1925–1928, Vernon Covell, and others, engineers; Stanley L. Roush, architect. 6th, 7th, and 9th sts. and the Allegheny River

The only coordinated set in town, these suspension bridges are particularly pleasing aesthetically and reminders that Pittsburgh played a major role in the history of bridge building. The "Three Sisters" bridges, as they are popularly known, were conceived in 1925 jointly by Pittsburgh's Civic Arts Commission and the Allegheny County Bureau of Bridges when the War Department required higher clearance on the river. These are self-anchored suspension bridges: the anchors to the suspension chains are not buried in the earth but are visible as the box girders separating the roadway from the sidewalks. The resulting structures are light and lyrical, among the best marriages of art and engineering in the country. Their names record three Pittsburghers who were creative in very different fields: baseball (Roberto Clemente Bridge [Sixth Street Bridge], AL13.1), art (Andy Warhol Bridge [Seventh Street Bridge], AL13.2), and ecology (Rachel Carson Bridge [Ninth Street Bridge], AL13.3).

AL14 Pittsburgh High School for the Creative and Performing Arts (CAPA)

2003, MacLachlan, Cornelius and Filoni. 111 9th St.

Among the brightest of recent buildings designed with Pittsburgh's riverfronts in mind is this six-story half-traditional, half-outrageous, cornerstone of the city's downtown cultural district. CAPA trains about 500 students each year. Partner in charge Albert Filoni and project architect Ken Lee produced a building that acknowledges the urban context stylistically and chromatically, and then expands on it. The long 9th Street facade takes its cue from the old brick office building next door (1915, Charles Bickel), six stories of which have also been appropriated for the new school. The shorter riverfront facade incorporates a gigantic electronic screen that presents student work and a curved six-floor-high glass

AL14 PITTSBURGH HIGH SCHOOL FOR THE CREATIVE AND PERFORMING ARTS (CAPA)

wall enlivened with whimsical polychromy. The wall reflects the contemporary ALCOA center (AL66) on the opposite bank of the Allegheny.

CAPA's program was complex: laboratories, a 400-seat proscenium theater, rehearsal space, shops, and studios for dance, painting, and sculpture classes, all of which had to fit within a 175,000-square-foot structure. In addition, CAPA needed classrooms for regular academic subjects. Filoni embraced this programmatic diversity in his loose amalgam of microfacade elements, which he quilted from white-glazed block, red brick, and glass, into a strikingly polyphonic and intentionally jarring exterior.

AL15 David L. Lawrence Convention Center

2000–2003, Rafael Viñoly, with Burt Hill Kosar Rittelmann Associates. 1000 Fort Duquesne Blvd.

Pittsburgh was no more sensitive in its treatment of its riverfront than were most American cities: the rivers of interest were rivers of commerce, and the only banks Pittsburghers cared about were made of marble and housed vaults. That was true for an earlier Lawrence Convention Center from the 1980s, a forbidding box that entirely turned its back on the Allegheny River. Since then, Pittsburgh created several new buildings that embrace and accentuate their riverside sites. The most intriguing of these is Rafael Viñoly's glazed catenary curve, which echoes three neighboring suspension bridges and eagerly thrusts its way toward the Allegheny River. The roof held by fifteen cables allows for unimpeded

AL15 DAVID L. LAWRENCE CONVENTION CENTER

AL16 THE PENNSYLVANIAN APARTMENTS (PENNSYLVANIA STATION, UNION STATION), rotunda

AL17 USX TOWER (UNITED STATES STEEL BUILDING)

space inside and draws in cooler river air at third-floor level, which is circulated through natural convection. Hot air rises and exits through a clerestory. Flag-topped masts externally express the building's structural tensions. The building earned a gold rating from the U.S. Green Council for site selection and use of nontoxic and recycled building materials.

Approximately half this complex is a parking garage, separated from the exhibition space by 10th Street, which still carries traffic through an arcade in the building. The upper part of the 10th Street arcade becomes a festive observation deck overlooking the river; the lower part is a ramp leading down to the water itself. The complex seems to reflect an awareness of its role as a historic nexus in American transportation history: here John A. Roebling's suspended aqueduct carried the barges of the old Pennsylvania Canal into the city 150 years before, and the main rail line between New

York and Chicago still snakes around the 11th Street end of the new building.

AL16 The Pennsylvanian Apartments (Pennsylvania Station, Union Station)

1898–1902, Daniel H. Burnham and Co. 1100 Liberty Ave.

The northern apex to the Golden Triangle had already served as terminus of the Pennsylvania Canal and home to three successive railroad stations when Alexander Cassatt commissioned Daniel Burnham for this stirring rail portal to Pittsburgh. It was Cassatt, a native Pittsburgher and brother of impressionist painter Mary Cassatt, who oversaw Burnham's later Union Station in Washington, D.C., and McKim, Mead and White's Pennsylvania Station in New York City. In 1898, Burnham was still riding his national fame as chief architect of the World's Columbian Exposition of 1893 in Chicago. In Pittsburgh he was also known for replacing the exposition buildings at the Point (1901, demolished). Among Burnham's surviving Pittsburgh buildings are the Engineers' Society of Western Pennsylvania (the original Union Trust Building, 1898; 337 4th Avenue), the Frick Building and Frick Annex (1902; 437 Grant Street), the Highland Building (1910; 121 S. Highland Avenue), and the Oliver Building (1910; 535 Smithfield Street) on Mellon Square.

At the last minute, what had been planned as a four-story building was expanded into a twelve-story tower. The impetus for the design change probably came from Cassatt, but one suspects also the hand of Henry Clay Frick, who was about to become the Pennsylvania Railroad's largest stockholder. The basic parti of the shelved plan later resurfaced as the key element in Burnham's Washington station. Here the tower is fronted by an elegant domed cab shelter, whose pendentive ornaments and the spelling as "Pittsburg" recall the twenty-year period (1891–1911) when Pittsburgh's name was spelled without a final "h."

Burnham manipulated standard Beaux-Arts stylistic devices for the main building and the rotunda, but employed them with restraint so as not to compromise function. The brown brick and terra-cotta facade has a smooth, even texture. The main block sits on a high basement, the better to provide more bulk for its vista down Liberty Avenue.

Curved entrance ramps give extra majesty to the low arches of the rotunda, which is often accounted the most captivating architectural element in Pittsburgh.

Preservation of so large and functionally specific a building was not easy. The Pennsylvania Railroad intended to tear down the station in 1966 as part of its 148-acre Penn Park redevelopment; then four years later, the merged Pennsylvania and New York Central railroads declared bankruptcy, imperiling the terminal a second time. The rotunda and office block now house a large apartment complex, while rail passengers catch their trains from a modest depot at the rear.

AL17 USX Tower (United States Steel Building)

1967–1971, Harrison and Abramovitz, and Abbe Architects. 600 Grant St.

At 64 stories and 841 feet, the tallest structure in downtown Pittsburgh, the USX Tower is symbolic of the city both in its triangular shape and its structural innovations in steel. The exterior features eighteen exposed vertical steel columns, each set three feet outside the curtain wall, such that columns and curtain wall connect at every third floor. The columns of Cor-Ten steel are self-oxidizing, hence unable to rust further. Every column circulates coolant inside, so should the tower ever be engulfed in flames, it would keep cool for four hours before surrendering to the heat.

AL18 Koppers Building

1927–1929, Graham, Anderson, Probst and White. 436 7th Ave.

The relocation of the Pennsylvania Railroad freight yards in 1927 gave new life to what for generations had been the blighted corner of Grant Street and 7th Avenue. In the space of five years, Andrew Mellon masterminded the construction of four key buildings at the corner: Koppers; the Art Deco building for the Pittsburgh branch of the Federal Reserve Bank of Cleveland (1930–1931, Walker and Weeks with Hornbostel and Wood); and the forty-four-story Gulf Building (1930–1932) by Trowbridge and Livingston, who also designed the massive U.S. Post Office and Federal Courthouse (1930–1934) on the remaining corner of the block.

Mellon could pull off this pharaonic-scaled patronage because he and his brother, R. B. Mellon, were chief shareholders in Koppers and Gulf, while he was at the same time secretary of the Treasury. To keep everything securely in the family, Mellon used his nephew Edward Purcell Mellon (1875–1953) as supervising architect for the Koppers Building and the family's Mellon-Stuart construction firm to build it. Mellon was probably also remembering the architectural ambitions of his friend Henry Clay Frick, who in the previous decade, had begun to line Grant Street with office towers. Even the choice of the architects was meaningful: they were the direct successors to Daniel Burnham, Frick's favorite architect.

But times had changed since Frick was building. In 1927, it was Art Deco and not Beaux-Arts that was the reigning style, so Koppers took on an appropriately streamlined image. Rising thirty-five stories with two setbacks, the first three stories of Koppers are polished gray granite, while the tower is Indiana limestone. Plain gray ribs exaggerate the building's height, and the spandrels sparkle with low-relief geometric designs. The final luster comes from a Chateauesque copper roof that is spotlighted at night in a dramatic green glow. The interior, too, is a jewel. The three-story lobby has cream-colored Italian marble walls veined in pale brown with a greenish tint, and a parquet floor in pink and gray Tennessee marble. A flowerlike design in cast bronze unifies elevator doors, directory panels, clocks, and balcony railings throughout the building. In the manner of the times, the cast-bronze mailbox is a miniature of the building, roof and all.

AL19 One Mellon Bank Center (Dravo Building)

1983, Welton Beckett Associates. 500 Grant St.

This was an early use of a framed steel tube structure, which uses the outer walls to reduce lateral sway. This was achieved by bolting one-quarter-inch-thick steel plates, one bay wide and three stories high, directly to the building's steel frame. Consequently, the interior columns could be relatively small and far apart, which gained the fifty-four-story tower more than eighteen inches around the

perimeter of its core; this translated into an impressive additional 1.7 million square feet of rentable space. Project director David Beer declared that the primary basis for his design was to contextualize it with the preexisting architecture of Grant Street, above all, Richardson's adjacent courthouse (AL1). This choice resulted in a melange of elements from the Courthouse, the neighboring Frick Building (1902, Daniel H. Burnham and Company; 437 Grant St.), the Union Trust (AL21), and the USX Tower (AL17). The intention proved finer than the result, but there was one definite improvement over the predecessor building: the new tower was canted far back from Grant Street, giving Pittsburgh its best view of the Courthouse since the Frick Building obscured it.

AL20 Omni William Penn Hotel

1914–1916, Janssen and Abbott; 1928–1929, Janssen and Cocken, and Joseph Urban. 530 William Penn Pl.

Henry Clay Frick conceived of this structure (though he later withdrew from its group of promoters) as the third of three in his private row along Grant Street, which at the time was a much less elegant thoroughfare than it is today. The first part of the hotel to open was the half that overlooks what is now Mellon Square (AL28.1); a decade would pass before Benno Janssen returned to add the Grant Street facade. Frick intended the William Penn Hotel to compete with the Plaza in New York City, which it does in technology if not in grandeur. The exterior cladding is brick (a colonial reference to William Penn, perhaps), while Renaissance Revival prevails inside in three handsome public spaces: the Terrace restaurant, Palm Court Lobby, and Grand Ballroom.

The lobby, a multitiered space with conversational seating groups enclosed in a deep arcade, is especially satisfying. The star of the Grant Street annex is the Urban Room, whose punning name recalls its author, renowned Art-Deco theater and set designer Joseph Urban. The sole survivor of a series of Urban Rooms that existed in the Congress Hotel in Chicago and the Bossert Hotel in Brooklyn, Pittsburgh's Urban Room is starkly different from the rest of the hotel. Its walls are pan-

AL21 TWO MELLON BANK CENTER (UNION TRUST BUILDING)

eled in strips of brass-bound black glass, leading upward to an elliptical pseudo-Persian ceiling mural of Urban's own design. Urban called the design "modernistic but gay," an apt summation for this Art Deco masterpiece.

AL21 Two Mellon Bank Center (Union Trust Building)

1915–1917, Frederick J. Osterling, with Pierre A. Liesch. 501 Grant St.

This structure carries downtown's most adventuresome skyline, with two ornate chapel-like structures crowning its elaborate Flemish Gothic roof. Urban legend holds that these are chapels, even though they are nothing more than penthouse offices and housing for mechanical services. Other legends insist that the Catholic Church obliged Henry Clay Frick to erect these pseudochapels as a remembrance of old St. Paul Cathedral, which had once stood on the site. The more prosaic probability is that the design conformed to the pattern of New York City's then new Woolworth Building, which had repopularized the Gothic Revival style and a terra-cotta skin. The design had two unexpected godfathers: art dealer Joseph Duveen (later Lord Duveen), Frick's art adviser, and the Luxembourg-born Pierre Liesch, Frederick Osterling's draftsman, who

worked in Pittsburgh for about a decade. For some years Liesch and Osterling battled in court over fees and artistic paternity of the design. Osterling advanced his claim through the styling of his studio building of 1917 at 228 Isabella Street, which still stands as a miniaturized Union Trust facade.

The interior is no disappointment: four broad corridors, basically interior streets, lead to a brilliant eleven-story central lightwell. Until 1923, these corridors were open to the fourth floor as a shopping arcade. Shutting down the arcade was not merely an aesthetic loss, it reduced the attractiveness of downtown Pittsburgh as a retail center and abetted the fragmentation of the city into zones of specialized function—something Pittsburgh planners have been fighting against ever since.

AL22 Macy's Department Store (Kaufmann's Department Store)

1898, Charles Bickel; 1913 addition, Janssen and Abbott. 400 5th Ave.

Opened in 1871 as a tailoring shop on the South Side by four immigrant brothers who had graduated from peddling, Kaufmann's Department Store found itself by 1885 at the best corner downtown, Smithfield Street and 5th Avenue, where it erected a replica of the Statue of Liberty. The building that stands now as the south half of the block-long Macy's store (since 2007), at Smithfield and Forbes Avenue, is a wing added in 1898 that combines Classical Revival, Romanesque Revival, and Chicago School motifs. In 1913, Edgar Kaufmann, of the second generation, tore down the original 1885 store on the north half of the block and commissioned its replacement: this delicate thirteen-story, white terra-cotta extension from Benno Janssen. In those same years, the store began leasing the wooded property southeast of Pittsburgh that would later host Kaufmann's weekend house, Fallingwater.

Kaufmann's brilliance as a retailer derived in large part from his commercial exploitation of architectural and technical innovation. Janssen and Cocken's ground floor redecoration of the store in 1930 (Kaufmann had demurred on a more radical Art Deco remake from New York's Joseph Urban) used state-of-the-art technology and contemporary design to create what architectural critics and retailing connoisseurs in the 1930s called the most beautiful store in the world. Along with his commission of Fallingwater from Frank Lloyd Wright in 1934, Kaufmann employed him to design his tenth-floor private office within the store. This was acclaimed as perhaps the most noble achievement ever rendered out of plywood, but following Kaufmann's death in 1955, the office was given to the Victoria and Albert Museum in London in 1974. The ground floor has not fared well, though Art Deco elements survive.

AL23 Park Building

1896, George B. Post. 355 5th Ave.

By the 1890s, brothers David E. and William G. Park had brought their father's Black Diamond Steel Works (c. 1870–1890; 2949 Smallman Street with remnants from 28th to 32nd streets) to world renown in specialty steel, and they sought to diversify their investments. Their goal was to put up Pittsburgh's most imposing office block, for which they chose the busiest corner in the city, opposite the Mellon brothers' bank and the Kaufmann brothers' giant retail store. This was the fourth steel-skeleton tower in Pittsburgh, and at fifteen stories, significantly taller than the Carnegie Building of a few years before. Today, it survives as the only downtown skyscraper of the nineteenth century. New York architect George B. Post was, at the time, the preeminent designer of commercial buildings within the Beaux-Arts style. The novelty of the Park Building has always been the thirty telemones, or atlases, that bear the top cornice on their shoulders. The overall design remains an excellent material lesson in early skyscraper packaging influenced by New York City's skyscrapers (as opposed to those of Chicago), which were reluctant to sacrifice decoration to the demands of modern function and utility.

AL24 PPG Place

1979–1984, Johnson and Burgee. 1 PPG Pl.

The ultimate glass house, PPG Place is both billboard and headquarters for a company founded almost on the same spot a century before as Pittsburgh Plate Glass. Today, it is one of the largest glass and chemical manufacturing companies in the world. Occupying five acres carved out of the heart of the eighteenth-century street grid of downtown Pittsburgh, PPG Place is the chief icon among the city's Renaissance II skyscrapers from the 1980s. Profusely pinnacled (231 in all, many glowing at night) and sheathed in one million square feet of PPG's own neutral silver Solarban 550 clear glass, the forty-four-story main tower and its five lower siblings give life— albeit rather stiffly—to Philip Johnson's vision of a glazed Place des Vosges of Paris. The plaza, laid out around an obelisk, is minimalist and austere, in stark contrast to the architectural hodgepodge of neighboring Market Square, an authentic if overrestored relic of the city plan of 1784.

The central tower is entered through a fifty-foot-high lobby paneled entirely in burgundy-colored glass. The glass motif is carried into the elevator cars, which are sheathed in crackled glass. Behind the tower, toward Stanwix Street, stands a large but underused Wintergarden that continues the pointed-arch motif of the surrounding arcades and reaches a height of forty feet, roughly scaled to match the height of the Gothic Revival St. Mary of Mercy Church (1936, William Hutchins) across 3rd Avenue.

Gothic veneer aside, PPG Place is a standard International Style product. Nonetheless it has a contextual quality much appreciated by Pittsburghers, since it echoes both Richardson's courthouse tower (AL1) a few blocks away on Grant Street and the Cathedral of Learning at the University of Pittsburgh (AL38), some two miles to the east. Citizens use PPG Place for outdoor concerts and the classic Pittsburgh event: Steeler pregame rallies. The open space was recently given some year-round excitement with an ice-skating rink that converts to a playful and user-friendly multiheaded fountain during warmer weather.

AL25 Burke Building

1836, John Chislett. 209 4th Ave.

A survivor as hardy as the Blockhouse next to Fort Pitt (AL6), the Burke Building must have always been one of the most handsome buildings downtown. Built of cream-toned

AL24 PPG PLACE

sandstone—luxurious for an office building—its Greek Revival design is taut and well proportioned. This five-bay, three-story pedimented structure, with its striking Doric-columned entrance, survived the onslaught of late-nineteenth-century revivals, escaped the ravages of the Great Fire of 1845 by not more than half a block, and, finally, has emerged as a surprisingly strong outbuilding to the PPG Place complex that engulfed it in the 1980s. In the 1990s, it was restored using renewable resources as the headquarters of the Western Pennsylvania Conservancy, which has since moved to 800 Waterfront Drive, thus opening a new chapter in the Burke Building's long history.

AL26 Industrial Bank

1903, Charles M. Bartberger. 333 4th Ave.

This is the most exuberant of the three bank buildings near the corner of 4th Avenue and Smithfield Street. Next door at 337 4th Av-

enue stands Daniel Burnham's coldly classical Union Trust of 1898, built for Henry Clay Frick. Beyond, at 341 4th Avenue, stands James Steen's overly fussy Fidelity Trust (1888–1889) in Richardsonian Romanesque.

German-trained Charles M. Bartberger (1850–1939) inherited his architectural practice from his father, Charles F. Bartberger, and passed it on to his son Edward. The three generations practiced architecture in Pittsburgh for well over a century (1845–1956). This bank is one of the most confident handlings of Beaux-Arts classicism in the city. Its facade consists of a huge granite arch whose voussoirs align with sharply cleft breaks in the horizontal coursing. Above, the windows are set in a dwarf mezzanine.

The two blocks of 4th Avenue between Market and Smithfield streets constitute the core of Pittsburgh's former financial district, once second in capital only to Wall Street. Fourth Avenue began life in the Woods-Vickroy plan of 1784, but gained importance only in the

AL28 REGIONAL ENTERPRISE TOWER (ALCOA)

1830s, when the Bank of Pittsburgh and the speculative Burke Building (AL25) located here. Other banks followed suit after the fire of 1845 and the financial panic of 1873. Imposing structures by George Post and Frank Furness are gone, but Dollar Savings Bank (AL27) remains. By the turn of the century, Pittsburgh's oil and stock exchanges and the headquarters of twenty bank and trust companies lined 4th Avenue. Eventually, bank mergers and the lack of room for growth forced many of the financial institutions to move. Today the dominant architectural style on the street is still Beaux-Arts, either in low-rise banking houses or high-rise office towers.

AL27 Dollar Savings Bank

1868–1871, Isaac Hobbs and Sons; 1906 wings. 348 4th Ave.

An endearing if hyperkinetic piece of Italianate froth by a major Philadelphia designer and architectural publisher, Dollar Savings Bank is an effective red sandstone facade superbly conserved. Although downtown Pittsburgh once had similar banks at every corner, today there is nothing like it in town. On what was formerly a restricted site, Isaac Hobbs set pairs of overscaled Corinthian columns to support

a high entablature of dramatically projecting stone brackets. The result is a facade that is virtually all detail and almost no wall.

AL28 Regional Enterprise Tower (ALCOA)

1953, Harrison and Abramovitz, with Altenhof and Bown. 425 6th Ave.

AL28.1 Mellon Square

1955, Mitchell and Ritchey; Simonds and Simonds, landscape architects

The ALCOA (Aluminum Company of America) building is one of the architectural icons of post–World War II America. The integration of windows within their spandrels, the simplicity of bolting the aluminum panels on their frames, the ease of cleaning the swivel windows, and the broad internal corridors that served as impromptu conference centers were all innovations that were supposed to forever change the art of building skyscrapers. Instead, ALCOA's influence was muted, and aluminum-clad office towers remain a rarity. The ALCOA corporation itself left the building in 1998 for a low-rise of a radically different configuration on the Allegheny shore (AL66). The thirty-story tower and its striking glass-walled entrance pavilion now house a consortium of city and regional planning agencies that hope to emulate the postwar synergy of Pittsburgh's Renaissance I.

Mellon Square was conceived to highlight ALCOA, to the north, and Mellon Bank, to the south, as two crown jewels of the Mellon empire. It still bespeaks the community spiritedness of cousins Paul and Richard King Mellon, who financed the project, and the ingenuity of the architects and landscape designers in consolidating a parking garage, fringe of retail stores, cascading fountain, and ample space for lunchtime patrons.

AL29 Trinity Cathedral and Graveyard, and First Presbyterian Church

1872 Trinity, Gordon W. Lloyd; 1905 First Presbyterian, Theophilus P. Chandler Jr. 328 and 320 6th Ave.

In 1787, the Penn family donated four lots on 6th Avenue for the congregations of Pittsburgh. Though several different churches have been constructed on the plot, an Episcopalian and a Presbyterian congregation worship on the site to the present day. The Episcopal congregation's first church, an octagonal structure, was at 6th and Liberty avenues. The second church, designed in 1824 by John H. Hopkins, the congregation's rector, was one of the earliest Gothic Revival churches on the continent, and the first in Pittsburgh. That structure was razed in 1869 to allow for the construction of the present stone building by English-born and trained, but Detroit-based, architect Gordon W. Lloyd (1832–1905). Lloyd's design derived from early-fourteenth-century English Decorated Gothic precedents. Glass from the second church was incorporated into this structure, although some was replaced after a fire in 1969. Most of the rib-vaulted interior was undamaged. A notable interior addition is the pulpit of 1922 by Bertram G. Goodhue. In 1927, the church was elevated to cathedral status and became the seat of the Pittsburgh Diocese.

First Presbyterian Church, though more recent, has a longer history on the site. The Presbyterians erected a brick structure in 1805, which was rebuilt in 1813 by Benjamin H. Latrobe during his Pittsburgh stay. That structure was replaced in 1851–1853 to a design by Charles F. Bartberger, which was in turn razed when the congregation sold the land for the construction of the Daniel Burnham–designed McCreery Department Store in 1904 (now 300 6th Avenue). The present church, a hybrid of thirteenth- and fourteenth-century English Gothic, clothes a single large meeting hall designed for preaching. First Presbyterian's thirteen Tiffany windows are its glory, while the glory of Trinity is the old graveyard, with tombs from the eighteenth century.

AL30 Duquesne Club

1889, Longfellow, Alden and Harlow; 1903, Alden and Harlow; 1931, Janssen and Cocken. 325 6th Ave.

Founded in 1873 and located on this site since 1879, the Duquesne Club's architectural setting is appropriate to its fame as the most influential business club in the region. Richardsonian Romanesque was a natural choice in the year following the opening of Richardson's nearby courthouse (AL1), as Longfellow and Alden had apprenticed with

Richardson. This commission made them one of Pittsburgh's leading design firms for two decades. The brownstone facade combines Richardson's bold materials and motifs with a more conventional classicism, which became the firm's hallmark as it recast itself into the local equivalent of New York City's McKim, Mead and White, Alfred Harlow's previous employer.

AL31 Benedum Center for the Performing Arts (Stanley Theater)

1928, Hoffman and Henon; 1987 restoration and addition, MacLachlan, Cornelius and Filoni. 207 7th St.

The Pittsburgh Cultural Trust was born in the 1980s with the goal of weaning eight central blocks of downtown Pittsburgh from pornography to high culture. The blocks were demarcated by the Convention Center (AL15) and Liberty Center on the east, Gateway Center (AL7) on the west, the Allegheny riverfront on the north, and Liberty Avenue on the south. The success of this transformation was almost immediate in terms of infrastructure improvements (sidewalks, signage, and lighting), facade restoration, and the new audience that was attracted downtown. The area's two theaters—the Penn, now Heinz Hall (AL11), and this, the Stanley—had declined along with their surroundings.

The Stanley (now the Benedum), the third largest theater in the country when built, was renovated as a performance space for the Pittsburgh Opera, Pittsburgh Ballet, Civic Light Opera, and Dance Council. To accommodate these arts groups, a new six-story backstage was added, which also includes two rehearsal halls. The old Stanley's exterior of off-white terra-cotta and brick was restored to its original appearance.

AL32 Theater Square (incorporating the O'Reilly Theater)

1999, Michael Graves. 621 Penn Ave.

The Pittsburgh Cultural Trust purchased and renovated several older structures between Liberty Avenue and the Allegheny riverfront, but Theater Square is its main venture in new construction. Consisting of a theater and parking garage by Michael Graves (an office tower remains an unfunded dream for the moment), plus a small plaza designed by Louise Bourgeois and Daniel Kiley in collaboration with Graves, the complex sits opposite Benedum Center (AL31) and Heinz Hall (AL11). Within a few minutes' walk are the Harris Theater and the Byham Theater (see AL12), also projects of the trust. As the home of the Pittsburgh Public Theater, the O'Reilly is the key element in Theater Square. It features a thrust stage and seats 650 people on three levels. Externally, the theater is boldly articulated as a glass and concrete half cylinder at ground level and a half-barrel-vaulted rehearsal hall above. The garage acts as an eleven-story pylon of brick and precast concrete.

The innovative part of the complex is the park. Bourgeois designed a twenty-five-foot-tall free-form bronze volcano through which water courses in rivulets. Spectators rest on smooth eyeball-shaped granite benches in a grove of trees.

OAKLAND

The Oakland plateau consists of several hundred acres at a much higher elevation than the Golden Triangle and three miles east of it. Crowded now by the buildings of the University of Pittsburgh and its medical center, the plateau, part of a tract of several thousand acres that once stretched from Lawrenceville to Squirrel Hill, lay virtually fallow until 1890. The land belonged to a single absentee owner, London-based heiress Mary Schenley, who had inherited it from her two Revolutionary-era grandfathers, James O'Hara and George Croghan. Schenley's land was topographically erratic, with a steep hill to the north and two gullies—the St. Pierre Ravine and Junction Hollow—cutting it from the south. In 1890, Schenley gave about four hundred of her acres for the making of Schenley Park, but Andrew Carnegie siphoned off the best twenty acres for the new library that he proposed to build between the two gullies.

No other part of Pittsburgh needed such dramatic changes to its natural topography before it could be settled. Between 1897 and 1915, the city artificially banked up the picturesque Flagstaff Hill in Schenley Park, bridged Junction Hollow once to carry an elegant drive into the park and then bridged it a second time to carry Forbes Avenue from the expanded Carnegie Institute to another of Carnegie's major benefactions, the Carnegie Technical Schools, now Carnegie Mellon University (AL43). (When Schenley died in 1903, Carnegie was expediently named an executor to her estate.) The city obligingly filled in the St. Pierre Ravine to render Schenley Plaza a proper entrance to Carnegie's library (AL41); it also rerouted Bellefield Avenue to funnel visitors to Carnegie Museum's new main entrance.

If Carnegie provided the money, then local land speculator, realtor, and developer Franklin Felix Nicola (1860–1938) provided the inspired vision for Oakland (the name derives from the estate of glassmaker William Eichbaum, German for oak tree). Nicola, who also owned a lumber company, dreamed of building a fine residential area adjacent to a civic center. He either lured institutions to build in Oakland—the University of Pittsburgh being his biggest catch—or he invented them. The result, in an inspired partnership with

Paris-trained designer Henry Hornbostel, was block after block of one of the more harmonious City Beautiful environments in the nation.

The interiors of Oakland's grand institutional buildings provide special delights as well. Not to be missed are Phipps Conservatory (AL42); the Carnegie Library and museums (AL41); the University of Pittsburgh's Cathedral of Learning (AL38), Heinz Chapel (AL39), and the Frick Fine Arts Building (AL40); the Carnegie Mellon Research Institute (AL37) and College of Fine Arts (AL43); two excellent churches and a synagogue (AL36 and see AL34 and AL118); and the flamboyant Soldiers' and Sailors' Memorial Hall (AL33). The statuary, landscaping, and visual linkage among Oakland's monuments are of the same high quality as the interiors.

There is, inevitably, a downside to all this magnificence. Decades before Carnegie fixed his eyes on Schenley's land, Oakland had provided thousands of modest homes for the ironworkers in the nearby Eliza Furnaces of Jones and Laughlin. The grand institutions and the modest residential neighborhoods have historically clashed in many a pitched battle, with the common citizen almost always on the losing side. The worst of the excesses came with the University of Pittsburgh's medical center, which by any measure is now overcrowded and overbuilt. There has been some recent improvement in Oakland's livability. Schenley Plaza redeemed itself by converting a

Aerial view of Oakland, c. 1980. Since this photograph was taken, the Cathedral of Learning (AL38; *center*) has been cleaned and the adjacent parking lot transformed into Schenley Plaza, a five-acre park modeled after Bryant Park in New York City, with a carousel, lawn, and food kiosks.

mammoth parking lot into a lovely greensward, and bit by bit some hospitals are leaving Oakland: Children's has relocated to Lawrenceville and other research centers have moved to Shadyside and Bloomfield. "People's Oakland" (as one advocacy group calls itself) is finally asserting itself.

AL33 Soldiers' and Sailors' National Military Museum and Memorial Hall (Allegheny County Soldiers' and Sailors' Memorial)

1907–1910, Palmer and Hornbostel. 4141 5th Ave.

In 1903, in the largest real estate transaction in Pittsburgh history to that point, Cleveland-born Franklin Nicola purchased a 103-acre enclave at the base of Oakland hill from the estate of Mary Schenley. This long-delayed tribute to local veterans of the Civil War stands on part of that land. After Henry Hornbostel, as the local favorite, won the competition against the much more senior Cass Gilbert, John Russell Pope, and Ernest Flagg, he faced a second hurdle: the siting. The building was to have faced east, toward Bigelow Boulevard, but Hornbostel convinced the county commissioners to rotate the plan, so it now faces south, fronted by a great lawn to 5th Avenue.

The sandstone memorial, an adaptation of the Mausoleum of Halicarnassus, stands on a high concave podium, with meeting rooms set at the corners of the base. Engaged Doric columns and a triplex of doorways give a heroic scale to the three main facades, but more prominent still is the cast-concrete pyramidal roof. The cornice is the best in Pittsburgh, its linked eagles furthering the memorial's histo-

AL33 SOLDIERS' AND SAILORS' NATIONAL MILITARY MUSEUM AND MEMORIAL HALL (ALLEGHENY COUNTY SOLDIERS' AND SAILORS' MEMORIAL)

ricizing aura with the Roman symbol for military power. Charles Keck's bronze statue of America stands above the main entrance.

AL34 Schenley Farms Residential District and Civic Center

1905–1930. Bounded by Centre, Bellefield, Forbes, and Parkman aves. and Bigelow Blvd.

The Civic Center portion of Franklin Nicola's dream continued with the construction of the Pittsburgh Athletic Association (PAA) (1909–1911, Janssen and Abbott; 4215 5th Avenue), which jump-started Oakland's building boom and Benno Janssen's lucrative career as a Pittsburgh society architect. Architectural critic Montgomery Schuyler deemed the PAA one of Pittsburgh's outstanding buildings and Janssen its best architect, when he wrote about the city in *Architectural Record* in 1911. Janssen produced this made-up Venetian Renaissance palace, with its learned quotes from Italian Renaissance precedents, as the first in a series of clubhouses envisioned by Nicola. A member of the New York Athletic Club, Nicola invented the PAA in 1908 as its Pittsburgh equivalent. For the limestone and terra-cotta clubhouse facade Janssen used stacked Corinthian orders: double-height paired pilasters for the lower floors and paired columns for the upper floors, each level set off by a prominent modillioned cornice. The rooms inside are triumphs of the same sophisticated historicism, not copies but stirring emulations of medieval and Renaissance interiors.

The PAA spawned numerous other commissions in the area for Janssen. The Masonic Temple (now the University of Pittsburgh's Alumni Hall; 4227 5th Avenue) went up next door in 1914 as a somber but stately foil; design cues from classical antiquity appropriately portray remoteness and secrecy, as the massive, Hellenistic side-gable temple coolly hovers above its exaggerated basement story. In 1916, Janssen produced an elaborate scheme for Henry Clay Frick of hundreds of apartments grouped around courtyards in the manner of the Palais Royale in Paris. This was

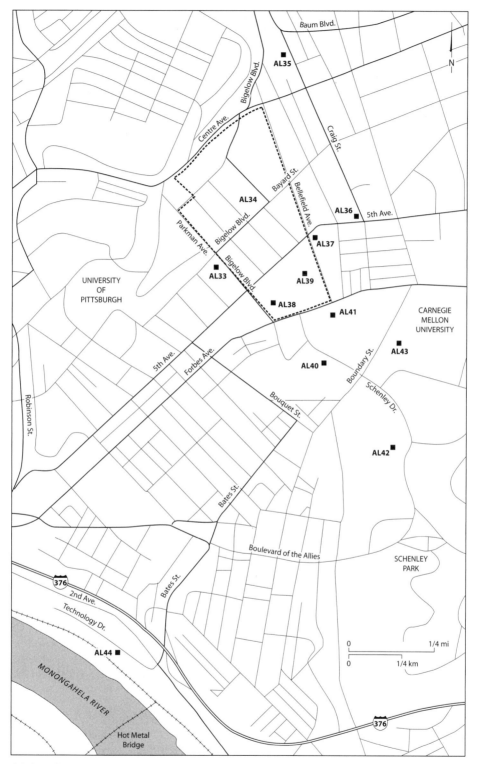

OAKLAND

to have occupied Frick's fourteen acres opposite the PAA, where the Cathedral of Learning now stands (AL38), but nothing came of it. Instead Janssen designed Eberly Hall (former Alumni Hall, 1920–1921) on the hillside portion of the University of Pittsburgh campus. In 1924, Janssen designed the Young Men and Women's Hebrew Association (now the University of Pittsburgh's Bellefield Hall; 315 Bellefield Avenue) on the eastern border of those same acres. An eclectic mix of Italian Renaissance and colonial Virginia, it works as well as the PAA on its modest budget. In 1930, Janssen was still designing for the same neighborhood, this time rebuilding the Twentieth Century Club (4201 Bigelow Boulevard) in a recollection of Michelangelo's Palazzo del Senatore in Rome. He also created the Mellon Institute (AL37) a few blocks to the east and several house designs for Schenley Farms. A richer or more varied production by a single architect for a single neighborhood can hardly be imagined.

In the meantime, Bertram Grosvenor Goodhue, working for Cram, Goodhue and Ferguson, designed the First Baptist Church (1910; 159 North Bellefield Avenue) after the congregation was forced to sell their downtown property in 1909 to make way for the City-County Building (AL2). The church relocated to an elevated corner overlooking Oakland's emerging civic center, from which, until the Cathedral of Learning changed Oakland's scale, it could be seen across the neighborhood. First Baptist reveals Goodhue's skill in manipulating traditional Gothic elements into a modern idiom for the specific needs of a Baptist meetinghouse. The church's cruciform plan accentuates the verticality of the elevations for an effect of uplift without intimidation. The four-bay nave is articulated externally by prominent buttresses between the grisaille windows designed by Charles J. Connick, while a 182-foot filigreed copper spire rises from the crossing. Inside, finely worked limestone arches alternate with Guastavino vaults in an unbroken space. As always in a Goodhue building, the carving and furnishings are rich and impeccable.

The residential portion of the Schenley Farms district is another product of Franklin Nicola's purchase of much of the Mary Schenley estate in 1898. By then Nicola had already built the ten-story Schenley Hotel (now William Pitt Student Union for the University of Pittsburgh, 1898, Rutan and Russell; 1983 renovation, Williams Trebilcock Whitehead; 5th Avenue and Bigelow Boulevard). The hotel was a key element in Nicola's vision of Oakland as Pittsburgh's cultural and social center. When it opened, Mary Schenley was still alive, and the eleven-story, steel-framed building towered over what remained of her farmland. Carnegie Institute (AL41) was the sole neighbor in a rural setting. For decades, the hotel served as a social center for Pittsburgh's monied class. Presidents from Taft to Eisenhower were among the celebrities who stayed there. The hotel was also popular with the major-league baseball players who played during the glory days of nearby Forbes Field. The University of Pittsburgh converted the hotel into a student center in 1956, but its renovation came three decades later. The lobby was returned to its original French Renaissance styling, with vaulted ceiling, mirrored walls, chandeliers, and detailed moldings. Postmodern touches include an invented classical colonnade on Forbes Avenue (to articulate the new basement rooms there) and slipped keystones at several minor entrances. The suites upstairs provide office space for student organizations and university administration.

In 1906, Nicola sold a separate forty-five acres for the university's upper campus. But the core of his vision was to transform this large patch of farmland into the best inner-city neighborhood in the nation. After an initial investment of $2.5 million, Nicola's Schenley Farms Company spent an additional $1.5 million to lay out streets, plant shade trees, landscape, and lay underground utility conduits—this last nearly unheard-of anywhere else in the city. Nicola hired leading Pittsburgh architects to design eleven sample houses on the west side of Lytton Avenue by 1906. Mostly Tudor Revival and Colonial Revival in style, the homes contained such luxuries as thirteen-inch-deep brick walls with insulating air pockets, brass pipes, hardwood floors, finished basements, under-window radiators, vacuum ducts, telephones, elaborate woodwork, and stained glass. Today, these homes would be prohibitively expensive to replicate. Forty-five more houses were completed by 1909, and a total of ninety-six by 1920. Around 1913, another forty homes, smaller but equally good in design and finish, were constructed in the adjoining Schenley Farms Terrace on Centre Avenue attributed to Janssen and Abbot.

Nicola never revealed the source of his vision for Schenley Farms, but connections to similar suburbs, such as Cleveland's Euclid Heights (1892) and Shaker Heights (1904), are likely. Nicola resided in Cleveland in 1892, and had close relatives in that city in 1904. Another contemporary of Schenley Farms was the Russell Sage Foundation's Forest Hills Gardens in Queens. Schenley Farms is smaller than these three neighborhoods, but, unlike the parallel developments, it contributed population to the host city rather than drawing residents to the suburbs. Nicola's vision was the city integrated, not segregated. He promoted Schenley Farms for the easy access it gave to good music, art, books, and companionship in the schools, concert halls, libraries, and clubs nearby. Like so many urban visionaries of great design, Nicola was nearly bankrupt at his death in 1938.

AL35 Arthur Lubetz Architectural Office

1982, Arthur Lubetz Associates. 357 N. Craig St.

Arthur Lubetz gained a steady national reputation in the 1980s and 1990s from an architectural philosophy that he defined as "active, interactive, and ongoing." Not lost on his clients was Lubetz's ability to fashion a workable program from the interface of low-budget materials and elegantly conceived designs. The 12,500-square-foot Lubetz studio reflects the designer's quirky style that does not compromise functionality. The offices group in the center of the plan, creating a building-inside-a-building effect that supplies privacy inside and whimsy outside. The exterior of this former garage is adorned with stucco, concrete, and glass, a distinctive but not haughty neighbor to a workaday streetscape. Especially beguiling is the set of miniaturized pavilions that greet visitors as they emerge from the parking lot on the side.

A near neighbor to the Lubetz office is his firm's William S. Moorhead Tower (1981; 375 N. Craig Street) for the blind and disabled. A triumph of functionality, the apartment block uses varied materials, natural lighting, and air movement to lead its residents through the halls. The focal point of the structure is the sequence of terraced roofs, which distribute light and air more broadly through their clerestory windows than would a traditional flat roof. The superficial postmodernism of these two buildings will not mislead, for it is clear that they are among the more thoughtful designs in the city.

AL36 St. Paul Cathedral

1906, Egan and Prindeville. 5th Ave. and N. Craig St.

This third version of St. Paul Cathedral (the other two were downtown, on Grant Street) is more than a single building: with its adjoining synod house and rectory and two neighboring schools, it constitutes a medieval grouping unto itself. The Chicago-based architects specialized in Catholic churches of a historicizing character. Here they imitated Cologne Cathedral's twin spires for the exterior, and its five-aisled nave for the interior. The impressively tall nave, with its pointed-arched arcade and rib vaulting, is imposing rather than alluring;

AL36 ST. PAUL CATHEDRAL

the best element is the immense pipe organ donated by Andrew Carnegie.

AL37 Carnegie Mellon Research Institute (Mellon Institute for Industrial Research)

1931–1937, Janssen and Cocken. 4400 5th Ave.

Founded in 1913 by brothers Andrew W. and Richard B. Mellon, the institute was one of the world's first centers for applied research in the natural sciences and industry. It became part of Carnegie Mellon University in 1967. This is its third site; an earlier home still exists on the University of Pittsburgh campus as Allen Hall (3941 O'Hara Street).

Planning for the building began in 1927, with the Mellons emphasizing the classical tradition and their wish to create a structure that would link science past with science present and future. The selected site also had to harmonize with two late Gothic Revival monuments: the Mellon-financed Cathedral of Learning (AL38), then under construction to the west, and St. Paul Cathedral (AL36) diagonally across the street. The Mellons' architect Benno Janssen proposed a severe Greek design that combined a grandeur appropriate to Oakland as the city's cultural center with a rational simplicity appropriate for a home of science.

The building's rectangular massing and imposing colonnade recall Robert Mills's Treasury Building in Washington, while the detailing echoes that of the small temple of Nike Apteros on the Acropolis in Athens. The fruit of this hybridization looks unlike any known Greek structure, yet the impact of that tradition is clearly perceptible. The exterior is made memorable by the sixty-two peripteral monolithic columns of Indiana limestone, each of which measures about six feet in diameter at its base and five feet at the neck. Their thirty-six-foot height is impressive in itself, but the fact that these are monolithic— even over the loading docks at the back— makes the Mellon Institute columns among the most remarkable ever erected.

The Mellon Institute faithfully adheres to its trapezoidal plot plan, roughly three hundred feet long on each side, subdivided internally into a center core and four connecting wings. This creates four interior courts, which are lined with glazed ivory terra-cotta and windows that illuminate the interior offices and laboratories. Only by standing at the bottom of the interior courts does a visitor comprehend the vast dimensions of the building.

Three of the building's nine stories were placed below ground to minimize vibration for sensitive laboratory equipment. The marble entrance lobby mediates between monumental exterior and utilitarian interior. Fourteen kinds of marble were used in construction, but Janssen, a traditionalist always intrigued by modernism, also put more aluminum in this building—for window frames, window grilles, doors, and stair rails—than had been used before in the United States, no doubt at the request of the Mellons, whose Pittsburgh-based ALCOA (Aluminum Company of America) dominated the world market. Janssen also insinuated Art Deco design into the pervasive Greek-inspired decor: pedestals in each corner of the lobby represent the traditional torches of science, while a marble bas-relief depicts the creation of scientific knowledge, beginning with the birth of the goddess Athena. Finely polished Slavonian and English oak, satinwood, and ebony provide accents to the library and main conference rooms. Anyone touring this sumptuous building must pause in its restrooms, where black Carrara glass walls and gilded faucets embellish some of the most luxurious public bathrooms in the nation.

AL38 Cathedral of Learning

1925–1937, Charles Klauder for Klauder and Day. Bounded by Bigelow Blvd. and Forbes, 5th, and S. Bellefield aves.

The University of Pittsburgh traces its origins to the Western Academy, established downtown in 1787. One hundred years later, it moved to a hilltop on the North Side. Realizing that the move was too isolated demographically and geographically, the university relocated twenty years later to Oakland Hill on land purchased from developer Franklin Nicola.

Henry Hornbostel's plan of 1906 for an academic Acropolis was transposed from Frederick Law Olmsted's plan for the World's Columbian Exposition of 1893 in Chicago—one of several points of impact of the exposition on Oakland. The top of Oakland Hill, where

AL38 CATHEDRAL OF LEARNING

the Veterans' Administration Hospital has stood since the 1950s, was to have repeated the Court of Honor, the Chicago exposition's centerpiece, but without the lagoon. The building layout on the slopes of Oakland Hill would have been in an S-shaped curve that approximated the informal lagoon setting in Chicago. Another precedent was the hillside pilgrimage plan that won the Prix de Rome in 1897 at the Ecole des Beaux-Arts in Paris when Hornbostel was studying there. What remains of Hornbostel's hillside campus today are Allen, Old Engineering, Eberly, and Thaw halls; several of the university's early buildings were demolished in the 1990s.

As enthusiasm waned for the vision of a Pittsburgh Acropolis, nationally prominent campus architect Charles Klauder of Philadelphia was hired to craft a skyscraper that would incorporate all academic departments of the university and create a symbolic rival to the downtown business interests. The program called for a kind of academic ark: 87 classrooms, 184 laboratories, 23 lecture rooms, 19 libraries, 80 conference rooms, and 60 faculty offices. Klauder and Chancellor John Bowman briefly toyed with the idea of erecting the world's tallest skyscraper, but settled for a 42-story, 535-foot Gothic Revival tower of a type repopularized by the Tribune tower then going up in Chicago. Mixed with the Gothic is plenty of Art Deco streamlining. In its basic external wall massing there is little to distinguish the Cathedral of Learning from the contemporary Rockefeller Center in New York City.

The Cathedral of Learning was meant to broadcast the importance of education to all of Pittsburgh, and its 360-degree visibility makes it a dominant, though benign, visual presence in every corner of the city. But the construction site was not ideal: a fourteen-acre trapezoid created by four streets oriented at four different angles and lying at four different levels. By 1924, the intended site was ringed by architectural prima donnas, ranging from Carnegie's library and museum (AL41) to the lordly institutional temples ranged along 5th and Bellefield avenues. To design a capstone for this prominent but heterogenous grouping was no simple challenge.

Klauder responded by placing the Cathedral so that a sheer rise of forty stories broken by just two setbacks greets one driving into Oakland from downtown Pittsburgh. This was the Cathedral's "business" face, no doubt made to demand attention from the corporate elite. The four corner views are all Gothic spires and pinnacles, which conversely presented the Cathedral as a guardian of spiritual values to the crowds at Forbes Field and the residential enclaves nearby. Yet, the outstanding Cathedral view comes not from any street but within the quadrangle on Carnegie Mellon University's (CMU) campus. What dominates any photo of that space is the University of Pittsburgh's Cathedral of Learning, and not CMU's buildings. A reminder that in architectural propaganda, sightlines are everything.

Klauder's Gothic fantasy works especially well in the Commons Room, a truly cathedral-like space of soaring vaults, brilliant sculptural detail, and some of Samuel Yellin's best ironwork. On the perimeter of the Commons Room, and also on the third floor, are nearly three dozen Nationality Rooms, many of them capturing the Arts and Crafts interests that had come back into fashion in the 1930s.

AL39 Heinz Chapel

1934–1938, Charles Klauder. 5th and S. Belle-field aves.

Heinz Chapel stands next to the towering Cathedral of Learning (AL38), but is not over-shadowed by it—a tribute to Charles Klauder's suave editing of Paris's Sainte-Chapelle into a nondenominational worship space. The exterior, which also alludes to Mont-St.-Michel and St.-Maclou in Rouen, is complemented by an interior of luminous stained glass windows by Charles Connick, who lived in Pittsburgh before moving to Boston. With the completion by 1940 of the Cathedral of Learning's tower, Heinz Chapel, and the nearby Stephen Foster Memorial, the university had given its campus an entirely new visual focus.

AL40 Henry Clay Frick Fine Arts Building

1965, [Burton] Kenneth Johnstone and Associates. 1 Schenley Plaza

This attractive replica of an Italian Renaissance palace was financed in 1925 by Helen Clay Frick as a memorial to her father, who had died six years before, but the building did not open until May 1965. The grueling

AL39 HEINZ CHAPEL

forty-year design review process that caused this wait involved the imperious Helen Frick and three different sites, five different teams of architects, and about fifty separate design schemes. Styles for the proposed building included Baroque, Arts and Crafts, Beaux-Arts, Gothic Revival, and Italian Renaissance, and an outside review team suggested Colonial Revival as well. As it now stands, it is a basic restatement of Ammannati and Vignola's Villa Giulia in Rome.

In 1962, Max Abramovitz produced a futuristic design for a research megastructure to fit inside Junction Hollow, a 150-foot-deep ravine behind the site that the university preferred to call Panther Hollow. Abramovitz called in as collaborators the New York firm of Eggers and Higgins, whose Gateway Center (AL7) had been such an important milestone in the rebuilding of downtown Pittsburgh. These architects saw the Frick building as the traditionalist tip for their modernist iceberg in the valley below. Otto Eggers and Daniel Higgins, who were both Beaux-Arts designers, nearly succeeded in satisfying Helen Frick's requirements for a showplace for her paintings and art books, but they ultimately withdrew in frustration. What we see now is a scandalously close reworking of the Eggers and Higgins design by Kenneth Johnstone, a Pittsburgh modernist who was the dean of the College of Fine Arts at Carnegie Institute of Technology from 1945 to 1953.

Though the design process was tortured, the building functions well as the penultimate gasp of the Beaux-Arts tradition in the city; the ultimate gasp is the Frick Art Museum of 1970 created by Helen Frick in Point Breeze (see AL107). Travertine walls, Italian Renaissance fresco reproductions, Vermont marble floors, cherry wood paneling, and noble proportions mark its public spaces, though artists, scholars, and students work in concrete-block cubicles behind the scenes.

In front of the Fine Arts Building is the Mary Schenley Memorial Fountain of 1918, titled *A Song to Nature*. Its siting is somewhat accidental, a by-product of the filling up of the St. Pierre Ravine to create Schenley Plaza, around 1915. The plaza became a parking lot for years, and in 2006, Sasaki Associates of Boston relandscaped it, creating seating, food kiosks, and a carousel in season. With the

AL41 CARNEGIE INSTITUTE AND CARNEGIE LIBRARY

ravine gone, the heavy stone bridge over it became superfluous, and the city recycled it into an invisible base for this stunning monument to the donor of Schenley Park. The work is a collaboration between H. Van Buren Magonigle, an important designer of Beaux-Arts civic monuments, and Victor D. Brenner, who also designed the Lincoln-head penny. The large, costly bronze, a stylistic cross between Art Nouveau and Art Deco, represents the sleeping earth god Pan being awakened by Harmony, who serenades him with his stolen lyre. Water pours from the mouths of four bronze turtles into Magonigle's granite basin below.

AL41 Carnegie Institute and Carnegie Library

1892–1895, Longfellow, Alden and Harlow; 1903–1907, Alden and Harlow; 1974 Scaife Gallery, Edward Larabee Barnes; 1993 Heinz Architectural Center, Cicognani Kalla Architects. 4400 Forbes Ave.

Along with Charles Klauder's Cathedral of Learning (AL38) and H. H. Richardson's courthouse (AL1), this sprawling complex is one of the irreplaceable buildings in Pittsburgh. The core of Carnegie's twelve-acre library and museum was a Richardsonian Romanesque structure that included twin towers (now gone)

that replicated those on the courthouse—a mark of loyalty by Longfellow and Alden, who came directly from Richardson's office. But other design influences were already at work on the first component, which fronted on Schenley Plaza rather than on Forbes Avenue. Although designed only four years after the triumphant reception of the courthouse, the first block (today Carnegie Library and Carnegie Music Hall) reflects the country's avid reception of the Beaux-Arts style, grandly announced in 1889 by McKim, Mead and White's design for the Boston Public Library. Alfred Harlow, one of the principal architects here, had formerly worked for McKim, Mead and White; it was probably he who led the way to making the Carnegie complex an amalgam of the two styles.

When two of the three partners returned a decade later to expand the museums of Art and Natural History along Forbes Avenue, the transition to Beaux-Arts style was complete, having become a national fixation after the World's Columbian Exposition in Chicago in 1893. The scale and detailing of the 1895 building—particularly the delicate interiors of the library and music hall—are beguiling, but the corresponding effects in this extension overwhelm with their lavishness. The building offers an exalted architectural experience,

AL42 PHIPPS CONSERVATORY

especially in five spaces that are exceptionally fine: the Early Renaissance interior of the Music Hall; the flood of gold leaf and Sienna marble in the adjoining Foyer; the vast Hall of Architecture, jammed with full-scale building fragments; the Hall of Sculpture, a replica of the Parthenon interior, complete with marble cut from the same quarries; and Andrew Carnegie's personal quarters in the exquisitely gilded Founder's Room.

The Carnegie complex was extended seventy years later with the addition of the Scaife Gallery on Forbes Avenue. This severe though grandly proportioned wing transforms the classicism of the main block into the abstraction of the late International Style.

In 1974, Edward Larrabee Barnes transformed an old gallery on the second floor into cold abstraction. Two decades later, in unexpected warmth and intimacy, the same space was reworked to house the Heinz Architectural Center by Pietro Cicognani and Ann Kalla. Working in a mere 40 × 100–foot footprint, they shoehorned three full floors of exhibition, storage, and office space beneath the old skylights. Their architectural inspiration draws from such diverse sources as the neighboring Hall of Sculpture and architect John Soane's house (now Museum) in London. The architectural unity of the center is highly personalized in the eccentric mix of saturated colors, cork floors, and mottled textures that pull the disparate elements together.

In 2007–2008, E. Verner Johnson and Associates inserted a three-story exhibition space for Dinosaurs in Their Time into a former lightwell, allowing the Natural History Museum's world class collection of dinosaur fossils and skeletons to be properly displayed.

At the base of the Carnegie Library's steps stands the gray granite stele of 1908 commemorating Christopher L. Magee, the local party boss whose machinations enabled Andrew Carnegie to take over this corner of Mary Schenley's new park. Henry Bacon (architect of the Lincoln Memorial) set up an unobtrusive marble enclosure for a pool of water, behind which rises the stele with Augustus Saint-Gaudens's bronze bas-relief. The relief represents Abundance or Charity, who holds an overfilled cornucopia below the branches of an oak.

AL42 Phipps Conservatory

1893, Lord and Burnham; 2005–2008 Welcome Center, greenhouses, Tropical Forest, and administration building, IKM Architects. 1 Schenley Park Dr.

This is the most prominent of a number of socially useful gifts made to Pittsburgh by Carnegie's partner Henry Phipps. This greenhouse, slightly earlier than the Enid A. Haupt Conservatory at the New York Botanical Gardens, is by the same Irvington-on-Hudson firm. It is located adjacent to Panther Hollow in Schenley Park.

The Phipps consists of a series of domed glass pavilions for tropical and desert plants, ferns, flowers, orchids, and palm trees. The palms grow in the central and largest room of the conservatory, which reaches 65 feet in height, is 60 feet wide, and 450 feet long. There are thirteen interior display gardens, two courtyards, an outdoor garden, two aquatic gardens, and a rose garden. The only loss to this otherwise perfectly preserved environment was the original Richardsonian

Romanesque entrance, which in the 1960s was supplanted by one in International Style. That insensitive intrusion was itself replaced in 2005, with a dramatic glass-bubbled welcome center and café, followed by growing houses, a 12,000-square-foot Tropical Forest conservatory, and an education/administration building, all models of sustainability and studied by architects for their energy efficiency and style.

AL43 Carnegie Mellon University (Carnegie Institute of Technology)

1905–present, Henry Hornbostel, and others. Bounded by Forbes Ave., Margaret Morrison, Tech, and Frew sts.

Conceived as Carnegie Technical Schools in 1900 by Andrew Carnegie, and opened in 1905, the institution was renamed Carnegie Institute of Technology in 1912 and renamed Carnegie Mellon University in 1968 when it merged with the Mellon Institute of Industrial Research. The campus of some 140 acres has been triply blessed: by the natural topography of the site itself, isolated from the rest of Pittsburgh by the Junction Hollow gully on the west, Schenley Park on the south, and the steep rise of Squirrel Hill on the east; by Henry Hornbostel's refined Beaux-Arts plan; and by astute choices in its later expansion.

Hornbostel won the competition for the Carnegie Technical Schools with a scheme that featured a pronounced axial quadrangle accentuated by technology at the west, with arts on a slight rise to the east. The College of Fine Arts (School of Applied Design, 1912–1916) was Hornbostel's tribute to his own classical but interdisciplinary education at the Ecole des Beaux-Arts in Paris. Named in cartouches atop the cream-colored brick facade are the five arts-related subjects originally taught. The structure also provided budding architects with three pedagogical displays. Five facade niches exemplify in bold relief major stylistic periods from ancient to Renaissance. Inside, four inlaid marble floor designs recall other great monuments of the past, and murals overhead depict additional great designs, not forgetting Hornbostel's design for Hell's Gate Bridge in New York. At the west end of the quadrangle, Hamerschlag Hall (Machinery Hall, 1906–1912), renamed for the school's first director, is an architectural silk purse made of a sow's ear. The building program demanded little more than a boiler plant below and workshops above, but Hornbostel decked it out in the guise of Leon Battista Alberti's S. Andrea at Mantua, with a high temple pediment surmounting an enormous ceremonial entrance arch. The crowning touch was the most poetic smokestack in the nation, an industrial brick, cylindrical Temple of Venus penetrated by a circular brick chimney, the whole further enriched by a helical staircase.

At the northeast corner of the original campus, Hornbostel designed a tribute to Carnegie's mother in Margaret Morrison Carnegie Hall (Margaret Morrison Carnegie School for Women, 1906–1907; 1914; 1990–1996, Bohlin Cywinski Jackson, with Pierre Zoelly). The Beaux-Arts-style building is fronted by a magnificent semicircular Doric portico that encloses an oval-shaped courtyard. The recent expansion, a fourth-story addition called The Intelligent Workplace, is a shimmering 7,000-square-foot glass penthouse. The offices

AL43 CARNEGIE MELLON UNIVERSITY (CARNEGIE INSTITUTE OF TECHNOLOGY), c. 1915.

and research labs are a living laboratory of futuristic office architecture and technology.

Hornbostel's work was essentially done by 1930, at which point the campus froze for more than fifty years, with new construction limited to benignly concrete Wean Hall (1968–1971, Deeter Ritchey Sippel) to plug a gap in the quadrangle, and to a few halfhearted buildings to strike a north–south axis (an equally long mall known as the "Cut") from the original quadrangle to Forbes Avenue.

This architectural lethargy ended overnight with the adoption of a new master plan in 1987, including the striking of a third axis, east–west this time, by urbanist Leon Krier, that points to Margaret Morrison Street and cuts the second axis at 90 degrees. Krier's axis became the southern edge for the East Campus (1987–1990, Michael Dennis for Dennis, Clark and Associates/TAMS), which is a new quadrangle with an athletic field linked to a range of dormitories on the south and a garage with attached stadium on the north. These buildings repeat the Hornbostel idiom of yellow factory brick laid with the same care as the old work, but here variegated in color. The buildings are crisp both in wall texture and detailing. The University Center (1989–1996), an Uffizi Gallery, Florence, look-alike in factory brick, strengthens the "Cut" as the campus's north–south axis. Designed by Michael Dennis and Associates and UDA Architects, this center for student life includes spaces for sports, lectures, a chapel, other student activities, and dining. These conflicting functions occasionally intersect, not always to the pleasure of the users, who often find them randomly juxtaposed. The Purnell Center for the Arts (1991–1999, Michael Dennis and Associates and Damianos + Anthony) mirrors the University Center on the west side of the "Cut," but with a simpler program.

The most neglected part of the campus had always been the slide into Junction Hollow, behind Hamerschlag, but this changed in 1987 with the addition of the volumetrically complex Facilities Management Services Building (Physical Plant Building) by IKM, Inc., which gives access to neighboring buildings at several different levels and compass orientations. In deference to Hornbostel, the architects employ the same yellow brick. Next door, George A. Roberts Engineering Hall (1993–1997, Payette Associates) was hung on the escarpment between the railroad tracks and the high exposed podium of Hamerschlag Hall. The resulting visual prospect either diminishes or enhances the old structure above, depending on one's purist or populist point of view.

A similarly awkward site on the west campus hosts the Gates Center for Computer Science designed in 2005–2007 by Mack Scogin Merrill Elam Architects of Atlanta. The starkly geometric building is complemented by Michael Van Valkenburgh's landscape architecture. He and artist and Carnegie Mellon alumnus Mel Bochner earlier collaborated on the Kraus Campo (completed 2004), an exquisite meditative garden space behind the College of Fine Arts.

AL44 High Tech Architecture and the Pittsburgh Technology Center (Jones and Laughlin Steel Company Site)

1990–2008. Technology Dr. between 2nd Ave. and the Monongahela River

One of the first buildings in Pittsburgh specifically designed for high-tech research was the Software Engineering Institute (SEI) (1987, Bohlin Powell Larkin Cywinski, and Burt Hill Kosar Rittelmann Associates; 4500 5th Avenue), a joint venture between Carnegie Mellon University and the Department of Defense. Its program called for a high-security environment, which dictated the building's three core elements: a public entrance pavilion, a controlled-access restricted office and laboratory block, and a parking garage. SEI is a neighbor to Mellon Institute (AL37) to the west and St. Paul Cathedral (AL36) across 5th Avenue to the northeast, with an exedra carved out of its facade picking up the axis of St. Paul Cathedral. The cathedral is reflected in SEI's glass curtain wall, whose two-tone vertical bands establish a secondary visual linkage with the giant colonnade of Mellon Institute. But there are limits to how self-effacing a large building can be, and SEI ultimately provides a cautionary tale of overcontextualization.

Two miles to the southwest, the office and research buildings on this forty-eight-acre riverside site had no such contextual demands when they were built. Their symbolism was

AL44 HIGH TECH ARCHITECTURE AND THE PITTSBURGH TECHNOLOGY CENTER (JONES AND LAUGHLIN STEEL COMPANY SITE)

almost palpable, since the shiny new structures were going up where the Eliza Furnaces of Jones and Laughlin (J&L) had stood for almost a century and a half. The complex remains significant and growing, in tribute to the competent manner in which Pittsburgh's Urban Redevelopment Authority (URA, a city-county agency) has nourished it. The development includes five buildings designed between 1990 and 2002 by Bohlin Cywinski Jackson and Burt Hill Kosar Rittelmann (later Burt Hill Architects) at 100, 200, 300, 550, and 700 Technology Drive. Bridgeside Point II (2007–2009; 450 Technology Drive) was designed by Dina F. Snider and John A. Martine for Strada, and Union Switch and Signal Research Center (1993–1995; 1000 Technology Drive) is by The Design Alliance Architects. True to their high-tech functions, the buildings look sleek and efficient with exterior surface materials of glass and metal panels. Still, to many Pittsburghers, the smoke-belching mills were a thrilling sight in contrast to the structures that replaced them. A Peter Eisenman design from the mid-1980s was originally intended for this site, but his deconstructivist recollection of the old J&L mills had spaces that were too eccentric to be rentable.

One important remnant of the river's industrial past near the Pittsburgh Technology Center (adjacent to 2nd Avenue and Bates Street) is the Hot Metal Bridge (c. 1887), which actually is two bridges with similar profiles sharing a set of stone piers. The upstream side held two tracks of the Monongahela Connecting Railroad; it was adapted in 2000 for automobile traffic. The downstream side held a single track underlain with metal plates protecting its wooden ties from sparks and the molten metal being shipped between the former steelmaking plant on one side of the river and the fabricating plant on the other. In 2007, it was adapted for bicycles and foot traffic.

In the North Hills, an innovative design for a similar high-tech company near I-79 at Warrendale (174-A Thornhill Road) was built for FORE Systems, Inc., in 1997, makers of ATM computer switches. As designed by Studios Architecture of San Francisco, the building distorts both perspective and form, leaving the viewer with a feeling of instability. The materials include brick with sides or ends of aluminum and glass in long three-story blocks. The high-tech, sleek character of this building in the suburbs outshines its cousins near the Monongahela River.

SOUTH SIDE AND THE MONONGAHELA VALLEY

Pittsburgh's South Side, occupying an extensive floodplain on the south bank of the Monongahela River across from the Golden Triangle, offers a completely different visual experience from the glitz of the downtown skyline or the flashy new sports stadia and office parks of Pittsburgh's North Side on the opposite bank of the Allegheny River.

An old Revolutionary-era farm turned workhouse, South Side was first named Birmingham, in the obvious hope that industry would flourish here as it had in Birmingham, England. The town was settled around 1810, and reached its peak population of some 45,000 around World War I. By then, E. Carson

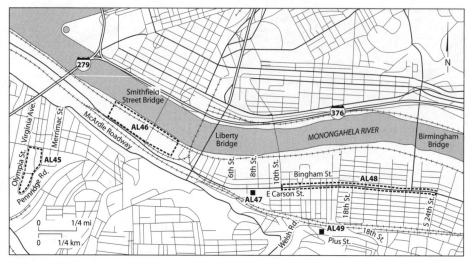

SOUTH SIDE

Street, its main spine, stretched for almost two miles with a continuous line of stores and apartments. Today, broken in only a few spots, E. Carson remains a fascinating thoroughfare. Streets could be laid in a more regimented manner over this floodplain than in most of Pittsburgh, which made it the most cohesive of the city's neighborhoods. This physical cohesion was then augmented by ethnic links (first Germans, then Poles, then immigrants from eastern and southern Europe) and an expressive architectural and visual collectivity.

The attraction of South Side was work, in a multitude of jobs in its glass-works, ironworks, foundries, and crucibles (critical components of iron making), that may be the perfect metaphor for this district of modest houses and ethnic churches and clubs. The Jones and Laughlin (J&L) steelworks was the biggest draw. Everything east of the Birmingham Bridge and the entire opposite shore from the Birmingham to the Glenwood bridges was occupied by J&L sheds and blast furnaces until the mid-1980s, when the economy and steelmaking fortunes changed.

A mill district such as South Side was effectively a company town that was devastated by the closing of the glasshouses and steelworks; by the 1980s and 1990s, its population had dropped to slightly more than 10,000, compared to double that in World War II. An eventual economic upturn came in the 1990s, not from any revival of industry but from the South Side's hundreds of lively nineteenth-century storefronts. Bars turned into gourmet restaurants, and mom-and-pop food shops resurfaced as antique stores, clothing boutiques, and nightclubs. Up on the slopes, there was a parallel move to rehab the wooden workers' homes into affordable housing for singles and young families. Today, South Side's economic troubles are not entirely behind it, but it has emerged as the undisputed entertainment center of Pittsburgh, and moved from just preserving its architecture to expanding it in vigorous new housing by the river and office and retail complexes at both ends of the restored Hot Metal Bridge (see AL44).

South Side was always a microcosm of the Monongahela River valley. Its rise foretold the later expansion of mill towns upriver, such as Homestead, Braddock, Duquesne, McKeesport, and Turtle Creek. Similarly, its fall announced their eventual fall, too, as metals processing was outsourced from Pittsburgh overseas. Those were the true company towns, and they lack South Side's diversification and nearness to the metropolis. Here and there one sees revitalization, particularly in historic preservation, but the new dawn for all of the Monongahela Valley mill towns remains elusive.

AL45 Chatham Village

1932, 1936, Clarence S. Stein and Henry Wright, planners; Ingham and Boyd, architects; Ralph Griswold and Theodore M. Kohankie, landscape architects; 1956 apartments, Frederick Bigger, planner; Ingham, Boyd and Pratt, architects; Griswold Winters Swain, landscape architects. Bounded by Bigham St., Virginia Ave., and Olympia and Pennridge rds.

The Buhl Foundation, in its brochure for the project, promoted this for-profit housing as the "First large scale, planned, residential community built from the ground up in one operation to be retained in single ownership and managed as a long-term investment." Chatham Village always had a national, and even international, impact out of proportion to its rather modest dimensions, deriving in part from the names of Stein and Wright, acclaimed planners of Sunnyside Gardens in Queens, New York, and Radburn, New Jersey. More notable is the complex's highly irregular contour; rarely had low-cost housing

AL45 CHATHAM VILLAGE

Seventeen inclines (also called inclined planes or funiculars) once operated on the hillsides of Pittsburgh. Funiculars are composed of counterbalanced passenger cars attached equidistantly along a single cable loop pulled at the top and tensioned at the bottom. Born out of pure necessity, the inclines were a crucial part of Pittsburgh's environment, some capable of carrying large trucks. In 1869, John Endres of Cincinnati teamed with Budapest-born Samuel Diescher to construct the Monongahela incline, the first in the city, lifting its passengers 640 feet up Mount Washington. The wire cable was furnished by John Roebling, an early landmark in his career that culminated in New York City's Brooklyn Bridge. The Monongahela incline operates all day between W. Carson Street and Grandview Avenue, adjacent to Station Square.

JOHNSTOWN INCLINED PLANE BRIDGE SPANNING STONY CREEK AT PA 3022, CAMBRIA COUNTY, 1997.

The Duquesne Heights incline, farther down W. Carson Street overlooking the Point, also reaches up to Grandview Avenue, opposite Oneida Street. Built in 1877 and rebuilt a decade later, this was the fourth of Pittsburgh's inclines. Diescher was again the engineer, this time operating with a track 793 feet long. The system is operated by the nonprofit Society for the Preservation of the Duquesne Heights Incline, which also oversees a collection of memorabilia in the upper station. The original hoisting drum and wooden drive gear are still in use, set at a 90-degree angle from the incline to save space. The cars on this incline are the originals, but the rails were early on converted from wood to iron and the power source was switched from steam to electric power in the 1930s. Neither incline has had a major accident.

Inspired by the inclined planes used at the Allegheny Portage Railroad (CA8), considered an engineering marvel in the 1830s, inclines were often built in response to the region's steep hillsides. Johnstown's incline (CA21) built just after the 1889 flood, was also designed by engineer Diescher, and, at 502.5 vertical feet, is one of the steepest in the world. It is the last of those in the region capable of carrying an entire vehicle from the lower city to the flood-proof suburb of Westmont.

dealt so successfully with steep slope topography. Helping its fame also was the decade in which Chatham Village went up; in the 1930s, governments everywhere in the nation were contemplating public-assistance housing. Chatham Village became a model for schemes across the country.

The complex fits 216 families on sixteen acres: 129 row houses date from 1932 and 68 from 1936; a three-story, 19-unit apartment building went up in 1956. The planners left four acres for playgrounds and commons, plus twenty-six adjoining acres of untouched woodland. Rented from the Buhl Foundation until 1960, the homes then became a cooperative and were privatized. Nonetheless, the complex retains strict restrictions on upkeep and changes.

At the south end of the development the Greek Revival former Thomas James Bigham mansion of 1849 is now a community center named Chatham Hall. Its original owner and builder was an avid abolitionist, newspaper publisher, and politician whose house was used as part of the Underground Railroad.

AL46 Station Square (Pittsburgh and Lake Erie Railroad Terminal)

1901, William George Burns; 1976 renovation, Landmarks Design Associates. Bounded by the Smithfield St. Bridge, W. Carson St., and the Monongahela River

This forty-acre rehabilitation of Beaux-Arts and industrial buildings constituted Pittsburgh's first recycling of an integrated complex of buildings. Initiated by the Pittsburgh History and Landmarks Foundation, the renovation and adaptive reuse had a profound effect on the revitalization of the entire South Side.

The centerpiece remains the seven-story former passenger terminal of the P&LE Railroad, which, though it made most of its revenue hauling iron ore and coal, lavished considerable expense on the waiting room. This elaborate space under a barrel-vaulted stained glass skylight was among America's more dramatic railroad station interiors. It was restored in the 1970s for use as a restaurant, which works well in that ceremonial space.

The adjoining office building, freight terminal, and warehouse also found new uses as office and retail space, in the process bringing thousands of suburbanites back into the city for work or entertainment.

AL47 St. John the Baptist Ukrainian Catholic Church

1895, 1917. 109 S. 7th St.

This grand monument at the western end of the E. Carson Street commercial district is the most striking reminder of eastern European heritage in South Side life. In 1895, the congregation, affiliated with the Catholic (not the Orthodox) Church, began to meet in the red-orange-colored brick narthex, the only part of the church then built. The maroon-hued brick main hall, in a traditional Ukrainian cross-in-square configuration, was added in 1917. The church is surmounted by six onion-shaped domes, and the central dome, with its covering of gold leaf, shines brilliantly. The two front domes fit less well on their towers, and were perhaps added as afterthoughts to reinforce the eastern European appearance of the church.

AL48 East Carson Street District

c. 1820–1900. E. Carson St. between 10th and 24th sts.

Any discussion of the buildings along E. Carson Street begins with the Bedford School Apartments (former Bedford School, 1850; 1997 renovation, EDGE studio; 910 Bingham Street), a three-story Greek Revival schoolhouse from 1850 that was retrofitted in 1997 with a dozen light-filled apartments, several with the original chalkboards still on the walls. The old school was a key element in stabilizing a neighborhood of rich architectural heritage that is under considerable development pressure from a growing population in the newly trendy South Side.

The apartments are two blocks west of Bedford Square (c. 1820–1893; Bingham and S. 12th streets), a relic of Nathaniel Bedford's plan for the settlement of Birmingham, drawn up in 1811. Evidently a copy of the Golden Triangle's Market Square, it works as a squared roundabout for the four arteries (two segments of Bingham Street and two of S. 12th Street) that would otherwise intersect here. Unlike Market Square downtown, Bedford Square retains its market house, South Side

Market. The first market on the site went up in 1813, when Bedford laid out the settlement. The current structure is a simplified 1915 reconstruction of Charles Bickel's original market of 1893, which was destroyed by fire. It currently houses a drop-in center for the elderly. The tiny homes and shops on the perimeter of the square, some in wood and others in brick, preserve the general Greek Revival massing if not the specific structures of the early nineteenth century, which makes this the oldest intact housing group in Pittsburgh.

E. Carson Street between 10th and 27th streets was the commercial spine of Bedford's borough of Birmingham. Connected to downtown Pittsburgh in 1818 by the first of the three Smithfield Street bridges (AL4), the street also functioned as a feeder road to the Washington Pike and the National Road (now U.S. 40), both south of the city. E. Carson Street's great boost came with iron making. By 1860, the Clinton Furnace (Station Square today) at its western terminus was balanced on the east by Jones and Laughlin's American Iron Works around 25th Street (the J&L company store survives as a Goodwill store). When the South Side became a mecca for immigrant steelworkers from western and later central and eastern Europe, E. Carson Street was stamped with their numerous churches and fraternal halls. The multidomed St. John the Baptist Ukrainian Catholic Church (AL47) is the most grandiloquent of the group, while the smaller, onion-domed former Cleaves Temple (1913) at 1005 E. Carson (now a café) is the most affecting.

The central mile of E. Carson offers one of the best collections of nineteenth-century commercial architecture in the country. Generally two to four stories in height, most of the standout storefronts are Italianate or Second Empire in style or have such late-nineteenth-century features as segmental arches and bracketed corbel tables, as in the Ukrainian Home at number 1113. The Pittsburgh National Bank of 1902 at number 1736, a Beaux-Arts study in contrasting yellow-gray sandstone and red brick, shows that a limited amount of capital investment came in the twentieth century, too. Rare and precious are examples of Art Deco, the last of the South Side's period styles: two of the best are Siegel's Jewelers at number 1510 and Dotula's Cafe at 1605 E. Carson. While most stores on the street had their lower stories altered over time, a community revitalization project of the late 1960s returned many storefronts to historical accuracy.

AL49 Angel's Arms Condominiums (St. Michael's Parish Complex)

1861–1890s, Charles F. Bartberger, and others; 2000–2006, Hanson Design Group. 1 Pius St.

This complex of Romanesque Revival buildings served the parish of St. Michael's (now part of Prince of Peace parish) on the slopes above the South Side. The first church of 1848 was demolished a decade later to make room for the current St. Michael's, designed by Charles F. Bartberger and completed in 1861. It is a stern and handsome red brick German-style Romanesque Revival building with a tall square entrance tower. Several impressive support buildings added over the decades include the rectory at the corner of Pius and Clinton streets (1889, Frederick C. Sauer), several school buildings, and a parish house known as the "Casino." All are in variants of the Romanesque Revival idiom. In the early twenty-first century, almost everything in this complex, church included, was turned into condominiums, though exterior changes were minimal.

The oldest surviving building of the group, higher still on Mount Washington, is Bartberger's St. Paul of the Cross Monastery (143 Monastery Street) of 1853, again in Romanesque Revival. This Passionist priory served the German immigrant workers who erected the hundreds of tiny frame houses that cover the hillside. The complex also includes St. Michael's Cemetery on S. 18th Street, at the brow of Mount Washington. This windswept slope is Pittsburgh industrial melancholy at its best. The gravestones, mainly chiseled in German, are evocative, but unforgettable is the view across the Monongahela River into Oakland, the Bluff, and the Golden Triangle. On a slope too daunting to be turned to industrial profit, the skilled German craft workers rest in the harshness of their adopted land.

AL50 John Woods House

1792. 4604 Monongahela St.

This three-bay, two-story farmhouse of random-cut sandstone has interior end chimneys and a two-over-two-room plan. The builder was probably lawyer John Woods (1758–1816), son of George Woods, who prepared the plan for the Golden Triangle in 1784. Located high on Hazelwood Hill, the house once enjoyed a view of the wooded Monongahela shore before it succumbed to the later Hazelwood coke works.

AL51 Episcopal Church of the Good Shepherd

1891, William Halsey Wood. 2nd and Johnston aves.

This church is a masterful demonstration of the power of a medieval idiom freely interpreted. The high Episcopal faithful who first met on this site in 1870 were probably summer residents of Hazelwood in its bucolic preindustrial days. By the time the existing church was replaced with this structure, Hazelwood was in the throes of industrialization. Nonetheless, the site itself remains verdant, and, in conjunction with Wood's choice of varied and highly textured materials—stone, brick, and shingles—and its louvered tower, the church beautifully captures the rustic feel that the congregation must have requested. William Halsey Wood (1855–1897) crafts almost nothing specifically medieval here, yet it is tangible in the tradition of the free interpretations by such British designers as William Morris or Philip Webb.

AL51 EPISCOPAL CHURCH OF THE GOOD SHEPHERD

AL52 St. Michael the Archangel Church

1925–1927, Comes, Perry and McMullen. E. 9th Ave. and Scotia Pl., Munhall

Few Pittsburgh architects around World War I were busier than John Theodore Comes (1873–1922), as a dozen local Roman Catholic churches and an additional fifty around the United States testify. A handsome home at 3242 Beechwood Boulevard in Squirrel Hill documents the profitability of his practice. Comes, born in Luxembourg, began his career in Pittsburgh in 1897 with several important projects for himself or for larger firms: St. Augustine's (1899, Comes for Rutan and Russell; 37th Street near Penn Avenue) and St. John the Baptist (1903, Comes for Beezer Brothers; 3501 Liberty Avenue), both in Lawrenceville (the latter now a brewpub); St. Anthony's in Millvale (1914, John T. Comes; 608 Farragut Street); and St. Agnes in Oakland (1917, John T. Comes; 120 Robinson Street)—all are Romanesque Revival variants. After Comes's death in 1922, the firm of Comes, Perry and McMullen put up such highly coloristic Gothic Revival works as St. Bernard's in Mount Lebanon (AL131). Along the way were occasional forays into modernism, such as St. Josaphat's Church (1909–1916; 2314 Mission Street), a kind of Polish folk-modern, or this church in Munhall, known as Kostol St. Michael to the Slovak community and now part of St. Maximilian Kolbe parish. The gable-fronted church is a stylized and modernized Italian Romanesque Revival constructed of factory-style brick and brightened by hundreds of colored tile inserts. The memorably tall square bell tower is topped with Frank Vittor's aluminum statue of St. Joseph the Worker (1966), which depicts the father of Jesus not as a carpenter but as a steelworker.

AL53 National Carpatho-Rusyn Center (St. John the Baptist Greek Catholic Cathedral)

1903, Titus de Bobula. 427 E. 10th Ave., Munhall

In their 1940s heyday, Homestead and neighboring Munhall were home to over fifty churches (about thirty survive), of which the former St. John the Baptist cathedral remains the most distinctive. It is that rarity in American architecture, a true Art Nouveau building, though of a peculiarly central European variety.

Located on the hill that characterizes much of Munhall, St. John's towers above the scores of worker houses in which its Carpatho-Rusyn parishioners lived. The facade of St. John's begins in walls of stone and brick on a raised stone basement, then soars into twin towers that have tall narrow windows under exaggerated sandstone voussoirs. The verticality of the towers is checked midway by the horizontal of a loggia in the center of the facade. The towers end in columned tholoi surmounted by Greek crosses. De Bobula created stunning textural discordances through jumps between smooth and rough-hewn stones. He overscaled the egg-and-dart molding and small modillion blocks under the eaves and cornices, to the point that a visitor eyes the whole church warily, as though it cannot be trusted. The architect's blend of historic styles is echoed in the adjacent two-story brick rectory, which incorporates fluted Corinthian columns and a cornice ornamented with acanthus leaves.

Little is known about Budapest-born Titus de Bobula (1878–1961). Long after he left Hungary, where his father and brother were well-known conservative architects, he maintained contact with the old country. In two of his surviving buildings, First Hungar-

AL53 NATIONAL CARPATHO-RUSYN CENTER (ST. JOHN THE BAPTIST GREEK CATHOLIC CATHEDRAL)

ian Reformed Church of 1903 at 221 Johnston Street in Hazelwood and Sts. Peter and Paul Ukrainian Orthodox Greek Catholic Church of 1906 at 200 Walnut Street in the suburb of Carnegie, as well as in a dozen sketches published in Pittsburgh, de Bobula quoted liberally from Art Nouveau and such Viennese pioneer architects as Otto Wagner. De Bobula is the most original force to have emerged from the many immigrant groups who enriched Pittsburgh with their artistic heritages.

AL54 Kennywood Park

1898, George S. Davidson, engineer. 4800 Kennywood Blvd., West Mifflin

Sprawling across forty acres along the west bank of the Monongahela River on the periphery of what was once a thriving mill town, Kennywood Park survived the Great Depression, two world wars, and several financial panics to become one of the leading trolley parks from late-nineteenth-century America.

In 1818, the site was the farm and coalfield of Charles F. Kenny. As early as the Civil War, its groves of oak and maple were a popular picnic area. By the time the Monongahela Street Railway Company extended out from Pittsburgh to reach the farm in the 1890s, the site was widely and popularly known as "Kenny's Grove." Soon after, the railway leased part of the land for a trolley park named Kennywood. George Davidson, chief engineer of the railway, was appointed the park's first manager, and he provided the first layout.

When the park opened to the public its only built attractions were a cafeteria, dance pavilion, and small bandstand surrounding a shallow lake. Kennywood's distinction among enthusiasts as "Roller Coaster Capital of the World" came only later, with the creation of the Racer, the Thunderbolt, the Jack Rabbit, and the Steel Phantom—once clocked as the world's fastest roller coaster. Today, the park maintains a good deal of its original landscape, including a lake and such early buildings as the Casino and Pagoda.

Historic preservation has long been a concern at the park, illustrated by Lost Kennywood, a re-creation of amusement parks of the past whose decorative arched entrance reproduces the arch of Pittsburgh's Luna Park of 1905, now demolished.

AL55 CHARLES SCHWAB HOUSE

AL55 Charles Schwab House

1889, Frederick J. Osterling. 541 Jones Ave., Braddock

Charles Schwab was Andrew Carnegie's most flamboyant associate. Beginning work as a common laborer, he became superintendent at Carnegie's Braddock works, then at his Homestead works, and, finally, president of Bethlehem Steel. Schwab's mansion, built when he was only twenty-seven years old, sits high on a hill above the dreary streets of Braddock, the mill, and the Monongahela. The house, like Schwab's own persona, suggests a prince among the people. It preceded Frick's rebuilding of Clayton (AL107) by three years, but Frick's aristocratic lifestyle was Schwab's probable model. A handsome house with compact massing, varied stonework, steep gables,

and towers and spires, it seems to speak to the millworkers of the glorious possibilities of labor and hard work. The house has been meticulously restored: the mahogany beams glow again, the stained glass windows sparkle, and a century of soot from the Edgar Thomson blast furnaces has been dislodged.

AL56 Carnegie Library of Braddock

1887–1889, William Halsey Wood; 1893 music hall, Longfellow, Alden and Harlow. 419 Library St., Braddock

A few minutes' walk from his Edgar Thomson steel plant (AL57), this is the first library Andrew Carnegie donated in the United States, though he built it solely for his workers, not the general public. Lively in design and elegantly executed inside with costly woodwork, this library, with additions in 1893 of a music hall, gymnasium, pool, and baths, is programmatically part of the mills.

The original library is designed in Pittsburgh's ever-popular Richardsonian Romanesque, but departs from the majesty of the downtown Courthouse and presents, instead, a picturesque silhouette marked by the two squat towers flanking the entrance. One imagines that William Halsey Wood, in choosing the light gray stone of the structure, envisioned the effect the then ever-present dust and smoke would have. The taller tower rising above the roofline was meant to unite Wood's library with Longfellow, Alden and Harlow's extensive addition, a device used by the firm at the Carnegie Institute (AL41) in Oakland.

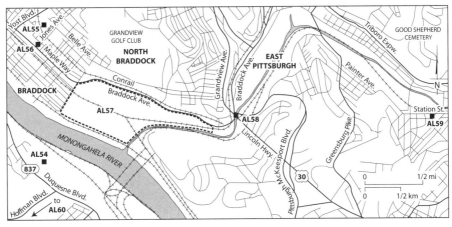

THE MONONGAHELA VALLEY

AL56 CARNEGIE LIBRARY OF BRADDOCK

After years of neglect, the library has been tended back to life by volunteers.

AL57 United States Steel Edgar Thomson Works

1873, Alexander Holley, engineer; many times rebuilt. 13th St. and Braddock Ave., Braddock

When Andrew Carnegie proposed construction of a Bessemer steel mill in 1872, his mentor William Coleman suggested as an ideal location the riverside meadow where General Edward Braddock met defeat at the hands of the French and Indians in 1755. Situated eight miles southeast of Pittsburgh, the land was cheap and situated on both the Baltimore and Ohio and the Pennsylvania Railroad lines. It was perfect for bringing raw materials on the Monongahela, and not far downstream of the Youghiogheny River, along which rail lines carried Connellsville coal and coke to the area.

Carnegie undertook the project with his customary enthusiasm, which did not flag even in the financial panic of 1873. To plan the works, he hired Alexander Holley, a preeminent mill designer, who brought with him the legendary Captain William Jones to help build and later manage the mill. Production of steel rails began in August 1875, and hung on through the mill closings of the 1980s to remain the last steel producer in the Pittsburgh area.

Edgar Thomson is best viewed at night, perhaps from a vantage point in nearby Rankin or atop one of the thrill rides in Kennywood Park (AL54), when the huge glowing plant, smoky and noisy and belching fire, evokes the grit and power of Pittsburgh a century ago.

AL58 Westinghouse Memorial Bridge

1931–1932, Vernon Covell and George S. Richardson, engineers, with Stanley Roush, architect. U.S. 30 over Turtle Creek Valley

From this bridge one sees the two most innovative industrial engines of Pittsburgh: Andrew Carnegie's Edgar Thomson Works (AL57) by the Monongahela River and George Westinghouse's immense electric works (AL59; today an incubator for start-up businesses) of 1894, about a mile inland. The bridge itself is noteworthy, with its elegantly proportioned piers and the seeming effortlessness of the semi-elliptical arches. It is the masterpiece of George Richardson's half century of bridge construction for Allegheny County. The five reinforced-concrete spans range in length from two hundred to nearly five hundred feet, and the center span was for decades the longest of its type in the world. From the roadway—part of the pioneering national Lincoln Highway (U.S. 30)—the excitement of the industrial landscape is heightened by the heroic severity of Frank Vittor's Art Deco reliefs on the bridge's four entrance pylons. Carved between 1934 and 1936, the scenes depict the development of the Turtle Creek valley and commemorate Westinghouse's contributions to industry. From the valley floor, the five semi-elliptical arches perfectly echo the natural drama of the valley itself.

AL59 Westinghouse Air-Brake Company Complex, and the Wilmerding Plan

1889, attributed to Frederick J. Osterling, and others. 325 Commerce St., Wilmerding

It was his need for a new air-brake plant that induced George Westinghouse to purchase five hundred acres of land in the Turtle Creek valley in 1888, a few miles from Carnegie's mill at Braddock (AL57). Both corporations enjoyed spectacular success over the next century, and their ultimate decline was a staggering blow to the region.

Westinghouse, the consummate inventor, earned the first of his more than 360 patents at the age of fifteen. He introduced the alternating-current system of generating and transmitting electricity, and in 1869, developed a compressed-air braking system for railroads, incorporating the Westinghouse Air-Brake Company a few months after the

AL58 WESTINGHOUSE MEMORIAL BRIDGE

patent was issued. Established first in the Strip, where its old factory still stands (AL91), the facility moved to an old cotton mill in Allegheny City. When the company outgrew those facilities in 1889, Westinghouse moved it to this sparsely populated place on the main line of the Pennsylvania Railroad.

Wilmerding, named for Joanna Wilmerding Negley, whose husband had owned the land, lies on the floor of a valley shaped by Turtle Creek. The 1889 plant was built on an island formed when the creek forked (one branch was later diverted). One building remains of the original plant, the handsome Machine Shop by Osterling, a tripartite structure with corbel-lined gable roofs flanking a squared-off facade. Segmental- and round-arched windows grouped in twos and threes extend across the facade. The foundry, east of and perpendicular to the Machine Shop, housed Westinghouse's innovative "traveling tables," the direct precursors of Henry Ford's assembly line in that product components were carried to workers, and not vice versa.

Westinghouse formed the East Pittsburgh Improvement Company to construct worker housing between 1889 and 1900. All the houses were relatively well constructed and could eventually be purchased at cost over a ten-year period. They ranged from eight-room, electrified, two-story houses with cellars and baths like those on Marguerite and Walsh avenues, to red brick row houses with double-height porches on Middle Street.

The Westinghouse Air-Brake Company General Office Building, situated midway up the southern hillside, dominates Wilmerding. Probably modeled after Carnegie's Braddock library (AL56), Library Hall (popularly known as the "Castle") opened in 1890 with a swimming pool, bowling alley, reading rooms, and public baths. Unlike Carnegie's steelworkers, Westinghouse employees worked only half days on Saturdays (they were among the first workers in the country to do so), and therefore had time to use these facilities. Osterling seems to have designed the original building as well as its 1896 replacement after a fire. By then, the library had become the administration offices, to which Janssen and Cocken added an east wing in 1926. Today the building houses the George Westinghouse Museum and the Education and Research foundation of the American Production and Inventory Control Society.

AL60 Allegheny County Airport (Allegheny County Municipal Airport)

1929–1931, Stanley L. Roush; 1936 additions, Henry Hornbostel. Lebanon Church Rd. at PA 885, West Mifflin

Being so involved in solutions to mechanical problems, Pittsburgh also took an early lead in American aviation: the first transcontinental plane was built here in 1910. As early as 1915, amateur pilots were taking off from the old racetrack in Schenley Park, and Pittsburgh

AL60 ALLEGHENY COUNTY AIRPORT (ALLEGHENY COUNTY MUNICIPAL AIRPORT)

Airways had regular commercial service by 1920. Early airfields, usually no more than grassy fields with steel hangers, were distributed all around town. Though boasting the first hard-surface runways in the United States, Allegheny County Airport was relatively primitive in function. Nonetheless, by 1937, the airport handled 70,000 passengers a year on Trans World Airlines (TWA) and the local Pennsylvania Central Airlines.

Architecturally, the airport marks a cautious essay in modernism by two Beaux-Arts designers who made clear where their real design loyalties lay. Published sketches for the airport show that Stanley Roush, Allegheny

County architect, was first thinking of something considerably more streamlined, akin to Erich Mendelsohn's widely published department stores of the 1920s in Germany. In the end, a more comfortable Art Deco triumphed. The airport makes no secret of its affinity for the Beaux-Arts, however. Architectural historian James D. Van Trump has likened it to a small Baroque country palace, with its horticultural allees turned into a starburst of runways.

The exterior's Art Deco, nationally popular in the 1920s and 1930s for transportation terminals of all types, has Mayan-style zigzag friezes in rich earth tones in a field of glazed white bricks that tie the building to the land and the sky. Roush's vivid green and black terra-cotta pots at the entranceway also represent the earth's clay, though the decoration on them represents banks of stylized planes. The building's taller central section, surmounted by the control tower, is symmetrically flanked by lower wings. Henry Hornbostel oversaw the design of their second stories and a one-story addition at the rear. The airport survives today as a notable instance of an Art Deco building almost unchanged physically or programmatically. Still busy, it is now restricted to corporate jets and private planes.

THE OHIO VALLEY

The Monongahela River led Pittsburghers upriver from West Virginia, and the Allegheny led them to upstate New York, but the Ohio River was their path to the larger world, via the Mississippi River to New Orleans and the Gulf of Mexico. The gateway to this prospect was McKees Rocks, the impressive hill on which, for centuries around 900 BCE, Native Americans lived and buried their dead.

There are no internationally significant buildings along the Ohio's banks in Pittsburgh today, but notably intriguing environments abound. The first of these is McKees Rocks itself, the best preserved of Pittsburgh's industrial satellites. The segregation of the immigrant workforce—not only by religion but also by ethnic origin—eventually produced an overabundance of churches here. The Roman Catholic St. Francis de Sales (810 Chartiers Avenue), designed by Marius Rousseau in 1899 as an exquisite miniature of S. Maria del Fiore, in Florence, Italy, is now a banqueting hall. Nearby churches include a Russian Orthodox and a Byzantine Catholic, but the synagogue has been demolished.

Factories were the old glory of the Ohio River valley's architecture in

Pittsburgh. Two of the region's most striking factories survive, unloved, in McKees Rocks. One, the Pittsburgh and Lake Erie locomotive repair shop (AL63), is traditionalist and massive; the other, the old Taylor-Wilson plant (AL62), is radical and gossamer light. Both are underused and serve as little more than storage facilities.

AL61 West End Bridge

1930–1932, Vernon Covell and George S. Richardson, engineers. U.S. 19 and the Ohio River

This and the McKees Rocks Bridge (1931, George S. Richardson, engineer; Ohio River Blvd., Termon Ave., and the Ohio River) went up as part of Allegheny County's energetic interwar program of improvements to its infrastructure, especially bridges and roads. The West End Bridge capitalizes on the 755-foot clear span of its steel parabolic arch to make an unforgettable impression as it bounds over the Ohio and simultaneously frames a view of Pittsburgh's Point. The McKees Rocks Bridge, a mere 2.5 miles northwest, unites five different units to achieve its length of nearly a mile over the "bottoms" of McKees Rocks and the Ohio. The engineering solution was to use a central through-arch of steel over the river itself, with vertical stays stiffening the deck and four severe stone pylons to give appropriate structural and visual support.

AL62 Pennsylvania Drilling Company (Taylor-Wilson Manufacturing Company)

1905, Robert A. Cummings, engineer. 500 Thompson Ave., McKees Rocks

One of a handful of buildings remaining in a barren industrial strip, the former Taylor-Wilson factory is an overlooked marvel of the pioneer generation of "daylight factories" that revolutionized industrial design at the turn of the twentieth century. By 1884, engineer Ernest L. Ransome and others had perfected a system of reinforcing concrete with iron rods to increase its strength. This reduced the need for structural support, and allowed the number and size of windows in exterior walls to be increased significantly. Industrial buildings could now consist of more window than wall, and, flooded with natural light, they provided a more productive and humane environment for workers. Significantly, Ransome built his first daylight factory in 1902 in nearby Greensburg (altered; 1225 South Main Street, Westmoreland County), and Cummings doubtless visited it. For Taylor-Wilson, Robert Cummings followed Ransome's patented mode of construction, which allowed exterior columns to intersect with projecting floor slabs, hence countering structural forces through a framework rather than through solid masses of wall.

Cummings designed Taylor-Wilson to be cheap and fireproof, and also to show artistic flair. Six bays wide, sixteen bays long, and three stories high, it encloses an enormous space (160 × 120 feet) with a gently arched roof, one-story projecting aisles, and a facade dominated by a round-arched window twenty feet in height, though now boarded over.

AL62 PENNSYLVANIA DRILLING COMPANY (TAYLOR-WILSON MANUFACTURING COMPANY)

AL62 PENNSYLVANIA DRILLING COMPANY (TAYLOR-WILSON MANUFACTURING COMPANY) interior

AL63 PITTSBURGH AND LAKE ERIE RAILROAD (P&LE) STEAM LOCOMOTIVE REPAIR SHOP

Wooden window frames were painted red to provide contrast with the intervening bands of gray concrete. Used originally for the production of custom-built machinery for heavy industry, the factory currently serves only as a storage facility.

AL63 Pittsburgh and Lake Erie Railroad (P&LE) Steam Locomotive Repair Shop

1885, with additions. Pittsburgh and Lake Erie Railroad Yards, 0.3 miles north of the intersection of Locust St. and Linden Ave., McKees Rocks

The Pittsburgh and Lake Erie Railroad put its locomotive maintenance and associated shops astride its tracks in McKees Rocks around 1885. Of the several buildings on this site that survive, the Erection Shop is the largest and most impressive. It was constructed in 1903 after a fire involving steam-powered motors. This magnificent brick basilica is twenty-four bays in length and four bays in width. The external structure, with its round-arched windows and decorative cornice, is entirely of brick, while the internal trusses and columns are iron and steel. Four locomotives could sit abreast during repairs; electric motors that powered overhead cranes picked up whole locomotives to place them for rebuilding. With the conversion of the line to diesel power in the 1950s, the Erection Shop became redundant. Only one-tenth of the building is used now (for an electrical reheating furnace), but this is one of the finest remaining buildings of Pittsburgh's industrial heritage, and every effort should be made to ensure its preservation. Its former companions, two

huge roundhouses and a powerhouse, have been demolished.

AL64 Newington (Shields-Brooks House)

1816; 1823; 1868 chapel, attributed to Joseph W. Kerr; c. 1870 gardens, attributed to Samuel Parsons; 1893 mausoleum, John U. Barr. Beaver Rd. at Shields Ln., Edgeworth

Certainly rare in the northern parts of the United States, this estate includes a chapel and a mausoleum. The house has served a single family without breaks in ownership since the 1770s. David Shields built the smaller two-story brick block in 1816 on land granted decades before to his father-in-law, surveyor Daniel Leet. The main house, two-and-one-half stories in height, followed seven years later in a more refined Greek Revival style. The gardens are the glory of the eleven-acre estate and they include an early-twentieth-century labyrinth, attributed to Bryant Fleming.

The Way family also prospered in Sewickley and Edgeworth for nearly two centuries,

AL64 NEWINGTON (SHIELDS-BROOKS HOUSE)

owning an inn and tavern (c. 1810, with later additions) located just inland from the Ohio River shore on Beaver Road at Quaker Road. At the same intersection, John Way's Federal-style brick house is three-bays wide with a central hall. Rebuilt after it burned in 1841, the house received several additions during the course of the nineteenth century. A block south, Abishai Way, an agent for the Harmonists, built his raised Greek Revival home in 1838 at 108 Beaver Road, giving it a pedimented portico supported on slender columns.

AL65 Wilpen Hall (William Penn Snyder House)

1898, George S. Orth. Bounded by Blackburn and Waterworks rds., Sewickley Heights

A steelmaker with excellent architectural taste, William Snyder hired George S. Orth (1843–1918) to build this brownstone and shingle Queen Anne–style home first, then a Beaux-Arts town house that still stands at the corner of Ridge and Galveston avenues in North Side. By the 1920s, automobile roads were improved, and the North Side had decayed so much that the family turned this summer retreat into their permanent home. This was the pattern as well for their neighbors, the Benjamin Franklin Jones family, whose adjacent Fairacres estate was even more lavish. Today, all that survives of Fairacres are a half-dozen servants' houses visible from Blackburn Road and a summary notion of the once lavish gardens.

NORTH SIDE AND THE ALLEGHENY VALLEY

Immediately opposite downtown Pittsburgh on the north bank of the Allegheny River is the district called North Side. (Local city planners are attempting to substitute the loftier "North Shore," but to date the term has not stuck.) This was originally Allegheny City, the most ambitious settlement of the early days of western Pennsylvania. Some correspondence survives between surveyor David Redick, on the site, and Benjamin Franklin in Philadelphia, but why Redick based his 1788 design on a New England model is not documented. The urban grafting worked surprisingly well, however, and the basic square-doughnut shape of Redick's town can still be seen. The central square carries institutional buildings as Redick planned, among them the Children's Museum (AL74) and a Carnegie Library (AL75). The surrounding eastern, northern, and western strips of common grazing ground are still verdant as small parks, and the housing stock in the outlying blocks remains for the most part intact. Just the southern strip of green on the river side is lost. Its fate was sealed when the Pennsylvania Canal cut its right-of-way immediately south of Allegheny in 1832; after the canal ceased operations in 1852, the Pennsylvania Railroad laid its tracks on the same alignment.

Allegheny City provides a cautionary tale against the advancement of metropolitan government. As the settlement prospered, it annexed Manchester and other contiguous towns. Then, in 1907, the comeuppance: it was itself ensnared by Pittsburgh, and then decayed for three-quarters of a century. What saved the North Side was historic preservation of residential and commercial properties in the 1960s, especially in the dozen blocks known as the Mexican War Streets (AL76). Along with its many handsome streets and hundreds of the best middle-class homes in Pittsburgh, the North Side is now a museum mecca. The Children's Museum (AL74), Carnegie Science Center (AL68), and National Aviary (1952, Lawrence Wolfe, with additions; West Park) present traditional museum fare, and the Andy Warhol Museum (AL67) and the Mattress Factory (AL77) exult in the contemporary and experimental. The North Shore Center and Allegheny Landing Park (1984, UDA Architects, with R. Jackson Seay Jr., landscape architect), bounded by Isabella, Federal, and Sandusky streets and the Allegheny River, combines one of the nation's first urban sculpture parks with an early attempt to exploit the recreational benefits of the city's waterfront for a commercial development. The three-acre park, containing a fountain, and sculptures by Ned Smyth, Pittsburgh's George Danhires, George Sugarman, and Isaac Witkin, lies between the riverfront office blocks and is an integral part of North Shore Center, in addition to being an important selling point to prospective tenants. A gently sloping meadow between the offices and the river also functions as an amphitheater, and overlooks the Three Rivers Heritage Trail and docks. Upriver on the Allegheny is a mixed and fascinating landscape of raw industrial satellites (Millvale and Etna), boating marinas, and the leafy suburbs of Evergreen Hamlet, Fox Chapel, and Oakmont.

AL66 ALCOA Corporate Center

1994–1998, The Design Alliance; Rusli Associates, architectural design consultant.
201 Isabella St.

The 1953 downtown home (AL28) of ALCOA (Aluminum Company of America) was an epochal corporate headquarters, but at thirty-two stories and 475,000 square feet, it no longer corresponded to corporate needs of the 1990s. This replacement downsized ALCOA to 340,000 square feet in a radically different configuration of just six stories.

The new ALCOA helps restore to the north bank of the Allegheny River the visual coherence lost after World War II through piecemeal destruction and construction. West of ALCOA stands the North Shore Center office park; east of it rises (rather awkwardly) Lincoln at North Shore, a maze of apartments and town houses from 1997. Behind ALCOA, at 100 Sandusky Street, is the elegant headquarters of SMS Demag (1994, UDA Architects). These are all important parts of the emerging urban fabric of the North Shore, but it is the wavelike ALCOA that best defines the district now.

The architects worked closely with the firm's employees to program the six-story building into three segments. The first is a

AL66 ALCOA CORPORATE CENTER, with Andy Warhol Bridge (Seventh Street Bridge, AL13.2) in foreground

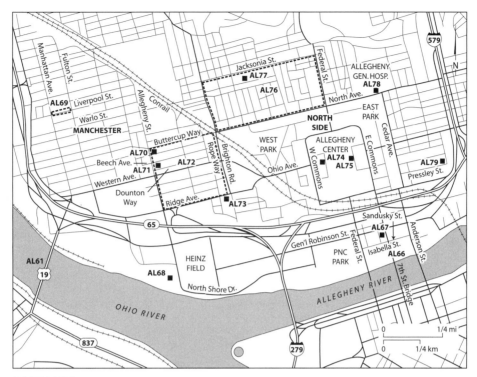

NORTH SIDE

small entrance and reception area on its north face, away from the river. The second, also on the north side, is a boxy housing of the heating, cooling, elevators, escalators, restrooms, restaurants, and a newsstand. Some of these elements are normally located on the roof, but architect Agus Rusli sought to shield the unattractive mechanics from the view of the downtown high-rises. The third element is the block-long serpentine curve of the headquarters itself. The skeletal frame of cantilevered sunscreens is aluminum, and the curtain wall is untinted glass to maximize both natural illumination and the striking views of the river and cityscape. The sunscreen accentuates the S curve of the building and fractures the base geometry into countless smaller shapes. The Three Rivers Heritage Trail cuts between the river and ALCOA's sandstone floodwall, with path and wall together muting the structure's bend.

AL67 Andy Warhol Museum (Frick and Lindsay)

1911, William G. Wilkins Co.; 1918 and 1922 additions, O. M. Topp; 1994 conversion to mu-seum, Richard Gluckman and Associates, and UDA Architects. 117 Sandusky St.

This cream-toned, terra-cotta-clad warehouse was a natural choice for conversion into a showcase for Pittsburgh's Andy Warhol, making it one of the world's largest museums devoted to a single artist. Its industrial character alludes to Warhol's use of industrial sites for his studios, while the mass production involved in industry reflects the mass production basis of Warhol's work. The building's original owners, William E. Frick (a distant relative of the magnate) and William G. Lindsay, lavished much care on their 1911 plumbing supply warehouse, not stinting on a bounteously ornamented Beaux-Arts cornice. Long gone, the cornice was replicated for the new museum, using high-technology lightweight fiberglass. Inside, virtually all nonstructural elements were removed from the seven-story building, leaving only the exterior walls, piers, and concrete floors. Richard Gluckman then split the warehouse into nineteen galleries on six floors for rotating shows of Warhol's thousands of paintings, graphics, videos, and personal archives. Visitors begin a tour by taking

AL68 CARNEGIE SCIENCE CENTER

an elevator to the top floor, then progress downward on the staircase inserted into the old freight elevator shaft. A new addition at the rear provides administration areas, an auditorium, and a theater for regular showings of Warhol's films. While the question, What would Andy have thought of all this? cannot be answered, the popularity of the museum suggests that the main design decisions were solved with uncommon sensitivity.

AL68 Carnegie Science Center

1989–1991, Tasso Katselas Associates. 1 Allegheny Ave.

Blessed with a dramatic site on the Ohio River just west of Heinz Field and prominently visible from the Point, the red and gray Carnegie Science Center stands as a guardedly populist temple to science and education. The Center is part of the Carnegie consortium, whose main museum and library stands in Oakland (AL41), but whose Andy Warhol Museum (AL67) lies less than a ten-minute walk away. Tasso Katselas gave the four-story building three major components: Omnimax theater, planetarium and auditorium space, and housing for specialized exhibits, all linked by a system of ramps and staircases to provide visual and physical unity. Somewhat brooding and somber despite color touches in red, the structure's domed Omnimax theater is on the city side, and a glass-skinned atrium and science theater are at the opposite end. Between the two sits the main exhibition block. The entrance is on the land side, reached by a

bridge from the parking lot. Busses use a second entrance below the bridge, which also allows direct access to the Omnimax theater.

A certain degree of disorientation seems endemic and possibly useful in science centers, and the lobby and attached atrium of this one do not disappoint, with a large and noisy gift shop, Aquabatics Fountain, and a restaurant overlooking the river. The three upper levels are each devoted to different themes. The interior is at its best with throngs of students climbing and descending its ramps, while the grounds are at their best when peaceful. Science education continues on the Ohio River with the USS *Requin,* a docked World War II diesel-electric submarine, and a barge that regularly navigates the three rivers as a floating marine laboratory.

AL69 Houses on Liverpool Street (originally Locust Street)

1880s. 1300 block Liverpool St., between Manhattan and Fulton sts.

Laid out in 1832, Manchester was already an important industrial center by the time it became part of Allegheny City in 1867. This block is one of the most impressive in Pittsburgh and the focus of one of the largest National Register Historic Districts in the city. At 1423 Liverpool Street, ironmaster James Anderson built c. 1830 a two-story, five-bay brick house with a central hall and a two-story pedimented portico that overlooked the Ohio River. The house recalls an era of almost unimaginable calm before men such as Anderson turned the North Side into a hellfire of industrialization. (Anderson's tiny public library, eagerly used by a young Andrew Carnegie, was the model for Carnegie's later worldwide library donations.) The 1300 block of Liverpool Street was originally settled in the 1880s by German-Jewish merchants and professionals. Edgar Kaufmann, the client for Fallingwater (FA28), was born around the corner in 1885. The rows of tall houses, coupled with the wide, tree-lined, red brick sidewalks, create an exhilarating and sophisticated urban streetscape. The nine double houses on the north side of the block are identical in their Second Empire styling, and were originally erected as rental properties on land owned by Letitia Robinson, scion of Allegheny's founding family. Houses on the block's south side were put up individually by such well-known merchants as Charles Aaron and Gustave Langenheim, whose freestanding house at number 1315 is the star of the block. The neighboring houses are mixed in style, but visual unity is maintained by similar mansard roofs, flat incised stone lintels, and the repetition of such basic design elements in the dormers, windows, and porch columns.

The decline of industry and the building of PA 65, which severed Manchester from other parts of the North Side, contributed to the severe decline of the neighborhood in the twentieth century. Since the late 1960s, however, the Manchester Citizens Corporation (MCC) and Pittsburgh History and Landmarks Foundation (PHLF) have played key roles in neighborhood revitalization. The PHLF rehabili-

tated most of the buildings on the north side of this block in the late 1960s in a program that later involved hundreds more homes throughout Manchester. The MCC continues to lead Manchester's redevelopment through initiatives designed to replace the neighborhood's dilapidated public housing with new units for sale and rental, and overseeing necessary social and community services.

AL70 Emmanuel Episcopal Church

1885–1886, Henry Hobson Richardson.
957 W. North Ave.

When the nascent Emmanuel church in prosperous post–Civil War Allegheny City created a building committee, it selected Malcolm Hay, a prominent Pittsburgh lawyer and politician, as its head. Hay possibly knew Richardson personally, but as an Episcopal layman, he had studied the designer's brilliant solution for the Episcopal liturgy in his Trinity Church in Boston. The committee selected Richardson for the commission in 1883. By the time Richardson committed himself to the work, he was also planning the Allegheny County Courthouse and Jail (AL1), in which Hay seems again to have played a role.

Richardson's first plans for Emmanuel were similar to his previous churches: Romanesque Revival in style but eclectic in detail. Richardson's first design adhered to the limitations of the plot (50 × 100 feet), but ignored the congregation's restricted budget. At $48,972, the projected cost was quadruple the budget, so the design was rejected. Eventually the building committee prevailed, and the church was built for only $12,300. In this budget fight—and not in some independent artistic source—lies the main reason for the simplicity of the plan and its reductionism from what until then had been Richardson's characteristically ornate style.

Emmanuel, massive and unadorned compared to the eclecticism of the other styles then present in Pittsburgh, is in no way visually poorer, thanks to the richness of its red brickwork and the striking comprehensiveness of its image. Five rows of voussoirs outline the three entrance arches and the tall windows that surmount and echo the entrance. The bricks outside the voussoirs are first laid in a basket-weave pattern, then in horizontal rows,

AL70 EMMANUEL EPISCOPAL CHURCH

and finally, in what the Dutch call "mouse-teeth" on the edges of the gable.

Neighbors have long referred to Emmanuel as the "bake-oven church" because of its un-broken transition to a semicircular apse. The interior is somewhat richer but still rustic, except for a white marble Tiffany-style glass reredos that was added in 1898 by Pittsburgh designers Leake and Greene. Richardson un-derestimated the thrust of the beams as well as the weight of the roof, which in just a few years gave the exterior aisle wall on Allegheny Avenue a picturesque but unthreatening bat-ter. Frank Alden of Richardson's Boston office was called in to evaluate the wall, which he found to be architecturally sound. It was Al-den, in 1888, who designed the adjoining par-ish house.

Though not an unsurpassed masterpiece, Emmanuel marks a significant turning point in Richardson's vocabulary. Given that a fa-mous architect was here incited to better work by a steadfast patron, Emmanuel stands as a good design lesson even beyond its local significance.

AL71 Calvary Methodist Episcopal Church

1892, Vrydaugh and Shepherd, with T. B. Wolfe. 971 Beech Ave.

The effusive academic detail of this society church contrasts markedly with Richardson's Emmanuel Episcopal Church (AL70) a block away. Calvary, whose Gothic Revival facade is marked by the enlivening contrast between the two differently sized facade towers, was almost a private devotional project for the four main families that backed it. So expen-sive was land in 1892 when Allegheny City was at its fashionable height that one-quarter of the budget is said to have been spent just for the site. Construction of the church cost another quarter of the budget, interior fur-nishings another quarter, and the last quar-ter went (by private subscription) into three of Louis Comfort Tiffany's best windows: the *Apocalypse, Resurrection,* and *Ascension.*

AL72 Allegheny West

1860–1900. Bounded by W. North, Allegheny, and Ridge aves. and Brighton Rd.

A large post–Civil War mansion on Western Avenue is one of the settings for Marcia Dav-enport's 1943 novel *The Valley of Decision,* about a family of Pittsburgh industrialists from 1873 to 1941. The Joshua and Eliza Rhodes House (c. 1866; 939 Western Avenue), in which the family of a traction czar lived from the 1860s through the 1920s, may have been the inspira-tion for that setting. Certainly it constitutes a fascinating remnant of late-nineteenth-century Pittsburgh. The Italianate house, of a simple sort, added florid hood molds and brackets to its plain brick walls. The vibrantly colored interior of the house, which is now a bed-and-breakfast, has original cabinetry, and a ballroom and servant quarters are located in a structure to the rear. The brick- and-stone-veneer houses in the 800 and 900 blocks of Beech Avenue, between Allegheny Avenue and Brighton Road, give a perfect idea of upper-middle-class Pittsburgh life after the Civil War. The blocks, unbroken and further unified by the roof cornice, are enlivened by the overlaying rhythm of prominent door and window moldings and punctuated by the oc-casional veranda. Two of the residents here were famous not for wealth but for their lit-erary talent. Gertrude Stein was born at 850 Beech in 1874; Mary Roberts Rinehart wrote a dozen of her mysteries in the solid house at number 954.

AL73 Community College of Allegheny County

1973, Tasso Katselas Associates. 808 Ridge Ave.

This megastructure of gray poured concrete and soft brown brick climbs the north slope of old Monument Hill. One of Tasso Katselas's stated objectives was to maintain the bulk of Monument Hill and not level it. The structure gently cascades in and out of the earth in a flow of movement that is also emphasized by the angularity of the escalator system.

Like many expressionist works of the 1960s and 1970s, Community College (CCAC) re-veals certain internal secrets externally, offer-ing viewers a glimpse into the inner workings of a building of this kind. Pipes, beams, and other internal elements become decorative as well as functional devices to offer visual movement to the viewer. Inside, the school has open circulation and free-flowing hall-ways. The criss-cross pattern of many of the hallways provides pedestrians with what

AL73 COMMUNITY COLLEGE OF ALLEGHENY COUNTY

Katselas calls a "series of discoveries," as they pass from classroom to classroom. Curving, and often looping, hallways bend through the school, providing kaleidoscopic views of the outside through the narrow slit windows cut into the walls.

Katselas sought to keep faculty and students in touch with each other by creating faculty cubicles that would be accessible and welcoming to students, while providing free zones where group interaction and discussion would foster the learning process. A design so strongly expressionistic is bound to have its detractors, and CCAC has many. Still, it succeeds in reclaiming a time when college campuses were not faceless education malls, but places of distinction and flair.

The college also owns Jones Hall (Benjamin Jones House, 1908; 808 Ridge Avenue), a forty-two-room reinforced-concrete Tudor Revival mansion designed by Frank E. Rutan and Frederick A. Russell of Rutan and Russell, a Pittsburgh firm that had its roots in H. H. Richardson's Boston office, for the heirs of Jones and Laughlin Steel. It remains a prime document to the time when Ridge Avenue was among the most glamorous Millionaires' Rows in the nation. The house was planned before Pittsburgh annexed Allegheny City in 1907, and wealthy families began to abandon the North Side for their country estates at Sewickley. (The Joneses stayed until 1931.) By 1912, though, the nature of this demographic shift must have been evident, because Thomas Hannah built Western Theological Seminary next door in the same style and scale as the

Jones house, but it was intended for institutional use from the first. Today both buildings serve the community college across the street. Another dozen neighboring mansions on Brighton Road and Ridge and Beech avenues have been restored from flophouses back to private residences.

Tasso Katselas Associates continued their North Side designs, a year after the college designs, with Allegheny Commons East (1974; 255 E. Ohio Street), a high-density complex of nineteen four-story brick town houses. The complex is part of the larger seventy-nine-acre Allegheny Center urban renewal project completed in 1978. This controversial redevelopment was intended to reverse the economic and social decay of the North Side, but it ended up obliterating much of it instead. Allegheny Commons East was built for low- and moderate-income tenants as a social counterbalance to the upscale apartment blocks and town houses elsewhere in Allegheny Center. In the end, the architectural quality of this subsidized complex was superior to that of its richer cousins.

AL74 Children's Museum of Pittsburgh (Buhl Planetarium and Institute of Popular Science and Old Post Office Museum)

1939, Ingham and Boyd; 2000–2004 addition, Koning Eizenberg Architects, and Perkins Eastman. 10 Children's Way

When Buhl Planetarium opened in 1939, it was the largest of the five planetaria in the United

AL74 CHILDREN'S MUSEUM OF PITTSBURGH (BUHL PLANETARIUM AND INSTITUTE OF POPULAR SCIENCE AND OLD POST OFFICE MUSEUM)

States. It occupies the site once occupied by Allegheny City's Italianate city hall, which became redundant after the city's forced merger with Pittsburgh. The Buhl Foundation, the planetarium's donor, also had links to the site: the Boggs and Buhl Department Store stood directly opposite the planetarium until the 1950s.

The Buhl's science exhibits, rooftop observatory, and astronomy workshops, as well as it planetarium, drew many visitors. Supplanted in 1991 by the Carnegie Science Center (AL68), the Buhl was given to the Children's Museum, which in the previous decade had taken over the Renaissance Revival Allegheny City Post Office (1894–1897, William Aiken).

The Buhl's exterior stripped classical walls, clad in gray limestone, hint at streamlining in their stylized quoins, and bold astronomy-themed Art Deco reliefs by Sidney Waugh provide a foretaste of the stylishly decorated interior. In 2004, an addition linked the Buhl to its neighbor, the former post office, to give convenient access between the two parts of the museum. The glass addition is sheltered by a gossamer-like screen of plastic petals that ruffles in the wind, yet allows light to enter the newly created space. A wind sculpture by Ned Kahn stands in the forecourt. Inside the museum is a replica of Mr. Rogers's Neighborhood House and puppets from his famous children's television show filmed locally at WQED (AL119).

AL75 Carnegie Library of Pittsburgh, Allegheny Branch

1889, Smithmeyer and Pelz. 5 Allegheny Sq.

This library enjoys the technical distinction of being the first Carnegie public library in the United States, since Carnegie's library in Braddock (AL56) was a proprietary gift to the steelworkers at his nearby plant. Andrew Carnegie made the gift offer in 1886 to Allegheny City, "the city which was my first American home." The national competition for the library was handily won by the firm of Smithmeyer and Pelz, who had just finished the Library of Congress in Washington, D.C. Taking no chances, the architects adhered closely to the detail and massing of H. H. Richardson's courthouse (AL1), especially in the massive square

tower that anchors the corner. The library included spaces for an art gallery, lecture hall, and a concert auditorium to accommodate an audience of 1,100. The library has closed and been replaced by a new building at 1230 Federal Street, but the auditorium serves now as a theater. In 2007, EDGE studio modernized the lobby, respecting the historic character of the building while bringing the box office and concessions area into the twenty-first century. In front of the library stands the central portion of Daniel Chester French's monument to James Anderson (1904, Henry Bacon), which Carnegie commissioned in memory of the man who, before him, made books available to a working public.

AL76 Mexican War Streets

1830s–1870s. Bounded by Jacksonia and Federal sts., W. North Ave., and Brighton Rd.

This core district of the North Side constitutes the largest area of development in uniform architectural style in the city and, with its brick herringbone sidewalks and new trees, it is one of the most pleasing neighborhoods visually. The North Side's oldest institutional building, an orphan asylum later purchased by the Allegheny Ladies' Relief Society to house Civil War widows and renamed the Allegheny Widow's Home preceded the residential buildings. Today known as the Renaissance Apartments, offering subsidized housing for the elderly (1838, John Chislett; 1873 additions; 1984; 2006 renovated, Landmark Design Associates; 1308 and 310–322 N. Taylor Avenue), the main brick building of the complex was

AL75 CARNEGIE LIBRARY OF PITTSBURGH, ALLEGHENY BRANCH

designed by Pittsburgh's second professional architect, John Chislett, in severe Greek Revival, five bays wide and three stories high, with a central pediment. It is located on land donated by William Robinson Jr., developer of the area.

Robinson, the first mayor (in 1840) of Allegheny City, around 1850, subdivided a portion of his inherited land just north of Allegheny Commons Park into approximately three hundred lots on twelve city blocks. Having just returned from military service in the Mexican War, Robinson named the streets after battles and generals of that conflict: Monterey, Palo Alto, Sherman, Taylor, and Resaca. Building followed, beginning in the 1850s with Greek Revival (mixed with some Italianate detailing) houses around Arch Street at the east, and ending in the 1870s in Richardsonian Romanesque around Brighton Road at the west. Unlike contemporary developments in Philadelphia or Baltimore, these houses went up independently, not in rows. They are of similar size (generally twenty feet wide and two stories high) and material (nearly always brick, though with a few standouts in wood frame or brownstone). There are some rare breaks between the homes.

By the early twentieth century, middle- and upper-class residents had abandoned these houses to renters and boarders. By the 1950s, the buildings had fallen into disrepair and the neighborhood was unsafe. Very few homes were torn down, however, as there was simply no economic incentive to do so. In the 1970s, these streets became one of Pittsburgh's earliest ventures into the historic preservation of a complete neighborhood, spurred by the new Pittsburgh History and Landmarks Foundation (PHLF). Today one of the premier preservation groups in the nation, the PHLF bought homes for resale either restored or as is, and also assisted landlords in maintaining their rental units. The result was, for the most part, an avoidance of the phenomenon of gentrification. The Mexican War Streets today have a growing and heterogeneous population, all concerned with preserving this gem of a neighborhood.

AL77 Mattress Factory

c. 1870; 1991 interior renovation, Joel Kranich; 2003 addition, Landmark Design Associates. 500 Sampsonia Way

This brick six-story former factory, which for about a century produced mattresses, was converted into a leading site for installation art in 1977, though the interior was not materially changed until a renovation in the 1990s. The ceilings and windows are high, the interior volumes capacious, and the galleries numerous enough that whole rooms can be dedicated to certain installations for decades. As well as its changing exhibitions featuring experimental artists, it has a growing permanent collection, including work by James Turrell. The gallery was expanded with an addition in 2003. A mesmerizing visual experience of art and architecture inside, Winifred Lutz created an interesting ruins garden outside beginning in 1993, using the foundations of homes and outbuildings that once stood next door.

AL78 Allegheny General Hospital

1929–1936, York and Sawyer. 320 E. North Ave.

The seventeen-story Art Deco tower of this 724-bed hospital building is topped by a penthouse in the guise of a Greek temple. Illuminated at night, it can be seen from many parts of town—Liberty Avenue in Bloomfield is the best viewing point—as a floating mirage. The same talent for combining function and fantasy emerges in the vaulted Byzantine-influenced entrance portico internally, which is supported on slender red and gray alternating granite columns with terra-cotta capitals. The numerous arches of the brick corbel table are filled with sculpted reliefs of major figures in the history of medicine.

AL79 The Priory and Grand Hall (St. Mary's Roman Catholic Church)

1853–1854 church; 1906 vestibule, Sidney Heckert; 1888 priory, Henry Moser. 614 Pressley St.

Father John Stibiel, second pastor for this parish of German immigrants, is the architect of record for this brick church. Externally, the twin-towered church is a melange of neoclassical features, but the interior betrays a far greater architectural talent. There, high barrel vaults held on four crossing columns intersect below a beautifully lit umbrella vault and skylight. Similar interior boldness marks Charles F. Bartberger's contemporary St. Paul of the Cross Monastery (148 Monastery Avenue), and St. Mary's may be his work as well. The church serves now as a busy banqueting hall; the Romanesque Revival priory next door is one of a handful of boutique hotels that Pittsburgh carved out of its Victorian white elephants at the end of the twentieth century.

AL80 Sixteenth Street Bridge

1923, Warren and Wetmore; James Chalfant, engineer. 16th St. and the Allegheny River

Like the "Three Sisters" bridges (AL13), the design of this span was overseen by Pittsburgh's Civic Arts Commission, which demanded a monumental aspect to what was the third bridge on this site. The New York architects had recently completed New York's Grand Central Terminal, and here, too, they employed oversized sculptures—in this case, giant bronze horses and globes by Leo Lentelli—to render the bridge a true civic monument. Two steel side arches flank a 437-foot center span, creating what has been described by bridge historian Steven Fenves as "an indeterminate hybrid, part trussed arch and part full-depth truss." The abutments consist of high stone piers carrying Lentelli's horses and globes.

AL81 Heinz Lofts (H. J. Heinz Company Factories)

1889, attributed to Frederick J. Osterling; various dates, additions, Robert Maurice Trimble, Albert Kahn, and Skidmore, Owings and Merrill; 2003–2005 loft conversions, Sandvick Architects and Developers. 300 Heinz St.

From this riverside site, Henry J. Heinz staged a revolution in food-processing and packaging techniques, ultimately building his food and condiment business into a global operation. The brand began modestly in 1869, with Heinz selling horseradish out of his family's house in Sharpsburg, three miles up the Allegheny. Twenty years later, Heinz consolidated his offices and plants in this model industrial complex, which grew to thirty-two buildings. Still standing are fine examples of late-

nineteenth-century industrial buildings and noteworthy newer additions

Heinz began life as a bricklayer, and these marvelous brick walls show the patron's understanding of the craft. Indeed, the old man caught his death of cold in 1919 while inspecting construction of a brick wall in this complex. Nearly everything that went up during his lifetime was in Romanesque Revival, probably designed by the local master of that style, Frederick J. Osterling. Utilitarian buildings executed in brick with stone trim, the structures feature corner spires, pronounced corbeling, and Roman arches, some structural and some decorative. Among the best-preserved older structures are the Bottling Building (1896; with 1905 additions), the Bean Building (1912), and Robert Maurice Trimble's Meat Products Building (1920).

Two of the early Heinz buildings depart from the Romanesque Revival idiom. Outside the complex, on E. Ohio Street, stands the Tudor Revival Sarah Heinz House designed by Trimble in 1913, a neighborhood youth center. And at the heart of the complex stands the five-story reinforced-concrete Administration Building (1906), by pioneer industrial architect Albert Kahn. Its neoclassical lines, rusticated Gouveneur granite facing, and white terra-cotta piers underscore its status as the seat of managerial power.

Kahn returned to the complex to add the four-story Employee Service Building, in close

AL81 HEINZ LOFTS (H. J. HEINZ COMPANY FACTORIES)

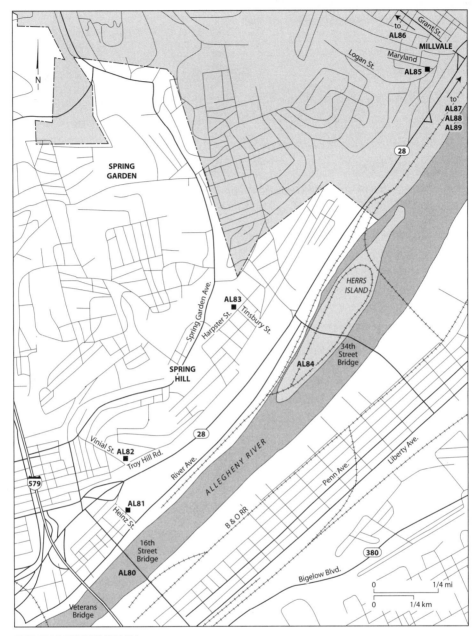

THE ALLEGHENY VALLEY

conformity with the earlier Romanesque Revival units. This housed dining facilities, auditorium, and other amenities for Heinz workers. Seeking to avoid the labor unrest that bedeviled other Pittsburgh industries, Heinz established benign but firmly paternalistic policies to encourage productivity among his employees. Kahn's other structure, an annex of 1930 to the Administration Building,

shows a clear stylistic break; it is a severe industrial block of light-colored brick, devoid of ornamentation.

In 1949, the company demolished seven obsolete buildings and commissioned Gordon Bunshaft of Skidmore, Owings and Merrill to erect a Vinegar Works and a central storage warehouse. The blue-colored glass curtain wall of the Vinegar Works marked the first

Western Pennsylvania hosts a stunning variety of planned communities, from utopian villages to company towns, several of which are included as individual entries in this volume.

HOUSE AND OUTBUILDINGS AT NORVELT, WESTMORELAND COUNTY, 1991.

The oldest of these communities was built by the Harmonists to meet their utopian ideals. Their villages included housing, farm buildings, mills, a hotel, a museum, and worship sites, all built according to the vision of George Rapp and his adopted son Frederick Reichert Rapp. Both Harmony (1804) in Butler County and Economy (1824) in Beaver County retain a remarkable number of their original buildings.

Vandergrift in Westmoreland County was designed by the nationally known firm of Olmsted, Olmsted and Elliott in 1895. The Apollo Iron and Steel Company provided the impetus, but Vandergrift is more than a company town. The houses were commissioned by their original owners and laid out along tree-lined curvilinear streets with a commercial district, a train station, churches, and a modified village green.

Chatham Village (1932), a National Historic Landmark and the best known planned community in western Pennsylvania, has only a vestigial commercial presence, but it has a variety of housing types and conforms to the master plan by Clarence S. Stein and Henry Wright (AL45). Two subsistence villages in southwestern Pennsylvania that also responded to the Great Depression are Norvelt (1933) in Westmoreland County and Penn-Craft (FA15, 1937) in Fayette County. While the economic focus of these two communities—the farm and the knitting mill—no

use of the International Style among Pittsburgh corporations, and an early and bold use of uncompromising modernism for industrial use anywhere in the country. While food processing does continue in some parts of the complex, the former Shipping, Meat, Bean, Cereal, and Reservoir buildings were converted to housing units between 2003 and 2005.

AL82 Penn Brewery (Eberhardt and Ober Brewing Company)

1894 brewhouse, Joseph Stillburg. 800 Vinial St.

Penn Brewery hugs the base of Troy Hill immediately across PA 28 from the Heinz plant (AL81). After the Civil War, German workers from the tanneries, breweries, and meatpacking industries gravitated to Troy Hill. In 1870, two brothers-in-law from Troy Hill, John Ober and William Eberhardt, took over this site in the hollow of the hill, where beer had been brewed since the 1840s, and built their brewery. It joined the Pittsburgh Brewing Company in 1899 and remained in operation until 1952, after which the buildings deteriorated.

In 1986, the North Side Civic Development Council initiated a program to revitalize the area's economy, using a mix of public and private funding. Part of the old brewery was restored for Penn Brewery and part was longer survive, the villages remain vibrant, as does Chatham Village, proving that good design and careful planning are always attractive and can retain residents.

The most recent (1989) in this long line of planned communities is Washington's Landing on Herr's Island in the Allegheny River (AL84). Here, Pittsburgh's Urban Redevelopment Authority and the landscape architects of Environmental Planning and Design have created a mixed-use development within minutes of downtown Pittsburgh.

Strictly residential planned communities found in western Pennsylvania date from 1851 (Evergreen Hamlet) to the New Urbanist development of Summerset at Frick Park (1995). Evergreen Hamlet (AL86) relied on the railroad to whisk into town those who resided in its frame Gothic Revival houses. Thornburg (AL134, 1900) and Schenley Farms (AL34, 1905) in Allegheny County were influenced by the trolley suburb ideal and the City Beautiful movement, respectively. Swan Acres, a unique reinforced concrete Moderne housing plan in Allegheny's North Hills initiated by Beck, Pople and Beck in 1934, has four houses designed by Quentin S. Beck and several more houses by architect Harry C. Clepper (c. 1938) along its curving streets. Taliesin fellows Peter Berndtson and Cornelia Brierly designed three houses in Meadow Circles (1959) on Lutz Lane in West Mifflin, Allegheny County, and Berndtson alone did two houses for Treetops (WE34, 1964), later dubbed Polymath Park. Both communities failed to fully develop, but the few flat-roofed, wood-sided Usonian houses that were built engage their natural settings.

The World War II town housing scheme for Aluminum City Terrace by Marcel Breuer and Walter Gropius in Westmoreland County (WE23, 1940) later became one of the first cooperative housing plans in the nation and remains fully occupied.

Summerset was developed on a former steel mill slag heap in Homestead by Pittsburgh's Urban Redevelopment Authority in 1995 and occupied in 2002. The grouping of traditionally styled houses and condominium units symbolizes the future of Pittsburgh, while building on its industrial past.

recycled into offices for the Brewery Innovation Center, an incubator of small start-up companies. The squat-towered brewhouse accommodates a restaurant and microbrewery, while some thirty tenant companies and their common support services use the brick office building (1897) next door. The Romanesque Revival–styled bottling building across Vinial Street is now independent of the brewery.

AL83 St. Anthony of Padua Shrine

1880; 1890–1891 addition. 1700 Harpster St.

In the late 1870s, Suibertus G. Mollinger, the Belgian-born pastor of Most Holy Name of Jesus Church in Troy Hill, faced a unique problem: he had to house the thousands of relics that he and his agents in Europe had acquired. In 1880, Mollinger used his personal inheritance to build St. Anthony's Chapel, a small domed cruciform structure. It attracted such throngs of pilgrims that it was enlarged in 1890 to its present size.

The chapel's brick and sandstone walls and twin square towers are a German version of the Romanesque Revival popular earlier in the century. Both the roof and octagonal spires are of slate-covered timber. The church fits comfortably in the neighborhood; it is attractive, solid, and substantial, if not spectacular. In contrast, the interior is flamboyant in

a dazzling Baroque explosion of gold leaf and stained glass windows, with yet more gold in the monstrances and reliquaries. Life-size figures of the Stations of the Cross, imported from Munich, line the walls of the chapel. Behind and to the sides of the altar stand massive walnut cabinets, fashioned by local craftsmen, to house more reliquaries.

After World War II, the numbers of pilgrims declined, and by the 1970s, the shrine had fallen into disrepair. Restored and refurbished in 1977, the shrine attracts a swelling number of visitors, with a catalogue of the relics now on a computer database.

AL84 Washington's Landing (Herr's Island)

1989–1999, Urban Redevelopment Authority of Pittsburgh, City of Pittsburgh Department of City Planning, and Environmental Planning and Design, master planners; LaQuatra Bonci Associates, landscape architects; Bohlin Cywinski Jackson, site planners; Montgomery and Rust, developers; commercial structures, Damianos Brown Andrews; The Design Alliance; and Kingsland, Scott, Bauer, Havekotte Associates; housing, Donald Montgomery and Bob Worsing. Allegheny River from 29th to 34th sts.

The forty-two acres of Herr's Island, two miles upstream from the Golden Triangle, entered history in 1753 when George Washington nearly drowned near here. A century later, Benjamin Herr made a fitful start at developing the island into a village of tree-lined streets, homes, shops, and recreational areas. But Herr's village was taken over by industry in the 1850s, and given its first stockyards by

tanner James Callery in 1885. In 1903, the Pennsylvania Railroad erected huge metal-roofed livestock pens on half of the island, turning it into one of the key livestock and slaughterhouse complexes in the nation. The railroad and the food processors abandoned Herr's Island in the 1960s, leaving behind a scrap yard, slaughterhouse, livestock auction house, soap works, rendering plant, and one hundred empty cattle pens.

After rusting for thirty years, the old installations were torn out as planners rebaptized the island Washington's Landing. The intent was to use neotraditional town planning to create a multiuse urban village, with adjacent areas for offices, light industry, and recreational use all within walking distance. Millions of dollars of public and private funds and intense collaboration between public and private planners and developers combined to create such a village fifteen years later, in 1989. Traditional house types and materials give a consistent architectural continuity to the sycamore-lined streets of the village at the southern end of the island, with its ninety town houses of brick and clapboard siding. The usual rows of identical town houses have been eliminated here by clusters of homes that are identified by distinctive bay windows, columned porches, and gabled roofs with cupolas.

Though Washington's Landing resembles such neotraditional projects as Duany Plater-Zyberk and Company's (DPZ) Florida town of Seaside, it differs from them by being located inside a major city, and being a true multiuse plan. Its commercial tenants were attracted to the island by its recreational facilities, and the homeowners—mainly ex-suburbanites or newcomers to Pittsburgh—extol their five-minute walks to work, or boating and rowing. The island's seven-acre public park provides bike paths and jogging trails, which in turn link to the north shore and the Three Rivers Heritage Trail by a converted nineteenth-century railroad bridge.

AL85 St. Nicholas Church

1901; 1922, Frederick C. Sauer. 24 Maryland Ave., Millvale

This yellow brick church's Colonial Revival exterior, with its twin towers (added by Frederick Sauer in 1922), gives no hint of the congregation's Croatian heritage, but inside lies an unforgettable portrayal of their former homeland in Maximilian Vanka's 1937 mural cycle. It depicts the Croatian experience in the New and Old Worlds in an eye-catching mix of Byzantine forms and social realist imagery in the manner of then dominant Mexican muralists José Orozco and Diego Rivera. Characteristic is the scene of a Pittsburgh millionaire, deathly pale, dining at a table outfitted with a stock ticker.

AL86 Evergreen Hamlet

1851–1852, Joseph W. Kerr; Heastings and Preiser, landscape architects. Rock Ridge Rd. just north of intersection of Babcock Blvd. and Evergreen and People's Plank Rd., Ross Township

This is one of America's first "romantic" suburbs, a few years before Alexander Jackson Davis's better-known Llewelyn Park in West Orange, New Jersey. Six families contracted to build on this hilltop five miles north of downtown Pittsburgh, in what must have been a reflection of the glorification of rural life in these years by poet Henry David Thoreau. In the end, only four houses rose on the eighty-five-acre site, for William Hill, William Shinn, Robert Sellers, and Wade Hampton. The Hampton (102 Rock Ridge Road) and Sellers (161 Rock Ridge Road) houses are boxy in shape, with their walls covered in shiplap siding. Hill's house (164 Rock Ridge Road) is more recognizably Gothic Revival in its gabled front and vaguely Tyrolean porch design—an amalgam of rural cottage designs found in Andrew Jackson Downing's three books on architecture and landscaping published between 1841 and 1852. Inside, the T-shaped disposition of the main rooms is more dynamic without being in any literal way Gothic. Only the cottage of the colony's founder, William Shinn (168 Rock Ridge Road), fully complies with the ethos, style, and environmental concerns of Downing. It is cruciform shaped, the walls covered with board-and-batten siding, and the bargeboards beautifully cut in intricate curves. Coming up to it on the deliberately winding road from below, one would be well prepared to meet the reclusive Thoreau himself.

AL87 Frederick Sauer Houses

1904–1930s, Frederick C. Sauer. 615–627 Center Ave., Aspinwall

These houses are a private fantasy by the otherwise restrained designer of a dozen staid Gothic and Classical Revival Roman Catholic churches around Pittsburgh (AL85). Though trained as an architect in Stuttgart, Frederick Sauer's hometown was Heidelberg, which was the likely model for this rugged and rambling group with their curved and angular forms, picturesque rubble walls, turrets, and chimneys (one of the units bears the name "Heidelberg"). The six rental properties in brick and random stone were built by Sauer with his own hands, and share something of the idiosyncratic glory (though none of the height) of Simon Rodia's contemporary Watts Tower in Los Angeles. This being Pittsburgh, though, Sauer's collection of fantastic shapes was and is commercially viable.

AL88 La Tourelle (Edgar and Liliane Kaufmann House)

1924–1925, Benno Janssen. 8 La Tourelle Ln., Fox Chapel

This exquisite eighteen-room fantasy seems more monastery or clubhouse than private residence, and not without reason. At least one of Benno Janssen's sketches refers to La Tourelle as a country house, which it may as well be, given its total isolation in spirit if not in mileage from Pittsburgh. The client was Edgar Kaufmann, an outsider to the clubby Pittsburgh elite for whom Janssen was designing mansions and clubhouses in the same years. Janssen's Longue Vue Club (AL89) stands a

AL86 EVERGREEN HAMLET, William A. Hill house

AL89 LONGUE VUE CLUB, entrance, clubhouse

few miles away on the opposite bank of the Allegheny, and La Tourelle can best be understood as a private Longue Vue. The roofs have the same high pitch and narrow gabled dormers as Longue Vue, and they are covered in the same Vermont slate. And though the walls here are brick, not sandstone, Janssen gives the massing the same artistic visual fragmentation, juxtaposing the turreted entrance—the estate's namesake—with the main house, the servants' wing, and the equally picturesque garage. Inside, the appointments were no less careful: master ironworker Samuel Yellin forged a wealth of wrought-iron decoration for the house right in the main fireplace. La Tourelle was greatly admired through the 1930s as a consummate achievement in the academic revivalism favored by the nation's rich, but the client's attention was by then wandering to modernism. It was in La Tourelle's rich fake-medieval living room, in 1934, that Kaufmann discussed with Frank Lloyd Wright the building of a radically different country house in nearby Fayette County: Fallingwater (FA28).

AL89 Longue Vue Club

1921–1923, Janssen and Cocken; Albert D. Taylor, landscape architect. 400 Longue Vue Dr., Penn Hills

This complex perfectly evokes the architecture and expansive spirit of the 1920s. On an inspiring site high above a wide bend in the Allegheny River, Benno Janssen created a miniature English-style Cotswold village of exquisite plan, profile, and materials for this golf club. The clubhouse rests between two hills, and its second story is carried via bridges, which allows automobiles to pass under the structure as it frames glimpses of the Allegheny River valley beyond. Though this picturesque device is certainly not restricted to Pittsburgh buildings, it had specific Pittsburgh precedents in H. H. Richardson's courthouse (AL1; the two arched entrances there were filled in around 1924) and in Henry Hornbostel's Carnegie Mellon campus (AL43). The bridges at Longue Vue allowed Janssen to skew the axes of his building and to compartmentalize its functions. They also work well with the timelessness expressed by the club's hand-hewn sandstone walls and high-pitched slate roofs. The golf course was designed by Scottish golf course architect Robert White.

PITTSBURGH NEIGHBORHOODS: A QUESTION OF PHYSIOGNOMY

Every city in the world is a city of neighborhoods, and Pittsburgh is no different. But neighborhoods seem more distinct here, and their hold on the residents is tenacious. The city's innate conservatism accounts, in part, for the endurance of and residential loyalty to Pittsburgh's neighborhoods, and its topography gives the city's ninety-one neighborhoods the hills, gullies, rivers, bridges, train tracks, and expressway traffic that create borders of striking prominence. Add to this mix Pittsburgh's traditional ethnic solidarity and the bonding that came from neighbors laboring side by side at death-defying jobs in the mills, and the result is the classic physiognomy of a Pittsburgh neighborhood.

The dozen neighborhoods presented here have visual and social cohesion, and a commonality of age, architectural styles, scale, color, and building materials. Mills that dominated many of these quarters are now gone, but certain places, such as Immaculate Heart of Mary Roman Catholic Church (AL92), distill and broadcast the essence of a neighborhood. The architectural glory of Pittsburgh may ultimately rest not in its buildings but in its neighborhoods.

THE STRIP, POLISH HILL, LAWRENCEVILLE, AND BLOOMFIELD

The Strip, Polish Hill, and Lawrenceville are three contiguous neighborhoods that are linked by topography and a shared involvement in early industry. The Strip got its name from its shape: a flat, long, narrow strip of three hundred acres hemmed in by the south bank of the Allegheny River and the steep rise of the Hill. Nearby transportation routes made it an area of intense industrial activity early in Pittsburgh's history, and the plentiful jobs attracted immigrant workers who built row houses and churches amid the commercial buildings. Early in the twentieth century, industry outgrew the Strip's natural confines, and the district fell into a decline that lasted to the 1970s. The decline has since been halted, and now wholesalers, food markets, nightclubs, and eclectic restaurants give the Strip its vibrant early hours and weekend street life.

If the Strip and Lawrenceville offered jobs, the isolation of Polish Hill offered domestic sanctuary to the thousands of Poles who settled here around 1885. The wood-frame homes clinging to this hillside are now attracting newcomers to settle here, though the majority of the neighborhood continues to be of Polish origin. Although Lawrenceville, upstream on the Allegheny, may be another extension of the Strip, it nonetheless has a separate character by virtue of its density along two spine roads, Butler Street and Penn Avenue, and its distinct central core in the old Allegheny Arsenal (AL93).

Like Lawrenceville, Bloomfield straddles two main thoroughfares, in this case, Liberty and Penn avenues, which here rise high above the Allegheny River, giving Bloomfield the aspect of a hill town. Buildings along Liberty Avenue are superior in architectural quality, and the secret of Liberty Avenue's animation lies in its unusual width as it passes through Bloomfield and in its social cohesion as the undisputed heart of the city's Italian-origin community. Italians began to arrive from the Abruzzi region in the 1880s; by World War I, they had settled in this neighborhood, which had been founded by German immigrants a half century before.

AL90 Senator John H. Heinz Pittsburgh Regional History Center (Chautauqua Lake Ice Company)

1898, Frederick J. Osterling; 1993–1996, Bohlin Cywinski Jackson; 2003–2004, Astorino Architects. 1212 Smallman St., The Strip

This former ice warehouse is a formidable seven-story red brick building, whose function dictated its enormous construction strength. The ground floor carries low masonry vaults between riveted steel beams, while upper-floor ceilings are of massive timber construction. Windows are narrow and recessed to protect the stored ice from sunlight. Ice blocks entered and left the building on railroad cars that ran directly into the building through the chamfered northeast corner. In 1993, the Historical Society of Western Pennsylvania chose the warehouse as a headquarters that could be equipped with galleries, archives, and meeting rooms. The remodeling presented the designers with numerous challenges. One of the most significant was to provide ventilation, access, and light in a structure built to prevent those things. Inner cagework was removed to form a seven-story atrium, which is topped by a new roof structure and partial clerestory. To the west, an elevator tower, clad in copper and steel and terminating in lattice-like steeple shape, was added to the exterior.

In 2004, the Center was expanded by a five-story red brick addition of a simple rectangular shape. It was designed to meet Leadership in Energy and Environmental Design (LEED) certification requirements, in keeping with Pittsburgh's leadership role in environmen-

AL90 SENATOR JOHN H. HEINZ PITTSBURGH REGIONAL HISTORY CENTER (CHAUTAUQUA LAKE ICE COMPANY)

tally sound architecture. The Center's exhibits celebrate Pittsburgh's heritage of industrial contributions and ethnic diversity—exactly the lessons visible in the streets around it.

AL91 2425 Liberty Avenue (Westinghouse Air-Brake Company)

1870–1871. 2401–2425 Liberty Ave., The Strip

This wooden-trussed, brick plant is a striking memorial to George Westinghouse, one of the nation's most important inventors. The legacy of Westinghouse—second in patent acquisition only to his rival Thomas Edison—has long been neglected in his adoptive city. Westinghouse came to Pittsburgh from upstate New York in the 1860s because it offered the industrial expertise, venture capital, and climate of aggressive entrepreneurship in which he could flourish.

Though Westinghouse branched out into switches and signals, electricity, turbines, appliances, natural gas, and even shock absorbers, the manufacture of railroad air-brakes was his first and central concern. It was for this enterprise that he supervised construction of this factory, an amalgam of three structures that eventually reached twenty-five bays in length and covered a full city block. In less than a decade, the plant proved too small for worldwide demand for his product. He then built a larger plant on the North Side in 1881, abandoning it nine years later to create a company town at Wilmerding (AL59). This Liberty Avenue building now accommodates office spaces.

AL92 Immaculate Heart of Mary Roman Catholic Church

1904–1905, William P. Ginther. 3058 Brereton St., Polish Hill

This church enjoys the best scenographic placement of any in the city, but not without cost. Its location high on Polish Hill affords it prominence both from Bigelow Boulevard above and from a wide sweep of the Allegheny below; but had the church burrowed headlong into the hillside, as it appears to, its apse would have been shrouded in darkness. Instead, William P. Ginther (1858–1933), of Akron, Ohio, set the church parallel to the hillside and designed a fake facade for one of

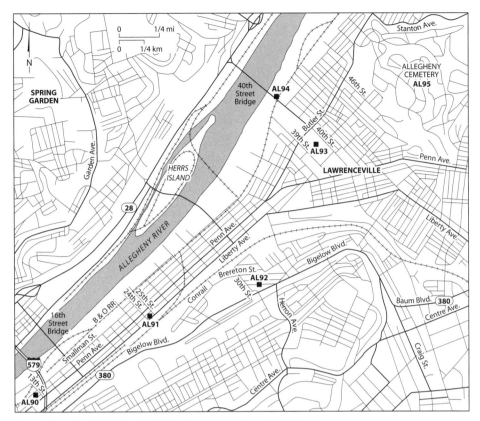

THE STRIP, POLISH HILL, LAWRENCEVILLE, AND BLOOMFIELD

the building's long sides. The moment worshippers cross the threshold they must make a 90-degree turn to enter the nave.

The original church was a small, wooden frame structure at the base of Polish Hill near the railroad tracks. In 1899, Polish immigrant millworkers gathered $10,300 to purchase property at the crest of Brereton and Dobson streets, just below the newly announced site of Bigelow Boulevard. Having resolved the problem of straddling the church across the brow of Polish Hill, Ginther appropriated various European precedents for his design. Francesco Borromini's S. Agnese on Piazza Navona in Rome appears to have contributed the high domed towers and the central dome (reaching almost one hundred feet in height on the interior), while the high attic with its prominent square windows and their flared moldings—so important for the dramatic effect on motorists on Bigelow Boulevard—is closely patterned after Michelangelo's St. Peter's in Rome.

AL93 Allegheny Arsenal

1814–1860s, Benjamin H. Latrobe, and others. Penn Ave. at 40th St., Lawrenceville

Although the Arsenal functioned until 1926, little survives of the buildings that once stood on the thirty-seven acres that stretch above and below Butler Street. Arsenal Park preserves the main vestige: an L-shaped powder magazine with cyclopean vault, half buried in the sloping ground. The more important buildings were those that stood for almost a century and a half before they were systematically destroyed by their then owner, a food distributor.

The layout of the Allegheny Arsenal was based on designs by English immigrant Benjamin Latrobe, the first professionally trained architect and engineer to practice in the United States. He came to Pittsburgh in 1813 to design and build steamships. When the U.S. Congress voted funds (eventually $300,000) for an arsenal in Pittsburgh, Latrobe drew up the required plot plans and details in a set of drawings that are today preserved in the Library of Congress. It appears, however, that neither Latrobe nor his protégé Thomas Pope stayed long enough in Pittsburgh to supervise construction of the buildings. Nonetheless, Latrobe's severe neoclassical imprint was unmistakable, both at the Arsenal and in the neighboring Greek Revival houses built for the munitions workforce. One of the best houses on the Arsenal grounds is on 39th Street, between Foster Street and the river: a three-story brick home with fanlight attic windows at both gable ends. The brick house at 257 40th Street, opposite the powder magazine, probably dates from the mid-nineteenth century, but keeps the severe forms and simplicity of proportions set by Latrobe. Other notable surviving outbuildings or worker houses stand on 38th, Carnegie, and Home streets, McCandless Avenue, and Modoc Alley.

The Allegheny Arsenal was among the first and most extensive of the nation's arsenals, a result of the federal government's concern for a permanent system of defense and supply that preceded the War of 1812 and was then much invigorated by that conflict. Pittsburgh was deemed a strategic locale for manufacture and storage of ordnance because of its established iron industry and its superior water access to military posts from Canada to the Gulf of Mexico.

The Arsenal manufactured ammunition, infantry and horse equipment, caissons, and gun carriages through the Civil War. Latrobe's layout drew on the quadrangle format of fort architecture, but it also reflects his proposal in 1800 for a national military academy. Roughly six hundred feet in length on each side, the quadrangle of stone and brick buildings was located between Butler Street and the river, with the entrance facing the street. The powder magazine was located southeast of the main site, in what since 1907 has been Arsenal Park. After 1868, the entire installation served as storage, and by 1926, the government had sold the last remnants. Portions of the Arsenal's perimeter wall and several of the stone piers from which iron gates once hung are visible along 39th Street, and nearby are some post–Civil War brick utility buildings.

AL94 National Robotics Engineering Consortium (Epping-Carpenter Company)

1898, Samuel Diescher, engineer; 1994–1996 adaptive reuse, Burt Hill Kosar Rittelmann. 10 40th St., Lawrenceville

Situated on five acres beside the Allegheny River, the Consortium is a joint venture undertaken by NASA, Carnegie Mellon University's Field Robotics Center, and private corporations to develop robotic technology applicable to industries ranging from mining to space exploration. The Consortium occupies 100,000 square feet in a rehabilitated steel-framed brick basilica that civil engineer Samuel Diescher (1839–1915) built in 1898 for the Epping-Carpenter Company. In 1925, the Pittsburgh Piping and Equipment Company added a four-bay pipe shop and shipping area facing the river.

When Pittsburgh's Urban Redevelopment Authority purchased the facility in 1993, it was structurally sound but its interior unsuitable for high-tech endeavors. The interior was gutted, mechanical systems were overhauled, and half of the addition of 1925 was demolished for parking and outdoor testing grounds. Diescher's original brick walls were fitted with thick, semiopaque windows for maximum heat retention and the original wooden roof was cleaned and reinsulated, giving the interior a striking rusticity for so futuristic an environment. The principal facade, facing the bridge on the west, was replaced with a glass curtain wall. Diescher's east facade on 43rd Street now has large plate glass windows illusorily fitted with small panes and set tightly in the wall plane.

AL95 Allegheny Cemetery

1844, John Chislett; 1848 Butler Street gatehouse, John Chislett, and 1868–1870, Barr and Moser; 1887 Penn Avenue gatehouse, Macomb and Dull; 1903, William Falconer. 4734 Butler St. and 4715 Penn Ave., Lawrenceville

Allegheny Cemetery is one of the earliest garden cemeteries in the United States. John Chislett laid out the grounds, designed the first structures, and then remained for some years as superintendent. Inspired by Boston's Mount Auburn Cemetery, Chislett, along with Dr. James Speer and merchant Charles Avery,

AL95 ALLEGHENY CEMETERY, Butler Street gatehouse

Chislett carved the original 100 acres from John Shoenberger's country estate. Superintendent William Falconer (creator of Schenley Park) landscaped the expanded acreage around 1903, augmenting the picturesque qualities of the natural topography with artificial lakes and new planting. The cemetery's architecture is just as rich. The Butler Street gateway is in Tudor Revival, the towered chapel behind it is Gothic Revival, and the huge gatehouse on Penn Avenue is Richardsonian Romanesque. The first burial took place in 1845. Among the more memorable monuments are the Gothic Revival chapel-like mausoleum with Tiffany glass windows for James Moorhead, designed by Louis Morgenroth in 1862, and a granite tree commemorating members of the Wilkins family. Songwriter-composer Stephen C. Foster, who grew up in Lawrenceville, and actress Lillian Russell Moore are among those who rest here.

had promoted the idea of a "romantic" cemetery as early as 1834. The goal was to alleviate overcrowding in Pittsburgh's graveyards and create a park for a city that had none. The city now surrounds the 300-acre cemetery, but the sense of an oasis is in no way diminished.

EAST END

Two Pittsburgh neighborhoods that could be said to live in a symbiotic environment are East Liberty and Highland Park. Highland Park was being farmed before the American Revolution, but was given its street patterns only after the Civil War. East Liberty was already a flourishing transportation and commercial nexus early in the nineteenth century. By midcentury, it was a pike town on the turnpike to Philadelphia and the prime crossroads for Pittsburgh's East End, a status augmented by the introduction of horsecars in 1859. By the early twentieth century, East Liberty was Pennsylvania's third most important commercial core, after downtown Philadelphia and downtown Pittsburgh. In the relationship of the two neighborhoods, it was East Liberty that sold goods and Highland Park that bought them, and the prosperity of the one was always dependent on the other.

Then in the 1960s, East Liberty was hit hard by urban renewal of the most rigid ideology. Its rabbit warren of streets and loading docks was bulldozed into a kind of suburban mall surrounded by a ring of high-rise subsidized housing projects that left it isolated. The decline of East Liberty badly afflicted Highland Park. Demolition of the high-rise in the early twenty-first century left gaping holes, which turned out to be big enough for a half-dozen big-box retail chains to move in, giving East Liberty a new hold on life as a kind of inner-city suburb.

AL96 BAUM BOULEVARD DODGE (CHRYSLER SALES AND SERVICE BUILDING)

AL96 Baum Boulevard Dodge (Chrysler Sales and Service Building)

1933–1934, Albert Kahn. 5625 Baum Blvd., East Liberty

Since its creation in the mid-nineteenth century, the two-mile length of Baum Boulevard has served as a modest but useful connector road between the Oakland and East Liberty neighborhoods. Around 1910, it became the regional center for the emerging automobile industry; a Ford assembly building still stands at the corner of Morewood Avenue. Dozens more gas stations and car dealerships emerged on Baum in the next decades. Albert Kahn's Chrysler showroom—one of many he designed in the nation—is a three-story modernist composition of finely cut stone and concrete, with a high-ceilinged showroom lit by plate glass windows. The dealership's distinguishing characteristic is its corner cylindrical tower, a recurring motif in Kahn's work for Chrysler. The building is marred only superficially by some gaudy signage. Its blueprints are in the Architectural Archives at Carnegie Mellon University.

AL97 Motor Square Garden/AAA East Central (Liberty Market)

1898, Peabody and Stearns. 5900 Baum Blvd., East Liberty

This is one of just two survivors of the dozen market houses that once served Pittsburgh; the other is in the South Side (see AL48). Its circular dome of metal, timber, and glass rises above a block of light and dark yellow bricks, colored terra-cotta, and geometric ornament, while enormous round-arched windows in gabled wall dormers on all four elevations illuminate the interior. It ceased functioning as a market in 1916, and, since then, has been used for various purposes, including an exhibition space.

AL98 East Liberty Presbyterian Church

1931–1935, Cram and Ferguson. 116 S. Highland Ave., Highland Park

This immense church is both visually and socially impressive. The congregation first assembled in a rural schoolhouse on this block in 1819, then built a succession of five different structures on the site. The wealthy congregation (the Negley and Mellon families were members) could afford a generous budget, so the church is luxuriously furnished with rib vaults, stained glass, a marble bas-relief of the Last Supper, a towering reredos of ivory-colored stone, and an elaborately carved pulpit.

Although Ralph Adams Cram believed that no other church in the nation achieved such completeness of utility and art, the design lacks the élan of his earlier (though scarcely much bigger) St. John the Divine in New York City. East Liberty works best as part of the urban fabric: its Spanish Gothic Revival

AL98 EAST LIBERTY PRESBYTERIAN CHURCH

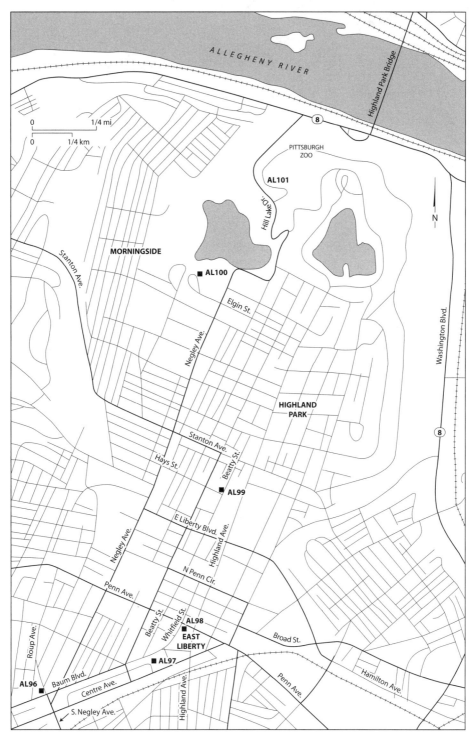

HIGHLAND PARK AND EAST LIBERTY

MARY SCHENLEY MEMORIAL FOUNTAIN IN 2008,
ALSO CALLED *A SONG TO NATURE* (H. VAN BUREN
MAGONIGLE, ARCHITECT, AND VICTOR D. BRENNER,
SCULPTOR).

Pittsburgh as we know it today was two cities in the 1890s, Pittsburgh east of the Point, and Allegheny west and north of it. The two entities constantly competed, even in the building of urban parks, until Allegheny was annexed in 1907. In Pittsburgh, Edward Manning Bigelow, director of public works from 1888 to 1906, arranged for the transformation of former farm lands into Schenley and Highland parks.

In 1889, Mary Schenley, an expatriate living in London, donated three hundred acres of her land to the city for Schenley Park and gave the city the option to buy one hundred additional acres. A log house on E. Circuit Road built c. 1787 for Robert Neill recalls the area's earlier history. By 1896, major roads within the park were completed, and the following year work began on Panther and Junction Hollow bridges that span the two gorges slicing through the park. William Falconer, park superintendent in 1896, and his successor George Burke implemented a massive program of picturesque improvements in the Olmsted tradition, from shady woodland trails to gently rolling pastures. Statuary by Guiseppe Moretti and reliefs by Daniel Chester French and Paul Fjelde are worthy complements to the park's verdant spaces. Moretti also designed heroic statuary for Highland Park. That park, which surrounds the city's 1879 reservoir, opened in 1893 after Bigelow assembled 380 acres of surrounding farmland, most originally owned by Jacob Negley.

Riverview Park, on the hills above what was old Allegheny and now Pittsburgh's North Side, has many features similar to its cousins across the river, including an early-nineteenth-century log house built for the Watson family, its original settlers. Riverview hosts the only remaining bridle trail in the city among its two hundred acres of woodlands. On the park's highest hill is a buff brick Renaissance-styled observatory. Its architect, Swedish immigrant Thorsten Billquist, arrived in Pittsburgh around 1893, after serving an apprenticeship with McKim, Mead and White in New York City. With fluted Ionic columns outlining one of its three domed sections and a pedimented portico marking the entrance, the building serves science and art equally well. Floors below two of the telescopes rotate, but each stands on an independent foundation of bedrock. An exquisite window designed by Mary Elizabeth Tillinghast (1903) depicts Urania, the Greek muse of astronomy. The telescopes are open to public use on select evenings.

Pittsburgh's fourth major urban park, Frick Park, was left to the city in Henry Clay Frick's will of 1919, and assembled in parcels purchased from 1919 to 1942. At six hundred acres it is the city's largest park. Between 1935 and 1957, it was laid out by the New York City landscape design firm of Innocenti and Webel. One the firm's first projects built in the park were stone entrance structures with conical roofs designed in 1935 by John Russell Pope.

crossing tower, a 300-foot massive tower of steel and concrete, dominates the East End as a pendant to the Mellon-backed Cathedral of Learning in Oakland (AL38).

AL99 Alpha Terrace

1880–1890s, attributed to James T. Steen. 700 block N. Beatty St., East Liberty

These two dozen row houses create a kind of private green between Stanton and Hayes avenues. The houses on the east side are in Queen Anne style of stone and wood, and those on the west side are Romanesque Revival of stone. On both sides, the uniform height is punctuated and enlivened by spires, miniature towers, and large gables. A building permit was granted to house builders Murphy and Hamilton for the west side of the terrace in June 1894, by which time the east side had stood for half a decade. James Steen is traditionally regarded as having designed both sides. Uniform terraces like this were once fairly common in the East End, and this survivor is still effective as a visual and social anchor to the neighborhood.

AL100 Baywood (Alexander and Cordelia King House)

1880s. 5501 Elgin St., Highland Park

Baywood sits on land that Virginian William Heth sold to Jacob Negley (ancestor to the Mellon family) in 1799. In 1856, it became the estate of Alexander King (grandfather to Richard King Mellon), who introduced soda ash to the glass-manufacturing industry. When the house that Negley built burned in 1879, King replaced it with this two-and-one-half-story red brick structure in a somewhat stiff Second Empire style, with a mansard roof, single- and double-arched dormer windows, and tall square tower. A greenhouse veranda across the front allowed Cordelia King to raise exotic plants and butterflies. Unfortunately, the two subsequent generations of the family who occupied the house allowed its lush planted terraces to go to ruin. Deeded in 1954 to the city of Pittsburgh as a cultural center, the mansion was sold in 1994 and was restored as a single-family dwelling.

AL101 Highland Park and the Zoo

1889, Berthold Froesch, landscape architect; later additions. Bounded by Antietam, Bunker Hill, and Butler sts. and Washington Blvd., Highland Park

Highland Park is both a park and a city neighborhood of the same name that stretches a mile from East Liberty to the Allegheny River. Park and neighborhood both illustrate the profound influence Edward Bigelow had on the urban development of Pittsburgh, a legacy that also survives in his three boulevards and in Schenley Park. Working here with the city's trolley czar Christopher Lyman Magee, Bigelow surreptitiously bought 360 acres of hilly woodlands bordering the river and conveyed them to the city as a park in 1893. Magee developed approximately one-third of the park into the Pittsburgh Zoo in 1898, then profited for years for his generosity by running trolley lines to the zoo through the newborn neighborhood.

The landscape architect was probably German-born Berthold Froesch. Bigelow was always careful to adorn his development projects with both fine plantings and good sculpture. Here, as at Schenley Park, his collaborator was Giuseppe Moretti, whose heroically scaled statuary in bronze and granite greets visitors at the Highland and Stanton avenue entrances to the park. These were restored in 2000 for the park's centenary.

In 2000, the PPG Aquarium (Indovina Associates Architects) opened in its splendid new 45,000-square-foot facility, a modernization and enlargement of the original aquarium of 1967. The same architects designed Water's Edge (2006–2007) for polar bears, walruses, and other water-loving animals.

AL102 Lincoln-Larimer Fire Station (Lemington Engine House No. 38)

1908, Kiehnel and Elliott. Lemington Ave. at Missouri St., Lincoln-Lemington-Belmar

Just before World War I, the firm of Kiehnel and Elliott was challenging Pittsburgh's orthodoxies in public architecture just as architect Frederick G. Scheibler Jr. (see AL105) was challenging housing orthodoxies. German-born Richard Kiehnel came to Pittsburgh from Cleveland, but he had worked in Chicago

AL102 LINCOLN-LARIMER FIRE STATION (LEMINGTON ENGINE HOUSE NO. 38)

during the early years of the Prairie School. He joined in partnership with Pittsburgher John Elliott in 1906. This simple fire station, with minimalist brick walls set off by exaggerated dark stone cornices, shows the influence of Frank Lloyd Wright. The placement of the windows on the main facade seems almost lifted from Unity Temple, a Chicago masterpiece of which Kiehnel was surely aware.

AL103 Lemington Elementary School

1937, Marion M. Steen and Edward Joseph Weber. 7060 Lemington Ave., Lincoln-Lemington-Belmar

This is the most successful of a number of Art Deco schools designed by Weber during Marion Steen's tenure as superintendent of buildings. Cincinnati-born architect Edward Joseph Weber (1877–1968), who trained in Boston and attended the prestigious Ecole des Beaux-Arts in Paris from 1903 to 1905, moved to Pittsburgh, where he designed many Roman Catholic buildings, most notably Central Catholic High School in 1926–1927 (4720 5th Avenue), for Link, Weber and Bowers. Weber also designed Pittsburgh's Art Deco Mifflin School (1932) at 1290 Mifflin Road for Link, Weber and Bowers, and later worked as an artistic designer for the Pittsburgh Board of Education. With Weber, Steen designed Schiller School in 1939 (1018 Peralta Street). The Lemington school's rather severe classical massing and factory brick is enlivened with vividly colored terracotta ornament representing the five human races. The three most successfully resolved Art Deco public buildings in Pittsburgh are the Lemington school, the New Granada

Theater (AL120), and the old Allegheny County Airport (AL60).

AL104 Holy Rosary Church

1928, Ralph Adams Cram for Cram and Ferguson. 7160 Kelly St., Homewood

This is the most inventive of Cram's three churches in Pittsburgh, with a powerful and idiosyncratic Spanish-inspired design for a congregation originally of German and Irish extraction and now African American. The surrounding blocks of identical frame houses are dwarfed by the church's tall and spiky spire. The numerous pinnacles on the sides and the crocketed spires on the facade make the vibrancy of this Iberian fantasy—a restatement of the Cathedral of Burgos in Spain—all the more powerful. Inside, Catalan Gothic provided Cram's precedent for a forest of slender columns and ribbed vaults that creates the most dramatic nave in Pittsburgh.

AL105 Old Heidelberg Apartments

1905, 1908, Frederick G. Scheibler Jr. 401–423 S. Braddock Ave., Point Breeze

Probably the most admired of Frederick Scheibler's many houses and apartments in the city, Old Heidelberg is a twelve-unit, three-story, concrete apartment block with cottage wings, strongly akin to his nearby Linwood Apartments (1907) at McPherson Boulevard and N. Linwood Avenue and The Whitehall (1906) at East End Avenue and Tuscarora Street. Scheibler is seen today as Pittsburgh's local prophet of modernism, especially in his Vilsack Row terrace of eighteen attached apartments (1912; 1659–1693 Jancey Street), with their absence of decoration, uncompromising horizontality, and contrast of solids and voids. A designer unschooled in architecture, he apprenticed with the local Barr and Moser firm and worked in traditional styles until breaking out on his own in 1901. He never left Pittsburgh, but traveled far stylistically. At Old Heidelberg, he used a more decorative treatment of openings and surfaces. The starkness of the white walls and the dramatic back-and-forth massing of the apartment volumes are resolutely modern, but the effect is rendered ambiguous by the pseudothatched profile of the massive, brooding roofs.

AL106 HOMEWOOD CEMETERY

AL107 FRICK ART AND HISTORICAL CENTER
(CLAYTON)

AL106 Homewood Cemetery

*1878; 1923 entrance buildings, Colbert T. A.
MacClure and Albert H. Spahr. 1599 S. Dallas
Ave., bounded by Forbes and Braddock aves.,
Point Breeze*

Founded in 1878, Homewood is named after
Judge William Wilkins's estate and his Greek
Revival mansion, which stood nearby from
the 1830s to the 1920s. The cemetery's 205
acres constitute about half of Wilkins's former estate, with the other half now Frick Park
and the residential streets in Point Breeze and
Squirrel Hill. The Romanesque Revival and
Beaux-Arts mausolea for the Fricks, Mellons,
Heinzes, Mestas, and Rockwells constitute a
true necropolis, whose visual and social order
mimics the nearby streets that the industrial
barons dominated when they were alive. The
cluster of buildings at the entrance includes a
Gothic Revival chapel and Tudor Revival gatehouse and administration building.

AL107 Frick Art and Historical Center
(Clayton)

*1860s; 1892 rebuilt, Frederick J. Osterling. 7200
Penn Ave., Point Breeze*

Following their marriage in 1880, Henry and
Adelaide Frick moved into and partially rebuilt
the Italian villa that still constitutes the core
of this mansion. In 1892, they commissioned
Frederick Osterling to expand the house again.
He transformed the two-story Italianate house
into a four-story French Chateauesque mansion, but the result inside and out was more
baronial than happy. Later additions are the
limestone Renaissance Revival Frick Art Museum (1969–1970, Thomas C. Pratt for Pratt,
Shaeffer and Slowik) and a Car and Carriage
Museum displaying Frick's sumptuous vehicles and a history of western Pennsylvanian's
love affair with the automobile.

More enchanting than the house are the
grounds, with Frick's private greenhouse and
the playhouse for his children. Immediately
across Reynolds Street begin the several hundred forested acres of Frick's estate. In 1935,
those acres became Frick Park, with John
Russell Pope adding pavilions at the park
entrances here and at the Forbes Avenue entrance. Currently a house museum, Clayton is
one of the best of its type in the nation, less in
artistic quality than in the obsessive retention
of every article of clothing and its accompanying documentation.

SHADYSIDE AND SQUIRREL HILL

From the 1850s, the Pennsylvania Railroad provided daily commuter trains
from the congestion and pollution of downtown Pittsburgh to the emerging
suburbs to the east. Shadyside evolved into a particularly distinguished suburb for an upper-middle class that now had the possibility of creating villas
within easy reach of the city. Succeeding waves of development (based on the
car and bus, since the Shadyside railroad station closed around 1950) kept to
the same standard.

Squirrel Hill is Shadyside's uphill neighbor, at least in its wealthy half. (Realtors call this district "North of Forbes," to distinguish it from the densely packed streets south of Forbes Avenue.) Rarely visually dull, the affluent north half contains striking houses by such modern architects as Walter Gropius and Richard Meier, local modernists, as well as many survivors in the various academic revivals from the 1890s to the 1920s. The names of many of the clients for these homes, such as Mellon, Thaw, Mesta, and Kaufmann, are renowned.

AL108 Calvary Episcopal Church

1906–1907, Ralph Adams Cram. 315 Shady Ave., Shadyside

Almost a dozen churches and a synagogue met the needs of Shadyside's newly rich and pious residents in the two decades around 1900. All survive today, with Calvary and Episcopal Church of the Ascension (1896–1897, William Halsey Wood; 1897–1898, Alden and Harlow; 4729 Ellsworth Avenue) standing like sentinels at Shadyside's east and west borders, and they are the two designs that are the most academically correct. With Henry Clay Frick among his patrons for Calvary Episcopal, Cram need not have worried about the budget. The church begins cool and almost brutal, then its limestone walls, emphasized by narrow vertical windows and prominent buttresses, culminate in a square tower and skyward-striving

AL108 CALVARY EPISCOPAL CHURCH

spire, one of Cram's best. The church turns rich and warm inside with its wood trim and stained glass. Compared with his erstwhile partner Bertram Grosvenor Goodhue's First Baptist Church (see AL34), the personality differences and approaches to church design and building that ultimately fractured their partnership are readily evident.

The former manse for Calvary, now known as the Sellers-Carnahan House and privately owned (1858; 400 Shady Avenue), was built by wholesale grocer and banker Francis Sellers. Sitting originally on ten acres of land, the sprawling L-shaped Italianate–Gothic Revival brick house likely had its origins in an architectural pattern book design. Immediately west of Calvary is Sacred Heart Roman Catholic Church (1924–1926, Carlton Strong; 310 Shady Avenue), which, like the adjacent Episcopal church, is thoughtful and dramatic both in concept and execution. Unlike Cram's Calvary Church, which is externally austere but rich inside, Strong captures the rich texturing of Gothic inside and out. The gable-topped facade, almost completely glazed, gives the church a sense of connection to the exterior that Cram's structure lacks. Particularly evocative is the forestlike wooden truss roof inside, its distinctive structure giving special meaning to the shiplike central volume of a church that we call a "nave."

AL109 Highland Towers

1913, Frederick G. Scheibler Jr. 340–342 S. Highland Ave., Shadyside

Of Frederick Scheibler's approximately eighty buildings in Pittsburgh, this four-story apartment block, designed for wealthy, progressive families, is the most confidently resolved. The usual influences Scheibler gleaned from architectural magazines and from the exhibitions of contemporary architecture held at the Carnegie Museum are evident in this stunning example of early modernism. Its two entrances on either side of the recessed central facade of this U-shaped building are elevated from the street level, pushing the apartments away from the noisy street. Scheibler composed the exterior in yellow tapestry brick, dark blue tile, glass, and stucco. Each of the recessed apartments has a solarium that opens into a balcony; the central apartments look over a garden terrace.

The interior is rich, beginning with the deep blue art tiles at the entrances from Henry Mercer's Moravian Pottery and Tile works in Doylestown, Pennsylvania. Originally, the floors were divided into four apartments, each with three bedrooms, two bathrooms, and servants' quarters. The apartments were equipped with the latest devices and had a safe, built-in oak and mahogany cabinets, and bookcases. The building had vacuum cleaning outlets, a prototype air conditioning system, and a Modulated Vapor System for heating. An earlier Scheibler-designed apartment block, which incorporated commercial space and is more overtly Art Nouveau, is the Minnetonka Building (1908; 5421–5431 Walnut Street).

AL110 Jerome and Joan Apt House

1951–1953, A. James Speyer. 40 Woodland Rd., Squirrel Hill

Among the older houses of the Squirrel Hill neighborhood are some of the most distinguished modern designs in the city. James Speyer was born in one of the old mansions in the Woodland Road district, but in 1938, just weeks after Ludwig Mies van der Rohe became dean at the Armour Institute of Technology in Chicago (now the Illinois Institute of Technology [IIT]), Speyer joined him for graduate studies and became a committed modernist. Speyer's achievements were fourfold: as teacher of architecture at IIT; as architect of some exquisitely detailed houses; as curator at the Art Institute of Chicago; and as famed exhibit designer there.

The background for the design of the Apt house was unusual. Joan Frank Apt had grown up across the road in a house designed by Walter Gropius and Marcel Breuer (AL111), and

she knew Speyer. The site is steeply sloped and a granite stairway descends the hillside to reach the house. The house's low rectangular base is Miesian, as are the great expanses of plate glass; the heavily wooded site affords privacy. Other design decisions seem to have been client driven, such as the two internal circulation systems, one for family members and one for servants. The architect's family summered next to the Kaufmanns at Fallingwater (FA28), and Frank Lloyd Wright's influence is apparent in the house's low ceilings and integration of the furnishings. The fireplace's dramatic arch is an H. H. Richardson influence.

Speyer also designed a house for his widowed mother, Tillie S. Speyer, in 1963 (Wightman and Northumberland streets). The severe templelike block turns its back on the adjoining busy intersection, and the entire property is ringed by a high brick wall for privacy, with the bricks stacked rather than bonded to indicate their nonbearing role. Large windows light the simple interior plan, which has a bank of rooms north and south off a two-story atrium. The theme of serenity and contemplation extends to the sunken garden and adjoining channeled rivulet of water, which gave his mother, a sculptor of biomorphic abstracts, the sense of a Japanese garden in the middle of Pittsburgh.

AL111 Cecelia and Robert Frank House

1938–1940, Walter Gropius and Marcel Breuer. 96 E. Woodland Rd., Squirrel Hill

Renowned modernist Walter Gropius, founding director of Germany's Bauhaus, emigrated to the United States, and to Harvard, in 1937; a year later, he invited his former student Marcel Breuer to follow. The commission to design a house for the Frank family, the largest and most comprehensive commission of Gropius's and Breuer's early American careers, gave them an unprecedented occasion to expand their ideas of a modernist house as total work of art, replete with an extensive program of specially conceived furniture that allowed Breuer to continue—for the first, and virtually the only, time in America—experiments in laminated plywood begun in the mid-1930s in England.

Robert J. Frank, a Pittsburgh industrialist,

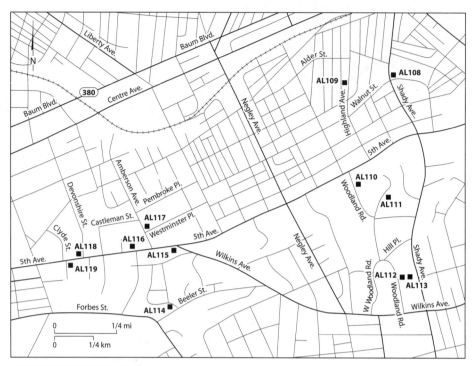

SHADYSIDE AND SQUIRREL HILL

heard Gropius lecture in 1938, and visited Gropius's and Breuer's own houses in Lincoln, Massachusetts, the following summer. By early 1939, he and the two Bauhaus masters had conceived a house, as modern in its systems and attention to family comfort and ease of entertaining and recreation as in its materials and appearance. With its cladding in sandy-pink Kasota stone over a welded steel frame combined with huge areas of glazing in plate glass and glass brick, the house appears at once grand and stylish as well as functional and open, particularly in the large-scale strip windows, huge sliding glass doors of the indoor swimming pool, and in the great open terrace that stretches through the block of the house above the pool. Gropius wrote his clients that the house would be "very noble" in appearance. The drama of the sweeping glass, curved stair window, linking the three principal floors, announces the flowing circulation within that would greet guests once they alighted under the cantilevered portecochere. A games room and the pool occupy the ground floor, while a stair sweeps guests up to a reception area from which the second-floor dining and living rooms, cloak room

and bar, and study with conservatory could all be reached at a step. A wishbone-shaped, travertine-clad fireplace core replaces conventional walls. The house is brilliantly integrated with its hillside site, so that the second floor is at grade with the rear garden, with its organically shaped lily pond and stepped retaining walls echoing the house's rustic stone base. The upper floor was given over to bedrooms, each with its own bath and dressing room, all accessed from the family living area at the center of the plan with its monumental granite fireplace.

Because of the family's interest in discretion and privacy, the Frank house, four-car garage, and grounds constitute one of the unsung masterpieces of American house design. They have been preserved intact by Alan [I W] Frank, the youngest of the Franks' three children.

AL112 Frank A. Giovannitti House

1979–1983, Richard Meier. 118 Woodland Rd., Squirrel Hill

The variety of architectural experiences a pedestrian might get from an inspection of Woodland Road is nowhere more pronounced than in the two postmodern residences standing at numbers 118 and 118-A (AL113). Richard Meier's Giovannitti House stands directly next to the roadway, with the Abrams House right behind. Meier's much-acclaimed design is, at first glance, a barely concealed reshuffling of his Smith House at Darien, Connecticut, of a dozen years before. Though keeping the Smith House's language of intersecting planes, solids, and voids, the Giovannitti three-story, neo-Corbusian white cube takes on extraordinary vividness as it tucks itself into the hillside. This affords privacy and a garden setting to the residents within the house, and a reconsideration of the relationship between man and nature to the streetside viewer.

AL113 Betty and Irving Abrams House

1982, Venturi, Rauch and Scott Brown. 118-A Woodland Rd., Squirrel Hill

The clients had previously lived a few blocks away in a ranch house next to the stringently modernist A. James Speyer–designed house (AL110), which may have spurred them to postmodernism here. Though they first considered postmodernist architects Charles Moore and Michael Graves for the commission, they chose the firm of Venturi, Rauch, and Scott Brown. The Philadelphia architects took as their point of departure the difficult setting of the proposed building site, slightly downgrade from Woodland Road, in a shallow valley split by a creek. The lot, one of five carved from the old Tudor Revival estate next door, contained an ornamental stone bridge from the 1920s that spanned the creek. The architects used the bridge as the main landscape incident that can be viewed from the oversized living room windows, and the creek's water fills ornamental pools at the front and rear of the structure.

The dynamic, curvilinear form of the Abrams House emerges from the green and white wooden clapboards and the colored enamel panels that form strident, raylike, decorative motifs from the center of the facade over a gray background. The left half of the facade is dominated by an oversized fan-shaped window that hints at a mill wheel—perhaps an allusion to the creek over which the structure is built. The interior plan of the house is simple, allowing the architects to syncopate

the large rectangles for the more important areas of the home with smaller squares for secondary bedrooms and storage and utility rooms. The most striking aspect of this interior is the changes in scale and the interplay of open and closed spaces. These effects are most notable in the living room, where a balcony extends the full width of the house to create a snug sense of enclosure for a narrow bar on the floor below it. This enclosure acts as a foil for the adjacent living room, underscoring the unexpected twenty-four-foot height of its gracefully curved ceiling.

The Abrams House represents the dynamic forms and dramatic juxtapositions for which the firm was acclaimed. By any measure, this quirky house on an inconvenient and waterlogged site is an exceptional addition to the architectural pedigree of Woodland Road.

AL114 Abraam Steinberg House

1951–1952, Peter Berndtson and Cornelia Brierly. 5139 Penton Rd., Squirrel Hill

This house for physician Abraam Steinberg is one of several Pittsburgh homes built from the 1940s through the 1960s by two designers who met and trained at Frank Lloyd Wright's Taliesin Fellowship. Peter Berndtson designed most of them, and his wife and partner, Cornelia Brierly, collaborated on several and designed others on her own. Certainly the close fit of a house and its surroundings is a textbook definition of organic architecture. The brick, redwood, glass, and concrete house stands on the edge of a long, narrow and steeply sloped lot. Two exterior walls of the house form a right angle to conform to the street grid, the

AL114 ABRAAM STEINBERG HOUSE interior

rounded rear wall echoes an inner circular garden that is open to the sky. This garden, visible from all the major rooms, provides the true facade for the house. Interior spaces flow visually from one to the next, analogous to the ramps that physically unite its three levels. The organic theme is carried through in the house furnishings, built-in where possible, and in the same redwood that provides structure for the house. Invariably but unfairly compared to their teacher Wright, Berndtson and Brierly were an important force in the adoption of modern architecture in postwar Pittsburgh.

AL115 Sunnyledge Hotel ("Sunnyledge," James McClelland House)

1886–1888, Alexander W. Longfellow for Longfellow, Alden and Harlow; 1996–1997 conversion, Raymond Schinhofen. 5124 5th Ave., Shadyside

James McClelland was a homeopathic doctor for Andrew Carnegie and the Frick, Mellon, and Scaife families. After rejecting a Queen Anne design for his house by a local architect, McClelland hired Longfellow, Alden and Harlow of Boston. The house sits easily on a narrow bench of land against a small hillside, which softens the bulky massing and austerity of the unadorned brick walls. The front elevation has a deeply inset arched door, irregularly spaced windows, and textured brickwork. Massive square chimneys with decorative brickwork and corbeling rise from the hipped roof. McClelland's medical office curves out at the northeast corner to form an oversized tower with conical roof. His patients entered through a separate porch with exposed rafters. Inside, the entrance hall is paneled in wood, and a forest of thin wooden spindles forms screens and the staircase banister. The spindles were fabricated simultaneously for Sunnyledge and Chicago's Glessner House, which the same firm completed after H. H. Richardson's sudden death in 1886.

The McClellands' younger daughter lived in Sunnyledge for ninety-four years, changing nothing. She endowed it as a private house museum, which would have had few equals for period authenticity, but her youthful curator survived her by very few years and the furnish-ings were auctioned. The family papers went to the Historical Society of Western Pennsylvania. Fortunately, when the home became a small hotel, the public rooms were kept intact, including samples of James McClelland's old medicine bottles from a century ago.

AL116 Gwinner-Harter House (William B. Negley House)

1871–1872; 1912–1923 additions, Frederick J. Osterling; 1996 restoration, Edge Architects. 5061 5th Ave., Shadyside

This is the second oldest home of what remains from the days when Pittsburgh's 5th Avenue rivaled 5th Avenue in New York City. After World War I, many of the mansions in the Oakland section of 5th Avenue were demolished or turned into apartments, and this occurred here in the Shadyside neighborhood after World War II. This three-story Second Empire–style house built for attorney and banker William B. Negley is one of the few survivors. Edward Gwinner, a stone contractor, purchased the house in 1911, and commissioned Frederick Osterling to design a three-story addition to the west side of the house, and a single-story classically inspired porch in order to update the, by then, old-fashioned house. Gwinner expanded the small central entrance hall into a lavish marble room with an extravagant staircase, reminiscent of mansions in Newport, Rhode Island. In 1923, Osterling returned to design the interiors of three reception rooms; each is paneled in English oak and walnut, and two have carved limestone fireplace surrounds that reach the ceiling.

Dr. Leo Harter acquired the house in 1963 and began a decades-long restoration. In 1987, a fire on the third floor caused extensive damage to the house. Then in 1995, Jo-edda Sampson, a major force in the renewal of Pittsburgh historic properties, bought and restored the house, and hired Edge Architects for a contemporary redesign of the burned-out third floor's interior. The reborn house is the third in a row of superb 5th Avenue mansions, after the coolly classical Hillman House (1924, Edward P. Mellon) at number 5045 and the Rococo-style Moreland-Hoffstot House (1914, Paul Irwin) at number 5057. Older is the Gothic Revival Willow Cottage

AL116 GWINNER-HARTER HOUSE (WILLIAM B. NEGLEY HOUSE)

(Howe-Childs House), dating to around 1867, seven blocks away at 5918 5th Avenue, which has been handsomely restored and is part of Chatham University.

AL117 Shadyside Presbyterian Church

1889–1892, Shepley, Rutan and Coolidge; 1937–1938 interior renovation, Eyre and McIlvaine. 807 Amberson Ave., Shadyside

Long one of Pittsburgh's wealthiest congregations, Shadyside Presbyterian was founded in 1867 by prominent landowners Thomas Aiken and William Negley. After constructing two unsatisfactory churches on the same site, the congregation turned to the Boston-based successor firm to H. H. Richardson, whose style then dominated Pittsburgh. The predictable outcome was a restatement of Richardson's Trinity Church in Boston. Here the muscular central block and pyramidal cap clearly recall Trinity, but Shadyside Presbyterian is broader and has a lower profile. In more densely packed city streets, the church's understated grandeur would be lost, but in this verdant setting amid nineteenth-century homes, the scaled-down facade, external narthex, and transept ends produce an unusually powerful neighborhood church. Another contextual touch is the inclusion of many windows, far more numerous here than in the Boston prototype, perhaps in response to Pittsburgh's dark and smoky skies.

AL118 Rodef Shalom Temple

1906–1907, Henry Hornbostel for Palmer and Hornbostel; 1989 renovation, The Ehrenkrantz Group and Eckstut. 4905 5th Ave., Shadyside

This synagogue is the best of Hornbostel's three religious structures in Pittsburgh—the other two are Smithfield United Church (1925–1926; 620 Smithfield Street) and the former B'Nai Israel Synagogue (1923–1924; 327 N. Negley Avenue). The congregation, which dates from 1856, used a synagogue in downtown Pittsburgh until it was attracted by the amenities of Oakland, coincidentally the same year that the neighboring St. Paul Cathedral relocated (AL36). The cream-colored brick structure has a square plan that culminates in a large squared dome of green tiles and glazed terra-cotta ornament. The synagogue's compact massing and bright coloring are reminiscent of Byzantine structures, which were popular precedents for synagogues at the time.

The interior, as expected from the exterior massing, is a huge, undivided volume underneath the Guastavino-tiled dome of light-colored herringbone tiles, which has an octagonal skylight. Stenciled color, gilded wood chandeliers, and oak paneling highlighted in gold leaf enrich the interior. A restoration in 1989 reversed water damage and improved the poor acoustics that had become an accepted but unloved attribute of the building.

AL119 WQED Studios

1969, Paul Schweikher. 4802 5th Ave., Shadyside

Created in 1952, WQED was the first publicly owned educational television station in the United States. As part of the cultural program of the Pittsburgh Renaissance I, it gained fame as home to Mr. Rogers, the much-loved children's television personality. The combined state-of-the-art studios and administrative facilities encompass 66,000 square feet. The hallmarks of New Brutalism are visible throughout the building, from the raw poured-concrete exterior to the unrestricted play of space inside. The plan of the complex is bilateral, with studios and conference rooms on the left side and offices housed in four blocks on the right. The subdued interior decor emphasizes texture over ornament, with rough concrete juxtaposed against polished oak and glass block partitions.

Paul Schweikher came to Pittsburgh in 1956 to head the architecture school at Carnegie Technical Institute (now Carnegie Mellon University). The Student Union at Duquesne University (1967; Vickroy Street) was his first Pittsburgh commission. The best external features of this massive, six-story poured-concrete Brutalist structure were the concrete scissor ramps at both ends of the rectangular building. But the Student Union's severe aesthetics were compromised when the entrance ramp was replaced by a double flight of steps, and the ground-floor interior resurfaced in brick in an attempt to make it warmer in tone. Schweikher's structuring of the Union has held up well, housing spaces for recreation, dining, and activities for both students and faculty. The two-story ballroom, illuminated by concealed clerestories, is a particularly grand space.

THE HILL AND THE BLUFF

The Hill and the Bluff offer another example of two Pittsburgh neighborhoods tightly linked. The first is oriented toward the Allegheny River and the second to the Monongahela, with 5th and Forbes avenues forming a corridor between them. Both neighborhoods are a world away from downtown Pittsburgh in topography, social function, scale, and architectural character, but anything that happens downtown for good or ill impacts these two communities that stand immediately uphill.

The Hill had farmhouses on it around 1800; then from the 1820s to the 1860s, immigrants from Ireland and Germany settled here; followed by eastern Europeans, notably Jews; and, from the 1880s to the 1920s, African Americans from the southern states. The Bluff was laid out on paper in the mid-nineteenth century. The rows of brick town houses surviving now date mainly from the 1860s to 1900.

AL120 New Granada Theater (Pythian Temple)

1927, Louis A. S. Bellinger; 1937, Alfred M. Marks. 2007–2013 Centre Ave., The Hill

In the 1920s, African Americans formed several chapters of the Knights of Pythias in Pittsburgh. A group of construction workers belonging to Union Local 111 commissioned Louis Bellinger, Pittsburgh's first African American architect of prominence, to design its lodge house. Born in South Carolina in 1891, Bellinger graduated from Howard University in 1914.

At first, the building flourished, with a dining hall on the first floor, a ballroom on the second, and offices on the third; but a downturn in economic conditions forced the sale of the temple in the 1930s to Pittsburgh theater impresario Harry Hendel. Having owned and lost an earlier Granada Theater, Hendel transferred its name to this building. The temple's dining hall became a theater, usually showing Yiddish movies, while the second floor housed the Savoy Ballroom, named for still another of Hendel's earlier businesses.

Bellinger's original design set three stories of windows in yellow brick below a cornice consisting of squared notches over a frieze of oval terra-cotta tiles. In 1937, Alfred M. Marks (1891–1970) added shimmering red, blue, and yellow glazed enamel panels to the ground floor. The marquee combines designs in blue, yellow, green, and red. The refur-

AL120 NEW GRANADA THEATER (PYTHIAN TEMPLE)

bished New Granada Theater remained the glory of the Hill for another three decades, hosting all the giants of the Jazz era: Count Basie, Cab Calloway, Ella Fitzgerald, Lionel Hampton, and Lena Horne. The New Granada closed after riots ripped through the Hill in the late 1960s. The Hill Community Development Corporation plans to rehabilitate it as part of Granada Square, a hub of educational, social, and artistic activities for the revived Hill of the future.

AL121 Crawford Square

1991–present, Urban Design Associates and Tai + Lee. Bounded by Crawford and Roberts sts. and Centre and Webster aves., The Hill

These attached town houses of tan brick and wood are set in short blocks with widened streets in the manner of the private streets of nineteenth-century St. Louis and Boston. Lively in detail and staggered in response to the sloped grade, these hundreds of units would be a standout in any neighborhood, and they certainly are here, between the desolation of the Lower Hill with its acres of parking lots around the Mellon Arena (AL122) and the unattended old buildings of the Middle Hill.

Probably the most successful of any public project in post-Renaissance II Pittsburgh, Crawford Square goes a long way toward healing the grievous urban wound inflicted by the Renaissance I of the 1950s: the destruction of the Lower Hill and the severing of its remnant from the Golden Triangle. The twenty-three-acre site holds 350 rental units and 140 houses of mixed-income housing. Three key groups were involved: Pittsburgh's Urban Redevelopment Authority (URA), a joint city-county agency; the developers McCormack Baron Associates of St. Louis; and Pittsburgh-based Urban Design Associates (UDA). The URA initiated the project in 1988, and hired McCormack Baron based on the firm's successful results in Cincinnati and St. Louis. The municipal agency enlisted UDA as designers based on their success in getting community involvement in turning around weakened neighborhoods. UDA provided site planning and design for the first 203 rental units, while the first forty houses were designed by Tai + Lee.

Since the Mellon Arena and Crosstown Expressway (I-579) block the site to the west, UDA designed a plan with a strong north–south axis, using the existing street grid as a guide to reinforce a traditional urban fabric and reintroduce connections to downtown. All buildings are two or three stories, each with front and rear yards. A pattern book codifies materials, colors, and facade elements, insuring that subsequent developers maintain a uniform look and feel in future expansions of the neighborhood.

Financing for this $55 million development came from the URA, the City of Pittsburgh, private lenders, and the philanthropic community. The reduced-rent units are provided by McCormack Baron, who gains tax benefits. Already in its short life, Crawford Square has begun to revitalize the Hill. Even more important, it provided a model for similar projects that are luring suburbanites back to the city, such as Washington's Landing (AL84), Lincoln at the North Shore, and Summerset at Frick Park.

AL122 Mellon Arena (Civic Arena)

1954–1961, Mitchell and Ritchey, architects; Ammann and Whitney, structural engineers; H. Rey Helvenston, superintending engineer. 66 Mario Lemieux Pl. (formerly 300 Auditorium Pl.), The Bluff

The Mellon Arena was, and still is, the subject of engineering admiration and urban regret. The project began when city council member Abe Wolk proposed an open-air tent to house summer performances of the Civic Light Opera. Edgar Kaufmann Sr. turned the concept into a glistening, retractable stainless steel dome. When its site was changed from Highland and then Schenley Park to the dense African American neighborhood of the Lower Hill, the result was controversy: engineering marvel or racial harmony. The marvel won out, and 1,600 African American families were dispersed throughout Pittsburgh's East End. The ninety-five-acre redevelopment of the Lower Hill constituted Pittsburgh's largest, costliest, and most fractious urban renewal project, with far more headache and far less to show for it than Gateway Center (AL7). After the leveling of nearly one thousand parcels of property, only Epiphany Catholic Church (1903, Edward Stotz) at 1018 Centre

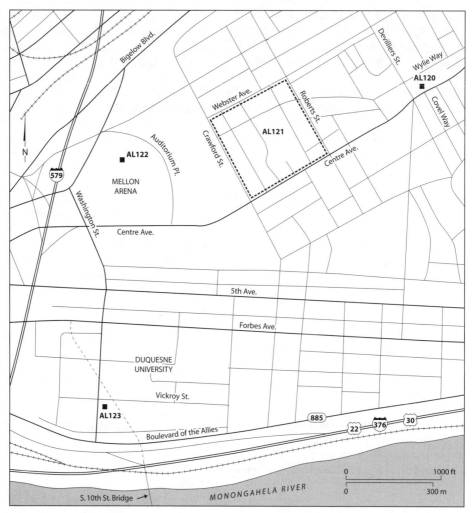

THE HILL AND THE BLUFF

Avenue and the rebuilt Beth Hamedrash Hagodol Synagogue (1964, Liff/Justh) at 1230 Colwell Street remained as witnesses to the old neighborhood.

The Civic Arena was one of four building complexes to emerge from the devastation: the others were I. M. Pei's Washington Plaza Apartments (1964), Edward Durell Stone's Chatham Center (1966), and the Central Medical Pavilion (1972). Only a few seasons were required to show the arena's impracticality for opera, though it remains a good venue for popular music and sports, and since 1967 has been home to the Pittsburgh Penguins hockey team. The arena has few betters in terms of clear-span roofs and retractable domes. The dome, approximately 417 feet in diameter and 109 feet high, is nearly circular in plan. The retractable shell is composed of six 220-ton steel leaves and two fixed leaves made of 7,800 stainless steel pieces, covering in all a total of 170,000 square feet. The leaves roll back on carriage wheels that ride on 3,000 feet of steel rails, coming to rest under the two stationary leaves that are supported by a 260-foot cantilevered space frame. Nonetheless, the dome has not been opened in years, and the hockey team is building a new arena across Centre Avenue (2007–2010, HOK Construction and Urban Design Associates; bounded by Centre and 5th avenues and Washington Place), for which Beth Hamedrash Hagodol Synagogue and the Central Medical Pavilion were demolished and replaced by a metal- and glass-clad trapezoidal hockey stadium that seats 18,000.

AL123 Richard King Mellon Hall of Science, Duquesne University

1968, Ludwig Mies van der Rohe. Duquesne University campus, Vickroy St., The Bluff

Duquesne University opened in 1878 as the Pittsburgh Catholic College of the Holy Ghost, occupying this site on the Bluff overlooking the Monongahela River. In the 1960s, Duquesne erected two notable buildings of complementary but different appearance on opposite sides of Vickroy Street: the Student Union (see AL119) and Richard King Mellon Hall of Science. Architect Paul Schweikher, an old Chicago friend of Mies van der Rohe, secured the Mellon Hall of Science commission for him. It stands opposite Schweikher's Student Union, close to the bluff of the Monongahela River. The rectangular four-story structure gives the impression of a horizontally oriented version of Mies's much-admired Seagram Building in New York City. It is based on a twenty-eight-foot module of bronze heat-absorbing glass that, on the upper three floors,

AL123 RICHARD KING MELLON HALL OF SCIENCE, DUQUESNE UNIVERSITY

is subdivided by thin steel mullions and black graphite-painted steel panels. The buff brick and glass first floor is recessed under the upper stories. Mellon Hall is visually adequate on the Bluff, but its power is best revealed when it is viewed from across the river on the slopes of South Side—another manifestation of Pittsburgh's abiding Acropolis complex.

The university recently expanded across Forbes Avenue into a new eight-story, Silver LEED-awarded recreation complex called Power Center (2006–2008, DRS Architects).

ON THE PARKWAY EAST

The boroughs of Wilkinsburg, Churchill, and Monroeville line up in a row extending east of Pittsburgh, but they have little in common beyond a shared growth pattern as pike towns. A settlement at what is now Wilkinsburg existed even before the American Revolution, but the town grew only after the turnpike to Philadelphia was cut through on the line of the current Penn Avenue, early in the nineteenth century. A second boost came in 1852, when the Pennsylvania Railroad's tracks reached Wilkinsburg and initiated a century of commuter service. A third transportation artery arrived in the early twentieth century, when the Lincoln Highway (U.S. 30) incorporated Penn Avenue as part of its cross-country route to downtown and points west. Wilkinsburg was so pleased with this extra attention and the revenue it generated that in 1916 it erected a life-size copper statue of Abraham Lincoln alongside the eponymous roadway. It still stands at the intersection of Penn Avenue and Ardmore Boulevard (U.S. 30).

But highways give and highways take away: in 1939, New York City's Robert Moses designed an expressway linking downtown Pittsburgh to the western extension of the Pennsylvania Turnpike. Locally called the Penn-Lincoln Parkway or the Parkway East (officially it is I-376), the post–World War II road bypassed Wilkinsburg, with severe economic consequences from which the borough has not recovered. In 2003, the Martin Luther King Jr. Busway, which runs busses alongside the Pennsylvania Railroad tracks, was extended to Wilkinsburg, but the impact of this link to downtown has been slight so far.

The original Pennsylvania Turnpike from Pittsburgh to Philadelphia was itself a direct successor to a Native American trail widened in 1758 by General John Forbes in his victorious march to dislodge the French from the Forks of the Ohio. The military trail gave birth to Churchill, a borough that profited in the post–World War II era from its positioning along I-376. Even rosier, at least superficially, was the postwar fate of Monroeville, which burgeoned in population and size as Pittsburgh's main interchange on the modern turnpike. But growth came too fast: farmland once plowed by early settlers, such as the Mellons, gave place to malls that are indistinguishable from those found anywhere in the nation.

AL124 C. C. Mellor Library and Edgewood Club

1916–1918, Edward B. Lee. 1 Pennwood Ave., Edgewood

This private swim and tennis club includes spaces for meetings and a library. Incorporated in 1904, the club purchased this site from the Charles Mellor family. While seemingly Spanish influenced in its stucco and elaborate tile roof, Arts and Crafts influences are much stronger, as seen in its cottagelike outline, steeply pitched roof, dormer windows, gardenlike atmosphere, and a pergola. The Mellor complex occupies a dramatic site on its own hill, the better to exploit the picturesque qualities of an exquisitely designed structure.

AL125 Edgewood Railroad Station

1902–1903, attributed to Frank Furness. 101 E. Swissvale Ave., Edgewood

This tiny station, with its passenger platform and adjoining baggage house, is all that remains of the Frank Furness legacy in Pittsburgh. Time has eliminated his bank on 4th Avenue, the elaborate Baltimore and Ohio (B&O) Terminal by the Smithfield Street Bridge, and two suburban railroad stations. The Edgewood station is a prosaic work, small scaled and utilitarian, with a hipped roof, but nonetheless showing an aging Furness still capable of wringing expression from brick and shingle. An 1876 example of his work in western Pennsylvania is the Fox Mansion Carriage House in Clarion County (CL25).

AL126 John F. Singer House

1863–1869. 1318 Singer Pl., Wilkinsburg

John F. Singer made his fortune supplying iron and steel to the Union army during the Civil War. Looking for a summer estate, Singer purchased thirty-five acres in what was then the rural village of Wilkinsburg. Singer began the house in 1863, and continued construction throughout the war. The architect could have been Joseph W. Kerr, Pittsburgh's dominant Gothic Revival designer in the 1850s and 1860s, but the house is too grand and too lavishly decorated to have come entirely from a pattern book, which was Kerr's usual mode of design.

AL126 JOHN F. SINGER HOUSE

With its finely cut stone construction, and thirty-five rooms, the Singer house achieved a degree of ostentation greater than any in Pittsburgh in that era. Austrian plasterers, English wood-carvers (some having just finished work on the Houses of Parliament), and German stonemasons were imported for the construction. Singer spared no expense to acquire hand-carved work, as in the hardwood vergeboards and the delicate natural motifs in low relief under each bay window. Two somber mahogany porches were painted with crushed sandstone and gesso to emulate the stone walls of the house. The house is cruciform in plan—typical of country houses at the time—with four steep gables and numerous dormers, each sumptuously decorated. The front steps, of Mexican slate, lead to an Italianate tiled foyer. The first floor's eighteen rooms feature elaborately carved mahogany window frames and doors, and every room has a mantel of a different imported marble.

The estate included an artificial lake, a gatehouse where a Russian farm laborer lived, a carriage house for Singer's "fine horse flesh," and a private chapel where Singer led Episcopal services. Singer's partner Alexander Nimick purchased adjoining property with the intent to build but he never did, and, instead, Nimick Place turned into speculative tract housing. After Singer's death in 1872, his wife and family left the estate. Westinghouse then used it as a boardinghouse for young executives, and after that, it was broken up into apartments. The current owner is returning the mansion to a single-family dwelling.

AL127 Sri Venkateswara Temple

1976, Shashi D. Patel. 1230 S. McCully Dr., Penn Hills

Those entering Pittsburgh on the Parkway West (I-376) are intrigued by their glimpse of the starkly white Sri Venkateswara Temple on its wooded hillside. It was the first Hindu temple in the United States built by workers from India and modeled after the seventh-century Sri Venkateswara Temple in South India. Constructed of white-stuccoed brick, the facade of the large rectangular edifice is dominated by a central stepped tower with massive teak doors at the base. Inside, the skylit hall is supported on pillars carved with intricate foliate designs and accommodates several shrines with images of various deities in its colonnade. At its center is the altar to Lord Venkateswara, to whom the temple is dedicated.

Pittsburgh architect Shashi D. Patel (b. 1942) also designed the first unified Hindu-Jain temple in the United States (1981–1990; 615 Illini Drive), five miles to the east. Here a clay-colored brick building follows the Nagradi architectural style of north-central India, with three massive central towers ringed by smaller versions. The exterior walls, articulated with horizontal brick bands, set off the windows with elaborately carved surrounds. Again, the interior is skylit, but has a central room featuring five free-standing altars honoring seven deities. Eleven master masons came from India to work on the project, using neither models nor scale drawings but instead proportioning all details of their carvings by religious formulas they had memorized.

EARLY SETTLERS AND TROLLEY SUBURBS

Were one to draw a crescent of about forty miles in circumference—from the Allegheny County Airport (AL60) near the Monongahela River, west to the Pittsburgh International Airport (1992, Tasso Katselas Associates; bordering PA 60) not far from the Ohio River, the crescent would encompass a number of important eighteenth-century settlements for Pittsburgh, together with suburbs that were born early in the twentieth century. The south half of the crescent is, today, thick with the bedroom suburbs collectively called the South Hills, while its southwestern component remains so spottily settled that it lacks any name at all (theoretically it would be the West Hills).

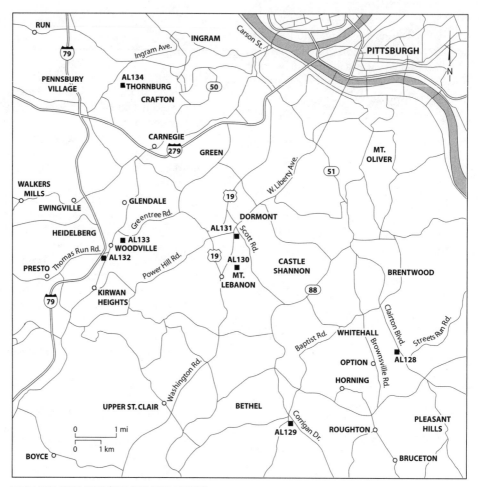

TROLLEY SUBURBS (SOUTH AND WEST)

In terms of development, this crescent marks the sleepiest part of the Pittsburgh orbit. Numerous farmhouses and selected isolated mansions survive from the early nineteenth century, but just a few of these nuclei transformed themselves into urban entities, compared to the dozens of parallel settlements east and north of Pittsburgh that did. The probable reason is the lack of access to major roads or rivers in this crescent. The South Hills had the Washington Pike to link it southward with the National Road (U.S. 40), but real growth came only with the opening of the trolley tunnel through Mount Washington in 1904. An even greater growth spurt came when the Liberty Tunnels, a second cut through Mount Washington, gave motorists similar access to the South Hills in 1924. The (theoretical) West Hills remained cut off from Pittsburgh a good deal longer. It was served by just a few trolley lines, and had no significant roadway until a parkway to the previous Pittsburgh International airport opened in 1952.

AL128 Holy Trinity Serbian Orthodox Cathedral

1967–1971, John V. Tomich. 450 Maxwell Dr., Whitehall

Churches once best expressed ethnic identity in Pittsburgh, as they did everywhere else in America, but have played a minor role in local architecture since World War II. This is one of the few postwar religious sites in Allegheny County that demands a visit, having liberated itself from denominational stereotypes while still deriving strength from architectural history. Holy Trinity uses uncompromising poured-concrete walls inside and out to evoke the ancient triconch plan of Byzantine architecture. What saves the church from being a mere pastiche of historic precedents and architectural clichés is what saved Richardson from falling into the same trap at his courthouse: a highly personalized vision coupled with the artistic authority to carry it out.

AL129 South Park and Oliver Miller Homestead

1927 park, with additions; before 1808 homestead; c. 1830 addition. PA 88 at Corrigan Dr., South Park Township

The Oliver Miller Homestead on Stone Manse Drive in South Park is one of a trio of early and impressive stone houses still standing around Pittsburgh, joining the John Woods House (AL50) and the John Frew House (c. 1790, c. 1840; 105 Sterrett Street). It is the

AL128 HOLY TRINITY SERBIAN ORTHODOX CATHEDRAL

best preserved of the three, and the only one open to the public. Five generations of the family lived here from the eighteenth century through the 1920s, although the dates and ownership of the house are a matter of some conjecture. Oliver Miller had a log house here from the 1780s, but it is uncertain whether it was he or his son James who replaced that house with this stone construction. James did add the larger portion c. 1830. Both sections are constructed of random rubble and are two stories in height.

The 2,000-acre park was established in 1927. About one-third of it is wooded, and the rest is greenspace and recreational areas. An eighteen-hole golf course is served by a clubhouse designed by Henry Hornbostel in 1938, when he was director of Allegheny County Parks between 1935 and 1939. The long rectangular structure's red brick walls are laid to create images of trees and golfers in relief designs. A stunning, concave corbeled arch that opens at the center of the building allows views across the landscape.

AL130 Mission Hills

1921, with additions. Along Jefferson, Orchard, and Parkway drs., Mount Lebanon Township

Mission Hills, one of the best of the interwar developments in Mount Lebanon, was promoted by local realtor Lawrence Stevenson in 1921, and modeled after its namesake, developer Jesse Clyde (J. C.) Nichols's subdivision in Kansas City. Stevenson put up three hundred homes on three-acre lots in the variety of styles preferred at that time. The street plan avoided replicating the regularity of Pittsburgh's street grid, and thus avoided a flaw in many other South Hills developments. Medieval Revival styles predominate, but one can find anything from Louisiana plantations to California bungalows. Visual continuity is maintained by the gently curving streets, common setback frontage, similarity of building materials, and design linkages through the employment of a limited number of architects. The landscaping is particularly noteworthy with houses sited on the hillside slopes. Marked by pillars and small parkways, the entrances from Washington Road give coherence and legibility to the street layout. The development is strictly a form of bedroom suburbia,

AL131 ST. BERNARD'S CHURCH

but the tight town center of Mount Lebanon is only a few minutes away on foot, where one can catch the trolley to Pittsburgh—renamed the "T."

AL131 St. Bernard's Church

1933–1947, William R. Perry for Comes, Perry and McMullen. 311 Washington Rd., Mount Lebanon

This Gothic Revival Roman Catholic church is highly visible thanks to its bulk, the vigorous coloring of its materials, and its location on the high spine of the old Washington Pike. It is the latest, and best, of a trio of churches built along the former pike during the interwar years. The others are the rock-faced Gothic Revival Mt. Lebanon United Methodist Church of 1923 by Charles Bier (3319 W. Liberty Avenue) and the twin-towered Gothic Revival Mt. Lebanon United Presbyterian Church (255 Washington Avenue) designed by J. Lewis Beatty in 1929. William Perry designed numerous churches and schools in western Pennsylvania and the Midwest. The most visible of Perry's local works today are this church and the former St. Philomena Church and School (now the Community Day School) of 1922 at 6424 Forward Avenue in Squirrel Hill.

St. Bernard's is constructed of coursed but rough-faced stones that range in color from gray to brown and red. Its interior is magnificent, thanks to Perry's firsthand knowledge of medieval architecture in southern France and Catalonia in northeastern Spain. Diaphragm arches in stone set up a rhythm along the wooden roof, and a ribbed dome covers the sanctuary. Especially impressive are the murals by Jan Henryk de Rosen that adorn the church and that include scenes from the New Testament and the life of St. Bernard. The church's capitals are by Frank Aretz, and the stained glass is by Alfred Fisher in the main church and by A. Leo Pitassi in the lower church.

AL132 Woodville Plantation (John and Presley Neville House)

c. 1780, c. 1785. 1375 Washington Pike (PA 50 E) at Thomas Run Rd., Woodville

This National Historic Landmark at the edge of Chartiers Creek is a mecca for student field-trips because it illustrates well the radically different way the region might have turned out had it not industrialized so soon after this house was built. When General John Neville built his log house (now the kitchen) on his 7,000-acre land grant, he registered the plantation as part of Virginia, since he refused to recognize Pennsylvania's claim to these lands.

This plantation aspired to be Mount Vernon, especially as its living room, entrance hall, parlors, and bedrooms were added to the kitchen nucleus. This was to be expected, perhaps, for John Neville was a blood relative of Martha Washington and an intimate of her husband, George Washington. Many Virginians visited Woodville, and in 1825, it was honored by a visit from the Marquis de LaFayette, a friend of John Neville's heir Presley Neville. Although Neville was one of the largest slaveholders in the area, no slave structures survive. The house remained in the ownership of Neville descendants until 1973, at which point the parlor wallpaper was sixteen layers deep.

AL133 St. Luke's Protestant Episcopal Church (Old St. Luke's)

1851–1852, attributed to John Notman. 330 Old Washington Pike at Church St., Scott Township

This may be the earliest Episcopal church site west of the Allegheny Mountains, beginning with services in a log garrison in 1765. A wood frame church was constructed in 1790 under the patronage of General John Neville and Major William Lea. This small Gothic Revival stone structure is the second on the site. The church was attributed to Philadelphia's John Notman by architectural historian James D. Van Trump because of the church's archaicizing appearance and the fact that Notman was working on the Episcopal church of St. Peter

(demolished) in Pittsburgh in 1852. Although the small wooden church is a modern reconstruction, the church and the pioneer burial ground, with graves dating from the early 1800s, are an excellent reminder of Pittsburgh's preindustrial era.

AL134 Thornburg

1900–1909, Samuel Thornburg McClarren, and others. Bounded by Baldwin Ave. and Hamilton Rd., Thornburg

Frank Thornburg and his cousin David established this trolley suburb on some 200 acres of their ancestor's 400-acre farm. The houses range in style from Queen Anne to Colonial Revival, Shingle Style, Spanish Mission, and Arts and Crafts. The last two styles were introduced after Thornburg's visit to California in 1905. Another cousin, architect Samuel McClarren, designed most of the suburb's houses, including Frank Thornburg's Shingle Style house at 1132 Lehigh Road in 1907. Other highlights are the Cobblestone House in Shingle Style with cobblestone garnish (c. 1905; 1137 Cornell Avenue), and a Colonial Revival mansion with a two-story Ionic portico (c. 1906, C. E. Willoughby; 1080 Stanford Road).

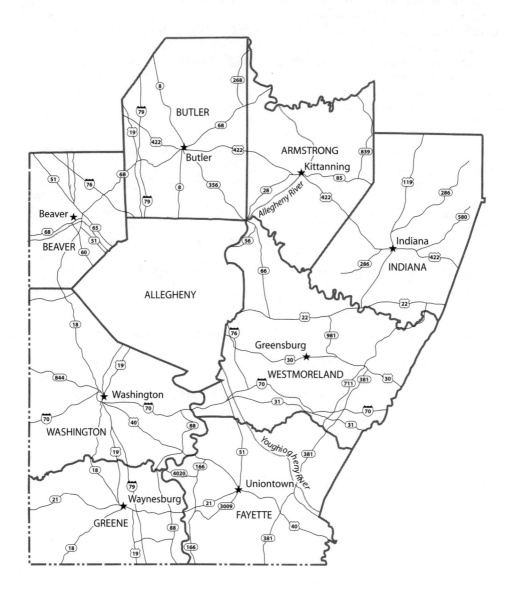

Rolling Hills and Rolling Mills

The southwestern counties (Beaver, Butler, Armstrong, Indiana, Westmoreland, Fayette, Greene, and Washington) surrounding Pittsburgh and Allegheny County share the topography of the Allegheny Plateau. Rolling hills created by erosion from thousands of streams reach to approximately 1,500 feet above sea level. Until 1769, the southern portions of Washington and Fayette counties and all of Greene County were the northwestern counties of Virginia. Settlers arrived as early as the 1750s, although after the territory was officially declared part of Pennsylvania in 1786, many slave-owning Virginians migrated farther west to Kentucky. All these southwestern counties sit atop one of the largest coal veins in the world, and share some of the most intensely industrial landscapes anywhere in the nation. Although iron and steel making did not originate here, these industries flourished and grew to international scale.

Building techniques and styles in this region are a true synthesis of the cultures that crossed it, from southern plantation houses to the modest homes of Quakers, German religious denominations, and Scots-Irish Presbyterians. The building types that originated here and became popular were exported westward to sites along the rivers, the early turnpikes, and the National Road (now U.S. 40). The areas closest to urban and suburban Pittsburgh have experienced considerable pressure for development and change in the course of the twentieth century. For those farther away, change has been less intense and their historic layers of growth are more evident, especially in the architectural styling of churches and monuments.

BEAVER COUNTY

Beaver County on Pennsylvania's western boundary and northwest of Pittsburgh is part of the large Appalachian Plateau now eroded by creeks and waterways into gently rolling hills. At its heart lies the confluence of the Beaver and the Ohio rivers. The county's most populous townships and boroughs line these rivers, as do its largest cities: Beaver Falls and Aliquippa. Farther from the rivers, Beaver County is almost entirely suburban or rural. A trading path for the Delaware, Shawnee, Seneca, and Mingo once roughly paralleled

Rochester–West Bridgewater Bridge (BE15.4), 1933. The third bridge north of the confluence of the Beaver and Ohio rivers, its profile resembles a beaver with its head to the left and tail in the foreground, according to local lore. Its heaviest traffic was diverted in 1958 with the completion of the Rochester–Beaver Highway Bridge (BE15.3) to the south.

the north shore of the Ohio River. By the mid-1700s, the rivers attracted European immigrants as well. Entrepreneur George Croghan opened his trading post as early as 1748 at what is now the town of Beaver. Beaver County's land was strategic to the frontier of the eighteenth century. The first federal military establishment north of the Ohio River, Fort McIntosh (1788), is marked by a series of plaques along River Road in what is now the borough of Beaver. The area remained dangerous for European settlement until U.S. troops, under General "Mad" Anthony Wayne, won the battle of Fallen Timbers near Toledo, Ohio, in 1794. General Wayne wintered and trained his soldiers in Beaver County at Legionville, now an archaeological site near Ambridge.

The easternmost segment of the county, adjacent to Allegheny County and bordered by the Ohio River, is known as the Ohio Corridor. Two company towns, Ambridge and Aliquippa, face each other across the river, and, although linked by a bridge, they have grown in different ways. Upriver and to the west around the confluence of the Beaver and Ohio rivers are four boroughs, one city, and a wealth of bridges that are important linkages between the various parts of the county. Beaver Falls, the only city (as opposed to borough) in the confluence region, retains its wide main street parallel to Beaver River, but since the decline of the steel industry, has lost much of its river-oriented shipping industry. The county lies atop the northwestern edge of the rich Pittsburgh coal seam and has abundant clay deposits, but little evidence of either industry remains. As transportation improved and mineral resources were depleted in the late nineteenth century, these resources were imported. Beaver County sandstone was used to build the county's numerous stone houses. The small town of Koppel, located along the Beaver River in the northern part of the county, supplied the large blocks of sandstone needed to construct many of the railroad and automobile bridges that cross the rivers. Most vernacular stone buildings were constructed with stone quarried and dressed on their sites or nearby.

Although Beaver and Allegheny counties have similar topography and mineral resources, Beaver has never rivaled Allegheny as a major industrial and banking center. The Beaver River is not as easily navigable as the Allegheny, and much of the Ohio River in Beaver County has steep shorelines and narrow river flats. Moreover, canals built along the Beaver River in the nineteenth century were too shallow to allow major barge traffic to pass. Only Ambridge, Aliquippa, Midland, and Shippingport have land areas that could accommodate large industrial development. Deliberate competition from established businesses in Pittsburgh was a third factor retarding growth in Beaver County; late-nineteenth-century entrepreneurs discouraged development to the west to protect their own interests. Several smaller towns retain buildings from the canal era, notably New Brighton and Bridgewater; and Hookstown, which, while not traversed by the canal, retains several houses from the simultaneous turnpike era.

Railroads made an indelible impact primarily along river banks where the grade changes were least. The little town of Conway has four miles of shoreline completely covered with rail lines and related structures where the Pennsylvania Railroad built one of the world's largest railcar sorting yards. The impact of the automobile on the county has also been dramatic. Major four-lane expressways, PA 60, PA 51, and PA 65, as well as the turnpike (now I-76), make Beaver County easily accessible from the east and south, but the principal roads from Pittsburgh are multiple-access highways with shopping strips and stoplights slowing traffic flow and making commuting difficult. Pittsburgh International Airport, alternatively, which is close to the Beaver County line, has proved a spur to the development of suburbs and industrial parks in Beaver County.

BEAVER AND VICINITY

Major trails west to Ohio and north to Erie made this area a popular Native American meeting place between 1730 and the late 1780s. It had several names, including Sawcunk, Beaver's Town, and Shingas Old Town. In the 1750s, warriors of the Delaware, Shawnee, and Mingo tribes gathered here in thirty-eight houses of square logs with stone chimneys built by their allies, the French. The defeat at Bushy Run in 1763 ended Native American habitation in the area.

In 1778, Fort McIntosh, named for General Lachlan McIntosh, was built on the site of present-day Beaver as a base for American attacks against the British forces at Detroit. The fort, believed to have been designed by French volunteer Louis-Antoine-Jean-Baptiste, Chevalier de Cambray-Digny, was particularly busy between 1780 and 1782, when native tribal warriors were constantly attacking. Archaeological studies indicate that the fort was an irregular quadrilateral shape, built of hewn logs and measuring approximately three hundred feet along the southern wall overlooking the Ohio River. Corner bastions were filled with earth and stone. The structure housed barracks, a blockhouse, powder magazine, and several smaller structures. By 1793, little remained of Fort McIntosh. Today, markers delineating the fort's footprint are preserved along River Road in Beaver. In 1783, the government designated 720,000 acres north of the Ohio River as Depreciation Lands. Before awarding these acres as payment to Revolutionary War soldiers, the lands had to be officially purchased from the tribes living on them according to the treaties of Fort Stanwix (1784) and Fort McIntosh (1785). The Treaty of Greenville, signed by General "Mad" Anthony Wayne in 1795, signaled the final defeat of the native tribes.

The borough of Beaver was authorized by legislative act in 1791. Situated strategically on a plateau well above the Ohio and Beaver rivers, it commanded a view in both directions and provided a good layover spot for boats. It was also accessible from the ridge roads in the rest of the county. State surveyor Daniel Leet surveyed the town in 1792, reserving eight lots for public use: four at each corner of the grid and four in the center. The town's high location saved it from the rampant industrialization that occurred along the river edges in the nineteenth century; as a result, the original town plan is still legible. Almost all the lots in the town were sold in a month. Due to its central location and early settlement, Beaver was chosen as the county seat

345 Commerce Street (c. 1874), Beaver Borough.

when Beaver County was formed from Washington and Allegheny counties in 1800.

During the canal era of the 1830s and 1840s, lands along the Beaver River were settled as Bridgewater and Rochester. The railroads accelerated the residential growth of the borough after 1851, and the majority of buildings date from 1850 to 1946. An early building is the Greek Revival Stokes House (1835; 1090 7th Street), with an Ionic-columned porch protecting its raised central entrance. More typical are the Italianate Anderson House (c. 1874; 345 Commerce Street), with elaborate cast-iron hood molds and an exquisite fanlight, and a large brick Queen Anne house (c. 1890; 404 Bank Street) with a wraparound porch. There has been little post–World War II development. The borough's main commercial and transportation corridor is 3rd Street. It is unusually wide at six lanes, and is lined with mostly two-story commercial structures. Since 1996, the central section of Beaver has been listed on the National Register of Historic Places.

BE1 Beaver County Courthouse

1974, Carl G. Baker and Associates; George Merges, project architect; 1989, Wallover and Mitchell; 2000–2003, WMB Architects and Associates. 810 3rd St.

This, the newest courthouse in western Pennsylvania, uses the geometry of classical forms to evoke the proper dignity, but it is stripped of their applied ornamentation. Built of beige limestone, the courthouse consists of two rectangular two-story sections flanking a central double-height curved portico that marks the entrance, above which is a domed cupola. The concrete and glass Brutalist-style annex northwest of the new courthouse was designed in 1974 by Beaver architects, and the newer sections were designed by architects from Beaver Falls.

BE2 Kwik Fill Gas Station

1955. 1499 3rd St.

Oil companies early realized the importance of brand identification using consistent packaging. The former Falcon Gas stations, found in several western Pennsylvania counties, illustrate this with their yellow and green, V-shaped rooflines and gracefully curved wooden supports. Recalling Marcel Breuer's Exhibition House of 1949 in the garden of New York City's Museum of Modern Art, the V-shaped, or butterfly, roofline symbolized the

speed of a falcon's flight, and was a popular design element in the 1950s. While other gas stations incorporated swooping canopies over their pumps, Falcon Gas's choice of this distinctive design as its brand's signature seems purely symbolic and aesthetic, as the wings do not cover the pumps or provide much shelter. In all of their stations, the rectangular office space is centered under the V and surrounded on three sides by plate glass, with a white concrete-block back wall.

BE3 Beaver Cemetery and Receiving Vault

1865 established; 1909 receiving vault. Buffalo and 3rd sts.

Beaver Cemetery was incorporated in June 1865, two months after the conclusion of the Civil War, when the town's existing cemetery was nearing capacity. Intended to emulate the rural cemeteries of the 1830s and 1840s, its plan is one of picturesque informality sur-

BE2 KWIK FILL GAS STATION

rounded by a low stone retaining wall. The Roman Revival receiving vault, located in the center of the cemetery, originally held bodies believed dead until the staff could be assured that this was so and that they were not merely comatose. Before the invention of sophisticated heart and respiration monitors, it was thought advisable to wait several days before burial. Today the structure is used as a chapel.

Two formal and traditional monuments include J. V. McDonald's Classical Revival brownstone tomb of 1869 built into a small hillock and with two wings projecting from a central round-arched entrance, and the tomb of c. 1884 for lawyer Lewis Taylor. The latter, one of the tallest in the cemetery, is crowned with a statue of a Roman goddess atop an eighteen-foot-high granite plinth; a bas-relief portrait of Taylor adorns the side of the shaft. One of the most interesting family mausoleums is that of engineer Colonel James P. Leaf designed in 1949 by Frank Polrio of Beaver Falls. Constructed of random stones, the rectangular fortresslike memorial's entrance is covered with a boulder that appears to have moved just enough to allow for the resurrection of the deceased. Colonel Leaf's antler trophy above the vaults is visible through portholes on the side walls.

BE4 Fort McIntosh Club (Riley Taylor House)

c. 1862. 374 College Ave.

The Fort McIntosh Club was originally the home of Dr. Riley T. Taylor, president of Beaver Female College, which was across the street. The white-painted brick Italianate house features paired elongated windows, central gables with deep eaves supported by paired brackets, and a cupola. At the southeast corner of this nearly square house is a windowed sun porch with shingling above. A classically inspired one-bay porch on the facade shelters double doors topped by a segmental-arched transom. Since 1926, the house has been used as a private club for retired men.

BE5 First Presbyterian Church

1890, James P. Bailey. 252 College Ave.

James Bailey practiced architecture in the area from the 1870s through 1900, and designed Old Main at Geneva College in Beaver Falls

(BE29), as well as the Butler County Courthouse of 1886 (BU1). From the rhythm of the arches and the design of the square corner tower to the foliated capitals, his design for this gray, rock-faced sandstone church recalls H. H. Richardson's Allegheny County Courthouse and Jail in Pittsburgh (AL1). Sculptural ornament in foliate and geometric patterns is integral to the design. A large educational wing north of the church is executed in stone in a compatible style.

BE6 Residential District

c. 1910–1955, John Henry Craner. 300, 700, 790, 1030, and 1050 River Rd.

This is an important collection of early-twentieth-century residential designs in an extraordinary setting overlooking the Ohio River. Designed by local architect John Henry Craner (1872–1955), the houses emphasize the texture and color of the shingles and bricks, the medieval half timbering, and leaded glass windows. Craner trained in the offices of Longfellow, Alden and Harlow in Pittsburgh before returning to his birthplace to open his own firm c. 1910. The large and small Tudor Revival houses he designed are characterized by steeply sloped roofs and irregular rooflines. Examples of his work are dotted throughout the borough, but are best seen here.

BE7 Beaver County Emergency Response Center and Beaver Area Heritage Museum (Pittsburgh and Lake Erie Railroad [P&LE] Passenger and Freight Depots)

1897; 1911, R. P. Forsberg. 250 River Rd. E.

These two stations, one for passengers and one for freight, are characteristic of such structures, with their brick and stone construction and deep overhanging eaves supported by oversized wooden brackets. Unlike the more elaborate station at Aliquippa (BE39), the Beaver passenger station has no second story, and its porte-cochere has been removed. Eyebrow dormers enliven the north and south elevations of the hipped roof, and a stone sill course joins the stone round arches above the windows and doors. The freight station is a simplified version of the passenger station, with stone lintels and sills. An undertrack tunnel joins the station with the platform on the east side of the tracks. Today, the Beaver County

BE7 BEAVER COUNTY EMERGENCY RESPONSE CENTER AND BEAVER AREA HERITAGE MUSEUM (PITTSBURGH AND LAKE ERIE RAILROAD [P&LE] PASSENGER AND FREIGHT DEPOTS), photo 1916

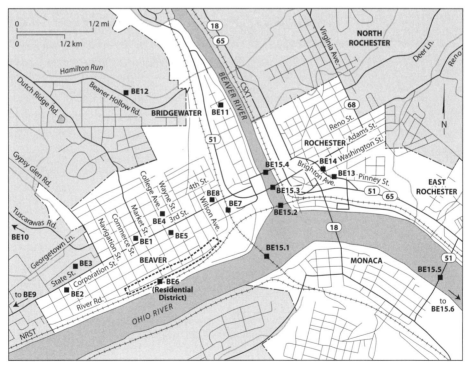

BEAVER, BRIDGEWATER, AND ROCHESTER

Bridges and dams are essential in a territory as riddled with streams and gullies as western Pennsylvania. The commonwealth's bridges are so renowned that every June more than 1,200 people attend the Engineers' Society of Western Pennsylvania's International Bridge Conference in Pittsburgh. The attendees visit several of the thousands of bridges in southwestern Pennsylvania, but given time, they could easily tour the central and northern tier counties as well, where there are bridges of immense beauty and utility. The terrain and the rampant industrialization of the nineteenth century made bridge building for roads and rail lines a vital part of doing business.

Pittsburgh led the way with the trio of experimental wire-cable suspension bridges erected by John A. Roebling, who settled in Saxonburg, Butler County, where his workshop still stands (110 Main Street). Roebling's first bridge for Pittsburgh was an aqueduct that carried the Pennsylvania Canal over the Allegheny River, in 1845; a year later, he replaced the burned Smithfield Street Bridge with a seven-span suspension bridge. Then in 1859, Roebling constructed the Sixth Street Bridge, where the Roberto Clemente Bridge (AL13.1) stands today. None of Roebling's bridges in Pittsburgh survive.

While earlier bridges served wagons, carriages, and canals, the next generation of bridges served the railroads. The Kinzua Viaduct (McKean County) ranked among the highest viaducts in the nation when it was built in 1882 (rebuilt 1900) to facilitate shipment of oil, lumber, and coal from Pennsylvania's north central counties to Buffalo, New York. Its size and scale, its beauty, and the opportunity to cross it by foot or by train made it a popular tourist destination. In 1963, it became part of the 316-acre Kinzua Bridge State Park. Then, in 2003, twelve of its twenty supports collapsed into the gorge after being pummeled by an F1 tornado. Even as a ruin it continues to attract tourists.

Controlling the water in the region has been a constant struggle for engineers. Extreme fluctuations in water level on the major rivers, caused by changing seasons and periodic droughts, made navigation uncertain. Beginning in the 1840s, the construction of locks and dams made rivers navigable year-round and flooding less frequent. Surviving structures from the earliest of these facilities include the former Merrill Station lockmaster's house (BE9) and another lockmaster's house at Rice's Landing in Greene County.

Large-scale dam sites are dramatic and can be controversial when villages are flooded for their construction. Cornplanter village north of Warren in Warren County, which belonged to the descendants of the Seneca chief Cornplanter, was inundated in 1964 as part of the Kinzua Dam project to regulate the Allegheny River's flow and prevent flooding downstream. The Conemaugh River flowing through Johnstown was tamed with a series of sixteen dams after World War II. Two dams near the confluence of the Conemaugh River and Loyalhanna Creek (forming the Kiskiminetas River) can be viewed from their surrounding parks. The Loyalhanna Dam (1951) in Westmoreland County, near Saltsburg, and the Conemaugh Lake Dam (1953) in Indiana County include hiking trails, boating, and scenic overlooks, all overseen by the U.S. Army Corps of Engineers.

KINZUA VIADUCT (NOW A RUIN) IN 1971, BUILT FOR THE ERIE RAILWAY, BRADFORD DIVISION, SPANNING KINZUA CREEK VALLEY NEAR MOUNT JEWETT, MCKEAN COUNTY.

Emergency Response Center is housed in the passenger station, and the Beaver Area Heritage Museum is in the freight station. In 1998, a log house for educational purposes was built adjacent to the museum using eighteenth-century logs salvaged from a nearby house.

BE8 Roman Catholic Church of Saints Peter and Paul

1972, Carl G. Baker and Associates; Tony Stichon, project architect. 200 3rd St.

This modern church uses local stone, wood, and slate with bands of stained glass windows to enclose and shelter its sacred space. Its asymmetrical and roundish shape is accented with stone buttresses and wide overhanging eaves that appear to hug the ground and then rise to soaring vaults in two places: at the altar paralleling 3rd Street and at the entrance opposite it. Slate-covered supports slant inward to emphasize the altar space within. Farther along the walls, gill-like sections of stained glass make the interior of the church remarkably light, emphasizing its vaulted ceiling, and they successfully tie the church to its corner site.

BE9 Lock 6 Landing Restaurant and Marina (Merrill Station Lockhouse)

c. 1905, Lt. Colonel William E. Merrill. 610 Midland-Beaver Rd. (PA 68), 2.5 miles southwest of Beaver

The Merrill Lock and Dam was the second in a series of ten locks and dams built along the Ohio River between 1892 and 1904. The isolated grouping was designed by and named for engineer William E. Merrill, supervisor of the Ohio River improvement, assisted by engineer William H. Chadbourn Jr. The complex, replaced in 1936 by the Montgomery Lock and Dam, has survived several owners and uses, most recently as a restaurant and marina. The orange-colored brick buildings perch on a narrow strip of land parallel to the Ohio River (29.5 miles northwest of Pittsburgh). The lockhouse's round-arched apertures and tower with flared and bracketed eaves lend it an Italianate flavor. The tower originally concealed a water tank for the lock buildings, and a semicircular bay at its base offers views up and down the river. Stone detailing at the imposts and sills sets off the patterned brick,

while a large five-bay, hipped-roof dormer on the river facade and a smaller version facing east complement the height of the tower and chimney. An oversized paneled chimney anchors the rear elevation with the coal storage area at its base. The interior formerly housed the machinery used to operate the lock gates, and retains a foliated metal stair rail to the south of the main entrance.

To the east of the lockhouse, a foursquare house, tied stylistically to the main building through the use of round-arched windows on the upper story, housed either the lockmaster's family or crews. An identical house west of the lockhouse was demolished.

BE10 St. Nicholas Chapel (Byzantine Catholic Church of the Greek Union)

1992, Thomas S. Terpack. 5400 Tuscarawas Rd., 6.5 miles west of Beaver

At the crest of a hill, its bulk relieved by the delightful interplay of its three onion domes, St. Nicholas Chapel is a unique sight in this suburban area. Its cedar logs and shingles resemble traditional village chapels in the Carpathian region of eastern Slovakia and western Ukraine, but they cloak modern features, such as structural steel framing, computer-controlled lighting, and air conditioning. Two massive carved wooden entrance doors are framed with logs and sheltered by the deep eaves of the roof; the eaves are supported by decoratively carved wood columns across the facade. Shingles cover the roof and domes. The chapel is small, seating only eighty people. A vestibule precedes the nave, and the sanctuary is separated from the nave by an iconostasis screen. The interior, designed by Michael Barbush Jr. of the Pittsburgh firm of Burke

BE10 ST. NICHOLAS CHAPEL (BYZANTINE CATHOLIC CHURCH OF THE GREEK UNION)

and Michael, is lined with random-width beveled oak planks stained progressively lighter, which prevents the upper dome from appearing too dark. Windows are located only in the upper areas to avoid weakening the log structure. Artists from Cleveland carved and painted the intensely colored modern icons in the church; the icon in the central dome is Christ Pantocrator.

Architect Thomas Terpack, a graduate of Carnegie Institute of Technology and of Carpathian heritage, designed several Byzantine Rite churches in Pennsylvania and Ohio. He calls this chapel "my private homage to my parents and my grandparents, who labored hard and long in the mines and mills to give me the opportunity to become a professional."

BRIDGEWATER AND VICINITY

The borough of Bridgewater, two blocks wide and eight blocks long on the western shore of the Beaver River, has been joined by a bridge to the eastern shore since 1816. The town was laid out in 1818 by innkeeper Joseph Hemphill, whose house still exists at 815 Market Street. When the Beaver River was canalized between 1834 and 1872, Bridgewater grew faster than its neighbors, Rochester and the borough of Beaver. Nearly thirty buildings from the canal era survive, including the Greek Revival mansion built for the Davidson family in 1835 (now Sweetwater Hill apartments; 1319 Riverside Drive). Tucked behind middle-class houses on Market Street, it overlooks the Beaver River and the site of the Davidsons' former sawmills and gristmills. The H-shaped two-story house has Ionic columns supporting double recessed porches on the west elevation, triple recessed porches on the east, and Flemish bond brickwork throughout.

After the canal closed and the railroad passed west of the borough in 1874, twentieth-century automobile traffic generally bypassed Bridgewater. Bridge

The Davidson family's Greek Revival house (now Sweetwater Hill apartments), 1319 Riverside Drive, Bridgewater.

Street became the site of most commercial development, and its red brick Greek Revival and Italianate stores give the town its distinctive appearance. Unfortunately, most of Bridge Street's south side has been demolished for new commercial construction. On two perpendicular streets, a handsome new fire station (2001; 619 Market Street) blends successfully with such older buildings as the red brick town houses at 905–911 Riverside Drive.

BE11 Samuel Dunlap House

c. 1840. 1298 Market St.

Sited on a bluff overlooking the Beaver River, the gable-roofed house has a pedimented portico supported by four Tuscan columns on both the front and rear elevations. It has a raised basement and paired corbeled, interior end chimneys, each with two pointed-arched windows in the gable ends. The white-painted brickwork is laid in a Flemish bond pattern. Fluted Ionic columns and Greek-style ornament flank the entrance doors. The first story has four rooms with a central hall. The kitchen in the raised basement is linked by a spiral staircase to the first floor and the attic. Built for James and Mary Arbuckle and their six children, the house was purchased in 1887 by Samuel R. Dunlap, who ran a brewery and hotel in Bridgewater; his name has come to be identified with the house.

BE12 Joseph Wray House

1835. 1020 Beaner Hollow Rd.

The Wray house, with its unique signature stone and scabble and drafted facade stones, retains the quiet solitude of its original forested setting at the end of a long wooded lane. The lintel above the entrance consists of a

BE12 JOSEPH WRAY HOUSE

single large stone hand-carved to resemble a flat arch with keystone, and is inscribed in a flowing script: "Erected in AD 1835, by Joseph Wray." Joseph Wray Jr., a stonecutter, was one of six sons of Joseph Wray Sr., a prosperous farmer of Irish descent. The remaining three walls are hewn stone. The three-part windows on both the facade and the rear elevation of the main portion of the house are elaborate and unique. Diamond-shaped four-light windows are the only fenestration in the gable ends. The house is similar in size to five-bay houses throughout Beaver County, but has unique detailing. In plan, the interior consists of four rooms over four rooms with a central hallway and curved banister.

ROCHESTER AND VICINITY

The town of Rochester sits on a rocky promontory above the confluence of the Beaver and the Ohio rivers. The steeply sloping site, characterized by radial streets and triangular lots, accommodates more than 4,000 residents. The floodplain along the Ohio River is defined by the six-story-tall, orange brick former Beaver Valley Brewery (1903) and smaller light industrial buildings and warehouses. Numerous railroad tracks traverse the area, and highway bridge ramps further divide this section from the town above. A linear riverside park and a marina west of the brewery and north along the Beaver River shore have substantially brightened the space, especially with the periodic mooring of the Louis Kahn–designed Point Counterpoint II barge (1964–1967).

Raised well above the tracks, most of Rochester's public and commercial buildings line two radial streets, Brighton and Harmony avenues, converging at Madison Street. Rochester's business district is characterized by three- to four-story stone and brick apartments, stores, and offices angled to meet the eccentricities of their sites. Two exceptions are the Masonic Temple and the Post Office. The Masonic Temple (1884; 197–199 West Park) is still among Rochester's tallest buildings, and overlooks one of the main squares. The dark red brick building has stone detailing and a tiny, mansard-roofed pavilion at the northwest corner of the facade. The side elevation resembles row houses, with six prominent corbeled chimneys and six separate entrances for bachelor accommodations. A handsome, golden brick Post Office (1932, James Wetmore, acting supervising architect of the U.S. Treasury; 257 Connecticut Avenue) employs the stripped classicism of the era in its design. The original street pattern of the commercial district has been altered to accommodate a new bridge across the Beaver River and parking lots for a modern shopping mall. Set back from the business district are the residential neighborhoods and their churches, such as the stone Grace Lutheran Church (1906–1907, William J. East) at 393 Adams Street, schools, and brick and frame housing dating from the 1870s to the 1920s. The Rochester Community Center (350 Adams Street), built as the Rochester High School in 1916, is a cream-colored Tudor Revival brick building delightfully bedecked with terra-cotta ornament.

Rochester was laid out by Ovid Pinney in 1835, but the town did not develop until after its incorporation in 1849. Its wide river plain allowed moorage for steamboats. By 1880, five railroads passed through the borough. A glass tumbler company, lumber yards, planing mills, and a casket company and door manufactory added to the growing industries of Rochester. The Fry Glass Company achieved international repute. Though no longer a major industrial center, the borough remains a transportation nexus for Beaver County, since the major entrance to the borough of Beaver from the east is through Rochester.

BE13 Young's Jewelry (First National Bank)

c. 1905. 181 Brighton Ave.

The distinctive flatiron shape of this stone bank was dictated by Rochester's radial avenues. The entrance on the chamfered corner of the lot is flanked by two colossal Ionic columns, with the name of the bank carved into the rusticated stone arch behind. On the long elevations, Ionic pilasters alternate with three elongated, round-arched windows, which are flanked by pavilion-like features, with triangular pediments topping square-headed windows. The attic zone, unlike the rich texture of the rusticated walls, is composed of smooth ashlar with three stylized acroteria above the entrance. The original occupant, the First National Bank of Rochester, was established in 1883 by Henry Clay Fry.

BE14 Hexagonal Building

c. 1895. Pinney St. and Jackson and Brighton aves.

On a small island directly across from the former First National Bank is a six-sided red brick Queen Anne office building whose plan has been determined by the irregular street pattern. To accommodate the slope, the office's two entrances are at different levels.

BE13 YOUNG'S JEWELRY (FIRST NATIONAL BANK)

The more prominent doorway, located on the narrowest face of the building, is set in a rusticated stone base and capped with a round hooded awning. The main facade on Brighton Avenue is the widest, with scalloped siding and a squat Palladian window within its large gable. The roof, composed of alternating bands of squared and fish-scale tiles, wraps around the various angles and projections of the building to unify it. The Queen Anne is primarily a residential style, and, indeed, with its two chimneys and prominent gabled roof, this building looks more like a home than an office. In its earliest years, the small building was home to a series of professionals: attorneys, doctors, dentists, a milliner, and even a tearoom have been among its tenants.

BE15 Confluence Bridge District

1908–1986. Ohio and Beaver rivers

The dramatic confluence of the Beaver and the Ohio rivers is a stirring natural spectacle, one that is enhanced by an unparalleled collection of bridges. From the Pittsburgh and Lake Erie Railroad Bridge (P&LE), described soon after it opened in 1910 as an engineering wonder of the century, to the Rochester-Monaca Highway Bridge, the area's six bridges are a visual catalog of twentieth-century bridge types. From the early nineteenth century, bridges spanned the narrower Beaver River and eventually the wider Ohio. By the 1890s, covered

wooden bridges were replaced by skeletal iron, then by the steel and concrete spans of today.

The P&LE Bridge (BE15.1; 1908–1909) was once the world's longest cantilever bridge (1,780 feet). German-educated design engineer Albert Lucius and A. R. Raymer, the railroad's assistant chief engineer, used 17,000 tons of steel to give their double-track steel bridge massive structural strength. At the time, it was criticized as too expensive and stronger than the weight demands of the day's trains, but the bridge continues to bear today's heavier burdens. The two-peaked profile, the long central span cantilevered over the river by the support of its counterbalancing piers, the structural refinement, and sheer visual presence of its blackened steel contrast sharply with the simple curved-outline twin spans of the nearby Conrail Bridge crossing the Beaver River since 1926 (BE15.2). Both can be viewed from the city of Beaver at the intersection of Beaver Road and East End Avenue or from the riverside park in Rochester at the foot of Water Street.

North of the Conrail Bridge is the Rochester-Beaver Highway Bridge of 1958 (BE15.3). This modern deck-arch bridge is the major automobile connection to the city of Beaver, and the busiest span in the county. North of it are the three steel trusses of the Rochester–West Bridgewater Bridge (BE15.4; 1933; see p. 132), a joint project of local gov-

BE15.1 P&LE BRIDGE

ernment and the Pennsylvania Railroad. The American Bridge Company (BE51) fabricated the steel superstructure. Local lore likens the distinctive profile of its three arches to the silhouette of a beaver, the county's namesake.

The newest bridge at the confluence, the Rochester-Monaca Highway Bridge of 1986 (BE15.5) reuses three stone piers and two abutments from an earlier span, and its through arch and flat profile are reminiscent of the long wooden bridges that first spanned the rivers of western Pennsylvania. Since 1988, the winner of the Monaca Indians/Rochester Rams high school football game is allowed to reorder the town names on the bridge's signs. The Monaca–East Rochester Highway Bridge of 1959 (BE15.6), farther up the Ohio River, is a steel cantilever bridge with a traditional profile and a heavy steel superstructure. It was a toll bridge until 1973.

NEW BRIGHTON

New Brighton lies along the floodplain of the Beaver River northeast of its confluence with the Ohio. The river drops steeply at this point, creating the waterfall that supplied waterpower to fuel many mills and manufacturing businesses in the early nineteenth century. The steamboat era stimulated boatbuilding in New Brighton, as did the completion of the Beaver and Lake Erie Canal that ran through New Brighton after 1834. The canal joined the two greatest canal systems of the early nineteenth century, the Erie and the Pennsylvania; however, it was undersized for large cargo and passenger boats. Traces of the canal survive along the river's edge behind 3rd Avenue's buildings in the commercial district. A few red brick houses date from the canal era, including Merrick House (1408 3rd Avenue), which was built in 1847 in the popular five-bay style with a central entrance. Two relatively modest c. 1840 red brick structures (1305 and 1317 3rd Avenue) stand out with handsome fanlights over the entrance doors. The southern section of the canal on the lower Beaver River continued to transport goods until 1872.

In 1851, the canal's northern portion was supplanted by what ultimately became the Pittsburgh, Fort Wayne and Chicago Railroad, stimulating a housing boom in New Brighton. A pair of stone churches mark the shift to the railroad era, Christ Episcopal Church (1851; 1217 3rd Avenue) and First

Presbyterian Church (1866–1872, J. M. Blackburn; 1199 3rd Avenue) in two different Gothic Revival modes. New Brighton retains a number of fine houses in popular domestic architectural styles from the 1830s to the 1920s. The Queen Anne and Colonial Revival houses set back from tree-lined streets are primarily located along 3rd Avenue between 13th and 17th streets and in the 1100 block of Penn Avenue. New Brighton's avenues run north–south and streets run east–west; so, for instance, the Fourth Ward Public School of 1894, now the Belltower Office Center (1011 6th Street), is located at the corner of 6th Street and 10th Avenue.

BE16 Standard Horse Nail Company Building

c. 1886. 5th Ave., bounded by 14th and 15th sts.

The Standard Horse Nail factory, founded in 1872 by Charles M. Merrick across the Beaver River, moved to New Brighton in 1882. Noted for its innovations in the forging of horseshoe nails, the company remains in the Merrick family. Today, they sell cotter pins, machine keys, and special fasteners for automotive, farm equipment, and appliance manufacturers. The administration building's bold round-arched entrance surround shows the influence of H. H. Richardson's Allegheny County Courthouse (AL1). The company's name, incised in a stone band above the door, highlights the projecting gable on the facade of the hipped-roof, one-and-one-half-story structure. A series of one-story, gable-roofed brick manufacturing buildings with segmental-arched windows fills the block to the south. Despite some brick infill to the windows, the buildings retain their charm and striking attention to detail.

BE16 STANDARD HORSE NAIL COMPANY BUILDING

BE17 Merrick Free Art Gallery

1847; 1880–1888 remodeled; 1901 second building; 1994, Landmark Design Associates; 1994 stair tower, John T. Regney. 5 11th St.

A pair of red brick, gable-roofed structures joined by a modern, glass-enclosed stair hall make up the Merrick Free Art Gallery. The building's main gallery illustrates the exhibition design techniques popular in early-twentieth-century art galleries. The east wing, dating from 1847, was built as a station for the Pittsburgh, Fort Wayne and Chicago Railroad. A fireplace, ticket window, and tin ceiling can still be seen in the present storeroom at the northern corner of the building. In 1870, the Merrick family purchased the property. Edward Dempster Merrick (1832–1911) altered and expanded the former station to hold his collection of paintings and art studio. He added a second story to the east building in 1888, lighting them with an innovative clerestory arrangement. His collection of European and American nineteenth-century paintings, especially the Hudson River School, continued to grow. In 1901, Merrick added a building to the west to accommodate the collection. This structure is a simple, red brick gable-roofed building of two by six bays with double-sash multipaned windows. At Merrick's death in 1911, paintings by him were destroyed by his descendants, but his remaining collection is open to the public free of charge.

BE18 First United Methodist Church (First Methodist Episcopal Church)

1903. 1033 6th Ave.

This Italian Romanesque Revival building of tan brick is distinguished by its striking square bell tower with three stories of triple arches. The arches are outlined with brick corbeling,

BE19 ESB BANK (PEOPLES HOME SAVINGS BANK)

and the two upper sets are separated by short composite columns. The church's entrance at the base of the bell tower facing 11th Street is sheltered by a round-arched portico supported on Corinthian columns. There is decorative brickwork around the windows and on the bell tower and cornice. The southeast facade has three large arched windows under the gable, while the southwest gable has a series of elongated segmental-arched windows. Two-story wings on either side of the 6th Avenue gable end have chevron-shaped eaves, brick belt courses, and smaller segmental-arched windows.

BE19 ESB Bank (Peoples Home Savings Bank)

1954, Louis G. Martsolf for Arthur L. Martsolf and Associates. 800 3rd Ave.

New Brighton's native son and third-generation building designer drew the plans for this bank with its sweeping stone arched window that terminates abruptly in a square, stone tower. Moderne metal overhangs accent the entrances on the facade and the southeast elevation. The tower is placed slightly off center and pierced by a narrow vertical window with geometrically patterned stained glass.

BEAVER FALLS

Beaver Falls grew from a tiny riverside community into a large industrial city over the course of the nineteenth century. Founded on the west side of the Beaver River in 1800 by brothers Daniel and William Constable, it was first named for their hometown of Brighton, England. In 1806, the original portion of the town was platted by Isaac Wilson and Company. These are now the diagonal streets named 1st through 5th avenues, which remain distinct from the grid of the town's later development.

The Beaver River drops nearly forty-two feet here, creating an early source of power for mills. The narrowness of the river channel and the width of its floodplain, as well as its proximity to the Ohio River, sparked intense commerce in the lower Beaver River valley. As early as 1808, David Hoopes of Philadelphia built an iron furnace on land settled by squatters. After suing the squatters in court, Hoopes was forced to buy the land and water-power a second time to secure his deed. The problem of ownership between government-sanctioned warrant holders and unsanctioned pioneer settlers continued into the first half of the nineteenth century in Beaver County, and delayed development. In 1815, a bridge across the Beaver River connected Beaver Falls to New Brighton. Philadelphian James Patterson bought 1,300 acres of the early town and established successful flour and cotton mills in 1829, using the Beaver and Lake Erie Division of the canal, then under construction, to navigate this treacherous length of the river.

The Pittsburgh, Fort Wayne and Chicago Railroad was built on a shelf of land west of the city, later shared with the Pittsburgh and Lake Erie Railroad (P&LE), which had substantial support from the Harmony Society in 1876. This allowed Beaver Falls's riverside industries to flourish. Today, 11th

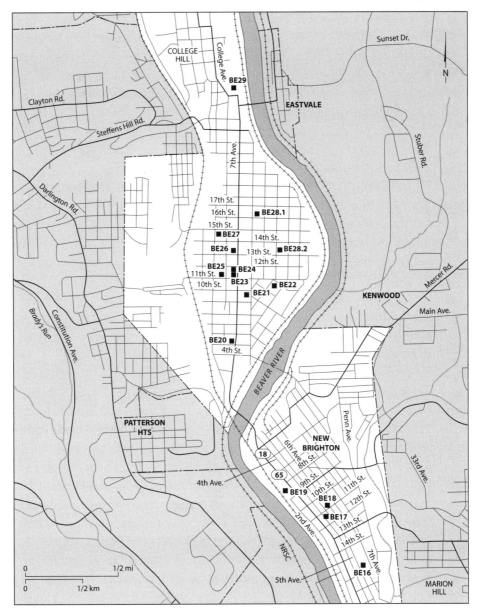

NEW BRIGHTON AND BEAVER FALLS

Street best illustrates this era, with the former P&LE railway station at its base, several churches, a handsome Italian Villa–style house and carriage house (c. 1870; 404 11th Street), and commercial buildings, such as the Penn Hotel (c. 1900; 235 11th Street) and Anderson Hotel (1894; 3rd Avenue at 11th Street).

Beaver Falls became an industrial city after the Civil War, when the Harmonists ordered a new survey of the area from Henry T. and John Reeves, real estate and land agents, which expanded the older grid. Seventh Avenue (PA 18) formed the spine of the city, which was renamed Beaver Falls and incorporated in 1868. The Harmonists actively recruited industries to build along the city's wide floodplain. Among these were the Beaver Falls Cutlery Company (1868–1886); Penn Bridge Company (1868 in New Brighton, 1878 in Beaver Falls); Economy Savings Institution (1868), which became the Reeves Bank; Emerson, Smith and Company, Ltd. (1871), manufacturers of saws and saw tools for mills; Beaver Falls Steel works (1875), which became Crucible Steel; Hartman Steel Co., Ltd. (1883), absorbed by U.S. Steel in 1901; Beaver Falls Glass Company (1887); and Union Drawn Steel (1889). The town grew rapidly under the communal organization's watchful eye and generous pocketbook.

In 1880, the Harmonists donated ten acres and the community raised $20,000 to entice Geneva College (BE29) to relocate from Ohio to Beaver Falls and serve as another stimulus to the town's growth. Two adjacent boroughs are closely tied to this development. The first, College Hill, a pleasant, residential area surrounding Geneva College was laid out in the 1880s by civil engineer J. C. Dodds, and incorporated into the city in 1892. Patterson Heights Borough, on a hillside southwest of Beaver Falls, has housing stock ranging from turn-of-the-twentieth-century frame houses to Tudor Revival and quaint brick cottages of the 1930s, especially along 7th Street Extension.

Beaver Falls prospered in the early twentieth century, adding the Carnegie Free Library (BE26) and several grand bank buildings, including the Farmer's National Bank (BE23). At six lanes wide and eleven blocks long, 7th Avenue has an architectural vitality despite many underused and vacant storefronts. The Union Drawn Steel Company encouraged the building of the $1.5 million Brodhead Hotel, now apartments, originally called the Union Hotel (1927, Emmet E. Bailey; 1965 remodeled, Michael Baker Jr.; 1985 remodeled, Roger A. Weaver; 712 12th Street). Since the decline of the steel industry, Beaver Falls has lost much of its river-oriented industry, but several industrial complexes remain, including the Mayer China Company building, now Royal Victoria China on 1st Avenue; Republic Steel at the entrance to Beaver Falls from New Brighton; and Moltrup Steel on 1st Avenue between 13th and 14th streets. Moltrup Steel has an office complex a block away from its mill, and the founder's house is only fifteen blocks away at 914 8th Avenue, a juxtaposition rarely seen today.

BE20 Hamilton Tool and Supply (First National Bank of Beaver Falls)

1891. 401 7th Ave.

Built by the Harmony Society in 1891, by 1918, this building had become the offices of the Union Drawn Steel Company, and functions today as retail and office space. It is an imposing four-story, mansard-roofed, brick and stone office building. The stone veneer of the facade, the march of arches across both

elevations, and the foliated capitals of its columns are all characteristic of Richardsonian Romanesque, at that time holding sway in western Pennsylvania.

BE21 Divine Mercy Parish (St. Mary's German Catholic Church)

1895–1896. 605 10th St.

With its picturesque central steeple topped by layers of copper sheeting and guarded by

BE20 HAMILTON TOOL AND SUPPLY (FIRST NATIONAL BANK OF BEAVER FALLS)

pinnacles at each corner, Divine Mercy Parish is a landmark in any aerial view of Beaver Falls.

The unusual roofline of the church consists of a main nave terminating in an apsidal dormer to the south and intersected by two parallel roofs, the first above the entrance is a hipped roof with chamfered ends, the other a gable at the midpoint. Gothic-arched windows and doors reinforce the verticality of the composition. The facade is a balanced three-part composition with side entrances flanking the larger central entrance at the base of the steeple. During a refurbishment in the 1950s, the profile of the steeple was altered to its present appearance, and stained glass windows with themes focused on Mary were added by Edward Hiemer and Company of New Jersey. This German Catholic parish purchased two lots from the Harmonists for $600 in 1869, and built an earlier church here. The present church (1896) was the nucleus for three Roman Catholic churches within three blocks that included a 1910 Polish church and a 1923 Hungarian church. They were recombined into this congregation in 1993.

BE22 First Congregational Church

1889–1890, John Snyder. 1024 4th Ave.

One of nearly three dozen churches built in Beaver Falls during the nineteenth and early twentieth centuries, this neat, white frame church originally served a German Evangelical Protestant congregation. A steep gable defines its simple massing, and on the bracketed entry facade, a small dormered doorway is flanked by paired triangular-topped windows. Five bays of similar peaked windows line each side of the church, and are trimmed with narrow decorative bargeboards echoing the horizontal wood siding.

BE23 National City Bank (Farmer's National Bank)

1928–1929, Uffinger, Foster and Bookwalter. 1101 7th Ave.

This bank is distinguished by bold classical details and lavish materials. Its opulence is evident, from the veneer of pink granite below the water table and the black granite columns on the limestone facade to the interior finishes of the original banking chamber. The restrained cornice is highlighted by stylized eagles perched on wheat sheaves and swags. A rich sculptural program of stylized animals and plants includes bulls' and rams' heads, corn cobs, and swans. Today, a dropped ceiling covers the original gilded, coffered ceiling, enormous brass chandeliers, a clock, and black marble pilaster strips. However, they can be seen from the mahogany-paneled boardroom on the third story of the stack of offices at the rear of the interior.

BE24 Granada Senior Center (Granada Theater, Colonial Theater)

1911; 1928 remodeled, M. J. DeAngelis. 1123 7th Ave.

The 300-seat Granada movie theater was opulent and exotic by Beaver Falls standards as designed by Rochester, New York, architect M. J. DeAngelis. The owner remodeled the modest Colonial Theater of 1911 into a pseudo-Spanish-style fantasy to offer the proper ambience for the new sound films. It is now the sole survivor of the four theaters once standing in Beaver Falls. The cream-colored glazed tile facade is replete with fanciful touches of gilding along the blind arches and small balconies that flank the marquee and line the irregular cornice. Foliated stone pilasters topped with owls complete the ensemble. The theater closed in 1960. In the early 1970s, new owners gutted the interior and converted it into a mini-mall and senior center.

BE25 Trinity United Presbyterian Church (First Presbyterian Church)

1928–1930, George Espie Savage. 1103 8th Ave.

This church, which became Trinity United Presbyterian Church in 1960, was designed by Scottish-born George Espie Savage (1874–1948) of Philadelphia, one of over three hundred churches that he and, later, his son, George D. Savage, designed, primarily on the East Coast. Although the church was commissioned just before the stock market crash of 1929, the congregation spent $750,000 to build it, testifying to the strong faith and prosperity of the Presbyterian community in Beaver Falls. The plan is L-shaped, with the nave of the main church opening onto 8th Avenue and the school and chapel oriented toward 11th Street. The church seats over 700 people in the nave, and the chapel seats an additional 160 people. Savage employed fifteenth-century English Gothic for this large church, which is constructed of schist from the Foxcroft quarry at Broomall, Pennsylvania, and trimmed with Indiana limestone. The stone is tool dressed and laid with open joints, giving it a colorful appearance. A four-story bell tower at the inner corner of the ell has lancet openings on all sides, with crocketed finials at the four corners. The nave rises sixty feet from the floor to the ridge of the open timber ceiling. It is lit by luminous windows designed by R. Toland Wright of Cleveland, Ohio, with sapphire tones predominating. In the chancel, Kentucky white stone furnishings and carved oak filigree and figurative sculptures are surrounded by oak rose-studded paneling.

BE26 Carnegie Free Library

1902–1903, Frederick Osterling. 1301 7th Ave.

Andrew Carnegie's letter announcing a grant of $50,000 to Beaver Falls for a new library was front-page news in the *Beaver Times* of September 1899. For sixteen years, a local library committee had been raising funds for the effort. Carnegie's usual conditions prevailed: the city must provide a site and fund the onoing maintenance of the building. Frederick J. Osterling had designed one library, several office buildings, churches, and houses for wealthy patrons like Charles Schwab by the time he received this commission. Set back on its site to allow for an imposing staircase, the library displays the Classical Revival attributes found in many Carnegie libraries nationwide. The heavy, squarish massing of the hipped-roof, yellow-orange brick building is dominated by a dentil-lined pediment supported by massive two-story stone columns. A large semicircular arched stained glass window highlights the two-story entrance bay and illuminates the interior stairwell, and stone belt courses and pilasters articulate each bay. The 13th Street elevation has three arched doorways (two now bricked in) with lunettes and keystones that marked the entrance to the former auditorium at the rear.

In plan, the library has a central room on each floor that is flanked by smaller rooms. The dark wooden interior trim is highlighted by fluted Corinthian columns delineating the entrances to the various rooms on the first story. There is a fireplace in the original children's reading room, which is used today as a

BE26 CARNEGIE FREE LIBRARY

BE27 MUNICIPAL BUILDING

general reading room. The upper stories were used as classrooms and offices for the local schools.

BE27 Municipal Building

1927–1928, Edward J. Carlisle and Harry P. Sharrer. 1425 8th Ave.

This large, dark orange brick structure houses the police and fire departments for the city of over 10,000 inhabitants. Dominated by a bell-shaped cupola atop the central tower, the building sits on a side street at the north end of the shopping district. The municipal offices occupy the east wing of the three-bay building and are accessed from the facade facing north, while the police department offices are entered from the east side. The west wing accommodates emergency vehicles with three oversized garage doors. Pairs of round-arched windows line the second story of each wing. The central tower, a former hose tower, has no entrance from the street, and houses sirens at the top. Architects Edward Carlisle and Harry Sharrer also designed parts of the former Beaver County Courthouse demolished in 2000.

BE28 Harmonist Houses

c. 1874. 1602 6th Ave. and 1314 3rd Ave.

These two simple, stone houses on 6th Avenue (BE28.1) and 3rd Avenue (BE28.2) were built for workers in local industries. They are visual reminders of the important part played by the Harmonists in the early development of Beaver Falls's industries, religious buildings, education, and housing. By 1859, the Harmonists held several large mortgages in the town, which they supplemented with purchases at sheriff's sales. In 1866, they owned so much of the town that they ordered a new survey, laid out a series of lots, and renamed it Beaver Falls. The small, two-story houses occupy narrow town lots, with their bracket-lined gable ends facing the street. A window and door on the first story and a single window centered under the gable on the second are the only fenestration. Later alterations, including porches, cannot hide the thick stone walls that identify these residences.

BE29 Geneva College District

1880–present. College Ave.

Geneva College, a Christian, coeducational college of 1,500 students, occupies a wooded fifty-five-acre campus on a bluff overlooking the Beaver River. Founded in 1848 by the Reformed Presbyterian Church in Northwood, Ohio, the college moved to Beaver Falls in 1880 at the invitation of the Harmony Society, which donated ten acres in their effort to reinvigorate the town. The college's buildings were built with a $20,000 donation from the community.

Old Main (1879–1881, James P. Bailey for Bailey and Anglin), the dominant landmark

BE29 GENEVA COLLEGE DISTRICT, Old Main

BE29 GENEVA COLLEGE DISTRICT, Johnston Gymnasium

of the college, is constructed of native gray sandstone quarried on the site. The facade features a central bell tower, gabled dormers, and alternating projecting and recessed wall planes, which give it a lively quality. A handsome three-bay entrance loggia on the principal elevation of the T-shaped three-story building is supported by columns with foliated capitals. The many pointed-arched or gabled windows on all elevations, the bracketed eaves, and the mansard roof draw attention upward to the roofline. Stylistically, Old Main is similar to a large number of college administration buildings of the era, which could be called "Collegiate Second Empire." "Fern Cliffe" (1879–1880) is a fine example of domestic Second Empire styling in wood, built for John L. McCartney, a professor of natural philosophy. The facade is dominated by a pentagonal bay with a bracketed mansard roof. A four-bay porch shelters the main entrance, and another wooden porch covers the northwest corner.

At the base of the hill, along the Beaver River, a small railroad station for the P&LE was designed by architect Joseph Ladd Neal of Pittsburgh and railroad engineer John Abiel Atwood in 1910. Named College Station, the two-story brick building with a seven-foot-wide canopy has been owned by the college since 1997.

W. G. Eckles Company Architects of New Castle designed four buildings for the campus. These include the two-story, red brick Johnston Gymnasium (1911) that is distinguished by a central projecting entrance bay, hipped roof, and tripartite segmental-arched windows. McKee Hall (1919–1921) is constructed of randomly coursed fieldstone, with tall exterior end chimneys at both gable ends. Its tiled roofline is broken by hipped-roof dormers and windows with stone surrounds on all three stories over the central entrance. The firm designed the Reeves Field south of Old Main and the two entrance pavilions along College Avenue (1923). The final campus building designed by Eckles is McCartney Library (1930–1931). Its L-shaped plan is highlighted by a square, three-story bell tower with lancet windows and stone coping defining the flat roofline. The stonework is similar to that of Old Main. The library's reading rooms have large stained glass windows by Henry Lee Willet that tell the stories of *Pilgrim's Progress* and *Paradise Lost*. Willet's other work includes windows for the chapel at West Point and the National Cathedral in Washington, D.C.

The Eckles firm also designed the nearby College Hill Reformed Presbyterian Church (1924; 3217 College Avenue), which, while not technically part of Geneva College, is located on a raised terrace west of the McCartney Library and complements the campus buildings of that era. The sandstone Gothic Revival church has a large stained glass window above the double entrance doors, stone coping and capstones defining the buttresses, and gable ends.

In 1953, Ezra C. Stiles (1891–1974), a landscape architect from Pittsburgh, drew up a campus master plan. While all of his recommendations were not implemented, it is an unusual document, since most of Stiles's work was either residential or for municipal parks, cemeteries, and schools. A preservation plan of 2007 prepared by the Pittsburgh History and Landmarks Foundation and the college recommends National Register listing for the core campus.

Among the several postwar buildings is Memorial Hall (1951–1952), which emulates McKee Hall, although without the chimneys and elaborate ornamentation of the earlier structure. It was designed by Arthur L. Martsolf (1895–1958) and his son, Louis G. Mart- solf. Later, Beaver Falls architect Joseph F. Bontempo designed three buildings for the campus: the Metheny Field House (1961; 1989 addition), Pearce Hall (1961), and Clarke Hall (1961). Alexander Hall (1971, Carl G. Baker and Associates) provided a flat-roofed din- ing hall in the brick and concrete materials popular at the time. All these buildings were upgraded in the 1990s.

FOMBELL

BE30 Samuel Hazen Farm District

1850–1920. PA 1008 from Celia Rd. to Hicker- nell Rd., 3 miles northwest of Fombell

The three Hazen farms illustrate rural life away from the rivers in late-nineteenth- century Beaver County. Samuel Hazen pur- chased land in the Connoquenessing Creek valley in 1854. His son, Nathaniel W. Hazen, inherited and added to it, running a dairy farm there into the 1890s. In 1876, Nathaniel divided the farm between his sons Ezra and Elsworth. Ezra added to his acreage and left the land to his two sons, Gilbert and Charles, in 1904. These farms, joined by proximity and family ties, now lie in the path of the ram- pant suburbanization overtaking rural lands in the counties surrounding Pittsburgh. The land rises gradually to the north along the east bank of the meandering Connoquenes- sing Creek, with the tracks of the Pittsburgh, New Castle and Lake Erie Railroad parallel to the creek. The Hazen-Perkins farmhouse and outbuildings (c. 1894) sit on a hillside distantly visible from the road. The other two farm complexes, the Hazen-Clyde (c. 1850) and the Hazen-Zeigler (c. 1920), surrounded by their fields, are adjacent to the road. The nearby Soap Run one-room schoolhouse of c. 1876 and a handsome five-bay stone house at 801 Hickernell, c. 1870, add to the rural au- thenticity of the area.

These farm buildings show the evolution of rural architecture from the mid-nineteenth to the early twentieth centuries. The oldest, the Hazen-Clyde farm built in the late 1850s, is at the core of the complex, and centers on a red brick, four-bay, gable-roofed house with a frame ell on the rear elevation. Originally owned by Nathaniel W. Hazen, it was pur- chased in 1876 by his son Elsworth. The house is oriented toward and slightly above the Connoquenessing Creek. A frame barn with a jerkinhead roof and peaked dormers is the only outbuilding remaining.

To the west is the Hazen-Zeigler farm, which was owned by Elsworth's half-brother, Ezra, who left it to his son Charles in 1904. Now owned by his granddaughter Mary Lynn Newell, it consists of a pyramidal-roofed brick house dating from the 1920s that replaced the 1890s house after a fire. The outbuildings are similar to those of the Hazen-Perkins farm: white frame structures on sandstone foun- dations. Hazen-Perkins Farm, on a hillside above the creek, was inherited by Ezra's other son, Gilbert. Its five-bay, white frame farm- house dates from 1894. The simple porch col- umns and window surrounds on the facade give way to a livelier east elevation dominated by a wraparound porch and a two-and-one- half-story ell with a bay window and large dormer. At the rear of the intersecting gable- roofed house is a summer kitchen, or "out house," not a latrine but a small house built for hired hands and nearly attached to the main house for convenience. A large white barn and outbuildings date from 1892. The barn was constructed by the Miller brothers, local carpenters who built timber-frame barns with mortise-and-tenon connections secured by barn pegs. The peaked framed vents, sand- stone foundation, and partially hewn tree trunks used for the framing are increasingly rare, as they compete with today's simple metal barns.

BE31 Clow-Schry House (James Beach Clow House)

1830. 243 Chapel Dr. at Ann St., 5.5 miles north- west of Fombell

Although Greek Revival farmhouses are not unusual in the area, intact frame versions are. James Beach Clow, scion of a prominent Allegheny County family, purchased over five hundred acres of land in Beaver County in 1821, and built this house on a 213-acre parcel called "Indian Camp." The L-shaped, two-story house is five bays across, with interior chimneys at each gable end and a central-hall, two-room-over-two-room plan. The fireplace mantels, door locks, flooring, and the rounded cherry handrail of the stairway supported by tapered balusters are all original, as are most of the white pine windows and shutters. The house is sheathed with rabbeted-bevel siding of eastern white pine (milled at Clow's sawmill along Brush Creek) applied directly over the studs, and the foundation is of sandstone blocks, some ten feet in length. To the rear, a privy covered with weatherboard has two windows. Nearby, an operating springhouse with a stone facade is banked into the hillside. The property stayed in the Clow family until 1893, and operated as a farm until 1950, when suburbanization began in the area.

BE31 CLOW-SCHRY HOUSE (JAMES BEACH CLOW HOUSE)

BE32 Shakespeare's Restaurant and Pub, and Stonewall Golf Club

1999 restaurant-clubhouse, Joseph J. Balobeck; golf course, Hurdzan/Fry, Golf Course Design, Inc. 1495 Mercer Rd., 6 miles northwest of Fombell

Southeast of the Lawrence County town of Ellwood City lies a surprising "medieval castle" made of textured light gray concrete block.

Situated on a 269-acre golf course, the rectangular two-story restaurant and clubhouse building has four square, sturdy-looking corner towers. Windows on the first story are appropriately small and barred, although there are solid panes above, and on the rear facade there are large plate glass windows that overlook the golf course and a formal garden. The entire structure is castellated. A simple stone belt course outlines the first story of the central entrance pavilion, with a pair of segmental-arched, twelve-foot-high wooden doors flanked by projecting two-story pavilions. The driveway and parking lot in front of the castle are lined with limestone boulders, each weighing from two to seven tons, quarried at nearby Medusa Aggregates. One enters the castle by crossing a wooden footbridge over a moat, expecting to hear the blare of welcoming trumpets. The interior is paneled with cross-cut oak, has New York blue stone floors, and is replete with faux medieval fittings and suits of armor.

DARLINGTON

The earliest inhabitants along Little Beaver Creek were primarily members of the Delaware, Mingo, and Shawnee tribes. The first European settlers were farmers who called the village Greersburg, after George Greer, one of the three original landholders. By the early nineteenth century, the village was a layover for stagecoach passengers traveling between Pittsburgh, Erie, and Cleveland, Ohio. Abner Lacock (1770–1837), a self-taught civil engineer, laid out the town in 1804, cutting the flat land into sixteen blocks, with eight lots to each block. Active in Beaver County politics and serving in the U.S. Senate from 1813 to 1819, Lacock supervised the building of the Pennsylvania Canal's western division from Johnstown to Pittsburgh, and lobbied successfully to bring segments of the canal up the Beaver River to Ohio via Beaver and Sandy creeks. Incorporated in 1820, Greersburg was renamed Darlington in 1830 to avoid confusion with Westmoreland County's seat, Greensburg.

Cannel, or slate coal, a popular alternative to English coal, was discovered near Darlington in 1832. Initially shipped to New York City via the canals, after 1850, it was transported by the Pittsburgh, Marion and Chicago Railroad, which used the Greersburg Academy (BE33) building as its train station. Nearby clay deposits prompted the founding of a brick company. Bricks from the Darlington area were used to construct two buildings in New York City: the Waldorf Astoria in 1930 and the United Nations in 1971. Both the clay and the coal mines are now closed. Yet, there has been an effort to retain old homes and academy structures that might otherwise have been demolished. The social influence of Scots-Irish Presbyterians can be seen in Mt. Pleasant Presbyterian Church of 1798 (1965 rebuilt; 718 PA 168); the Reformed Presbyterian Church (1847; 140 1st Street); the red brick Jonathan Morris House (1837; 463 Cannelton Road); and Buttonwood, home of abolitionist Arthur B. Bradford (1837–1840; 137 Bradford Road). Today, the village of Darlington is a small crossroads community with late-nineteenth-century houses providing a charming bedroom community for Ellwood City, located to the north in Lawrence County.

BE33 Greersburg Academy

1802. 710 Market St. 1883. 803 Plumb St.

Greersburg Academy, the oldest extant building in Beaver County, and affectionately called the "stone pile," has sophisticated stonework for such an early frontier building. Built under the direction of Reverend Thomas E. Hughes, pastor of nearby Mt. Pleasant Presbyterian Church, it was the first Presbyterian academy north of the Ohio River. The building is nearly thirty-three-feet square, and has an entrance on each side. It features corner quoins, a stone segmental-arched entrance on the east elevation, and stone arches above the first-story windows. Two interior brick chimneys with paired chimneypots flank the central portion of the pyramidal roof. On the interior, three rooms surround an enclosed stair in the center of the first floor; the second story has five small adjoining rooms. When Greersburg Academy moved to new premises in 1883, the building was sold to the Pittsburgh, Marion and Chicago Railroad Company. Its days as a rail station are evidenced by the reinforced floor in the freight room, the ghost of a porch on the north wall where the platform stood, and a ticket window in the largest room on the first floor.

The Greersburg Academy of 1883 on Plumb Street is a tall, dark red brick rectangle, with two bays of segmental-arched windows at the gable ends and four windows on each side. It functioned as a Presbyterian Academy until 1908, and then as the local public school until 1957.

The two buildings indicate the importance of education to the Presbyterians of western Pennsylvania, a theme echoed in the many local colleges founded by the denomination. Among the eminent Pennsylvanians who attended Greersburg Academy was William Holmes McGuffey (1800–1873), whose readers and spellers sold nearly thirty million copies in the mid-nineteenth century. The Little Beaver Historical Society now operates both former Greersburg academies as museums.

BE33 GREERSBURG ACADEMY

Aerial view of Crucible Steel Company's Midland works, c. 1952.

MIDLAND

BE34 United Steelworkers of America, Local 1212

1950–1951, Robert F. Beatty. 617 Midland Ave.

The United Steelworkers Local 1212 is a three-story rectangular structure sheathed in coral-pink marble inside and out. Located only two blocks north of Midland's enormous former Crucible Steel plant, the town's commercial district saw more work shirts and steel-toed shoes than coral-pink anything. The restrained detailing of the structure and its open, glass-fronted lobby and meeting hall suit the needs of its sponsor, despite the seemingly incongruous color scheme.

BE35 Carnegie Library of Midland

1916, Frederick J. Merrick. 61 9th St.

This is a classic Carnegie branch library, essentially one large room with a fireplace nook to the right of the entrance in the children's library and an adult reading room to the left. The librarian's office is located in the center at the head of the entrance stair.

A local couple, William and Lucy Hart, applied to the Andrew Carnegie Foundation in 1914 for a $20,000 grant to build the library. The land was donated by the Midland Improvement Company, the real estate arm of Crucible Steel, which between 1906 and 1936 owned nearly all the homes in Midland. Set one block north of the commercial street in town, the library is a transitional site from the commercial to the residential portions of Midland. When the school board agreed to manage the library and the borough to

BE35 CARNEGIE LIBRARY OF MIDLAND

support it with tax dollars, the design of the library's basement was raised to allow larger windows so it could be used as the library for the Midland High School. The structure has a residential scale and Tudor Revival touches in the leaded glass and casement windows, and in the building's crisp angles. Irregularly coursed sandstone trimmed with limestone and the steeply gabled roof lend the building the air of a chapel.

SHIPPINGPORT

BE36 First Energy (Duquesne Light, Beaver Valley Power Station)

1976 Unit No. 1, 1987 Unit No. 2, Stone and Webster, contractors. PA 168 at Shippingport Rd.

With steam billowing from their hulking curves, the 505-foot hyperbolic cooling towers of the Beaver Valley nuclear power station dominate the Ohio River shore twenty-two miles northwest of Pittsburgh's Point. The power station, one of approximately 104 nuclear facilities in the United States, generates nearly 1,643,000 kilowatts of power at peak capacity. It was the site of the first commercial nuclear power plant in the nation, and its opening in 1957 was viewed as a renewal of American's faith in science: "The force that blasted Hiroshima will light our Christmas trees this year," stated the *Pittsburgh Press* newspaper in December 1957. The plant was a joint project of the United States Atomic Energy Commission and Duquesne Light Company. Construction was overseen by Rear Admiral Hyman G. Rickover and the Westinghouse Electric Company. The station was retired from service after twenty-five years of operation in 1982, and all but the office structure was dismantled between 1984 and 1989.

The plant of 1957 was replaced by the 185-foot-high dome-shaped concrete reactor containment buildings of Units No. 1 and No. 2. These are designed to withstand earthquakes, floods, and tornados, while protecting against the release of radioactive material. Each is 126 feet in diameter and constructed of four-and-a-half-foot-thick steel reinforced concrete walls with ten-foot-thick bases. An inner steel liner is three-eighths of an inch thick. The site was listed as a landmark by the Society of Mechanical Engineers in 1980. To the east, the coal-burning power plant of the Bruce Mansfield Power Station adds to the drama of the site with three more hyperbolic cooling towers and two enormous smokestacks.

HOOKSTOWN

Hookstown, about three miles south of the Ohio River, is a simple farming community and crossroads town with a preponderance of nineteenth-century red brick houses. An 1817 map shows roads from Pittsburgh and Washington, Pennsylvania, converging just below Hookstown. The road through Hookstown leads to Georgetown on the Ohio River and Dawson's Ferry on the north shore, and the community's location on this major route kept its inns, taverns, and wheat and flour mills busy. The town was named for two brothers from Maryland, Mathias and Benjamin Hook. Both were salt dealers, and Mathias was a Revolutionary War soldier. They came to western Pennsylvania c. 1786, patented the land in 1806, and laid out Hookstown over the course of the next three years. The earliest settlers were from Maryland and Delaware, and most were Scots-Irish Presbyterians, as evidenced by the two Presbyterian churches in this small town. Largely settled before the Civil War, Hookstown maintains its historic appearance despite minor alterations to many of its buildings. It was incorporated in 1843 at the peak of its population of 350. Never on a rail line, Hookstown avoided the industrial development that so

Hookstown Main Street (PA 168), looking north from Pittsburgh Grade Road.

dramatically altered neighboring towns. The undulating land surrounding the village continues to support working farms. Closely spaced, gable-roofed houses line Main Street and one block west. They are two stories in height, with four to five bays across the facade and a variety of chimney placements. Notable is the McLaughlin house (c. 1840; 464 Main Street), with a Georgian-styled fanlight and sidelights at the entry.

RACCOON CREEK STATE PARK AND VICINITY

BE37 Raccoon Creek State Park Recreation District

1935–1937, 1939–1941, Civilian Conservation Corps. PA 18

Raccoon Creek was planned as a Recreation Demonstration Area by the National Park Service in an attempt to reforest and preserve exhausted timber and farmland and provide underprivileged city dwellers, especially children, opportunities for outdoor living.

These 6,909 acres of wooded parkland in southwestern Beaver County are dotted with campsites accessed by gravel roads. Eight administrative and service buildings adjacent to PA 18 include the park office, a conference building, storeroom, carpenter shop, blacksmith shop, repair shop, garage, and open shed. The standardized, prefabricated utilitarian structures were built to serve the Civilian Conservation Corps (CCC) workers on a temporary basis. The nearly 120 log buildings built by the CCC between 1935 and 1941 are west of PA 18. All are in their original locations in groupings illustrating prewar ideas of family camping. The hand-worked log and stone construction recalls America's pioneer past, but influences from Bavarian and Swiss chalets and the camps of the Adirondacks are also evident. They have new asbestos-shingled roofs, or new chinking and mortar.

Group Camp No. 1, with its unique wane-edged siding and log construction, was featured in Albert H. Good's *Park and Recreation Structures*, a 1938 National Park Service publication. This camp's fifty buildings were designed to hold 120 civilian campers and are the oldest and most architecturally interesting. The logs are salvaged telephone poles sharpened at the ends and laid on a stone foundation. Gable roofs are standard, and the larger unit cabin and lodge have massive stone chimneys. These units are not used or maintained. While seemingly random in plan, they were laid out with careful consideration given to shade, safe water supply, vehicular access, and minimal damage to the environment. The central administrative unit is located at the top of the hill, with four smaller cabin groupings in the woods below.

Camp No. 2 consists of forty-five buildings arranged around a central administrative unit with four smaller camps around it for 120 civilian campers. The gable-roofed buildings are wood frame with rough, wane-edged siding and stone chimneys on the larger buildings. Some board-and-batten siding and rows of multipaned and double-sash windows offset the horizontality of the siding. Camp No. 3, the smallest of the older camps, contains one administrative unit and two unit camps with twenty-two buildings designed to accommodate 56 civilian campers. The cabins, unit houses, and shower houses are clapboarded or board and batten and have gable roofs. The main lodge has a brick chimney.

In 1945, the National Park Service turned the Recreation Demonstration Area over to the Commonwealth of Pennsylvania, at which time it was renamed Racoon Creek State Park.

BE38 David Littell House (Chestnut Flats)

1849–1851, Hayward and Cains, builders. 2039 Littell Dr., 3.5 miles north of Raccoon Creek State Park

This is a fine example of a house type common in western Pennsylvania in the 1850s: a central-hall, five-bay, gable-roofed red brick house. Not quite as common are its paired interior end chimneys and single window in each gable end. Solid and large, the austere house reflects the values of its owners. The house sits on land obtained by William Littell, a Presbyterian from Hazelhatch, Ireland, as a land grant in 1796. The present structure, built by William's grandson David Littell, is the fourth home on the property. Several ancient trees nearby contribute to the integrity of the setting. The interior cedar woodwork was cut on the property. The fireplace surrounds are cast iron. There is a central stairway with a plain gooseneck railing. Back stairs lead up to the second story from the kitchen in the southeast corner. The datestone at the base of a column supporting the facade's portico bears the date 1851.

ALIQUIPPA AND VICINITY

Located on the Ohio River's west bank twenty-two miles northwest of Pittsburgh and known as Woodlawn until 1928, Aliquippa was sparsely populated as late as the mid-1870s, when the area began to attract railroad speculators. In 1878, the Pittsburgh and Lake Erie Railroad laid its route to Youngstown on the west bank of the Ohio River, and laid out Aliquippa Park, a popular attraction, to boost ridership on its new line. The name "Aliquippa" commemorates a Seneca woman who died in 1754.

By 1905, Woodlawn's proximity to Pittsburgh, easy rail and water access, large tracts of undeveloped land, and available natural resources attracted the Jones and Laughlin Steel Company (J&L), which had outgrown its Pittsburgh factories. The company purchased five-and-one-half miles of land along the river, including the former park, and by 1907, its first blast furnace was under construction. The Aliquippa Works of J&L manufactured raw and finished steel in its integrated plant. Its workforce grew to 14,000 laborers, larger than the neighboring American Bridge Company across the Ohio River. J&L not only transformed Woodlawn's waterfront from light agriculture to heavy industry, it also engineered the layout and management of the town. The

Woodlawn Land Company, a subsidiary of J&L, designed and built worker housing and managed the company store, the local trust company, and many of the public offices. More than 1,500 homes were built in the ten years following 1907; the first year averaged one finished home a day. By 1913, there were twelve housing plans, each sensitively sited according to natural boundaries, although the houses within the plans were typically arranged in straight rows. Each plan was designated for a different ethnic group, including Italians, Serbians, African Americans, Croatians, Slovaks, Russians, Poles, Ukrainians, and Greeks. The ethnic enclaves proved convenient for the immigrants, who could preserve their languages and customs, and, even more convenient for the company, which could better control its workers by setting each group in opposition to the others: no joint demonstrations of unity could occur to oppose company proclamations. The houses, noted for their efficiency and modernity, were constructed primarily of brick or concrete with anywhere from six to ten rooms, and were sold on easy terms to steel mill employees. Paul M. Moore, contractor, and R. E. Murray, architect, have been credited with some of the buildings. Plan 6 High, including Larimer Road, was reserved for management; here the houses are set atop the hillside, with larger lots and an overlook to the steel mill below.

Through the late 1960s, Aliquippa grew with and because of the steel industry. Thus, when the mill, then owned by LTV Steel, shut down in the early 1980s, the city suffered greatly. Today, the workers' housing remains in tight clusters, but suburbs to the west, with easier access to major highways, have drawn many residents from the town. The throngs of shoppers once patronizing Franklin Street were drawn first to suburban strip malls and then to the regional megamalls accessed by Beaver County's superhighway, PA 60.

BE39 LTV Structural Steel Offices (Pittsburgh and Lake Erie Railroad Station)

c. 1915, attributed to Joseph Ladd Neal. 111 Station St.

The first station of the Pittsburgh and Lake Erie Railroad (P&LE) at Woodlawn (Aliquippa) was little more than a shed, but with the dramatic growth of the town in the early twentieth century, a grander building was needed. Joseph Neal, originally from Maine and educated in Boston, apprenticed with Shepley, Rutan and Coolidge, and practiced in Pittsburgh between 1893 and 1917. He is linked with P&LE engineer John Abiel Atwood and credited with several stations for the railroad (see BE29). This station, the largest and best preserved of Beaver County's train stations, has a cruciform plan with its long edge parallel to the railroad tracks. With broad overhanging eaves to protect waiting passengers from the elements and the warm brown tones of its brick and stone walls, the building shares some stylistic motifs with other P&LE stations. The station's eclectic mix of medieval-inspired details include Dutch gables with ball finials, flat stone window moldings, oversized wooden brackets, and a castellated bay. The tiled roof and elaborately corbeled chimney are atypical of local rail stations. The building now houses the offices of LTV Structural Steel.

BE40 Towne Towers (Pittsburgh Mercantile Company)

1910. 434 Franklin Ave.

Built in 1910, Pittsburgh Mercantile, a subsidiary of the Jones and Laughlin Steel Company, provided the mill workers with five sto-

BE39 LTV STRUCTURAL STEEL OFFICES (PITTSBURGH AND LAKE ERIE RAILROAD STATION)

ries of shopping, including departments for home furnishings, clothing, and food. It was the largest and most complete department store in its day for miles outside Pittsburgh. The steel-frame, pale brown brick building originally had large plate glass windows and a canopied entrance on the first floor; these are now obscured by brick and tile panels. Only an ornamental band with stylized cresting waves and budding flowers remains at this level. The three middle stories are grouped into vertical bays and accented with molded brick in the fashion of the Chicago School. A bracketed hollow tile roof caps the attic zone of decorative brickwork and green terra-cotta panels. The interior was once equally as impressive, with high ceilings and mahogany trim. A refrigerating plant in the basement served primarily for meats, vegetables, and other grocery items displayed on the first floor. Despite the loss of its first-floor windows, the building retains its monumental presence on Aliquippa's main street. It has been converted to an apartment building.

BE41 Benjamin Franklin Jones Memorial Library

1929, Brandon Smith for Bartholomew and Smith. 663 Franklin Ave.

This library was a gift to the citizens of Aliquippa from Elisabeth M. Horne in honor of her late father, founder and a director of the Jones and Laughlin Steel Company for over fifty years. Benjamin Jones spent his boyhood in nearby New Brighton, and advanced from part ownership in a canal and transportation company to full-fledged steel baron. Designed by Brandon Smith while with the firm of Bartholomew and Smith of Pittsburgh, the library's sumptuous style emulates a Renaissance palazzo. A cast-bronze cornice relieves the austerity of the Indiana limestone facade. The central entrance is softened slightly by the recess of the flanking wings, with each showcasing four Ionic columns below a scrolled entablature; windows are recessed behind the columns, adding depth to the facade. Swags flanking the entrance are repeated on the door surrounds. Not to be outdone by the Carnegie Library in Pittsburgh (AL41), which lists the names of male artists, authors, scientists, and poets along the cornice, Aliquippa's library lists subjects: Philosophy, Biology, Astronomy, Fiction, History, Science, and the Fine Arts on its cornice. Inside, the central librarian's desk oversees book stacks behind it and the two flanking reading rooms. The east room has a coffered ceiling and Kasota marble walls, and in the west room, children's scenes are depicted in stained glass windows by Henry Hunt of Pittsburgh. A walled garden southwest of the building retains the stone wall and ornament specified by Smith.

BE42 Physical Education/Recreation Complex, Community College of Beaver County

1976, Carl G. Baker and Associates. Community College Dr., 4 miles northwest of Aliquippa

This aluminum geodesic dome anchored by a steel continuous ring and attached to raked concrete block walls and concrete piers is the school's gymnasium. The entrance facing the campus is a rectangular glass box. The interior has an apex of 65 feet and maximizes its nearly 32,000 square feet of usable space with a minimum of materials. The clear span of 232 feet is suitable for basketball games and large gatherings. Although there are more than 200,000 geodesic dome structures around the world, this is one of the few modern buildings of this scale built in Beaver County in the 1970s.

FREEDOM

BE43 Vicary House

1826–1829. 4th Ave. at Harvey Run Rd.

Philadelphia sea captain William B. Vicary purchased one thousand acres of land along the Ohio River in 1826, and commissioned contractor John Moore to build his substantial house. The beauty and size of its stones are noteworthy, even in Beaver County where sandstone houses were numerous well into the late nineteenth century. The massive, honey-colored blocks of the Vicary House were quarried and dressed on the property. A foliated pattern carved in the stone threshold of the facade's smaller door appears to be a mason's mark. Vicary replaced Moore for failing to complete the house in the proposed time. The two-story house has a lower two-story wing to the south and measures seventy-seven feet in width. It has a familiar five-bay central-hall plan, with four rooms per story. The three-bay south wing appears to have accommodated the kitchen, with bedrooms above. Massive bridged chimneys, unusual

BE43 VICARY HOUSE

for Beaver County, and a distinctive round-arched oak entrance door sheltered beneath a columned portico add to the mansionlike appearance of this house, which was restored in 1999 by Charles L. Desmone and Associates. Opposite the house, across Harvey Run Road, architect John Comes used a similar stone to construct the Gothic Revival St. Felix Chapel (1906).

CONWAY

BE44 CONWAY AUTOMATIC CLASSIFICATION RAILYARD (PENNSYLVANIA RAILROAD CLASSIFICATION YARD), photo c. 1950

BE44 Conway Automatic Classification Railyard (Pennsylvania Railroad Classification Yard)

c. 1954–1956, Hunting, Larsen and Dunnells. Between the Ohio River and PA 65

Stretching nearly four miles along the Ohio River shore, the Conway Automatic Classification Railyard looks, in an aerial view, like a pair of forks with interlaced tines. An average of 6,000 freight cars coming from east or west are sorted here onto 107 separate tracks for destinations from St. Louis to Montreal. With 181 miles of track, the yard is one of only five or six this size in the United States.

Upon entering, a long freight train is pushed to the top of a slight hill called "the hump," then each car is separated by hand when one of the crew pulls the coupling. The cars roll down the hump to the designated track, which is opened by an electronic switch. The buildings reflect the yard's evolution from a railyard for the Pittsburgh, Fort Wayne and Chicago line in the 1880s to a freight classification yard for the Pennsylvania Railroad after the turn of the twentieth century. The latter built the roundhouse in 1910, northwest of the administration building. Its timber construction is visible on the interior, though the building has been altered over the years. In the early twenty-first century, it had eight tracks and enough workers to sand (for traction), refuel, and repair an average of eleven locomotives per day. Nearby, the carpenter shop, formerly the administration building, is of red brick and has round-arched windows that are still visible through many coats of ruddy paint.

More tracks were added to the site over the years, and a renovation of the site in 1956 added five yellow-orange brick buildings dotted across the acreage. The three-story administration building, the largest structure, lies in the center of all the activity, and its five-story tower offers a view of the entire yard. This building initially housed train crews, who were fed and entertained by the YMCA under contract to the railroad. The former sleeping quarters now house training classrooms and an engine simulator. Similar but smaller buildings lie at both the east and west entrances of the yard and adjacent to each hump. They are simple brick buildings with metal-framed, green-tinted windows slanting in at the base to reduce reflections in the towers. Their interiors are finished with enameled tile and linoleum.

AMBRIDGE

Sixteen miles northwest of Pittsburgh, the borough of Ambridge stretches for two miles along the east shore of the Ohio River. At this point, the Ohio flows almost due north. The borough occupies the wide floodplain close to the river's edge and a relatively flat shelf of land approximately forty feet above the shore.

In 1824, George Rapp and his Harmonist followers returned to Pennsylvania after ten years in southern Indiana, purchasing three thousand acres on the Ohio River (BE46; and see Harmony, Butler County). Though the Harmonists had their greatest material success in Economy, their social and intellectual influence on the development of Beaver County and western Pennsylvania throughout the nineteenth century was profound. They are perhaps America's most important and successful experiment in early-nineteenth-century Christian communal living. While no major new Harmonist buildings were built in the area after 1834, the group brought observers to the region from around the world.

In 1900, the American Bridge Company, then a subsidiary of Carnegie Steel, bought the Berlin Iron Bridge Company and constructed what evolved into the largest bridge-building plant in the world. The American Bridge Company became a subsidiary of United States Steel c. 1901. Located downstream from some of the largest steel producers in the world, the big, new plant had plenty of available material to fabricate. The company imported thirty thousand cars of slag from the Carnegie furnaces at Homestead to bring the floodplain up to the level of the railroad tracks. Within two years, fourteen buildings were erected, including the enormous Main Bridge Shop (270 × 776 feet), and the Engineers' Offices on the hillside above. The American Bridge Company's 4,000 workers needed housing. Using a contraction of the company's name as its title, the Ambridge Land Company graded and paved streets with firebrick, set curbs and sidewalks, and built sewer and gas lines to 970 lots on the plateau above the plant. The company offered discounts on the lots and bonuses to those who could complete a new house in less than a year. Most of the brick houses are two-and-one-half-story vernacular versions of the Colonial Revival style.

The borough's plan extended south from the grid pattern already established in Economy. The Ambridge Land Company arranged for a two-story, hipped-roof police and municipal building (1910; 1003 Merchant Street) of cream-colored brick, with pedimented dormers on all elevations. Foliated and classical ornament, including dentils, swags, lintels with keystones, and corner quoins, enliven its facade. The company also reserved lots for churches, parks, and schools. Free lots had been reserved in 1903 for the Lutherans, Presbyterians, Methodists, and Catholics. The supervisory personnel lived on Park Road between 4th and 8th streets because of its river overlook and larger lot size. Foremen and skilled workers generally lived on Maplewood Avenue, one block east of the river. East of Merchant Street along Melrose Avenue, Irish laborers occupied houses similar to middle management's but on smaller lots. Unskilled German and Slavic workers tended to live on Glenwood Drive and Olive Lane, often in row houses. While the design of the housing stock does not reflect national origins, the borough's two dozen churches by their numbers and their architecture reveal the workers' various ethnic and religious backgrounds, especially Holy Ghost (Russian) Orthodox Church of America (1907–1914; 210 Maplewood Avenue) and St. Stanislaus Polish Roman Catholic Church designed by W. Ward Williams (1926–1927; 558 Beaver Road).

In 1926–1927, the Woodlawn-Ambridge Bridge (BE49), built by the Ambridge Land Company, opened the area south of the river to Ambridge employees. The new borough was also linked with heavily populated Allegheny County to the south via a small streetcar system that began operating in 1906 using the Harmonists' empty laundry building as the generating plant. Ultimately, Ambridge's shopping district served 35,000 people, and its commercial district prospered. Ambridge lost population during the Great Depression, but during World War II, the Ambridge Navy yard, built on sixty-four acres of reclaimed marshland adjacent to the plant, employed 12,000 people. During the late 1950s, temporary wartime housing was removed and the population began to move farther from the dense commercial areas. Shopping malls and convenience stores nearer to the new homes brought steady decline to Ambridge's retail street. Yet, few other communities in western Pennsylvania retain such distinctive physical traces from each phase of their economic development as Ambridge. Today, heritage tourism at Old Economy and brownfield reuse of the former industrial sites are reinvigorating the riverside town.

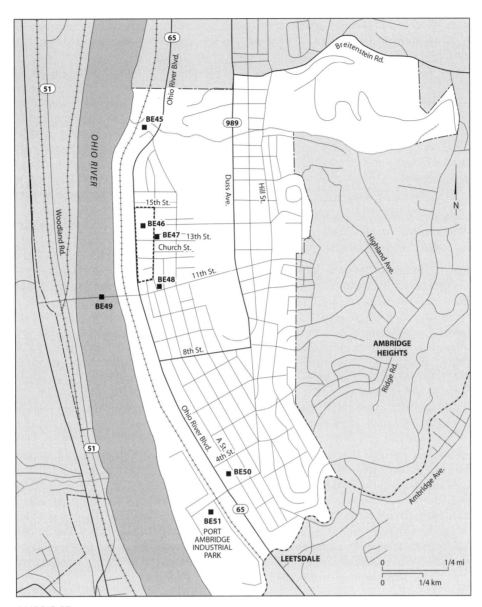

AMBRIDGE

BE45 Ambridge Borough Water Softening Plant

1933–1934; 1952–1954 addition, J. N. Chester Engineers. 1901 Brier Rd.

This plant is tucked away on a shelf of land cut off by PA 65 on the west and a large industrial park on the east. Employing horizontal bands of orange bricks and stacked windows, the Ambridge Borough Water Softening Plant is a rare instance of sleek Art Deco design in a community known for the early-nineteenth-century buildings at Old Economy and large industrial sites. Considering its strictly utilitarian function, the detailing of the building is extraordinary. The octagonal lobby is lined with pale green and jewel-toned glazed tiles and showcases an Art Deco chandelier above its central fountain-planter. The original 1933–1934 portion of the plant treated water from deep wells along the Ohio River. By the late 1940s, these wells were contaminated with minerals. The Chester engineering company was again called on to find a source of clean water and to design a system to deliver it for treatment. The company attached a pipeline to the Woodlawn-Ambridge Bridge (BE49) to carry water from the south side of Beaver County six miles away, and designed an addition to the west side of the original plant compatible in every way with the earlier section.

BE46 Old Economy Historic District and Visitor Center

1825–1830, Frederick Reichert Rapp; 2003 Visitor Center, Susan Maxman and Partners. Historic district west of Church St. between 15th and 11th sts.; Visitor Center at 270 16th St.

The Harmonists, founded by charismatic George Rapp (born Johann Georg Rapp, 1757–1847), fled Germany in 1804 for the United States to escape religious persecution. They grew to become one of the most influential communal societies in America, a model of industrialization yet with a rich spiritual life. They were internationally known, discussed in England and Germany and mentioned by Lord Byron in his 1819 epic satire *Don Juan*.

The Harmonists established two towns before returning to the region of their first settlement, western Pennsylvania. In 1804, they established their first American commune in Harmony in Butler County, and in 1815, they moved to southern Indiana and built New Harmony. In Beaver County, the Harmonists founded two cities, Economy and Beaver Falls. Here at Economy in 1824, they purchased three thousand acres along the Ohio River, the smallest acreage of their three

BE46 OLD ECONOMY HISTORIC DISTRICT AND VISITOR CENTER, typical Harmonist house

settlements. The celibate members aged and the organization fragmented after the 1830s, but their productivity and wealth allowed them to function until 1905, guided by a series of savvy business leaders. The Harmonists ran several companies, built housing for workers, and introduced new industries. They also operated a museum and a hotel that were open to the public. Between 1824 and 1832, they built more than one hundred houses; a large sawmill; planing mill; cotton, woolen, and flour mills; and a church. Especially after the Civil War, they invested in oil, timber, and railroads in western Pennsylvania. The mark they left on Ambridge is apparent at every turn, not only in the red brick and frame structures that have been preserved by the Commonwealth of Pennsylvania since 1916 but also in eighty other houses and businesses around the village dating from the period of the Harmonists' habitation (1825–1905).

The Ambridge site was named a National Historic Landmark in 1965. In 1990, architectural historian Michael J. Lewis, working for the Clio Group, and Marianna Thomas Architects produced a multivolume Historic Structures Report that is quoted in the following paragraphs. In 2003, an energy efficient Visitor Center opened to provide an orientation theater, classrooms, archives, and exhibition space. The gabled brick portions of the one-story building have espaliered grape vines similar to those on the Mechanics Building, discussed below. Sandwiched midblock northeast of the picket-fenced village, the center enhances the neighborhood rather than dominating it.

Frederick Reichert Rapp, adopted son of George Rapp and a stonemason by trade, designed most of the more elaborate Harmonist buildings and supervised the construction of all three towns, Harmony, New Harmony, and Economy. His drawings are preserved at the Pennsylvania Historical and Museum Commission's archives in Harrisburg. Rapp's architecture is unique, a product of conscious thought and decision making. He invented a new visual and functional system to balance the contradictions inherent in the Harmonists' existence. Their buildings had to accommodate a communal identity while allowing privacy for married couples and familylike groupings of adults; they had to show an

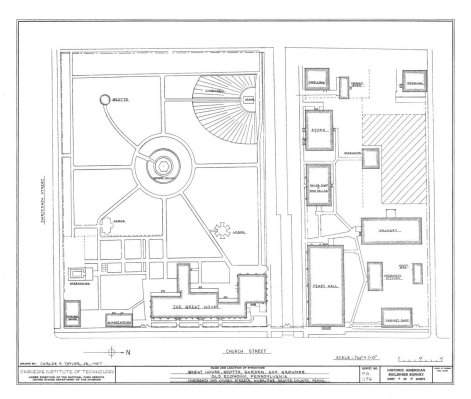

BE46 OLD ECONOMY HISTORIC DISTRICT AND VISITOR CENTER, HABS site plan, 1967 (*above*) and Visitor Center (*right*)

American identity without losing their distinct Germanic character; and they had to illustrate prosperity without losing the sense that the millennium was imminent. Rapp and his builders called on various sources to achieve this balance. They used vernacular German sources for their half-timbered houses and the granary, and the fashionable Georgian or Colonial style for Rapp's house, their public face. They used international pattern books for the Grotto and the Fountain, and some buildings are invented artifacts, like the Feast Hall that reflects Harmonist theological doctrine.

The Feast Hall facing Church Street em-bodies the Harmonists' communal and educational ideals. Accommodating offices below and a massive feast hall above, it resembles, in both form and plan, those of other pietist groups, especially the Moravians, whose buildings were an important model for the Harmonists. It is clear that the lower stories were meant as offices and spaces devoted to the mind, while the second floor was mystical and spiritual. With its elliptical ceiling and dimensions of 96 × 50 feet, there is still much to learn about how the Harmonists used this fantastic space flanked by balconies leading nowhere. The hall's first story held a collection of "natural curiosities," and, as such,

BE46 OLD ECONOMY HISTORIC DISTRICT AND VISITOR CENTER, the Grotto (*Einsiedeley*)

ranks as one of the earliest museums in the country. An 1832 schism in the denomination precipitated by the withdrawal to Louisiana of a third of the members with the charismatic, self-styled Count von Leon (Bernhard Mueller) left the Feast Hall underused and one-third of Economy's buildings vacant.

The Harmonist community always honored its leaders with special residences. The house, as the parlor for the town of Economy, illustrates the richness of the immigrant experience by expressing an American identity but defiantly retaining its German character. George Rapp's house was built in 1825, and Frederick Rapp's by 1832. They were made to be joined and appear as one, illustrating the close relationship of subordination and affectionate attachment between the denomination's spiritual leader and its chief administrator-architect. The exterior of the house uses elements of the American Georgian (portico) and Federal forms (fanlight) with the German vernacular (jerkinhead roofline). Because the houses were constantly inhabited by Rapp's successors, they have been altered more than any of the buildings preserved in the village. Behind the formal facade, the rear elevation is irregular and dominated by a two-story veranda focusing on the river and the garden.

The garden west of Rapp's house was more than a source of herbs and flowers for the Harmonists. Each of the garden's four quadrants has different characteristics that may reflect the theological program of the communal society. All three of their towns focused on a garden, a grotto, and a maze. Here the Grotto

(*Einsiedeley*) is a hermitage in the wilderness. Built of local yellow sandstone and granite with mud-pack mortar, the exterior of the cylindrical building with its conical thatched roof was deliberately primitive, but its interior reveals a smoothly plastered circular Greek Revival space, with a plaque honoring George and Frederick Rapp. Openings are located at each of the four compass points with a curved door fashioned from white oak bark.

The Granary, built in 1824 and one of the first buildings at Economy, is located within one hundred paces of the master's home. The Harmonists believed that the second coming of Christ was imminent, and, as such, they were vigilant about keeping a year's grain supply on hand for any disruption during the "transition to the new Jerusalem." At 90 × 38 feet and four-and-one-half stories, the huge half-timbered building with rubble foundation was one of six granaries the Harmonists built in the United States, and one of only two remaining; the other is in New Harmony, Indiana. While a new building type was created for the Feast Hall, the Granary adheres to the conventions of late-eighteenth century vernacular German building types. The narrow southern facades and masonry first story kept the building cool; the frame upper story had louvered apertures to disperse moisture from the stored grain. By the 1890s, the granary had been remodeled twice.

A rare survivor of the brick structures that the Harmonists used for their factories is the Mechanics Building, which housed a wine cellar, tailor, shoemaker, and printing shops. The wine cellar, "a masterpiece of Harmonist masonry," has deeply splayed light shafts, stone vaulting, and cut-stone floor slabs. Parallel tracks lining the exterior basement stairs allowed kegs to be rolled into place. The upper story has a central-hall plan with two rooms on each side.

A typical Harmonist house in Economy was made of brick or frame with three rooms inside: living room, sleeping room, and kitchen; corner stairs were in a separate vestibule, and most houses had a central chimney. Entrance doors faced the kitchen garden rather than the public street. Forty-three houses were built in Economy between 1825 and 1830. The Romulus L. Baker house, for example, was built for a prominent Harmonist, the storekeeper, and

BE46 OLD ECONOMY HISTORIC DISTRICT AND VISITOR CENTER, George Rapp's house

it overlooked the Ohio River and the garden. In the earlier Harmonist towns, some single, adult members lived in dormitories, but in Economy most members lived in assigned houses.

At first glance, one might assume that the Harmonists' impact on the architecture of western Pennsylvania was regional and vernacular. Harmonist-trained carpenters built structures in Harmony, Beaver Falls, and Monaca; they built barns and utilitarian buildings to serve the industries they funded and housing for workers in those industries. Their stylistic choices were limited to the time of Frederick Rapp, and little new design work followed his 1834 death. Yet during the 1830s and 1840s, were widely studied here and abroad for their adaptations to the Industrial Revolution. Their buildings are, as architectural historian Michael J. Lewis remarked in the Historic Structures Report of 1990, "an amazing collision of German vernacular building, modern neoclassical sources, American Georgian tradition and contemporary mill-building technology," unique and amazingly well preserved.

BE47 St. John's Lutheran Church (Harmony Society Church)

1828–1831, attributed to Frederick Reichert Rapp. 1320 Church St.

The Harmonists' former church was redundant even as it was built, since the Harmonists held worship services in the nearby Feast Hall. Perhaps Frederick Rapp was nostalgic for the churches of his youth in southwestern Germany, or thought that a church was a fitting complement to George Rapp's house across the street. By the early 1830s, when the Harmonist community was wracked by internal turmoil and dissent, the familiar image of a Lutheran church would have been a reassuring symbol. Architectural drawings show Frederick's thought process as he designed the church. The building's rectilinear form and tower imply a longitudinal plan, but instead, he placed a pulpit at the center of the south wall and organized the pews around it to create a communal preaching space. Entrances at the tower end (women's) and the opposite, east end (men's) kept the sexes segregated, a common characteristic of pietist groups. The church's location on Economy's main street signaled to visitors the industry and success of the society. Its four-story, square bell tower, visible for miles, was used to mark the hours of the work day and summon the fire company. Today, under Lutheran ownership, the church has the processional plan that its exterior suggests, with the pulpit at the east end lit by a stained glass window.

BE48 LAUGHLIN MEMORIAL FREE LIBRARY

BE48 Laughlin Memorial Free Library

1929, Eric Fisher Wood. 99 11th St.

The library was built in memory of Major Alexander Laughlin Jr., president of the Central Tube Company and a major in the American Expeditionary Forces of World War I, who died in 1926 from an infected tooth extraction. His grieving family commissioned Pittsburgh architect Eric Fisher Wood (1889–1962) to design this Italian Renaissance–style building of Indiana limestone. A tall flight of stairs leads to the round-arched, flat-roofed entrance portico supported on four slender Doric columns. Oversized, round-arched windows at each corner are set off by bands of limestone. All exudes a rather tomblike dignity. The interior is warmly lit and pleasantly open due to the clerestory windows illuminating the central square above the information desk. Sixteen monolithic black and gold composite Italian marble columns rise thirteen feet above the marble floor.

BE49 Ambridge-Aliquippa Bridge (Woodlawn-Ambridge Bridge)

1926–1927, T. J. Wilkerson, engineer. Ohio River at 11th St.

This elegant cantilever bridge across the Ohio River is truly a local product. Designed by a Beaver County engineer, it connects two major industrial centers: Ambridge, home of the American Bridge Company, and Aliquippa, home of Jones and Laughlin Steel Company (J&L). In a unique partnership of competitors, J&L produced much of the necessary metal, while the American Bridge Company (a subsidiary of United States Steel) fabricated the bridge superstructure; even the sand and gravel for the piers and abutments were excavated from the local riverbed. The bridge's span of 1,907 feet includes an extension above the railroad tracks on the west bank of the river. This is one of the most beautiful of Beaver County's major bridges, and second only to the P&LE Bridge (BE15.1) for sheer impact. Its graceful metalwork that culminates in four pinnacled towers is a filigree of thin struts and intricate trusswork in a pale blue-green coloring that lends the bridge an almost ethereal quality. Among the first to span the wide Ohio River, the bridge has required more than its share of repairs and expenditures over the

BE49 AMBRIDGE-ALIQUIPPA BRIDGE (WOODLAWN-AMBRIDGE BRIDGE)

years. A pipeline added in 1953 runs along its length carrying water to the Ambridge Borough Water Softening Plant (BE45) from a reservoir six miles away.

BE50 Engineers' Office Building of the American Bridge Company

1903. 341 Park Rd.

This large, handsome office building is a telling symbol of the influence of the American Bridge Company in Ambridge, as befits the company that drew the plans for the Panama Canal's gates and the bridge over the Mackinac Straits. This rust-colored brick structure once oversaw the vast bridge works from its hillside terrace. The H-shaped building is highlighted by a full cornice, stone trim, and pediment-shaped gables over the central entrances on both sides, facing the river and the town. The grilles in the entry transoms have the company's initials, and elaborate light fixtures flank the doors. Windows, evenly spaced on each elevation, gave the drafting tables natural light. Keystones embellish the windows on the two lower stories, and stone lintels those on the third story.

BE51 Port Ambridge Building (Main Bridge Shop, American Bridge Company)

1903. PA 65 at Ambridge Industrial Park

Stretching 776 feet along the shore of the Ohio River below the town of Ambridge, the

BE51 PORT AMBRIDGE BUILDING (MAIN BRIDGE SHOP, AMERICAN BRIDGE COMPANY)

American Bridge Company works employed 12,000 people at its peak. The company built trusswork for the San Francisco Bay Bridge, Empire State Building in New York City, and Sears Tower in Chicago, among its many projects. The exterior of the Main Bridge Shop mimics half timbering, but uses exposed steel and concrete instead of wooden timbers and plaster. Daylight floods the cavernous interior through the glazed sawtooth pattern of the roofline and long, multipaned windows. The site, now an industrial park that accommodates other large metal buildings, also includes the original launches for the landing ship tanks made in the factory during World War II.

BUTLER COUNTY

Formed out of Allegheny County in March 1800, Butler County covers 789 square miles, with the city of Butler located at its approximate geographical center. The county was named after General Richard Butler, who was killed in 1791 by Native American warriors during St. Clair's Defeat near what became Fort Wayne, Indiana. The two most important Native American trails crossing this county—the Venango Trail and the Pittsburgh-Franklin Pike—intersected a dozen miles north of the city of Butler.

The first European settlers were of German and Irish descent. They came from Westmoreland or Allegheny counties to the headwaters of Bull Creek in the southeast corner of Butler County in the 1790s, seeking better farmland for their families. Their numbers increased after General Daniel Brodhead's expedition to the headwaters of the Allegheny in 1796 burned Native American villages and essentially ended attacks in the region. It was only after lots were sold at the county seat beginning in 1803 that the county's population began to grow. One of the most influential early German settlers was Dettmar Basse, who came to southwestern Butler County in 1802 and sold land to the Harmonists in 1804. German influence continued when the Mennonites succeeded the Harmonists near Zelienople, and John and Karl Roebling arrived in Saxonburg with a group of German neighbors in 1831.

On August 27, 1859, William "Uncle Billy" Smith, a native of Butler County, became the first to successfully drill an oil well in Venango County. Over the course of the next forty years, oil drilling spread into Butler County and dominated its northern half, making it one of the largest producers in the world for a short time. Nearly a dozen boomtowns sprang up, including Petrolia and Karns City. Small amounts of oil continue to be pumped by wells, such as the Diviner Well (1874) southwest of Chicora. A second major industry, the Standard Steel Car Company, produced railcars and employed nearly 4,000 Butler residents at its peak in the mid-twentieth century. In 1982, the enormous railcar factory abruptly closed, wreaking havoc on the county's economy. Fortunately, specialty steelmaker AK Steel is operating at full capacity, and the petroleum operators near Karns also offer employment. From 1914 to 1937, a series of automobile manufacturers operated in Butler, beginning with the Standard Steel Car Company and including the Bantam Car Company.

Eight miles northwest of the city of Butler is the enormous (3,225 acres) reclaimed glacial Lake Arthur, created by the damming of Muddy Creek in 1968. The land had been deep mined, strip mined, and drilled for oil and natural gas. Its reclamation as part of 16,000-acre Moraine State Park is a fine example of environmental engineering. One of the park's attractions is the two-story cedar-log Davis house (c. 1798, 1920s; N. Shore Drive, northeast of Davis Hollow Marina) built of local sandstone. Today, the house is leased by the North Country National Scenic Trail Association, which uses it as their Pennsylvania headquarters.

Butler County Community College (College Drive in Butler), founded in 1965, was the first community college in western Pennsylvania. It opened with three buildings donated by Armco (now AK) Steel's Butler Works. Today the campus has sixteen buildings, including an award-winning Science, Technology, and Cultural Center designed by DRS Architects of Pittsburgh, with the 446-seat, state-of-the-art Succop Theater in one wing. During the last decades of the twentieth century, with the completion of I-79, southern Butler County has become a suburb of Pittsburgh. Numerous farms were sold for housing developments and strip malls, which has transformed and continues to change the rural character of Butler County.

BUTLER AND VICINITY

Butler was laid out in 1803 on a hillside above Conoquenessing Creek on land donated by John and Samuel Cunningham. Butler flourished immediately.

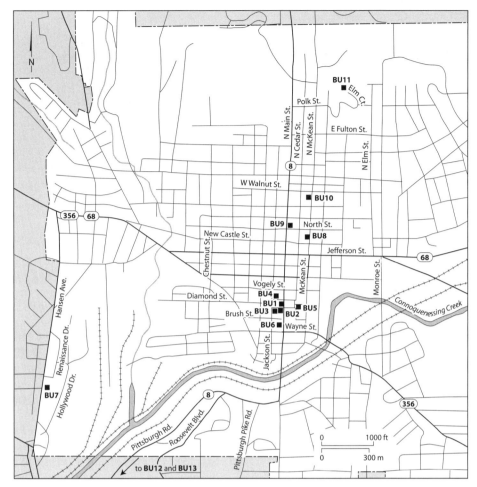

BUTLER

By 1805, there were five taverns, followed by churches: Presbyterian (1815), Roman Catholic (1822), Episcopal (1824), and United Methodist (1827). John Negley established a woolen factory and carding works in 1810, the William Borland brickyard was established in 1823, and iron and steel manufacturing began in the 1840s. The fastest growth occurred during the late-nineteenth-century oil boom. North Main and N. McKean streets are lined with large Second Empire, Italianate, and Queen Anne houses built with oil wealth, notably the brick, Second Empire house for William Timblin (c. 1874; 6 W. Diamond Street), now occupied by law offices. The grandest of the houses built by an oil heir is the forty-room Tudor Revival Elm Court (BU11).

During the first half of the twentieth century, manufacturing plants for railcars, automobiles, and the Bantam Jeep, of World War II fame, sustained the city's prosperity. Butler's industrial base declined after the war, the steel industry floundered, and the oil wells ran dry. Despite this, the downtown business district remains alive with the activities of the county seat.

BU1 Butler County Courthouse

1886, James P. Bailey; 1907 remodeled, J. C. Fulton Architect. Main and Diamond sts.

The county's courthouse sits at the highest point in Butler, looming over the town square with its 190-foot-tall, square central tower. Butler sandstone from the Hobaugh quarry at the end of E. Boyd Street was used for the exterior. The building is enlivened by a variety of arched window shapes, from pointed to semicircular and segmental. Since 1958, some architectural detailing has been lost to exterior repairs, and the interior has been remodeled. James Bailey practiced in Pittsburgh from the 1870s to 1900, and designed a number of buildings influenced by H. H. Richardson, notably the First Presbyterian Church in Beaver (BE5). Another prolific regional architect known for his churches, John Charles Fulton modernized the Butler Courthouse in 1907. Today, there are two courtrooms in the building and each has been restored. A skywalk joins the older courthouse to the Government Center of 1991 designed by Foreman, Bashford Architects.

BU2 LAFAYETTE APARTMENTS (BUTLER COUNTY NATIONAL BANK)

BU2 Lafayette Apartments (Butler County National Bank)

1902–1903, Mowbray and Uffinger. 302 S. Main St.

Built as the Butler County National Bank, this Renaissance Revival six-story, steel-frame, red brick building was designed by a New York City firm. Advertised for years as "The Big Bank by the Court House," it accommodated a bank and post office on the first story, and offices for oil and gas companies above. Late in the twentieth century, the building housed county offices before being converted into apartments. The rounded corner entrance framed by columns and an architrave is the focal point of the first story. This corner building's two facades are enriched with limestone detailing, including prominent voussoirs and cartouches over the first-story windows and pediments above the second-story windows. Pressed-copper spandrels and limestone surrounds delineate each bay on the upper stories, and a full copper cornice supported by elaborate brackets crowns the building. Unfortunately, the interior has lost most of its mahogany, bronze, and marble in two major remodelings. The architects also designed the National City Bank (former Butler Savings and Trust Company, 1925–1926; S. Main Street at W. Jefferson Street). This sleek, eight-story limestone building features eleven grotesques at the base of the V-shaped pilasters, which provide an unexpected note of lightheartedness in the otherwise fairly somber bank.

BU1 BUTLER COUNTY COURTHOUSE

BU3 Lowrie-Shaw House Museum (Senator Walter Lowrie House, Shaw House)

1828. 123 W. Diamond St.

Scottish immigrant Walter Lowrie was a county commissioner, justice of the peace, and a Pennsylvania and later a U.S. senator. Built three years after his term in the Senate, this two-story, five-bay house has a four-over-four plan. A kitchen and a scrub room were added at the rear of the house in the 1870s. In 1986, Isabella Shaw left the house to the Butler County Historical Society, which has restored the building as the Lowrie-Shaw House Museum and the society's office. Nearby, at 209 W. Diamond Street, is a log house built c. 1840 on land once owned by Lowrie; it has been restored by local attorneys.

BU4 Butler Eagle Building

1924, Edward B. Lee. 114 W. Diamond St.

This handsome limestone, ornamented Art Deco building opposite the courthouse provides space for the newspaper's newsroom and business offices. Architect Edward B. Lee (1876–1956) trained at Harvard and at the Ecole des Beaux-Arts in Paris, and worked in the architectural firms of McKim, Mead and White; Cram, Wentworth and Goodhue; and Alden and Harlow in Pittsburgh. From 1910, Lee was the resident architect in charge of the Pittsburgh projects of Palmer, Hornbostel and Jones. This commission, though, is credited to Lee alone. The dark brick, two-story building's three-bay facade is outlined with a limestone decorative frieze in a Greek key motif punctuated by rosettes and plaques, and crowned by a spread-winged eagle with the paper's name flanking it. The effect is a blend

BU4 BUTLER EAGLE BUILDING

BU5 GRACE AT CALVARY LUTHERAN CHURCH (CALVARY EVANGELICAL PRESBYTERIAN CHURCH)

of stylized classical elements stripped to their essential components.

BU5 Grace at Calvary Lutheran Church (Calvary Evangelical Presbyterian Church)

1897–1902, attributed to William Boyd and Sons. 123 E. Diamond St.

The sandstone church on the town square opposite the Courthouse (BU1) is credited in the church minutes to William Boyd and Sons, contractors. However, a church history written in 1902 gives credit to Thomas Boyd and Son of Pittsburgh. Thomas Boyd died in 1902, but his firm may have completed the commission. This is quite a progressive Romanesque Revival design showing the influence of medieval architecture from southwestern France. The dominant feature of the sandstone building is the solidly proportioned circular tower over the crossing that is topped with a conical roof. Its form is echoed in a smaller stair tower to the left of the entrance. A gable roof extends over the choir to the north, with a much shorter transept oriented east to west. The main entrance on the square opens directly into the Akron plan sanctuary. To the west and hidden behind the bulk of the building is an education wing built in 1960.

BU6 Masonic Temple

1908, Albert L. and Carroll C. Thayer. 346 S. Main St.

This Masonic Temple is affiliated with the system of degrees called the York Rite. Designed by a New Castle firm, the temple's limestone Greek Revival facade is capped by a fully ornamented pediment with the Masonic symbol at its center. The meeting rooms are meant to be exotic and to transport the members from their everyday lives, thus they are on the upper floors with windows above eye level to minimize distractions and keep down street noises. The Greek key–patterned cornice above the first-story storefront was also used by Edward B. Lee in his design for the *Butler Eagle* newspaper (BU4). Multiple Masonic chapters serving hundreds of members use the building as their headquarters.

BU7 Pullman Factory Office Building

1909, Thomas H. Scott. Hansen Ave. south of Renaissance Dr.

Pittsburgh architect Thomas H. Scott (1865–1940) designed this main office building for what was then the Standard Steel Car Company. It is the only structure remaining from the plant. The Renaissance Revival design contrasts with the workers' housing it overlooks. The U-shaped, buff brick building has hipped-roof pavilions lined with segmental-arched windows, with keystones separated by pilaster strips. Its three stories rest on a raised basement.

The Standard Steel Car Company built passenger railcars and automobiles intermittently between 1916 and 1923. Construction of the factory buildings began in April 1902. The first all-metal railcar rolled off the line in October of the same year. In the next year, 12,337 railcars were produced. Machine, blacksmith, and pattern shops were all housed in old pickle factory buildings on the property. Standard Steel spawned a subsidiary, the Lyndora Land and Improvement Company, to build hundreds of workers' houses adjacent to the plant. The town of Lyndora, originally consisting of one hundred frame flats that each housed six families, was constructed almost overnight in the winter of 1902–1903. It became a hotbed of labor unrest. In 1930, Standard Steel merged with the Pullman Company, but by the 1980s, the railcar industry was shrinking. The entire works closed in 1982, putting over 3,000 Butler residents out of work. Today, a shopping center and office park are located on the acreage of the former plant.

BU8 Saint Paul's Roman Catholic Church

1909–1911, John T. Comes. 128 N. McKean St.

Saint Paul's was built to provide services in English for the rapidly growing first- and second-generation Irish and German Roman Catholic population of Butler. The long nave, transept, tall slender steeple at the southeast corner, and generally restrained decoration are all hallmarks of the English Gothic style employed by John Comes. The church was constructed of Butler sandstone quarried within the city limits and laid by local mason John Hobaugh. The extraordinary jewel-toned stained glass windows were designed by Leo Thomas for his uncle, George Boos's Munich firm. All the interior furnishings and statuary were specified by the architect. Comes designed over sixty buildings, including churches, schools, convents, and rectories from California to New York. The majority of his works are in Pittsburgh and the surrounding areas. Although best known for his revival of Italian Romanesque, Comes did not confine himself to any particular style.

BU9 Phillips Gas and Oil Company Building

1929, Janssen and Cocken. 205 N. Main St.

Built in 1929 between the completion of T. W. Phillips Jr.'s mansion (BU13), south of Butler, and the groundbreaking on Elm Court for Benjamin D. Phillips (BU11) in town, the T. W. Phillips Gas and Oil Company Building is another example of the company's success and the Phillips brothers' architectural patronage. Pittsburgh architect Benno Janssen created a subdued and elegant limestone office building reminiscent of a Florentine palace, characterized by a heavy cornice and few recessions or

BU9 PHILLIPS GAS AND OIL COMPANY BUILDING

BU11 ELM COURT

projections from the main body of the building. The offices echo the tradition of major clubs and public buildings, such as the Philadelphia Athenaeum and the Pittsburgh Athletic Association (see AL34).

BU10 Maridon Museum

2003–2004, Paul Rosenblatt and Bill Szustak for Springboard Architecture Communication Design. 322 N. McKean St.

Using an empty car dealership and a c. 1900 frame house, the architects created a small modern museum to display Mary Hulton Phillips's personal collection of Asian jade and ivory sculpture, furniture, and tapestries. Mrs. Phillips's husband, Don, thus the combined name "Maridon," was the grandson of the founder of T. W. Phillips Gas and Oil Company. The one-story facade of transparent, translucent, opaque, and reflective glass contrasts with the ornate artifacts within, but reflects the streetscape of the residential neighborhood. The adjacent, renovated two-story frame house anchors the cultural institution firmly to the surrounding houses. A glass atrium joins the two disparate pieces harmoniously.

BU11 Elm Court

1929–1931, Janssen and Cocken; 1985–1995, Charles T. Young Architects. Elm St.

Benjamin D. Phillips (1885–1968), apparently impressed with Janssen and Cocken's design for the company office building (BU9), commissioned the firm to design his house,

one of the finest estates in Pennsylvania. The two-story limestone house is centered on a courtyard, and the heavily slated, steeply gabled roof is dotted with dormers, chimneys, and spires. The architects, with project architect Roy Hoffman and Nicolet and Griswold as landscape architects, succeeded in fitting a grand house and gardens into a relatively small, uneven space without overfilling the property, while at the same time shielding the house from the surrounding city.

Forced to sell by the Great Depression, the house had a series of short-term owners until 1985, when Frederick Koch, heir to a different oil fortune and an art and architecture connoisseur, purchased the house and began to restore and expand it. The New York City firm, with project architects Elaine Felhandler and Sue Steeneken, designed the additions, expanding the house eight thousand square feet down the hill on the southern elevation. The line between the 1920s work and the 1990s work is almost indistinguishable. Young allowed two places where his work would stand out rather than integrate into Janssen's earlier work. The first is a glassed pavilion overlooking the swimming pool and the second is a colonnaded stone gazebo perched at the southwestern corner of the house.

BU12 Succop Conservancy (Marcraig Farm, Maharg Farm)

c. 1830; 1934; c. 1950, Brandon Smith. 185 W. Airport Rd., 6.5 miles south of Butler

At the heart of this fifty-acre site is the nineteenth-century Maharg family farm and its brick, two-story house that once had a two-story porch oriented toward PA 8, the main highway. A nearly perfect cube, the hipped-roof house has been updated several times since its purchase in 1921 by the Phillips family. When Margaret Phillips and her husband, Craig Succop, took possession of the house in 1934 after their marriage, they made some changes, and then sixteen years later, commissioned Brandon Smith to reorient the entrance and add modern conveniences. Margaret grew up in The Mansion (BU13), east of the Conservancy, and had a special attachment to the farm. Her son donated the land to the Butler County Community College in 2001.

A large frame Pennsylvania bank barn remains on the complex, and is to be used along with the greenhouse, former chicken hatchery, and rental house as educational buildings for the Conservancy. The grounds will be used for hiking trails, environmental education, and event rentals.

BU13 The Mansion (Ernie's Esquire, Phillips's Hall)

1927, Walker and Gillette, J. Walter Ketterer, project architect. 657 Pittsburgh Rd. (PA 8), 8 miles south of Butler

Sited at the top of a hill at the end of a long curving drive, this house built for T. W. Phillips Jr. is a rare local example of a large estate with grounds still intact. The forty-seven-room brick house was designed by a New York City firm famous for its Wall Street bank designs. Here, they produced a sleek interpretation of the Georgian style, employing undulating two-story window bays and an entrance recessed behind two-story Corinthian columns to enliven the facade. The house is reminiscent of the Newport, Rhode Island, home of 1886 designed by McKim, Mead and White for the Edgar family. It is solidly built, using fireproof materials and cement floors throughout, as in the firm's banks. Befitting a mansion, there is a calling system, multiple rooms for the servants, and appropriate outbuildings. The complex includes a red brick, two-story multicar garage and carriage house, a large L-shaped, two-story guesthouse adjacent to the pool, and an octagonal brick water tower. The surrounding 130 acres were planted with a variety of species native to western Pennsylvania. The Phillips family owned the estate until 1970, when it became a restaurant and hotel called Ernie's Esquire. A ceramics engineering company now owns the property and rents it for private functions.

STONE HOUSE

BU14 Old Stone House

1822; 1963–1964 reconstructed, Charles M. Stotz; Ralph E. Griswold, landscape architect. 2865 William Flynn Hwy., 11 miles north of Butler on PA 8

The reconstructed Old Stone House is located at the junction of the first two major roads in the county, the Pittsburgh-Franklin Pike and the Venango Trail, later the Butler-Mercer Pike. John K. Brown built the house in 1822 as a tavern and stagecoach stop. By the beginning of the twentieth century, the house was a ruin. In 1963, when little was left but the crumbling north wall and chimney, a major rebuilding project was initiated by the Old Stone House Restoration Committee and the

Western Pennsylvania Conservancy. Pittsburgh architect Charles M. Stotz undertook reconstruction of the building. Using original materials when possible, they rebuilt the two-story, six-bay sandstone house with a full, two-story wooden porch tucked under the eaves of the facade. The house is one room deep and the first story has three rooms, each with a fireplace and an exterior entrance. The second story is one large dormitory divided only by curtains. The interior was completely updated for use as an educational facility by its present owner, Slippery Rock University of Pennsylvania. To the west, across PA 8, is the Jennings Environmental Education Center, with hiking trails that connect to the Moraine State Park to the southwest.

BU15 Slippery Rock University of Pennsylvania (Slippery Rock State Normal School)

1891–present. Bounded by Maltby Ave., Main St., and Keister and Harmony rds.

Slippery Rock University, like many of the small regional colleges in the state, began as a teachers' college. Founded in 1889 as Slippery Rock Normal School, today the university provides over 7,000 students with a choice of sixty-four academic programs.

From 1888 to 1906, Sidney Winfield Foulk (1848–1932) of New Castle designed a total of eight buildings for the campus, of which three remain. Old Main (1891–1893) on Maltby Avenue has Richardsonian Romanesque features, but is constructed of brick rather than stone, perhaps to save costs. Foulk's freewheeling designs always have distinguishing features. Here, the facade is a lively arrangement of abstract geometric volumes: a square tower emerges between two projecting bays, one polygonal and one curved, which dramatically offset the cavernous round-arched entrance below. West Hall (now Paul and Carolyn Carruth Rizza Hall) was completed in 1902, and is the work of Frank H. Foulk (1874–1929), Sidney's son. The father and son practiced together from 1900 to 1907, and Frank, who trained at the Armour Institute in Chicago, continued to practice in New Castle until his death. Constructed of yellow brick, West Hall continues the Richardsonian Romanesque style and has heavy stonework around the doors and windows. To update the mechanical systems and improve handicapped access, a major renovation (2003) moved the stone-

work around the main door on the south elevation to a more accessible entrance on the north elevation. The West Gym (1906) is the last of Sidney Foulk's buildings on campus and is located at the intersection of S. Main Street and Keister Road. The gym uses a classical vocabulary for the porticos on the north and west elevations, although the massing of the building remains Richardsonian.

Between 1929 and 1939, seven major campus buildings all designed by the W. G. Eckles Company Architects of New Castle were added to the campus in red brick Georgian Revival style. They include the two-story President's House (1937) at 251 Maltby Avenue; the one-story Maltby Center (1938), with its cupola and broken pediment; and the three-story dormitory North Hall (1938). Seventeen buildings on campus date between 1958 and 1977, and are generally utilitarian brick rectangles. The half-dozen buildings constructed since 1980 have been designed with more attention to detail and architectural flair, notably the Aebersold Recreation Center designed in 1998–2000 by RDG Bussard Dikis, and new residence halls among which is Watson Hall (2006) designed by WTW architects of Pittsburgh in traditional red brick but using green building techniques.

BU16 Lee Ligo House

1994–1996, Lee Ligo and Associates. 500 Bretkur Ln., off Forrester Rd., 1.5 miles north of Slippery Rock

Lee Ligo of Slippery Rock designed his house overlooking Wolf Creek with an asymmetrical floor plan accented by contrasting roof shapes over the various wings. The gabled roofs at varying heights and small hipped-roof projections are tied together by a wide band of scalloped slates on each roof section. Ligo incorporated salvaged items into the design, including logs from a nineteenth-century house and a rose window from a small church. Stylistically, the house is reminiscent of Benno Janssen's Long Vue Club (AL89) and La Tourelle in Allegheny County (AL88), yet has a maximum amount of interior open space. Ligo's nearby architectural offices are in a red brick house and office built in 1828 for Dr.

BU15 SLIPPERY ROCK UNIVERSITY OF PENNSYLVANIA (SLIPPERY ROCK STATE NORMAL SCHOOL), North Hall

DeWolf at 262 Grove City Road. Following DeWolf's death in 1848, the house was sold and remained a private residence until 1968, when Ligo purchased it.

KARNS CITY AND PETROLIA

The Karns City and Petrolia area smells like oil even today. The first well was drilled in 1872, and within three years, both Karns City and Petrolia were thriving towns with telegraphs, post offices, and hotels. Today, the landscape is intensely industrial, with storage tanks, metal and brick utilitarian buildings, and pipelines for the three major plants spreading up the western side of the valley for two-and-one-half miles. Penreco on Main Street (PA 268) in Karns City and Sonneborn Refined Products and Indspec of Petrolia form a nearly unbroken chain of heavy industry, with only small patches of residences nearby. Penreco, producing mineral oils and petrolatum (Vaseline and baby oil) products, is the oldest of the three and in its original nineteenth-century location. Sonneborn, originally known as W. H. Daugherty and Sons and later Witco, also produces petrolatum products. Both companies formerly used local oil, but today import oil by pipeline, railroad, and truck. Indspec is a chemical plant that produces an additive for the manufacture of tires, dyes, and medicine.

CHICORA

BU17 E. F. Hays and Son Hardware Store

1892. 106 W. Slippery Rock St.

Entering Hays Hardware is like time traveling back to the 1890s: the owner prides himself on being able to sell a single nail rather than the prepackaged allotments sold in the big box stores. Edward F. Hays opened his business in 1882, but that store burned to the ground ten years later. He reopened in 1892 on the same site in the present building. The store's false front has a bracketed cornice with a semicircular "pediment" in the center, and is shaded by a deep overhang sheltering the two entrances. Between them is a windowed office, complete with its original safe. Toward the rear of the store is a working hand-powered, rope-operated elevator. The back room is still heated with a wood stove and is piled high with the tools accumulated from more than one hundred years in the hardware business.

BU18 Chicora Community Center (English Lutheran Church)

c. 1874. 211 Main St.

Halfway up the hill in Chicora is the frame former English Lutheran Church. It has a cross gable and incorporates both Stick and Shingle Style elements. The slate roof is laid in alternating bands of diamond- and rectangular-shaped slate shingles, and a small faceted bell tower with a hexagonal spire and elongated paired brackets marks the corner entrance. Pointed-arched windows indicate a Gothic Revival influence. For nearly 130 years, there was a German Lutheran Church opposite this building, but it was demolished in 2003.

COYLEVILLE VICINITY

BU19 McGrady Farm

1970 house. 1403 Hardwood Ln. 1973 barn; 1980 house. 691 Clearfield Rd.

Rita McGrady, her son, and neighbors have built three of the most distinctive pieces of vernacular architecture in Butler County. Using stones from old barns, and the mechanical aid of only a tractor and a forklift, she designed and they built her home, a round barn, and a smaller house. Inspired by the numerous farms she visited with her father as a

Penreco Refining, from PA 268 in Karns City, near Petrolia, Butler County.

child, the McGrady barn is one large circular space with two oversized doors on opposite sides and a roof supported by a central post. A small one-and-one-half-story gable-roofed house was built adjacent to the barn, which is used for storage. Her house on a separate property north of U.S. 422 nestles into a gently sloping hillside, and is constructed of old barn stones and huge recycled barn beams.

SAXONBURG AND VICINITY

Saxonburg was founded by a group of three hundred Lutheran families organized and led by John and Karl Roebling, brothers from Mühlhausen in central Germany. In 1831, John Roebling (1806–1869) purchased 1,582 acres and began to farm and manufacture bricks. As a trained architect and engineer, he took an interest in laying out the community, first called Germania, then Sachensburg, and later anglicized to Saxonburg. In 1837, John Roebling became the Pennsylvania state engineer, which included among other duties oversight of the canal system. He had witnessed the frailty and unwieldiness of the enormous hemp ropes used to pull loaded canal boats up the steep inclines in the Allegheny Mountains, and he experimented with alternatives at his shop in Saxonburg, which is preserved in a park dedicated to him at 199 N. Rebecca Street. In 1841, he developed the twisted-wire cable to be used on the Pennsylvania Canal and, later, the Brooklyn Bridge. The use of the steel cable revolutionized bridge building and enhanced Roebling's reputation, beginning with the suspension bridge-aqueduct he designed in 1844–1845 for the Pennsylvania Canal to cross the Allegheny River in Pittsburgh (demolished). Roebling moved his wire rope factory to Trenton, New Jersey, in 1848 to facilitate shipping the heavy cabling internationally.

Saxonburg's main street is lined with white frame buildings, such as the Hotel Saxonburg of 1832 (220 Main Street) and the Saxonburg Memorial United Presbyterian Church designed by Roebling in 1837 (100 Main Street).

Many of these buildings dating from the 1830s and 1840s are of heavy timber construction, with brick and straw used as insulation between the framing in the Germanic manner. Unfortunately, Roebling's own house at 110 Main Street, which now serves as the office for the Saxonburg Memorial United Presbyterian Church, as well as many other frame buildings in town, has been sheathed in aluminum siding.

BU20 Cooper Cabin

c. 1810, with additions. 199 Cooper Rd., 1.5 miles northeast of Saxonburg

Cooper Cabin, one of the oldest houses in Butler County, is an excellent example of the log structures that once dotted this landscape.

BU20 COOPER CABIN

Sam Cooper bought the land with the shell of the unfinished house in 1811 or 1812, and added the doors, windows, roof, and other essentials. Soon after 1812, he built a spinning house behind the main house. After the Civil War, descendant John Cooper added a two-story addition to the main house on the north elevation. Several generations of the family remained here until 1963; nine years later, the house was purchased by the Butler County Historical Society. The society installed a new floor in the main room, replaced the clay chinking with cement and the water-damaged logs at the base of the south and west elevations, and removed the raw lumber partition that divided the first floor between living area and bedrooms. It is used as an educational facility and to host a Cooper family reunion every year.

HARMONY

George Rapp, the charismatic leader of the Harmonists, purchased four thousand acres along Connoquenessing Creek from Dettmar Basse in 1804. Over the course of the next few years, the village grew to about 850 people from Württemberg, who built log and brick houses accommodating forty-six families on lands they called Eidenan, or "Beautiful Meadows." Harmony is laid out around a small oval central square lined with the important buildings, including the store, church, and George Rapp's house. Though the Harmonists believed that the Second Coming was imminent, they built more than 130 buildings, and, by 1814, had evolved from subsistence farmers into exporters of woolens. The Christian and Elizabeth Waldmann log house (1804; 516 Main Street) represents the earliest and least expensive building technique employed by the Harmonists. The house began with a two-story log structure, then had a one-story brick in-filled, half-timbered dining and congregation room added to the north elevation c. 1807, the year a brick yard was established in the village. The Harmonist architecture changed over time as the group continued to absorb the culture around them. While their early log and brick houses and barns reflect their German heritage, the materials available at the time, and the rural buildings of their native Swabia, their later

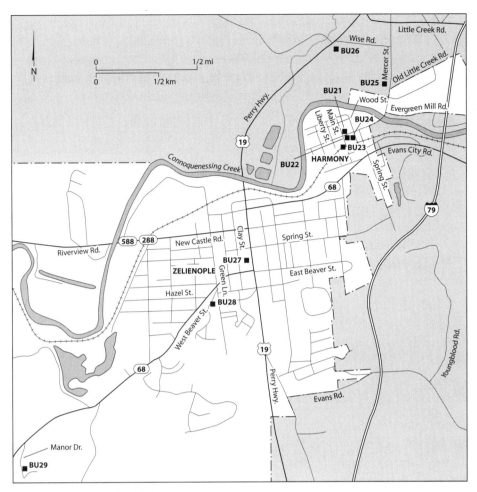

HARMONY AND ZELIENOPLE

houses show a Georgian influence, evidenced by the Flemish bond brickwork and fanlight on Rapp's house.

One of the first Harmonist buildings is a sheep barn at 303 Mercer Road, built in 1805 just north of Connoquenessing Creek and away from the residential center. The barn's stone foundation and lower level insulation of Dutch biscuits, sometimes called paling, which is clay and straw encased in boards and slid in between floor joist grooves as insulation, show Harmonist workmanship, and the upper level employs their framing techniques. In the 1850s, probably due to tornado damage, the roof was replaced by the Mennonites. The silo was constructed c. 1950.

The Harmonist cemetery, on a rise at the southeast edge of town, holds only unmarked graves, reflecting their belief that all are equal in death. The surrounding stone wall and a finely carved stone gate that revolves on a metal pin were built in 1869 by contractors to Harmonist specifications. Ironically, the cemetery gate has become a symbol of the town of Harmony, even though it was not actually built by the Harmonists, but for them.

By 1815, the community had left Harmony and built the town of New Harmony on the Wabash River in Indiana. They sold their Butler County land and buildings to Mennonite Abraham Ziegler, who in turn sold farms and lots to others, thus changing the religious and architectural traditions of the area. The Mennonites built in their own symmetrical and slightly more decorative style, often adding on to Harmonist buildings and changing their character. The Langenbacher-Ziegler House of c. 1810 (539 Main Street) was altered by Abraham Ziegler after he purchased it in 1815. He added two windows beyond the door and a double porch. Prominently sited, this house shows the transition from the Harmonist to the Mennonite building style.

Harmony's Mennonite period ended early in the twentieth century, and other than losses to fire in the 1850s, little changed in the town until the 1960s, when the zeal for modernization demolished or completely altered over fifty Harmonist buildings. To reverse this, local historic district guidelines were added to the zoning code, creating a Historic Architectural Review Board that oversees the preservation and restoration of Harmony's buildings. A group of log houses dotted throughout the village reflects the earliest heritage (546 Main and 245 and 248½ Mercer streets), while the rural beginnings are reflected in the Knauf's Feed Mill (formerly the Harmony Cereal Mill) of c. 1900 at 326 German Street. A modern housing development, Jackson Manor, at Mercer and Aise roads shows dramatically the area's change from rural to suburban.

BU21 Frederick Reichert Rapp House

1811–1812, Frederick Reichert Rapp. 523 Main St.

Frederick Reichert Rapp, the adopted son of George Rapp, was a stonemason as well as the Harmony Society's business manager. He designed a number of buildings in Harmony and in the Harmonists' later towns of New Harmony and Economy (BE46). His house here, modeled after town houses in Philadelphia with its Flemish bond brickwork and fanlit

BU21 FREDERICK REICHERT RAPP HOUSE

doorway, is by far the most elaborate in the borough. The glazed brickwork is highlighted by a subtle geometric pattern of a cross on a hill on the southern gable end. The house is larger than the average Harmonist house, with an extra bay on the northern end, matched in size only by the Mueller house (1810; 233 Mercer Street), which acted as both a residence and doctor's office. Opposite Frederick Rapp's house is that of George Rapp (c. 1811; 528 Main Street), which has the standard three-bay Harmonist plan but lacks the decorative touches of Frederick's house.

BU22 Harmony Museum

1809. 218 Mercer St.

The Harmony Museum displays furniture and artifacts from Harmonist history and, as an artifact itself, embodies that history. Built as a warehouse and granary, much of the building remains as the Harmonists left it, including the recessed Virgin Sophia (symbol of chaste and holy wisdom) doorway attributed to Frederick Reichert Rapp. The original windows had stone surrounds, which are gone, but

the building retains its vaulted wine cellar. A similar cellar can be found in the recently restored Harmonist store building of 1807 (534 Main Street) diagonally across the town square from the museum, which also contains the only remaining example of a Harmonist-era wooden casement window, which has now been duplicated on the facade.

BU23 Neff and Schmidt Houses

c. 1810. 550 and 538 Main St.

The Neff and Schmidt houses are standard Harmonist houses, that is, simple, two-story brick houses with three-bay facades of two windows followed by a door. The interior consists of a single large room on both the first and second floors. The Harmonists used locally available materials like log, brick, and stone, instead of the traditional German building technique of half timbering with stucco-covered wattle and daub walls. The Harmonists in Butler County favored solid brick exterior walls and heavy timber, with brick-infill interior walls covered with plaster. They did, however, continue to use Dutch biscuits (as in the 1805 Harmonist barn at 303 Mercer Road). With the exception of renovated windows and other minor changes, both houses maintain their architectural integrity.

BU24 Harmony Inn (Austin Pearce House)

1856. 230 Mercer St.

Built as a summer residence for Austin Pearce, founder of the Pittsburgh, New Castle and Lake Erie Railroad, the brick, two-story Italianate house has been sensitively remodeled as a restaurant. While the lack of brackets and elaborate turnings were unusual for the period, the elongated windows topped by round arches and the building's asymmetrical organization are typically Italianate. Across Mercer Street is the former Bank of Harmony (c. 1860; 239 Mercer Street), another Pearce-run business. The brick building has a handsome wooden fanlight over the central doorway and round-arched windows similar to those on the Harmony Inn framed by elongated pilaster strips.

BU25 Mennonite Shantz-Wise Barn

1835; 1948 addition. 339 Mercer Rd.

The Mennonite Shantz (Shontz) brothers built this unusually solid gable-roofed barn almost entirely of stone. The barn has double stone sheds on the banked side and its original interior joinery and truss work. Stone barns are rare, and a rapidly dwindling resource in western Pennsylvania, unlike eastern Pennsylvania, where they are prevalent. Though no longer an integral part of a working farm, the large frame additions indicate that it served a thriving dairy farm in the mid-twentieth century.

BU26 Mennonite Meetinghouse

1825; 1815 cemetery. 114 Wise Rd.

Located on the outskirts of Harmony, this is one of the oldest unchanged Mennonite meetinghouses in North America and the oldest west of the Alleghenies. The Mennonite sect is named for sixteenth-century Dutch reformer Menno Simons, who advocated adult baptism by choice, nonviolence,

BU26 MENNONITE MEETINGHOUSE

and the teachings of the New Testament. This stone meetinghouse originally had three bays; the fourth, of brick, was an early addition. The fading Mennonite congregation ceased meeting in 1902, but, inside, the original bleacher-style benches, a desklike pulpit, and the original window sash and doors remain. The congregants were segregated by sex; men and women not only sat separately, they entered through separate doors. One-half mile east is a two-story, four-bay stone house built in 1816 for the first local Mennonite bishop, John Boyer (295 Perry Highway, U.S. 19). It, too, serves as an example of the Mennonite's stone building techniques.

ZELIENOPLE AND VICINITY

Dettmar Basse dreamed of building a barony for himself and his family in the forests of Pennsylvania after his finances were ruined in revolutionary France. As ambassador from Frankfurt to Paris during the Napoleonic era, he was a respected and powerful man. When he purchased ten thousand acres of Depreciation Lands (see Beaver and Vicinity, p. 134) in 1802, he assumed other German citizens would also be interested in emigrating. He built a three-story frame house, "Bassenheim," and owned and operated a brickyard, sawmill, iron furnace, and forge in the area before he returned to Germany in 1818, where he died in 1836. His influence far outweighed his relatively short stay in Butler County.

Situated on an elevated plateau south of a bend in Connoquenessing Creek in southwest Butler County, Basse planned Zelienople in 1803, naming it for his daughter Zelie, who was married to Philipp L. Passavant. The village of Harmony is adjacent to Zelienople on the east. The Germanic influence was strong in the Connoquenessing valley, especially between 1826 and 1840 when immigration was at its height. Basse was industrious and brought Merino sheep and a gristmill to the farming community. As a miller who knew something of medical practices, Basse was sometimes referred to as Dr. Basse Miller (Muller). Zelienople became a market town for the surrounding farms through the efforts of Philipp Passavant and his son, who ran a general store. Basse worked to ensure that a major road connecting Pittsburgh and Erie would pass through the village, and U.S. 19, also called the Perry Highway, does this. By 1816, Zelienople consisted of a half-dozen log houses and shops. It grew significantly in the 1870s, when the Pittsburgh and Western Railroad and repair shops opened and the first passenger train reached Zelienople in 1879.

Today the town of 4,000 has a lively commercial district of solid, two- and three-story brick buildings with a sampling of 1830s two-story, five-bay brick houses remaining from the earlier pike town. The three-story, red brick Kaufman House (1902; 105 S. Main Street), now a popular restaurant, and the Strand Theater, a small performing arts center (1914; 119 N. Main Street), attract visitors from throughout the region.

BU27 Passavant House

1808–1810. 243 S. Main St.

Zelie Basse and her husband, Philipp L. Passavant, built a two-room-over-two-room brick house on S. Main Street, which they promptly outgrew. An addition was made to the east elevation in 1810 and, subsequently, the double porch of this addition was enclosed. In c. 1910, the family hired Pittsburgh architect Frederick J. Osterling, who had relatives in the area, to add bay windows and a grand Colonial Revival porch to the north elevation. It was probably at this time that all the windows were enlarged. The name Passavant, synonymous with philanthropy in Lutheran circles, refers to Zelienople native William A. Passavant (1821–1894), Philipp L. and Zelie's son, who founded hospitals, orphanages, and homes for seniors in a dozen places in the United States between 1849 and 1893, including the Orphans Home and Farm School, now Glade Run (BU28), in Zelienople.

A few doors north, another German émigré, Christian Buhl, built a two-and-one-half-story brick house in 1805, which, with the exception of the 1940s two-story addition to the west (rear) elevation, has not been substantially altered (221 S. Main Street). The interior is unusually spacious for the period, with wide stairwells and a full third floor. Both houses are open to the public under the auspices of the Zelienople Historical Society.

BU28 Glade Run Lutheran Youth and Family Services Public Relations Office (Superintendent's House)

1853–1854. 70 W. Beaver St. at S. Green St.

The brick Gothic Revival cottage on the campus of Glade Run was built to house an early superintendent of the Orphans Home and Farm School. It was the first building on the grounds, and for many years was listed as a staff house. The steeply pitched roof, intersecting gables, and decorated bargeboards in the gable ends highlight the careful construction by local craftsmen. Several additions

BU29 BENVENUE MANOR (GEORGE HENRY MUELLER HOUSE)

have today provided office space for Glade Run's Resources and Development and living quarters for a Lutheran deaconess.

BU29 Benvenue Manor (George Henry Mueller House)

1815–1817. 160 Manor Dr.

Benvenue Manor, the estate of George Henry Mueller, was designed at the suggestion of his friend and mentor Dettmar Basse, who played a major role in recruiting Germans to the Connoquenessing valley. Basse's house, "Bassenheim" (burned 1842), was regarded by his neighbors as a model. While the Mueller house is technically in Beaver County, it is grouped with Zelienople in Butler County to acknowledge its close proximity and social ties. This house is one-and-one-half stories with a raised basement overlooking the valley and set into the hillside at the rear. Here, the combination of the gambrel roof usually associated with a barn and the formal, two-story, colonnaded, curved porch on the north facade are an amalgamation of elements from the German homeland and the adopted country. The heavily mortared irregular fieldstone contrasts with the fanlight and transoms atop the main doors, again illustrating the tension between "proper" Philadelphia and Germanic traditions. As if the house were not already odd enough, a later owner added the large, one-story crenellated cistern and patio wall on the east elevation.

ARMSTRONG COUNTY

Armstrong County, formed in 1800 out of parts of Allegheny, Westmoreland, and Lycoming counties, has completed a difficult transition from heavy industry to lighter, more technical manufacturing. Since 2003, when it was made part of a Metropolitan Statistical Area (MSA, a federal census designation), the Armstrong County Tourist Bureau has marketed the area as a suburb of Pittsburgh. The borough of Kittanning, the county seat, is a mere fifty minutes by car from downtown Pittsburgh.

From the riverside camp at what is now Kittanning, the French and their Native American allies the Delaware sent raiding parties against English and German settlers. Colonel John Armstrong led a successful retaliatory attack on the French and the Delaware in 1756, and the county is named for him. The region was not secure from periodic attacks until the mid-1790s, when permanent settlements began. In 1826, the Pennsylvania Canal opened in the southern part of the county along the Allegheny and Kiskiminetas rivers, spurring the growth of such towns as Freeport, Leechburg, and Apollo. By the mid-1800s, the county was exporting coal, sand, gravel, limestone, salt, and timber, and simultaneously producing glass, iron, steel, gunpowder, pottery, and brick for use in the area and for export. Drawing upon local coal and iron ore deposits, as well as trees for charcoal, iron manufacture began in northern Armstrong County in 1839 with the opening of the Great Western Iron Works, later reorganized as the Brady's Bend Iron Works (see AR7 and AR8). Industry benefited when the Allegheny Valley Railroad connected Kittanning to Pittsburgh in 1856. Oil was struck in the county in 1865, and for ten years Armstrong County was a major producer with oil exchanges in Parker City and Kittanning. Parker City was a typical boomtown, its population peaked at 15,000 in the late nineteenth century, although today it is less than 800. Closure of the wells in the late 1870s virtually halted further growth. After the canal closed in 1857, the Pennsylvania Railroad used a similar route through the same towns, maintaining their prosperity. Building stock in these towns reflects the periods of growth that followed the opening of the canal and the railroad. Although Armstrong County is still considered rural by the Center for Rural Pennsylvania, in recent years, the region has begun to develop small businesses in places like Parks Bend Industrial Park, and suburban housing. Good highway accessibility in all directions, east to west on U.S. 422 and north and south on PA 66 and PA 28, allows over 25 percent of the county's residents to commute to work in nearby counties.

KITTANNING

As the Delaware were steadily forced out of eastern Pennsylvania, they settled on the east bank of the Allegheny River, calling their village Kittanning, meaning "at the great stream." In the 1750s, the French and their Native

American allies used the village as a staging area for raids and a holding camp for English prisoners along what was then the northern frontier of European settlement. Under General John Forbes's orders, Colonel John Armstrong set out with three hundred militiamen from Fort Shirley in Huntingdon County to capture the settlement. Outnumbering the Native Americans and French by at least three to one and armed with the element of surprise, Armstrong launched a successful and bloody attack, and burned the entire village, consisting of about thirty cabins, to the ground. The battle restricted Native American movements south of the Kittanning Trail. The village remained the farthest outpost of European settlement for many years.

Judge George Ross (1778–1849) laid out the borough in 1803 as the county seat for Armstrong County. He used Philadelphia's town plan as a model, duplicating such street names as Water, McKean, Arch, and Jacob. As a trading post and stop on the Kittanning Trail, the town grew steadily during the early nineteenth century. In 1856, the first bridge across the Allegheny River at Kittanning was built at the end of Market Street on the same site as the present bridge of 1932. The river provided cheap transportation for goods, and a level bank to accommodate the Allegheny Valley Railroad after 1856. Later, coal-hauling railroads, including the Buffalo and Pittsburgh and the Pittsburgh and Shawmut, served the county. Between 1928 and 1930, the Dravo Corporation built Lock and Dam No. 7 north of town, making seventy-two miles of the river navigable and lifting barges and towboats thirteen feet to the next river level.

A visitor to Kittanning today gravitates toward Market Street, which continues the path of the old Kittanning Trail as it slopes down from the courthouse to the river and the Citizen's Bridge. It is lined with late-nineteenth- and early-twentieth-century storefronts, such as the restored three-story, corbeled red brick Rosebud Mining Company Building (former Poundstone Building, c. 1900) at 301 Market Street and the tiny limestone-fronted Kittanning National Bank (c. 1890; 224 Market Street), with lions guarding its pediment. Next door, at 222 Market Street, the stylish former Arcade Department Store, now Merchants National Bank (1886), has a pressed-copper cornice and spandrels. River View Park, designed by Urban Design Associates in 1998, has opened the riverfront to recreational uses.

AR1 Armstrong County Courthouse

1858–1860, Barr and Moser. 500 E. Market St.

The Armstrong County Courthouse, dramatically sited against a steep hillside at the eastern terminus of Kittanning's Market Street, is one of eight remaining Greek Revival courthouses in western Pennsylvania. Constructed by Hulings and Dickey for Barr and Moser, the courthouse includes features usually found late in the style's popularity. The pediment and four columns, the tall windows on the second floor, the roundels above, and the ornate cupola that crowns the building are all typical of the Greek Revival. However, the Roman Corinthian columns and the ground-floor windows topped with semicircular arches are characteristic of a newer fashion. The cruciform plan building has a wide stairway at the east, or rear, elevation. The interior was ex-

AR1 ARMSTRONG COUNTY COURTHOUSE (*right*) and **AR2** ARMSTRONG COUNTY JAIL (*left*)

AR3 GRACE PRESBYTERIAN CHURCH

tensively and unsympathetically remodeled by Kittanning and Ford City architect Tillman Scheeren Jr. in the mid-twentieth century. The courtroom ceiling, originally twenty-three feet high and covered with frescoes, was unfortunately lost in this remodeling. The courthouse is Kittanning's third courthouse, and the second on this site. It has a fairly discrete wing of 1991 at the south; to the north is the jail.

AR2 Armstrong County Jail

1873, James McCullough Jr.; 1981–1982, L. Robert Kimball and Associates. 500 E. Market St.

While most Gothic Revival buildings attempt to recall the graceful, spiritually uplifting forms of a medieval cathedral, this jail is modeled on a castle. The heavily crenellated build-ing of Clarion County golden sandstone has two projecting towers on the facade and a high watchtower in the center. The main entrance is recessed between the two towers. Special features are incorporated into the design to prevent prisoners from escaping. Between a convict and freedom are two-and-one-half feet of brick threaded with steel bands to prevent tunneling, and a series of iron plates in the floor to prevent digging. The roof has been reinforced since its original construction. A brick version (1873–1874) of this building, also designed by James McCullough, stands in Clarion (CL2), and the 1868–1869 prison in Hollidaysburg, Blair County, designed by Edward Haviland, may have been the model (BL3). In 1981, L. Robert Kimball redesigned the cell blocks, guardrooms, control center, and visiting area, turning what was originally the warden's apartment into offices and installing modern security devices.

AR3 Grace Presbyterian Church

1910–1911, Vrydaugh and Wolfe. 150 N. Jefferson St.

This is a fine example of Richardsonian Romanesque, a style popular in the region in the late nineteenth and early twentieth centuries. Although Martin U. Vrydaugh (dates unknown) and Thomas B. Wolfe (1860–1923) were known for their Gothic Revival designs, the tower, the rough-hewn stone of the door and window surrounds, and the roofline all follow H. H. Richardson and his imitators. Inside are exquisite Tiffany windows, most notably the superb Jane Ross Reynolds Memorial Window on the north wall of the sanctuary that depicts the figure of Truth in luminescent blue tones surrounded by jewels. An education wing added in 1956 to the N. Jefferson Street side of this corner church had little effect on the exterior appearance of the older building. However, the church's groin-vaulted interior was almost completely remade in 1968 with new lighter woodwork and plastered ceilings.

AR4 Calarie and Owen Law Offices (Colwell House, Old Library)

1860. 200 N. Jefferson St.

This two-story brick house was originally the estate of railroad magnate John A. Colwell, commissioned during the railroad boom in Kittanning. In 1933, the building was sold to the borough and converted into a public library; it now serves as offices. The building retains its stately and substantial window and door surrounds, stone quoins, pediment-like central gable, and bracketed eaves. Alterations to the house include interior remodeling, the loss of an original ell wing at the rear, and the removal of a full porch along the facade, although a section survives as a columned entrance portico. A carriage house and stable once existing on the grounds have been demolished.

AR5 North Water Street District

Mid-19th to late 20th centuries. Between Market St. and Union Ave.

North Water Street, parallel to the eastern bank of the Allegheny River and visible from both the bridge and the opposite shore, is a showpiece for the city. Most of Kittanning's largest, impressive houses are found on this quiet street, as are a number of religious structures. As the area has developed continuously from the mid-nineteenth century, no single architectural style dominates. The YMCA (138 N. Water Street), for example, is housed in a brick Chateauesque house; Elks Club No. 203 (1876; 140 Arch Street) is located in a Second Empire former residence; the former Simon B. Truby House at 280 N. Water Street is a large Colonial Revival (1864); an English cottage–style house, the C. H. Ferne House, with faux thatching (c. 1920) anchors Water Street's corner with Vine Street; and a red brick Italianate house c. 1880 (340 N. Market Street) completes the collection of interesting houses on the street. Three significant religious structures are also found in the district: St. Paul's Episcopal Church (1912–1913) at 112 N. Water Street is a stone Gothic Revival church; and the First United Methodist Church (c. 1950; 332 N. Water Street) was originally a synagogue (Knesset Israel) designed by Alexander Sharove of Pittsburgh in a Frank Lloyd Wright–inspired style. In sharp contrast to the long, low shape of Sharove's geometric design is Saint Mary, Our Lady of Guadalupe Roman Catholic Church at 101 W. High Street (1962–1963, Elmer Dattola Jr. and George Ruscitto), which, while also dating from the mid-twentieth century, emphasizes the vertical with its bell tower and two-story entrance window. At the north end of the street, a c. 1940 group of ten trailers, all of the same general appearance, has an exquisite riverside view. Trailers comprised 5.1 percent of the commonwealth's housing units in 1990, and are one of the most prevalent forms of shelter in rural areas.

WORTHINGTON VICINITY

AR6 St. Patrick's Roman Catholic Church

1806. PA 4007 west of St. Patrick's Rd., 6 miles northwest of Worthington

Constructed by Irish immigrants who settled in 1795 in Donegal Township across the nearby Butler County line, St. Patrick's may be the oldest Roman Catholic church in western Pennsylvania. Using squared logs and V-shaped notching at the corners, the simple rectangular, gable-roofed structure

AR6 ST. PATRICK'S ROMAN CATHOLIC CHURCH

AR8 ST. STEPHEN'S EPISCOPAL CHURCH AND PARSONAGE HOUSE

symbolizes the rugged persistence of faith on the frontier. The building was renovated and rechinked in 1987. The church continues to function as a place of worship, with the altar at the eastern wall and a small balcony in the rear for additional seating. The surrounding graveyard, which predates the church, has headstones dating as early as 1798. Just over the rise to the west at 422 PA 4007 is the new St. Patrick's Church (1929–1930), with round-arched windows, irregularly coursed stonework, and a hipped roof with a gabled projection above the central entrance. It has replaced the log church for Sunday worship.

BRADY'S BEND

AR7 Superintendent's House

1868. 280 Foust Rd. (PA 68)

The Brady's Bend Iron Works built numerous tracts of worker housing, most of which have been demolished or absorbed by suburban development. The iron works also built several more extravagant homes, of which this large two-and-one-half-story superintendent's house is one of the few remaining examples. The highlight of the building is the front entrance with its Italianate portico, impressively displayed at the top of a flight of stairs. Narrow horizontal wood siding, bay windows on the side elevations, heavy window surrounds, and corner quoins distinguish the house. Three successive superintendents' families lived in this house before the company closed in 1873.

AR8 St. Stephen's Episcopal Church and Parsonage House

1867 church, Joseph Minteer; 1869 house. 107 Foust Rd. (PA 68)

This church and its associated parsonage are reminders of the glory days of Brady's Bend.

Great Western Iron Works and its successor Brady's Bend Iron Works employed hundreds of people and supported the entire area economically between 1839 and 1873. The company donated land for six churches. When the iron works closed, most of the village's population, recruited from England, Wales, and Belgium, left. This church's congregation disbanded, and since then, the building has been used as an American Legion Post and is now the property of the Brady's Bend Historical Society, which has restored and preserved the church as a museum. St. Stephen's was the only local congregation to build in stone. To make this financially possible, undressed golden sandstone was used for most of the construction, and red brick, instead of expensive ashlar stone, for the window surrounds; the contrasting color and materials create a decorative effect. The parsonage, completed two years after the church, remains a private residence. It has excellent board-and-batten siding, decorative window surrounds, and handsome carving around the double entrance doors.

AR9 ROBINSON HOUSE AND FARM, ROBINSON UNITED METHODIST CHURCH (ROBINSON MEMORIAL CHAPEL), Robinson House

AR10 ROUND BARN

PARKER CITY VICINITY

AR9 Robinson House and Farm, Robinson United Methodist Church (Robinson Memorial Chapel)

1872–1874 house; 1902 chapel. 210 Robinson Rd. (take Bennertown Rd. from PA 268), 0.8 miles north of Parker City

In 1865, after years of running a successful tannery and farm, the Robinson family discovered oil on their farm, and in the following years, Samuel M. Robinson built a fine home and farm complex at the top of a winding hill north of Parker City. The complex includes a large Italianate house, a stone chapel built by Elisha Robinson II, a barn, carriage house, ice house, granary, mill house, and other associated outbuildings. The house, constructed of a warm orange brick, maintains its original segmental-arched windows and slate roof. Paired brackets under the eaves, the flared porch roofs, and the elongated windows are all Italianate in style. Water pipes throughout the house are wooden. Small as it is, the Gothic Revival chapel is an impressive display of religious devotion. It has a polygonal apse, and an unusual pinnacled belfry consisting of two stone uprights and a cross beam over the main entrance. The remaining buildings are utilitarian, but the early-nineteenth-century board-and-batten barn is particularly handsome.

DEANVILLE

AR10 Round Barn

1912. Reedy Mill Rd. at Deanville Rd.

Dew Mar Dairy Farm's working barn is truly round, not octagonal, as are so many barns that are described as round. It was built by Homer H. Shoemaker into the bank of land, so that there are ground-level entrances to the haymow above and the animal stalls below. The exterior is sheathed in red corrugated metal. The interior of the haymow illustrates the advantage of a round barn over a rectangular structure, as it allows for capacious storage unrestricted by interior beams. There is a large corrugated-metal addition on the north side of the building.

DAYTON

This small rural community serving the surrounding farms maintains a feed mill, and hosts an agricultural fair each year in August. Since 1962, when the first of eleven congregations of Amish families moved to the area, farming and its support industries have had a resurgence in northeastern Armstrong and northwestern Indiana counties. The tiny borough of Smicksburg, four miles east in Indiana County, hosts artists' studios and several shops selling Amish crafts and baked goods.

In 1976, the Dayton Area Historical Society bought and restored the Thomas H. Marshall house as a bicentennial project. Marshall, a farmer who ultimately expanded into lumber, tanning, and milling, built his house (now Marshall House Museum, c. 1865; 107 State Street) at the center of his farm, along with several adjacent barns, now demolished. A drawing of 1883 shows the house without the several porches that were added later, with such stylish extras as paired brackets and turned porch posts. The house has a four-over-four plan with a two-story off-center rear wing. Two blocks north, the Buffalo, Rochester, and Pittsburgh Railroad (BR&P) built a small passenger station in 1898 (W. Railroad Avenue at Poplar Street), later purchased by the Baltimore and Ohio line. The one-and-one-half-story frame and shingled station features deep eaves, a rectangular bay window under a hipped-roof dormer, gracefully curving brackets, and a steeply pitched, flared hipped roof. Other stations by the BR&P were designed by the Rochester, New York, firm of Gordon, Bragdon and Orchard, at Dubois in Clearfield County (see Dubois, p. 474) and Bradford in McKean County (demolished); but by 1898 that firm had dissolved, and Bragdon, whose name is on the earlier drawings, was a partner in the firm of Bragdon and Hillman, which may have designed the station. Dayton became the transportation center for the surrounding coal mines during the boom years between 1890 and 1910, when the population more than doubled.

APOLLO

AR11 Drake Log House

Between 1816 and 1836. William's Alley

The town of Apollo grew around this log house, which was occupied until the 1970s, when the Apollo Area Historical Society purchased it. They replaced the decayed logs at the base with logs from the same period, and rechinked the entire house. The interior, initially three rooms with a ladder to the loft, has been altered to one large common room with a pull-down ladder. The fireplace was completely rebuilt using some original stones. Water is carried from a recently rebuilt springhouse to the west. The house is named for longtime resident Mrs. Sarah Drake.

AR12 Apollo United Presbyterian Church (First Presbyterian, Westminster Presbyterian)

1905–1907, J. C. Fulton Architect; 1965 addition. 401 1st St.

This church, the third built at this site, is constructed of native white sandstone quar-

ried nearby. John Charles Fulton, of Uniontown, designed a number of courthouses in western Pennsylvania and West Virginia, and hundreds of churches nationwide, including those in Ellwood City, Lawrence County, and Connellsville, Fayette County (see FA23). His penchant for using domes and adaptations of the Akron plan in his Protestant church designs is well documented. Here, a squat central tower with an octagonal peaked roof is surrounded by various elements, including

AR12 APOLLO UNITED PRESBYTERIAN CHURCH (FIRST PRESBYTERIAN, WESTMINSTER PRESBYTERIAN)

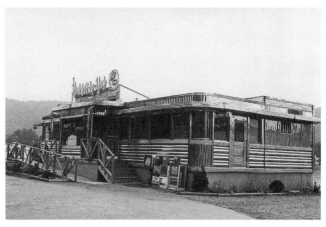

AR13 WOMAN'S CHRISTIAN TEMPER-
ANCE UNION (WCTU) BUILDING

AR15 YAKKITTY-YAK DINER

four small towers, crenellated corner tower, and intersecting gables. The interior of this church had some minor alterations in 1917, but it retains its square vaulted sanctuary.

In 1970, the congregation of the Calvin United Presbyterian Church joined with this congregation, and the Calvin church building of 1885 (423 N. 2nd Street) was acquired by Sovereign Grace Baptist Church. That Stick Style structure has white woodwork outlining the windows and doors and forming the gable-end decoration.

AR13 Woman's Christian Temperance Union (WCTU) Building

1909. 317 N. 2nd St.

This frame, two-story meeting room and library has a number of decorative elements that raise it above the strictly utilitarian, notably the row of five narrow Ionic pilasters, with plinth and architrave, that frame the second-story windows. A fanlight in the pedimented gable is repeated in the transom of the main door, and a basket-handle arch above the first-floor window completes the ensemble. The result is an asymmetrical yet cohesive facade. This building demonstrates the aspirations and achievements of the WCTU, among the oldest voluntary, nonsectarian women's organizations in continuous existence (since 1874). The substantial brick Romanesque Revival WCTU building in Bellefonte, Centre County (CE7), shows what the organization was able to achieve in an urban setting. The Apollo Area Historical Society purchased the Apollo building from the state WCTU in 1997.

AR14 Nellie Bly House

c. 1864. 505–507 Terrace Ave.

Elizabeth Cochran (1864–1922), writing under the pen name Nellie Bly, was an internationally known journalist who wrote major articles for the *Pittsburgh Dispatch* and the *New York World* newspapers, supporting labor and exposing the social problems of her era. She lived in this sprawling, three-story frame Colonial Revival house until her father died, leaving the family of fifteen children nearly destitute. A pair of pseudo-Palladian windows on the first story of this private home are sheltered beneath a porch supported on slender Ionic columns. The upper windows have sawtooth ornament and scrollwork.

AR15 Yakkitty-Yak Diner

1956, Jerry O'Mahony Co. 2104 River Rd.
(PA 66)

This diner was the last built by the Jerry O'Mahony Company, which had been operating in Bayonne, New Jersey, since 1914. The classic stainless-steel diner has horizontal siding and curved corners with windows along the entire facade. This diner opened as the Gateway in 1956 in Wilkins Township, Allegheny County, and operated until 1978. The diner moved to Vandergrift, Westmoreland County, in 1978, and served as a video store until 1992, when it was moved to its present location and returned to its original purpose. The building is now permanently sited, but could be moved again with a minimum of labor, simply by undoing a series of carriage bolts and loading it onto a truck.

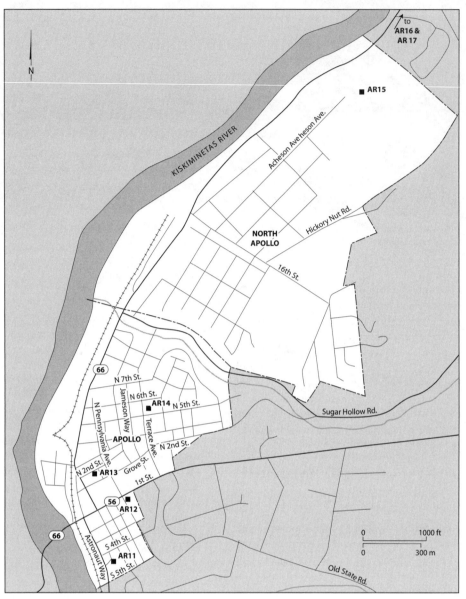

APOLLO

LEECHBURG AND VICINITY

Located on a floodplain in a deep gorge, Leechburg is surrounded on three sides by the northwesterly-flowing Kiskiminetas River on its way to the Allegheny River near Freeport. Because of frequent flooding, there was no permanent Native American settlement until a Delaware Indian named White Mattock bought land here in 1793. The area, then called White Plains, became a market center for the surrounding farms. Its transformation began in the 1820s with the decision to build a portion of the Pennsylvania Main Line Canal's western division parallel to the river. The town was named for civil engineer David Leech of Sharpsburg, who secured the contract to design and build the lock and dam adjacent to the site. He also built a sawmill, gristmill, and woolen mill using waterpower supplied by the dam. With the advent of canal shipping in 1829, Leech opened a boat yard and ran a packet line in the 1830s and 1840s, supplying salt and coal to Pittsburgh and beyond. His house (c. 1827; 118 1st Street), a two-story brick house with a hipped roof and a pair of entrances on the facade, is the oldest remaining in Leechburg.

When the Pennsylvania Railroad bypassed the Kiskiminetas River valley, canal shipping slowly waned. The establishment of an iron rolling mill up-river at Apollo in 1855 maintained a steady stream of workers into the valley, and when the Western Pennsylvania Railroad company built a rail line along the west bank of the river in 1865, it became a fertile site for iron makers. In 1872, William Rogers Sr. opened a second tin plate mill at Leechburg, using natural gas for the first time in an industrial capacity, and imported hundreds of Welsh and English skilled workers to man the plants at Leechburg and Apollo. But in 1873, one of the nation's worst financial panics closed banks and called in loans. The company declared bankruptcy in 1876, and was purchased by Pittsburgh ironmaster J. C. Kirkpatrick a year later. Leechburg's commercial district is typical of the area's other boroughs, with the exception of the Moderne limestone facade of the First National Bank of Leechburg (c. 1929; 152 Market Street). In the residential area, a handsome brick, late-nineteenth-century Second Empire house at 292 Pershing Street speaks to the pretensions of the tin plate mill era.

AR16 Armstrong County Bridge No. 13 (Hyde Park Walking Bridge)

1886 piers; 1955 deck. Terminus of Canal St.

This rare pedestrian-only steel deck suspension bridge is mounted on the heavy stone piers built for an 1886 railroad bridge that was damaged in the Johnstown flood of 1889. The bridge joins Hyde Park on the Westmoreland County side of the Kiskiminetas River with Leechburg. It continues to be used daily by those who live in Armstrong County and work for Hyde Park industries and vice versa. The steel grating reverberates with each footfall.

AR17 New Ventures Center (Parks Bend Farm and Industrial Park)

1990, Charles L. Desmone and Associates. 1129 PA 66, 1 mile north of Leechburg

New Ventures Center sits on eighty-two acres of what was once the Parks Bend dairy farm

AR17 NEW VENTURES CENTER (PARKS BEND FARM AND INDUSTRIAL PARK)

and Parks Bend Industrial Park. Two barns, one gambrel roofed and the other gable roofed, adjacent to a pair of silos, mark the site of the original farm to the north. This type of development, called a small business incubator, is proliferating in the rural counties closest to Pittsburgh, where land is relatively inexpensive and access to major highways is available. Charles L. Desmone and Associates designed the large cement-block and corrugated-steel building to blend with the rural landscape. While larger in scale, the basic elevations are similar to a barn, including the silo-shaped element on the facade that houses a metal circular stair. The exterior mimics board-and-batten siding in steel, reminiscent of agricultural rather than industrial buildings. Parks Bend Industrial Park has received numerous architectural commendations at the local, state, and national levels.

FREEPORT

Freeport sits on land settled by William and David Todd in 1796 at the confluence of the Allegheny River and Buffalo Creek. The site was such an ideal spot to moor river craft that David Todd decreed that no wharf fee could ever be charged; thus, the town became known as a free port. It was incorporated as a borough in 1833. As early as 1816, a gristmill and, later, a sawmill were built on the west side of Buffalo Creek in adjoining Laneville. The present mill (AR18) dates from a later period. The town grew as the woolen mill, distillery, and brickyard began to ship their goods via the canal in 1831. Several two-story, five-bay-wide, red brick houses from this era resemble the fine example at 619 High Street. The small borough at one time hosted nine churches; five remain today, including the brick Gothic Revival Freeport Methodist Church (1877; 209 4th Street), which is festooned with corbeling and buttressed pilaster strips. The DeBlasio House at 319 4th Street (1875) was built during the county's oil boom, when the railroad dominated transportation. Architectural styles like this vernacular interpretation of the Second Empire swept into town along the rails. As the brick industry and local distillery prospered in the 1890s, several grand houses went up, including the large Queen Anne, Turner house (c. 1890; 104 Buffalo Street) and the Truby house (c. 1900; 317 4th Street), a substantial brick, Colonial Revival dwelling with a two-tiered, double-columned porch. The small commercial district contains a series of three-story brick buildings, including a former hotel at 401 Market Street (1852) and the Keystone Building at 201–205 5th Street (1898).

AR18 Valley Mills (Mickey's Mills)

c. 1871. Old Mill Rd.

After the first mill on the site burned to the ground during the Civil War, the Mickey family bought the property, rebuilt, and began operating the present three-story wooden mill by 1871. It continued in operation until 1965 under three different families and a number of names. The mill ground mainly winter wheat and buckwheat. Power was provided by a water turbine, now lost. The mill and its nineteenth-century equipment, which include a scale,

AR18 VALLEY MILLS (MICKEY'S MILLS)

stone burr mill, and separators and sifters, are still in place, preserved by the Freeport Area Historical Society and open for tours by appointment.

FORD CITY AND VICINITY

Ford City, on the Allegheny River, is more intensely industrial than Kittanning its neighbor four miles to the north. With easy access to sand, coal, gas, and cheap transportation, Ford City was ideally situated for glass manufacturing. The enormous Pittsburgh Plate Glass (PPG) plant, built along 3rd Avenue in 1916, was reputedly the largest plate glass plant in the world until 1950 (see AL24). The borough also produced ceramics and brick. Architecturally, the finest building in town is the stone, Gothic Revival St. Mary's Roman Catholic Church (1911–1915; 738 4th Avenue), designed by an architect of German heritage, Edmund B. Lang, for a predominantly German parish. A row of one-and-one-half-story workers' housing in the 800 block of 4th Street was built in the 1890s for PPG workers. The wide, squat profile and steeply gabled roofs of the houses are reminiscent of early workers' housing built by the Pennsylvania Salt Manufacturing Company at Natrona in Allegheny County.

AR19 Ross House

1807–1809. 723 Ross Ave., 2 miles southwest of Ford City

This very early stone house is so named as one of the William Penn family's forty-four original manors. Built by George Ross, the house is only a few hundred yards from the Allegheny River and its confluence with Crooked Creek. The gable-roofed, two-story house has returning eaves, multipaned double-hung windows, and elegant porches that date c. 1870s. The frame portion on the west elevation was probably added shortly after the original house was completed. The Ross family maintained the house and land throughout the nineteenth century with income from the saw and grist mills.

INDIANA COUNTY

The southern half of what is now Indiana County came under European control with John Penn's Land Purchase from the Six Nations of 1768, and the northern half followed with the purchase in 1784. The county was established in 1803, but the first settlers traveled over the Kittanning Trail through the middle of the county and along the Conemaugh River from the south c. 1769. Most of them were Scots-Irish Presbyterians, moving into what was then old Westmoreland or Lycoming County from Cumberland Valley.

Although the town of Indiana was the county seat, Blairsville was the county's largest town in the first half of the nineteenth century. It was a principal stop on the Pennsylvania Canal and, later, the Pennsylvania Railroad. Rivers and creeks were early transportation routes, but ice jams stalled traffic on them for many months of the year. After the Pennsylvania Canal was completed through the southern part of the county in 1829, large-scale boatbuilding and regular packet services developed. Saltsburg, another canal

Conemaugh Generating Station No. 2, Power Plant Road (PA 2008) near Huff, West Wheatfield Township, Indiana County. This plant, which opened in 1970, uses over four million tons of coal each year on its 1,750-acre site along the Conemaugh River.

town at the southern end of the county, was known for its salt mining, a profitable industry in the nineteenth century. In 1852, the Pennsylvania Railroad supplanted the canal, and by 1860, the canal was abandoned. Blairsville remained the busiest city until 1864, when the Indiana Branch Railroad opened to the county seat. The former Buffalo, Rochester and Pittsburgh Railroad (BR&PRR) station (1904; 1125 Philadelphia Street) is now a restaurant.

After the Civil War, networks of small roads facilitated the movement of produce and coal to the larger market towns of Blairsville and Indiana. Covered bridges built between 1870 and 1910 spanned small creeks to make this possible. Indiana County has three Ithiel Town truss (patented in 1820) covered bridges, an unusual number considering there are only eighteen remaining in the commonwealth, thirteen of them in Bucks County in eastern Pennsylvania. All three are easily accessible from the county seat and each other: Harmon's Bridge (1910) and Trusal Bridge (1870), 2 miles and 3.3 miles northeast of Creekside, and Thomas Ford Bridge (1879), 3 miles southwest of Creekside. A Town truss uses timber lattice pinned with wooden pegs at the intersections for ease of construction. The fourth extant covered bridge here in Indiana County (IN8), even rarer, is one of only four Howe truss types remaining in the state. Modern highways, notably U.S. 119 that runs centrally from north to south and the newly expanded U.S. 422 that stretches from east to west, have stimulated growth in the town of Indiana.

Before 1850, the main industries were agriculture (corn and dairy), salt refining, iron smelting, coal mining, the distillation of alcohol, hide tanning, and lumbering. Today, most Indiana County residents are employed on farms, in education (Indiana University of Pennsylvania, IN6), in power plants, or in the service industries. Tree farming began here in 1918, and now Indiana County leads the commonwealth in their harvesting. However, the county has lost one-third of its manufacturing base since 1990, and mining employment has dropped by half. In the late 1960s, nine power companies from four eastern states and the District of Columbia pooled their resources to construct a billion dollar power station at four separate facilities, three in Indiana and one in Westmoreland County. The Indiana County plants at Homer City, Huff, and Shelocta have awesome coal-burning and electrical-generating capacities, over 1,000-foot-tall smokestacks, and 370-foot cooling towers. Together, the stations employ 1,100 and supply over 21 million people with electricity.

INDIANA

Soon after Indiana County was formed in 1803, debate began as to where the county seat should lie. There were two possibilities, the first at the fork of Two Lick and Yellow creeks (present-day Homer City), and the second at the geographical center of the county. The latter was chosen after land for the town was given to the county by George Clymer. A wealthy Philadelphia Quaker and a signatory of the Declaration of Independence, Clymer was also a land speculator who sought to improve the value of his surrounding property. With little settlement before 1810, the borough was not incorporated until 1816.

The town was laid out on five acres with two large public squares, one containing the courthouse and the other designated for several churches (IN4). Unfortunately, in the mid-nineteenth century, the public squares were sold as lots, what historian William H. Egle called an "unpardonable blunder" in his 1880 *History of the Commonwealth* (p. 795). With no river or canal nearby, the importance of a railroad to the borough of Indiana was clear. After a branch of the Pennsylvania Railroad connected Indiana to Blairsville and Pittsburgh in 1856, transportation of coal and timber became a vital part of the area's economy. The wealth generated during this period can be seen in the many Second Empire and Italianate houses in Indiana, styles popular in the 1860s and 1870s when the railroads boomed. Coal mining created a second economic boom in the early twentieth century, as evidenced by the handsome Beaux-Arts-inspired Old Borough Hall, now the Municipal Building (1912; 39 N. 7th Street), designed by New Jersey architect Herbert King Conklin. He won the borough's c. 1910 competition for this building that combined fire department, jail cells, fire call box, and a truck scale to measure coal shipments. The facade is dominated by a stepped and arched parapet, and three large windows with fanlights; a hose tower rises above the roofline.

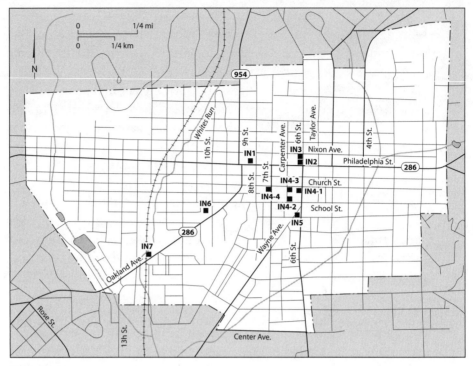

INDIANA

Indiana hosts a college campus in the southwest corner of the borough, which nearly doubles the population when classes are in session. While the town-and-gown relationship is strong, the borough's long main street has suffered from the lack of a preservation ethic, despite the excellent restoration of the former courthouse by the National Bank of the Commonwealth (IN2). Both the borough and the township surrounding it show signs of unplanned and unsympathetic development.

IN1 Indiana County Courthouse

1970, Lawrie and Green; George Shea, project architect. 825 Philadelphia St.

The architects' efforts here yielded what architectural historian James D. Van Trump labeled "neo-neo-Georgian," according to his papers at the Pittsburgh History and Landmarks Foundation. The rectangular brick building has lost the fine proportions of earlier Georgian two- to three-story buildings, and rises to four stories without considering their impact on the aesthetics. Only a simple Greek Revival porch and brick quoins break up the boxlike appearance of the courthouse. A 1983 statue of Indiana-born actor Jimmy Stewart, by sculptor Malcolm Alexander, stands in front of the courthouse. Stewart,

who graduated with a degree in architecture from Princeton in 1932, has a museum dedicated to his memory on the third floor of the Indiana Free Library Building (1913, E. M. Lockard; 845 Philadelphia Street).

IN2 National Bank of the Commonwealth (NBOC), Eastern Division Headquarters (Indiana County Courthouse)

1871, James W. Drum. 601 Philadelphia St.

The former Indiana County Courthouse, now a bank headquarters (see also IN3), is a red brick, four-and-one-half-story Second Empire building with a mansard roof, pedimented window surrounds, and Corinthian columns, with cast-iron capitals surrounding the heavily proportioned square clock tower.

When the new courthouse was built and this one slated for demolition, NBOC leased the building from the county for ninety-nine years. Renovations by Millan Kerr Architects earned the Excellence in Design-Extended Use award in 1977 from the Pittsburgh chapter of the American Institute of Architects. Opposite, at 600 Philadelphia Street, is the large, limestone-clad First Commonwealth Bank (originally First National Bank) of 1934, with handsome Art Deco touches and a classically ornamented interior. These two buildings are the architectural highlights of the borough's main street.

IN3 National Bank of the Commonwealth (NBOC), Eastern Division Headquarters (Sheriff's House and Jail)

c. 1871, C. H. Sparks. 22 N. 6th St.

Architect C. H. Sparks designed this pair of buildings, adjacent to and in a bold style complementary to James W. Drum's former courthouse (IN2). Both are connected to the old courthouse and were included in the NBOC restoration. The twelve-room house facing 6th Street was the county sheriff's residence and offices. The cut-stone quoins, window surrounds, and ornate woodwork are typical of the decoration found on houses of the era, and the addition of pedimented wall dormers creates here an amalgam of Italianate and Colonial Revival elements. The former jail across the courtyard to the west is more severe, and

IN2 NATIONAL BANK OF THE COMMONWEALTH (NBOC), EASTERN DIVISION HEADQUARTERS (INDIANA COUNTY COURTHOUSE)

has a rusticated stone base and corner quoins. It retains the bars on its tall and narrow windows, but they have been blocked off from the inside and natural light enters through two large skylights added at the time of the renovations.

IN4 Church District

1923–1931. Church St., between 6th and 7th sts., and School St.

Despite having addresses on adjoining streets, Zion, Calvary, and Graystone churches stand together facing what was once the church square (1808) of Indiana. Much of the land was later sold as commercial and residential lots, but the three churches remain on one block of the aptly named Church Street. A fourth church, Grace United Methodist, is two blocks to the west.

Zion Lutheran Church (IN4.1), the earliest (1922–1923; Church and 6th streets), was designed by Philadelphia architect George C. Baum, who trained with an eminent designer of Roman Catholic churches, Edwin F. Durang, but specialized in Lutheran churches in his own architectural practice. This rusticated sandstone Gothic Revival building replaced a church of 1880. A square corner tower flanks the buttressed triple-arched entrance that opens directly into a traditional nave and aisle plan. A large stained glass window fills the area above the portico. The manse next door is attributed to Leo A. McMullen from Apollo, Pennsylvania.

At the other end of the block and built a year later, in 1924, Calvary Presbyterian Church (IN4.2; 695 School Street) was designed by J. C. Fulton and Son. Constructed of an unusual deep red Hummelstown brownstone, the heavy, solid stonework contrasts with the lightness of the Gothic-arched openings. A prominent square corner tower separates the two entrances on the north and east elevations. The deep porches and squat columns of these entrances are not imposing and have an inviting human scale. Fulton's design has his trademark stained glass domed ceiling, this one designed by the Rudy Brothers Company of Pittsburgh, rising above the Akron plan sanctuary. The large east window is by Dodge and Company of New York, but the remaining art glass is by Rudy Brothers.

Graystone United Presbyterian Church (IN4.3; 640 Church Street), a separate branch of Presbyterianism, but now under the same administration, was built two years after Calvary Presbyterian, in 1926. With its buttresses along the side walls, simple pinnacles at the roofline, and more elaborate ones at the corners, Graystone is the most obviously Gothic Revival of the three churches. Its Scottish-born architect George Espie Savage designed over three hundred churches, mostly Presbyterian, during his long career.

Grace United Methodist Church (IN4.4; 712 Church Street) is removed from the rest of the group in size, date, and style. It is the largest of the four, occupying nearly an entire city block. The Colonial Revival church was dedicated in 1931, replacing an older 1870s building. Designed by John T. Simpson in red brick, it has a soaring steeple above the main entrance that is sheltered by a pedimented porch supported on cast-marble Corinthian columns. In 1974, a major fire damaged the kitchen and the roof, both of which were replaced.

IN5 Historical and Genealogical Society of Indiana County (Silas M. Clark House)

1869–1870, attributed to James W. Drum. 200 S. 6th St.

This house was built for lawyer Silas M. Clark, who lived here during his appointments to a number of local and state positions, and, in 1882, his election to the Supreme Court of Pennsylvania. The design of the house is attributed to James W. Drum of Punxsutawney and Pittsburgh, architect for the former Indiana County Courthouse of 1871 (IN2), Sutton

IN5 HISTORICAL AND GENEALOGICAL SOCIETY OF INDIANA COUNTY (SILAS M. CLARK HOUSE)

Hall at Indiana University of Pennsylvania (IN6), Miller Hall at Waynesburg University (GR3), and a number of significant buildings of the 1870s in the region. The two-story brick house is a textbook example of the Italian Villa, with two gabled sections intersecting at a central three-story tower, segmental-arched windows in groups of two, prominent brackets supporting deeply overhanging eaves, bay windows, and a veranda. The house remained in the Clark family until 1917, when it was sold to the county and the interior was altered to suit its new use as offices. In 1951, the Historical and Genealogical Society of Indiana County moved here, and, in 1996, completed a major renovation of both the interior and exterior.

Diagonally opposite Clark's house, J. P. Carter built a large house (1870; 209 S. 6th Street) to compete with him. When Clark obtained the services of the architect that Carter had wanted (assumed to be James W. Drum), Carter deliberately made his house larger than Clark's. J. P. Leach, a local architect, gave the house all the essentials of the Second Empire style: a mansard roof, dormer windows, and bracketing under the eaves. The only alteration to the house appears to be the removal of a square, mansard-roofed tower at the center of the facade.

IN6 Indiana University of Pennsylvania (IUP) Campus

1868–present. 1011 South Dr., bounded by School and S. 13th sts. and Oakland and Wayne aves.

Founded in 1875 as Indiana Normal School, Indiana University of Pennsylvania (IUP) is a liberal arts college with 14,000 students. The campus has suffered from a lack of planning, as is evident in the randomly placed brick buildings of the 1950s. The administration has initiated several projects to create clusters, or minicampuses, for each of the university's seven colleges. There are two fine buildings in the center of the campus. The oldest, Breezedale (1868; School Street between 7th and Oakland), was commissioned by local dry goods entrepreneur James Sutton as his home. The two-story red brick Italianate house features paired brackets, first-story bay windows, and stone corner quoins. Now an

IN7 SAINT THOMAS MORE PARISH

alumni and conference center, it has served the university as a dormitory, offices, and classrooms. Breezedale was extensively renovated by MacLachlan, Cornelius and Filoni between 1984 and 1989. Sutton Hall was the entire college when constructed near South Drive in 1873. Designed by James W. Drum in a subdued Italianate style, it has a cupola above the pediment of the central wing of its E-shaped plan, brick corner quoins, and rows of double-sash windows on each of its four stories. Drum also designed the former courthouse (IN2), and the Silas M. Clark House (IN5) has been attributed to him. In 1960, Price and Dickey architects of Philadelphia made repairs to Sutton Hall.

IN7 Saint Thomas More Parish

1968, Francis O'Connor Church. 1200 Oakland Ave.

DIXONVILLE VICINITY

IN8 Kintersburg Bridge

1877. Off PA 1005 near TWP 612 over Crooked Creek, 4 miles west of Dixonville

Built by J. S. Fleming, this is one of four Howe truss bridges remaining in Pennsylvania. With its trapezoidal shape, vertical siding, and narrow windows along the eaves, it is similar to the three Town truss, covered bridges in the county, but a Howe truss system was favored nationally by railroad engineers from 1842 to the 1880s. The Howe truss added iron rods

Built as the Newman Center for the students of Indiana University of Pennsylvania, the church was designed by Greensburg architect Francis O'Connor Church (1910–1992) as an architectural and artistic teaching tool. Its kidney shape symbolizes the spiraling journey of faith as it flows toward the altar. The shallow domed roof is constructed of a lightweight acoustical plaster requiring little structural support. Skylights and high small windows bring abundant natural light into the sanctuary while allowing a smooth uninterrupted curve of brick on the exterior. The church seats over 600, with no congregant farther than forty feet from the altar, giving a sense of community encouraged by the liturgical reforms of Vatican II. The unusual structure is enhanced by carefully chosen religious art by Ed Carlos and Armento Liturgical Arts of Buffalo.

IN8 KINTERSBURG BRIDGE

as a primary structural member to what was essentially a timber bridge. These adjustable wrought-iron rods replaced vertical timbers, adding invaluable strength. The bridges were simple and quick to build, and relatively long lasting. Massachusetts millwright William Howe (1803–1852) patented the bridge plan in 1840.

COMMODORE

Commodore was one of several coal patch towns built by the Clearfield Bituminous Coal Corporation (CBCC) to supply their holding company, the New York Central Railroad. At one time, Indiana County alone supplied three-fourths of the New York Central's coal needs. The coal-carrying rail line, the Cherry Tree and Dixonville Railroad, was established in 1904. Now abandoned, the line originally followed one side of the Two Lick Creek valley, and then with a horseshoe curve reached a higher point on the opposite side to avoid an abrupt grade. Laid out by the CBCC's engineer Paul Gill in 1919, the town was named for Commodore Cornelius Vanderbilt, founder and one of the principal stockholders in the parent company. At the Commodore mine's peak in 1922, it produced more than one thousand tons of coal a day, and continued operation until shortly after World War II. Today the mine is almost completely dismantled, with one much-altered repair shop remaining. However, dozens of the workers' houses still stand. This was considered a model community for the coal company, its fourth in Indiana County, after Rossiter (1900), Clymer (1905), and Barr Slope (1905). The two-story houses with either pyramidal or gable roofs were constructed of hollow pressed-clay tile block made in the company's brick plant. Each has indoor plumbing, and shed porches on the facade. The 1924 company store now serves as a community center, but the school has been demolished. The town remains active despite the mine's closing, since most residents own their own homes.

CHERRY TREE AND VICINITY

Cherry Tree is named for a large wild black cherry tree that marked the site known to the local Native Americans as Canoe Place. This was as far upstream on the West Branch Susquehanna River as a canoe could navigate. With the Land Purchase from the Six Nations of 1768, this same tree marked the point on the John Penn family's land where the boundary stopped following the Susquehanna and turned west to follow a straight line overland to Kittanning on the Allegheny River. The tree also marked the point at which Indiana, Clearfield, and Cambria counties met. The landmark tree ultimately washed away in a flood, but it is commemorated in the borough by a rusticated stone column designed by the E. R. Carr Company of Quincy, Massachusetts, in 1894.

Logging, the first major industry in Cherry Tree, peaked in 1870. When the Pennsylvania and the New York Central railroads collaborated to build the Cherry Tree and Dixonville Railroad to service the rich coal fields of Indiana County, Cherry Tree prospered, as did such other towns along the rail line as Commodore, Starford, Clymer, Dixonville, and Heilwood. Today, the railroad is owned by Conrail and remains in use. Flooding had long been a problem for Cherry Tree, which straddles the confluence of the West Branch Susquehanna River and Cush Cushion Creek. A flood control project consisting of a series of levees and earthworks begun in the 1940s was rehabilitated in the 1970s, and again in the 1990s. The grass-covered slopes of the earthworks are more parklike than intrusive.

Cherry Tree remains a residential community with a small commercial core centered on the intersection of Cherry and Main streets and anchored by First Commonwealth Bank in a handsome two-story brick building with arched windows (c. 1900; 11 Main Street). Reflecting the prosperity of the lumbering era are a number of frame Greek Revival and Italianate houses with distinctive wide, paneled corner boards with capitals and bracketed eaves, such as the Porter Kinports House (c. 1872; 161 Front Street). At least four other buildings in Cherry Tree have similar details: 131 Main Street, Main Street at the Creek, 10 Maple Street, and Cherry Tree Presbyterian Church (1856; 121 Front Street). In addition, the triangular window in the attic gable end, unusual for its size and shape, on the Kinports House, is found on two other houses in town: 110 and 101 Main Street.

IN9 Living Waters Camp

1935 established; 1939 tabernacle. PA 240 at Redwood Rd., 0.3 miles west of PA 580, 2 miles southwest of Cherry Tree

The Living Waters Camp opened in 1935 as a tent camp and spiritual retreat for the Assembly of God congregations. Today it is an independent Christian camp. During the 1920s and 1930s, David McDowell, an engineer in the ministry, developed the prototype for the Assemblies of God rural retreat tabernacles, one of which forms the nucleus of the Living Waters Camp. Constructed in 1939 of wooden trusswork and covered with tongue and groove vertical siding, it has wide folding doors on the side elevations so that the congregation can open the walls to increase air circulation. Clerestory windows provide natural light and ventilation. In 1959, asphalt replaced the straw that had been strewn over the dirt floor. The original straight-backed wooden benches are still in use. There are over two dozen single-family cottages on the property, built and rebuilt over the years. Most of them are simple one-room clapboard cabins with a few two- and four-room buildings as well. Assorted modern buildings such as a dormitory and cafeteria lie to the southeast.

HOMER CITY

IN10 Two Lick Farm (Ross House)

1820, with additions. 150 Two Lick Farm Ln.

John Ross, a carpenter from eastern Pennsylvania who worked on Indiana's first courthouse and jail (demolished), purchased the 270-acre farm in 1811. The family lived in a log house on the property until they finished the substantial springhouse, which stands east of the main house. They occupied the main house in 1820. Originally two rooms over two

IN10 TWO LICK FARM (ROSS HOUSE)

rooms, with a small off-center kitchen wing at the rear, this latter was enlarged to a full two stories by 1840. When the present owner purchased the house in 1983, he restored the stone portion and added another floor to the kitchen extension. The five-bay rough-cut stone facade retains its original windows, while the shutters are reproductions made in 1983. The main entrance was also reproduced from a photograph of the main entrance of the earlier courthouse by Ross. It has a distinctive fanlight, a small pediment, pilasters, and a round-arched, recessed entrance.

BLAIRSVILLE

James Campbell and Andrew Brown laid out Blairsville in 1819 along the northern bank of the Conemaugh River. The village prospered when the western division of the Pennsylvania Canal was completed in 1828, and boat-building and packet services were founded. Only a few buildings from the canal era remain, located at 302 and 312 S. Liberty Street and 123–127 W. Market Street. They are simple, two-story red brick buildings of four and five bays, typical of canal housing in the region. The arrival of the Pennsylvania Railroad, which connected Blairsville to Pittsburgh in 1856, quickly made the canal obsolete, and by 1860, it was abandoned. Blairsville became the terminus of a branch of the Pennsylvania Railroad main line, and therefore home to a large number of offices and mechanics shops. The line traversed Main Street and stretched to a wharf on the river. Two buildings mark the railroad's impact on the town: the board-and-batten former Station House (1851; 55 Old Main Street) and the Italianate Artley House (1852; 304 S. Walnut Street), built by and for Daniel Artley, a master carpenter for the Pennsylvania Railroad. Today, ten blocks of Market Street contain two- and three-story brick and frame commercial buildings that successfully compete with the large chain stores along U.S. 22.

IN11 BLAIRSVILLE ARMORY

IN11 Blairsville Armory

1909, W. G. Wilkins Company, with Joseph Franklin Kuntz, supervising architect. 119 N. Walnut St.

The Blairsville Armory's main purpose was to serve as a meeting, training, and storage place for the B Node 43 of the Twenty-eighth Signal Battalion of the Pennsylvania National Guard. Its broader goal, like that of the other armories in the commonwealth, was to protect the citizens and property of Pennsylvania. The stone building has a floor plan that was the standard for armories built between 1879 and 1938: basically a T shape with two stories of administrative offices in the front and a drill hall that was lit by a clerestory behind. The Wilkins company designed a number of armories in the western half of the commonwealth, and Joseph Kuntz was the architect in charge of armory commissions for the firm. Kuntz specialized in office buildings, armories, railway stations, and gas stations. He also designed Linden Hall (FA22), a large estate in Fayette County.

CLARKSBURG VICINITY

IN12 Evergreen Estates (Miller-Marshall House)

1790s. PA 286 at Tunnelton Rd., 0.4 miles south of Clarksburg

The Evergreen Estates house, overlooking Blacklegs Creek, was built by Christian Miller, and is reputed to be the oldest house in the county. The five-bay stone house has a four-over-four plan, central stair hall, two interior end chimneys, and a c. 1900 frame unheated summerhouse that is now attached at the southwest corner. The house has randomly laid stonework and rudimentary quoins. Originally, the main entrance faced the creek to the north, but in 1984, the area enclosed by the ell of the house was paved, effectively moving the main entrance to the southern elevation. The barn and several outbuildings remain north of the house.

SALTSBURG

Located at the point where the Conemaugh River and Loyalhanna Creek meet to form the Kiskiminetas River, Saltsburg was settled in 1766. The town was laid out in 1817, three years after the first salt well was bored by William Johnson. Salt production peaked in 1838, when more than thirty wells produced over 70,890 bushels. The largest well, the Great Conemaugh Salt Works, was two miles east of the village. Fuel to power the pumps for the saltworks sparked the coal mining industry in the southern part of the county.

The Pennsylvania Canal and the Pennsylvania Railroad both traversed the borough. Three five-bay stone houses dating from the 1830s and early 1840s line the canal's former path, which today is a borough park. The Saltsburg Historical Society (105 Point Street) is located in a house built between 1830 and 1839 that is typical of these canal-era houses: flush with the sidewalk, two stories, five bays, and a central door. The stone house at 214 Washington Street is also in excellent condition. The third stone house, known as the McIlvain house at 519 Salt Street, has a Greek Revival portico that was added in 1910. After the railroad withdrew in 1954, business slowed. Most of the nineteenth-century building fabric survives and is preserved as a historic district. Saltsburg's location at the confluence of two water systems has made it both a tourist attraction and a frequent victim of floods. Eight large dams

South facade of 105 Point Street, Saltsburg.

throughout the county (on Conemaugh River and Loyalhanna, Yellow, and Little Mahoning creeks) have helped to regulate the waters and create recreational facilities nearby.

IN13 George Altman Mill (Patterson Mill)

1911–1912. 111 Point St.

This flour mill replaced the original 1885 structure after a fire destroyed it. It is rare to find a flour mill so close to its original condition and so well integrated into its village, and retaining most of its original equipment. The large frame building is three-and-one-half stories, with paired windows on each elevation. Previous mills on the site used hydraulic power from a dam upstream. The Patterson Mill, however, generated its power from a steam engine. Eventually, this engine was replaced by electric motors, which were in use when the mill closed in 1980. The various outbuildings were added in the 1950s.

WESTMORELAND COUNTY

Created from Bedford County in 1773, Westmoreland was the last Pennsylvania county formed under British rule. Its first European colonial settlers were Scots-Irish and German, with smaller numbers of Irish and English. Several other counties were formed later from Westmoreland's original boundaries, including Allegheny, Armstrong, Fayette, Greene, and Washington. Two forts from the French and Indian War are the reconstructed Fort Ligonier of 1758 (U.S. 30 and PA 711) and the National Historic Site of Colonel Henry Bouquet's 1763 defeat in Pontiac's Rebellion at Bushy Run, 1.3 miles east of the intersection of PA 130 and PA 993. The original county seat of 1773 at Hanna's Town was moved to Greensburg in 1786.

Agricultural products and natural resources were the first cargoes on the rivers, the Pennsylvania Canal, and the roads, which superseded Native American pathways. In the late nineteenth century, coal mining and railroads transformed the agrarian landscape to one of scattered mining towns and industrial complexes populated by a workforce of European immigrants. Salina, founded in the Kiskiminetas valley in 1874, is one example of a company town, and retains a pair of tunnel kilns from its early fire-brick plant, as well as a grouping of two-story, single-family frame houses. Between 1890 and World War II, the promise of inexpensive land and larger spaces enticed many Pittsburgh and Allegheny County companies to build new factories and housing in Westmoreland County. Glass manufacturing and the production of iron, steel, and aluminum flourished at a number of sites, such as Jeannette, Vandergrift, and New Kensington.

The county's architecture reflects these important economic eras: the agricultural economy of farms, mills, and distilleries; the industrial age of mining towns, factories, railroad buildings, and large industrial complexes; and since the middle of the twentieth century, suburban growth, especially in the central part of the county, where many townships serve as bedroom communities to Pittsburgh. Today, Westmoreland County has the sixth largest population and the seventh largest area in Pennsylvania.

GREENSBURG AND VICINITY

Sited on rolling hills near the geographic center of Westmoreland County, Greensburg has served as the county seat since 1786, supplanting Hanna's Town northeast of the city. Three reconstructed log houses and a log fort on Old Hanna's Town Road (PA 1032) mark that site. Christopher Truby of Bucks County and William Jack laid out a sixty-acre grid of streets in the 1770s, reserving a two-acre site for the new courthouse. Truby named the settlement Newtown, but in 1799, it was incorporated as the borough of Greensburg to honor Nathanael Greene, a general in the American Revolution under whom many local men served.

Located along the historic Forbes Road between Ligonier and Pittsburgh, Greensburg became the commercial center for this largely agrarian county. The first turnpike connected Harrisburg to Pittsburgh via Greensburg in 1821. In the late nineteenth century, approximately twenty-five coal and coke operators worked the rich coal deposits in the surrounding area, reaching peak production between 1916 and 1919. Consequently, Greensburg became a banking center with seven major banks. Today, it is a shopping and professional center focused around the activities of the courthouse and local colleges. Surrounding the courthouse (WE1), the centerpiece of downtown, are several major buildings, including the Westmoreland Museum of American Art designed by Sorber and Hoone in 1958 (221 N. Main Street); the Palace Theater, formerly Manos Theatre, a Renaissance Revival design of 1926–1927 by Leon H. Lempert and Son (21 W. Otterman Street); and the Classical Revival former Barclay-Westmoreland Trust, now Mellon Bank, of 1928 (1 N. Main Street). Since the 1990s, the Westmoreland Cultural Trust has been actively restoring handsome buildings and returning them to use, notably the Stark-James

1 N. Main Street, the former Barclay-Westmoreland Trust building (1928), in Greensburg.

Building, home to the Westmoreland County Historical Society (1889; 33–41 W. Otterman Street). Greensburg's YMCA is a four-story brick Renaissance Revival building (1913, Paul A. Bartholomew; 101 S. Maple Avenue).

Residential areas remain near the courthouse hilltop. The 300, 400, and 500 blocks of N. Maple Avenue have a fine collection of brick Queen Anne and Colonial Revival two-story houses dating from 1890 to 1910. West of downtown along W. Pittsburgh Street and neighboring streets between Division and Westminster streets is another group of substantial brick Colonial Revival houses, including the Barclay House of 1904 by Alden and Harlow and the c. 1840 Jeremiah Burrell House (133 Morey Place), with Greek Revival and Italianate details.

WE1 Westmoreland County Courthouse

1906–1908, William Kauffman; 1978 addition, Roach Walfish Lettrich Bohm. 2 N. Main St.

This 175-foot-high domed courthouse rises above the skyline of Greensburg from the site of three previous courthouses. The Beaux-Arts building is constructed of steel and faced with granite. The ground floor is rusticated, geometric terra-cotta ornament adorns the upper floors and dome, and the roofline has personifications of Justice, Law, and the People. Inside, the dome covers a four-story rotunda enriched with marble mosaics, San Domingo mahogany, and bronze railings along the grand staircase. This ornate interior is the work of decorator Paul Hoffman, with murals by French muralist Maurice Ingres. Pittsburgh artist Carroll Westfall restored the murals. The courthouse was restored and expanded with a six-story addition to the west in 1978 by a Greensburg-based architectural firm. Although lacking classical decoration, the addition's similar granite surfaces and landscaped courtyard blend with the original building.

The courthouse's architect, Pittsburgh's William Kauffman (1857–1945), is often associated with his contemporary Edward M. Butz (1851–1916) in designing large public buildings, including two Pennsylvania courthouses, in Fayette (FA1) and Clarion (CL1) counties. They designed buildings together between c. 1882 and c. 1910.

WE2 Pennsylvania Railroad Passenger and Freight Stations

1910–1911, William Holmes Cookman. 101–109 Station Pl.

Cookman, architect and engineer for the Pennsylvania Railroad, designed these elaborate passenger and freight stations on the main line between Philadelphia and Pittsburgh. While the rectangular shape of the brick buildings, their wide overhanging eaves

WE1 WESTMORELAND COUNTY COURTHOUSE

with brackets, and the porte-cochere for the passenger station are typical features of other railroad stations, the classical details of sandstone quoins, water table, coping, pedimented dormers, and belt courses are atypical. The passenger station features an unusual square, ogee-domed clock tower accented with finials. The railroad first arrived in Greensburg in 1852, but the construction of the present buildings in 1910 represented the increased importance of the passenger trade. RWL Architects and Planners restored the two buildings in 1998 as shops, and Gerard Damiani designed the restaurant, while retaining Amtrak access.

WE3 Seton Hill University

1886–1889, Joseph Stillburg; 1920–1928, Carlton Strong; 1956–1958, Philip Johnson. Seton Hill Dr.

Founded in 1883 by the Sisters of Charity and named for St. Elizabeth Ann Seton, Seton Hill University evolved from a private academy to a four-year degree-granting college in 1918, and, finally, a university in 2002. A large, rambling brick Romanesque Revival administration building designed by Joseph Stillburg and built between 1886 and 1889 crowns the hilltop campus overlooking Greensburg. A series of additions over the years allowed the

WE2 PENNSYLVANIA RAILROAD PASSENGER AND FREIGHT STATIONS

WE3 SETON HILL UNIVERSITY, Sullivan Hall

building to house a variety of functions, from dormitory to chapel. North of the administration building are three two- to four-story-high brick buildings designed by Carlton Strong of Pittsburgh, which were added as enrollment increased. Outstanding among them is the Tudor Revival gymnasium, Sullivan Hall (1928), with stone and half-timbered corner towers and a steeply pitched slate roof. In the early 1950s, then president Monsignor William Granger Ryan, advised by Strong's successor firm and his friends Dominique and Jean de Menil (patrons of Philip Johnson), consulted Johnson in the building of a new library, and ultimately had his firm design Havey Hall, a three-story concrete-frame dormitory with brick infill. Greensburg architect Francis O'Connor Church acted as supervising architect. Johnson was commissioned again in 1990 to design an art quadrangle, but the plans were never realized. The college purchased two former mansions in the 1970s, along Mt. Thor Road (WE11).

WE4 Cole House (Dee Miller House)

1950–1952, Peter Berndtson and Cornelia Brierly. 629 Oakhill Ln.

Berndtson and Brierly's houses always draw their character from the nature of the site, and, consequently, from the aesthetic of Frank Lloyd Wright, their mentor. Here, the house of dark russet–colored brick and cypress is one story in height and is oriented to the south to capture sunlight throughout the seasons. The long horizontal lines of the roof are offset by the mitred-glass corner windows, which further distinguish the house from the surrounding suburban housing. A central chimney anchors the composition. The plan comprises a combination living and dining room, kitchen, three bedrooms, and two bathrooms. As in other houses by these architects, there are a number of built-ins, and exposed brick walls and wood as a backdrop. The dramatic windows in the southeast corner of the living room open to a flagstone terrace, while the north elevation of the house uses smaller clerestory windows. Dee Miller, an insurance executive, sold the house to Dr. Cole before it was completed. Dr. Cole's sister Catharine married Mario Celli, who, with his brother Raymond and with William V. Flynn, founded the Pittsburgh architectural firm Celli-Flynn Associates. Celli designed his family's modern house (1955; 839 Harrison City Road) of redwood and sandstone west of Greensburg shortly after the Miller-Cole house was completed.

WE5 Tribune-Review Building

1958–1962, Louis Kahn. 622 Cabin Hill Dr.

What initially appears to be a square, unadorned, concrete block building comes to life with Kahn's square keyhole windows that create a continuous rhythm across the north facade. Windows abutting the cornice line allow light to penetrate the interior, while their narrow proportions reduce glare for the adjacent desks. Louis Kahn (1901–1974) addressed a difficult program dictated by the multiple needs of a newspaper within a single story and basement. The newspaper required warehouse space, an industrial printing plant whose vibrations needed exceptional structural support, and space for journalists to write and research. The prestressed concrete beams of the roof are supported on concrete block piers, creating a busier rhythm on the

WE5 TRIBUNE-REVIEW BUILDING

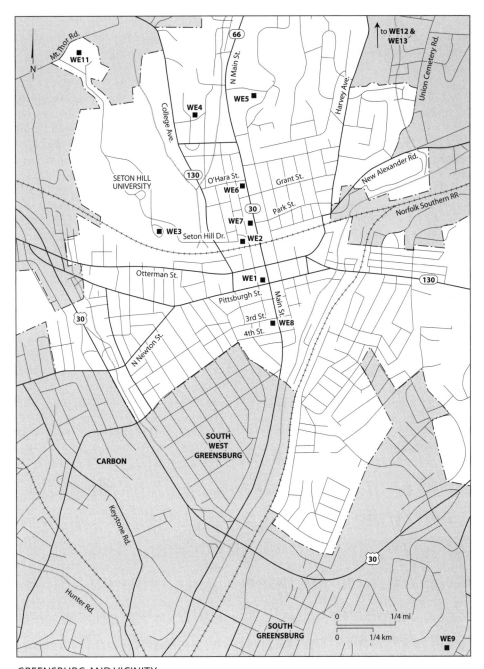

GREENSBURG AND VICINITY

side elevations. The dark glassed openings contrast with the nearly square, rough-faced concrete blocks to give depth and drama to the symmetrical exterior, which has been altered by the addition of loading bays on the facade and a large addition to the south.

WE6 YWCA (William Augustus Huff House)

1899–1900, Cram, Goodhue and Ferguson, consulting architects. 424 N. Main St.

This Colonial Revival house was designed for industrialist William A. Huff by an unidentified local architect (possibly Beezer Brothers, twins from Altoona who earlier had designed Colonial Revival houses for Huff's brother and nephew), but the design was refined by Cram, Goodhue and Ferguson. The L-shaped red brick house has a hipped roof, pedimented portico supported by four Ionic columns across the symmetrical facade, pedimented dormers, columned porte-cochere, and two brick chimneys unusually placed on the facade rather than at the end walls. The exterior clearly shows the influence of Goodhue's Charles Grosvenor house (1899) in Athens, Ohio. Cram recommended a symmetrical and open plan allowing for a "long straight vista" between living room and library. The commission is documented in letters between Cram and Huff written in 1899 and preserved at the Boston Public Library.

A number of red brick Colonial Revival houses were built in the early 1900s in the adjacent 300 and 400 blocks of N. Maple Avenue, which have been designated the Academy Hill National Register Historic District.

WE7 Blessed Sacrament Cathedral (Most Holy Sacrament Church)

1923–1928, Comes, Perry and McMullen. 300 N. Main St.

Two buildings dominate Greensburg's skyline: the county courthouse (WE1) and Blessed Sacrament Cathedral. This Gothic Revival sandstone church has a massive, 125-foot-tall

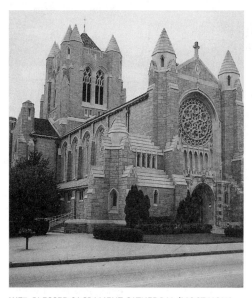

WE7 BLESSED SACRAMENT CATHEDRAL (MOST HOLY SACRAMENT CHURCH)

square tower rising from the intersection of nave and transepts. Windows outlined in Indiana limestone accentuate the finely detailed exterior. The stained glass windows were made by the Franz Mayer Company of Munich, Germany. The present building is the fourth Roman Catholic church on the hilltop site. Its name was changed in 1951 when the Greensburg Diocese was formed. The cathedral is similar in detailing, plan, and style to St. Bernard's Church in Mount Lebanon, Allegheny County (AL131) designed by William R. Perry. In 1971, Mario Celli (1910–1998) designed the alterations to the sanctuary to address the new liturgical guidelines of Vatican Council II. Next door to the cathedral is Aquinas Academy (1880), an Italianate brick school building of three stories, with dual cupolas on the facade.

WE8 First Presbyterian Church

1916–1919, Ralph Adams Cram for Cram and Ferguson. 300 S. Main St.

Cram designed this Massachusetts seam-faced granite church with a gracefully proportioned square tower at the crossing and a pair of slender hexagonal towers flanking the W. 3rd Street main entrance. The interior is distinguished by spare rough-plastered walls with fumed oak woodwork in the church and chestnut in the chapel. A dramatic Gothic arch soars above the altar at the east, lit by a large stained glass window. The windows in the chancel and above the rear balcony are by Pittsburgh-trained Charles Connick of Boston, a frequent Cram collaborator. Cram chose five Pennsylvania churches to illustrate in *The Work of Cram and Ferguson, Architects* (1929). Three are in western Pennsylvania, Holy Rosary (AL104) and Calvary Episcopal (AL108) in Pittsburgh and this church, which is illustrated on plates 41–44 of Cram's book.

WE9 University of Pittsburgh at Greensburg's Lynch Hall (Charles McKenna Lynch House, "Starboard Light")

1923, Bartholomew and Smith; 1929 addition, Paul A. Bartholomew. 150 Finoli Dr.

Starboard Light is coal magnate Charles McKenna Lynch's former secluded country estate built in the revival style popularly referred to as

WE10 HARROLD ZION EVANGELICAL LUTHERAN CHURCH interior

"stockbroker Tudor." Lynch purchased a dairy farm in a valley near Greensburg, and hired Paul Bartholomew and his partner Brandon Smith to design his sprawling Tudor Revival house of brick, with stone trim and faux timbers in the stucco gable ends. An addition in 1929, designed by Bartholomew, included an arched stone bridge over the adjacent stream that meanders through the 104-acre site. The grounds included a pool and pool house, tennis court, and gatehouse, as well as a Colonial Revival house (1940) for his daughter.

Paul A. Bartholomew (1883–1973) was a 1909 graduate of the University of Pennsylvania, who during his prolific and extended career designed such varied projects as the six-story former Troutman Department Store (c. 1921–1923; 202–226 S. Main Street), Westmoreland Hospital (532 W. Pittsburgh Street), and the New Deal community of Norvelt (see Norvelt and Vicinity, p. 230). Starboard Light was purchased in 1964 by the University of Pittsburgh at Greensburg as the first part of its satellite campus. Since 1976, when the entire regional campus moved to the estate, the school has transformed itself into a four-year college with brick student residences, faculty building, library, and nearly a dozen other buildings, most designed by Bartholomew's successor firms and the Warren, Pennsylvania, firm of Creal Hyde and Lawson, Architects.

WE10 Harrold Zion Evangelical Lutheran Church

1964, Roach Walfish and Lettrich. PA 136 at PA 3097 (Baltzer Meyer Pike Rd.), 2 miles southwest of Greensburg

Built to house a long-established Lutheran congregation, the Greensburg architectural firm gave a fresh interpretation to Gothic forms with a dramatic, eye-catching roofline that sweeps upward at both ends of the nave. The church is clad in dark brown brick and has steel beam buttresses along the side elevations. The interior has a central aisle flanked by smaller side aisles, and is highlighted by the soaring beams of the roof.

WE11 Coulter Family Houses

Henry W. Coulter House. 1922, Alden and Harlow; 1970s chapel, Mario Celli. Skara Glen–Margaret Coulter House. 1925–1926, Walter T. Karcher and Livingston Smith. 447 and 461–465 Mt. Thor Rd.

The Coulter family moved from their late-nineteenth-century Main Street residence in Greensburg to more spacious Tudor Revival houses outside the city in the 1920s. Henry Coulter commissioned Alden and Harlow to design his two-and-one-half-story sandstone house. The firm continued to design solid estate houses for the upwardly mobile in and around Pittsburgh after Frank Alden's death in 1908, but its work had become predictable.

WE13 WILLIAM STEEL FARM

The house has a slate roof, porte-cochere at the front entrance, and limestone window surrounds on the facade. Mario Celli added a chapel in the 1970s.

Henry Coulter's unmarried brother and sister William and Margaret hired the Beaux-Arts-trained Philadelphia architects Walter Karcher and Livingston Smith to build their brick Tudor Revival mansion immediately adjacent to Henry's stone house. This brick house has similar limestone window surrounds, but lacks the hipped-roof dormers found on Henry's house. Both properties were subsequently purchased by the Sisters of Charity as their headquarters and as offices for Seton Hill University (WE3). A third house on College Avenue for the Coulters' brother Richard was also designed by the firm of Karcher and Smith. All three of these large, asymmetrical houses have steeply gabled slate roofs, and supporting outbuildings and stables on their generous grounds.

WE12 John Coulter House

1963, John Pekruhn. 30 Glenmeade Rd.

At the end of a slightly curving drive, the John Coulter House emerges from its wooded site behind unassuming rough stone walls fronting a gravel parking court. The rectangular house, designed by John Pekruhn (1915–

1998) of Pittsburgh, is an excellent example of 1960s styling and craftsmanship. The house is integrated into the site through a series of enclosed courtyards with native stone walls, expansive floor to ceiling glass windows opening to the courtyards, and a horizontal, flat-roofed profile. Despite the modernist appearance of the exterior, the house has a surprisingly symmetrical room arrangement, evidence of Pekruhn's Beaux-Arts training at Carnegie Institute of Technology. A large living room and dining room are separated by a shared massive stone fireplace. Service rooms adjoin the dining room to the north, while private family accommodations are off the living room to the south. Interior detailing includes slate floors and built-in cabinetwork.

WE13 William Steel Farm

1866, with additions. 295 Hannastown Rd., Fire Station Rd. at PA 1055, 4 miles north of Greensburg

The William Steel farm is Westmoreland County's most intact nineteenth-century farm complex. The elaborate farm buildings were financed largely through Steel's lucrative contract to provide wheat and beef to the Union army during the Civil War. The south-facing complex has a brick, two-story Italianate farmhouse with a cupola, brick and frame agricultural and domestic support buildings, rock-faced stone retaining walls, and farm lanes. In 1890, Steel built a separate overseer's house and kitchen building west of the main complex. Profits from the sale of the farm's mineral rights and railroad right-of-way in 1912 insured its survival. The complex was sold out of the family in 1992. In the early twenty-first century, the village of Totteridge Estates and golf course abutted the farm to the north. The Jamison Coal Company developed the nearby mining towns.

JEANNETTE AND VICINITY

WE14 Jeannette Glass Company and McKee Glass Company Housing

1907, J. E. Myers. Chambers Ave. and 300 blocks 5th, 6th, and Mill sts.

Remains of Jeannette's once thriving late-nineteenth- and early-twentieth-century glass

industry include approximately one hundred brick company houses, the only brick company housing in Westmoreland County. Erected on adjoining streets between Bullit and Cassatt avenues, these flat-roofed duplexes and row houses have decorative brick parapets and brick corbeling at the cornice.

Similar to other company towns, the housing is built along a simple grid of streets with consistent spacing. Although the accompanying Jeannette Glass Company factory buildings have been removed, the McKee Glass Company factory buildings remain and now house an architectural metals company.

WE15 United States Post Office

1933, Charles Sorber. 223 S. 5th St.

Construction of this classically derived post office, by Greensburg architect Charles Sorber, coincided with President Franklin D. Roosevelt's massive government-financed building effort in which more than forty thousand new public buildings were built across the country. In a style often described as "starved classical"—in reference to their economical design and minimal detailing—the lean and hungry look suits this buff brick and sandstone-trimmed post office. Its recessed entrance is flanked by two-story windows and guarded by a colonnade of six Greek Doric columns. To remind patrons of pre–Great Depression events, heroic murals at either end of the long rectangular lobby depict local glassmaking and the battle of Bushy Run. The murals were mandated by the Treasury Department of the 1930s that earmarked 1 percent of a building's cost for public artwork. Carnegie Institute of Technology–trained mu-

WE17 BRUSH HILL

ralist T. Frank Olson of Pittsburgh was chosen after a competition. Unfortunately, he died before the murals could be executed, but his colleagues Robert L. Lepper and Alexander J. Kostellow completed the painting and gave the fee to Olson's widow.

WE16 Brush Creek Salem United Church of Christ (Brush Creek Salem Church)

1816–1820. 177 Brush Creek Rd., 1.2 miles southwest of Jeannette

Stylistically influenced by Anglican church buildings of eighteenth-century Virginia, this is a two-story, symmetrical, red brick church. It is characterized by square-headed windows on the first floor, compass-headed windows on the second floor, and entrances on both gable-end walls. Interior finishes are restrained and simple. Six square columns support the balcony, which is accessed by stairs in the northeast and southeast corners of the church. In addition to Brush Creek, two similar churches for German Lutheran congregations were constructed nearby: Harrold Zion (1815) of stone and Bee Hive Church (1820) in Greensburg (both demolished). Deliberately choosing the name Salem, meaning "peace," the church was originally built to house two separate denominations, German Lutherans and German Reformed. They held it jointly, if not always amicably, until 1958, when the Lutherans moved out. A large cemetery surrounds the present church.

WE17 Brush Hill

c. 1798. 651 Brush Hill Dr., 0.5 miles west of Jeannette

Colonel John Irwin erected Brush Hill along the historic Forbes Road after Native Ameri-

WE16 BRUSH CREEK SALEM UNITED CHURCH OF CHRIST (BRUSH CREEK SALEM CHURCH) interior

cans burned his log house and lightning struck and destroyed his subsequent frame house. This stone house differs from the square vernacular stone houses erected by many settlers, as it is a large (35 × 54 feet), rectangular, Georgian-influenced two-story house with a central passage plan. Brush Hill was the center of a 700-acre working plantation, which included a gristmill along nearby Brush Creek. The borough of Irwin encroached on the Brush Hill property in the twentieth century, and the house is now surrounded on all sides by twentieth-century tract houses.

NEW KENSINGTON

WE18 John Wood Logan House

c. 1876. 427 6th Ave.

John Logan built this architecturally distinctive house as a testament to the family's success in the lumber and banking industries. The southern section of New Kensington, once owned by the Logans, was called Parnassus. The substantial Italianate brick house has oversized bracketed eaves, wide fascia boards, segmental window caps, and two-over-two double-hung sash windows with louvered shutters. An elaborate porch of grouped Tuscan columns and wide fascia boards with additional brackets accents the facade. It is likely that the house was designed by an architect or a skilled builder influenced by period pattern books. Nearby, Logan's Ferry (Parnassus) Presbyterian Church (1885; 730 Church Street) is a frame Gothic Revival church in a T shape, with an elaborate bell tower that rises in stages to a steeple over an open arched belfry. The building is highly textured with a variety of wood treatments and slates on the steeply pitched gabled roof, and a wooden truss ceiling on the interior.

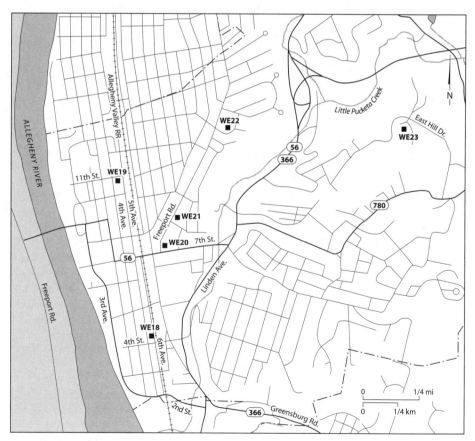

NEW KENSINGTON

WE21 ALCOA ALUMINUM CLUB

WE19 Kensington Arms Apartments (ALCOA/Wear-Ever Building)

1914, J. H. Giesey. 400 11th St.

Aluminum Company of America (ALCOA), once the largest employer in the area, commissioned several architecturally distinguished buildings in this industrial boomtown, founded in 1891 eighteen miles northeast of Pittsburgh on the Allegheny River. The Wear-Ever Division, ALCOA's cooking utensil company, expanded rapidly in the early 1900s, and commissioned Pittsburgh architect J. H. Giesey to design these distinctive and substantial offices. Giesey's inspiration was English Tudor, evidenced by the twin domed towers flanking the oriel window above the recessed entrance and the grouped windows with limestone window surrounds. The brick building was sold to the city of New Kensington in 1968 and transformed into apartments, retaining much of its original exterior appearance.

WE20 Mount St. Peter Roman Catholic Church

1942, Enos Cooke. 100 Freeport Rd.

Sheathed in red Michigan sandstone from the demolished mansion of Richard King Mellon on 5th Avenue in Pittsburgh, this church sits on a hillside above New Kensington. Architect Enos Cooke was a pupil of noted church architect John T. Comes. St. Peter's congregation, organized in 1902, outgrew its small frame building during New Kensington's industrial boom. World War II caused a shortage of materials that mandated an imaginative reuse of scrap items. And since the Mellon family no longer needed a grand mansion in Pittsburgh and no one was found to purchase or accept the house as a donation, they reluctantly con-

tracted to demolish it. Seventy-five percent of the exterior material and interior fittings of the mansion, including steel beams, oak and bronze doors, marble, bronze stair railings, carved wood, and a granite porch balustrade, were moved from Pittsburgh to New Kensington and reused in this tall, severe basilica plan church with tall narrow nave windows. Setbacks at the entrance suggest the Art Deco style. A convent, parish house, and school that complement the style of the original building were added to the complex in 1946.

WE21 ALCOA Aluminum Club

1915–1918, Benno Janssen and Franklin Abbott. 200 Freeport Rd.

A two-story brick residential and recreational facility designed for male employees and visitors to ALCOA's nearby research facilities, this flat-roofed structure consists of nine central bays distinguished by an arcaded entrance, with flanking three-bay projecting wings. Side wings have three-sided bay windows in their first story's central bays, stone quoins, and window and door architraves. The interior retains some aluminum light fixtures and furniture, and a formal staircase. A one-story arcaded section extends the facade to the south. Presently, the building is unused.

WE22 ALCOA Research Center

1928–1930, Pierre R. L. Hogner and Henry Hornbostel. 600 block Freeport Rd.

Henry Hornbostel and ALCOA's in-house architect Pierre Richard Leonard Hogner (c. 1887–1966) designed the limestone-faced research laboratory overlooking the company's plant made of the local industrial, cream-colored Kittanning brick. The central project-

WE22 ALCOA RESEARCH CENTER, photo 1989

ing entrance bay with a shallow pediment is decorated with aluminum acroteria and a Greek key motif at the cornice, giving it a monumental presence. Fluted pilasters separate the recessed windows and doors, which have ornate pressed-aluminum spandrels between the floors. To promote ALCOA's products, Hornbostel embellished the interior as well as the exterior with abundant aluminum decoration. The marble-lined lobby's elevator doors were brought from ALCOA's Gulf Building headquarters in downtown Pittsburgh. The Research Laboratory closed in 1986, but other utilitarian buildings in the complex continue in use as shipping and receiving departments for the metals division.

WE23 Aluminum City Terrace

1940–1942, Walter Gropius and Marcel Breuer. Terminus of East Hills Dr. north of PA 780

Aluminum City Terrace was one of hundreds of projects across the country built to solve the housing crisis created by the demand for workers in defense-related industries. The government engaged prominent architects across the nation to design similar dwellings, including Richard Neutra, Eliel Saarinen, and George Howe. Aluminum City Terrace's 250 one- and two-story units have flat roofs, con-

WE23 ALUMINUM CITY TERRACE

crete block foundations, stretcher bond brick facades, rear elevations of cedar siding, and long bands of second-floor windows. Windows on the north elevations are small and rectangular with vents. The units were laid out on the irregular forty-five-acre site to face south for the best sun and air circulation. The townspeople, despite initial opposition to the project, deemed Aluminum City Terrace extremely successful. In 1947, the government sold the complex, and it became one of the first cooperative housing projects in the country. The units have been continuously occupied and have a waiting list of several years. In 1983, local architect Michael Shamay renovated the exteriors.

VANDERGRIFT

Vandergrift stands in striking contrast to most of Westmoreland County's company towns. Apollo Iron and Steel Company founder George G. McMurtry hired the firm of Olmsted, Olmsted and Eliot in 1895 to create a landscape plan for his ideal company town. By that year, Frederick Law Olmsted's health had failed, and so his partners drew the plans. The client and planners stipulated that residents would build or commission their own houses and alcohol manufacture or sale would be banned in the borough. The town would have paved curvilinear streets lined with trees and dotted with parks, buildings with consistent setbacks, running water, sewers, low-priced lots to entice workers, incentives for businesses to open stores in town, and donations of land and money for local churches. The expense of the initial planning and infrastructure construction ultimately caused the company to cut the lot sizes and decrease the green spaces provided, but nonetheless the lots sold well.

Several of the corner buildings in the business district were given curved facades following the streets' configurations. James E. Allison designed the Classical Revival Casino Theater (1900; 145 Lincoln Avenue), which has

Northeast corner of Grant and Columbia avenues, Vandergrift.

flanking wings housing the borough offices and the library. At the entrance to the former Apollo Iron and Steel Plant (since 1988 owned by Allegheny Ludlum Steel Company), a small train station (c. 1896; 75 Washington Avenue) was initially meant to anchor the south end of the village green. By 1903, seven churches took advantage of the company's offer of a free lot and $7,500; the stone Gothic Revival First Evangelical Lutheran Church designed by Alden and Harlow (1896–1897; 101 Washington Avenue) was among the first. Its square crenellated tower and the gable end ornamented with a rose window reflect Frank Alden's debt to H. H. Richardson. Housing for the borough's 6,000 residents follow late-nineteenth- and early-twentieth-century revival styles, including Queen Anne, Romanesque Revival, and Colonial and Classical Revivals in frame and brick. A group of larger homes lines Washington Avenue, and the business district on Grant Avenue has substantial two-story brick buildings.

WE24 St. Gertrude Roman Catholic Church
1911, John T. Comes. 305 Franklin Ave.

Within ten years of the first (1898) Catholic church in Vandergrift, a larger facility was needed. This John Comes design has a strong Italian Romanesque flavor, with its horizontal limestone belt courses contrasting with the red brick walls and clay tile roof. The basilica plan is unusually narrow (54 feet) compared with the 104-foot-high landmark twin towers arcaded with sandstone columns in the belfries. The nave is lit by clerestory windows and an elaborate wheel window above the entrance.

LATROBE AND VICINITY

Latrobe lies at the base of Chestnut Ridge, the westernmost ridge of the Allegheny Mountains. Although the town is situated just north of the historic Forbes Road, its development is closely tied to the subsequent rise of the railroad in the 1850s. Oliver Barnes, a civil engineer and agent of the Pennsylvania Railroad (PRR), purchased the Thomas Kirk farm in 1851, built rail lines across it, and then laid out lots on the flat plain adjacent to Loyalhanna Creek. He named the town for his classmate and friend Benjamin Henry Latrobe Jr., an engineer for the Baltimore and Ohio Railroad and son of the eminent architect. Three years later, the town became a borough. By the late 1870s, a second rail line, built by the Mellon family, extended into Ligonier Valley from Latrobe. Increased passenger traffic led to the construction of a handsome, eclectic, c. 1903 passenger station and support buildings on McKinley Avenue, designed by the Pennsylvania Railroad's chief engineer William H. Brown. In 1904, Latrobe became a stop on the interurban trolley line that linked many isolated coal patch towns. By the 1930s, Latrobe had become a center of alloy steel production and home to the Latrobe Brewing Company, manufacturer of Rolling Rock Beer until 2006, when the company was purchased by City Brewing.

Two iconic figures are native sons of Latrobe: Fred Rogers of public television children's program fame, who in his youth was a member of the brick Romanesque Revival Latrobe Presbyterian Church (1891–1892) designed by William Kauffman at 428 Main Street, and professional golfer Arnold Palmer, whose name is attached to the local airport. Rogers's boyhood home of Colonial Revival style stands at 737 Weldon Street. Other notable buildings in town include the Queen Anne–inspired Samuel Miller house at 414 Baker Hill Road, which reflects the exuberance of the late-nineteenth-century railroad era. The majority of the suburban streets are lined with modest houses dating from 1900 to 1960. The multistory brick and stone veneer business and commercial district includes the 1892 iron-fronted Columbus Building at 908 Ligonier Street and the six-story Classical Revival Bank Building of 1926 at 816 Ligonier Street by Bartholomew and Smith.

WE25 MOZART RESTAURANT (MOZART HALL)

WE25 Mozart Restaurant (Mozart Hall)
c. 1890. 340 Main St.

Mozart Hall's exotically detailed cast-iron facade with two onion-domed turrets is a distinctive contribution to Latrobe's Main Street. George Seiler erected the brick building in 1890 as a music and dance hall. Seiler's European heritage apparently influenced him to build a hall similar to those in Austria, and to name it for Salzburg's native-born musician, Mozart. The brick building was designed with space for two businesses on the first floor and an adjacent entrance to the second-floor concert hall. The hall has a pressed-metal ceiling, stage, and balcony. It was used for musicals and operettas until the Showalter Opera House (demolished) opened on Depot Street.

WE26 ST. VINCENT ARCHABBEY BASILICA, MONASTERY, AND COLLEGE COMPLEX

Mozart Hall is still used for community functions and a restaurant occupies the building's ground floor. A second building with a cast-iron front is the Columbus Building, located at 908 Ligonier Street.

WE26 St. Vincent Archabbey Basilica, Monastery, and College Complex

1891–1905 church, J. William Schickel; 1999 steeple, Tasso Katselas; 1967–1969 campus buildings, Tasso Katselas. 300 Fraser Purchase Rd., 1.5 miles southwest of Latrobe

In 1846, Bavarian monk Boniface Wimmer came to western Pennsylvania to serve the large German-speaking population and establish the first Benedictine monastery in North America. Wimmer also shared King Ludwig I of Bavaria's vision of creating a center for German art in North America inspired by traditional European techniques. Five abbeys across the United States emerged from his work here, in addition to this liberal arts college. As a profound statement of their German identity, the monks hired German-born architect J. William Schickel (1850–1907) to design their sacred space, the magnificent St. Vincent Archabbey, which is visible for miles. Schickel trained at the Ecole des Beaux-Arts in Paris and came to the United States at the age of twenty. He then worked in the New York City office of Richard Morris Hunt, and ultimately, he designed approximately three hundred projects with his partners Isaac E. Ditmars and Hugo Katka before his death in 1907.

The red-orange brick basilica is the focal point of the St. Vincent College campus, and its twin-towered facade and spires are inspired by twelfth-century Romanesque churches of the Rhineland. However, the initial fourteen-year building effort stopped short of the architect's original design. Financial difficulties reduced Schickel's massive twin towers on the east elevation from 250 to 120 feet. Like medieval cathedrals that took centuries to complete, shorter, simpler versions of the design's original crowning towers were finally added in 1999, overseen by Carnegie Institute of Technology–educated and Pittsburgh-based architect Tasso Katselas.

The college was originally a self-sufficient complex, with its own farm and power source, as can be seen in the number of support buildings surrounding the archabbey. The most prominent survivor of these utilitarian buildings is the operational steam-powered gristmill of 1854 northwest of the basilica and now used as an environmental education center. A devastating fire in 1963 destroyed nearly the entire college quadrangle and monastery behind the archabbey. To replace these buildings, Katselas developed a master plan and oversaw the design and construction of two major buildings, the monastery of 1967 and the sprawling Science Center of 1969. The Brutalist design of the monastery building, with five stories of concrete boxes projecting from its stepped back facade, allows the monks light and privacy in their rooms. The Science Center is a complex of four interconnected brick and concrete buildings with a courtyard and rounded amphitheater. A series of red brick student residences surround the athletic fields southwest of the campus, and the Fred Rogers Business Center

(2007–2008, Davis Gardner Gannon Pope Architects) will complete a large quadrangle around the fields.

The twenty-five-acre Winnie Palmer Nature Reserve connects to the St. Vincent campus and features hiking trails and the c. 1879 George Smith barn that was moved from another location on the property and converted to a nature center by architect Joseph Bleehash of Foothills Architecture and Consulting. Also on the property is the restored Lochrey Blockhouse of 1780.

WE27 Office Building (Johnston's "Kingston House")

1815, 1830. 3435 Lincoln Highway (U.S. 30), 2 miles southeast of Latrobe

Alexander Johnston's "Kingston House" was named for the original land patent. Its three-part plan, composed of a two-story central block flanked by one-story wings, was featured in Charles Stotz's *The Early Architecture of Western Pannsylvania* (1929). Originally, the centerpiece of Johnston's iron plantation, its location on the southern bank of Loyalhanna Creek near the Greensburg-Stoystown Pike (now U.S. 30) prompted its owner to enlarge the house with a one-story stone addition to the west in 1830 and convert it to a tavern after abandoning the unsuccessful forge he had built along the creek. A dentiled cornice, transomed front door, and end chimneys highlight the symmetrical Georgian Revival facade. The stonework is of high quality, especially the eastern facade, which has rough-cut stone in regular courses, quoins, keystones above the first- and second-floor window openings, and stone lintels over the door openings. The house has a central-hall plan, with one room flanking the hall on both floors. It has been converted to offices.

LIGONIER VALLEY

Ligonier Valley encompasses the area between Chestnut Ridge and Laurel Hill, and includes Ligonier, its primary commercial center; Cook Township; and the towns of Laughlintown, Rector, and Stahlstown. The valley's dramatic, mountainous setting only fifty miles east of Pittsburgh has made it a destination for affluent city dwellers since the late nineteenth century, when the Mellon brothers built a spur from the Pennsylvania Railroad at Latrobe east along Loyalhanna Creek to access the valley's timber and limestone resources. From the early to mid-twentieth century, the valley attracted secluded estates and private clubs designed by such notable architects as Marcel Breuer (WE30), Roger Cesare Ferri (WE31), Benno Janssen, and Peter Berndtson. The 6,200-acre Rolling Rock Club was founded c. 1916 as a shooting preserve for the Mellon family. Edward Purcell Mellon designed the original c. 1925 brick clubhouse. Janssen, who designed some of the club's interior rooms, is lauded for his picturesque Hunt Stables and Kennels built of stuccoed stone, which were converted to condominiums in 1984 by MacLachlan, Cornelius and Filoni. Only the Rolling Rock stables and farm administration buildings are visible along PA 381.

Ligonier Valley is a private and secluded area where many of the estate houses are set well back from public roads. However, the growing campus of the Valley School of Ligonier, a private elementary school on Linn Run Road east of Rector, is visible from the road, and its main building, the former house of William C. Carnegie (Andrew's nephew), may be attributed to Brandon Smith (1932; Lupine Lane). A recent addition to the environmentally conscious building movement is the Carnegie Museum of Natural

History's field station at the Powdermill Nature Reserve. The nature center building addition, which expands the exhibition and education space, is itself a tool to teach sustainable building techniques (2007, Pfaffmann + Associates; PA 381, south of Rector). The Southern Alleghenies Museum of Art has one of its four branches in a newly built structure of historic logs at 1 Boucher Lane along PA 711. The other branches are in Altoona (see BL10), Loretto (see CA5), and Johnstown (see CA28).

WE28 Idlewild Park

1878–present. 2582 U.S. 30, 2.2 miles northwest of Ligonier

Spread under tall oak and evergreen trees, Idlewild Park began in 1878 as a 300-acre picnic destination for Judge Thomas Mellon's narrow-gauge Ligonier Valley Railroad, which closed in 1952. Conversion to standard-gauge lines allowed families, schools, and church groups to travel directly from Pittsburgh to the park beginning in 1881. Among the park's oldest buildings are the frame train station (1878) and a white frame carousel pavilion (1896) with a cupola, which houses a Philadelphia Toboggan Company carousel built in the 1920s and brought to the park in 1931. The Rollo Coaster by the same company opened in 1938. Other features at the park include manmade lakes, water slides, fishing areas, and mature shade trees. In 1956, the park opened Story Book Forest, a collection of fifteen life-size displays of nursery rhymes, and in 1989, Mister Rogers' Neighborhood of Make-

WE28 IDLEWILD PARK, carousel pavilion

Believe was built to honor Latrobe native Fred Rogers and his popular public television children's program. Taliesin-trained architect Peter Berndtson designed the entrance gates, now modified, along U.S. 30 in 1956. The Darlington Station (c. 1878), located at the western end of Idlewild Park, is one of the few surviving stations of the Ligonier Valley Railroad and is being restored to house the Ligonier Valley Rail Road Museum.

LIGONIER AND VICINITY

Situated along Loyalhanna Creek with dramatic views of Chestnut Ridge and Laurel Hill, Ligonier is the commercial center of Ligonier Valley. Laid out in 1817 by Colonel John Ramsey, Ligonier was named for the French and Indian War fort of 1758, which was reconstructed in the 1960s and is marked by the stone Fort Ligonier Museum of 1961, designed by Charles Morse Stotz, at the intersection of U.S. 30 and PA 711. The town's grid plan includes a central square (called a diamond in the region) at the junction of its main roads, similar to the Holmes plan of 1682 for Philadelphia. Originally used for open markets and hitching horses, the diamond became a green space with a bandstand during the City Beautiful movement of the 1890s. The chamber of commerce commissioned architect Charles Stotz to design a town hall, library, new bandstand, and other commercial buildings around the diamond in the late 1960s and early 1970s in a colonial style. The blue stone Romanesque Revival Heritage United Methodist Church (1902–1903; Main and S. Market streets) anchors one corner of the square. Farther west along Main Street are two former Ligonier Valley Railroad stations, a frame passenger station of 1878, and to the northwest the glazed terra-cotta station (1909–1910) at W. Main and S. Walnut streets, which, since 2002, has housed the Ligonier Valley School District Central Administrative offices. Across Main Street is an Art Deco armory of red brick with limestone trim (1938; 358 W. Main Street).

While the railroad spurred the growth of coal mines and lumbering, the desire to retreat to the country, coupled with the freedom provided by the 1915 opening of the Lincoln Highway, inspired the construction of Ligonier Beach, a unique roadside establishment east of Ligonier. The complex, along a bend in Loyalhanna Creek, consists of a 400 × 125–foot pool surrounded by sand and grass beaches built in 1925. A white frame concession stand, bathhouse, and pumphouse, dating to the 1950s, were followed by a band shell, adjoining dance floor, and miniature golf course. Although the popularity of dining and dancing at the beach waned, the stream-fed cool water still draws many to this neon-signed oasis. Residential styles in Ligonier run the gamut, but most of the building stock dates from 1870 to 1910.

WE29 Laurel Ridge ("Stornoway," Donald McLennan House)

1965, Winston Elting. 305 Country Club Rd., 3 miles south of Ligonier

Renamed Laurel Ridge, the house originally known as "Stornoway" for a town in the Scottish Hebrides, was designed by Princeton-trained Winston Elting (1907–1968), who studied for three years at the Ecole des Beaux-Arts in Paris before partnering for nearly twenty years with Paul Schweikher in Chicago. In 1957, Schweikher came to Pittsburgh as the dean of architecture at the Carnegie Institute of Technology. It is possible that he may have introduced insurance broker Donald R. McLennan to the architect. Elting integrated the house into its site by using narrow layers of native stone and redwood trim. He placed

WE29 LAUREL RIDGE ("STORNOWAY," DONALD MCLENNAN HOUSE)

it near the highest point of the sixty-acre property, oriented to the west toward views of neighboring Chestnut Ridge. A low roof and recessed second-floor windows visually lessen the impact of the seven-bedroom house on the site. The restrained interior spaces are linked through a series of long hallways around an interior courtyard. The landscape designers, Franz Lipp and Associates, used plantings and blue stone–paved outdoor living areas to extend the indoor living spaces outdoors. The house shelters a pool and pool house on the southwest side from public view.

WE30 Wonderwood

1947–1948, Marcel Breuer with Rolland Thompson, Harry Seidler, and William Landsberg. 234 Country Club Rd., 3 miles south of Ligonier

Marcel Breuer designed two houses in western Pennsylvania, a city house—the Cecelia and Robert Frank House in Pittsburgh (AL111) with Walter Gropius—and this country house for the mother of Rolland Thompson, a draftsman in Breuer's New York City office. Thompson, who studied at Harvard's Graduate School of Design and held an engineering degree from MIT, joined Breuer's newly formed New York City firm just after World War II. The site specified by the client offers an exquisite view of Ligonier Valley. After much correspondence, Breuer designed a long, one-story stone house that blocks the view from the approach, but reveals it magnificently upon entering the living room with its wall of glass. Breuer agreed to use oak windows and mullions to complement the narrow, squared sandstones of the walls specified by the client. The house, with its characteristic flat roof, glass walls, and sunscreens, hugs the hillside. Breuer also helped design the terraced landscaping defined by low stone walls. A second story, not designed by Breuer, was added later. The second owners sympathetically restored the house in 1995, using the more than two hundred drawings in the Syracuse University archives, many by Breuer associates Thompson, Seidler, and Landsberg, overseen by architect Laura Nettleton.

LAUREL MOUNTAIN AND VICINITY

In the lush woodland landscape at the base of Laurel Ridge off U.S. 30 on Nature Run Road (PA 1023) nestle approximately one hundred simple vernacular cottages originally used as summer retreats. Beginning in 1926, developers L. W. Darr and Company laid out streets, constructed a pool and tennis courts, and subsequently sold lots to many Pittsburgh-based businessmen, professionals, and their families. The cottages are grouped around eight, short, grid-patterned streets, and are typically one- to one-and-one-half stories, of frame or stone construction with screened porches, stone end chimneys, and rustic wane-edged siding materials. Many cottages are now winterized and used year-round. Stone gates, walls, split rail fences, a pool, and picnic shelter dot the community. The tennis courts have been converted into a community garden. Laurel Mountain became a borough in 1982.

WE31 Walton House

1984–1985, Roger Cesare Ferri. Grounds of Rolling Rock Club, 1.5 miles west of Laurel Mountain

Screened by woods on secluded grounds, the clients requested only that their architect create a work of art with all the major rooms on one floor. New York City architect Roger Ferri (1948–1991), trained in architecture at Pratt Institute, combined his talents in painting, sculpture, and design with an architectural philosophy focused on reharmonizing man and nature. His study of Italian architectural masters and the natural world could be described as "Bernini meets Frank Lloyd Wright." The U-shaped house, which opens from a low terrace to a fast-flowing trout stream, has fieldstone walls and cedar siding to tie it to the site. Smoothly flared columns support deep eaves that brilliantly contrast with these natural elements. A two-story square tower houses the entrance and stairway to a single second-story guestroom. The architect described the living room ceiling as "vaulted in a compound curve not unlike an ocean wave breaking and rushing up the shore." The vaulted ceilings in the bedrooms and the furnishings (also designed by Ferri) create a weekend pavilion that can best be described as sensuous for its flowing curves. Ferri's first architectural commission is open to the public in nearby Loretto, Pennsylvania, where he transformed a 1920s gymnasium into the Southern Alleghenies Museum of Art (1975; St. Francis University Mall; see CA5).

WE32 Compass Inn Museum

1799; 1820; 1862; 1970s restoration and additions, Charles M. Stotz. U.S. 30 and California Ave., 0.5 miles northwest of Laurel Mountain

The Compass Inn, strategically located at the western base of Laurel Hill in Laughlintown, was a popular overnight stop on the historic Pennsylvania Road between Bedford and Pittsburgh. The evolution of the inn reflects the rise and fall of commerce along the road. The V-notched log portion (1799) is a typical roadside inn that used a common pre-1860 construction method. Hoping to attract affluent stagecoach travelers of the newly privatized turnpike, Robert and Rachel Armour purchased the property in 1814, built a stone wing in 1820, refined the simple existing interiors, and named it for an inn they knew in Chester County. By the 1860s, use of the road had declined, and the inn was converted to a house and store. A frame addition was constructed at the rear of the log portion for a second kitchen. In 1966, the Ligonier Valley Historical Society purchased the property, and in 1970 commissioned Pittsburgh architect Charles M. Stotz to restore the inn based on his knowledge and research of similar buildings in western Pennsylvania. Stotz made sympathetic additions to the rear for its planned conversion to a museum and supervised reconstruction of a log barn, blacksmith shop, and summer kitchen.

Laughlintown hosts a second roadside inn east of the Compass Inn. Built in 1827 of log covered with weatherboarding, the Yellow House or Naugle Inn retains its two-story drover's porch from which its patrons could watch their cattle in the barn (demolished) on the north side of U.S. 30.

PLEASANT UNITY

WE33 David Pollins Farm, "Sewickley Manor"

1790s; 1849 barn; 1852 house; 1880s. 272 Pollins Rd., 2 miles southwest of Pleasant Unity

Seven generations of the Pollins family have worked this 192-acre farm, among the most beautiful in western Pennsylvania, which has buildings dating from the late 1700s to the 1880s. The handsome red brick Greek Revival house sits on a shelf of land sheltered on the northwest by the crest of a hill and overlooks a rural vista to the southeast. The large, white frame posted forebay Pennsylvania barn is of timber-frame construction with an unusual triple-braced center post. Turned walnut posts supporting the forebay are unique to this barn. A remarkable number of intact

WE33 DAVID POLLINS FARM, "SEWICKLEY MANOR," Pollins barn

outbuildings remain, including a smokehouse from the 1790s, springhouse (1820s–1850s), chicken coop, machinery shed, wagon shed, utility shed, pig pen, sheep barn (all 1880s), and tenant house (c. 1900).

NORVELT (WESTMORELAND HOMESTEADS) AND VICINITY

Norvelt is one of two government-assisted housing projects of the New Deal era in Pennsylvania (see Penn-Craft, FA15). It provided industrial workers, who were unemployed after mines closed in the 1920s, an opportunity to own their own homes, grow subsistence crops on a small plot of land, and work in a garment factory or on the cooperative farm. In 1933, the government purchased 1,492 acres of farmland and hired Paul A. Bartholomew to plan the community, then named Westmoreland Homesteads. By 1937, a central area, with a school, athletic fields, community buildings, and a factory designed by Alfred M. Marks of Pittsburgh, was surrounded by 254 Cape Cod–style houses on curvilinear streets. The remaining 720 acres formed the cooperative farm, with two handsome barns remaining on Kecksburg Road. In contrast to the minimally sized duplexes in most mining towns, the houses ranged from four to six rooms and had indoor plumbing. Each house had one to seven acres of land, with a garage, poultry house, and grape arbor.

After Eleanor Roosevelt's tour of the completed Westmoreland Homesteads in 1937, residents voted to honor her by renaming the community Norvelt, combining the last syllables of her first and last names. The community's continued popularity and success are evident in the many additions to the houses and subdivisions of original plots of land for subsequent housing.

WE34 Polymath Park (Treetops)

1957–1965. Dillon Rd. north of Evergreen Rd., 4 miles southeast of Norvelt

In 1962, Peter Berndtson, a former Taliesin fellow, drew a master plan for a residential development that he named Treetops and Mountain Circles. Only two of the twenty-four houses planned for the wooded site were built, for Pittsburgh industrialists James Balter (1964) and Harry Blum (1965). In 2006, the new owner of the site, Thomas D. Papinchak, a local builder, disassembled the Frank Lloyd Wright–designed Duncan House (1957) from Lisle, Illinois, and moved the pieces to the renamed Polymath Park for reconstruction in 2006–2007.

Wright had sold three prefabricated house designs to the Erdman Builders of Madison, Wisconsin. The Duncans purchased Style 1 as a kit. (Nine houses of this design are scattered across four states.) While its shallow gable roof is not typical of Wright's designs, the composition anchored by a heavy stone chimney and thinly layered stone walls that emphasize the house's horizontality is quintessentially Wrightian. The house uses Maryland ledge rock, an alternative foundation material specified by Wright, rather than the original cement block chosen by the Duncans.

The Berndtson designs vary considerably. The Balter House is the larger of the two, with a shallow hipped roof above deep eaves, a fieldstone base, and redwood board-and-batten walls surrounding the ribbon windows. The great room and screened porch are cantilevered into the woods surrounding the house. Redwood beams outline the cathedral ceiling inside. The Blum house, which overlooks a pond and a twenty-acre meadow, is much smaller. Its hipped roof shelters stuccoed walls with redwood trim, and the interior has mitred corner windows and several built-in cabinets. There is also a farmhouse on the property that Berndston lived in while the two houses were built. Today, the Duncan and Balter houses are available for rental and the Blum house serves as a visitors' center.

MOUNT PLEASANT

Lots were laid out for Mount Pleasant in 1797 by Alexander McCready. Sited on a plain west of Chestnut Ridge along an early Indian path, Mount Pleasant became a commercial center for southern Westmoreland County and was incorporated in 1828 as the county's first borough. The commercial district flanks historic Glades Road and has a central square, or diamond. In 1924, a doughboy monument to the soldiers of World War I replaced the troughs and hitching posts at S. Diamond and W. Main streets. The two- to three-story brick commercial district includes several red brick churches along Main Street (PA 31) between Braddock Road Avenue and Hitchman Street. A few early-nineteenth-century buildings, such as the Shupe-Pritts Mill, remain along Main Street, but most of the historic commercial buildings have been modernized. Church and College avenues are composed of late-nineteenth-century houses, including the brick Second Empire Warden House (1886; 200 S. Church Street), now housing the Braddock Trail Chapter of the Daughters of the American Revolution, and the brick Colonial Revival Mullin-Harmon House (c. 1910; College and Church streets). Frick Hospital is a large, orange brick complex on Eagle Street adjacent to Ramsay High School (now Elementary School) in a Spanish Mission Revival style with a red tile roof. Middle Presbyterian Church (PA 981 at PA 2007) is an eighteenth-century congregation housed in a c. 1854 church. The church, the fifth on the site, has a traditional rectangular plan, gable roof, and two entrance doors opening into a sanctuary with two side aisles. The Italianate brick parsonage south of the church was built in 1876. The nearby cemetery reinforces the relative isolation of the complex.

WEST OVERTON

This exceptionally well-preserved, mid-nineteenth-century agricultural and industrial community northeast of Scottdale was founded in 1800 by a group of Mennonites from Bucks County led by Henry Overholt. When Overholt purchased his farm, it already had two small distilleries, since making rye whiskey was already well established in western Pennsylvania. Henry Overholt's son Abraham added a gristmill to process grain for distilling and to serve the adjacent farms. The West Overton of today is primarily his work. Abraham and his son Henry arranged the vertical integration of their own farm by manufacturing what they needed, such as barrels, and reusing whatever they could, for example, mash from the distillery to feed the pigs. These lessons were well learned by Henry Clay Frick, who was born in the stone springhouse adjacent to the large main house (1838–1839), and ultimately were applied by him and Pittsburgh's industrialists to the steel industry. The West Overton barns are enormous brick buildings that rival the six-story red brick distillery (1859) for pride of place in the village. The two larger barns

West Overton Distilling Company, north elevation of the red brick distillery building, PA 819, East Huntingdon Township.

were used for livestock (1826) and as a dairy barn (1832). Although they do not have decorative brickwork, the dairy barn has an arched loggia supporting its forebay. Brick barns, often found in southeastern and south-central Pennsylvania, were more expensive to build than the log or timber-frame barns prevalent in western Pennsylvania. The technically difficult masonry of the smaller stable (1838) with the wheatsheaf or hourglass designs required a considerable investment. The brick openwork allowed ventilation and some light into the haymow.

Mennonite farmers were progressive and often used up-to-date machinery, crop rotation, and fertilization. A line drawing of the village in the 1876 *New Illustrated Atlas of Westmoreland County, Pennsylvania* depicts the coke works as secondary to the farm, but this was a nostalgic and idealized vision. In fact, by 1880, West Overton had become a coal patch town dominated by coke ovens and a rail line. Of the nineteen structures visible in the drawing, sixteen remain intact. The distilling business ended here in 1919 with the onset of Prohibition, although Old Overholt whiskey is still made in Kentucky. Forty-five acres of the village are now part of a museum complex established in 1927, when Helen Clay Frick donated the house and distillery to the Western Pennsylvania Historical Society.

SCOTTDALE

Bordering Jacobs Creek and spreading over low hills to the northwest, the borough, originally called Fountain Mills, was first laid out in 1873 on the adjoining farms of Jacob and Peter Loucks, German Mennonites and cousins of Henry Clay Frick. The town's strategic location in the emerging coal and coke region between Connellsville and Uniontown to the south and Greensburg to the north, and the building of the Pennsylvania Railroad, prompted its incorporation as a borough in 1874, and a name change to Scottdale, after Thomas A. Scott, president of the Pennsylvania Railroad. The Henry Clay Frick Coal and Coke Company, Scottdale Iron and Steel, and other coal companies and industries located in or near the borough.

Broadway and Pittsburgh streets intersect as the primary commercial district, with the former Frick office, a four-story rectilinear brick building (1906; 100–300 S. Broadway), one of the few remaining Frick-related buildings in the commercial district. The large buff brick former Scottdale High School on S. Chestnut Street (c. 1910, Allison and Allison, Architects) overlooks its playing field below. Handsome late-nineteenth-century Queen Anne and Colonial Revival housing built for the owners and managers of local industries line Loucks, Arthur, and N. Chestnut streets. The A. K. Stauffer House (c. 1880; 701 Loucks Avenue) represents the wealth and sophistication achieved by Scottdale's industrial owners and managers in that era. Local builder Samuel J. Zearly designed and constructed Stauffer's Queen Anne house with a wraparound porch, two turrets, and a similarly styled carriage house.

WE35 LUSTRON HOUSE

WE35 Lustron House

c. 1950. 804 Arthur Ave.

This Lustron house is a rare artifact of the post–World War II era. The steel-paneled houses were intended to ease the housing shortage after the war, and were promoted as economical and of low maintenance. Built of two × two–foot squares of porcelain enamel-clad steel, Lustron houses typically were assembled in five working days. Influenced by protoypes shown at Chicago's Century of Progress Exposition in 1933, Chicago architect Morris H. Beckman designed a model where the entire house, including the roof, exterior and interior walls, kitchen cupboards, bookcases, and built-in vanities, is steel. The company produced 2,492 houses in the Midwest and Northeast between 1948 and 1950, when they went out of business. There are only a handful of Lustron houses remaining in western Pennsylvania.

WEST NEWTON VICINITY

Isaac Robb laid out West Newton in 1796 on a southwest slope along the Youghiogheny River, naming it for his hometown, Newton, New Jersey. Prior to the construction of the National Road in the early nineteenth century, West Newton was a shipbuilding port on the river. The Pittsburgh and Connellsville Railroad brought further growth in 1855, with West Newton serving as a midpoint between the two towns. West Newton is laid out on a grid plan with Main Street perpendicular to the river and lined with frame and brick late-nineteenth-century Queen Anne and Italianate houses and brick commercial buildings. Notable among these are the mansard-roofed house of c. 1870 at 303 Main Street, the brick commercial building at the corner of Main and 4th streets, and the brick First United Methodist Church, an early J. C. Fulton commission (1883; 106 N. 2nd Street).

A bridge company was created to build a three-span covered bridge with stone abutments across the Youghiogheny c. 1834. In 1906, the present three-span Parker truss bridge replaced the covered bridge, using what appear to be the original stone abutments and piers. John Plumer's house overlooking the Youghiogheny River (131 Water Street) shows the evolution of his fortunes, the frame portion built just after his marriage in 1814 and the brick portion in 1846 after his success as a mill owner, justice of the peace, and contractor for the covered bridge nearby. West Newton's Baltimore and Ohio passenger station (1893, Ephraim Francis Baldwin for Baldwin and Pennington; Vine and S. 1st streets), with irregular roofline, wide eaves, large wooden brackets, and canted bay, draws from the late-nineteenth-century Queen Anne and Shingle styles. The railroad continues to use the passenger station as well as the freight station on Water Street.

WE36 Concord School

1830. 100 block Port Royal Rd., 4.9 miles south of West Newton

The well-loved golden sandstone Concord School was built just as public schools were being mandated by state decree. Its primary entrance on the long wall rather than the short gable-end wall sets it apart from most one-room schools. The building has a simple wooden plank door, wood shingle roof with a slight overhang, exposed rafter ends, and windows with plain wooden lintels and sills. In use until 1870, the school subsequently served many other functions until 1947, when it was restored with financial assistance from local schoolchildren and their parents. Nearby, the Daily House (c. 1797) is among the earliest of Westmoreland County's brick houses and was built with fine Georgian details and interior appointments. It lies at the intersection of PA 51 S and Fells Church Road.

WE37 Bel Ange

1992, Michael Marquez. 333 Castle Dr., 3.3 miles southwest of West Newton

This enormous 17,000-square-foot gray stone and stucco house dominates a hilltop in an area of modest suburban houses. The sprawling postmodern design, by Los Angeles architect Michael Marquez, uses the typical Queen Anne vocabulary of historical elements, such as turrets, towers, quoins, multiple chimneys, conical roofs, and a porte-cochere. Large gates further distinguish the house from its neighbors overlooking the Willowbrook Golf Course. The name "Bel Ange" merges the hometowns of the original owners, Belle Vernon, Pennsylvania, and Los Angeles, California.

WE38 Bells Mills Covered Bridge

1850, Daniel McCain. PA 3061 off PA 136, 3.2 miles east of West Newton

This is Westmoreland County's only surviving wood truss bridge. Spanning Sewickley Creek, the ninety-five-foot-long and fourteen-foot-wide structure is covered with a low-pitched gable roof, and features pediments and Tuscan piers at the portals. Burr's truss system was patented in 1804. Here, McCain added arches to the multiple kingpost truss to create a longer and stronger bridge. Modern engineers believe that the multiple kingpost truss is a system for keeping Burr's slender arches properly aligned and preventing them from buckling. Daniel McCain (1810–1891) was for a time the superintendent of bridge construction in Allegheny County, working on the Ninth Street (AL13), Sixteenth Street (AL80), and 43rd Street bridges in Pittsburgh, as well as bridges for the Pennsylvania and West Penn railroads. Transportation advances have caused demolition of similar bridges on well-traveled roads of the commonwealth. In the late 1980s, the Beamery, a local firm known for reconstructing historic structures, made extensive repairs to this bridge. Nearby are the stone Sewickley Presbyterian Church of 1831 and a large, red brick, five-bay house at 211 Bells Mills Road.

FAYETTE COUNTY

Fayette County is a study in contrasts: farms interspersed with coal patches and vernacular buildings between architect-designed houses. It contains many architectural delights, from the Isaac Meason House (FA27) to Frank Lloyd Wright's Fallingwater (FA28) and Kentuck Knob (FA29). In addition to Wright, three nationally known architects—Daniel Burnham, Richard Neutra, and theater designer Thomas White Lamb—designed buildings in the county.

Named for the Marquis de Lafayette, French hero of our Revolutionary War, Fayette County, southwest of the Youghiogheny River, was carved from Westmoreland County in 1783; the northwest corner was added in 1784.

Geographically, the land is mostly rolling hills typical of the Appalachian Plateau of western Pennsylvania. It is crossed from southwest to northeast by Chestnut Ridge, a 2,000-foot-high spine of land that looms over Uniontown and Hopwood and is referred to by locals as "the mountain." Following the rivers and such Native American trails as the Nemacolin Path, explorers and traders were joined by European settlers beginning in the 1750s. Virginia's Ohio Land Company induced eleven families to settle in what became Fayette County, led by Christopher Gist, their scout, who built a log house at Mount Braddock in 1753. In the 1780s and 1790s, flatboat and keelboat trade began on the Monongahela River from Brownsville, utilizing a river network that extended through the interior all the way to New Orleans. Items manufactured in western Pennsylvania thus found markets to the west and south.

However, confusion over land titles and which state, Pennsylvania or Virginia, would take precedence hindered settlement. And the area's isolation from the eastern coastal states fostered an independent attitude that continued after the American Revolution. In 1791, when the newly formed federal government levied a tax on whiskey, one of the largest income-producing items in the western farmer's inventory, federal troops were called out to quell the rebellion that ensued. To bind the western counties to the eastern seaboard, a road extending from Cumberland, Maryland, to the Ohio River was needed. Between 1810 and 1850, the National Road brought prosperity to several Fayette County towns: Hopwood, Uniontown, and especially Brownsville, the point of departure for travel on the Ohio River. Initially bypassed by the Pennsylvania Railroad, Fayette County eventually secured rail service from Pittsburgh to Connellsville in 1855, although it was not joined directly to the national lines until 1871, when the Pennsylvania Railroad extended south from Greensburg, Westmoreland County, to Uniontown. In 1875, the Baltimore and Ohio Railroad finally established itself in Fayette County by leasing three feeder lines. The two major railroads monopolized transport of the county's exceptionally pure coal.

While coal was mined for personal use from the late 1700s, commercial coal mining boomed only after 1843, when it became common to use coke (hard-baked coal) in the production of iron and, eventually, steel. One-hundred-and-fifty coal patch towns existed in Fayette County c. 1900. Eighty survive, which is surprising because the towns were isolated and intended to last only as long as the mines they supported. Many have become communities of closely knit families who now commute to other jobs in the region. Some villages were absorbed by neighboring towns or cities. For example, the small coal patch of Leith became a suburban neighborhood of Uniontown. Today, its double-chimneyed patch houses abut the Uniontown County Club and golf course, which is connected by footbridges to the former patch. The grid pattern of the company town was expanded with middle- and upper-middle-class housing dating from the 1930s to today.

In the twentieth century, the beauty of Fayette County's landscape and its relative isolation from urban sprawl have made it a desirable spot for rural retreats, with locations such as Fallingwater and the lesser-known Deer Lake (1938), a development on 107 wooded acres near Chalk Hill. Tourists continue to stop at inns dating from the 1790s to the 1990s located along the National Road.

UNIONTOWN AND VICINITY

Uniontown lies in a valley west of Chestnut Ridge at the intersection of several former Native American routes. Looking east from the valley, "the mountain," or ridge, is a panorama of woods punctuated dramatically by the approximately sixty-foot-tall white Jumonville cross (see FA33). Uniontown, the county seat, was laid out in 1776 by Henry Beeson, a Quaker from Berkeley County, Virginia (now West Virginia). With his brother Jacob, Beeson built log houses and a mill just south of the confluence of Coal Lick and Redstone creeks. Named Beeson's Town for its founder, the name "Union" was used on deeds as early as 1780. Uniontown became a borough in 1796.

Bisected by the old National Road (now Main Street), Uniontown profited from the surrounding rich rural land and the stagecoach lines along the road. But it was coal and its extraction that brought wealth to the city. After 1883, railways linked the surrounding coalfields with Connellsville and ultimately Pittsburgh. The town's development can be traced through its domestic architecture, beginning with the modest two-story brick houses on Union Street dating from the 1840s. Large Colonial Revival and Tudor Revival houses followed in the 1890s, especially along Ben Lomond Street and South Beeson Avenue. Substantial churches, such as the stone Gothic Revival St. Peter's Episcopal Church (1884–1885, Charles Marquedent Burns; 60 Morgantown Street) and the handsome brownstone Asbury United Methodist Church (1913–1919, Andrew Cooper; 20 Dunbar Street), enhanced their surroundings. The town continued to expand to the south in the twentieth century with substantial suburban housing, many with the tall gabled roofs and Palladian windows that became popular later in the century. The largest employer today is the hospital, but tourism is a growing industry.

FA1 Fayette County Courthouse

1891, William Kauffman and Edward M. Butz.
61 E. Main St.

In 1891, only three years after H. H. Richardson's Allegheny County Courthouse (AL1) was completed, Kauffman and Butz designed the third Fayette County Courthouse. As a student at the Massachusetts Institute of Technology from 1879 to 1881, William Kauffman (1857–1945) was familiar with Richardson's work, as evidenced by his other building in Uniontown (FA4). Edward M. Butz (1851–1916), active in

Pittsburgh's German community since the 1870s, would have witnessed the construction of the Allegheny County courthouse. The architects created what architectural historian James D. Van Trump described (in his papers at the Pittsburgh History and Landmarks Foundation) as "the Allegheny County courthouse . . . disassembled and rearranged in a smaller version." Uniontown's courthouse differs from Richardson's in its asymmetrical plan, its use of yellow-gray sandstone rather than pink granite, and the elimination of a lobby space; the last of these was a suggestion made in 1884 by Judge Thomas Mellon to the Allegheny County commissioners not to provide space "for loafers and hangers on." Uniontown's small lobby only provides space for access to the stairways. It is illuminated by a stained glass dome. Murals in the upper lobby were painted by Ohio artist Alice Schille (1869–1955) in 1905. Courtroom No. 1 retains most of its original fittings, but the other major courtroom has been altered. The "bridge of sighs" connecting the jail to courtroom No. 1 was added in 1902. It is uncertain whether its design was provided by the same architects.

A four-story Italian Renaissance Revival county office building designed by Emil R. Johnson and Clarence F. Wilson was added to the east in 1927–1928. Its central section echoes the courthouse's triple-arched entrance, which is topped by a row of arched windows. Set into the smooth limestone walls above the entrance are stone relief panels commemorating agriculture and coal mining, Fayette County's two main industries.

FA2 State Theatre Center for the Arts (State Theatre)

1922, Thomas White Lamb. 25–35 E. Main St.

Designed by renowned theater designer Thomas White Lamb (1871–1942), architect

FA1 FAYETTE COUNTY COURTHOUSE

of a half-dozen theaters on New York City's Broadway, the 1,600-seat State Theatre has hosted everyone from the Dorsey Brothers and Cab Calloway to Conway Twitty and Johnny Cash. Although initially designed for movies and vaudeville, the stage now accommodates full theatrical productions. The exterior, fashioned from a soft brown–colored brick, has Renaissance-style arches crowning three terra-cotta-trimmed windows above the marquee. A foliated entablature of green and blue highlights the parapet at the roofline. The original ticket windows remain, and much of the original restrained classical interior decor has been maintained.

FA3 Fayette Bank Building (First National Bank)

1901–1902, Daniel H. Burnham. 50 W. Main St.

The First National Bank was commissioned by Josiah V. Thompson (see FA7), who made his fortune buying coal rights in southwestern Pennsylvania. Thompson competed with coal magnates like Henry Clay Frick, but he also emulated Frick's architectural patronage by hiring one of the country's best-known architects, Daniel Hudson Burnham, who had been designing buildings for Frick since 1898. To construct the eleven-story bank, the building (1828) previously on that corner was demolished. A year earlier, Thompson and a partner had built the smaller domed Thompson-Ruby building across the street to serve as bank headquarters during construction of the Burnham building. The First National is a severe, classically derived building that wraps around the former Grand Opera House (now called the Masonic Building). When the Opera House could not be purchased at Thompson's price, the bank building was simply designed around it. The bank's entrance on the curved corner is ornamented with engaged Doric columns and framed by large windows. The two lower stories and the eleventh story are sheathed in limestone, and the eleventh story concludes with modillion blocks at the cornice; the central eight stories are brick. Within, the circular banking chamber is faced with marble, and a central Tuscan column supports an unusual ceiling with foliate-decorated beams creating pie-shaped coffers. Leading from the cavernous banking

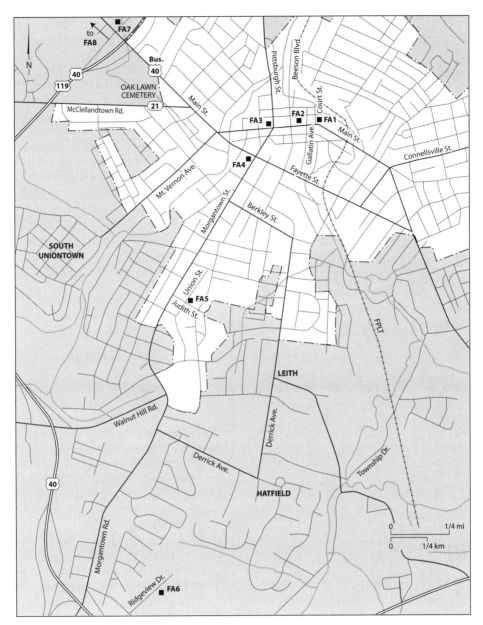

UNIONTOWN

chamber, a small, mahogany-lined manager's office retains its fireplace and mirrored overmantel.

FA4 Trinity United Presbyterian Church (First Presbyterian Church)

1894–1895, William Kauffman. 79 W. Fayette St.

The sandstone exterior of this church, with its massive central tower, conceals the warmth of its interior, which is enlivened by the brilliance of seven large Tiffany windows. The model for this church was H. H. Richardson's Trinity Church in Boston. Although Richardson's Trinity is a more compact composition and more suavely executed in its details, William Kauffman has deftly captured the intent of the design. The church's cross plan focuses attention on the sanctuary. Large pointed arches at the crossing are decorated

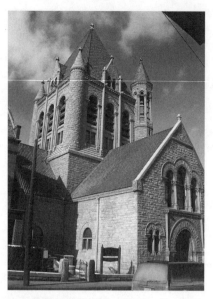

FA4 TRINITY UNITED PRESBYTERIAN CHURCH (FIRST PRESBYTERIAN CHURCH)

entrance. At the rear, the house opens to a garden off the living room and to a valley view of Chestnut Ridge, a view now compromised by the adjacent house. Neutra had advised the Parisers to buy the then inexpensive lot to preserve the vista, which he considered a critical component to human well-being. The large kitchen is a tour-de-force of attention to the little lauded ergonomics of cooking, storage, and cleanup without fuss. It contains a glassed breakfast area separated from the work space with cabinetry and a low book shelf, an area in turn leading to a screened porch adjacent to the garage and used for casual meals. Neutra designed six buildings in Pennsylvania between 1955 and 1969, and this is the only one in western Pennsylvania. The Parisers chose Neutra as their architect after seeing him on the cover of a 1949 *Time* magazine and reading about his work in a Museum of Modern Art catalogue.

with carved florets interspersed with floral fixtures designed to hold lightbulbs, which, at the time of building, would have been technological wonders. Details such as the carved mahogany end pieces on each curved oak pew and the mosaic floors in the vestibule add to the richness of the design. The windows, installed in 1895, are by Tiffany Glass and Decorating Company. They depict major events in Christ's life and, with the other small ornamental windows, light the sanctuary in an extraordinary way.

FA5 Pariser House

1959–1960, Richard Neutra. 27 Judith St.

Despite its mature shroud of plantings, this modern house, like many Neutra dwellings, instantly stands out from its suburban neighbors. Richard Neutra used walls of different heights and textures to differentiate the public space from the private spaces on the side elevations. A reddish-brown-stained board-and-batten wall with a short curve at its end effectively hides the garage opening on the west elevation. The small but effective gesture gently scoops up visitors to propel them to the entrance, where golden sandstone walls surround the recessed front door. The wall then steps forward to shield the long bedroom wing and the skylit hallway from the

FA6 House (Dr. Holbert J. and Beatrice Nixon House)

1948, H. Wesley "Hap" Altman Jr. 10 Ridgeview Dr.

Although from the street this house appears to be a one-story ranch house, it is one-and-one-half stories in height in the living room. There an east-facing window wall takes advantage of a magnificent view of Chestnut Ridge. The shallow gabled roof soars out over these windows, as does the roof on the north elevation, where it shelters a patio that overlooks the landscaped yard. The interior is distinguished by its linearity and detailing, including solid wood doors with stainless steel doorknobs, built-in furniture, and radiant heat in the floors. The house was designed by "Hap" Altman for his in-laws.

Many of the handsome post–World War II houses in Uniontown were designed by the Altman firm. H. Wesley "Hap" Altman Jr. (1916–1994) began practicing with his father, Harry W. Altman, in 1946. Both graduated from the University of Pennsylvania, Harry c. 1908 and Hap in 1940. Harry trained with Wallace Frost and Albert Kahn, and opened his Uniontown practice in 1909, where he designed the Central High School (1916; Church and Gallatin streets). The firm's third generation is Hap's son, Mark Nixon Altman, who began work after graduation and became managing partner in 1986. Over the years, the firm has completed dozens of schools, hospitals, public buildings, and private residences, including the Frazee house at 40 Ridgeview Road, and houses at 43 and 117 Belmont Circle. Houses designed by Hap Altman take full advantage of their natural sites and views. His work is best seen in the stone-sheathed houses he designed at 20, 40, and 50 Bailey Lane. The rectangular Robert W. Miller house of 1949 (50 Bailey Lane) is anchored to its site by an eight-foot-wide stone chimney, and its variegated sandstone is dressed and cut in long, narrow blocks. The low profile, ribbon windows, deep eaves, and flat roof are reminiscent of Frank Lloyd Wright's work. The living room's fourteen-foot-high wall of windows opens to a patio and a view of the rolling hills and Chestnut Ridge.

FA7 Mount Saint Macrina Retreat Center (Josiah V. Thompson House, "Oak Hill")

1903–1904, Ernest Woodyatt. 500 W. Main St. (U.S. 40)

Josiah Thompson commissioned Daniel H. Burnham to design his bank building in downtown Uniontown (FA3) and a mansion for his second wife, "Hunnie" Hawes. Burnham sent drawings for a Chicago residence by his deceased partner Charles Atwood, calling them in a July 1903 letter to Thompson, "the most exquisite ever made since a hundred and fifty years ago." Thompson rejected them, and Burnham, already overcommitted, suggested that he hire his nephew-in-law, fellow Chicagoan Ernest Woodyatt, to design a new mansion. The lavish Flemish bond, red brick house in a Classical Revival mode has an overscaled, semicircular, Ionic-columned portico facing south toward a wooded hillside and the National Road. A porte-cochere at the rear welcomes guests from the driveway. Stone quoins, splayed lintels, cornices, and balustrades define all the elevations; viewed from any side, each could be mistaken for the facade. The interior was designed to encourage circulation for the many social events hosted by the couple. The main rooms open off a large T-shaped hall furnished with oversized pieces and Tiffany floor lamps and light fixtures. Most of the original mahogany woodwork survives, but the wall coverings and fabrics have been replaced.

In 1915, after his 1913 divorce, Thompson's bank failed, and by 1917, he was bankrupt. He sold his holdings to Andrew Mellon's Piedmont Coal Company, which hired him as a salesman and allowed him to continue to live in the house. For the final two years of his life, the Sisters of St. Basil, a Byzantine Rite Greek Catholic order, owned the house and also consented to him living there. Today, they use the estate as a retreat center, nursing home, and school. At one time, the grounds of Oak Hill encompassed two thousand acres, and included a power plant, pumping station, racetrack, swimming pool, greenhouse, and stables, the last of these connected to the main house by a tunnel. Today, the order owns approximately one hundred acres. Also on the grounds and west of Oak Hill is the former Fox Hill (c. 1904), a smaller Colonial Revival brick house built for the Howell family and purchased for Andrew Thompson, Josiah's son. Its architect is unknown.

FA8 Searight's Tollhouse Museum

1835, Captain Richard Delafield. U.S. 40, 5 miles west of Uniontown

The former Searight's tollhouse is a small, red brick octagonal building with a one-story rectangular wing on the south elevation. Built by the U.S. Army Corps of Engineers, it was one of six tollhouses located every fifteen miles along the National Road between Pennsylvania's southern and western borders and was in use until 1905. Only two tollhouses remain; this one and another in Somerset County (SO15). Searight's, now a museum, was restored in 1966 under the supervision of the Pennsylvania Historical and Museum Commission and is listed on the National Register

FA7 MOUNT SAINT MACRINA RETREAT CENTER (JOSIAH V. THOMPSON HOUSE, "OAK HILL")

of Historic Places. The tollhouse was designed by Captain Richard Delafield, assistant engineer of the Army Corps of Engineers. He used noted British engineer and architect Thomas Telford's design for the tollhouses along the Holyhead Road (1819–1826) through Shropshire, England, later illustrated in *Atlas of the Life of Thomas Telford* (1838). This tollhouse has a two-story octagonal bay, which offers several angles for viewing the road. The neoclassical architectural details paid homage to the ancient ideals of government and democracy. By making the tollhouses large enough to live in, the corps' engineers hoped to attract responsible family men to run them.

FA8 SEARIGHT'S TOLLHOUSE MUSEUM

The buildings were auctioned for private ownership in 1877.

SHOAF

Shoaf is one of four company towns built between 1904 and 1917 in southwestern Fayette County by the Henry Clay Frick Coal and Coke Company. Although the Frick company owned many patch towns, most were built by various operators and then purchased by Frick. Shoaf was also the last operating small-size coke works in the nation and the best preserved when it closed in 1972. About thirty houses of the original forty remain. They line the 100 and 200 blocks of Shoaf Road and a parallel street above it, just west of the mine and coke works. Shoaf's drift mine No. 1 opened in 1902, and the company built the houses and a company store. The houses were sold to individual residents in the early 1950s, and the works were sold in 1958 to Max Nobel, who once every year relit a coke oven to celebrate the county's once great industry. More than three hundred ovens survive, the most intact

View of coke ovens at Shoaf, with larry cars (which carry coal from storage bins to the coke ovens) above.

group of beehive ovens in the region, consisting of one battery of double-block ovens and one battery of bank beehive ovens. The lorries, or coal cars, that delivered coal to the ovens from the hillside above still stand on their tracks. A Baltimore and Ohio rail line links Shoaf to other coke ovens in the lower Connellsville region. The surviving brick powerhouse, the supply house, and a machine shop date from c. 1905. The coal tipple was moved here by the Menallen Coke Company in 1963. Because they did not meet clean air standards, the coke ovens were required to burn out in 1972

FRIENDSHIP HILL

FA9 Friendship Hill (Albert Gallatin House)

1789–1791, with many additions. 1 Washington Pkwy., off PA 166

Friendship Hill represents life on the early frontier and during the coal boom years at the beginning of the nineteenth century. The house was commissioned by Swiss immigrant Albert Gallatin (1761–1849), who rose from local legislator to become secretary of the treasury under presidents Thomas Jefferson and James Madison. Gallatin reduced the national debt and arranged financing for the Louisiana Purchase, the Lewis and Clark expedition, and the building of the National Road. This rambling house was built by local craftsmen in five stages, three during Gallatin's forty-six-year tenancy, and two in the late nineteenth century. Gallatin built a modest side-hall plan brick house in 1789, with one large room on the first floor and one bedroom upstairs. After the death of his first wife and his involvement with national politics, he spent little time on this Fayette County estate. Following his second marriage, he added a two-story clapboarded addition in 1798, one room downstairs and one upstairs, to the north side of the original house. A second addition of 1821, built by Scots-Irishman Hugh Graham and supervised by one of the two sons

from his second marriage, Albert R. Gallatin, included a sandstone kitchen to the west and a grand two-over-two house of three bays to the northeast. He apparently was less than satisfied with the aesthetics of either, saying in an 1823 letter to his daughter Frances that "the outside of the house, with its porthole-looking windows has the appearance of Irish Barracks, whilst the inside ornaments are similar to those of a Dutch Tavern." In 1825, his family, tired of provincial life, moved east. Gallatin sold the house in 1832 to Swiss immigrant Albin Mellier and moved to New York City, where he remained active in business and politics. The Charles Speer family added a formal dining room and upstairs bedrooms in 1895 that linked the 1798 and 1821 additions. And between 1901 and 1903, a brick bedroom and servants quarters were added.

The National Park Foundation acquired the house in 1979, and it was restored by the National Park Service in 1984 to its early-nineteenth-century condition. Nearby coal mine tunnels have been filled to avoid subsidence (the sinking of land above an abandoned mine), and later alterations to the house were removed. The Park Service has incorporated museum exhibition spaces into the house with little disruption to its original outlines.

BROWNSVILLE AND VICINITY

Laid out in 1785 by Thomas Brown, Brownsville was a natural strategic point known then in the western counties as Redstone Old Fort. A major land to water transfer point for the westward journey, it was heavily used by early settlers traveling the Nemacolin Path (Front Street) and, later, the National Road (Market Street). After 1844, a series of locks and dams on the Monongahela River allowed nearly 300,000 passengers a year to set off upriver from

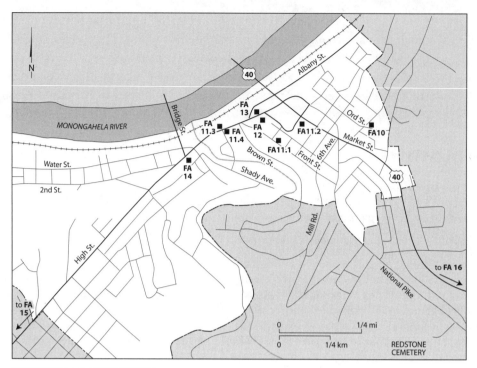

BROWNSVILLE AND VICINITY

Brownsville. Water access made Brownsville a center for boatbuilding, first
for keelboats and later for steamboats. It served the western frontier as a
commercial and industrial center during the National Road's heyday. After a
rail line between Pittsburgh and Philadelphia opened in 1852, Brownsville's
population peaked with just over 2,300 residents; it never reached that level
again. Instead, it stagnated for nearly thirty years, dependent on the transport
of coal and coke to Pittsburgh's foundries and mills between 1907 and 1930.

Brownsville's earliest buildings are several handsome stone houses, dating from the 1790s. They are located in the six square blocks of the Northside
neighborhood, a hilltop section adjacent to the major highway bridge carrying U.S. 40 across the Monongahela River. A brick commercial block built between 1815 and 1840 on the north side of Market Street between 4th and 5th
streets is a vernacular version of merchant shops and residences seen often
in such seaports as Baltimore. Nine churches (1845 to 1920) reflect the early
English, German, and Irish influences in this neighborhood, which survived
its time as outfitter to the westward migrants, and its later incarnation as the
middle-class residential area after commercial interests moved closer to the
river into the area known as "the Neck." This latter was named when a cause-
way was built to link the higher ground with the river plain and the bridge
crossing Dunlap's Creek. Later, landfill gave the area its present dimensions,
and the coal-hauling Monongahela Railway prompted an early-twentieth-
century building boom along this lower portion of Market Street.

FA10 St. Peter's Roman Catholic Church

1843–1846, W. R. Crisp. 300 Shaffner Ave.

The most surprising aspect of this church is how early it reflected the latest trend in English church design and for a mostly Irish congregation. Resembling most closely A. W. N. Pugin's St. Oswald's Roman Catholic Church in Liverpool, England (1839–1842), St. Peter's represents Pugin's ideals that a church should function well without artificial symmetry and that the medieval period represented the perfection of church architecture. W. R. Crisp, a draftsman in Thomas Ustick Walter's Philadelphia office in the 1830s, supervised construction. Perched on a hillside above the Monongahela River, the square central tower has a spire rising ninety feet and visible for several miles. Referring to the rough-hewn stonework in praising St. Peter's "unostentatious charm," architectural historian Talbot Hamlin wrote in *Greek Revival Architecture in America* (1944), "Hardly anywhere else have basically Gothic forms been so thoroughly Americanized." The church represents one of the first tangible symbols of Catholicism in southwestern Pennsylvania. The single nave interior is simple, but appears richly ornamented from the rough-hewn stone to the exposed rafters. A carved stone spiral staircase leading to the choir loft and an exquisite baptismal font in the southwest corner are further evidence

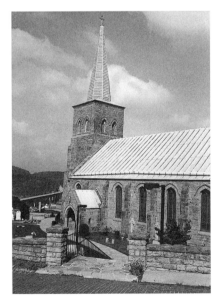

FA10 ST. PETER'S ROMAN CATHOLIC CHURCH

that a skilled practitioner was at work here. Stained glass windows represent the history of the Catholic Church since 1754.

FA11 Monongahela National Banks (Four Generations)

1812–1925. Front and Market sts.

To find buildings of four successive generations of an American bank, spanning two centuries, in one small town is remarkable. The first bank (FA11.1), at 221 Front Street, was built in 1812 only a block from the home of its first president, Jacob Bowman. It is a brick, three-bay, two-story house with a central entrance, similar to the other houses and shops along Front Street at the time. The bank's second building (FA11.2), at 320 Market Street and built in 1873 and in operation to 1900, is a large, Italianate two-story brick structure with round-arched windows and a pyramidal roof located on the National Road. The third generation (FA11.3), which dates to 1900 and is located at 39–41 Market Street in the river plain section of Brownsville called "the Neck," reflects the relocation of the commercial district here from the Northside neighborhood. This is a four-story, brick row building with a storefront at the first story and round-arched windows above, and, originally, it had a cupola on the roof. It is distinguished by red and pink terra-cotta trim and a pseudo-Palladian window on the second story. The storefront from this building has been reused as the facade of the Brownsville Public Library nearby. The final bank building (FA11.4), located on the east side at 46 Market Street and built in 1925, reflects the twentieth-century conception of a city bank; it was designed by a New York firm specializing in banks, Morgan French and Company. Sheathed in Indiana limestone and marked by forty-ton, paired Ionic columns, its size befits Beaux Arts ideals, popular for banks at that time.

FA12 Nemacolin Castle (Jacob Bowman House)

1789, with many additions. 136 Front St.

When Maryland merchant Jacob Bowman opened a trading post in the late eighteenth century, Brownsville was known as Redstone Old Fort. Bowman built a log house in 1789, and, as the family's fortunes increased in his

FA12 NEMACOLIN CASTLE (JACOB BOWMAN HOUSE), photo 1963

ing constructed of Flemish bond brickwork has the round-ended shape of an eighteenth-century clothing press iron. An addition was made to the east end of the building c. 1903. Its position on the National Road made it a popular office space. In 1990, the building was donated to a nonprofit group and became the Heritage Visitor Center, with a 1,500-square-foot museum on National Road topics.

FA14 Dunlap's Creek Bridge

1836–1839, Captain Richard Delafield. Market St. across Dunlap's Creek

This bridge is both a National Historic Civil Engineering Landmark and the oldest cast-iron bridge in the United States. It cost nearly seven times more than a wooden bridge to construct. The federal government was renovating the National Road (also called the Cumberland Road) to turn it over to the states for maintenance. As one of the largest inland ports in the country at the time, Brownsville was a starting point for traffic along the National Road and a busy boatbuilding town with skilled foundry workers. The bridge was heavily used and necessary to continued progress along the road. The U.S. Army Corps of Engineers procured more than 300,000 pounds of iron from Portsmouth, Ohio, and leased a foundry and its workers to make the 250 castings required. The foundry owner, English immigrant John Snowden, and engineer Richard Delafield, a West Point graduate trained in French engineering concepts, together represented "an American amalgamation of both the contemporary British and French engineering traditions," according to

various industries, grander and more idiosyncratic additions were made to the homestead. At its core is a chimney from the log house, a single room from the stone house that replaced it in 1805, and three rooms from the three-story stone house dating from 1822. When Jacob's grandson Nelson Bowman married in 1857, he enlarged the house, surrounding the stone portions with brick. This addition included a crenellated Gothic Revival turret, and draws on illustrations in Andrew Jackson Downing's popular pattern books. Between 1875 and 1880, a bracketed, gable-roofed study was added by the last Bowman family member to live here. The two c. 1859 brick towers, one Gothic Revival looking west to the Monongahela River and the other Italianate facing Brownsville's Northside neighborhood, prompted the family to call the house "Nemacolin Towers," after the Delaware Indian guide who had a cabin on nearby Dunlap's Creek in the 1700s. "Bowman's Castle," as it is locally known, is the architectural anchor for the surrounding residential neighborhood. As it grew from a rustic commercial establishment to a wealthy family's mansion, it encapsulates the various eras of Brownsville's growth. The house is open for tours.

FA13 Brownsville Heritage Visitor Center and Frank L. Melega Art Museum (Flatiron Building)

c. 1835; 1903; 1990 renovated, Albert L. Filoni for MacLachlan, Cornelius and Filoni. 69 Market St.

When built on this triangular sloping site, the Flatiron Building housed Brownsville's first post office and library. The three-story build-

FA13 BROWNSVILLE HERITAGE VISITOR CENTER AND FRANK L. MELEGA ART MUSEUM (FLATIRON BUILDING)

the Historic American Engineering Record survey of the bridge. Delafield was assisted by Lieutenant J. K. F. Mansfield. There were delays in the construction caused by decisions about which government body had jurisdiction, selection of the best location for the crossing, and uncooperative weather. The townspeople living on the south side of the creek won the decision about location, despite Delafield's warning that it would necessitate a sharp turn onto the covered bridge then crossing the Monongahela, and would create a traffic bottleneck, which it ultimately did. It is not a large bridge, spanning eighty feet across Dunlap's Creek, and is now almost concealed by two abutting twentieth-century buildings. A pair of sidewalks has been cantilevered from the sides since the 1920s, but the bridge remains a landmark for its material, design, and antiquity.

FA15 Penn-Craft

1937; 1946, William Macy Stanton, and others. Penncraft Rd. off PA 4020, 5.4 miles south of Brownsville

In the 1920s, when most of the coking operations that employed many county residents were consolidated and moved to Pittsburgh, a crushing economic depression began with unemployment as high as 30 percent in the nearby coalfields. The American Friends Service Committee (AFSC), the service branch of the Quakers, who were determined to give people a new way of life, hired architect William Stanton, a Quaker from Philadelphia, to design model subsistence-homestead communities. Stanton, architect for several Atlantic City hotels in the 1920s and meetinghouse restorations, also designed two communities for the Norris and Cumberland Homesteads Communities for the Tennessee Valley Authority; the latter most resemble Penn-Craft. Its fifty houses are arranged along four cul-de-sacs accessed from Penncraft Road, each occupying a one- to three-acre site. The rural settlement is distinct from neighboring coal patches and early river towns because it looks like a 1930s suburban housing development. Each family chose their floor plan from the five available designs and customized them. This custom design took more of the architect's time than the AFSC had antici-

FA15 PENN-CRAFT, knitting factory/community center

pated, so fifteen houses in the phase II addition of 1946 used floor plans from the Farm Security Administration's publication *Small Houses* (1939). The complex was designed around Isaiah N. Craft's original farmhouse purchased in 1937 and initially used as a community center; today it is a private home. Residents had a subsistence garden and were encouraged to work on the cooperative farm, the produce from which was sold in the cooperative store. They built a knitting factory in 1939, which was run by women and children during World War II; the stone building is now a community center. The cottages were built of stone quarried on an adjacent property by the prospective homeowners, who laid it themselves. Unlike most coal patch towns of the era, Penn-Craft's small stone houses had indoor bathrooms, garages, and cellars. So that community life could begin while the houses were under construction, Penn-Craft settlers built temporary wooden homes that were later converted to chicken coops. A few of the poultry houses remain.

Two-thirds of the community's present residents descend from the original families. Numerous additions to the original houses give the complex the suburban quality it has today. Penn-Craft was more an example of small house construction than a model of town planning. The AFSC has repeated its subsistence farming social experiment many times nationally and internationally. In 1989, the community was placed on the National Register of Historic Places.

FA16 Peter Colley Tavern

1796; 1842 addition. U.S. 40 near Brier Hill, 3.5 miles southeast of Brownsville

This three-bay stone inn was built by Peter and Hannah Colley along what was then the Nemacolin Path from Cumberland, Maryland, to Brownsville. The original eighteenth-century portion of the house is the quintessential stone house of the region, and was the centerpiece of the family's considerable holdings. It operated as a tavern from 1801 until 1824, when Peter retired seven years after the National Road replaced the earlier path. George, the youngest of the eleven Colley children, reopened the tavern in 1842, after adding the five-bay stone addition to the south.

The fourteen-room, L-shaped inn is one of the largest stone inns along the National Road and the oldest in Pennsylvania. The Colleys sold it in 1880, but the building was always used as a home in addition to its commercial functions. The Brier Hill Coke Company, which built a company town nearby, purchased it in 1902. The bank barn east of the house was built in 1848 using queenpost construction and no ridgepole. Tax records indicate that the house and barn were built by Welsh, English, and Scots-Irish masons and carpenters. The building has been abandoned for many years.

FAYETTE CITY VICINITY

FA17 Colonel Edward Cook House

1774–1776. 347 Cook Rd., 2 miles north of Fayette City

Edward Cook came to western Pennsylvania from Lancaster in eastern Pennsylvania in 1770, and began construction of this house two years later from limestone quarried on his property. It was one of the largest houses on the frontier, measuring fifty-eight feet in width and twenty-eight feet in depth. The stone, laid in a random pattern popular in eastern Pennsylvania, was intended to be stuccoed. The house has a central hall and four rooms on each floor, two larger rooms at the front (south) and two smaller chambers at the rear. Chimneys are interior end, and the chimney on the west elevation marks two fireplaces in a "turkey breast," or triangular, arrangement. Many of the double-sash windows retain their original glass, eight by eight on the upper story and twelve by eight on the first story. A one-story, one-room stone addition built before 1798 contains a twelve-and-

FA17 COLONEL EDWARD COOK HOUSE

a-half-foot-wide cooking fireplace. Cook, who served in the Revolutionary War, was a member of the Provincial Congress and counseled moderation during the 1794 Whiskey Rebellion. This house and its stone springhouse are extraordinary artifacts of the eighteenth century, and have been restored by Cook's descendants, who operate the neighboring farm from a large Colonial Revival red brick house and frame Pennsylvania barn.

PERRYOPOLIS AND VICINITY

Perryopolis lies on land purchased by George Washington in 1769. Washington made seven trips to western Pennsylvania over a period of forty-one years, and purchased thousands of acres, many through his close friend and agent William Crawford, who fought in the French and Indian and Revolutionary wars. Washington's lands were never as productive as he hoped, and when Crawford was killed in 1782, Washington leased and then finally sold his holdings near Perryopolis in 1795 to Colonel Israel Shreve. Thomas and Nathan Hersey, Samuel Shreve, and Thomas Burns laid out the town of Perryopolis in 1814, with Independence, Liberty, Union, and Social streets as the spokes of the wheel. A one-story, one-bay, gable-roofed stone bank (1816; 312 Liberty Street) remains from this period. An example of the area's early building types is the reconstructed log Gue house (c. 1820; 1976 rebuilt; 311 Independence Street).

The area had abundant natural resources, including waterpower, iron ore, coal, and timber. Streams provided power for grist and fulling mills; William Searight's simple, stone fulling mill (1815; Strawn Road) remains on Washington Run. In the 1990s, George Washington's gristmill on Layton Road near the Youghiogheny River was reconstructed using prison labor for the stone foundation and Amish carpenters for the waterwheel and its housing. The farms surrounding Perryopolis gradually gave way to coal mines and patch housing. Similar frame patch houses lining the road leading to Perryopolis from PA 51 are a remnant of the Jameson Coke Company town. South of Perryopolis, Star Junction had one of the largest runs (999) of beehive coke ovens in the county. Several red brick mining buildings remain. In the small commercial center of Perryopolis, a local miner, Mike Karolcik, built a Craftsman-inspired red brick and glazed terra-cotta combined theater, bowling alley, butcher shop, and apartment building in 1921 (115–117 S. Liberty Street). A World War II–era housing development southeast of Perryopolis is one of hundreds commissioned by the federal government during that conflict.

Nearby, Layton Bridge and Tunnel (Layton Road at the Youghiogheny River), built in 1899 by the A. and P. Roberts Company and Pencoyd Iron Works, is a rare nineteenth-century survivor. The pin-connected steel bridge has an 811-foot Pratt half-through truss, with the deck raised well above the bottom chords. The bridge's two main spans rest on ashlar piers and lead directly into a one-lane tunnel exiting to Layton Road and Perryopolis.

FA18 Samuel Cope House

1839. PA 201 at TWP 494, 3.5 miles west of Perryoplis

FA18 SAMUEL COPE HOUSE

The Cope house incorporates elements of Gothic Revival and Greek Revival. The T-shaped intersecting gable plan of the brick, two-story house, and the bracketed porch are typical of a Gothic Revival cottage, and the attic window on the facade has a pointed arch. Greek Revival features are at the entrance with in antis piers and the transom and sidelights that surround the door. The piers have stepped capitals to complement the geometry of the porch's surround. Three remaining frame outbuildings indicate that the house was part of a working farm.

Nearby, a two-and-one-half-story, three-bay stone house (c. 1800; 286 Cope Road)

was the original homestead of John Cope, the West Chester, Pennsylvania, Quaker who first came to Fayette County in 1785 and helped establish the Providence Meeting that was in session from 1793 to 1880.

FA19 Providence Quaker Cemetery and Chapel

1895. PA 4036 and PA 4038, 2.5 miles southwest of Perryopolis

This small, rectangular, gable-roofed building commemorates the home of the Providence Meeting of the Society of Friends. The meetinghouse is on the site of a log meetinghouse of 1789 that was replaced by a 1793 stone meetinghouse. By 1893, the stone meetinghouse was in disrepair, and its ruins were used to construct this three-bay structure that has exterior chimneys at the gable ends. The central entrance leads into a single large room that provided a chapel for burials and a refuge for mourning relatives. The stone is laid irregularly, and there are large, almost rudimentary, quoins at the corners. A metal standing-seam roof shelters the structure. The barred windows originally were covered by wooden shutters. The cemetery contains the remains of approximately five hundred Society of Friends members, many in unmarked graves. The site has a dramatic view of the countryside.

DAWSON AND VICINITY

FA20 James Cochran House

1890. Main St. at Railroad St.

James Cochran's two-and-one-half-story, frame Queen Anne house dominates the streetscape of tiny Dawson. The house has multiple turrets, porches, a horseshoe-shaped recessed porch hood, and faceted chimneys. Surrounded by workers' houses, the building reflects the philosophy that the owner should live near the works. James and his son Philip G. Cochran owned the nearby Washington and New Florence mines and the Jimtown and Clarissa coke works. The borough benefited from, or at least witnessed, the success of their endeavors in the fairgrounds, the United Methodist Church (FA21), and the manager's houses, all built from Cochran family largesse. The former First National Bank (1897; 200–206 Main Street) housed the offices of Cochran's Washington Coal and Coke companies. Its gabled wall dormers, reminiscent of the Cochran house, rhythmically culminate in a rounded turret at the corner entrance.

FA21 Philip G. Cochran United Methodist Church

1926–1927, Thomas Pringle. Howell St. at Griscom St.

Scottish-born Thomas Pringle (1881–1951) came to Pittsburgh in 1903, attended the Carnegie Institute of Technology, and worked with several of the best local firms, including Alden and Harlow and Janssen and Abbott. Sarah Cochran (see FA22) commissioned Pringle in 1926 to build this Gothic Revival church to honor her deceased husband and son. The tower at the crossing of the nave and transept is marked with a smooth spire with small lancet dormers and a pent-skirted base. Exterior walls of variously sized sandstone are textured by adze marks, and the roof is covered in irregularly shaped slate shingles. Ralph Adams Cram's book *American Church Building of Today* (1929) features four illustrations of the church on pages 225–28. The parish building attached at the southwest has the half timbering and leaded glass windows characteristic of domestic Gothic architecture.

FA22 Linden Hall (Sarah Boyd Moore Cochran House)

1911–1913, W. G. Wilkins Company, with Joseph Franklin Kuntz. 432 Linden Hall Rd., 5.9 miles northwest of Dawson

Linden Hall, named for the trees once lining the driveway, was built for Sarah B. Cochran,

FA20 JAMES COCHRAN HOUSE

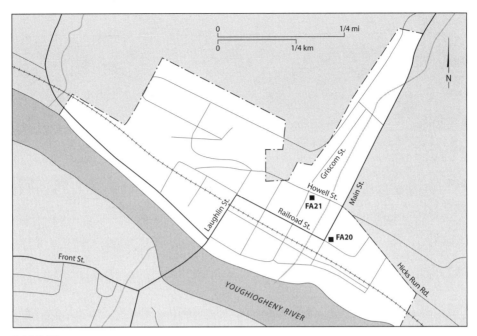

DAWSON

widow of coal and coke magnate Philip Galley Cochran. Cochran was the son of "Little
Jim" Cochran, who ran the largest coal and
coke operation in Fayette County in the mid-
nineteenth century. Following the deaths
of her husband and son, Sarah traveled in
Europe and Asia before returning to Fayette
County to continue the family business. She
hired Pittsburgh architect and industrial designer Joseph Kuntz to build a monument to
her travels. The house, shaped like a faceted
crescent, has several Tudor Revival elements,
including a random-laid limestone first story,
stuccoed second story, clipped gables, heavy
bargeboards, and massive brick chimneys.
The wings have gabled projections at the intersections, and hipped-roof dormers line the
roofs. Sixty Italian stonemasons worked the
local limestone used on the thirty-five-room
house. Mrs. Cochran had the simple adage

"East, West, Home's Best" etched above her
front door. Stained glass family crests from
the estates she visited adorn the conservatory.
The gingko trees, hydrangea, and hollyhocks
that adorned her garden are re-created on the
Tiffany Studio windows in the stairway landing. The house has an Aeolian pipe organ, central vacuum system, twenty-seven fireplaces,
and an Otis elevator. The 785-acre estate had
its own generator, gas wells, and fire-fighting
equipment. East of the estate house and north
of Dawson, the Cochran fairgrounds have several frame exhibition sheds, barns, and silos
(PA 1002 and PA 819). After Sarah Cochran
died in 1936, the home had a sequence of
owners until purchased by the United Steelworkers of America, who restored it in 1976
and opened it the following year as part of a
resort, including a modern motel, swimming
pool, and golf course.

CONNELLSVILLE AND VICINITY

Connellsville, on the east bank of the Youghiogheny River, was laid out in
1790 as 180 quarter-acre lots by surveyor and land agent Virginian Zachariah
Connell; it was incorporated in 1806. Initially, Connellsville's growth centered on the west bank village of New Haven, the location of Isaac Meason's
large woolen factory and paper mill. In 1812, a wooden bridge connected
Connellsville to New Haven and the two communities were combined in

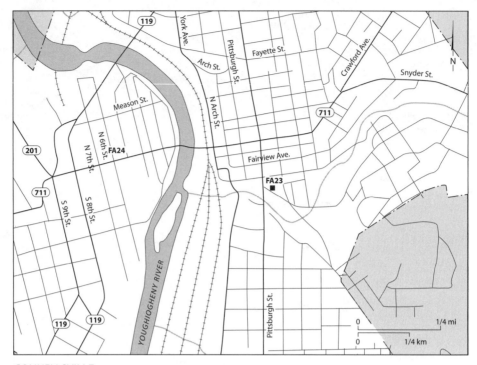

CONNELLSVILLE

1909. In 1833, an English immigrant named Nicholls supervised construction of the first beehive coke oven in Fayette County on Connell Run. It used the pure, low-sulfur coal that distinguishes the area. Connellsville became a major site in the history of local coal mining. The need to transport coal brought the railroads. Both the Baltimore and Ohio and the Pittsburgh and Lake Erie railroads served Connellsville after 1883. Today, part of their rail bed from McKeesport has become a portion of the Great Allegheny Passage rails to trails system. The heyday of Connellsville is reflected in its large brick houses dating from the 1890s, substantial brick and stone–faced banks, and nearly a dozen churches. The St. Emory Hungarian Roman Catholic Church, now Faith Bible Church (1904–1905; 425 S. Arch Street), was designed by Titus de Bobula, and while it has undergone some unsympathetic alterations, it is a rare work by this idiosyncratic architect. The high-rise Aaron Building (1906; 139 N. Pittsburgh Street), a popular furniture store until 1978, has an unusual recessed domed entrance.

FA23 Carnegie Free Library

1903, J. M. McCollum. 299 S. Pittsburgh St.

Connellsville's Carnegie Library is one of the more than 1,600 Carnegie-endowed libraries in the United States. Although it was built before Carnegie's design review requirement, it nonetheless has the restrained classical quali-

ties so admired by his New York foundation. The square-shaped building is faced with Ohio buff stone and has a pediment above the central entrance on the west facade. Windows throughout are double sash and separated on the second story by columned pilasters. While only two stories on a raised basement in height, the building seems taller due to its hillside site. The second story housed the auditorium. A large square chimney on the north elevation vented the coal-fired furnace. The interior has dark woodwork, but is not highly ornamented. The rather severe building is surrounded by a small city park and several of Connellsville's many churches, Trinity Evangelical Lutheran Church (1908–1911, J. C. Fulton Architect; 126 E. Fairview Avenue), First Christian Church (1897–1898; 212 S. Pittsburgh Street), First Baptist Church (1900; 301 S. Pittsburgh Street), and St. John's Evangelical Lutheran Church (1901; 144 E. South Street).

FA24 Youghiogheny Station Glass and Gallery (Pittsburgh and Lake Erie Railroad [P&LE] Passenger Station)

1911. 900 W. Crawford Ave.

The deeply overhanging eaves and low hipped roof of this depot are typical of train stations throughout the United States. What sets this station apart is its blue-green tile roof, central square tower decorated with blind arcades, brick laid in English bond, recessed brick panels, and bays defined by a stone water table. The tower's top floor was used as a teletype room and originally gave access to a bridge connecting to elevated tracks north of the station. The interior's marble flooring, wainscoting, and oak woodwork appealed to passengers. Ridership peaked in Connellsville between 1912 and 1939. Lack of revenue caused the building to be sold in 1939. The P&LERR Freight Station c. 1900, a single-story clapboard rectangular building with the requisite overhanging eaves, stands nearby at the intersection of PA 119 and PA 201.

FA25 Abraham Overholt and Company Distillery

1899, with additions. Youghiogheny River at Broad Ford off PA 1038, 2 miles northwest of Connellsville

Although only the remnants of the Abraham Overholt and Company Distillery remain, the buildings evoke a sense of the size and scale of the distillery, which operated here from 1855 until the Old Overholt label was transferred to the Jim Beam Company in the early 1960s. Visible today are buildings dating from 1899 to the 1940s, including the five-story brick boiler house and engine room with round and segmental arches, corbeled cornices, and pilaster strips; a 1930s yellow brick, three-story office building; a six-story grain elevator complex; and warehouses in varying states of disrepair. One year before Abraham Overholt's grandson Henry Clay Frick began work as an office boy at the distillery in 1868, he began investing in the local coke industry. Adjacent to the distillery along the western shore of Galley Run are one hundred coke ovens dating from the 1870s, built into the hillside by Frick. Barely visible even in winter when the vegetation dies back, it is one of the longest runs of coke ovens accessible by car in Fayette County. The proximity of the coke ovens and distillery tangibly encapsulates the early career of Henry Clay Frick.

FA26 Newmyer House and Barn

c. 1794 barn; 1820 house. 316 Richey Rd. (PA 1027), 5.5 miles north of Connellsville

This is one of the region's earliest stone barns called a Pennsylvania barn, not for its location

FA23 CARNEGIE FREE LIBRARY, photo 1989

FA24 YOUGHIOGHENY STATION GLASS AND GALLERY (PITTSBURGH AND LAKE ERIE RAILROAD [P&LE] PASSENGER STATION)

FA26 NEWMYER HOUSE AND BARN

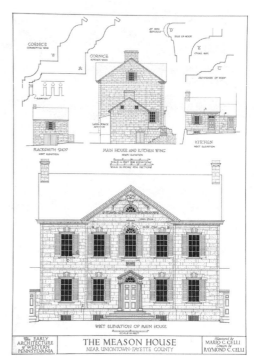

FA27 ISAAC MEASON HOUSE (MOUNT BRADDOCK), elevation, c. 1933

but for its architectural attributes: a forebay and a banked entrance. Also called a Sweitzer (Pennsylvania German variant of Schweitzer) or Swiss barn, this type was commonly built into a hillside by German farmers in the eighteenth and nineteenth centuries and given a saltbox roof. This barn has an earthen ramp, projecting frame forebay, and simple slit ventilators in its stone side walls. An interesting hybrid, the roof framing is English, while the barn shape is Germanic. As was typical, the barn was more substantial than the original farmhouse, which was a log house rather than the five-bay brick house on a raised basement found on the premises today.

FA27 Isaac Meason House (Mount Braddock)

1802, Adam Wilson. 135 Cellurale Rd., 5.5 miles southwest of Connellsville

The Isaac Meason House has a Palladian plan of wonderfully lavish scale that reflects the wealth and sophistication of one of western Pennsylvania's leading early industrialists, as well as his attraction to the styles then prevalent in his native Virginia. Meason was likely aware of similarly detailed houses in eighteenth-century Philadelphia, New York City, and Boston. He commissioned architect-builder Adam Wilson from the British Isles to design the rigidly symmetrical house of sandstone that demonstrates his elite status, despite his isolation on the frontier. This is one of two dressed ashlar houses designed in a seven-part Palladian plan remaining in the United States (the other is Mount Airy in Richmond County, Virginia). The 20,000-acre slave-owning plantation of which this mansion was the center began the long history of iron production and coal extraction in the region. A summer kitchen, blacksmith shop, and barn remain on the four acres comprising the present estate; no slave houses survive. The two-and-one-half-story house is flanked by small one-story passages (hyphens) leading to single-story end pavilions. Two unattached dependencies north and south of the pavilions create the seven-part plan and flank the encircling carriage road. At the center of the symmetrical facade, a trio of arches rises from the fanlight over the entrance to the arched second-story window. A fanlight in the central pediment is highlighted by foliated ornament. The formal planning of the knoll on which the house sits reinforces its prominence.

OHIOPYLE AND VICINITY

From the Native American "ohiopehhele," which means "white, frothy water," Ohiopyle was laid out in 1868 as the town of Pile Falls by Andrew Stewart, whose family held the land formed by a large loop in the Youghiogheny River.

As it rounds the curve, the river drops ninety feet in less than two miles. It was hoped that the area could be developed for its hydraulic power, but its steep banks and turbulent rapids prevented the large-scale industrial development that occurred farther north. During the 1850s, the falls powered small mills for flour, tanning, and lumber; one of the mills manufactured barrel staves. A post office opened in 1856, and the first hotel opened in 1858 near the gristmill. Following the opening of the Pittsburgh, Washington and Baltimore Railroad (later the Baltimore and Ohio [B&O]) in 1871, Stewart opened a hotel in his large farm building, naming it Ohio Pile House. Subsequently, four more hotels and several frame houses were built, and in 1880, the town was renamed Falls City. The borough was renamed Ohiopyle in 1891 to avoid confusion with another Falls City stop on the rail line. During this time, the B&O shipped lumber and other wood products from the surrounding farms and lumber camps. The simple frame train station built in this era remains as a visitor information center (c. 1880; 7 Sheridan Street).

The Ohiopyle United Methodist Church, built in 1893 for a congregation that was formed in 1840, is a white frame cross-gable church with Queen Anne windows (691 Mill Run Road). A square tower with a spire marks the entrance, which is similar to white frame Methodist churches in Greene County.

Since 1971, the area has been a trailhead for hiking paths that cross several state parks, including Ferncliff Park, Keister Park at Cucumber Falls, and Ohiopyle State Park, covering 18,719 acres. Enthusiasts of whitewater rafting, hiking, biking, and nature trails enjoy the rushing rapids, waterfalls, picturesque rocks, wooded valleys and gorges, and rhododendron thickets in the summer months.

FA28 Fallingwater

1934–1937, Frank Lloyd Wright. PA 381 S, 4.7 miles northeast of Ohiopyle

Fallingwater is considered the most important American house since Monticello and one of the most important buildings of the twentieth century. It is the dramatic synthesis of a remote natural site, innovative design, and dynamic relationship between architect and patron. The house was built between 1934 and 1937 as a weekend retreat for department store owner Edgar J. Kaufmann, his wife, Liliane, and son, Edgar. Frank Lloyd Wright cantilevered the house over Bear Run's waterfall on a tract of wooded mountain land formerly used as the Kaufmann Department Store's employee summer camp. He mimicked the local layered rock strata with quarried sandstone defined by smooth concrete cantilevers separated by plate glass and steel. A boulder near the waterfall was incorporated into the basement walls of the house to make a rugged hearth for the living room fireplace. A canopy, guest house, and servant's quarters extend like an outstretched arm up the hillside behind the main portion of the house. Wright's internationally renowned design gave the Kaufmanns an intimate union with nature and the waterfall they loved. Forty years after Fallingwater's completion, the Western Pennsylvania Conservancy, given the house by Edgar Kaufmann Jr., commissioned furniture designer Paul Mayen to design a visitors' center relating to the house, but not conflicting with it. Mayen worked with architects Curry, Martin and Highberger to build a concrete, cedar, and glass design raised above the ground and ecologically mindful. Its trio of pavilions houses a restaurant, museum shop, and permanent exhibition space.

FA28 FALLINGWATER

Near the entrance to Fallingwater, on the east side of PA 381, two older Kaufmann barns were adapted as sustainable offices and a community center by Bohlin Cywinski Jackson for the Conservancy. The reuse was given a Green Design Citation and awarded the Pittsburgh Chapter of the American Institute of Architects 2005 Silver Medal as an extraordinary work of architecture. Further information on Fallingwater can be found in the numerous publications on this house.

FA29 KENTUCK KNOB/HAGAN HOUSE, with I. N. and Bernardine Hagan at the entrance, photo 1985

FA29 KENTUCK KNOB/HAGAN HOUSE, photo 1985

FA29 Kentuck Knob/Hagan House

1954–1956, Frank Lloyd Wright. 644 Kentuck Rd., 3.2 miles northwest of Ohiopyle

Kentuck Knob represents a handful of customized houses the architect designed that drew from his Usonian model. Bernadine Hagan, in her 2005 memoir, *Kentuck Knob*, described Wright's instruction for choosing their house site: use land no one else wanted. She preferred to be on the knob since she would often be alone in the house and wanted to see visitors arriving. Wright said, "My clients are either perchers or nesters, and you are perchers" (p. 8). This house is the mature culmination of Wright's modular designs based on an equilateral triangle. The half-hexagon-shaped house angles around a west-facing courtyard, blending comfortably into the contours of the land. The anchor of the design is a hexagonal core of native stone that rises from the long, low profile of the copper roof at the intersection of the living room and bedroom wings. The cantilevered cypress eaves have hexagonal openings that allow the low rays of the winter sun to penetrate the interior, while blocking the higher angle of the summer sun. Wright crafted the interior finishes and built-in furniture from tidewater red cypress. The Hagans, who visited Wright's Fallingwater, owned by their business friends the Kaufmanns, also purchased Hans Wegner and George Nakashima furniture. The present owners, Lord and Lady Palumbo, bought the house and seventy-nine forested acres from the Hagans in 1985, and opened it to the public in 1996. They have added acreage and over three dozen modern sculptures to the grounds.

FARMINGTON VICINITY

FA30 Nemacolin Woodlands Resort and Spa

1960; 1987 Chateau LaFayette, Rothschild Architects and DRS/Hundley Kling Gmitter; 2003–2004 Falling Rock Hotel, David R. Merritt. 1001 LaFayette Dr., north of U.S. 40, 1.4 miles southeast of Farmington

The nineteenth-century inns along the National Road were joined by the twentieth-century Nemacolin Woodlands Resort and Spa when it opened in 1997. What began as Willard Rockwell's 1,759-acre hunting lodge, wildlife preserve, and 26-room corporate getaway of 1960 was transformed in 1987 by Joseph A. Hardy Sr., owner of 84 Lumber, into a 2,800-acre, four-star resort dominated by the 124-room extravaganza Chateau LaFayette, which was inspired by the Ritz Hotel in Paris. Visible over the treetops from the National Road, the five-story mansard-roofed building is one of the largest projects ever sheathed in glass-fiber reinforced concrete (GFRC), tinted to mimic limestone. Architectural details of the GFRC were poured into molds to achieve the decorative effect of carved stone. The product is said to age like stone, but drip edges were added to protect the material from water runoff. Falling Rock, a forty-two-room boutique hotel on the eighteenth green of the Pete Dye–designed golf course Mystic Rock, was designed by architect David Merritt of Maine as an homage to Frank Lloyd Wright. The stone and stucco hotel has carving and details reminiscent of Fallingwater and Kentuck Knob, including cherry wood and triangular window projections. Golf, spa and equestrian facilities, and skiing keep a year-round clientele busy. An airstrip on the grounds allows visitors to avoid the ninety-minute drive from Greensburg or Pittsburgh.

FA30 NEMACOLIN WOODLANDS RESORT AND SPA

In the hilly terrain of western Pennsylvania, road building takes on an almost mythic quality. Native Americans used narrow pathways along ridges and through natural passes, trails often first blazed by large animals like the buffalo. Consequently, the path from the Upper Potomac River to the Ohio River was named for a chieftain and a local tribe: the Nemacolin or the Mingo Path. George Washington and his Virginia militiamen used it in 1754 to establish British rule at Pittsburgh's Point. General Edward Braddock expanded the road, using legions of axmen to fell trees and heavy wagons to mark the trail. The road was then named Braddock's Road. Yet none of these paths was paved, and even Braddock's Road was little more than wagon tracks through the forest.

THE CENTURY INN, 2175 EAST NATIONAL PIKE, SCENERY HILL, WASHINGTON COUNTY, IN 1997. OPENED AS STEPHEN HILL'S STONE TAVERN IN 1794, THE BUILDING IS ONE OF THE OLDEST ALONG THE NATIONAL ROAD, AND ACTUALLY PREDATES THE ROAD ITSELF.

Western Pennsylvania's participation in the Whiskey Rebellion of 1794 showed that the frontier needed to be tied more closely to the eastern coastal cities. During Thomas Jefferson's presidency, both he and his secretary of the treasury, Albert Gallatin, who owned property in Fayette County, urged Congress to fund a road connecting the two regions. The National Road, begun in 1806, three years after repeal of the whiskey tax, took five years to build, and, by 1852, stretched over six hundred miles from Cumberland, Maryland, to Vandalia, Illinois. The sixty-six-foot-wide right-of-way had a twenty-foot-wide graveled portion, and was mostly built by Irish laborers.

The first section from Cumberland to Brownsville, Fayette County, opened in 1817, and by 1818, reached Wheeling, West Virginia. While the National Road was the first federally funded highway and the only highway built entirely by the federal government, its maintenance became too burdensome. In 1822, President James Monroe decided that the road's operation must be turned over to the states through which it passed. Pennsylvania refused to agree until repairs were made, which took the federal government thirteen years. Meanwhile, federal employees built tollhouses with large iron gates crossing the road to stop traffic. Two of these early tollhouses survive: Searight's in Fayette County (FA8) and at Addison in Somerset County (SO15), but neither retains its gate. What does remain are ten of the three-foot-tall, two-sided, cast-iron mile markers first placed along the road in the 1830s by the commonwealth. In 1982, fiberglass duplicates of the obelisk-shaped markers replaced the missing signposts along the north side of the road.

Traffic along the National Road waxed and waned as methods of transportation evolved. In the 1850s, traffic to Pittsburgh shifted from the road to the railroad, but road use picked up again in the 1880s, when coal mining grew to feed the burgeoning steel industry. When automobile touring became popular, the National Road was named part of the National Old Trails Road in 1912. In 1925, it was designated U.S. 40, part of the federal system of interstate highways. After 1956, modern interstate highways such as I-70 replaced the older two-lane versions. But nothing can replace the unique collection of forts, inns, tollhouses, gas stations, tourist cabins, and pike towns along the National Road.

FA31 Mount Washington Tavern

1827–1828. 1 Washington Pkwy., off U.S. 40,
1.2 miles northwest of Farmington

The Mount Washington Tavern was one of the largest inns on the National Road. Built by Judge Nathaniel Ewing of Uniontown, it was named for George Washington, who owned this land until 1799. It was the site of the battle of Great Meadows, Washington's first major battle and only defeat, and today is part of Fort Necessity National Battlefield. The tavern was a luxury inn, or a stagecoach inn, as opposed to a wagon stand built to accommodate drovers, and was run by the Sampey family to accommodate travelers on the Good Intent Stagecoach Line. It has a typical five-bay facade with a handsome doorway surmounted by an elliptical fanlight. Four windows in the gable ends light each of the first-story rooms and the hallways above. The seven guest rooms on the second floor open into a central hall that runs parallel to the facade, unlike most five-bay houses in the area, which have four rooms and a hall perpendicular to the facade; the tavern's scheme allowed more rooms in the available space. The Flemish bond brickwork on both the north facade and the east elevation, which is the first elevation seen by most travelers, and handsome bridged chimneys at each gable end distinguish the inn. The pretensions of Judge Ewing overreached the capabilities of his builders, as several details reveal, for instance, the fanlight's arch was laid without using pie-shaped bricks.

An even earlier inn two-and-one-half miles to the west, the Stone House restaurant (1822, 1909; 3023 National Pike, U.S. 40) has undergone several large additions to give it the appearance of a Colonial Revival house, including a single-story porch across the facade. It was originally known as the Fayette Springs Hotel.

SUMMIT

FA32 Summit Inn Resort (Summit Hotel)

1906–1908, J. Edward Keirn. 101 Skyline Dr.,
south of U.S. 40

This hotel, designed with Spanish Mission exterior details, became a favorite of automobile travelers for its dramatic views and healthful mountain air. Wide porches, some now fenestrated for dining spaces, take advantage of these splendid views. The gabled entrance is flanked by square, pyramidal-roofed towers with round-arched windows. The lobby, dominated by a grand cypress staircase, contains Craftsman woodwork, stained glass windows, and a massive stone fireplace. The 800-acre grounds include the original carriage house, barn, and staff dormitory.

JUMONVILLE

FA33 Jumonville Methodist Training Center (Soldier's Orphan School)

1874, 1941. 887 Jumonville Rd. (PA 2021)

Now occupied as a Methodist summer camp, this 275-acre site on Chestnut Ridge was named for the ensign killed in 1754 when George Washington and his troops surprised a party of French soldiers at the start of the French and Indian War. The site was used later as an orphanage and school for Civil War soldiers' children until 1908, then as a summer hotel until 1941. In the 1870s, the orphanage and school moved to this site from Uniontown with about 150 children ages three to sixteen. Several of the surrounding buildings remain from this period, including the stone office called Fleming Lodge and the stone Ann Murphy Building to the east. The stone chapel of 1882 was dedicated as a Lutheran church. In 1972, it was enlarged slightly, changed to a nondenominational space, and then renamed for coke operator Harry Whyel, who donated the entire property to the Methodists for use as a camp. The other camp buildings, primarily frame, were built during the late 1940s and 1950s with periodic updates.

The idea to erect an enormous cross on Dunbar's Knob (2,480 feet above sea level) east of the camp was first suggested in 1942. Louis C. Steiner, of the Latrobe Foundry and Machine Company, donated the material in

1950 to make the over sixty-foot-high steel-plated cross, which has twelve-foot-long arms supported by an interior armature. The six-foot-deep foundation for the cross is made up of 183 tons of concrete. Illuminated at night, the cross is visible throughout the valley to the west. Warren "Bud" Parkins was the architect, and H. M. Logan of Philadelphia, the project engineer. Attempts to landscape around the base of the cross have not survived the harsh winters on the knob, and the cross itself has been the victim of vandals. As a result, today its base is surrounded by a chain-link fence.

HOPWOOD

Located on the National Road (U.S. 40) four miles east of Uniontown, Hopwood was named Woodstock when settled in 1791. It was renamed Monroe in 1816 after a visit from President James Monroe, and received its present appellation in 1881 to honor its founder, John Hopwood from Virginia, an aide-de-camp to George Washington. Hopwood patented 450 acres of land at the foot of Chestnut Ridge and recorded a town plan for 400 quarter-acre lots. He deeded property for an academy of higher learning. When the proposed route for the National Road did not correspond to the main street of Woodstock, John's son Moses laid out a new section and made the name change of 1816. The village served as a resting stop before the ascent of Chestnut Ridge, and at one time, had seven inns to accommodate acres of wagons and animals overnight. Six gray sandstone buildings dating from 1816 to 1839 were houses, inns, or stores that served the National Road. The first building upon entering Hopwood from the east is now the fire station (1818; National Pike at Paul Street). It is two stories in height, with a tablet reading "William Morris, September the 7th—1818." At 1208 National Pike is the former Monroe Tavern c. 1825, and at 1187 National Pike, a restaurant is located in the former Moses Hopwood Tavern c. 1816. The Benjamin Hayden House (1225 Main Street) on the north side of the road is now Dean's Barber Shop, and two stone houses in the same block at 1223 (built in 1823) and 1213 National Pike complete the ensemble of stone houses from the early nineteenth century.

The two-and-one-half-story rambling James R. Barnes house at the southeastern edge of Hopwood blends Colonial Revival with Shingle Style elements and is surrounded by a low cobblestone wall and the remnants of a garden. It was built in 1906–1907 by one of Josiah V. Thompson's partners, who lost his fortune with Thompson's bankruptcy a decade later.

GREENE COUNTY

Greene County, at the southwest corner of Pennsylvania, has been a crossroads for millennia. Round stockaded villages of prehistoric tribes preceded the Shawnee and Delaware, who later encountered the early English and French explorers. Colonial British settlement began in the mid-eighteenth century after the last major Native American uprising. Virginians and Marylanders moved into the area with their slaves, seeking to extend the plantation system through the Monongahela River valley and to claim the area as a Virginia county. Virginia encouraged settlement by offering larger land patents for lower prices than Pennsylvania and by sending troops to fend off Native American attacks. When Greene County was officially declared a part of Pennsylvania in 1784, the 1780 law limiting slavery in Pennsylvania prompted many of the area's southern families to move to Kentucky. The John B. Gordon House (GR7) is an excellent example of a Virginia farm whose family chose to remain. Greene County was formed in 1796 and named for Nathanael Greene, one of George Washington's generals during the Revolutionary War; a statue of Greene stands atop the courthouse in Waynesburg (GR1).

Greene County's landscape is breathtaking: ridges, valleys, and streams contribute to the wild natural beauty. Creeks in the eastern two-thirds of the county drain into the Monongahela River, while those in the west flow through the panhandle of West Virginia into the Ohio River. The Monongahela River on Greene County's eastern border acted as a major highway for the developing country, especially after 1856 when locks and dams could maintain a constant water level to provide longer shipping periods. Several older houses oriented to the river's edge provide evidence that Greene County's river towns preceded the canalization of the river and served as early trading centers. Because of the hilly topography, transportation has often been problematic in Greene County, although certain parts of present-day PA 218 and PA 18 have been in continuous use since before European contact. Seven late-nineteenth- and early-twentieth-century wooden covered bridges (GR14), many of which are rebuilt and maintained by local landowners, facilitated transportation; an annual festival throughout the county celebrates their survival.

In 1807, the first glassworks was founded at Greensboro and the industry operated until the Civil War. Later, locally made salt-glazed stoneware Greensboro and New Geneva crocks were shipped nationwide via the Monongahela, Ohio, and Mississippi rivers. During the mid-1800s, livestock farming, primarily sheep, was the main source of revenue for Greene County. By 1840, there were nine fulling mills and four woolen manufacturers, all now demolished. Greene and Washington counties together continue to have the largest number of sheep of any county in Pennsylvania, although today's numbers are greatly reduced. Poor transportation systems in the early twentieth century, cheap imported wool, and a reduction in demand for wool all contributed to the industry's decline.

Below the tree-covered hillsides of farms and small villages lies the greatest concentration of natural gas pipelines and coal mines in western Pennsylvania. The coal reserves in Greene County alone exceed all the coal in the remainder of the state. The largest underground mine in the United States, the Bailey and Enlow Fork Mine owned by Consolidation Coal, is located near Wind Ridge. Bobtown and Nemacolin are model coal patch towns. Greene County's gas industry began with a well drilled at Rice's Landing in 1860, only one year after the discovery of oil at Drake's Well in Venango County. By 1906, over 1,300 gas and oil wells had been drilled in Greene County. However, the large-scale discovery of oil in Texas overshadowed Greene County's oil production, and the largest drillers went south. During World War II, two pipelines were laid across the county to protect the United States from disruptions to its oil supply. They were converted to carry natural gas after the war when Texas and Oklahoma gas companies began to ship gas to Greene County, where it was stored and distributed as far as New England. Natural gas continues to be stored today in an enormous formation of gas "sands" called the Holbrook Reserve in Aleppo Township.

There were no major railroads through the county until the early twentieth century, when the Baltimore and Ohio Railroad acquired the right-of-way. The coal companies added a branch of the Pennsylvania Railroad along the Monongahela River and up Tenmile Creek to Mather in 1917–1918 to transport coal to Pittsburgh's steel mills. The completion of I-79 through Greene County in the 1960s and 1970s was the biggest influence on twentieth-century development. It opened the county to Pittsburgh to the north and Morgantown, West Virginia, to the south. As a result, several suburban developments spread over the rolling hills east of Waynesburg in the 1980s. While coal mining remains a major industry in Greene County, it employs fewer and fewer people, relying instead on mechanized mining. Today, one of the largest employers in Greene County is the maximum security state prison east of Waynesburg.

WAYNESBURG AND VICINITY

The county seat of Waynesburg was founded in 1796, less than a year after the county's formation and located within five miles of its geographical center. It is named for General Anthony Wayne, the tireless warrior of the Revolutionary War who was dubbed the "man who never sleeps" and "Mad Anthony Wayne" by Native Americans. Bounded on the west and south by Tenmile Creek, Waynesburg is eleven miles west of the Monongahela River. The town was laid out on a grid pattern with green space between Waynesburg College and the commercial district. The low-scale, brick commercial corridor, ten blocks along High Street between East and Richhill streets, consists of a group of handsome two- to three-story, five- to seven-bay red brick buildings from the 1830s and 1840s, the courthouse of 1850 (GR1), and the Fort Jackson Hotel (1926, Bartholomew and Smith; 19 S. Washington Street). High Street's commercial character remains intact despite fast food emporiums and shopping centers east of downtown. The Emerald Mine Cleaning Plant at the western edge of town is a sprawling industrial complex and a constant reminder of the primacy of coal to the county's economy. It contrasts with the human-scaled Waynesburg Milling Company at Tenmile Creek south of the courthouse. This flour mill, operating since 1881, now produces animal feed

North side of E. High Street, Waynesburg.

from grains. In the 1890s, Waynesburg's only connection to Pittsburgh was via the narrow-gauge Waynesburg and Washington railroad (the "W and W") that made two trips daily.

GR1 Greene County Courthouse

1850, Samuel and John Bryan, contractors. High and S. Washington sts.

This Greek Revival courthouse is the most beautiful representative of its era in western Pennsylvania. The commissioners asked Samuel and John Bryan, contractors from Harrisburg, to build a courthouse similar to their earlier work in Fayette County (now demolished). The red brick building features a portico with six two-story fluted Corinthian columns supporting a dentil-lined pediment. A tall domed and colonnaded cupola is topped with a statue of General Nathanael Greene doffing his hat; it was carved in 1998 by Miles Davin Sr. The courthouse's side elevations are articulated by brick pilasters springing from stone bases and display wide entablatures and simple dentiled cornices. Double wooden entrance doors are surmounted by a multipaned transom topped by a smaller version of the dentil-lined pediment. The courthouse has one large airy courtroom on the second floor that can be accessed by a curved set of double stairs located at the front of the building. The

central hallway of the first story is lined with offices.

Directly behind the courthouse to the south stands a large two-and-one-half story, c. 1870 mansard-roofed sheriff's house, with a slightly projecting central bay, stone lintel, and sill bands. The red brick jail (c. 1880) southeast of the courthouse was recently demolished and replaced with a large three-story red brick office building.

GR2 Observer-Reporter Building (Democrat Messenger Building)

1939, Frederick G. Scheibler Jr. 32 Church St.

This two-story, buff brick office building with ribbon windows, a flat unadorned cornice, and a recessed central entrance is one of Frederick Scheibler's severest designs. The Moravian tile medallions on the facade and the doorway surround are the only ornamental details. Scheibler was commissioned by Washington County's Monongahela City newspaper magnate Robert H. Robinson to design this building with unusual programmatic demands including a printing plant,

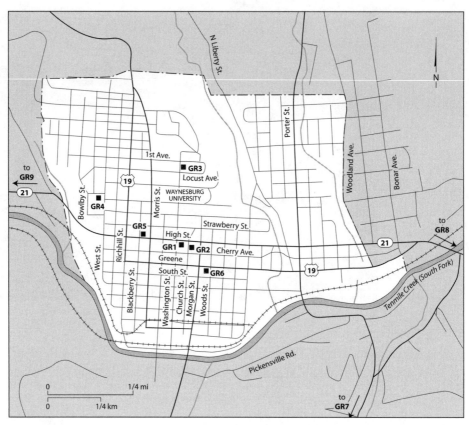

WAYNESBURG

shipping facilities, and offices, all branching from a central hallway.

GR3 Waynesburg University

1850–present. Washington St. at Locust Ave.

First called New College, then Waynesburg College, this university was founded in 1849 by the Cumberland Presbyterian Church. Hanna Hall at College and Washington streets was the first building constructed, in 1850. It was later named for Reverend William Hanna, who paid for a new roof in 1899. Similar to the courthouse, although without a portico, this tall Greek Revival structure has a simple pediment above the facade and a domed cupola, which has lost much of its original exterior detail. Originally, Hanna Hall housed a second-floor chapel that was reached by a pair of dogleg stairs at the south front of the building. Today, it is used as a classroom building.

In 1872, increased enrollment from returning Civil War veterans and the expansion of the five other colleges within a fifty-mile ra-

dius prompted the board of trustees to authorize the building of Miller Hall (1874–1890, James W. Drum; 51 W. College Street), ultimately named for the college president A. B. Miller. The student body made over 800,000 bricks between 1875 and 1877 for the building's construction. But the devastating economic depression of 1873, and a determination to build only what could be paid for in advance, delayed the building's opening for nearly twenty-five years. The commanding Second Empire structure of three-and-one-half stories has a mansard roof and central five-story tower. It is the tallest building in Waynesburg, as well as the symbol of the university. By the time it was completed, the Second Empire style was out of fashion, and its architectural details reveal the building as the product of an earlier time. On the third floor, a vaulted room called Alumni Hall can accommodate 1,000 people, and its stained glass windows, donated by alumni, depict the college's history. The adjacent five blocks of city parkland lend a picturesque quality to the campus and visually link it to Waynesburg's commercial section.

Additional buildings were constructed in the mid-twentieth century. Then, in 1992, the administration hired Carl Johnson, landscape architect of the Michigan firm, Johnson, Johnson and Roy, to create a twenty-year master plan, which the school implemented in five years. Two new campus buildings designed by Valentour English Bodnar and Howell of Pittsburgh began the most recent building campaign and changed the appearance of the college. The award-winning angular Performing Arts Center (PAC) of 1996 blends with the older campus in its use of banded red brick throughout and a tall pyramidal roof. The PAC's complex plan includes a 250-seat auditorium fitted with state-of-the-art electronic light and sound systems for lectures and conferences. To the east across a newly defined quadrangle lies the student center, Stover Hall (1998). Its postmodern design is highlighted by the oversized fanlight and colonnade on the west facade.

GR4 Adam Hewitt–Huffman House

c. 1883. 175 N. West St.

This frame house has an unusual W-shaped plan, with a foreshortened central wing that is repeated in only one other house in the Greene County village of Nineveh (c. 1880; 1800 block of Browns Creek Road). It is not known if a local carpenter favored this style and adapted it from a favorite pattern book, such as E. C. Hussey's *Home Building* of 1875. A mansard roof, zigzag-shaped moldings across the windows, corner boards, and a

GR3 WAYNESBURG UNIVERSITY, Miller Hall

GR6 GREENE COUNTY LOG COURTHOUSE

front porch linking all three sections complete the ornament. A frame carriage house stands to the west. The house was originally built for Adam Hewitt and has been owned by the Huffmans for nearly forty years.

GR5 Denny House

c. 1850; 1907 addition. 145 High St.

This is one of several surviving residences along Waynesburg's commercial corridor. E. L. Denny added a Dutch-gabled brick facade to his two-and-one-half-story home in 1907. The facade, with stone coping around the shaped parapet and a round-arched entrance, is unique in Waynesburg. An older portion dating from the 1850s lies to the north and is set off by a rounded portico. The kitchen wing at the rear was bricked over and enlarged sometime after 1910, and a garage was added. E. L. Denny, entrepreneur and coal rights buyer, died young but left a small fortune to his wife and three young daughters. They maintained the house with its turn-of-the-twentieth-century aggrandizements for over eighty years.

GR6 Greene County Log Courthouse

1797, George Graham and George Ullom, builders; 2002 addition, Ellis Schmidlapp for Landmark Design Associates. 144 E. Greene St.

This two-story log house served as Greene County's courthouse from 1797 to 1800. The court moved to a brick courthouse on High Street and into the present courthouse (GR1) on the same site in 1850. The building has been restored after years of being masked behind siding and serving a series of commercial establishments. The interior has a "turkey breast," or triangular, chimney base that pro-

GR7 GEORGE W. GORDON FARM (JOHN B. GORDON HOUSE)

vides an angled fireplace to serve two rooms with one stone stack. Court was held in the upper room, which was originally reached by an exterior stair and balcony. A one-story frame addition on the courthouse's south elevation accommodates the Cornerstone Genealogical Society's library.

GR7 George W. Gordon Farm (John B. Gordon House)

1843. Gordon Hill (TWP 786) and Longwoods (TWP 542) rds., 4.3 miles southeast of Waynesburg

Virginian John Gordon's house is one of the finest examples of Greek Revival in the region. Set within a notch of land near the top of a ridge, it is protected from north winds and has a wonderful view of two valleys below. The symmetrical one-and-one-half-story stone house has a central recessed porch flanked by a pair of Ionic columns. The exquisite sandstone is scabble and drafted. Corner blocks flank each lintel, and two stone balls mark the semicircular steps leading to the entrance. Chimneys are at each of the gable ends, and the roof has a pair of segmental-arched dormers. The house's U-shaped plan incorporates a stairway in the side hall to the west and a brick kitchen to the east. A one-and-one-half-story frame house and another outbuilding lie northeast of the stone house. The remaining frame barns and storage sheds line both sides of Gordon Hill Road, mimicking a small rural village.

GR8 Greene County Historical Society Museum (Greene Hills Farm, Rinehart House)

c. 1860; 1886 and 1990 additions. 918 Rolling Meadows Rd. (PA 2026), 3.2 miles southeast of Waynesburg

This is a very large version (nine by four bays) of the typical western Pennsylvania farmhouse. The extravagance of its size prompted Jacob Rinehart to sell it a year after it was built to Robinson Downey, who three weeks later sold it to the county for ten times as much as he paid, ironically for use as a poor farm, a home for paupers. The county's indigent adults (approximately sixty per year) were housed in this facility from 1861 to 1964. In the early years, alcoholics, unmarried mothers, and mentally ill and mentally challenged adults were mixed together and, before 1900, often abused. The national campaigns of Dorothea Dix from the 1850s to the 1880s and the Russell Sage Foundation after 1907 raised the standard of care for all the wards of the commonwealth.

The county made two large additions, first to the south of the original house in 1886, then to the west in 1900. The two-story, hipped-roof west wing with a central cupola has the appearance of a large school building and is equal in size to the original large farmhouse. A barn and carriage house on the property date from the time of the original Rinehart house. The boiler house and smokehouse were built for the poor farm.

The Greene County Historical Society moved to the property in 1969, and opened it as a museum in 1971. A log house, located southwest of the main building, was constructed in 1981 from the ruins of two separate cabins to demonstrate a dogtrot house form. The historical society holds several other properties in the county: the Coal Lick one-room school c. 1870 at this site; the W. A. Young Foundry and Machine Shop in Rice's Landing (GR16); and the Crouse Schoolhouse (1900; PA 21, Furman Highway at Rush Run Road) in Center Township, a classic one-room schoolhouse used from 1900 to 1959. Constructed of red brick, it has a cupola, front porch, and the distinctive wooden sunburst attic vent seen on several Greene County buildings. The building's contents are preserved, and it is maintained as a museum.

GR9 Ely Faddis Farm

c. 1870. PA 21 at Barton Hollow Rd., 2.3 miles west of Waynesburg

One of the most handsome nineteenth-century farmsteads remaining in Greene County, the red roofs on the house and out-buildings attract attention. The classic western Pennsylvania red brick farmhouse of five bays, two stories, and a gable roof continued to be built locally from 1800 through the 1880s. The only variations here from the standard form are the segmental-arched windows and Eastlake porch ornamentation. The wooden farm buildings close to the house are rapidly disappearing on other farms, since they no longer meet the needs of modern agricultural operations. Here, they are attractively preserved.

WIND RIDGE

GR10 Jacktown Fairgrounds

c. 1890, c. 1920. Furman Hwy. (PA 21) at McNay Ridge Rd.

The Richhill Agricultural Society has operated the Jacktown Fair, one of the oldest continuously running fairs in the country, since 1866. Their slogan, "You can't die happy, if you haven't been to the Jacktown Fair," captures the fun of the July-held produce and livestock contests. The fairground's half-dozen buildings of various ages are grouped atop a hillside just west of the village of Wind Ridge (popularly called "Jacktown"). Two gable-roofed, white frame exhibition buildings from c. 1890 and c. 1920 and a small frame office at the gate were built to replicate the nineteenth-century style.

GARARDS FORT

Garards Fort, named for a family home that had been fortified and used as a fort in the late eighteenth century, has an interesting combination of buildings typical of the county's rural villages. At its western edge is the former farm of Andrew Lantz, with two handsome white frame barns from 1877. The smaller of the two barns is a board-and-batten structure with a fanciful cupola. The larger barn is sheathed with tongue-and-groove siding and has a peaked cupola at the ridgepole. Both have multiple framed louvers on their side walls. The barns now mark the entrance to the State Game Lands No. 223. South of Garards Fort Road (PA 2011) on Warren Roberts Road, the White covered bridge crosses Whitely Creek. This is the longest queenpost bridge in the county at just over seventy feet. Garards Fort has the smallest post office in Greene County (1942–1943; Garards Fort Road), a miniature white frame gable-roofed structure approximately the size of a large walk-in closet. The large red brick Gothic Revival Corbly Baptist Church (originally Goshen Baptist Church, c. 1900; 107 John Corbly Lane) at the eastern edge of the village is named for the Reverend John Corbley [*sic*], a Scots-Irish preacher whose family was killed before his eyes by Native Americans in 1782. Corbley spent his remaining years preaching and opposing what he saw as unfair proclamations by an inept federal government. He was imprisoned for his role in the Whiskey Rebellion in 1794, asking his neighbors why they should pay taxes to a government unable to protect them. Baptist churches, whose preachers needed neither formal education nor ordination, appealed to subsistence farmers in remote areas and greatly outnumber all other denominations in Greene County. Corbley established more than thirty Baptist churches in western Pennsylvania, Ohio, and West Virginia.

BOBTOWN

Bobtown is a self-contained mining village, and one of the largest coal patches in Greene County. It was built between 1924 and 1928 by the Shannopin Mining Company (GR11) on the former Titus and South farms. The Shannopin Mine was one of the last operating mines in the county connected to a company town. Bobtown ultimately had 354 simple, frame, gable-roofed houses of three by two bays in four styles, with running water, flush toilets, and electricity. Most are one story, although two-story versions exist. The inset porches and central chimneys, as, for example, at 6 Crescent Circle, are unique to Bobtown. The houses were built by the Ward and the Fink brothers.

The village is reached by climbing the hillside on a winding road past the empty mine company locker rooms and administration buildings adjacent to Dunkard Creek. Bobtown was built on the plateau at the top of a hill, with streets conforming to the landscape and the houses ranged tightly along them. The former Circle Theater (1925) in Bobtown is a large, blockish red brick structure, much altered over the years. Originally used as a theater, it is now the fire station. The village has one Roman Catholic church, St. Ignatius of Antioch (1974; Larimer Avenue at Bobtown Hill Road) and two Methodist churches; a library reading room (1927; 777 Larimer Avenue) in the former frame school building; jail (1924; Larimer Avenue at Bobtown Hill Road); and several stores. The arrangement of the theater, jail, war memorial, and Catholic church at the intersection of Bobtown Hill Road and Franklin and Larimer avenues creates a central space, almost a town square. Brick corbeling at the cornice line ornaments the rectangular company store at the corner of Main and Franklin avenues, while the former jail is embellished

Larimer Avenue, Bobtown, Greene County; typical coal-patch frame housing with two stories, gable roofs, and simple porches set on the facades.

with a pediment, wide cornice, brick corner quoins, and a brick arched door surround. As an ensemble, the village is representative of a pre–World War II way of life that was tied to a single industry.

GR11 Shannopin Mining Company Administration Buildings

c. 1930. Bobtown Hill Rd.

The Shannopin Mines Nos. 1 and 2 were drift mines over a portion of the Pittsburgh seam in Dunkard Township. In 1927, the company, a subsidiary of Jones and Laughlin Steel Company, began transporting coal overland along Dunkard Creek to the Monongahela River for shipment to Pittsburgh's steel industry. The mine closed in 1992. This group of six red brick mine buildings of one and two stories is located in the flatland adjacent to the creek. The General Office, a hipped-roof one-story building with a pedimented three-bay porch on the facade, is the only building with touches of style, including segmental arches over the windows, running bond brickwork, and patterned roof shingles. The other one- and two-story buildings are gable roofed, and their brick walls are reinforced and articulated with pilasters. The bathhouse, like the office, has a hipped roof and deep overhanging eaves. Although the houses in Bobtown had running water and flush toilets, most did not have showers, and residents were allowed to use the company showers on weekends. The complex is the only group of buildings along Bobtown Hill Road between Dunkard Creek and the village on the plateau.

GREENSBORO

Located on the west bank of the Monongahela River, Greensboro was laid out in 1787 by Elias Stone. The original town plan included eighty-six lots of one-half acre each on flat land along the high banks of the river. A gradually rising hillside allowed expansion to the west. The town's population has remained between 300 and 400 people for most of its history. By 1807, a glass company, founded by Swiss immigrant Albert Gallatin in 1797, had moved to Greensboro from New Geneva east of the Monongahela River to take advantage of the coal beds. Incorporated as Reppert and Company in 1808, it closed in 1821. However, it spawned other glass manufactories, which became Greensboro's primary industry for almost forty years. Local glass cutter James Jones built a two-story red brick house c. 1879 (429 Front Street) with round-arched window and door openings, each with a keystone and corner blocks. Honoring his trade, the house has a ruby-colored, floral-etched, round-arched transom above the front door, and frosted glass transoms on the first-floor interior. The Ionic-columned porch with a sunrise carving in its small pediment was added around 1900.

From 1856, steamboat packet service to Pittsburgh offered a more efficient means of shipping the local pottery, which, by the 1860s, replaced glass to become the dominant industry. Clay roof tiles made by Star Pottery works and crockery manufactured in Greensboro were distributed across the nation, reaching peak production in the 1870s. Painted with advertisements, they held food and whiskey and dispersed Greene County products nationwide. Few glass- and clay-making industrial buildings survive, making the Hewitt pottery site in Rice's Landing all the more important (see Rice's Landing, p. 273). Several houses built by people who worked in the industries survive

The lion's share of electricity in the United States continues to be generated by coal-fired power plants. Although coal in western Pennsylvania has been mined since the 1750s, only about eighteen of the estimated eighty-four billion tons of the Pittsburgh coal seam have been extracted. Mining this wealth of coal, while no longer requiring a huge number of employees, is nonetheless dark, dirty, and life-threatening work. To extract coal from western Pennsylvania mines, nineteenth-century mining companies needed a workforce willing to live in isolated areas. They built towns, often called patches or patch towns, to house labor near the mine heads. Hundreds of these towns survive in western Pennsylvania. Surprisingly, given that many mines and other industries have closed, scores of the patch towns remain fully occupied. Subsequent generations purchased their houses from the companies, expanded and upgraded them, and continue

COKEBURG COAL PATCH FROM FAVA FARM ROAD, WASHINGTON COUNTY, 1997.

to live in the patch, commuting to work in urban areas. Small patch towns today are distinguishable by their tight rows of one- and two-story, gable-roofed frame houses lining the streets.

Muriel Earley Sheppard's *Cloud by Day: A Story of Coal and Coke and People* (1947) captures the danger and dankness of the mine, the isolation of the patch town, and the tyranny of the company store. Comparing the towns of Shoaf, in Fayette County, and Ellsworth and Marianna, in Washington County, one can see the evolution of the patch town and the ways in which mine owners either ignored workers' welfare or sought to enhance their lives.

Mining supplies needed power, but it can affect people in negative ways. Subsidence (the sinking of land above an abandoned mine) and longwall mining (mechanical removal of coal that causes the land to drop several feet) have disrupted streams and several historic houses, especially in Greene County. One of the largest sources of water pollution in the region is acid mine drainage. Once a deep mine is abandoned, water fills its tunnels, leeching out heavy metals that cling to the rocks in creek beds, creating what locals call "yellowboy," an iron-based metallic pollution that kills aquatic life. Several campaigns have been initiated to reclaim area streams. For example, at Vintondale in Cambria County, a model thirty-five-acre water treatment park along the Ghost Town Trail has been created around an abandoned mine site (see CA29). Remediative plants and settling ponds neutralize acid mine drainage, and the park includes recreational sites and landscaping that commemorate the area's history.

in and around Greensboro. Transporting coal by river barge was the last major industry in Greensboro, peaking between 1900 and 1920 before trucking became the preferred method of shipment. The Colonial Revival and the Queen Anne houses at County Street and the Monongahela River are two of the largest houses in the village, while to their west, a reconstructed log house (110 Front Street) and the two-story, red brick I-house at 222 County Street represent the earliest buildings in town.

In 1996, the U.S. Army Corps of Engineers relocated Lock and Dam No. 7 three miles north of Greensboro to Gray's Landing, which caused the river level to rise fifteen feet in Greensboro, inundating its two-hundred-year-old cobblestone wharf. The townspeople rallied to save their many interesting historic buildings. In combination with its proximity to the river, the preserved buildings retain the village's charm.

GR12 Riverrun Books and Prints (Reppert and Williams Store and House)

c. 1870. 1874 County St.

An artifact from Greensboro's prosperous 1870s, this unusual and intact storefront and residence is adjacent to a small creek at the rear and one building away from the Monongahela River. The dry goods store served river travelers as well as locals, advertising that they accepted produce for goods. The building is two-and-one-half stories tall and built of red brick, with wooden brackets lining the shaped parapet and the six bays of the basically rectangular building that abut the sidewalk. Round-arched windows on the upper stories and segmental-arched windows at street level are complemented by impressed brick panels.

GR12 RIVERRUN BOOKS AND PRINTS (REPPERT AND WILLIAMS STORE AND HOUSE)

GLASSWORKS

GR13 Reppert-Gabler House

c. 1810; c. 1880 addition. 300 block PA 2014

This house was built in two parts by two generations of glassworkers. The original c. 1810 portion was built by George Reppert as a three-bay, two-story red brick house with a side stair and two rooms on each floor. At the time, he was helping to relocate the New Geneva glassworks to Greene County from Fayette County. John C. Gabler, son of one of Reppert's glassmaking partners, constructed the c. 1880 addition. The Gabler family bought the house in 1832, and owned it for 150 years. A fine Federal doorway and back-to-back triangular fireplaces distinguish the earliest, southern portion of the house. The northern portion consists of two-and-one-half stories with three rooms on each floor under a gabled roof. The house's two sections intersect to create a T-shaped plan. Across the road at 363 PA 2014, cooper John Minor Crawford built an Italianate brick house c. 1878 with the money earned shipping pottery in his barrels.

NEMACOLIN

This company town, built in 1917 for the Buckeye Coal Company, a subsidiary of Youngstown Sheet and Tube Company in Ohio, contains over four hundred cedar-sided private residences constructed by Stone and Webster Construction Company between 1918 and 1925. Because it was laid out on curving streets and had electricity, indoor plumbing, toilets with baths, and underground sewage, Nemacolin was touted in coal industry publications in 1924 as a model mining community. In contrast, a standard coal patch town was isolated and had cheaply built bungalows and double houses without necessities like electricity or water, and with subsistence-level utilities such as public pumps, coal stoves, and outhouses. In 1920, the company added a theater, bowling alley, pool, restaurant, and barber shop, and the Pennsylvania Railroad arranged passenger service the following year. Larger mines and a mobile workforce ended the patch-town phenomenon, and Nemacolin's houses were offered for sale to their respective occupants in 1946.

CARMICHAELS

GR14 Carmichaels Bridge

1889. Old Town Rd. over Muddy Creek

One of seven covered bridges in Greene County able to bear vehicular traffic, this single-span queenpost truss bridge is sixty-four feet across and fifteen feet wide and rests on stone abutments. The exterior is sheathed with vertical planks in a board-and-batten pattern, and the gabled roof is shingled. All but one of the covered bridges in Greene County are queenpost trusses, a type that has been popular for short spans since its inclusion in Andrea Palladio's *Four Books on Architecture* (1570). The stone house at 303 Market Street on the east side of Muddy Creek and the brick house at 401 Old Town Street on the west date from the early 1800s and complete this nineteenth-century vignette.

GR15 Greene Academy of Art (Greene Academy)

1791, 1810. 310–314 Market St.

The 1791 fieldstone portion of Greene Academy was built as an Episcopal church on land owned by James Carmichael during a time when the threat of Native American attack was ever present. The brick extension of 1810 housed the only post-elementary-level school in Greene County until 1849, when the school moved to Waynesburg College (now University, GR3). Women were accepted to Greene Academy in 1837. The academy housed the local public school from 1865 to 1893. Subsequently, the building has housed the local post of the Grand Army of the Republic, three apartments, and, after restoration, a community center. Greene Academy is a plain, two-and-one-half-story rectangular building. The stone portion at the north end is two bays in length and three bays across the facade. First-

GR14 CARMICHAELS BRIDGE

floor openings have segmental stone arches, as does the entrance, with double doors facing Market Street. The brick addition is three bays on all elevations and has a more regular fenestration. The gable roof has been replaced with a standing-seam metal roof topped with a cupola. The building now houses the local center for the arts.

RICE'S LANDING

Named for John Rice, the landholder in 1786, this once thriving borough sat at lock No. 6 (constructed in the 1850s) on the Monongahela River. Today, it is a village of sixty-three buildings, including two c. 1930 brick lockkeepers' houses (133–135 Main Street) that overlook the river. The parklike riverfront and banks of Pumpkin Run lend the village today a more pastoral appearance than it had in the nineteenth century. The Pittsburg [*sic*], Monongahela and Southern Railroad reached Rice's Landing in 1907, occupying a ledge above the narrow shelf of the town's main street. It served the Dilworth Coal Mine, once one of the busiest shippers on the Monongahela, which also opened in 1907 and closed in 1927. Today its path is the Greene River Trail, a 3.8-mile hiking and biking trail connecting Greene Cove Marina at Tenmile Creek with Rice's Landing.

The former Rice's Landing National Bank (1914; Main Street at Dry Tavern Road) is a one-story, flat-roofed buff brick building with green and purple terra-cotta ornament that sits on the river's edge. Many of the borough's frame buildings have similar window surrounds and corner boards due to local access to heavy machinery, planing mills, and the great number of precut sections shipped by river and rail. For example, former Excelsior/Hewitt Pottery (c. 1870; 112 Water Street), built and operated by former schoolteacher Isaac Hewitt Jr., is a six-bay, gable-roofed structure now converted to housing, but the clapboarded building retains its stone foundation and boxed cornice and eaves returns, as well as its river's edge location.

GR16 W. A. Young Foundry and Machine Shop

1900; 1908–1910 addition. 114 Water St.

Housed in a long, one-story clapboarded building, this foundry and machine shop are an excellent example of a small-scale turn-of-the-twentieth-century industrial enterprise built to serve the surrounding agricultural community, as well as nearby coal mines and riverboats that plied the Monongahela River. Inside, the power for the twenty-five pieces of machinery (including extant drill presses and lathes) was furnished by a twenty horsepower electric motor attached by means of a complex system of driveshafts and leather belting. The foundry section features the large cupola that held the molten metal that was cast into various shapes, as seen in the hundreds of wooden patterns hanging from the walls.

GR16 W. A. YOUNG FOUNDRY AND MACHINE SHOP

To keep up with changing times, the Youngs added a hardware and automotive repair shop before closing the business in 1965. The Greene County Historical Society bought the building and its contents in 1985 to preserve its historical integrity, and occasionally they open it for special events.

GR17 Thomas Hughes House

1814. Hatfield St. at Hughes St.

Thomas Hughes's slaves quarried and hand-cut the sandstone used to build this house. Hughes was one of fifty Virginia and Maryland settlers who emigrated to what they considered to be western Virginia in 1767. The datestone on the south gable end bears the initials of Thomas and his wife, Elizabeth. Hughes freed his slaves before the Civil War, and his home became known as a stop on the Underground Railroad. Three bays wide, the house is built into a hillside overlooking a tributary of the South Fork of Tenmile Creek. It is two stories on the east facade and drops to three stories on the creek side. The two-bay dependency on the north has porches front and back sheltered under eaves. There are interior end chimneys at both ends of the ridgepole. Note the incised marks in the facade's stonework and the carefully cut quoins on front and rear. Side walls are of irregularly coursed stone.

Across the creek, the Jefferson Presbyterian Church (1845; 208 Pine Street) was the Hughes' family church, and its eighteenth-century cemetery holds their graves. It is a classic rural brick church with two doors on the south facade and three double-sash windows along each side. An octagonal cupola is perched on a square base above the entrances.

GR18 John Rex House

c. 1874. 1565 PA 188, 0.8 miles northeast of Jefferson

This is an excellent example of a pattern book house built in the cottage style as promulgated by Andrew Jackson Downing between 1840 and the 1880s. Originally, the five-bay, one-and-one-half-story house was T shaped in plan, but additions at the rear have expanded it. The house has a single-story porch with bracketed eaves and post supports, and above it, a tall central gabled dormer trimmed with sawn ornament. The first building on the property was the c. 1865 summer kitchen, which today houses an office. The smokehouse, barn, and carriage house, all clad in vertical wood siding, were built c. 1874. The house is at the center of a 115-acre farm set in rolling hills and woods that adjoin the South Fork of Tenmile Creek.

GR18 JOHN REX HOUSE

RUFF CREEK

GR19 Benjamin Ross House

1858. 190 PA 221

Benjamin and Hannah Ross and their twelve children ran a livestock farm on their 290 acres, and had this house built as the centerpiece. The windows on the south-facing facade are organized in groups of three and echo the central entrance with its sidelights. A filigreed iron balcony highlights the second-story doorway with datestone and shelters the principal entrance below. Stone window lintels on the facade have decorative carvings at their corners. Returning eaves are typical of the style, as are paired interior end chimneys. The interior has a full front and back stair in the central hall and four rooms per floor. There is a stone fireplace in the basement, as well as water supplied by a spring. A frame two-story house with its own large, stone fireplace may predate the brick house, and is attached to its east side by a modern breezeway.

Another five-bay, red brick house at 105 PA 221 and the brick Bethlehem Baptist Church (685 Washington Road), with its crenellated tower, illustrate that Ruff Creek aspired to be more than merely the crossroads of U.S. 19 and PA 221.

Washington County was part of the land granted to the Plymouth Land Company by James I of England in 1606. Virginia claimed jurisdiction over it from 1752 to 1783, even after it became a Pennsylvania county in 1781, the first county in the United States named after George Washington. The boundary dispute caused confusion over property rights, and anger among the settlers delayed development. The county's earliest industry was the processing of grains milled for flour and whiskey, and by 1817, there were more than one hundred mills along the streams of Washington County. Streams supplied power and a means of shipping the finished products to outside markets via the Monongahela River. During this early period (1818–1850), the National Road was a major factor in the county's economy; its route was altered to pass through Washington County. Centerville, Hootman, and Malden grew as pike towns along the road's original path. Larger pike towns such as Scenery Hill and West Alexander now attract tourists. Sheep farming was introduced in 1820, and the county continued to have the largest number of sheep of any Pennsylvania county as late as 1997. Several large, handsome, brick, pre–Civil War farmhouses are indicative of this industry's early success. The county also hosts the largest number of covered bridges in the state, with twenty-four kingpost or queenpost bridges spanning local creeks.

Washington County residents rebuffed the Baltimore and Ohio Railroad's (B&O) proposal in 1828 to bring a rail connection, fearing it would cut into commerce along the National Road. By spurning these early advances, the town of Washington missed its chance to compete with Pittsburgh in having the shortest link to the East Coast. Washington connected to Wheeling, West Virginia, in 1857, but the Pennsylvania Railroad fought a rail connection to Baltimore and denied the B&O a direct connection. Further isolating Washington was its relatively late connection to Pittsburgh; they were finally linked in 1871 by the Chartiers Valley Railroad. Nevertheless, mine operators understood the advantage of shipping coal by rail rather than by riverboat, and specialized coal-hauling rail lines were established throughout the region as early as 1865.

Washington County is characterized by its many farms set among picturesque rolling hills. The southwestern section of the county features forested state game lands, and the southeastern section, away from the industrialized riverbanks, has preserved its rural landscapes along scenic winding roads. Interspersed with the many farms are coal patches that are so compact and isolated that they do not affect the general rural appearance of the county. Since the coal in Washington County is deep, strip mining, which mars surfaces and rural ambience, is not usually practical, except in the county's northwest corner. The larger mining towns are located along the Pigeon Creek Railroad, southwest of the town of Monongahela.

In the 1880s and 1890s, oil and gas deposits were discovered in northern Washington County. The result of this oil boom is visible in the superb collection of frame Queen Anne houses throughout the city of Washington. Because of the intersection of two major highways—I-70 and I-79—Washington County is easily accessible from all directions by car and is rapidly suburbanizing on the northern border between McDonald and McMurray. The impact of such development on the many older buildings farther south remains to be seen. One example of compatible development is the town of Charleroi, which built a mall adjacent to the original main street. In this way, both the mall and the main street were strengthened. Charleroi is one of several industrial towns along the Monongahela River that are now discovering the recreational value of their beautiful riverfronts.

WASHINGTON AND VICINITY

Chief Catfish of the (Kuskee) Delaware Indian Tribe was the first to settle on this land c. 1750. In 1769, David Hoge of Harrisburg bought three tracts in the region, and, in 1781, his son built a log house on the site of the present-day city of Washington. First called Bassettown for Hoge's friend Richard Bassett, the village was renamed Washington in honor of George Washington in 1784, and incorporated as a borough in 1810. The town was laid out in a grid pattern across rolling hills typical of the Appalachian Plateau. Located midway between Brownsville and Wheeling, West Virginia, Washington lobbied to be on the National Road. From 1811 to the mid-nineteenth century, the town thrived as a transportation hub, county seat, and college town. But it suffered from its relative proximity to Pittsburgh and from the rivalry between the Baltimore and Ohio and the Pennsylvania railroads. Washington achieved a rail connection to Wheeling in 1857 and to Pittsburgh in 1871 when the Chartiers Valley Railroad opened. Rail connections to Pittsburgh increased in numbers and frequency as coal, oil, and natural gas businesses grew. The Waynesburg and Washington Railroad (the "W and W"), a narrow-gauge line, joined the two county seats and operated from 1877 to 1929. Two distinctive rail stations from the turn of the twentieth century remain at the south end of the commercial district (ws8).

Washington Academy, later Washington College, founded here in 1787, was joined with Jefferson College in 1869 (ws4). A female seminary in existence between 1835 and 1875 prompted the names "Beau" and "Maiden" to be assigned to parallel streets four decorous blocks from each other (they ultimately do intersect on the west side of town). In 1879, a military academy, Trinity Hall (ws9), was added to the educational mix in Washington.

The town centered on the intersection of W. Beau and Main streets at the courthouse (ws1), one of the most beautiful in western Pennsylvania. Perhaps Washington's role as county seat and college town, its orientation toward Virginia, and the wealth from coal and oil stimulated the relatively sophisticated stylistic choices for its buildings. Many of the town's major buildings show

45 S. Wade Street, Washington, typical of the large, handsome, Queen Anne–style houses prevalent in Washington, Pennsylvania.

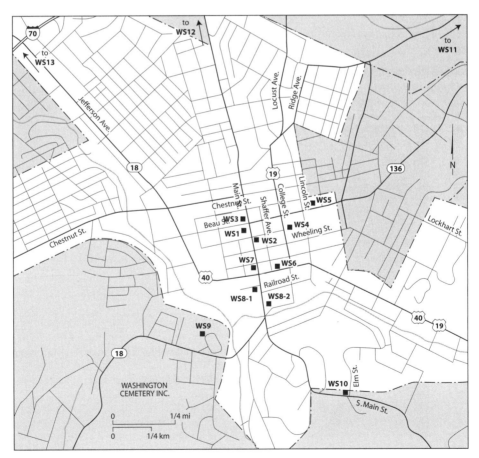

WASHINGTON

an attention to detail and sense of style not apparent in nearby counties. For example, the Baird-Acheson house (1826; S. Main and W. Maiden streets) has a magnificent four-story, elliptical interior stairway. A unique collection of exuberantly styled frame Queen Anne houses along East Avenue and Grant, E. Wheeling, and E. Beau streets adds to the architectural eclecticism. Three c. 1890 houses with rounded turrets, wraparound spindled porches, and five square windows in their front gables (48 S. Wade Avenue, 411 E. Maiden Street, and 104 E. Prospect Street) are the work of an unknown local carpenter-builder, who adapted the designs from one of the popular architectural style books. The brown brick, six-story Washington Trust Building (6 S. Main Street), designed in 1902 by Frederick J. Osterling, hosted professional offices, a dime store, and the Elks Club, and with its ten-story addition (1921–1923, Jay W. Percowper), remains the tallest building in Washington. Percowper also designed the Art Deco *Observer-Reporter* newspaper offices at 122 S. Main Street. Although Washington's suburban sprawl now extends outward to the interstate highways, an older shopping district adjacent to the college and the courthouse remains vibrant.

WS1 Washington County Courthouse and Jail

1898–1900, Frederick J. Osterling. Main and W. Beau sts.

One of Frederick Osterling's most impressive designs, this courthouse admirably represents the beauty and dignity of the law. The exte-

WS1 WASHINGTON COUNTY COURTHOUSE AND JAIL, courthouse interior

rior, of cut Columbian sandstone with South Carolina granite trim, is adorned with thirty-six-foot-tall Ionic columns supporting porticoes on each elevation. The porticoes are rectangular on the side elevations and rounded on the facade. Smaller domes flank a central dome, which is topped with an eighteen-foot cast-bronze statue of George Washington. The original terra-cotta statue was decapitated by a lightning strike; lightning rods protect this statue from its predecessor's fate. The courthouse's interior has a central lobby and staircase lit by a grand dome lined with stained glass in golden hues. Beautifully restored foliate-patterned murals highlight the pendentives. Marble columns and florid iron railings add to the grandeur. The three courtrooms on the second story are also restored, and each echoes the lobby with smaller, circular stained glass skylights.

The jail, behind the courthouse, is a suave rendition of Richardsonian Romanesque, surmounted by a hexagonal lantern with an open arched colonnade above its cruciform plan.

WS2 George Washington Hotel

1922–1923, William Lee Stoddart. 60 S. Main St.

The local chamber of commerce, seeking to meet the needs of the motoring public along the National Road, funded this ten-story hotel

WS4 WASHINGTON AND JEFFERSON COLLEGE (W&J), Old Main

by selling stock to those who had previously hosted travelers in their homes—the city's women. New York City architect William Lee Stoddart (1869–1940), who specialized in hotels, banks, and federal buildings, chose a tripartite base, shaft, and capital formula for this high-rise structure, which has limestone trim highlighting the maroon-colored brick. The murals (1935) in the Pioneer Grill, by Washington County resident Malcolm S. Parcell (1896–1987), depict travel on the old National Road. Across the street, Citizen's Bank of c. 1930 at 40 S. Main Street is a white marble–faced bank inspired by classical forms.

WS3 Smith's Iron Hall

1861. 3 N. Main St.

This three-story Renaissance Revival commercial building has a rare, fully cast-iron facade. Because of its corner location, the ironwork and arched windows continue for one bay onto the south elevation. The facade is reminiscent of a Venetian palazzo with its large, paired, round- and flat-arched windows that are separated by paired, fluted Corinthian columns. On the third floor, they illuminate a ceremonial meeting space. Owner William Smith was born in western Pennsylvania in 1800, but spent time in the early 1820s in Philadelphia before returning to Washington County to open a general store. A smaller, two-story, cast-iron-fronted com-

mercial building at 14–16 N. Main Street has similar detailing.

WS4 Washington and Jefferson College (W&J)

1793–present. Bounded by E. Maiden, N. College, and E. Chestnut sts. and East Ave.

Two rival late-eighteenth-century Presbyterian academies for the training of frontier clergy (Washington Academy in Washington, and Jefferson College in Canonsburg) merged after the Civil War (1869) to form Washington and Jefferson College (W&J). Land for a college in Washington had been donated in 1787 when the city was laid out. W&J emulated men's Ivy League colleges, shifting its educational focus from religious training to emphasize a liberal arts curriculum, preprofessional studies, and athletics. In 1970, women were admitted to W&J. The picturesquely landscaped campus consists of six groupings of buildings on forty acres east of Washington's commercial district. The Administration Building (1793–1794), constructed of native limestone, had brick wings added in 1818–1820. Old Main, begun in 1836, assumed its present ornate appearance in 1875 after a series of additions designed by John Upton Barr and Henry Moser. Old Main's facade has twin mansard-roofed towers flanking a central entrance similar to the facade of Old Main at California University of Pennsylvania (WS23) designed by Barr and Moser five years earlier.

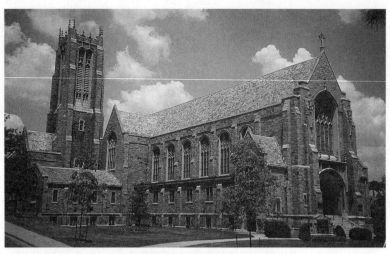

WS5 CHURCH OF THE COVENANT (SECOND PRESBYTERIAN CHURCH OF WASHINGTON)

Other nineteenth-century buildings include the Greek Revival Davis Memorial (former Reed House, 1846) and two Queen Anne–style houses: the President's House, (former Duncan House, 1892), and the Admissions House (former Andrew Gardner Happer House, 1894). The Colonial Revival McIlvaine Hall (1897), designed by Elise Mercur (her later, married name was Wagner), was demolished in 2008 to make room for a new science center. The Romanesque Revival gymnasium, Swanson Hall (1893), which features an impressive bell tower, was designed by Arthur B. Jennings of New York City.

Twentieth-century buildings include the Beaux-Arts-influenced Thompson Memorial Library (1904) designed by Rutan and Russell. Austere for its time, Thistle Physics Hall (1912), designed by Thorsten E. Billquist, was modeled on progressive building designs of the English and German university systems. Colonial Revival buildings of the 1930s and 1940s, notably the Jesse Lazear chemistry building (1939–1940, named for the physician who allowed himself to be bitten by yellow fever–infected mosquitoes as part of Walter Reed's pioneering experiments and died of the disease), were designed by Jens F. Larson (1891–1982) of Hanover, New Hampshire, a noted architect of college buildings. His 1933 book, *Architectural Planning of the American College,* and his role as official architect of the Association of American Colleges convinced over thirty colleges nationwide to seek out his plans and designs. Since 1956, the college

has hired architects affiliated with Edward Stotz and his successor firms of Stotz, Hess and MacLachlan and MacLachlan, Cornelius and Filoni to design a number of red brick Colonial Revival and modern buildings. The former firm designed the Student Activities Center (1956), the Commons Building (1967), and the Residential Center and ten fraternity houses (1968). The latter firm designed the modern Olin Fine Arts Center (1982) and the russet brick Rossin Center (1992).

Beginning in 2001, the college has added a new quadrangle of buildings to the east of Old Main consisting of the stone-clad Burnett Center (2001) and a new technology center (2003), Bica-Ross dormitory (2004), and ten Colonial Revival houses on E. Chestnut Street (2006), all designed by the Pittsburgh firm of MacLachlan, Cornelius and Filoni.

South of the Administration Building's front lawn is the First Presbyterian Church of Washington (1868), with a towering Gothic Revival spire. Washington and Jefferson continues to expand into the city of Washington by acquiring properties in the nearby residential neighborhoods.

WS5 Church of the Covenant (Second Presbyterian Church of Washington)

1930, Nicklas and Rodrick. 267 E. Beau St.

William H. Nicklas (1867–1960) and Jesse L. Rodrick (1884–1963) of Cleveland laid out this Gothic Revival granite church on a basilica plan with side aisles; it can accommodate 900 congregants. A chapel and a large square tower west of the intersection of the chancel and nave add to the bulk of the church. The focal point of the interior is the oak communion table with a carved and canopied reredos behind. The floors are of multicolored, handmade Nemadji tiles from Minnesota. Beautiful, blue-toned windows, designed by the Pittsburgh Stained Glass Studios, include a traceried rose window in the chancel. A large addition, which includes an auditorium-gymnasium, classrooms, and a kitchen, was added in 1999, using stone from the same quarry for the major facades. Two Washington and Jefferson College buildings, Vilar Technology Center and the Burnett Center (ws4), south of the church are faced with similar stone.

WS6 Dr. John Julius LeMoyne House

1812. 49 E. Maiden St.

This handsome early Greek Revival house for physician John LeMoyne was designed and constructed by a Mr. Wright, about whom little is known. The house originally had an open gallery across the facade at the third floor, indicated by the offset chimney. This area was enclosed with stone c. 1840 and now has a band of windows across its seven bays. The coursed stonework of the facade contrasts with the rubble side and rear elevations. Two entrances on E. Maiden Street allowed separate access to the family home (door with columns) and the doctor's offices (smaller door to the west). The house remained in the LeMoyne family until 1943, when it was donated to the Washington County Historical Society. John's son, Francis, also a physician, was instrumental in building the crematory located at S. Main and Elm streets (ws10). However, Francis LeMoyne was best known as an early and outspoken abolitionist who ran for governor of Pennsylvania on the Abolitionist ticket. The house, now open to the public and housing the Washington County Historical Society's archives, was frequently used as part of the Underground Railroad.

WS7 David Bradford House

1788. 175 S. Main St.

Washington's two finest early stone houses (ws6) were built twenty-four years apart, but within a block of each other. They form the core of Washington's historic district, and illustrate the growing stylistic sophistication of the trans-Appalachian territory after the American Revolution. This house is typical of its period and many other houses throughout western Pennsylvania, with its four bays and side-hall plan with two rooms per story. While such houses are often of sandstone, the Bradford House is unusual for its limestone exterior. This early house has an elegant mahogany staircase and finely crafted interior cabinetry, yet it does not approach the styling seen in the later LeMoyne house. But by 1812, when the LeMoyne was built, what was once frontier had become a landscape of permanent settlement. The Bradford house's facade was restored c. 1936 from its storefront configuration to its present appearance by Charles M. Stotz. David Bradford is best known for his support of the Whiskey Rebellion in 1794.

WS8 Washington Train Stations

1892–1906. S. Main St.

The stone Baltimore and Ohio (B&O) station (ws8.1; 1892; 273 S. Main Street) is one of five Richardsonian Romanesque railroad stations designed by Ephraim Francis Baldwin (1837–1916) and Josias Pennington (1854–1929), who produced more than one hundred railroad buildings during a twenty-year stint with the B&O. The slate hipped roof forms porches over the platforms on all sides and is pierced by a variety of shingled dormers, including hipped, gabled, and faceted. The brick Waynesburg and Washington station (ws8.2; 1905–1906; 404 S. Main Street), designed by William L. Price (1861–1916) and M. Hawley

WS7 DAVID BRADFORD HOUSE

McLanahan (1865–1929) on the east side of S. Main Street, is highlighted by an ornate round-arched portico with a steep roof. Price worked for the Pennsylvania Railroad earlier in his career, and McLanahan was a graduate of Washington and Jefferson College. This might explain their interest in designing for a narrow-gauge rail line in western Pennsylvania when their practice was headquartered in Philadelphia. The windows lining the side elevations are sheltered by deep eaves and echo the round arches of the facade. The "Waynie," as locals fondly called this line, ran in a steep and circuitous route between the county seats of Greene and Washington counties. It closed in 1929, when it was no longer able to compete with buses and automobiles.

WS9 Trinity High School (Trinity Hall Boys' School; Joseph McKnight House, "Spring Hill")

c. 1866; 1881 addition, McKim, Mead and White; 1960 addition, C. Garey Dickson. 231 Park Ave.

The grand, brick Italianate house "Spring Hill," built for Joseph McKnight, is at the core of the present high school. In c. 1869, banker, soldier, merchant, and philanthropist William W. Smith purchased the house, and in 1879, founded a private boys' military academy here, which he named Trinity Hall. He commissioned the New York City firm of McKim, Mead and White to design a large addition to the north in 1881. The original house had a library, parlor, high ceilings, and fine woodwork; the kitchen was in the raised basement. The addition consisted of a large, two-and-one-half-story classroom and dormitory with a monitor roof lighting the alcoves in the attic and a half-timbered end bay. Regrettably, nearly all traces of the McKim, Mead and White addition were covered when George W. Brugger, architect for the school district, fireproofed the building in 1925. Today, both the original "Spring Hill" house and the McKim, Mead and White addition are attached to a 1960s high school designed by C. Garey Dickson. The grounds were landscaped by Robert Morris Copeland (1830–1874) of Boston, probably during Smith's tenure. He employed 125 varieties of trees and shrubs, but little is visible today. The school has a sloping, grassy hillside with rings of trees, but not the elaborate plan shown in earlier engravings.

WS10 LeMoyne Crematory

1876, Dr. Francis J. LeMoyne. S. Main and Elm sts.

This crematory is the oldest in the United States. It was designed by Francis LeMoyne (see ws6) and built to his specifications by John Dye. Measuring 20 × 30 feet, the three-bay, gable-roofed, brick building with the simplest of ornament sits at the top of Gallows Hill. The extra chimney on the east elevation reveals the building's purpose, as does the 6 × 10–foot oven above the coke-fired furnace, which reaches ceiling height in the cremation room on the east side. The reception room on the west side contains much of the furniture used in LeMoyne's time. A total of forty-one private cremations were performed in the building before it was permanently closed in 1901. LeMoyne was cremated here in 1879 and is buried nearby.

WS11 The Shoppes at Quail Acres (William M. Quail House)

1837. 1445 Washington Rd. (U.S. 19), 4 miles northeast of Washington

Used today as offices and shops, the stately Quail house was built by a successful farmer and stock dealer with considerable wealth and architectural savvy. From the bridged chimneys to the two-story pedimented projecting porch and the symmetrical fanlit central entrances on the first and second stories, the details of the house have been influenced by James River plantation houses in Virginia and by Thomas Jefferson's first version of Monticello. The Quail house is large, with three interior stairways and a large ell on the south elevation. Several original outbuildings remain on the four-and-one-half-acre property: a brick springhouse and carriage house close to the southwest corner, a handsome frame barn with a storm shed and a stone foundation, and three c. 2005 wooden commercial buildings. All are rented to commercial enterprises. The Linn house (1848; 27 Brehm Road), of similar design and grandeur to the Quail house, but in poor condition, is located nearby.

WS11 THE SHOPPES AT QUAIL ACRES (WILLIAM M. QUAIL HOUSE)

WS12 John White House

1804–1806; 1814 or 1851 brick addition. 2151 N. Main St., 4.8 miles northwest of Washington

The John White house, built by a Scots-Irish miller between 1804 and 1806, was originally the heart of a 360-acre farm. The house illustrates the progress made by a rural family at the beginning of the nineteenth century as the area shifted from subsistence farming to a market economy. The original stone structure was a substantial thirty-two-foot square sited on a rise, with the land sloping away from the house on all sides for drainage. It had a side hall and two rooms on each story. Later, the house was almost doubled in size by the addition of two rooms on each story. The Whites built a flour mill in the early nineteenth century, but all the outbuildings are demolished. In 1916, the farm became the Washington County Fairgrounds and the house became an office and caretaker's residence. Since 1993, the house has been restored and leased by the Washington County History and Landmarks Foundation.

The Pennsylvania Trolley Museum, collecting and interpreting urban and interurban railcars for over fifty years, is directly across the street at 1 Museum Road. Another well-interpreted, two-story, brick house that opens for tours upon request was built by Enoch and Rachel Wright, a prosperous farm family with Virginia roots. It is located fifteen miles northeast of the fairgrounds and owned by the Peters Creek Historical Society (1816; 815 Venetia Road).

WS13 Haney Farm (Matthew Morrow Farm)

c. 1820. 471 Haney Rd., 4 miles west of Washington

A simple three-bay brick house and a rare German forebay stone-end barn of 1821 set this farmstead apart. The barn is a modified Sweitzer (Pennsylvania German variant of Schweizer or Swiss) style, with a frame forebay and a single stone out-shed adjacent to the ramp on the south elevation. The Morrows were Scots-Irish Presbyterians and farmed for several generations in Canton Township. This barn is similar to the much earlier Newmyer barn of 1794 in Fayette County (FA26) with the ventilating slits in the stone end walls and very little alteration to its original form. More study is needed to understand exactly how long this barn type persisted in the region, but this barn illustrates that it was popular for at least twenty-five years. The two-story gable-roofed house has Federal touches, including scored stone lintels with bull's-eye corner blocks, small paired brackets, a lunette in the gable end, and a simple but elegant fanlight above the entrance.

CLAYSVILLE

John Purviance opened the first tavern on the future site of Claysville in 1800. As soon as news of the National Road's route through Washington County was disclosed in 1817, he laid out lots for the town and named it for Henry Clay, Kentucky's representative in the U.S. Congress and a champion of western interests, who facilitated the construction and completion of the road. Claysville grew slowly as a rural market town catering particularly to the wool trade. At its population peak of just over 1,000 in 1890, the town had ten stores, two livery stables, and six physicians. Its importance as a commercial hub grew after the Baltimore and Ohio Railroad connected it to Wheeling, West Virginia, and Claysville became the only point between Washington and Wheeling for shipping livestock. Its commercial district continues to grow.

WS14 Robert Porter House

1883–1885. 1274 W. Main St.

The single most elaborate and fanciful house in Washington County, Robert Porter's house is known for the amount and imagination of its decoration. From the multitiered and mansard-roofed tower to the front and back porches festooned with sawn ornament, the three stories of elaborate window surrounds, and the bracketed eaves, every inch of this house is decorated. This monument to the skills of the planing mill run by Porter served as excellent advertising. A Gothic Revival cottage (1860s) was moved from W. Main Street to the south of the house, and is now used as a stable-garage.

WEST MIDDLETOWN AND VICINITY

West Middletown, laid out in 1796 as a stopover for travelers along the Wellsburg Pike, lies midway between Washington, Pennsylvania, and Wellsburg, West Virginia, an Ohio River departure point. West Middletown became a borough in 1823, and developed into a thriving nineteenth-century rural commercial center. The Ralston grain threshing machine was invented

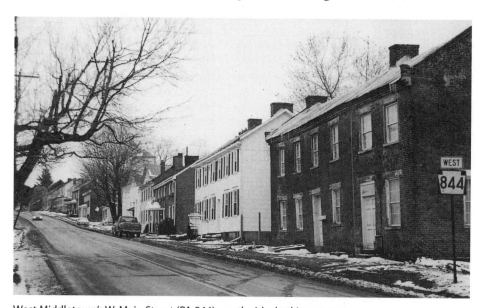

West Middletown's W. Main Street (PA 844), north side, looking west.

nearby and made in West Middletown until the manufacturer's bankruptcy c. 1859. The borough was also a major stop on the Underground Railroad, establishing an Anti-Slavery Society in 1834 and an African Methodist Episcopal Church in the late 1860s at 40 E. Main Street. Situated on a ridge overlooking rolling farmland, the small village has attractive red brick and white frame houses lining E. Main Street. Many of the houses were built before 1850, and the simple vernacular structures are flush with the sidewalk. A two-story red brick, five-bay Greek Revival house (c. 1850; 17 W. Main Street) has a standing-seam metal roof, pressed-stone corner blocks in its window surrounds, and a dogtooth course of brickwork at the cornice. A neighboring house (c. 1870; 1 W. Main Street) has bracketed eaves, segmental-arched windows, and sawn ornament on its porch. The National Register nomination for the borough states that "modest prosperity and a conservative Scots-Irish heritage" have preserved the town's homogeneity and that "the nineteenth century formed it, and the twentieth century froze it."

WS15 Isaac Manchester House, "Plantation Plenty"

1799–1815. 52 Manchester Ln. at PA 231, 3 miles west of West Middletown

One of the best preserved and most architecturally significant farms in the region nestles into a well-watered scoop of land with space for cultivation and grazing. Isaac Manchester, a carpenter from Newport, Rhode Island, traveling along the Wellsburg Pike (PA 844), spotted the site already called "Plantation Plenty" and purchased it in 1797. The Manchester descendants have farmed it ever since. The house was built by 1815, with the joinery completed by Philadelphian John McGowen. The two-and-one-half-story red brick house has Flemish bond brickwork on all elevations, dressed stonework at the foundation, massive brick chimneys at each gable end, and a captain's walk on the rooftop. The interior has a central-hall plan, with a basement kitchen at the downhill corner and a large single room under the eaves. The farm is sited in its valley not for the aesthetics, but to keep it out of the wind and close to spring-

WS15 ISAAC MANCHESTER HOUSE, "PLANTATION PLENTY"

water. The Pennsylvania-type timber-frame barn dates from 1803, with some alterations over the years. Outbuildings contained within stone boundary walls house many early farm implements, including carpentry tools used in the construction of the house and barn. Despite its sturdy utilitarian functioning, the house is a sophisticated eastern seaboard transplant far from the shores of Narragansett Bay. Acknowledging his accomplishment, Manchester's initials and the date the house was completed are carved in the stone parapet at the roofline.

AVELLA VICINITY

WS16 Meadowcroft Museum of Rural Life (George Miller Sr. Farm)

1850, with additions; 2007 shelter, Pfaffmann + Associates. 401 Meadowcroft Rd., 3 miles northwest of Avella

The Miller family has lived on this land since 1795. Over the years, the farm, noted for raising harness racehorses since the 1880s, was denuded of its foliage and strip-mined. After World War II, brothers Albert and Delvin

WS16 MEADOWCROFT MUSEUM OF RURAL LIFE (GEORGE MILLER SR. FARM), Meadowcroft Rockshelter enclosure

Miller planted over 300,000 trees, and, in 1962, began to collect regional artifacts and buildings in danger of being demolished. More than twenty buildings have been moved to the 800-acre site as a means of preserving them and making them accessible to the public. Meadowcroft's structures include three log houses dating from 1795 to the 1850s, an 1834 one-room schoolhouse, an 1865 blacksmith shop, and an 1870s covered bridge. The Fairview South Methodist Episcopal Church (1869–1870), a large log church covered with clapboard siding, was moved here from outside of Jollytown in Greene County.

Three barns on the property could, if restored, interpret rural life in three settings: a 1790s farmstead, an 1860s sheep farm, and an 1890s village. The c. 1790 Patterson Barn, one of the oldest in western Pennsylvania, was moved to Meadowcroft in 1962 from a farm called "Oddity" five miles away. The double-crib log barn is supported by stone piers and has floor timbers of rounded logs. The two sections of the barn are separated by a threshing aisle. The second barn, the C. H. G. Beall barn (c. 1860), is a two-and-one-half-story timber-frame ground barn with louvered windows and a round window in the gable end. It once served a 600-acre merino sheep farm on the Pennsylvania–West Virginia border. The third barn (c. 1890) is from the Hodgkin farm and

was moved to the site from south of Claysville in Washington County. It is a Pennsylvania barn, a type of barn built against a hillside using the mortise-and-tenon or timber-frame method, allowing access to the upper level for hay storage on one side and to the ground floor on the other. Animals live on the ground level, where the entrance doors are sheltered by the porchlike overhang, or forebay.

In 1955, Albert Miller discovered the Meadowcroft Rockshelter, dating to 14,000 BCE, on the property. The archaeological site, a massive rock overhang that sheltered Native American hunting parties, is now recognized as one of the earliest documented sites of human habitation and one of the longest continually used sites in eastern North America. In 2007, Pfaffmann + Associates met the challenge of anchoring a new enclosure around the National Historic Landmark archaeological site to protect it and to provide safe visitor access. The structure has three carefully located foundations that are laterally supported by the original rockshelter outcropping, which collapsed thousands of years ago into Cross Creek. The new enclosure's shed roof is composed of pairs of fifty-five-foot, glue-laminated pine beams. The slatted Douglas fir walls are suspended from the roof and lined with clear polycarbonate, allowing soft natural light into the excavation.

John Canon bought this land from the state of Virginia and established a sawmill and a gristmill along Chartiers Creek in the 1770s. Ten years later, he laid out lots on the land, and his name became permanently attached to it. Since that time, there has been a Presbyterian presence in the region, as evidenced in the establishment by John McMillan of Jefferson Academy (later College) in 1780 in the small log building now at 25 E. College Street. In 1865, Jefferson College merged with Washington College, and four years later all college activities moved ten miles south to Washington (WS4). The strong denominational presence is also apparent in the brick Canonsburg United Presbyterian Church (1870; 112 W. Pike Street) that has evolved from four separate Presbyterian churches within blocks of one another. The church's massing, ebullient corbeling, and bracket-lined cornice are reminiscent of several other United Presbyterian churches in Washington County, including Westminster United Presbyterian in Burgettstown (1873; 1325 Main Street) and Emmanuel United Presbyterian Church (1869–1871; 480 PA 519) in Eighty Four.

With the loss of the college, the area's economy shifted to coal and steel manufacturing in the late nineteenth and early twentieth centuries. During the 1820s, Canonsburg was a stagecoach stop on the Washington and Pittsburgh Turnpike, but it took rail access to Pittsburgh via the Pennsylvania Railroad's Chartiers Branch, established in 1871, to spark an economic recovery. The brick passenger station remains at Murdock and Jefferson streets (c. 1870). The railroad, combined with access to coal, spurred the development of ever-larger factories making sheet iron, bridges, pottery, and stoves, in addition to mining and coal shipping. By 1902, there were twelve trains a day through Canonsburg. The large brick PNC Bank (1903; 4 W. Pike Street) illustrates the commercial success of these enterprises. The borough's commercial core suffered through a period of demolitions in the late 1950s, leaving the brick Colonial Revival Municipal Building and Library of 1963 to act as a town center until the new library, at the corner of N. Jefferson Avenue and Murdock Street, designed by L. D. Astorino, is completed.

WS17 John Roberts House

1798, 1804, 1809, c. 1840. 225 N. Central St.

This beautiful stone and brick house was built in increments during the first half of the nineteenth century. The first section, a large log house of 1798, has been incorporated into the brick portion of 1840, while a stone addition of 1804 remains at the rear of the house. In 1809, the house received a second and more sophisticated stone section facing N. Central Street, which has elegant Flemish bond stonework on the east and south elevations. The exterior woodwork continues this high level of design: stars line the wooden cornice, a simple fanlit doorway retains its original paneled surround, and the southern eaves feature a gable pediment. The c. 1840 brick addition completes the N. Central Street facade at the north end, and duplicates the size and scale of the 1809 stone portion. This addition of two bays makes the house—ironically—the most typical house type in western Pennsylvania: the five-bay. The house commemorates the name of John Roberts, during whose twelve-year ownership, the 1804 and 1809 portions were built. The house was important to Canonsburg's former Jefferson College (see ws4), since for over thirty years it housed either its president or faculty members.

BENTLEYVILLE

WS18 Bentleyville Camp Meeting Grounds

c. 1890; 1907 tabernacle, George W. Yohe. 5 Camp Meeting Ground Rd., off Washington St.

Dotting thirty acres of wooded hillside northeast of Bentleyville, the Union Holiness Camp Meeting Association is a complex of white frame cottages dominated by a large, open-air tabernacle designed by local architect George W. Yohe (1880–1968). An early pastor is said to have exclaimed "God is here!" when he saw the property. Vertical wood siding encloses the tabernacle's west facade, which is ornamented with Gothic-arched double-sash windows flanked by a pair of double doors with wooden strips that mimic the Gothic tracery above. In the gable end, a rose-patterned attic vent and three tiny Gothic-arched vents complete the simple, elegant composition. The other three walls of the gable-roofed building are open, with brick posts supporting wooden trusswork. On the interior, the open trusswork emphasizes the height of the ceiling, and the sloping floor focuses attention on the pulpit and choir. The white frame cottages range from one to two stories. Most have porches and are grouped close to each other and around the tabernacle. A two-story board-and-batten dormitory is set apart from the main rows of cottages. Decorative touches are limited to corner boards, some sawtooth woodworking, and railings. The cottages, extraordinary in number and condition, are simple, as they are intended for use for only one or two weeks each summer, not as permanent shelter.

ELLSWORTH AND COKEBURG

James William Ellsworth, a shipping entrepreneur from Hudson, Ohio, bought 16,000 acres of coal land in southeast Washington County in 1898, and studied the organization of mining towns in Wales. Ellsworth built his model mining community of locally fired red brick, rather than the more commonly used wood. The town's highlight is the administration building, distinguished by its three stories, cupola, and bridged chimneys. Ellsworth spent approximately $100 million to open four mines, two at Ellsworth and two at Cokeburg three miles to the southwest. He provided rail service from the city of Monongahela along Pigeon Creek. During his ownership, 1.5 million tons of coal were mined at the two sites. Miners were assigned to small, three-bay, one-and-one-half-story brick houses. Despite the amenities Ellsworth offered his miners, they went on strike in 1905. In disgust, he sold his Washington County holdings to the Lackawanna Steel Corporation, and offered funding to his hometown of Hudson to create a model community. Nevertheless, the four mines continued operation until 1982. The 238-acre Cokeburg coal patch consists of four-bay, frame duplex houses rhythmically marching up and down sloping hills. Today, their location close to Bentleyville on PA 917 has allowed them to survive, even without the mining operations. An excellent view of Cokeburg may be seen from TWP 441 north of Scenery Hill.

Marianna, yellow-brick row houses.

MARIANNA AND VICINITY

This model mining town, built by the Pittsburgh-Buffalo Coal Company between 1906 and 1912, was noted for its progressive attitude toward its workers' safety and living standards. The company's president, John H. Jones, from Monongahela, specified that the 250 houses be constructed from the yellow brick made in his brickworks at Freeport in Armstrong County, and that the houses have indoor plumbing—among the first miners' housing to do so. Ranging from two to three stories in height and generally two bays wide, the houses have decorative brickwork in the gable ends and originally had turned posts and balustrades supporting their porches. The houses line long straight and curved streets on the now wooded hillside. Marianna had a company store, school, movie theater, and church. At its peak in 1910, its population of 2,000 included White Russians, Italians, Scots, English, and Slavic miners. The 2000 census listed the population at 626 residents. The shuttered mine buildings, located along the wide floodplain of Ten Mile Creek, consist of a tipple and washer, in use until 1988, and brick beehive coke ovens that had closed earlier. Ironically, despite Jones's emphasis on safety, Marianna was the site of a disastrous explosion in 1908 that killed 154 men.

WS19 Valentine Kinder Farm

c. 1769, 1785, 1975. 113 Barnard Rd., 5.6 miles northeast of Marianna

One of the oldest structures in western Pennsylvania, the Kinder house has grown in three sections from the eighteenth to the twentieth centuries. The small original section, said to date from the late 1760s, is a rectangular gable-roofed room with a door on the south elevation and a single window on the north elevation, smaller than many log houses of that period. The second section, built in 1785, is two stories in height and four bays wide, with a gable roof and two attic windows in the upper west-facing gable; its peaked wooden window surrounds appear to date from a later era. The large rear addition dates from 1975, but was built in the style of the 1785 addition, using stone from the same quarry on the farm. The three sections form an ell, and the two older sections were restored in the 1970s. The earliest portion has an original three-layer door, composed of finely detailed wooden sections sandwiching an inner layer of lead. On the interior are a walk-in hearth and a sleeping loft. This working farm has several large outbuildings, including a gable-roofed frame c. 1840 barn with a stone foundation. The family's gristmill (c. 1790) half a mile to the southwest on PA 2011 has similar rubble stonework and corner quoins, is three stories and gable-roofed, and is adjacent to Plum Run, which supplied the waterpower.

WS20 Stephen Ulery Farm

1780–1787, 1857. 34 Cranberry Marsh, off PA 2011, 2.6. miles southeast of Marianna

This elegant, four-bay stone house is one in a colony of buildings constructed by the Ulery family dating from the early to mid-nineteenth century, all sited on the original 500-acre farm in southern Washington County. Included are two houses, a school, a gristmill, and the Zol-larsville Methodist Church. The farmhouse is prominently sited on a knoll overlooking pastureland. The stonework, most noticeable on the gable ends, is laid in a pattern similar to common bond brickwork, twelve courses of smaller stones separated by a course of larger stones. Quoins are quite large and smooth, while the facade windows and door have flat arches with raised keystones. A two-story brick ell was added to the north elevation in 1857. That year, a timber-frame bank barn was built and given a fan-shaped gable-end louver, dentilled cornice, and eaves returns, which add a Greek Revival touch to the utilitarian building. Once a dairy farm, today the owners raise cattle. A one-story, frame guesthouse was built with materials purchased through the Sears and Roebuck catalogue.

CLARKSVILLE

WS21 Yablonski House (Mary Ann Furnace Ironmaster's House)

c. 1820. 5 Polly Ave.

Sited at the border of Greene and Washington counties, overlooking Ten Mile Creek, this large stone ironmaster's house is set well back from the confluence of the creek and the river. It is a two-and-one-half-story golden sandstone gable-roofed house with an equally large addition at the rear. In 1969, it became notorious as the site of the murders of Joseph "Jock" Yablonski and his family, as ordered by the president of the United Mine Workers at the time, Tony Boyle.

WEST BROWNSVILLE

West Brownsville was laid out by Ephraim L. Blaine, whose wife's family, the Gillespies, were the first European owners of the site in 1784. A ferry crossed the Monongahela River here until 1833, when a wooden covered bridge was built to accommodate coaches on the National Road. The present bridge, the second on the site, was built in 1914 reusing the stone piers of the covered bridge. Constructed by the Fort Pitt Bridge Works, its 519-foot span is an unusually long example of the Pennsylvania (Petit) type truss perfected in the 1870s by engineers of the Pennsylvania Railroad; it has an inclined top chord and substruts to resist and transmit stresses.

The village's largest industry was the Pringle Boat-Building Company, which, with its successor firms, built well over five hundred boats between 1844 and 1912. A rail connection to Charleston, West Virginia, by the Pittsburgh, Virginia and Charleston Railroad (PVCRR) opened in 1881, and, later, the Pennsylvania Railroad developed an extensive rail yard just below West Brownsville, prompting another growth in the town's population. A stone, four-bay house built for the ferry operator is one-and-one-half-stories on the west elevation that is flush with the old route of the National Road (c. 1825;

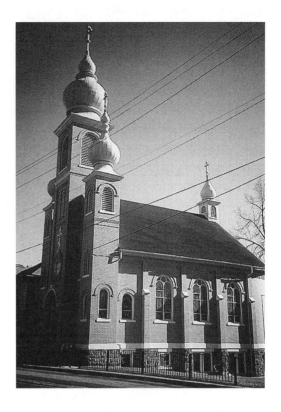

Holy Resurrection Russian Orthodox Greek Catholic Church, West Brownsville. Onion domes are common in western Pennsylvania, but are usually not as well maintained as those seen here.

4 Main Street), but is two-and-one-half-stories on its east elevation toward the river. Today, this one-time home of the Krepps family, who also ran the Malden Inn (ws22), is overshadowed by the hulking, brick, derelict Samuel Thompson distillery buildings surrounding it. The board-and-batten Gothic Revival St. John's Episcopal Church, was under construction in 1860, but only completed in the 1870s after the Civil War. Later, it became the mission for Slovak Methodists, and was often called the Coke Mission, after the coal product manufactured nearby; today it is the Apostolic Temple (132 Main Street). The Holy Resurrection Russian Orthodox Greek Catholic Church (1915; 118 Main Street) brought services to the Carpatho-Rusyns who came to work in the nearby coal mines, summoning them with a quartet of onion domes.

Driving south along PA 88 and following the course of the Monongahela River takes one through several other small river towns. At Fredericktown, the only surviving ferryboat service on the Monongahela River transports about 150 cars per day across the water in three to four minutes.

WS22 Pacis Lounge and Malden Inn (Kreppsville Inn)

1822, 1830. 384 Old National Pike. (U.S. 40)

The inn was built in two phases by the Krepps family of West Brownsville. It is known for its unique datestones, the older (1822) of which is located between the chimneys on the west elevation, and is decorated with wheat sheaves, a plow, and a flying eagle carrying arrows in its talons. The second datestone (1830), located on the facade, is inscribed with the name "Kreppsville," in the hope that a town would grow around the tavern. This 1830 datestone also has the word "Liberty" and similar images to the 1822 datestone. Despite the sign on the inn, the area has continuously been called Malden. The two-story sandstone inn, six bays wide and with distinctively wide bridged chimneys, has seven bedrooms and several public rooms. One-story wings on the north elevation create a U-shaped plan and have been expanded to two stories over the years. A handsome stone, gable-roofed, one-story stable, and a walled stable yard to the west are home to a restaurant and bar.

CALIFORNIA

WS23 California University of Pennsylvania (California State Teachers College, South Western Normal School)

1868–present. 250 University Ave.

California in Washington County was founded in 1849, and named for the California gold rush of the previous year. In the following decade, the borough successfully competed to be the site of one of the commonwealth's ten teacher training, or normal, schools. The first campus building was not completed until 1870. Old Main and its flanking men's and women's dormitories North (demolished 1969) and South halls were designed by John Upton Barr and Henry Moser. Old Main has twin brick mansard-roofed towers, differentiated by clock faces on the southwest tower and the college's bells in the northwest tower. Windows throughout are round arched, with bull's-eye windows above the second-floor windows. In 1900 and 1907, J. C. Fulton Architect of Uniontown designed additions to the east and west elevations. His design for the Library Annex included a stained glass interior dome, a feature he used repeatedly in his churches. John Charles Fulton also designed the First Presbyterian Church of California (1900; 303 4th Street). The round arches of Old Main are echoed in the striking entrance of the Old Science Hall (1890–1892), now the Watkins Academic Center, designed by Frederick J. Osterling. Stylistically, Vulcan Hall (also called Watkins Academic Center, 1892) appears to be by Osterling as well. Red brick Colonial Revival buildings dating from 1930 to 1938 fill out the quadrangle on the south and east, among them the Industrial Arts Building of 1939 by C. C. Compton, who also designed the boiler plant. A quadrangle runs east toward the Monongahela River behind the Herron Recreation and Fitness Center of 1932, designed by Emil R. Johnson and Clarence F. Wilson, terminating in the concrete block and aluminum New Science Hall (1956–1961, Slater, Cozza and Critchfield).

In the 1950s and 1960s, the campus plan called for the demolition of the older structures, and, in anticipation of this event, buildings were crowded around Old Main. Most of the campus buildings were built in this period, until a recent spate of new building. A campus plan of 1996 proposed to make Old Main the focal point again, and this resulted in the demolition of the Reed Arts Center (former library, 1962) and several older dormitories north of the Natali Student Center (1992, WTW Architects). The bold, three-story Manderino Library (1980), sheathed in a warm peach-colored stone, was designed by Norman Frey Associates, the successor firm of Slater, Cozza and Critchfield. The Eberly Building of 1998, designed initially by Mac-Lachlan, Cornelius and Filoni, was built by Hayes Large Architects and is in keeping with the new campus plan to create a primary entrance at the northern facade of Old Main. The Kara Alumni House (2002; 611 2nd Street) also was built after the designs of MacLachlan, Cornelius and Filoni in a similar red brick Colonial Revival style. Since 2000, more than half-a-dozen new building projects continue to upgrade the campus. An entirely new quadrangle of dormitory buildings, or-

WS23 CALIFORNIA UNIVERSITY OF PENNSYLVANIA (CALIFORNIA STATE TEACHERS COLLEGE, SOUTH WESTERN NORMAL SCHOOL), Old Main, rear addition

ange brick with hipped roofs and gabled dormers, surrounds Natali Student Center. The Steele Auditorium is being expanded and renovated by Tasso Katselas (2007), and a New Duda Hall (2007, MacLachlan, Cornelius and Filoni) will be a Welcome Center at 3rd Street and University Avenue.

CHARLEROI

Charleroi sits on the west bank of the Monongahela River, approximately forty-two miles southeast of Pittsburgh. Access to coal and natural gas and a wide floodplain made the site ideal as a manufacturing center after a rail connection was made c. 1880 via the Pittsburgh, Virginia and Charleston Railroad (PVCRR). James S. McKean, postmaster of Pittsburgh and an influential banker, who grew up in the area, realized this potential and formed a consortium that began selling lots in 1890. They named the city Charleroi after the industrial city in southwestern Belgium known for its glass factories. The effort attracted several manufacturers to the new Charleroi, including the Charleroi Plate Glass Company. Later known as Pittsburgh Plate Glass, it produced Carrara glass, a pigmented structural glass substitute for marble, in the Charleroi works. The Hussey-Binns Shovel Works, located in two gable-roofed brick buildings that remain adjacent to the river, and the Macbeth-Evans Chimney Works, one of the world's largest chimney glass manufacturers, also established factories here. Charleroi's growth was so rapid that in 1895, a local newspaper dubbed it the "Magic City."

The Charleroi Land Company attracted developers and merchants, and by 1910, the community included eleven churches and one synagogue representing a dozen ethnic groups. As rail access for passengers to Pittsburgh and the adjoining towns increased accessibility, Charleroi's population tripled between 1890 and 1910. The commercial and residential portions of the town were laid out in a grid pattern on the hillsides to the west. There are two parallel main streets that host the handsome classically inspired former post office, now the John K. Tener Library, by James Knox Taylor, supervising architect of the U.S. Treasury (1909–1912; 638 Fallowfield Avenue). Two banks in the same mode are William L. Stoddart's First National Bank (1919–1922; 210–214 5th Street) and the former Bank of Charleroi and Trust Company by Hopkins and Dentz (1925–1927; Fallowfield Avenue at 5th Street). The Coyle Theater, with its marquee and vertical sign, designed by Victor A. Rigaumont (1927–1928; 311 McKean Avenue), is one of several theaters designed by the architect along the Monongahela River in Donora, Monessen, and Pittsburgh. The brick water filtration plant (1911; McKean Avenue) shows attention to detail in the civic buildings, as does the Fire Department building of 1917 at 328 Fallowfield Avenue. Two cottage-style gas stations designed by local architect Benjamin D. Trnavsky have steeply gabled roofs, testifying to petroleum company attempts to create stations resembling quaint cottages that would fit into the fabric of residential neighborhoods in the 1920s and 1930s; they are at 9th Street and McKean Avenue and at 10th Street and

McKean. Charles W. Bolton and Son designed the Christ Lutheran Church (1908–1909; 400 6th Street) in a Collegiate Gothic mode using native blue stone with Indiana limestone trim.

DONORA

Located in a deep valley along a curve of the Monongahela River and approximately thirty-seven miles south of Pittsburgh by river, this local farmland was called "Walnut Bottom," c. 1769, and by 1815, was known as the village of Columbia, later West Columbia. Even today, the area is isolated by its geography, two miles east of the road connecting Monongahela with Charleroi and reached by a long, winding street descending to the river plain. When the Pittsburgh, Virginia and Charleston Railroad (PVCRR) passed through in 1881, the possibility of using the wide, three miles of floodplain for industry was recognized by William Henry Donner and Andrew Mellon. They built the Union Steel Company here and, ultimately, the American Steel and Wire Company. Andrew Carnegie purchased the steel plant in 1905 and integrated their operations: one plant produced the steel, the other molded it into rods, nails, and wire. By 1915, the Donora Zinc plant was making anticorrosion coating for these steel products. The plants took raw materials into Donora and shipped them as finished products.

The town's name is a contraction of the names "Donner" and Donner's partner Andrew Mellon's wife's first name, "Nora." When the town was laid out in 1900, there were four houses on the farmland and 12 residents. By 1903, there were more than one thousand buildings and 6,000 residents. Like Charleroi, which earned the moniker "Magic City" for the rapidity of its growth, Donora was a city that sprang up due to the power and industry of its major employers. At the peak of production, the town's population swelled to 13,000. To facilitate transportation, Washington and Westmoreland counties built the Donora-Webster Bridge in 1908. William Wylie, a local civil engineer, designed the 1,547-foot, five-span Parker truss.

Ethnic churches were important to the workers of Donora, including St. Michael's Byzantine Church (1911; 511 Murray Avenue), designed by Donora architect Conrad C. Compton for a Greek Catholic parish. The church is a handsome amalgam of elements, from octagonal brick towers supporting domes topped with Greek crosses to a Romanesque Revival round-arched entrance and windows to suit this multiethnic steel town. On an adjacent hillside, the cruciform St. Nicholas Russian Orthodox Church (1951–1959; 1 St. Nicholas Drive) displays the turquoise onion domes and elongated arches of eastern Europe, which contrast with sleek 1950s design elements, such as cream-colored brick and narrow windows. Architect Roman N. Verhovskoy (also Verhovskoi) applied multiple arches and richly carved door surrounds to add depth to the surfaces. The church was built by its congregants during evenings and weekends away from the mills, and, as a result, was eight years in the building.

Industrial success led to tragedy when, on Friday, October 29, 1948, thick smog settled in the river valley creating a temperature inversion that trapped toxic smoke in the town. Six thousand people were sickened and twenty died. Despite the disaster, the factories reopened two days later after a rain. This incident precipitated the first organized efforts to document the impact of air pollution on the populace, which eventually prompted federal regulations and, ultimately, the Clean Air Act of 1970.

Despite a boom around World War II, Donora's factories began layoffs soon after the war ended and they were closed completely by 1967. That year the Donora-Monessen Highway Bridge opened, the borough's second over the Monongahela River. Small-scale industry has opened along the river's edge in a new industrial park, but most of Donora's 5,500 residents now commute to work out of town.

WS24 Cement City District

1916–1917, Louis D. Brandt. Bounded by Walnut and Chestnut sts., Beeler Alley, and Modisette Ave.

Cement City is what its name implies: a group of eighty concrete buildings that the Lambie Concrete House Corporation built for American Steel and Wire Company's middle managers on a steep hillside overlooking Donora. The builders used steel forms to mold the wet, reinforced, poured-in-place, Portland concrete. For the first time, the concrete included 6,650 tons of blast furnace slag from local steel mills. Eight different plans with low-pitched roofs and wide overhanging eaves were offered to meet the needs of one hundred families. The houses were finished with stucco and painted one of four prescribed colors. The company's "Ellwood Style" fencing enclosed the backyards. Because these houses were for managers, Cement City offered indoor plumbing and electric lighting, wood floors over the concrete slabs, and gas-fired hot-air heat. The company provided a flower garden and tennis courts to make living in Donora more desirable. At the time of their construction, the houses of Cement City created a great deal of interest and were visited by engineers and technical students as models of affordable, sanitary, and fireproof housing on a mass scale, a lifelong interest of Louis Brandt. After 1943, the houses were purchased by individual tenants.

MONONGAHELA AND VICINITY

Monongahela grew around a ferry crossing on the Monongahela River. By the 1780s, the town was situated on a direct overland route to Washington, Pennsylvania, via what today is PA 136. One of its earliest settlers was Joseph Parkinson, who operated a ferry and an inn, and hosted several meetings during the Whiskey Rebellion of the 1790s. For brief periods, the locality was called Parkinson's Ferry. Parkinson laid out the town in 1792, naming it Williamsport for his son William. Due to the Virginia–Pennsylvania title disputes, the first public sale of lots was unsuccessful. But four years later, in 1796, twenty-four lots were sold in an area between what is now 1st and 3rd streets. In 1838, a bridge across the Monongahela boosted the city's status as a major commercial center and important boatbuilding site that rivaled Brownsville and Pittsburgh. Political pressure from these rivals delayed railroad service into Monongahela until 1873. The town as it looks today reflects

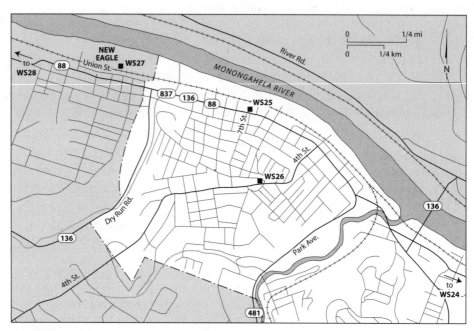

MONONGAHELA

the building boom that accompanied the rail connection and the founding of large-scale industry in the Monongahela River valley.

Architects well known in Pittsburgh and Philadelphia, as well as local architects, were hired to design buildings in Monongahela, testifying to the community's aspirations. John Chislett of Pittsburgh laid out a portion of the Monongahela Cemetery in 1863. Joseph C. Hoxie of Philadelphia designed the First Methodist Church of Monongahela (now altered; 430 W. Main Street) between 1864 and 1873 in a German Romanesque style. Nearly a dozen brick Italianate and Second Empire houses and three Gothic Revival churches on Monongahela's Main Street were designed by local architect John Blythe. Contracting-building firm Yohe Brothers supplied the valley with talented designers and carpenters from the 1880s through the 1920s. And architect Frank Perry Keller designed several handsome houses in Monongahela between 1894 and 1911, before migrating to Los Angeles. Since it was never dependent on a single industry, unlike many other Mon Valley (as the river valley is locally known) towns, Monongahela did not experience a precipitous decline at the collapse of the steel industry in the 1980s. A notable feature of the modern city is the Aquatorium constructed of Flexicore concrete slabs and corrugated metal. This riverside auditorium seats 3,000 people and was built in 1969 by the Frank Irey Construction Company.

WS25 Longwell House

c. 1872, John Blythe. 711 W. Main St.

This two-story, brick, L-shaped house was designed by Monongahela architect John Blythe

(c. 1839–1901), for a riverboat captain, which may explain the porthole in the gable end. Since Blythe co-owned a planing mill, there are heavy wooden molds over the windows, a full bracketed cornice, and a bay window on the Italianate facade. Blythe began his career in Monongahela as a carpenter in the 1860s. During the railroad boom of the 1870s, Blythe designed three churches, notably First Presbyterian Church (1871–1872; 609 W. Main Street); six commercial buildings, including that at 208 W. Main Street (c. 1870); and at least a dozen Italianate and Second Empire brick houses, among them the Mrs. James Kerr House of 1889 (717 W. Main Street). Blythe based his house designs on pattern books of the era, especially A. J. Bicknell's *The Village Builder* (1870), adapting the patterns to meet local needs and his own imagination. The *Monongahela Valley Republican* in 1872 noted that the homes were "better and finer than they might have been, because Mr. Blythe has contributed his advice and skill and taste toward their erection."

WS26 John Robinson House (Daily Republican Model Home)

1939–1940, Frederick G. Scheibler Jr. 522 4th St.

Frederick Scheibler designed this model home sponsored between September 22, 1939, and June 1, 1940, by the *Daily Republican,* the Monongahela newspaper, as a prototype to solve the shortage of inexpensive housing in Mon Valley, and, not coincidentally, as a promotional scheme to sell newspapers. The design centers around a polygonal stair tower highlighted with overlapping brick corner joints, an oxidized copper pyramidal roof, and a glass block window. The house blends modern smooth walls and minimal decoration with a cottage ambience by using Moravian tiles around the door and window and polychrome slates on the gable roof. When com-

WS26 JOHN ROBINSON HOUSE (DAILY REPUBLICAN MODEL HOME)

pleted it was open to the public for two weeks, and the newspaper devoted sixteen pages to the gala event.

WS27 Therm-o-Rock Buildings (Wightman Glass Factory Buildings)

c. 1900. East of Pennsylvania Railroad tracks at Union St.

Remnants of the Pittsburgh region's enormous glass industry are rapidly disappearing, which makes the three remaining Wightman Glass factory buildings in New Eagle, the small town north of Monongahela, a rare find. They lie between the former Pittsburgh, Virginia and Charleston Railroad (PVCRR) tracks and the Monongahela River. The largest brick building is an enormous gable-roofed structure with a gabled monitor at the ridgeline. Corbeling along the cornice of the monitor's gable end distinguishes a circular window vent, with three elongated rectangular windows below. A second brick, gable-roofed building has corbeling at the cornice line, gable ends, and chimney. The tiny office building looks like a train station, although lacking the characteristic deep overhanging eaves. Its hipped roof is broken by large double-windowed dormers. The first story has wide paired windows and a handsome central door with sidelights and transom facing the railroad tracks. Therm-o-Rock has been combining and packaging organic additives and mineral aggregates and powders here since 1948.

WS28 Allegheny Power (West Penn Power, Mitchell Station)

1948 north section; 1963 south section. PA 837, 3 miles north of Monongahela

This power station coal electrification plant is a commanding presence at the shoreline of the Monongahela River along PA 837. The enormous brick rectangular block was built in two parts—the northern section in 1948 and the southern portion in 1963—by Sanderson and Porter, engineers and constructors. A huge smokestack, added in 1982, is painted red and white to warn low-flying planes. The coal that fuels the station arrives by barge from West Virginia. The plant is linked to the hillside by a cable system carrying coal combustion by-products west from the generating plant to the landfill on the top of the hill.

Ridge and Valley

This region (Cambria, Blair, Centre, Huntingdon, Fulton, Bedford, and Somerset counties) encompasses the south-central portion of Pennsylvania west of Blue Mountain. It includes the geographic center of the commonwealth, in the appropriately named Centre County. The region's eastern section is characterized by valleys embedded with limestone or shale and surrounded by sandstone ridges that curve gently from southwest to northeast; from the air, the ridges appear as frozen waves of land. The western area is considered part of the Allegheny Plateau landform. However, unlike the area around Pittsburgh, it belongs to the foothills of the Allegheny Mountains and has higher altitudes and cooler temperatures. Laurel Hill marks the western boundary of this region. Mount Davis, the highest point in Pennsylvania at 3,213 feet, is in Somerset County. The Juniata River and its branches flow through most of the region, heading eastward into the Susquehanna River. This riverine system provided the earliest transportation routes.

Much of the region has remained largely rural despite the early development of iron plantations and coal mining. Remains of many iron plantations survive, especially in Centre and Blair counties. They were rural industrial villages where an iron furnace and those who worked it lived self-sufficiently by integrating agriculture and industry. Coal was an important part of later iron making, and though it continues to be mined here, increased mechanization has reduced the labor force, resulting in fewer human employees. Networks of abandoned coal mine tunnels lie beneath the surface, their presence only apparent when a stream turns orange as rainwater leeches minerals exposed by the mines into the ground water. A model reclamation program designed by D.I.R.T. Studio, a team consisting of an artist, a historian, a landscape designer, and a hydrogeologist, has addressed the acid mine drainage from the former Blacklick Creek Mine No. 6 at Vintondale in Cambria County (see CA29). A series of bioengineered settling ponds and cleansing marshes has changed what was once an ecotragedy into a community-building, water-restoring ideal.

Farming remains important in this region. The fertile farm valleys, each slightly different from the next, offer a secure feeling, as they are sheltered by ridges on the east and west. Because of the relatively high elevation, there is a short growing season here. Dairy farms dominate, although their number is constantly dwindling. Local farmers are often aided by scientists from the Pennsylvania State University (PSU) who experiment with new agricultural and animal husbandry techniques. Farms in this region are generally larger than elsewhere in western Pennsylvania, and focus on a single crop or animal. Increasingly, farms closest to the cities are giving way to residential development and mining interests.

Several early Native American tribes, such as the Shenks Ferry people from the fourteenth and fifteenth centuries, lived throughout the lower Susquehanna. By 1600, they were overrun by the Susquehannocks, who migrated from southern New York and lived in settlements with as many as 3,000 people. Nothing aboveground remains of these cultures. The Iroquois defeated the Susquehannocks, and European contact brought permanent settlers and disease. By the 1770s, Scots-Irish and German settlers moved into the territory. The architecture in this part of Pennsylvania shows two major external influences. In the southern halves of Somerset, Bedford, and Fulton counties, red brick construction and full-facade porches were inspired by Marylanders. Eastern Pennsylvania influences, seen in the stone ironmasters houses and farmhouses in Centre and Blair counties, were brought by immigrants traveling along the Susquehanna and Juniata rivers.

Traversed by the Pennsylvania Canal, Railroad, and Turnpike during the course of the nineteenth and twentieth centuries, these counties stayed generally rural and forested. The growth of PSU and the suburban growth between State College in Centre County and Altoona in Blair County are increasing at such a rate in the early-twenty-first century that it is beginning to rival Pittsburgh in the west. Late-twentieth-century construction in this I-99 corridor includes housing, commercial developments, shopping centers, a convention center, and stadium.

CAMBRIA COUNTY

Cambria County was formed in 1804 from parts of Huntingdon and Somerset counties. Topographically, it is part of a ridge and valley formation, bounded by Laurel Hill on the west and Allegheny Mountain on the east. Straddling the Continental Divide, Cambria's streams drain into both the Gulf of Mexico and the Chesapeake Bay. The area's earliest settlers came in three waves in the 1790s: Roman Catholics traveled from Maryland and settled in the area around Loretto; Pennsylvania Germans from Somerset County settled in the Johnstown area; and immigrants from Wales founded Ebensburg and named the area Cambria after the Welsh mountains of that name.

Lumbering, iron, and steel production dominated the county's economy by the mid-nineteenth century. Small-scale coal mining began in Cambria County in the 1840s with the opening of iron furnaces. While most initially used charcoal, needing 150 acres of trees per year, by the 1850s, most fur-

Cambria Iron Company, Blast Furnaces Nos. 5 and 6, Johnstown, remains of the lower plant.

naces had switched to coke (hard-baked coal) as their fuel source. By the 1920s, Cambria County mines were producing sixteen million tons of coal annually. Johnstown was the headquarters of the Cambria Iron Company after 1852 (CA16). At its peak, in the 1870s, the company employed over 7,000 people, many of whom were immigrants from southern and eastern Europe. Industrial success prompted the growth of a local dairy industry needed to supply the coal miners and ironworkers. Ebensburg, the county seat, and Johnstown took advantage of the various means of transportation: water, turnpike, canal, and rail. Railroads sparked the growth of summer resorts, allowing heat-exhausted city dwellers to enjoy the cool mountain breezes at sites like Cresson. Today, the county is quartered by major highways: U.S. 22 bisects the county from east to west, and U.S. 219 from north to south.

The demise of coal mining and steel manufacturing caused household income to decline by almost 20 percent between 1980 and 1990. To offset this downturn, the county has embraced tourism by commemorating one of its darkest moments, the Johnstown Flood of 1889, with two museums (CA14, and in the village of St. Michael), and a memorial at Grandview Cemetery. This has successfully drawn visitors back to the county, where they can enjoy hiking and biking along the Ghost Town Trail (CA29), Prince Gallitzin State Park on PA 53, and the Allegheny Portage Railroad National Historic Site (CA8), as well as the Johnstown Heritage Discovery Center in the former Germania Brewery building (1907 and 1995–2001) at 7th and Broad streets in Johnstown, and two of the four locations of the Southern Alleghenies Museum of Art in Johnstown (see CA28) and Loretto (see CA5).

Southeast of Johnstown at the confluence of Paint and Little Paint creeks, artist George Hetzel in 1866 found a place of great natural beauty called Scalp Level. The name derives from the farmers' wish that the local lumbermen would harvest all the local timber, that is, cut the trees to ground (or scalp) level, in order to clear the fields for farming. The following summer Hetzel convinced the entire faculty of the Pittsburgh School of Design to join him there and to immortalize these scenes from nature on canvas. Today, this region west of Windber and straddling the Cambria and Somerset county borders has been strip-mined beyond recognition, but the paintings of the Scalp Level painters preserved in museums and private collections nationwide depict the late-nineteenth-century glories of the territory.

EBENSBURG

The Reverend Morgan J. Rees, a Welsh Baptist minister, laid Ebensburg's grid plan over a rounded hill in the early 1790s, naming it after his eldest son, Eben. It was settled mostly by Rees's followers in 1796, who arrived in the second wave of Welsh immigration after the colonial era. The town became the county seat in 1805 by virtue of its proximity to the geographical center of the county, and in 1825, was made a borough. As late as 1873, Welsh descendents were still the largest ethnic group in Ebensburg and the surrounding township.

Less industrial than Johnstown, Ebensburg's economy revolves around the courthouse, which sits atop a hill visible for miles and was donated by the Lloyd family of Welsh ancestry. A six-block area north of the courthouse between Beech and Poplar streets contains a good representation of handsome houses. The Bissell-Kimball house, for example, built for Annie M. Bissell in 1890 (615 W. Highland Avenue) and mistakenly attributed to McKim, Mead and White because of its Colonial Revival sophistication and handsome interior fittings, is more likely a design by Beezer Brothers of Altoona or another regional firm. Today, the house is occupied by the architectural engineering firm of L. Robert Kimball and Associates, who built a large addition at the rear. The Cambria County Historical Society (615 N. Center Street), which resides in an orange brick Queen Anne house built in 1889 for bank president A. W. Buck, has a wraparound porch, turret, and round-arched windows.

CA1 Cambria County Courthouse

1880–1882, Milton Earl Beebe; 1913–1924 additions, James Riely Gordon. 200 S. Center St.

The Cambria courthouse is one of six courthouses Milton Earl Beebe (1840–1922) of Buffalo designed in Pennsylvania and New York. Its French Renaissance Revival appearance with the stone quoins and a slate mansard roof echoes the Warren County Courthouse (WA1) that Beebe designed five years earlier. Both courthouses have similar stonework surrounding their main entrances and had similar cupolas, although Cambria's was removed soon after construction. In 1913, James Riely Gordon (1863–1937), educated in San Antonio but with a national practice out of New York City, was engaged to enlarge the building. He had designed nearly seventy courthouses and government buildings around the country. Work was delayed until 1916 due to World War I. The additions are

curved hyphens attached to rectangular wings at the north and south, and a balcony level within the original courtroom that greatly increased its seating capacity. The main lobby of the building was enhanced by a three-story domed stained glass rotunda in the space originally occupied by Beebe's failed cupola. Murals funded by the Works Progress Administration adorn the walls.

CA2 Noon Collins Inn

1834. 114 E. High St.

When Philip Noon's house was completed in 1834, the Federal style was in its twilight. One of the few pre–Civil War buildings remaining in Ebensburg, the randomly coursed stone house is around the corner from the courthouse, a convenience for its original owner, a judge. By the 1970s, the house had suffered several modernizations, which were undone when the present owners purchased it. Once restored, the five-bay, two-story gable-roofed house looks as it did when it was built, with delicate fanlights in the gable ends and a fanlight above the central entrance.

CA3 Old County Jail

1870, Edward Haviland; 1910 addition. 201 N. Center St.

Like most buildings of its kind, the county prison in Ebensburg is foreboding. The section completed in 1870 is a boxy stone Gothic Revival fortress with cell blocks at the rear and a central tower on the facade. Edward Haviland, son of famous prison architect John Haviland, designed it with massing similar to that of his Blair County Prison (BL3), but with more powerful rectilinear projections on the facade. In 1910, a long brick cell block was added to the west. The addition's resemblance to a large, barred barracks only increases the dreary mood of the building.

LORETTO

CA4 Carmelite Monastery of St. Therese of Lisieux

1929–1930, A. M. Tadejeske. 201 Loretto Rd. (PA 1001)

This red brick Discalced (barefoot) Carmelite monastery, loosely based on a convent in Lisieux, France, sits on fourteen acres in the Allegheny Mountains. The front of the two-and-one-half-story building is a shallow U shape; at the rear is an enclosed courtyard. Eighteen cells face this interior cloister for the nuns who withdraw from the world to focus intensely on God's work. The steeply sloping roof, diaper-patterned brickwork in the gable end above the chapel, and bell tower evoke the forms of the French monastery. The Discalced Carmelites came to the United States in the 1790s, but when this monastic group was exiled from France in the 1920s, they were invited to the Diocese of Altoona. Charles Schwab's sister, Mary Jane, who took the name Mary Cecelia of the Blessed Sacrament, joined the "barefoot nuns," and area industrialist Schwab financed this convent in Loretto. Pittsburgh architect Lucian Caste made alterations to the chapel in 1967.

CA5 Mount Assisi (Charles Schwab Estate, "Limestone Castle")

1919, Dana and Murphy; Charles Wellford Leavitt Jr., landscape architect. PA 1001 and Manor Dr. NW (PA 1005)

Now home to an order of Franciscan monks, this was first the summer home of Charles Schwab, Andrew Carnegie's trusted lieutenant and the first president of the United States Steel Corporation. Eager to occupy the new property he named "Immergrun" (CA7) in the town where he grew up, Schwab commissioned a frame Queen Anne house from architect Frederick J. Osterling in 1898. In 1915, the Osterling house, now known as Bonaventure

Hall, was hoisted over a group of trees and moved to make way for the stone mansion designed by the New York City firm of Dana and Murphy. The new house was half the size of Schwab's New York City mansion, forty-four rather than eighty-three rooms. Richard Henry Dana Jr. (1879–1933), the grandson of poet Henry Wadsworth Longfellow, attended the Ecole des Beaux-Arts in Paris from 1904 to 1906. He is presumed to have been the primary designer of the Schwab house since his partner Henry Killam Murphy (1877–1954) was working on Sinling College in China between 1913 and 1918. The house itself, known as "Limestone Castle," is an austere Renaissance Revival design of smooth buff-gray stone with tiled roofs and gabled dormers on the east and crenellation at the west end, both ends punctuated by towering chimneys. Despite a massive two-story bay window and wraparound porch, the house has the formal qualities of an urban mansion rather than a summer home. Stone carriage and gate houses are visible from Loretto Road.

It is the layout of the gardens that truly distinguishes the estate. The grounds were sculpted by the nationally known landscape engineer Charles Wellford Leavitt Jr., whose works ranged from country estates, colleges, and town plans to racetracks and sewage plants. (Leavitt was hired by the owner of the Pittsburgh Pirates to design Forbes Field in Pittsburgh in 1909—his only design for a baseball stadium.) He designed the elaborate Italian Renaissance sunken gardens south of Schwab's mansion to cascade down the steep hillside in a series of nine falls ending in three reflecting pools. While much of the original statuary was auctioned after Schwab's death in 1939 to pay his considerable debts, four pieces and many of Leavitt's horticultural choices remain.

Nearly 250 acres and a dozen buildings of the original 1,000-acre estate were purchased for the Franciscans for less then $50,000. The mansion now accommodates a monastery, and the original house, Bonaventure Hall, is a home for novices. The gardens have been restored mostly by Father Ronald Bodenschatz, who added religious statuary, and are the only part of the property that is open to the public at 105 St. Francis Drive.

South of Loretto Road, St. Francis University, a small, coeducational, liberal arts school hosts the headquarters of the Southern Alleghenies Museum of Art, an American art museum in four parts in Altoona (BL10), Johnstown (see CA28), Ligonier Valley (see Ligonier Valley, p. 227), and here in Loretto. Architect Roger Cesare Ferri transformed a former gymnasium, using black steel members in a grid, to create a grand entrance and interior space fit for displaying art.

CA6 Basilica of St. Michael the Archangel

1899, Frederick J. Osterling. 321 St. Mary St.

St. Michael's church is a product of the convergence of the two most influential and diametrically opposed denizens of Loretto: one born a prince who lived as a pauper, the other born a pauper who aspired to live as a prince. Father Demetrius Augustine Gallitzin, son of a Russian prince and Prussian Catholic mother, went to Baltimore in 1792 to study under Bishop John Carroll. He gave up his title and became a Roman Catholic priest and missionary in the Allegheny Mountains after 1799. He founded and built the first church here in 1800, and after forty years of tending his flock, he died in Loretto, known simply as "Father Smith" (his mother's maiden name was Schmettan). Fifty-nine years later, the other major name in Loretto's history, Charles Schwab, commissioned this stone church and a black marble statue to mark Gallitzin's grave.

The Romanesque Revival church was designed by Frederick Osterling, Schwab's favorite architect, who designed Schwab's house in Braddock ten years before (AL55) and his first summerhouse in Loretto, now called Bonaventure Hall (see CA5). The immense square tower pierced by two layers of round-arched windows and topped by squat pinnacles does more to tie the church to earth than raise it heavenward. As such, it is a fitting symbol of Schwab's all-too-earthly life.

The adjacent three-story Italianate manse is also attributed to Osterling. At 357 St. Mary's Street, Gallitzin's two-story simple home and attached private chapel, built to replace his log house in 1832, have been preserved, along with some of his effects.

CA7 Norman Village, Klein Immergrun

1920, Dana and Murphy; Charles Wellford Leavitt Jr., landscape architect. 439 Brick Rd.

Charles Schwab, an uneasy combination of small-town boy and wealthy industrialist, asked his New York City architects Dana and Murphy to design a mansion and a farm in the village of Loretto. The farm, called the Norman Village, is located southeast of the mansion on rolling hills cascading away from the ridge. Five ivy-covered buildings completed in 1920, with stuccoed walls and steeply pitched, slate-covered pointed roofs, comprised a working farm where pigs, sheep, and horses were raised. The sculpted landscape design was conceived by Charles Wellford Leavitt Jr., whose varied career included designing estates for the Whitney and Jewett families, and working closely with Schwab on the design of Lehigh University in Bethlehem, Pennsylvania. The farm buildings enclose a courtyard on a hillside, with the smoke house, butcher shop, carriage house, and forge on the upper level, and a piggery and sheepfold at the base of the slope. Today, the complex is the summer estate for a local architect-engineer who has designed a cottage as his art

CA7 NORMAN VILLAGE, KLEIN IMMERGRUN, former farm complex

studio on the hillside overlooking the farm complex. His extensive family enjoys the five-bedroom house, swimming pool, and several golf holes. Schwab, who took up golf in 1915, commissioned eminent golf course architect Donald J. Ross (1872–1948) to design a nine-hole golf course south of the former farm. Immergrun Golf Course is owned and maintained by St. Francis University and open to the public. The farm and the town of Loretto were serviced by the 1.5-million-gallon reservoir dressed as a stone medieval tower on the hillside east of Klein Immergrun.

CRESSON AND VICINITY

Cresson, on the path of the Huntingdon, Cambria, and Indiana Turnpike in the late 1790s, lies one-half mile west of the summit of the Allegheny Mountains on tableland between Allegheny Mountain and Laurel Hill. Medicinal spring waters were discovered on the land, and Philadelphia philanthropist John Elliot Cresson convinced the locals that a resort would prosper here.

In an effort to compete with New York's Erie Canal, Pennsylvania built its own canal, but the Allegheny Mountains were a major obstacle. Engineering ingenuity led to a combined system of water and rail transportation, where canal boats were loaded onto rail beds and pulled by hoists or engines through the mountains. Ten inclines were built along the Allegheny Portage Railroad. Incline No. 6 reaches the summit (CA8; and see CA11) near Cresson.

Inns were built along the pike and, later, the canal, but the era of large resort hotels began with the railroads in the 1850s. Established in 1854, the Allegheny Mountain Health Institute in the Mountain House Hotel was linked to the railroad by a plank sidewalk. The hotel, which ultimately housed 1,000 guests and was surrounded by three hundred forested acres, vied with Saratoga and Bedford Springs as a celebrated watering place in the 1880s. Demolished in 1916, the sole surviving element from the Mountain House Hotel is a conical tower preserved on a frame house of 1862 at 1220 Cottage Street.

Several of the eight cottages remaining on the Mountain House grounds were built by the Cresson Springs Company in 1862.

The large frame house at 1225 3rd Street, with Shingle Style and Queen Anne elements, was built c. 1887 for Benjamin Franklin Jones, founder of Jones and Laughlin Steel Mills. Named "Braemar" (Scottish for "on the hill above the spring"), it is derelict but is an extremely important artifact of the resort era and an architecturally significant house for central Pennsylvania. Andrew Carnegie, who worked for the Pennsylvania Railroad in nearby Altoona, summered with his mother in Cresson during the 1880s to escape the heat of New York City. Carnegie's cottage was one house east of Jones's. After his mother died there in 1886, Carnegie never returned to Cresson, despite his extensive land holdings on a nearby hillside. In 1913, he donated his five hundred acres of land to the Pennsylvania State Sanitarium for tubercular patients. The sanitarium functioned for over fifty years, and today is a state correctional institution.

In the 1890s, coal mining and coke making became a major local industry, and with seaside resorts replacing mountain retreats in popularity, the stink of coke making replaced the fresh air of the grand hotels. Instead of shipping passengers, the local transportation industry began shipping tons of coal to Pittsburgh and Philadelphia. By 1925, the Pennsylvania Coal and Coke Company, which had a local office in Cresson, counted 2,723 employees in Cambria County. The former office building (c. 1910) remains at the northwest corner of Ashcroft Street and 2nd Avenue, now called the Calandra Building. A new set of corporate executives built brick houses in Cresson; the coal executives concentrated on Webster Hill. Cresson native Admiral Robert Edwin Peary (1856–1920) in 1909 was the first American explorer to reach the North Pole.

CA8 Allegheny Portage Railroad National Historic Site (Samuel Lemon Tavern)

c. 1834; c. 1910 addition. U.S. 22 Gallitzin exit, 0.5 miles east of Cresson

Samuel Lemon had the good fortune to own the land and operate a tavern at Cresson Summit along the Huntingdon, Cambria, and Indiana Turnpike when the Allegheny Portage Railroad (APRR) came through in 1834. The original log tavern was quickly replaced with a larger stone building, which served as both an inn and residence. Built at the top of incline No. 6 of the APRR system as it made its way over Allegheny Mountain from Hollidaysburg to Johnstown, the seven-bay, two-story stone house faces the tracks within a hundred yards of the stationary engine house. Built on the traditional Pennsylvania five-bay,

central-hall plan, the house was enlarged with two smaller-scaled bays at the west in the first decade of the twentieth century. The main entrance has a delicate fanlight above the door, while two simpler entries have rectangular transoms.

The house is now the centerpiece of a National Historic Site, which includes the path of the inclined plane, the preserved foundations of the engine house, and a stone bridge over the incline. These elements provide a tangible impression of what the area looked like in the 1830s and 1840s.

The stone skew arch bridge (technically in Blair County) was built 1832–1833 by J. Fenton, A. and J. Darling, and R. Kinimouth to carry the Huntingdon, Cambria, and Indiana Turnpike over the Portage railway. The bridge marked the intersection of two technologies:

the bridge representing the old transportation route crossing the Portage Railroad representing the newest technology in the 1830s. To allow for the steepness of the turnpike's grade, the bridge was changed from its original design, perpendicular to the tracks below, to the present skewed configuration, where each course of stone along the length of the bridge was stepped so that it rises at a gentler grade over the tracks.

In 1992, a visitors' center opened in two gable-roofed, stone-faced buildings joined by an archway that mimics the opening of the Staple Bend Tunnel (CA11). A short walk east, the modern wheelhouse, sheltering the remains of the stationary engine that formerly pulled railcars up the incline, was designed by Ken Bennet with technical review by Harold LaFleur, both of the National Park Service. The structure resembles the original wheelhouse.

CA9 Mount Aloysius College

1892–present, Longfellow, Alden and Harlow, and others. 7373 Admiral Peary Hwy. (PA 2014)

Mount Aloysius's main building was Longfellow, Alden and Harlow's largest commission in western Pennsylvania after the Carnegie Institute in Oakland (AL41). Architectural historian Margaret Henderson Floyd (1993) has noted that the styling here combines elements of a medieval Flemish character with classical ornament. For more than ten years following groundbreaking for the main building, the architects were active on the campus, making additions and alterations. The building, oriented east toward the railroad, is a beautifully proportioned, large, red brick, L-shaped structure with a tall square tower anchoring the center. Heavy dormers and distinctive arcading in the tower enliven the upper portion of the hipped roof. The first story is connected to flanking five-bay wings by a loggia that is punctuated by roundels reminiscent of Filippo Brunelleschi's arcades in fifteenth-century Florence. In 1902, Charles Schwab funded a small, brick gable-roofed Romanesque Revival music hall, called Alumnae Hall, attached to the north elevation. Windows in the hall depict musical instruments and were designed by Willet Stained Glass and Decorating Company.

CA8 ALLEGHENY PORTAGE RAILROAD NATIONAL HISTORIC SITE (SAMUEL LEMON TAVERN), stone skew arch bridge, photo 1987

The school's origins lie in an academy for girls in Loretto in 1853. Construction began on the Cresson campus in 1892, and the school moved to the new campus in 1897. Mount Aloysius became a junior college in 1939, and advanced to a four-year college in 1990. The campus consists of eleven buildings arranged along a gently sloping hillside. The chapel (1923) attached to the administration building's southwest corner was designed by William R. Perry for John Comes's successor firm Comes, Perry and McMullen in what they called a "Lombardy Romanesque" style. After World War II, two simple, brick, flat-roofed dormitories were designed by Johnstown architect Art Hornick. Between 1964 and 1997, five classroom and laboratory buildings designed by Hayes Large Architects were added west of the administration building. A gable-roofed health and fitness center was designed by Don Lenger in 1990. The postmodern brick library, designed by L. Robert Kimball and Associates in 1995, completed the quadrangle west of the main administration building, echoing its form in the central entrance and projecting end wings. The entrance portico has huge concrete columns supporting a stylized entablature and a pediment-shaped window above that is a reinterpretation of classical forms.

CA10 Elmhurst (Mary Thaw House)

1901–1902, George S. Orth and Brother. 365 McConnell Rd., 1.5 miles west of Cresson

Mary Sibbet Copley Thaw, widow of William K. Thaw, commissioned this grand half-timbered house in 1901, according to a reference in *The American Architect and Building*

CA10 ELMHURST (MARY THAW HOUSE)

News of that year. The area was popular with Pittsburgh industrial moguls such as Andrew Carnegie and Charles Schwab, and it is not surprising that the Thaws would choose an architect well known to that set. George S. Orth (1843–1918) and his brother, Alexander Beatty Orth (1868–1920), formed their partnership in 1900, but George, while in solo practice, had already designed two houses for William Penn Snyder of Pittsburgh (AL65).

The design of Elmhurst is often attributed to Stanford White, but research into the McKim, Mead and White archives disproves that assertion. The rumor persisted, however, and grew in dramatic license after 1906, when White was murdered by Mary's son, Harry K. Thaw, although that grisly coincidence did nothing to reveal the name of the architect of this house. The work was also mistakenly attributed to Beezer Brothers of nearby Altoona, especially when they designed buildings for Mary Thaw in Pittsburgh. However, the design can be credited to the Orth brothers, with contractors John H. Trimble and Brother of Allegheny, who were paid $75,000 in August 1901.

Its history aside, the Tudor Revival house is well designed and equally well appointed. Not only is the hand of the architects obvious in the house's siting and the design, it is also evident in the fittings and details, such as the heavy banisters, fine cabinetry, and oak woodwork. The first floor has four rooms with a slightly off-center central hall, and the upper floors are laid out to accommodate numerous guests and servants, with a fifty-foot-long corridor running parallel to the ridgepole. The main entrance has a heavy, 5 × 8–foot Dutch door that opens onto a porch overlooking a wide valley below. The estate includes a springhouse and timber-frame bank barn with two cupolas.

ST. MICHAEL AND VICINITY

Serving as a base for the fishing and hunting trips of its wealthy clientele, the village of St. Michael was the original home (established 1879) of the South Fork Fishing and Hunting Club. Built by the members of the club, the cottages overlooked Lake Conemaugh, the man-made lake that burst its dam and flooded Johnstown in 1889. Although the lake, dam, and powerful industrialists are gone, the village remains. It retains only three of the original frame cottages, although these Queen Anne and Stick Style buildings were significantly larger than cottages. The three-story frame clubhouse has seventy-four rooms and a wraparound porch (1889; 186 Main Street). Completed just before the flood and owned by the group who bought the land originally, including Andrew Carnegie, Henry Clay Frick, Henry Phipps Jr., Robert Pitcairn, and Andrew Mellon, the clubhouse has been restored and is now a hotel.

For several years after the flood, refugees from Johnstown resided here, until the properties were sold piecemeal. After the club disbanded, coal was discovered under the former lake bed, and in 1907, the Maryland Coal Company opened a coal mine and built company housing in the village, giving it the name of St. Michael. The building stock of this small town consists mostly of clapboard single-family homes.

The National Park Service restored the small, three-bay, gable-roofed frame cottage owned by Colonel Elias J. Unger, manager of the South Fork Fishing and Hunting Club, and built an interpretive center nearby, northwest of St. Michael at 733 Lake Road, north of PA 869. This site explains the creation of the lake from the Little Conemaugh River and the failure of the dam, while the Johnstown Flood Museum (CA14) documents the city's devastation when twenty million tons of water came barreling down the valley.

CA11 Staple Bend Tunnel

1828–1834. Beech Hill Rd. (PA 3035), 7.2 miles northwest of St. Michael

The Staple Bend Tunnel, built for the Allegheny Portage Railroad, sits atop the first of ten inclines—five up the mountains, five down—that took railcars bearing canal boats from Hollidaysburg to Johnstown, where they could reenter the canal. It was a groundbreaking enterprise, both literally and figuratively. According to the National Park Service, this is believed to be the first railroad tunnel in the United States. It was blasted out of solid bedrock at the rate of about eighteen inches per day to create a tube 901 feet in length and 20 feet in diameter. Portals at the east and west entrances are lined with cut sandstone to protect the tunnel from rock slides and other weather-related accidents. The sandstone ashlar west portal resembles a Roman triumphal arch and is embellished with paired Doric pilasters on each side of the arch. The eastern portal is roughly horseshoe-shaped and lined with cut stones. The tunnel is open to the public as part of the Staple Bend Tunnel rail trail run by the National Park Service.

JOHNSTOWN

For a town so thoroughly defined by its disasters, Johnstown has a remarkably productive and optimistic history. The city developed in a steep valley where the Little Conemaugh River joins Stony Creek to form the Conemaugh River proper. The topography lends itself to flooding, and Johnstown has been inundated numerous times. Between 1881 and 1889 alone, the city was flooded seven times. On May 31, 1889, when the dam across the South Fork of the Little Conemaugh River failed and sent twenty million tons of water crashing down the narrow valley into Johnstown, 2,209 people died, and only a handful of buildings were left standing. The engineers of the Pennsylvania Railroad earned fame when the only bridge left standing in the flood's path was of their design. It was also the first large, stone, arched bridge they had constructed west of the Susquehanna. Downstream from Johnstown's confluence, the bridge caught and held the massive piles of debris without collapsing. The town rebuilt and continued to prosper because of the many iron industries based here, especially the largest, the Cambria Iron Company (CA16). Its Lower Works are located slightly to the west of the city center and stretch more than a mile along the north bank of the Conemaugh. The multitude of churches in the town reflects both the devotion of people well acquainted with disasters as well as the rich ethnic stew of residents created by the importation of workers for the coal, iron, and steel industries.

The main urban areas lie in a triangle of land just upstream from the confluence of the Little Conemaugh River and Stony Creek. In 1916, the Johnstown City Planning Commission hired a team of architects to develop a

Johnstown from the top of the incline, a valley between the Little Conemaugh River and Stony Creek.

comprehensive plan for the city, which they published the following year. Henry Hornbostel, George Wild, and Johnstown architect Victor A. Rigaumont constructed a detailed plan based on Beaux-Arts principles, some of which was implemented. Designs for both the Washington Street and Napoleon Street bridges were realized, as was the scheme to restructure the flow of traffic through the use of one-way streets. A proposed major thoroughfare on the south bank of Stony Creek was instead routed along PA 56 on the north bank. The plan's suggestion of a riverside park was not realized.

Johnstown was hit hard by the industrial decline of the mid-twentieth century, and the population declined almost 60 percent between 1930 and 1990. However, infused with money from the state government and rejuvenated by a bustling tourism industry, the city is reviving. The Cambria City Heritage Discovery Center highlights the life of ethnic workers at the ironworks. The University of Pittsburgh Medical Center has expanded, the Crown American Corporation (CA20) has maintained a downtown presence, and heavy industry has returned to the Cambria Iron Company site (CA16).

CA12 City Hall

1890–1900, Charles M. Robinson, with Walter R. Myton, project architect. Main St. at Market St.

The City Hall, a monumental Richardsonian Romanesque building, was designed to anchor the center of Johnstown when it resurrected after the flood of 1889. The building's rectangular two-story mass is capped by a dormered and hipped roof, and a central clock tower.

An octagonal tower stands at the building's northwest corner. Plaques at the corner of Main and Market streets show the levels that water reached during the disastrous floods of Johnstown's history.

Charles Morrison Robinson (1867–1932) had a career that spanned thirty-eight years and took him from Altoona, to Pittsburgh (1901–1908), to Richmond, Virginia, where he designed several hundred school buildings and became the staff architect for several colleges, including William and Mary. Walter R. Myton (1872–1929), a talented and prolific architect who studied at Cornell, practiced first in his hometown of Huntingdon and then in Pittsburgh before arriving in Johnstown in 1900, where he remained until his death.

CA13 The Professional Building (United States Post Office)

1912, James Knox Taylor, supervising architect of the U.S. Treasury. 131 Market St.

The design of this Greek Revival former post office adheres to supervising architect James Knox Taylor's proclamation in 1901 that government buildings should return to the "classic style of architecture." The Market Street elevation, clad in Pennsylvania white marble with a terra-cotta cornice, has a portico of eight fluted Doric columns, while the triglyphs and metopes of the full-facade entablature are appropriate to the Doric order. The post office occupied this building until 1937, when it moved to the larger Boxler Station (CA17). Between 1938 and 1968, the building housed a variety of government offices, including the Works Progress Administration, Internal Revenue Service, and Bureau of Mines. In 1968, Crown Construction (later Crown American Corporation; CA20) purchased the building and occupied it until 1989. Company architect Carl Barefoot renovated it by converting the mezzanine into a full second floor. Today, the building houses various offices.

CA14 Johnstown Flood Museum (Johnstown Carnegie Library)

1890–1892, Addison Hutton. 304 Washington St.

As a member of the South Fork Fishing and Hunting Club, which was partially responsible for the maintenance and subsequent failure of the South Fork dam, Andrew Carnegie funded this library in 1890 after touring the disaster area in 1889. Architect Addison Hutton (1834–1916), a Westmoreland County native and Quaker, trained under and, for a time, shared a practice with Samuel Sloan in Philadelphia. The three-story tan brick Chateauesque building has been refitted as the Johnstown Flood Museum. The steeply pitched roofline, intricate gabled dormers,

and tall narrow chimneys give the building an elegance beyond the grammar of its plaque that states: "Rebuilded, Enlarged & Improved by ANDREW CARNEGIE, 1891."

CA15 Walnut Street Station, Pennsylvania Railroad

1916, Kenneth M. Murchison. 301 Washington St.

In 1916, the Pennsylvania Railroad began a series of improvements at Johnstown, including elevating the right-of-way by several feet. This had to be accomplished without interruption to the more than two hundred trains that ran daily through the city. The construction also included this reddish brick passenger station designed by the Beaux-Arts-trained, New York City architect Kenneth M. Murchison (1872–1938). A flat-roofed one-story section surrounds the raised portion on all sides and provides a recessed entrance fronted with Tuscan columns and pilasters. The facade columns are echoed on the side elevations as engaged columns on the east elevation and pilaster strips on the west. Arched windows on all four elevations flood the two-story waiting room with light.

CA16 Bethlehem Steel Corporation (Cambria Iron Company, Cambria Steel Company)

1852, S. A. Cox, supervising engineer; many additions. 317 Washington St.

With such innovations as the three-high rolling mill and the perfection of the Bessemer process, the Cambria Iron Company contributed greatly to the foundations of the iron

CA14 JOHNSTOWN FLOOD MUSEUM (JOHNSTOWN CARNEGIE LIBRARY), photo 1988

There is a glamour about the making of steel. The very size of things—the immensity of the tools, the scale of production—grips the mind with an overwhelming sense of power.... Bessemer converters dazzle the eye with their leaping flames. Steel ingots at white heat, weighing thousands of pounds, are carried from place to place and tossed about like toys.... The display of power on every hand, majestic and illimitable, is overwhelming; you must go again and yet again before it is borne in upon you that there is a human problem in steel production.
—John A. Fitch, *The Steel Workers*, 1911

The above quotation evokes equal parts unabashed wonder and cautionary observation, as it applies to the entire region of western Pennsylvania. The sights, sounds, and smells of an active steel mill dramatize both the dangers to the mill's workers and the activities that bonded men together in a common struggle. The region west of the Allegheny Mountains has physical remnants of every step in the growth of the iron and steel industries, from the earliest form of iron making in the 1770s in the Juniata Valley to the decline of the steel industry in the mid-1980s in the Monongahela Valley.

Iron furnaces, relying initially on charcoal for fuel and later on coal, proliferated as the demand for iron grew. Blair and Cambria counties together had nearly one-fourth of the early iron furnaces in Pennsylvania. Their remains, especially those of the Mt. Etna Furnace and Iron Plantation (BL28), are a fascinating lesson in the early technology of iron making.

The railroad build-up of the mid-nineteenth century caused the demand for iron rails and, later, steel rails to explode. By 1886, the United States was the largest steelmaker in the world, even before the demand for steel expanded with the proliferation of automobiles, appliances, skyscrapers, and tin cans (originally steel sheathed in tin).

Structures to accommodate these industries evolved from the small, domestic scale of iron plantation buildings consisting of stone houses and barns, to brick, gable-roofed sheds often with round-arched windows and monitor roofs dominating their riverside sites, and, finally, to

BLAST FURNACES NOS. 3 AND 4 OF THE CARRIE FURNACE, UNITED STATES STEEL CORPORATION, IN RANKIN, ALLEGHENY COUNTY, 1964.

today's steel-sheathed behemoths with scrubbers catching the bulk of their particulates and mechanization taking the place of thousands of workers. The entire region was devoted to making steel and making things out of steel, including structural elements, tubes, wire, and sheet, and to providing the services needed to support the industry, from making refractory bricks to building the trucks and machinery used in the mills.

Towns grew up around the large, fully integrated plants, with river docks and rail yards bringing in the raw materials and removing the finished products. Two novels written in the 1940s capture the human anguish and energy of these times in western Pennsylvania: Thomas Bell's *Out of this Furnace* (1941) and Marcia Davenport's *Valley of Decision* (1942).

The surviving iron and steel plants, especially the Cambria (CA16) and Edgar Thomson (AL57) works, each have an assemblage of buildings, many now encased in metal sheathing, with enormous machinery hidden from view. But only remnants remain of the once mighty mills in Beaver County, at Midland's former Crucible Steel works and Aliquippa's enormous former Jones and Laughlin plant. The hulking carcasses of the region's industrial infrastructure are often worth more as scrap than as machinery.

The puzzle for today is what should be saved to illustrate this legacy and how to pay for it. The America's Industrial Heritage Project founded in 1986 published studies of nine Pennsylvania counties: Bedford, Blair, Cambria, Fayette, Fulton, Huntingdon, Indiana, Somerset, and Westmoreland. In 1988, the name changed to the Southwestern Pennsylvania Heritage Preservation Commission, and since 1998, it has been known as the Westsylvania Heritage Corporation, which works to record and interpret the industrial history of these central and southwestern Pennsylvania counties.

The Regional Industrial Development Corporation (RIDC), in Allegheny County, took charge of several brownfield sites and is marketing and facilitating their reuse. The Steel Industry Heritage Corporation, and its Rivers of Steel National Heritage Area, documents steel towns and their customs, oral histories, and crafts, while preserving and giving tours of their landmark buildings and structures, such as the former Carrie Furnaces downriver from the Edgar Thomson works (AL57).

While U.S. Steel continues to operate the world's largest coke works at Clairton in Allegheny County, the former Jones and Laughlin Coke Works in the Hazelwood neighborhood of Pittsburgh (opened in the 1880s and rebuilt periodically until the 1960s) ceased production in 1999, ending the last element of the manufacture of steel within the city (Braddock and Clairton are outside the city limits). In Hazelwood, the Almono Project—a consortium of foundations—has purchased these old coke works and plans to develop a mixed-use project, including research space and housing on the 178-acre site.

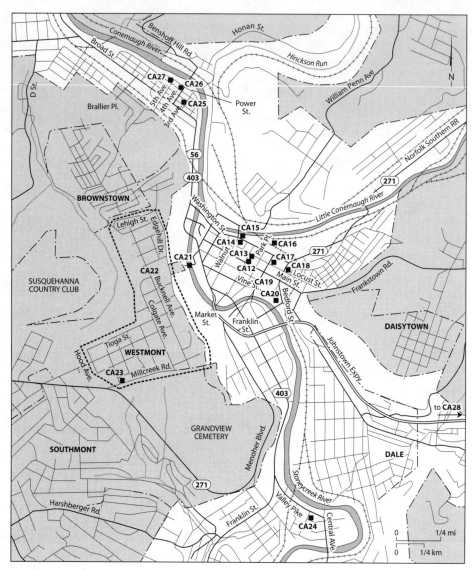

JOHNSTOWN

industry. The company reached its peak in the post–Civil War era when the demand for iron and steel rails was immense, providing 10 percent of the rails produced in the nation, with over one million miles of rail between 1880 and 1890 alone. George King and Peter Shoenberger founded the company in 1852 to supply rails to the Pennsylvania Railroad. However, the cost of putting the plant into operation and a drop in the price of iron pushed the company close to bankruptcy. A reorganization of ownership and management in 1862 allowed continued production of top quality iron and rails. Between 1852

and 1862, the company made the first thirty-foot rail produced in the nation. By 1873, the Cambria Iron Company was the largest iron and steel works in the United States. Renamed the Cambria Steel Company in 1898, it continued to expand, building mills along the floodplains of the Conemaugh and Little Conemaugh rivers between Morrellville and Franklin.

In 1923, the Bethlehem Steel Corporation acquired the company, modernizing and running it for nearly seventy years. Bethlehem Steel closed the plant in 1992, and sold the property as individual pieces rather than as an integrated mill. Republic Steel and Standard Forging, which produced railcar axles in the rolling mill during the 1870s, bought properties at the far end of the Lower Works downriver from the city. At the upper end of the works, Johnstown Welding and Fabricating now operates in the cavernous, corrugated-metal, hangar-sized buildings known as the eleven-inch mill and the manganese shop. Fortunately for the city of Johnstown, the most historic part of the works containing the blacksmith shop (c. 1864), rolling mill office (c. 1874), pattern shop (c. 1870), and machine shop (1906) remain. These are the most architecturally significant brick buildings, designed in a Romanesque Revival style, and located in the middle of the property. Bethlehem Steel is donating the four buildings, along with a large parcel of the surrounding land and the road leading into the area, which will be developed for commercial use, tourism along the river, and possibly some light industry in the machine shop.

CA17 Johnstown Post Office, Boxler Station

1937, Louis A. Simon, supervising architect of the U.S. Treasury, and Lorimer Rich. Franklin and Locust sts.

In 1937, the U.S. Post Office moved out of its original building on Market Street (CA13) into this modern, polished black granite building designed by Lorimer Rich (1891–1978). A graduate of Syracuse University, Rich designed several buildings for his alma mater. He served in World War I, then worked for New York architect Charles A. Platt and studied at the American Academy in Rome. From 1922 to 1928, he was in the office of McKim, Mead and White. After leaving that firm, Rich won his most famous commission: the design for the Tomb of the Unknowns at Arlington National Cemetery with sculptor Thomas Hudson Jones. While in private practice, Rich designed at least eight post offices in New York City, including what he felt was his best work, the Brooklyn Station. The Johnstown building is so similar to his design for the Forest Hills Post Office in Queens, New York, that one set of plans may have been used for both.

This building is a smooth black box with stylized eagles on heavy pedestals at the edge of the entrance, and six three-story strips of recessed windows across the facade. The windows are spaced along the facade and side elevations with the same even rhythm as the columns on older Greek Revival post offices, like the post office on Market Street that this one replaced. The starkly stylized exterior is a superb Moderne expression.

CA18 St. John Gualbert Cathedral

1895, Beezer Brothers. 117 Clinton St.

St. John Gualbert Cathedral is one of the highlights of Johnstown, and a landmark in the early architectural careers of the Beezer brothers. By using structural steel in the walls to support the roof, the architects could use lighter materials, including decorative terra-cotta, for the walls. The church measures 124 feet in length and rises 47 feet. The 165-foot-tall square corner tower is, as the architects intended, reminiscent of the Campanile of San Marco in Venice in both form and decoration. Ironically, this tower is older than the tower so often photographed in Venice. The original tenth-century Venetian tower collapsed unexpectedly in 1902, and its replacement was not completed until 1904, by which time the Johnstown tower had been standing for nearly a decade. The church's interior space was modernized after Vatican II, but retains its single-span coved and coffered ceiling, round-arched windows, and fluted pilaster strips with Corinthian capitals.

CA19 First United Methodist Church

1912, Boyd and Stewart. 436 Vine St.

This First United Methodist Church replaced a stone chapel that had survived the flood of 1889 with survivors clinging to its roof, some for as long as two days, but it could not survive a growth in membership. The rusticated brownstone church, one of the largest in the city, has a cruciform plan with a broad central polygonal tower that almost engulfs the arms. Squat pyramidal-roofed towers mark each corner of the church and are roofed in clay tile. Inside, the domed central tower rises above the Akron plan sanctuary. This church has played a pivotal role in the formation of modern Methodism. It was the site of the 1946 merger between the Evangelical and the United Brethren churches. On the fiftieth

CA20 CROWN AMERICAN BUILDING

anniversary of that event, the First United Methodist Church was made a Heritage Landmark of the United Methodist Conference, one of only thirty-nine worldwide and the only one in western Pennsylvania.

CA20 Crown American Building

1986–1989, Michael Graves. 1 Pasquerilla Plaza

Frank Pasquerilla commissioned Michael Graves to design a new headquarters for his multimillion dollar real estate conglomerate after seeing Graves's Humana Building in Louisville, Kentucky, completed in 1985. The Crown American shares the warm tonality and basic geometric vocabulary of the Humana Building, since both the client and the architect shared an interest in Italian art, Tuscan coloration, and classical forms. The building consists of three parts: a main office block, a porte-cochere, and a rotunda. The office block's lower two floors are faced with brown agate granite from South Dakota, and the upper floors are of lighter-colored Kasota limestone. A Doric-columned structure suggestive of an ancient temple crowns the building. The massive four-story porte-cochere's heavy square pillars extend two stories in height, concluding in a steep truncated pyramid. The porte-cochere repeats the color scheme of the main block. A three-story, freestanding Doric rotunda in front of the building has columns cast of resinous concrete that are enormous versions of those in the rooftop arcade. The building's unusual silhouette fits well within the context of downtown Johnstown, primarily because Graves kept the edifice in scale with its surroundings, even though some of its individual parts are on a monumental scale.

CA21 Johnstown Inclined Plane

1890–1891 incline, Samuel Diescher; bridge substructure, Sparks and Evans; bridge superstructure, Phoenix Bridge Company. Incline base at Vine and Union sts. and summit at 711 Edgehill Dr.

An unparalleled engineering feat for its day, the inclined plane that rises above Johnstown is the steepest vehicular inclined plane in the world, traveling 502.5 vertical feet at a 71.9 percent grade up Yoder Hill. Access to the railway is via a truss bridge over Stony Creek, which flows along the base of the hill. The inclined plane was designed by Hungarian engineer Samuel Diescher, who assisted in the design of the Monongahela incline and designed the Duquesne Heights incline (see **Inclines: A Trio of Diescher Inclines** on p. 76), the only two still operating in Pittsburgh. He designed many other inclines throughout the United States and abroad.

Construction was prompted by the need for an escape route to high ground during floods, and for real estate profits to be made by the Cambria Iron Company from their development in Westmont (CA22). The plane proved useful during the flood of 1936, when nearly 4,000 citizens rode it to safety after boarding it from both the bridge and the rescue boats on rising Stony Creek. The plane has twice been saved from bankruptcy by community action and has been refurbished many times by volunteers. The most recent project was a government-funded, year-long restoration of tracks, cars, and both stations in 1984 that returned the plane to its place as a major tourist attraction in Johnstown. In 2001, the wrought-iron and steel, pin-connected and riveted 232-foot-long truss bridge over Stony Creek was refurbished. The inclined plane, built so soon after the devastating flood of 1889, is a symbol of the city's resilience.

CA22 Westmont Residential District

1889–1949. Bounded by Lehigh St., Edgehill Dr., Millcreek Rd., and Hood Ave.

Westmont borough, immediately southwest of downtown Johnstown, was conceived as a pastoral suburb separated by the 1,694-foot-high Yoder Hill from the noise, stench, and mud of the ironworks. The Cambria Iron Company owned much of the land surrounding

Johnstown. Immediately after the 1889 flood, the company hired Charles Miller, of Miller and Yates, a Philadelphia landscape architecture firm, to design a model suburb on these former farmlands where the horses and mules used in the company's mills and mines grazed. The company opened the land for sale to the residents of Johnstown soon after, and completion of an inclined railway in 1891 rapidly increased lot sales. Miller's grid plan extending from Edgehill Drive to Hood Avenue followed the contours of the hill's crest. The area was popular as a place to picnic, spend a day at the Johnstown Driving Park, a horse track in operation from 1893 to 1903, or play golf or tennis at the Westmont Tennis Club of 1895. As housing developments crowded these recreational activities, the company revoked their leases, and after 1907 they moved farther outside the city.

Unofficially, the borough was divided into two neighborhoods: the southern more affluent section, the "Dinner Side," and the northern blue-collar section with company-owned housing called the "Supper Side." The Dinner Side is best represented by the Shingle Style house of Cambria Iron Company general manager Charles S. Price (1892; 510 Edgehill Drive). The Supper Side houses are dispersed throughout the area and date from three periods: first, the gable-roofed single and double frame houses for laborers and millworkers on Wyoming and Lehigh streets built c. 1891; second, the pyramid-roofed, single-family frame houses on Tioga Street built c. 1901 for middle management employees; and third, the middle management homes on Colgate Avenue and Tioga Street built between 1909 and 1911. Two frame Queen Anne houses at 140 and 146 Colgate Avenue, both dating to 1911, were built by the Cambria Iron Company, using kits from Sears and Roebuck. Most of the houses were modest but well constructed, and the Cambria Iron Company was known for excellent maintenance of its rental properties.

CA23 Beth Sholom Synagogue

1951, Alexander Sharove. 700 Indiana St.

Jewish settlers first came to Johnstown in the early 1850s, when the Cambria Iron Company opened and merchants were needed to serve the community. Since 1905, Orthodox, Conservative, and Reform congregations have all built synagogues here. In 1950, two synagogues were built for the Beth Zion (Reformed) and Rodef Sholom (Conservative) congregations in Westmont. Both congregations followed their members to the suburbs, and both synagogues were designed by Alexander Sharove (1893–1955) of Pittsburgh. The combined synagogue Beth Sholom uses the former Beth Zion building, while the Rodef Sholom at 100 Dartmouth Avenue is now the Ferndale Elementary School. Sharove's two buildings are flat roofed, and the horizontally laid stone of the walls is emphasized rather than the windows. At this synagogue, exterior decorative elements are restricted to a smooth stone cornice and a stone menorah frieze on the facade. The windows by artist A. Raymond Katz depict scenes of Jewish holidays.

CA24 Masonic Temple

1927–1933, J. C. Fulton and Son. 130 Valley Pike at Linton St.

Between 1923 and 1925, the Johnstown Masons purchased a lot in the southeastern trolley suburb of Moxham, and commissioned a meeting hall from the Uniontown firm of J. C. Fulton and Son. The temple serves more than 1,000 members in two lodges. The Art Deco facade focuses attention on the tall central entrance section, where staggered recesses alternate with fluted pilaster strips that resemble the pipes of a church organ. This central bay rises almost a full story above the rest of the building and projects from the facade. The vibrantly colored Egyptian-influenced meeting space on the third floor is typical of Masonic temples.

CA25 Immaculate Conception Church of the Blessed Virgin

1906–1908, William P. Ginther. 308 Broad St.

Home to a congregation established by immigrant German steel workers in 1859, this church was originally called St. Mary's. It is one of the first churches that a visitor sees when leaving downtown Johnstown and one of the largest in Cambria City. The contrast between the light yellow brick and the dark brownstone trim adds drama to the Gothic Revival facade. The niche holding a statue of Our Lady of Grace, the gabled portals be-

CA25 IMMACULATE CONCEPTION CHURCH OF THE BLESSED VIRGIN, photo 1988

low, and the gargoyles guarding each door are all in the darker stone to great effect. A tall, square tower with a spire at the southeast corner has a rose window on each elevation. William Ginther, of Akron, Ohio, was a popular church architect who designed over 250 churches in the region.

CA26 St. Mary's Greek Catholic Church

1921–1922, John Comes. 401 Power St.

St. Mary's is one of a dozen ethnic churches in the grid plan of Cambria City, a 10 × 4–block neighborhood of Johnstown on the opposite side of the Conemaugh River from Cambria Iron Company's Lower Works (CA16). Settled a year after the company's founding in 1852 by Irish and German workers, the neighborhood of modest row houses and single-family residences is dotted with spires and domes from a remarkable group of churches. Pittsburgh-based John Comes designed this Byzantine-derived Catholic church for its Carpatho-Rusyn, or eastern Slavic, congregants. The building is cruciform in plan, with a multi-colored dome at the crossing that is echoed by two similarly colorful domed towers at the corners of the facade. Glazed brick, foliated stonework, and richly colored mosaics and tiles at the door surrounds further enliven the building's mottled brick of yellow, brown, and tan. The interior has round-arched vaults and a central aisle.

Ten years earlier, in 1913, Comes designed St. Columba's for a largely Irish congregation (918 Broad Street). The chocolate-brown brick, tile roof, and limestone trim are configured in what Comes called his "Lombard Ro-

manesque" style: a gable-roofed facade with a single tower to the west, and elaborate corbeling at the roofline and in the gable end.

CA27 St. Casimir's Roman Catholic Church

1902–1907, Walter R. Myton. 500 Power St.

St. Casimir's was completed for a predominantly Polish congregation in 1907. The rough-faced stone Gothic Revival structure was partially financed by money taken from Polish employees' paychecks by the Cambria Iron Company and in exchange for the priests' help in securing labor from the congregation. The company is said to have donated the bricks and steel. The squat square twin towers at the facade have gables on each side and miniature turrets at each corner, which are echoed in the hexagonal central tower. Rose windows at the facade and transepts light the interior. Walter Myton's interpretation of the Gothic Revival here differs from William Ginther's more vertically emphasized approach at the Immaculate Conception Church (CA25). St. Casimir's has been combined with a former Hungarian parish, St. Emerich's, whose church was only a few blocks away (1913, demolished 2003), and was also a Myton design.

A third Myton design, St. Stephen's Slovak Catholic Church (1911; 414 4th Avenue), was the mother church for these parishes. Myton, who designed in different styles according to the fashion and his clients' tastes, drew on Renaissance forms for St. Stephen's. The buff brick church is a composition of triangles, circles, and rectangles unified by a cornice at the base of the soaring twin towers. Its facade is composed of bricks laid in courses to

CA26 SAINT MARY'S GREEK CATHOLIC CHURCH, photo 1988

resemble cut stone. In the 1940s and 1950s, St. Stephen's was one of the largest Slovak congregations in the United States.

CA28 University of Pittsburgh at Johnstown

1966–present. 450 School House Rd.

The University of Pittsburgh at Johnstown is a four-year degree-granting institution with over 2,000 students on its suburban 650-acre campus. It began in 1927 as a two-year feeder college that was housed in a former high school and in several commercial buildings in downtown Johnstown. In the mid-1960s, a local coal company donated 136 acres of wooded land in Richland Township to the university, and the architectural firm of Hunter, Campbell and Rea of Altoona designed a student union, two gable-roofed classroom buildings, and three dormitories of wood and stone veneer. Between its opening in 1967 and 1993, nine new dormitories, library, sports center, aquatic center, chapel, and performing arts center were built, bringing the total number of buildings on campus to thirty-two and the acreage to 455. Landscape architects Sasaki Associates of Boston developed a master plan in 1990 to organize the growth process and take advantage of the unique natural environment.

In 1976 and 1978, Urban Design Associates of Pittsburgh designed seven "lodges," or small living units, with kitchenettes. Zamias Aquatic Center (1990) was designed by L. Robert Kimball and Associates from Ebensburg. Certainly the crown jewel of the wooded campus, and the building used regularly by the general Johnstown population, is the Pasquerilla Performing Arts Center, designed by Damianos Brown and Andrews of Pittsburgh from 1990 to 1991. The 1,000-seat theater borrows directly from Frank Pasquerilla's Crown American headquarters designed by Michael Graves (CA20), with its rhythmic fenestration and columned entrance rotunda. The building also houses the Johnstown branch of the Southern Alleghenies Museum of Art, which has three other sites, in Ligonier (see WE31), Loretto (see CA5), and Altoona (see BL10).

VINTONDALE

CA29 Ghost Town Trail

1991 established; 1995–2002, D.I.R.T. PA 3045 at County Line

Ghost Town Trail links former coal patch towns in the Blacklick Creek valley in Indiana and Cambria counties. The biking and walking trail follows a thirty-six-mile route, part of which runs along former railroad tracks. Historical markers along the trail interpret the valley's history. In Vintondale, the adjacent Blacklick Creek, polluted by acid mine drainage, is being reclaimed by the work of D.I.R.T. Studio (an acronym for both Design Intelligent Research Terrain and Dump It Right There), composed of landscape architect Julie Bargmann, historian T. Allan Comp, hydrogeologist Robert Deason, and sculptor Stacy Levy, using natural systems to treat the water in a thirty-five-acre floodplain, and creating a community park for Vintondale in the process. Bioengineered settling ponds and cleansing marshes have been created adjacent to the walking/biking trail, which is lined with native plants and trees.

Vintondale came into existence to serve the Vinton Colliery Company's six mines and coke works in the Blacklick Creek area that operated from 1892 to 1968. Built much earlier (1845–1846), the Eliza furnace happened to be on the land purchased by the coal company. It was built by David Ritter and George Rodgers without mortar between the stones, but for a variety of reasons operated only until 1849. It stands in the community park along the trail and is kept in excellent repair by the Cambria County Historical Society. The series of cast-iron pipes at the top of the structure functioned as a heat exchanger and allowed for the preheating of the air that was blown into the furnace. This is one of the few furnaces with its hot blast coils intact.

BLAIR COUNTY

European settlers first filed land patents in 1755 in what later became Blair County on land purchased a year earlier from the Iroquois. The latter had sold it, despite the presence of their allies the Shawnee, Delaware, and Seneca tribes living in the territory. Nearly a hundred Scots-Irish, German, and English families moved to the region between the end of the French and Indian War in 1763 and 1776, the start of the Revolution. Their presence incited the tribes, prompting settlers to build a series of forts. Fort Roberdeau (BL25), for example, erected in Sinking Valley in 1778, was designed to protect lead mines from the British and their native allies.

Juniata Valley was a fine source of limestone and a seemingly endless supply of timber. The region's many streams powered bellows to heat furnaces for the production of iron used for household goods and machine parts, and later for railroad rails. Twenty iron furnaces and twelve forges were constructed between 1807 and 1850, with an entire iron plantation developing around them. After the War of 1812, the "Northern Turnpike" connected Pittsburgh to the Susquehanna River through the towns of Ebensburg, Hollidaysburg, and Huntingdon. Until the 1830s, nearly all the iron made in Blair County was carried to Pittsburgh on this route, rather than to towns along the East Coast. The completion of the Pennsylvania Main Line Canal in 1826 expedited the trip from western to eastern Pennsylvania. In 1832, a settler named John Blair ensured that the canal's last stop before the Allegheny Mountains was in Hollidaysburg on the Juniata River. The state legislature, recognizing his local prominence, named the county for him in 1846. Canal traffic peaked in 1852, just as the railroad was establishing itself across the state. From Hollidaysburg westward, the Allegheny Portage Railroad (APRR) replaced canal transportation. Fully loaded canal boats were lifted onto wheeled flatbeds. Ten inclined planes, five on each side of the mountains, connected the two segments of the canal by rail. Canal boats were attached to cars, which were raised up the inclined planes powered by steam engines and transported between planes by teams of mules. Engineered by Moncure Robinson, the APRR opened to regular traffic in 1834 and was double tracked in 1835. The PRR completed a line to Hollidaysburg from Harrisburg, Dauphin County, in 1847, and two years later, Pittsburgh and Johnstown in Cambria County were connected by rail. Although the canal and rail systems coexisted for over twenty years, the railroad proved itself consistently superior with its year-round operation. The Pennsylvania Canal essentially closed by 1872.

The fate of the iron industry in Blair County paralleled waning canal usage. By the 1870s, coke manufacturers were mining cheaper ore farther west, and improved manufacturing methods made it possible to use steel rather than iron for railroad rails, leading to the death of the iron industry by 1885. Blair County's major industry then became the Pennsylvania Railroad. Enormous service shops were built in Altoona. The railroad's peak years were between 1924 and 1928 and from 1943 to 1946. As late as 1952, the Pennsylvania Railroad built one of the largest freight-car building and repair facilities in the world at Hollidaysburg. Diesel power and highway construction after World War II crimped the railroad's growth, and air travel sounded its death knell. The last steam locomotive was built in 1946, and by the 1950s, old locomotives were often cut into scrap.

Recovery from the devastating loss of the railroads has been under way since the late 1960s. During the 1980s and 1990s, the county added such attractions as the Railroaders Memorial Museum (BL7), a new baseball stadium and park (BL22), and a convention center (BL23) in Altoona. The town of Hollidaysburg is proving to be an attractive alternative to big-city living and has several designated historic districts. Tourism continues to grow, offering bike trails and the Horseshoe Curve (BL24) to attract visitors.

HOLLIDAYSBURG AND VICINITY

The town of Hollidaysburg is located at the midpoint of early Native American seasonal migrations from Michigan to Virginia. As such, the area was often the burial site for those who died during the journey. Its strategic location also prompted the fledgling United States government to designate several fortified houses as forts to protect the early colonists: Fort Fetter, Fort Holiday, and Fort Titus (all demolished). The first European landholders whose names are identified with the site were Adam and William Holliday, northern Irish immigrants who fought in the French and Indian War. They purchased the land in 1768, and had the town surveyed and plotted c. 1793. It was a farming community until the Huntingdon, Cambria, and Indiana Turnpike opened in 1819. It was among the more than one thousand miles of turnpikes in Pennsylvania whose usage waned after the opening of the canal in 1832.

The Pennsylvania Main Line Canal dominated the trading and industry of Hollidaysburg from 1832, the year the town was incorporated, until the 1870s. This was the holding point for cargo continuing into the western territories, and, after the APRR opened in 1834, for the raw materials being shipped east from the forests and farms of western Pennsylvania. As canal traffic was seasonal, storage was an important component of the system, and large warehouses grew along the canal's edge. The canal was popular with human cargo, as well and as many as one hundred passengers arriving in Hollidaysburg aboard several packets would need overnight accommodations. The canal's influence on the town remains visible in many ways, from the name of the neighborhood Gaysport to the south—commemorating canal engineer John Gay—to the commercial buildings lining the canal's former path, such as the U.S. Hotel (1835; 401 Wayne Street). The focus of the town was initially at the diamond, a four-block rectangle of land at the intersection of Montgomery and Allegheny streets. During the canal era, however, the town's focus shifted to the canal path with its inns and warehouses.

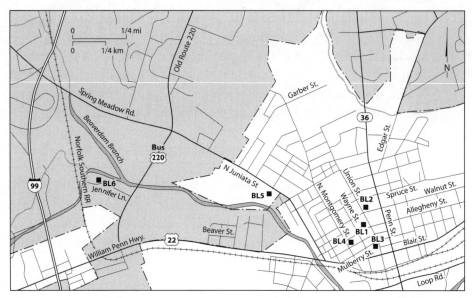

HOLLIDAYSBURG AND VICINITY

In Hollidaysburg, the railroad followed the canal's path, and even the addition of streetcars did little to interrupt the town's gridded street pattern. The railroad's impact on Hollidaysburg was softened by the building of Altoona just four miles to the north in 1850. But this changed in 1952, when the Pennsylvania Railroad built one of the world's largest classification yards, rail service, and construction facilities in Hollidaysburg's southeastern section. The Samuel Rea yards were a major employer in this town of 5,368 until new owners, Norfolk and Southern Railroad, closed them in 2001, eliminating almost four hundred jobs.

With few development pressures and successful preservation programs, Hollidaysburg has maintained its attractive nineteenth-century appearance and the many handsome single-family houses built between 1890 and 1930. Recognizing this as a tourist attraction in the early 1960s, the borough's chamber of commerce implemented Project 60, an award-winning preservation program designed by Milton S. Osborne, then head of Pennsylvania State University's College of Arts and Architecture. Since 1988, the borough has operated under a Historic District Ordinance to preserve its architectural assets and counsel homeowner's on appropriate ways to preserve their buildings.

BL1 Blair County Courthouse

1875–1876, David Smith Gendell; 1906 addition, William Lewis Plack; 1981 addition, L. Robert Kimball and Associates. 423 Allegheny St.

Ironically, while the cathedral in Altoona (BL15) looks like a courthouse, the courthouse in Hollidaysburg looks like a cathedral.

Constructed of smoothly finished stone, the courthouse blends Ruskinian Gothic Revival with the Second Empire style. Two square mansard-roofed towers flank the entrance, and a clock-bearing steeple rises at the building's center, the point in a church that would be the crossing. David Smith Gendell of Philadelphia is credited with the design, although in 1875 he was still in practice with his father, John A. Gendell, a carpenter-builder and foundry owner. An extension in 1906 on the east elevation added two bays at the intersection of the north and south wings in the same style as the original building. In 1981, the Kimball firm of Ebensburg designed an 80,000-square-foot addition to the west, using the same beige and peach sandstone. By alternating the forward thrusting towers with the recessed mansard-roofed sections, the size of the new wing is downplayed and the original portion of the courthouse is highlighted not overshadowed.

The second-floor courtrooms in the original courthouse are stylistically at odds: the south courtroom is Stick Style with exposed wooden rafters, while the main courtroom is classical with arched stained glass windows, ceiling and wall murals, heavy moldings, and paired marbleized pilaster strips with Corinthian capitals.

BL2 Highland Hall

1867–1869, Samuel Sloan; 1911, Price and McLanahan. 517 Walnut St.

When the town's Presbyterians decided they needed a private school, they turned to Philadelphia's well-published architect Samuel Sloan, whose book *Model Architect* (published from 1851 onward) was about to be reissued for the fourth time. He designed this large, three-story, Colonial Revival building with a

BL1 BLAIR COUNTY COURTHOUSE

central pedimented block flanked by mansard-roofed wings to the east and west. The building has pronounced extruded mortar between the irregularly laid golden-toned stone that had been quarried on the site. The school's philosophy was to "shun mere display and affectation, and to give practical knowledge." It was coeducational for only one year, after which the boys were banished for misbehavior. Highland Hall became a well-known girls' school in 1906, with John King McLanahan as the major stockholder. In 1911, his son, architect Martin Hawley McLanahan, in partnership with William Price, oversaw extensive renovations and designed an addition with practice rooms, an infirmary, and sleeping porches, as well as a separate gymnasium and boiler house–laundry. The McLanahan family remained involved with the school through 1940, as long as their daughters attended it. After several post–World War II uses, including as a Franciscan preparatory school and a courthouse annex, the building is awaiting its next function.

BL3 Blair County Prison

1868–1869, Edward Haviland; 1983 addition, L. Robert Kimball and Associates. Mulberry and Union sts.

Employing a formidable Gothic Revival castellated style, thought best to impress the wayward with its awesome power, this prison is a condensed version of the Eastern State Penitentiary in Philadelphia by the architect's father, John Haviland. A three-story central watch tower above the entrance is flanked by two-story-high polygonal bays. The one-story side wings of the stone edifice are greatly foreshortened compared to those of the Philadelphia prison. The rear addition in the 1980s brought the prison into the twentieth century. A second golden-colored cement block addition on the west elevation is more recent.

BL4 Mellon Bank (Hollidaysburg National Bank)

1903, Price and McLanahan. 312 Allegheny St.

When Martin Hawley McLanahan's father opened a bank, he commissioned his son's architectural firm to design it. This, the second commission for the Philadelphia firm of Price and McLanahan, is a jewel box of a commer-

BL4 MELLON BANK (HOLLIDAYSBURG NATIONAL BANK)

cial building, with colorful tiles from Henry Mercer's Moravian Pottery and Tile Works in Doylestown around the entrance and walls of a warm red-orange brick. This one-story building has an oversized facade with a tiled, gabled parapet, and is highlighted by variegated brickwork and tile insets. The recessed entrance is flanked by columns and elaborate metal grilles. Pilaster capitals on the interior are carved with owls and animals. A vestigial balcony shielding recessed lights surrounds the interior's banking space. Price and McLanahan's commissions reached a national audience through their PRR stations, a series of resort hotels, and small commercial buildings across Pennsylvania and in Indiana.

BL5 Sill House (William and Caroline Jack House)

1856–1860. 1111 N. Juniata St.

Banker William Jack and his wife, Caroline, came to Hollidaysburg in 1852, and four years later commissioned this twenty-two-room, well-proportioned Italian Villa house. Its two-foot-thick walls of slate block were in place by 1860, when the Jacks prepared for the coming Civil War. The four bull's-eye windows on the rear elevation have gun rests that overlook the Beaverdam Branch of the Juniata River. William Jack was active in the Underground Railroad, and a large brick room beneath his carriage house was accessible via a tunnel

from the riverbank. The wood floor of the front hallway has a north-facing arrow inlaid in the wood, pointing the way to Canada and freedom for escaping slaves. The house remained in the Jack family until 1953, after which it had various uses, including for more than thirty years as the Evangelical Methodist Manahath (Hebrew for "God's resting place") School of Theology. Purchased in 1996, the new owners restored the house to its 1890 appearance. Although the architect and contractor are unknown, the house clearly shows an architect's hand at work, and takes advantage of its site with a glazed belvedere on the roof and unique attic windows at the rear.

BL6 Sunbrook Farm

1795, with additions; 1897–1904, Beezer Brothers. 2 Jennifer Rd., off U.S. 220 Business

This idyllic farm complex includes a large, yellow brick Colonial Revival house c. 1897 at the top of the hill, with an adjacent gambrel-roofed carriage house, and a smaller Shingle Style cottage nearby. Below, on the flat land along the creek, the original farmhouse of 1795, incrementally added to in 1825 and the 1930s, adjoins a spectacular barn and matching outbuildings. This is a combination of three farms, one from the eighteenth and two from the nineteenth centuries, which were made into a summer estate for John Lloyd Sr. by the Beezer twins. Lloyd was president of a litany of local businesses, including the Altoona and Logan Valley Electric Railway, the First National Bank of Altoona, and the Allegheny Water Company, whose water source was three springs on the Sunbrook farm property; and he had strong financial ties to the PRR and its president Alexander Cassatt. The deeds were in Caroline B. Lloyd's name, and her name is on the drawing of the aforementioned Colonial Revival house in the 1897 architectural catalog of Beezer Brothers' Altoona work.

Lloyd bought four hundred acres from three farms between 1880 and 1890, and asked the architects to glamorize the barns adjacent to the older four-bay, red brick house. In 1900, the timber-frame barn, originally covered with vertical siding still visible inside, was covered with horizontal siding painted yellow to match the yellow brick of the Lloyd house

BL6 SUNBROOK FARM, barn

at the top of the hill. The more fashionable horizontal siding, round-arched vents, and charming rooftop ventilators made the farm a showplace. Now painted white with green trim, the weight of the extra siding, slate roof, and added gabled wall dormers, in combination with a persistent snow one winter, nearly destroyed the barn. It was repaired by an Amish crew from Bellville. An icehouse and railroad station have been demolished, but a springhouse, machine shed, corn crib, milk house, goat shed, and hay shed survive.

ALTOONA AND VICINITY

When the Pennsylvania Canal breached the Allegheny Mountains in the 1830s, it used a rudimentary railroad to haul cargo, passengers, and canal boats over the mountains. Twenty years later, PRR engineers decided they needed a central location for trains to regroup and add locomotives before continuing the arduous journey over the mountains. They found their site at David Robeson's 233-acre farm, where the Little Juniata River carved a relatively flat valley, and purchased it in 1850. Within four years Altoona grew from a town with a population of 50 people to one with more than 2,000, and to over 10,000 by 1875. The name was chosen by the railroad to commemorate Altona, a sixteenth-century Danish town that hosted an important railway hub after 1844 and is now part of Hamburg, Germany. The extra "o" was added purposely to distinguish the two towns. While engineers improved the tracks from Altoona westward, the PRR used the old portage railroad to link to Pittsburgh until it could craft a better route. Chief engineer J. Edgar Thomson recommended that the railroad build the Horseshoe Curve (BL24), but it was not constructed until 1854, after he became president of the PRR. In 1857, the PRR dismantled the portage railroad.

By 1852, the Altoona shops were repairing railway cars, making parts for locomotives, and constructing cars, cast-iron bridge parts, boilerplate, and track. The PRR began building entire locomotives in Altoona in 1862, and by 1884, the local works were producing over five hundred per year in an indoor facility large enough to test a full-scale locomotive. They also built several specialty cars for refrigeration and overnight passengers. The PRR founded the Altoona Hospital and the Mechanics Library, and sponsored a company

View of Altoona with the Cathedral of the Blessed Sacrament (BL15) in the foreground and Brush Mountain in the misty background.

band, athletic events, and a symphony orchestra. The railroad and its successors were Altoona's major employer until well into the 1980s, when they were superseded by the Altoona Hospital. But by 2000, when Norfolk Southern controlled the railroad, all but the shops in north Altoona had closed, and the city's population was nearly 40 percent less than it had been at its peak in 1929. The fate of the PRR can be summarized as follows: it was merged with the New York Central in 1968 to become the Penn Central, which failed in 1970. Many of Altoona's shops and its passenger station were razed in 1972. In 1976, the government created the Consolidated Rail Corporation (Conrail), which in 1998 was split between Norfolk Southern and CSX, the track's operator. The Altoona and Hollidaysburg shops went to Norfolk Southern.

The city learned from its initial dependence on a single industry and has diversified. Today, Altoona is the urban core for the central part of the commonwealth, with shopping, entertainment, and cultural sites, as well as a branch of Pennsylvania State University (since 1939). In addition to the usual array of suburban big box stores and malls, Altoona maintains several historic districts and unique historical sites. The Railroaders Memorial Museum founded c. 1979 moved in 1998 to the PRR's Master Mechanics building (BL7). The largest employers are now city, state, and federal governments and service industries, such as Altoona Hospital (1995; 620 Howard Avenue), which opened a four-story concourse and atrium designed by Hayes Large Architects to improve access and circulation for the increasing patient load.

Unlike most company towns, Altoona has a history of home ownership, due in large part to the PRR, which encouraged it. Local architectural firms include Beezer Brothers, active in Altoona from 1892 to 1896 and in Pittsburgh until 1906. Their homes and the streetcar station at Llyswen introduced

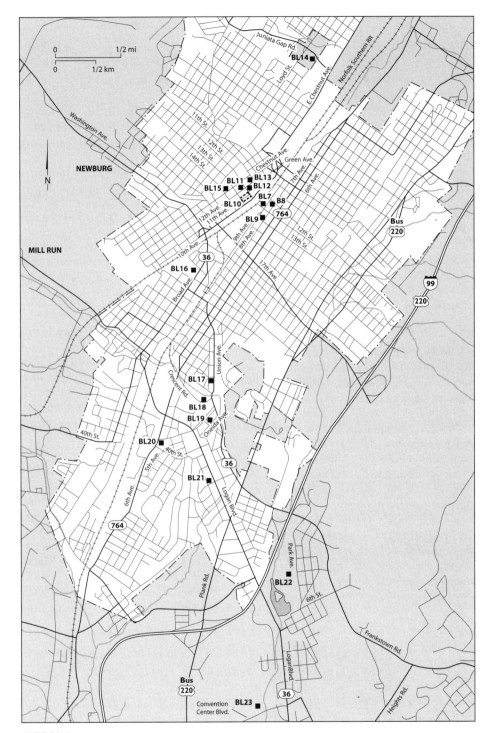

ALTOONA

elements of Shingle Style and classicism to the area. The Hayes Large architectural firm, founded in Hollidaysburg in 1922 by John Hunter (1898–1993), has grown from a single individual to a firm employing 136, with offices in Pittsburgh, Harrisburg, and on N. Logan Avenue in Altoona.

BL7 Railroaders Memorial Museum (Pennsylvania Railroad Master Mechanics Offices and Testing Department)

1882–1906, Pennsylvania Railroad engineers; 1998, Wallace Roberts and Todd. 9th Ave. and 12th St.

After 1850, the daily rhythm of Altoona was regulated by the whistles of the Pennsylvania Railroad (PRR). Even after a series of mergers, buyouts, and failures, the railroad remains the city's heart. At its peak, 17,000 Altoonans worked for the railroad in three separate shops and one foundry. There have been hundreds of railroad buildings constructed here, but most have been demolished, altered, or reused. For example, all the roundhouses have disappeared. This museum is located in the former Master Mechanics building, part of the original Altoona works of 1882 adjacent to 12th Street. It is one of only three remaining buildings in that complex, and was adapted by Wallace Roberts and Todd of Philadelphia for its present use as a focal point for the city. As a railroad known for its standardization and efficiency, the PRR engineers allowed the machines to dictate the design of the buildings. Just as the locomotives and cars were standardized, so too were the buildings, which are invariably red brick and gable roofed with slightly depressed bays of segmental-arched windows separated by brick pilasters, and with brick corbeling at the cornice line and

in the gable ends. The two rail shops remaining in Altoona are the Juniata Shops, which stretch for nearly a mile north of downtown and east of Chestnut Street, and the South Altoona Foundries, now an industrial park west of 6th Avenue. Only the Juniata Shops (which include some of the Altoona Car Shops) still operate as part of the Norfolk Southern Corporation.

BL8 Our Lady of Mount Carmel Church

1912, 1922–1923, David George Puderbaugh. 806 11th St.

Altoona's Italian community lived for the most part within a seven-block radius of this church. They commissioned Altoona-born architect David Puderbaugh to design this, his first Altoona commission, only three years after his graduation from the Drexel School of Architecture in Philadelphia. After the basement was dug and the foundation and cornerstone were laid, the bishop halted construction due to the congregation's heavy debt. Construction resumed in 1922. The rough-faced brownstone church in a Florentine Renaissance style uses smooth-faced brownstone on the clerestory and upper apse and as trim on the facade. A tripartite central entrance leads to the sanctuary with a tall, rounded apse at the west. The interior's basilica plan was ornately decorated in 1953, after the church's mortgage was retired, and was restored in 2006.

BL9 St. Luke's Episcopal Church

1881–1882, Frederick Clarke Withers. 806 13th St.

This stone church stands today as silent testimony to the sophistication of the Protestant Episcopal congregation that commissioned it from Frederick Clarke Withers (1828–1901), an English-trained devotee of the Ecclesiologists who had come from London to work with Andrew Jackson Downing, practiced for a short time in New York City with Calvert Vaux and Frederick Law Olmsted, and who wrote books on church architecture. Built

BL7 RAILROADERS MEMORIAL MUSEUM (PENNSYLVANIA RAILROAD MASTER MECHANICS OFFICES AND TESTING DEPARTMENT)

within blocks of the then sprawling, noisy PRR shops, its walls are rough-faced Ohio sandstone trimmed with smooth-finished sandstone. The ridgeline of the gable roof is pierced by a steeple on a square base at the south end, and a small triangular version to the north. Entrances are on both 8th Avenue and 13th Street. Withers also designed the interior's ash pews and reredos. The roof's truss system is exposed in both the nave and aisle ceilings. Between 1915 and 1917, local architect Julian Millard (1866–1951) added a parish house in a vaguely Tudor Revival style along 8th Avenue, containing classrooms and a gymnasium.

BL10 Office Building District of Altoona

1905–1933. 1200 block 11th Ave.

These five, classically derived buildings define Altoona's downtown and create a sophisticated urban quality rarely seen in towns of this size. The oldest building, the Central Trust Company (1905–1906, Charles M. Robinson and George Winkler) at 1218 11th Avenue has a Romanesque Revival facade of white glazed brick with ornate, brownstone trim. The south elevation's seven bays have simple paired windows with belt courses of darker brick. One door to the north at 1210–1216 is the former Brett Department Store (1922–1924) designed by Julian Millard of Altoona. To build on this north side of the Central Trust Company, the Brett store owners agreed to make their building's upper stories accessible to Central Trust. The Brett building has Chicago-style windows and ornate blue and white terra-cotta ornament at the cornice. It hosts the Altoona branch of the Southern Alleghenies Museum of Art.

The grand Corinthian-columned, four-story First National Bank Building (1924–1926; 1206 11th Avenue) designed by John A. Dempwolf (1848–1928) of York, Pennsylvania, has a stylized steam engine in the bronze cartouche above the entrance, reminding visitors of the local economic role of the Pennsylvania Railroad. The Silverman Building (1924–1925) anchors the corner at 1200–1204 11th Avenue. It is sheathed in white glazed terracotta, and has fluted pilasters with Corinthian capitals. The building was used by the Penn Central Light and Power Company from 1926 to 1965. Across the street at 1201 11th Avenue, the post office (1931–1933, James A. Wetmore, supervising architect of the U.S. Treasury, with David A. Royer and Ronald C. Anglemyer, project architects) is in the severe classical style popular at the time. The project architects were University of Pennsylvania trained, graduating in 1921. On the east and west walls of the lobby are two large murals by Lorin Thompson depicting Altoona's history. Large cast-aluminum eagles and cresting were removed in the 1950s.

BL11 Mishler Theater

1906, Albert E. Westover; 2000, Hayes Large Architects; A. Raymond Goodman, project architect. 1211 12th Ave.

Named for its founder, Isaac Charles "Doc" Mishler, the theater has an unusually large and glamorous auditorium and proscenium stage for its time. The limestone first story has ornate poster display windows on each side of the central entrance. Columns on the second story flank colorful representations of the muses and culminate on the third story in statues of Terpsichore and Melpomene, the muses of song and dance, and tragedy. Mishler initially worked for the Pennsylvania Railroad, but turned to theater management, eventually running three theaters in Trenton, New Jersey; Johnstown in Cambria County; and Altoona. Philadelphia theater designer Albert Westover (d. 1919) designed the grand 910-seat theater, whose location on the Pennsylvania Railroad's main line made it an excellent venue for premiering shows headed for Broadway, and, as a result, nationally known entertainers often performed here. The theater was used for stage productions and movies until 1965 when it closed. The Blair County Arts Foundation initiated its restoration in 1967, and owns the theater, which is home to the Allegheny Ballet Company, Altoona Community Theatre, Altoona Symphony Orchestra, and Blair Concert Chorale.

BL12 Altoona Alliance Church (First United Presbyterian Church)

1897–1898, William J. East; 1926 addition, George Espie Savage. 1314 12th St.

The First United Presbyterian Church is a handsomely proportioned stone corner

BL14 JUNIATA GAP ELEMENTARY SCHOOL

church. Its Richardsonian Romanesque design has a large, square central tower crowned with a pyramidal roof rising ninety feet above the crossing and pierced by eyebrow dormers. Architect William J. East (1865–1936), who trained in the offices of Charles Bartberger of Pittsburgh, designed over 150 churches in the region, and ultimately moved to North Carolina, where he continued to specialize in ecclesiastical architecture. He used sandstone from Scalp Level in southern Cambria County for the exterior of this church. The windows throughout were designed by Rudy Brothers of Pittsburgh. The cruciform-shaped church has interior furnishings of red oak. In 1926, a three-story addition containing a gymnasium, meeting rooms, and classrooms was designed by the Scottish-born George Savage, who designed dozens of churches in a career spanning the years 1897 to 1929.

BL13 M&T Bank (Altoona Trust Building)

1901–1902, Mowbray and Uffinger. 1128–1130 12th Ave.

Louis M. Mowbray and Justin M. Uffinger of New York City designed many banks in western Pennsylvania, in addition to their numerous New York commissions. They specialized in a classical style, using the base-shaft-capital formula for their high-rise banks, as they did here for Altoona Trust. After being in business for only one year, the bank commissioned this building and leased the offices above. This round-cornered building's first story is sheathed in Bedford limestone highlighted by the granite columns flanking the corner entrance. In contrast to the red brick typically used in Altoona at the time, the upper four stories are of gray Pompeiian bricks.

BL14 Juniata Gap Elementary School

1999, Hayes Large Architects; Grace Oh, project architect. Juniata Gap Rd. and E. Chestnut Ave.

This sprawling school has a three-story central core, with one-story wings at the north and south ends. Its warm reddish brick alternates with occasional bands of buff brick, which, with the ribbon windows, lend the building a streamlined look. A two-story window wall lights the library, as it projects at the northern end of the building like the prow of a ship. Two circular windows delineate the entrances on the west elevation. A rounded single-story wing at the southeast corner houses the kindergarten with a drop-off entrance. The gymnasium, kitchen, and mechanical spaces are set slightly below grade at the rear of the building, where they subtly blend into the hillside. The corridors are curved in response to the arc in nearby Juniata Gap Road, allowing for gathering spaces along their length. The school accommodates 600 students in grades K–6, with two levels on each story.

BL15 Cathedral of the Blessed Sacrament

1924–1931, George Ignatius Lovatt Sr.; 1959–1960 interior, Alfred Reid. 1 Cathedral Sq.

Like a medieval European cathedral, the exterior of Altoona's cathedral took many years to complete, and its interior stood unfinished for twenty-eight additional years while services were held amid bare brick and rough concrete walls. The building sits on a rise and is raised further on a basement, making it visible for miles. The domed crossing gives the massive Indiana limestone cathedral the appearance of a state capitol. Forty-eight stone steps, separated into smaller groups by broad terraces, lead to the entrance portico with its six fluted Ionic columns in antis supporting a balustrade. Above this, the central pedimented portion over the nave is reminiscent of the church of S. Maria Novella in Florence, while the dome incorporates elements from St. Peter's in Rome and Filippo Brunelleschi's cathedral dome in Florence. Philadelphia architect George Ignatius Lovatt (1872–1958) had completed dozens of churches nationally by the mid-1920s, most of which were in Philadelphia and Delaware.

The cathedral's cruciform plan has three aisles separated by six massive piers on each side, and a dome at the crossing of transept and nave. A continuing program of embellishment and remodeling gives the cathedral its evolutionary quality: the exterior and interior obviously date from different eras. The pews and much of the interior, dedicated in 1960, were designed by Alfred Reid of Pittsburgh, using a modern vocabulary in contrast to the historical appearance of the exterior. Since 1986, several stained glass windows by Hunt Studios of Pittsburgh have replaced earlier colored and frosted glass windows. In addition, engraved glass panel doors by Baut Studios of Pennsylvania have been installed on the facade.

BL16 Jaffa Shrine

1928–1930, Frank A. Hersh and Frederic James Shollar. Broad Ave. at 22nd St.

Operated by the Shriners, this building looks like a golden brick Middle Eastern fortress, with circular towers topped by elongated domes similar to minarets at the corners. Instead, the building is a 3,400-seat auditorium and conference center. The eleven-acre complex occupies an entire city block in Altoona, enclosing an acre of space under one roof. The central entrance facing Broad Avenue is topped with diapered bricks surrounding a large curved scimitar, the symbol of the Shriners.

Frank Hersh, a member of the Jaffa Shrine, and Frederic Shollar were popular Altoona architects in practice between 1904 and 1930.

In their design for the limestone-sheathed city hall (1925–1927) at 1301 12th Street, they employed a stripped-down classicism in a formal composition of elongated windows and arched entrances. A quartet of fluted columns supports the namestone above the 12th Street entrance, conveying the dignity appropriate for a civic building. Altoona architect David B. Albright earned a Preservation Pennsylvania award in 2002 for his renovation of the city hall's interior.

BL17 Temple Beth Israel

1924, Morris W. Scheibel. 3004 Union Ave.

This domed synagogue on a green lawn in a wooded suburb of Altoona brought Altoona's Jewish congregation away from the clamor of the railroad shops and into suburban tranquility. The temple's polished smooth surfaces were, perhaps, influenced by Henry Hornbostel's often published Rodef Shalom Temple in Pittsburgh (AL118). Here, the Youngstown, Ohio, architect Scheibel chose a dome to distinguish his work.

The congregation's earlier temple, designed by Charles Morrison Robinson, is now Holy Trinity Greek Orthodox Church (1898; 1433 13th Avenue). It is one of the few remaining nineteenth-century synagogues in western Pennsylvania designed in the Moorish Revival style, one of the most popular architectural styles for American synagogues in that period.

BL18 Woman's Club of Altoona (Allegheny Furnace)

1811; 1837 office-storehouse; 1939 furnace restored. 3400 Crescent Rd.

The stone, pyramidal, iron furnace in the backyard of what was Elias Baker's stone

BL16 JAFFA SHRINE

office-storehouse, approximately one-tenth of a mile from Baker's mansion (BL19), is now surrounded by suburban houses and yards, making it a most unusual lawn ornament. When built, the furnace was adjacent to Mill Run, which supplied the power to turn the bellows. The other plantation buildings, such as workers' housing, and barns have been demolished. The three-bay, gable-roofed office building has rudimentary corner quoins and an exceptionally long lintel over the entrance.

BL20 KNICKERBOCKER

BL19 Blair County Historical Society (Elias Baker Mansion)

1844–1849, Robert Cary Long Jr. 3500 Bake Blvd.

Elias Baker moved to Blair County from Lancaster County in 1836, only one year before a six-year economic depression hit. This poor timing appeared to plague him throughout his business life. He expanded the Allegheny Furnace iron plantation (BL18), already on his land, and then commissioned this mansion on a knoll overlooking it. In 1844, he commissioned drawings from Robert Cary Long Jr. (1810–1849) of Baltimore, son of the renowned architect of the same name. Long drew up plans, but was so tardy in supplying specifications that Baker fired him. His contractor, Charles B. Callahan of Bellefonte in Centre County, completed the project in five years. Baker's dreams were larger than his income, and building the house strained the family's fortunes. Several changes, often for reasons of cost, were required. The Greek Revival styling and central-hall plan remain unchanged from Long's plans, but Baker's constant financial woes caused the contractor to specify that the columns, which originally were meant to be cast iron, should be made of cheaper materials. The base, capital, and bottom third of each column are cast iron, while the upper portion of the shafts is brick parged with Johnstown cement and fluted by hand. The entablature and pediments are all covered with cement, painted to imitate stone. The gray limestone used to face the exterior was quarried nearby. The stones are set with strips of lead at the joints. The north elevation, the principal facade, has a pediment supported by six fluted Ionic columns, while the rear elevation has a similar two-story pedimented portico, but with square columns, simple capitals, and a second-story porch. Family members lived in the house until 1914. It was leased to the Blair County Historical Society in 1922, and purchased by the society in 1941. In 2000, the house underwent an extensive exterior renovation.

There are several iron plantation houses extant in western Pennsylvania. The Isaac Meason House of 1802 (FA27) is the most architecturally significant, but the Baker House is the best ironmaster's mansion from the mid-nineteenth century. Between this complex—which includes the Allegheny Furnace located one and one-half blocks north—the Daniel Royer House (BL29), and the Mt. Etna Furnace complex (BL28), a complete story of early iron making can be told in Blair County.

BL20 Knickerbocker

1904–1929. 3900–4000 blocks Burgoon Rd. and 6th and 4th aves.

These 153 brick row houses were built by New Jersey developer William Genther to house railroad employees. The six rows of units were built between 1904 and 1929, with the majority completed by 1910. The curved commercial section at the intersection of 6th Avenue and Burgoon Road sets the tone, with its bay windows and prominent parapet. Most of the original forty-two-acre development is devoted to two-bay, Colonial Revival row houses, each with shaped parapets above the second-story bay windows and front porches. Approximately two-thirds are now individually owned and one-third is rental, and they vary in condition and architectural integrity. The grouping's distinctive scale and rhythm of repetition make this dense urban setting unique.

BL21 H. Dean Allison Insurance Agency (Llyswen Station)

1895–1896, Beezer Brothers. Whittier Ave. at Logan Blvd.

The suburb of Llyswen was designed to take advantage of the Altoona and Logan Valley Electric Railway Company's six-mile line between Altoona and Hollidaysburg that was completed in 1892. The Altoona Suburban Home Company, founded in 1894, purchased the land from the Elias Baker heirs and built Altoona's first streetcar suburb. Winding tree-lined streets and generous lot sizes were sought after by the doctors, bankers, store owners, and skilled railway workers who settled here. Constructed of rounded river rock, the streetcar station's upper story is capped with a pyramidal tower whose flared eaves are echoed in the stone supports of the porch. The building served as the land office for this railway suburb.

The Beezer brothers were given two lots at 306 and 308 Logan Boulevard to the southeast as payment for the station's design, and they built their family homes on them. Their mirror-image cottages were ultimately sold to settle their bankruptcy c. 1900. On each house, the brick first stories and shingled second and attic stories are highlighted by a steeply sloping roof and Colonial Revival detailing.

BL22 Lakemont Park and Blair County Ballpark

1893 park; 1999 stadium, Louis D. Astorino and Associates. Frankstown Rd. (PA 1009) at Lakemont Park Blvd.

In 1893, the six-year-old Altoona and Logan Valley Electric Railway Company opened Lakemont Park on 113 acres. The park included a thirteen-acre artificial lake and a wood-framed casino. It was accessible to both Altoona and Hollidaysburg residents by a trolley that ultimately expanded into an interurban line linking several central Pennsylvania cities. Today, the park has over thirty rides and a waterslide park. Lakemont Park is also home to Leap the Dips of 1902, a National Historic Landmark and the world's oldest and the last remaining

side-friction roller coaster. The ride begins with a push from the attendant and reaches a rollicking ten miles an hour at its fastest. It was restored by private donations between 1997 and 1999, and reopened. The park is adjacent to the Blair County Ballpark, home of the Altoona Curve baseball team that is affiliated with the Pittsburgh Pirates. The stadium, designed by Louis D. Astorino and Associates, seats 6,200.

BL23 Blair County Convention Center

2001, L. Robert Kimball and Associates. 1 Convention Center Dr.

Set among suburban commercial buildings, overlooking a golf course and the mountains of central Pennsylvania, the Blair County Convention Center has the large meeting spaces, business resource center, and high-tech communications systems required of a modern hall. Parking for eight hundred cars and an attached hotel help draw conventions from around the state and the region. The center's red brick base with limestone trim is considerably lightened by the ribbon of windows along the hallways and the upper portion of the stone walls lining the patio. A round-arched glass canopy marks the main entry.

BL24 Horseshoe Curve National Historic Landmark

1852–1854, J. Edgar Thomson, chief engineer; 1992 visitors' center, Richard Glance and Associates. Kittanning Point Rd., 3 miles west of Altoona

The main line of the Pennsylvania Railroad needed a relatively flat route to penetrate the Allegheny Mountains. To achieve this, large earthen bridges or embankments were built across two streambeds at the former Kittanning Point, which allowed the trains to curve 275 feet up the mountainside at the proper grade. Ultimately, the right-of-way of this engineering marvel was expanded to accommodate four tracks. A model of the curve was displayed at the World's Columbian Exposition of 1893 in Chicago, increasing interest in the site to the point that in the first half of the twentieth century, the Horseshoe Curve was considered one of the engineering "Wonders of the World." In 1940, the railroad gave permission to the city of Altoona to operate

Railroads had an immense impact on western Pennsylvania, changing what had been a network of small commercial towns into an industrial powerhouse. They generated high-profile passenger stations like Daniel H. Burnham and Company's Pennsylvania Station in Pittsburgh (AL16) and hotels in several cities. But railroad-related buildings ranging from the simple vernacular Dayton railroad station in Armstrong County to William Holmes Cookman's brick Jacobean Revival station of 1911 in Greensburg (WE2) may be found in nearly every town. Today, these buildings are reused as everything from restaurants to daycare centers.

The railroad evolved from earlier technologies used along the Pennsylvania Canal system. The canal's Allegheny Portage Railroad, built between 1828 and 1834, hauled loaded canal boats up the Allegheny Mountains on a series of inclined planes. The technical prowess needed to master this undertaking acted as fertile training ground for future railroad engineers.

Pushing railroads through western Pennsylvania's hilly terrain was a major engineering feat. The entire town of Altoona was built to service the needs of the Pennsylvania Railroad. What survives today, the reused Master Mechanics building that houses the Railroaders Memorial Museum (BL7) and the magnificent Horseshoe Curve National Historic Landmark of 1854 located three miles west of Altoona along Kittanning Point Road (BL24), encapsulates the drama of railroading. Locomotives are no longer built in Altoona, but they continue to be built in Erie at the General Electric plant (ER34).

Today the railroads' biggest impact is what has been left behind: the nearly level former track beds that have been reused to great advantage as hiking and biking trails, such as the Great Allegheny Passage from Cumberland, Maryland, to Pittsburgh, now capable of transporting generations who may have never ridden the rails.

PENNSYLVANIA RAILROAD CAR SHOPS, ALTOONA, BLAIR COUNTY, AS PICTURED IN T. M. FOWLER'S 1895 COLOR LITHOGRAPH PANORAMIC MAP 109.

BL24 HORSESHOE CURVE NATIONAL HISTORIC LANDMARK

a park at the site, since tourists were driving to it by car. The horseshoe curve was closely guarded during World War II as a prime strategic target. In 1992, a new interpretive center and single-rail funicular were built to allow visitors to see the curve from above and read about the site's history and significance in a hipped-roof building at the base

CULP AND VICINITY

BL25 Fort Roberdeau

1858 barn; 1976 fort reconstructed, N. Grant Nicklas, project architect; 1989–1991 White Oak Hall; A. Raymond Goodman, project architect. PA 1013, 0.7 miles south of Culp

Fort Roberdeau was built in 1778 to protect the miners and local farm families who were supplying George Washington's troops with lead, from attack by the British and their Native American allies. During the Revolutionary War, lead for bullets was at a premium, so Philadelphian Brigadier General Daniel Roberdeau traveled to Sinking Valley, at his own expense, to mine and smelt the lead needed by the new nation. Rangers patrolling the frontier were also garrisoned here from 1778 to 1782. The place name points to the valley's creek that disappears into a sink hole and then reappears at Arch Spring, thus the names Sinking Run and Sinking Valley.

The fort is built with the logs of its outer walls stacked horizontally from the ground up between vertical posts because bedrock in the valley is close to the surface. The fort fell into disuse by the nineteenth century, and its parts were reused or left to decay. In the late 1930s, under the Works Progress Administration and

the National Youth Administration, the fort was excavated and the footer laid for reconstruction using the archaeological and documentary evidence available. In 1976, to honor the nation's bicentennial, the stockade and six of the log cabins within its walls were rebuilt. Forty-seven acres of land surrounding the fort provide nature trails and enhance its rural atmosphere. A group of supporters continues to accrue land around the property, including a timber-frame, Pennsylvania bank barn of 1858 and a white frame farmhouse c. 1866. White Oak Hall, a simple board-and-batten structure with a gable roof, was built between 1989 and 1991 on a hillside overlooking the fort to provide space for educational programming.

BL26 Jacob and Elenor Isett Farm and Store

1799 store; 1805 house. PA 1013, 0.3 miles south of Culp

The entire Isett complex illustrates the evolution of a late-eighteenth-century farm into a small settlement and back again, with a sampling of nineteenth-century vernacular buildings added to maintain its operation. When Jacob Isett, from Berks County, first arrived in Sinking Valley in 1785, Fort Roberdeau was already abandoned, and Scots-Irish and German settlers were establishing farms in the sheltered limestone valley. Although trained as a cobbler, Isett set up a store, sawmill, and gristmill (the latter two demolished) along Sinking Valley Run. A small village flourished around these enterprises, including three millworkers' houses (all demolished). Isett's restored limestone house is seven bays across with doors in the first and fifth bays from the south. Its datestone is distinctive for listing the name of Isett's wife, Elenor. A simple gable roof, corner quoins, and jack arches above the double-sash windows distinguish the main house. A small (16 × 20 feet) summer kitchen at the rear southwest corner is constructed of irregularly coursed limestone two feet thick, as in the main house and store. The store, east of the house across PA 1013, is an elegant rectangular building with a gable roof, fanlights at the gable end and above the double entrance doors, and large double-sash eight-over-twelve windows throughout. Five vertical-board-sided farm buildings c. 1870 dot the landscape south of the main house. They include a timber-frame barn with double outsheds banked at the rear and a weigh shed with the scales intact.

ARCH SPRING

BL27 Sinking Valley Presbyterian Church (Arch Spring Presbyterian Church)

1885. PA 1013 at Church Hill Rd.

In a relatively isolated place like Sinking Valley in the 1870s, a pattern-book church was usual for most congregations. The squat proportions of the corner tower, its flared roofline, and the jerkinhead dormers on the side elevations and over the entrances on the facade all indicate self-assurance and the builder's willingness to tweak the expected forms. The church's first level is irregularly laid stone interrupted by paired Queen Anne windows and two portholes on the side walls. The upper story is red brick, and its windows are Gothic arched. The ornamental woodwork includes carved brackets below the eaves and diamond-patterned shingling on the gable end of the rear elevation. Classrooms on the first story and a second-story sanctuary seating three hundred are traditional for the period. The second-story sanctuary symbolizes the biblical Upper Room where Christ and the apostles held the Last Supper. The Arch Spring Cemetery surrounds the church on three sides.

WILLIAMSBURG VICINITY

BL28 Mt. Etna Furnace and Iron Plantation

1805–1809, 1827–1846. Casselberry Rd. and PA 2017 NW, 6.4 miles north–northeast of Williamsburg

This is the most remarkable collection of early-nineteenth-century iron furnace plantation buildings in western Pennsylvania. The ironmaster's home and office, workers' housing, and a working farm survive. More remarkably, all continue to be used as either homes or farm buildings. The entire complex is relatively isolated along Casselberry Road adjacent to Roaring Run. A canal lock survives one mile to the south at the Juniata River. The pyramidal stone furnace, built between 1805 and 1809, operated until 1877. Most of the limestone, gable- or pyramidal-roofed buildings were constructed during the ownership of Henry S. Spang between 1827 and 1846. The entire complex was owned by the Isett family of Sinking Valley (BL26) until World War II, when the farm portion with its handsome stone barn was sold. It is an astonishing assemblage of buildings embodying the core story of the industrial development of western Pennsylvania.

BL29 Daniel Royer House

1815. 59 Piney Creek Crossing Rd. (PA 866), 2.6 miles southwest of Williamsburg

Dotted throughout the forests of Blair County are remains of the once booming iron industry. The Royer house was the mansion for an iron plantation begun in 1814. Three Royer brothers came to Blair County in 1811 and purchased land. One brother farmed, but Daniel and John opened a forge to hammer raw iron bars, "pigs," into smaller, thinner bars that could be hammered by blacksmiths into horseshoes, locks, and other small items. Within three years, they branched out and built the Springfield Iron furnace and ore mine to supply a steady stream of iron for their forges, establishing a strong, local, family-based industry. Daniel's son Samuel moved into the two-and-one-half-story random-laid stone house in 1821 and raised ten children here, expanding the house several times. From a three-bay side entrance house, it became a five-bay central entrance. A two-story wing added to the rear has a two-story porch along its inner (south) elevation, and a two-story log wing with clapboard sheathing was added at a lower level on that elevation. Various family members worked for the Royer family empire, founding not only the first iron forge operating in the county but also the last, which closed in 1885.

ROARING SPRING

The borough takes its name from a great spring that could be heard roaring a mile away, and though the roaring stopped when several large stones were removed from the spring's base, the name continues. Located at the southern end of Morrison's Cove, the earliest European settlers were German Brethren farmers in the 1780s. By the 1820s, the Spang family had opened a mill, store, and two forges. As a commercial center, the village, then called Spang's Mills, attracted a steady stream of teamsters, as it was located midway between the source of iron ore and a large iron furnace at McKee. In 1863, Daniel Bare and his son, Daniel Mathias Bare, purchased ninety acres, and two years later, in partnership with two others, they founded a paper mill and expanded it twice. In 1880, they built an additional and even larger paper mill in Tyrone. The family wisely declined the dubious honor of naming the village "Baretown," choosing instead to commemorate the Roaring Spring. Connected to Altoona in 1871 by the Morrison's Cove Branch of the Pennsylvania Railroad, the community grew large enough to become a borough in 1888. A one-story, hipped-roof brick train station (c. 1905; Main Street), three bays wide and with a long covered platform, is the only historic passenger station continuing to operate in Blair County, and represents the connection of the paper mill and the planing mill to larger markets.

Two large churches from the 1890s flank the town center, the gray stone Gothic Revival Trinity United Methodist Church (1898; 434 E. Main Street) and the red brick Romanesque Revival Bare Memorial Church of God (1889, 1930; 508 E. Main Street). The blue limestone Colonial Revival mansion with a large colonnade across the facade at 604 Oakmont Place was built for Dr. W. A. Nason. Today, the employee-owned Appleton paper mill and the Roaring Spring Blank Book Company (BL30), with their Roaring Spring Premium Spring Water division (1980), are the major industries. Another significant employer is the New Enterprise Stone and Lime Quarry, north of the borough.

BL30 ROARING SPRING BLANK BOOK COMPANY

BL30 Roaring Spring Blank Book Company
1888, with additions. 740 Spang St.

Certainly the most dramatic site in Roaring Spring belongs to the three-story, blue limestone warehouse and office building of the Blank Book Company. Circular crenellated towers at the corners flank three recessed central bays, with a semicircular arched entrance. Daniel Mathias Bare began producing paper at this site in 1865. In 1886, the family founded the Blank Book Company, using their paper to make account books. With convenient rail service and abundant water, the factory thrived. All the factory buildings built between 1888 and 1914 survive. The later buildings are brick and range from three to five stories. Today, the company continues to manufacture ledgers, day books, memos, school composition books, and tablets, which are sold in the former Roaring Spring Planing Mill (1905) adjacent to the factory. The family also owns the Roaring Spring Premium Spring Water Company (founded 1980), which processes sixteen million gallons of water annually and ships it regionally. Its headquarters are in the same complex.

CENTRE COUNTY

Centre County is named for its location at the state's geographic center. The county's southern section is part of the ridge and valley terrain, and on its northern side is the Allegheny Plateau, running southwest to northeast. Shawnee and Delaware peoples inhabited the area in the colonial period, but few archaeological sites remain. By the late eighteenth century, Europeans began to settle the area, a process stimulated by the discovery of iron ore and coal deposits in the 1780s. Settlers came into the county (established in 1800) via Bald Eagle Creek, a tributary of the Susquehanna, and settled in Penns, Brush, Half Moon, Bald Eagle, and Nittany valleys. Germanic settlement was mostly in agricultural Penns and Brush valleys, while Irish, Scots-Irish, and Anglo-Americans settled throughout the region.

Iron making, in addition to agriculture, was a mainstay of the economy, and by the 1830s, the industry included furnaces, forges, rolling mills, and slitting mills producing pig iron, bar iron, and nails. The discovery of coal in Centre County's northern region added another dimension to the local industry. Canal service was established in 1848, linking Bellefonte and Lock Haven in Clinton County, and rail service opened in 1857 from Bellefonte to Tyrone, Blair County. Aside from Bellefonte, the county seat and business center, iron plantations such as Centre Furnace (CE21) were the most densely populated settlements. The plantations were practically self-sufficient, consisting of imposing stone ironmasters' houses and stone furnace stacks surrounded by a scattering of farm buildings, workers' houses, stores, churches, and the occasional school. By the late nineteenth century, however, technological innovations in iron and steel production were pushing small-scale iron operations to the margins, except for such endeavors as the Scotia iron ore mines southwest of State College, which shipped ore to Andrew Carnegie's mills in Pittsburgh.

In Bellefonte, the courthouse and a few stone Federal-style residences stood alongside mostly wooden row houses. In the countryside, log construction was the norm, and construction techniques often followed ethnic patterns; buildings typically were small and spare. Later in the nineteenth century, balloon framing and milled decorative elements were added to the local architectural vocabulary, notably in Bellefonte. Much of the wood for building was supplied locally, and lumbering became a thriving industry, especially in the northern part of the county. Agricultural production for local markets was also a significant part of the economy. While many farm families struggled, others were wealthy enough to erect the large Pennsylvania barns that now appear in the county, especially along PA 45 (CE12). Agriculture-dependent villages, such as Aaronsburg and Boalsburg, updated existing buildings with Victorian trim or porches rather than build anew.

In the late nineteenth century, the expansion of Pennsylvania State College (CE16) shifted growth to the State College area. The college (which became a university in 1949) increasingly was a driving force in the county, especially in the twentieth and twenty-first centuries, engendering an ever-expanding campus, as well as suburban sprawl and commercial buildings to serve the university population. The loss of prime farmland to commercial and residential development is a growing public concern.

BELLEFONTE

Bellefonte was laid out by Colonel James Dunlop and his son-in-law James Harris on hilly terrain adjacent to Spring Creek in 1795. Located near a major gap in Bald Eagle Ridge, it lay at the main entrance to the fertile Nittany Valley. Farms had been developing in the region for at least ten years, and a flour mill was built as early as 1785. The region's high quality iron ore encouraged the establishment of iron furnaces and forges in the early 1790s. The iron industry and, after 1857, the rail lines that carried its raw materials and finished products spurred Bellefonte's economic growth. However, the slowdown of industrial development meant that Bellefonte retained a large number of handsome nineteenth- and early-twentieth-century buildings. Houses built in the various revival styles popular at the turn of the twentieth

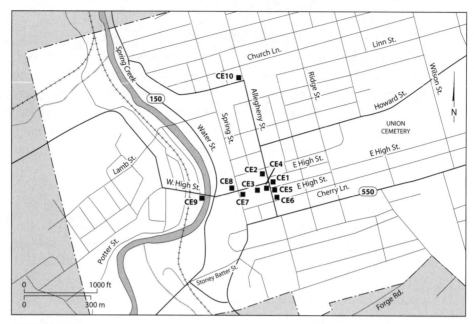

BELLEFONTE

century line the streets that are laid out in a grid over the hilly terrain. The Miles-Humes House (203 N. Allegheny Street) epitomizes the local evolution of architectural taste. Built by ironmaster Joseph Miles between 1814 and 1816, it was acquired by banker E. C. Humes in 1895, who added Colonial Revival trim and enlarged the dormer. At 120 W. Lamb Street, the stone Gothic Revival St. John's Episcopal Church (1871) emphasizes verticality with its elongated corner steeple and lancet windows. The former Gamble Mill at W. Lamb and Dunlop streets, now converted to a restaurant, points to Bellefonte's industrial origins. Bellefonte's commercial prosperity in the last decades of the nineteenth century is reflected in the highly textured Queen Anne–style Crider Exchange Building (c. 1889; 103–117 N. Allegheny Street) and the neighboring stone First National Bank (1889; W. High and N. Allegheny streets).

Several buildings designed by the commonwealth's first female registered architect, Anna Wagner Keichline, survive in Bellefonte (CE3). To her credit are houses at 177 E. Curtin Street (1916) and 412 E. Linn Street (1930), a model house at 440 N. Spring Street (1936), and the B. O. Harvey houses of 1935 and 1939 at 121 E. Curtin and 518 N. Allegheny streets.

The town square, or diamond, at Allegheny and High streets is the town's centerpiece. However, the shores of Spring Creek have taken on a new life since the 1960s, when plans were drawn to create Talleyrand Park here. Bellefonte is said to have received its name from French diplomat Charles-Maurice Talleyrand-Perigord, who visited the area during his two-year banishment in the United States (1794–1796). As he traveled the forested regions in search of commodities and real estate, he was shown the local spring and is said to have declared, "La belle font!" After a period of industrialization, the banks of the creek were obscured by undistinguished buildings, but in the 1970s, local citizens and their representatives commissioned a gazebo and, later, footbridges and the George Gray Barnard Sculpture Garden. In 2006, they restored the stone pump house of 1926 to create a welcoming water feature at the base of the town. George Barnard, another Bellefonte native, is best known as the collector of medieval architectural artifacts that make up the core of the Metropolitan Museum of Art's Cloisters collection.

CE1 Centre County Courthouse

1805, attributed to Ezra Ale; 1835; c. 1855, George W. Tate; 1909, Newman and Harris; 1963–1964, Dean Kennedy. High and Allegheny sts.

Now an imposing two-story templelike building, the courthouse began in 1805 as a modest limestone structure. The Ionic portico and pediment were added in 1835. Around 1855, the building of 1805 was replaced by a longer structure, although the portico was retained. The tall, domed cupola with classical detailing was added at this time. The rear of the building was further extended and the interior completely refurbished in 1909. On the interior, a central hall on the first floor is flanked by offices, and courtrooms are located on the second floor.

The colonnade in the courthouse square was designed in 1906 by Joseph M. Huston of Philadelphia, architect of the Pennsylvania State Capitol in Harrisburg. In the center of the colonnade is William Clark Noble's c. 1913 bronze statue of Andrew G. Curtin, Pennsylvania's governor during the Civil War and one of five commonwealth governors from Bellefonte.

CE2 Bellefonte Museum (General Philip Benner–Henry Linn House)

1810, attributed to Samuel Wetzel. 133 N. Allegheny St.

Commissioned by Revolutionary War general Philip Benner, this house was built as a rental property and owned by various members of the Benner family until 1954. The

Crider Exchange Building on North Allegheny Street, one of many high-style commercial buildings in Bellefonte, the county seat of Centre County.

CE3 PLAZA CENTRE (PLAZA THEATER)

CE4 BROCKERHOFF HOTEL

name Linn became attached to the house when Benner's granddaughter Mary Wilson married John Blair Linn, and they lived in the house for seventy-six years, until 1907. Built of coursed limestone, the two-and-one-half-story house is three bays wide. The delicacy of the broken pediment on slender pilasters at the entrance is typical of the Federal style. An elegant fanlight over the door, surrounded by restrained molding, is echoed in the two dormer windows. A two-story rear ell, also made of limestone, was constructed after the Civil War. The house is occupied by the Bellefonte Museum.

CE3 Plaza Centre (Plaza Theater)

1925, Anna Wagner Keichline. 124 W. High St.

Five bays of maroon brick with a central gabled pediment mark this two-story theater, a few doors west of the courthouse. Commercial spaces with wide transoms flank the first-story central entrance under the marquee. Anna Wagner Keichline (1889–1943), a 1911 graduate of Cornell's architecture school, began her design career in high school by crafting furniture in her Bellefonte home workshop. By 1912, she was designing buildings for private clients, and became the first female registered architect in Pennsylvania in 1920, when the commonwealth began certification of architects for the first time. Another maroon brick building, c. 1916, by Keichline at the southwest corner of S. Allegheny and W. Bishop streets initially served as the Cadillac dealership and apartments. She was an early auto enthusiast who enjoyed servicing and repairing her own car.

Keichline invented a precursor of the concrete block in 1927, called the "K brick," a light, fireproof clay brick that was intended

to be filled with insulation and used in hollow wall construction. Her reputation as an architect, inventor, suffragist, and World War I Army Intelligence agent prompted the commonwealth to erect a historical marker in her memory in 2002 in front of the theater, which is now used as an antiques cooperative.

CE4 Brockerhoff Hotel

1864–1866; 1890, John R. Cole. 100–119 S. Allegheny St.

Constructed by German immigrant Henry Brockerhoff, this three-story building is embellished with drip moldings around the windows, recessed two-story wall arcading, and ornate wooden brackets along the eaves. As Bellefonte prospered with the coming of the railroad, the hotel was enlarged and renovated with a steeply pitched mansard roof, complete with fanciful dormers, and polychrome slate roof tiles. In the 1980s, automobile traffic had rendered the hotel obsolete, and the town's aging population prompted its conversion into senior citizen apartment housing. John Robert Cole (1850–1916), a local designer, trained at a Bellefonte planing mill. He also designed the earliest buildings of the Pennsylvania Match Factory, a group of red brick industrial structures west of Spring Creek, which produced matchsticks between 1900 and 1947. Today, the American Philatelic Society is headquartered in one of the former administration buildings at 100 Match Factory Place.

CE5 Courthouse Annex (W. F. Reynolds and Company)

1887, Charles Shuster Wetzel. 108 S. Allegheny St.

This building is an excellent example of a traditional corner bank, a three-and-one-half-story structure with a two-story banking room lit by large arched windows. Constructed of red brick above a brownstone base and with a copper-clad wooden roof and wood trim, the building was designed by Charles Shuster Wetzel (1822–1898) from Danville. The square massing and the detailing of the dormers, cornice, and corner turret are typical of the Queen Anne style. Its central location adjacent to the courthouse recalls Bellefonte's role as the county's financial center in the late nineteenth century.

CE6 Temple Court Building

1894, John R. Cole. 116 S. Allegheny St.

This four-story Romanesque Revival building is constructed of golden-orange-colored Pompeiian brick on the upper stories, with a heavily rusticated brownstone base. Tall round-arched windows span the second and third stories, and the cornice is a mixture of such classically inspired elements as dentils, pediments, sunbursts, and a blind arcade. The building has commercial stores on the first story and is adjacent to the courthouse annex.

CE7 WCTU Petrikin Hall

1901, John R. Cole. 136 W. High St.

This substantial Romanesque Revival building for the local branch of the Woman's Christian Temperance Union (WCTU) is constructed of red brick on a rusticated brownstone foundation. Seven fenestrated arched bays, each with prominent voussoirs, extend up the first two stories of the facade; the third story is punctuated by a row of narrow windows. The vertical emphasis of the bays is balanced by a massive projecting cornice, supported by muscular scroll bracketing. Italianate details include a large, central segmental-arched pediment and low relief decoration of festoons and wreaths on the frieze. Petrikin Hall illustrates the power and popularity of the WCTU, which by 1901 was one of the most prominent women's organizations in the country (see also AR13). Though later often dismissed as a rigid "bluestocking" organization, at the turn of the twentieth century, the WCTU embraced many progressive reform causes, including women's suffrage, and became an important political and cultural force. This WCTU building originally included a large public meeting room with apartments on the upper stories to provide rental income. When theaters and other venues proved too much competition, the building was given over to commercial and residential tenants.

CE8 Centre County Banking Company Building

1881–1882, George W. Tate. 201 W. High St.

A colorful addition to the Victorian eclecticism of Bellefonte's High Street, this Ruskinian Gothic building displays brick quoins, a heavy brownstone foundation, decorative polychrome brick window lintels, and a projecting corner turret. A pair of corbeled chimneys rises through the dormers on the third story, adding to the building's eccentricity. George Tate established himself in Bellefonte by replacing most of the county courthouse and adding the portico (CE1).

CE9 Gamble Mill Restaurant (Gamble Mill)

1894. 160 Dunlap St.

This former mill, which replaced two industrial buildings destroyed by fire, is a brownish brick structure on a stone base. The tallest section of the asymmetrical structure is distinguished by its prominent stepped end gable. Iron star-shaped tie rods and arched and lunette windows provide the only decorative touches. The roller mill was used until 1947, and then deteriorated nearly to the point of demolition before being rescued and renovated in 1985 for its new purpose.

CE10 W. F. Reynolds House

1884–1885. 101 W. Linn St.

This imposing house, home of banker W. F. Reynolds, was built in the heyday of Bellefonte's prosperity. The building's massive proportions and heavy brownstone blocks point to Romanesque Revival, while the mansard roof and spire, wooden bracketing, cornice work, bargeboard, and porch all hail from different stylistic vocabularies to give the house a playful eclectic character. This is one of many large, imposing mansions lining N.

Allegheny and Linn streets, and is balanced on its block by the handsome brownstone St. John's United Church of Christ (1880; 145 W. Linn Street).

CURTIN

In the mid-nineteenth century, Curtin's economy revolved around the Eagle Iron Works founded in 1810 by Roland Curtin, father of the Civil War–era governor Andrew G. Curtin. The complex comprises wooden industrial buildings (reconstructions), original worker housing, company store, grist and saw mills, a church, and a school. Curtin's house (251 Curtin Village Road), located at the center of the complex, dominates the industrial plantation spatially and symbolically. Built in 1830, the two-and-one-half-story, stucco over brick fifteen-room house, with its symmetrical facade, central arched entrance, and smooth surface, communicated order and refinement in this relatively remote spot. The building's role as the center of an active workplace required space for large-scale cooking and for a continual round of visitors and business associates. The Curtin family remained in residence until the 1950s. Nearby, a wooden tenant house accommodated furnace managers and their families. Still standing, a few hundred feet away, is the furnace stack of 1847. The village of Curtin and sixty acres around it are state owned and open to the public.

AARONSBURG AND VICINITY

Immigrant entrepreneur Aaron Levy laid out Aaronsburg in 1786 on a grid plan with two wide intersecting streets. Although Levy intended an industrial and perhaps political future for the town, the lack of water in the immediate vicinity, development of other towns, and demise of road transport destined Aaronsburg to remain a small agrarian village. Consequently, the village has an unusually strong visual coherence. Typical housing includes four- or five-bay buildings executed in log, brick, or stone, especially in the 200 block of Aaron Square. Most have end chimneys, while a significant number also have double doors or side-hall plans. Levy was also noteworthy for his ecumenical vision. Though Jewish, he set aside land to be available to any religious association, and he donated a pewter communion set preserved at the Salem Lutheran Church (138 E. Plum Street). The larger town of Millheim to the west had grist, planing, and woolen mills along Elk Creek in the nineteenth century, and retains a variety of brick and frame residences from that period.

CE11 Centre Mills Bed-and-Breakfast (Centre Mills)

c. 1800. 461 Smullton Rd., 4 miles north of Aaronsburg

This massive stone grain mill, erected at the beginning of the nineteenth century, was a focal point for agriculture-related industry and trade in the early history of Brush Valley. For the entire nineteenth century, a millrace supplied waterpower to the wheel located under an archway. Now, the fieldstone structure, bracketed at the corners by stone quoins, is crumbling away. The nearby house complements the mill in its stonework, featuring courses of larger stones for the window lintels and sills. Nine-over-six sash windows and a transomed, paneled entrance door contribute to the balanced facade.

CENTRE HALL

The village of Centre Hall, situated along Nittany Mountain where PA 192 and PA 144 now intersect, was linked to Bellefonte and Lewistown. By the mid-nineteenth century, Scots-Irish and German families had settled here. Laid out in the typical Pennsylvania manner with a grid plan and a central square, the village functioned as a business center for the Penns Valley region, with many farm landlords in residence. The arrival of the Lewisburg and Tyrone Railroad in 1885 launched Centre Hall into a period of growth that included agricultural processing and chick hatcheries. The architecture reflects the conservatism evident elsewhere in the county in its five-bay, rectangular houses, such as those at 220 and 315 N. Pennsylvania Avenue, both dating c. 1865. Later houses, for example at 251 S. Pennsylvania Avenue (c. 1880), experimented with projecting gables, bays, and ornate spindlework, but still within the original five-bay format. Three churches served the Protestant population: the brownstone Gothic Revival Trinity United Church of Christ of 1895 at 108 N. Park Avenue; the red brick St. Luke Lutheran Church built c. 1900 at 301 N. Pennsylvania Avenue; and the red brick Centre Hall Grace United Methodist Church, built for a Presbyterian congregation in 1888 at 127 S. Pennsylvania Avenue. The Grange Encampment grounds, southwest of town (237 S. Hoffer Avenue), host thousands of tents and RVs during the weeklong Grange Fair, held every year since 1876, when it was devised as a means of introducing rural families to the Grange organization.

CE12 Calvin Neff Round Barn

1910, Calvin Neff, designer; Aaron Thomas, builder. 2519 PA 45, 2.3 miles south of Centre Hall

In 1910, farmer Calvin Neff and carpenter Aaron Thomas introduced the round plan to barn construction in Centre County. During the late nineteenth century, this type of barn appeared sporadically in the Northeast and the Midwest, where Neff was first exposed to it during a train trip in 1892. The round plan was utilized for its labor and space-saving characteristics. The barn measures 88 feet in diameter, 56 feet in height, and has an area of over 6,000 square feet. Built on a limestone foundation with board-and-batten siding on the first floor and lap siding on the second floor, the red and white barn is topped by a cedar-shingled roof with tin at the very top. Six dormer windows and a cupola cap the

CE12 CALVIN NEFF ROUND BARN

structure. The barn's interior has a cattle floor and a mow floor, each resting on one of three concentric sills. Radiating rafters support the roof and floor. Though no longer an active agricultural site, the round barn is a popular and enduring landmark in the rural Centre County landscape.

BOALSBURG

Boalsburg began as a post village in the early nineteenth century, and flourished because of its location along the major stage routes leading to both

Pittsburgh and Harrisburg. The town is named after Captain David Boal, who settled in the area after emigrating from Ireland in 1789. In 1809, land speculator Andrew Stroup officially laid out the village along two main thoroughfares, Pine and Pitt (now Main) streets. The grid-patterned streets and the main town square, or diamond, are lined with excellently preserved examples of Federal and late-nineteenth-century architecture. The buildings represent a wide range of construction techniques, including log (now covered with clapboard, c. 1815 at 110 W. Main Street), plank, and balloon framing. Several taverns catered to travelers (CE13), and many residences served as workplaces for artisans. After the eclipse of stage transportation, Boalsburg became an agricultural village, as its Odd Fellows Hall (1895; 101–109 W. Main Street) testifies. At the same time, residents modernized their older buildings with expansive porches and other fashionable features.

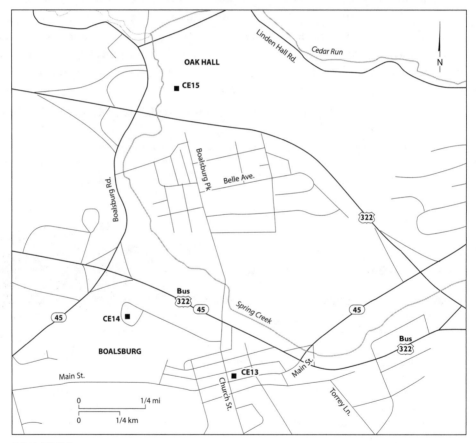

BOALSBURG

CE13 Duffy's Boalsburg Tavern

1819, with additions. 113 E. Main St.

This imposing tavern was constructed by Colonel James Johnston Jr. and his wife, Hannah, to cater to traveling gentry. The Johnstons inscribed their initials and the date of construction above the main doorway of this seven-bay Federal structure that dominates the town's main square. Although the roof and the third floor were lost to a fire in 1934, it was painstakingly rebuilt. The original part of the tavern consists of the five easternmost bays, which are notable for fine stonework, decorative limestone and sandstone keystones over the sash windows, and cornice trim. The two western bays were added in the mid-nineteenth century, and may have housed the tavern keeper and family. Other rear extensions and dormers were added over the years, resulting in the present appearance. In 1830, Johnston constructed a house on a hillside overlooking the small town (204 S. Church Street). Its elaborate fanlight, decorative exterior pargeting, and slender proportioned details show excellent workmanship. Federal features include the double-hung sash windows, steeply pitched roof, strict symmetry, and double chimneys. In plan, the building has a central hall and is one room deep.

CE14 Boal House

1789, 1898, 1900. 300 Old Boalsburg Rd.

Captain David Boal constructed the first portion of this house, a one-and-one-half-story stone cabin in 1789. His son, also David, added a two-story, three-bay stone section north of

CE14 BOAL HOUSE

the original cabin in 1798. This Federal-style portion has a side-hall plan, interior end chimneys, a dramatic interior stairway, dormer windows, and an arched transom over the doorway. A century later, in 1898, Colonel Theodore "Terry" Boal, who trained at the Ecole des Beaux-Arts in Paris, and his wife, Mathilde, began to enlarge the family estate. Preserving the character of the earlier Federal north facade, they added two recessed bays west of the 1798 section of the house. The new work included classical details and a greater sense of symmetry. After 1900, the Boals continued to enlarge the estate, adding barns and stables, and embellishing the grounds with arbors, formal gardens, and fountains. A small stone chapel built in 1912 houses the furnishings of the Columbus family chapel that were imported from Olviedo, Spain, the home of Mathilde's relatives, direct descendants of Christopher Columbus. After Colonel Boal's death in 1938, the estate was unoccupied until 1952, when restorations began and the grounds were opened to the public. Today, the barn is used as a theater, and the house and chapel are museums.

OAK HALL FARM

CE15 Irvin House and Barn

1822. Boalsburg Pike at Linden Hall Rd.

John Irvin Sr. built this stone, five-bay Federal house in 1822, which, at the time, was one of the largest buildings in the entire county. It has fine coursed stonework, a central doorway with fanlight, and stone end chimneys. Irvin also built grist and saw mills in the small transport and mill center of Oak Hall. A bank barn of uncoursed limestone masonry with evenly spaced louvered openings and a cupola

echo the house's sense of order and dignity. Irvin's son, General James Irvin, was an early ironmaster, and his family's farm reflects the close relationship of industry and agriculture in the early iron and mill sites. When General Irvin experienced financial losses after the financial panic of 1857, the farm was purchased by the Reverend Robert Hamill of the Spring Creek Presbyterian congregation (see the next section on Lemont). Most likely, he undertook the addition of the ironwork porch with flaring eaves.

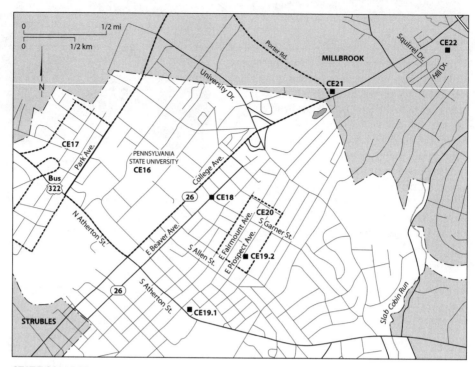

STATE COLLEGE

LEMONT

This crossroads village was laid out by local iron entrepreneur and business-man Moses Thompson. After the arrival of the railroad in the mid-1880s, the village developed a modest commercial district and new houses. The Dale-Mayes house of 1871 (1890 renovated) at 918 Pike Street shows this prosperity vividly, with its cross gables, wraparound porch, and decorative ironwork along the roof ridge. The John I. Thompson Jr. house (c. 1870; 821 Pike Street) is built of local limestone, and with its five-bay facade and three projecting dormers, it has an anachronistically Georgian appearance. The Spring Creek Presbyterian Church (c. 1870; 144 Mary Street) also makes use of local stone, and has a fine buttressed tower, a rose window and stained glass windows, and arched entrances. Other notable houses include 913 Pike Street (c. 1886), which has uncoursed stone, a circular window in the gable end, and project-ing eaves with brackets. Next door at 907 Pike Street, I. J. Dreese built a center-gable, five-bay I-house at about the same time, with decorative win-dow lintels and a spindlework porch. The railroad station (c. 1885; 140 Mary Street) is reused as an architectural office and shops.

STATE COLLEGE

CE16 Pennsylvania State University (PSU) (Farmer's High School of Pennsylvania)

1887–present. Roughly bounded by College and Park aves., N. Atherton St., and Porter Rd.

In 1855, the trustees of the Farmer's High School of Pennsylvania (later the Pennsylvania State College, and today, the Pennsylvania State University) chose two hundred acres in

Centre County for the school. Currently, more than two hundred buildings occupy PSU's University Park campus. Old Botany is the most significant of the early buildings. Designed by the college's staff architect Frederick L. Olds in 1887, this Richardsonian Romanesque two-and-one-half-story hipped-roof building of stone and brick presents the squat, massive volume typical of its style. Among the several buildings added to the campus between 1899 and 1906, under the presidency of George W. Atherton, were the first buildings financed by individual donors (Charles M. Schwab and Andrew Carnegie). These were Schwab Auditorium (1902, Edward Hazlehurst) and the Carnegie Library (1903, Davis and Davis). Both are rectangular Beaux-Arts-inspired buildings with hipped roofs and faced with light-colored, smooth stone. Farther east on "Ag Hill," the Patterson (1903), Armsby (1905–1907), and Weaver (1914) buildings surround the agriculture quadrangle. All designed by Edward Hazlehurst (1853–1915), these Renaissance Revival buildings create a harmonious ensemble. All are executed in warm-colored (deep red, tan, or brown) stone, with a massive first story and progressively lighter-detailed second and third stories. Round-arched windows, tile roofs, wide projecting eaves, and dormers are shared architectural features.

In 1914, Charles Z. Klauder (1872–1938) developed a master plan for the PSU campus. Klauder decided to make a new Old Main the focal point and to create a set of symmetrical quadrangles in the spirit of Beaux-Arts planning, one of which would evolve into a mall stretching to Allen Street in downtown State College. Klauder's Old Main (1930) is constructed from limestone blocks reused from the campus's original College Building. The Georgian Revival, H-shaped building has an eight-columned portico supporting a tall entablature, and a domed cupola of slender proportions and simple geometric lines. With Klauder as university architect, a building boom in the 1930s resulted in many new laboratories, an expanded agriculture campus, and student residences. Klauder designed many of these buildings, including the Pattee Library (1938) at the head of the mall. Its plain, massive square-columned portico, topped by a glassed-in second story, can be categorized as the "starved Classicism" of the 1930s. A row

of historic elm trees line the mall. Additional designs by Klauder include the West Halls dormitory group, a Georgian Revival ensemble facing open quadrangles, and the Mineral Industries Building (now Steidle Building) of 1929–1931 that has a projecting domed entrance supported by a semicircle of columns.

Expansion after World War II included the long, rounded one-story building (1930; 200 W. Park Avenue) adjacent to the Nittany Lion Inn. Designed in 1974 by Venturi, Scott Brown and Associates as a faculty club, the building's wood shingles blend with the surrounding woods. Unfortunately, the faculty club never materialized, and the interior fittings have been removed. Increasingly, football became a focus of Penn State life. Beaver Stadium was constructed in 1960 out of materials from the old Beaver Field. Its horseshoe shape, with bleacher sections on the long sides, was eventually filled in with bleachers added to the end of the horseshoe (1999–2001, John C. Haas Associates/HOK Sport). In scale, the stadium dwarfs all other campus structures. Its exposed steel framework, concrete ramps, scoreboard, and spiky lights (added in 1984) are often seen on national television when the Nittany Lions play football here. The stadium seats 107,000 people. The neighboring Bryce Jordan Center (1993–1996, Haas/Rosser Fabrap/Brinjac, Kambic) claims it is the largest covered arena between Pittsburgh and Philadelphia; it seats 15,261 people for basketball events, graduation ceremonies, and concerts. Its rounded profile, red brick facade, and imposing, white curved and segmented roofline are eye-catching.

Across Park Avenue, the Agricultural Arena (1986, Dagit/Saylor) features an over-

CE16 PENNSYLVANIA STATE UNIVERSITY (PSU) (FARMER'S HIGH SCHOOL OF PENNSYLVANIA), Agricultural Arena

CE16 PENNSYLVANIA STATE UNIVERSITY (PSU) (FARMER'S HIGH SCHOOL OF PENNSYLVANIA), Information Sciences and Technology Building

sized and creatively ornamented barn shape. Another notable addition to campus architecture is the Palmer Museum of Art on Curtin Road, built in 1972, and given an addition and major renovation, completed in 1993, by Charles W. Moore (1925–1993) in association with Arbonies King Vlock. Moore was the first out-of-state architect to design a building on the Penn State campus. The new entrance, with its arched, angled front transformed the museum. It faces an expansive loggia whose geometric patterns echo those on the entrance windows. The brick arches refer to neighboring buildings on the Ag quad, and each arch, supported by white columns topped with colorful glazed-tile capitals, frames a view from a different point on campus pathways to create inviting vistas. An imposing two-story lobby with giant corbeled projections angles the visitor to the gallery spaces. These rooms have projecting portals placed at slight angles to the gallery walls, thus creating visual interest and a sense of movement.

In 2003, the Student Union and library were renovated, and more than a dozen red brick residence halls and buildings devoted to the applied sciences were built on the west campus. The Information Sciences and Technology Building (1999–2003), by Rafael Viñoly with Perfido Weiskopf, spans Atherton Street (U.S. 322), linking the central and west campuses in a graceful sweep of glass anchored by red brick. The new brick, steel, and glass Smeal College of Business at the corner of Park Avenue and Shortlidge Road was designed by Robert A. M. Stern with Bower Lewis Thrower (2003–2005). In 2005, the Architecture and Landscape Architecture departments moved into the Stuckeman Family Building, a gold LEED-rated, copper-sheathed building south of Park Avenue and west of Shortlidge Road. It was designed by Overland Partners of San Antonio, Texas, and WTW Architects and Landscape Architects La Quatra Bonci of Pittsburgh.

CE17 College Heights District

1920–1960. Roughly bounded by Holmes St.; Park, Ridge, Hillcrest, and Mitchell aves.; Woodland Dr.; and Sunset Rd.

The College Heights neighborhood, adjoining Pennsylvania State University (PSU) campus to the north, reflects the robust economy of the university town during the Depression years, when other regions of the commonwealth could afford little new construction. Enrollment at the college doubled during the 1930s, and with this expansion came an infusion of people and money. College Heights was laid out in the early 1920s, and by 1940, over 270 houses had been built in the neighborhood. Early deed transfers required that houses built here cost at least $5,000. This was a boon to the local building trades, since low prices for labor and materials meant that

CE18 GRACE LUTHERAN CHURCH

even faculty members could erect architect-designed houses. For example, at 721 and 722 Holmes Street, local architect Clarence Bauchspies designed homes in Tudor and Colonial styles. The former features cross gables with decorative half timbering, casement windows with stone lintels, and a corbeled brick chimney. The latter has a simple three-bay design with a hooded porch and door with fanlight. Bauchspies's own house at 608 Sunset Road (1935) is similar. At 154 Ridge Avenue, the multigabled Tudor Revival residence of 1928 by Frederick C. Disque has false half timbering in a fanciful lozenge pattern. Brick and stucco-finished walls and irregular fenestration add to the building's cottage ambience. At 335 Arbor Way, P. Boyd Kapp and Dean Kennedy, together with local contractor John Henszey, landscaped and built a charming Tudor Revival house in 1935. Cross gables, multiple chimneys topped with terra-cotta pots, projecting bay windows, and a slate roof combine with beautifully textured masonry of local hammer-worked stone. More than a dozen houses are authenticated as mail-order houses. For example, the Sears "Colchester" (1932–1933; 750 Holmes Avenue) has rounded stone arches, rustic clapboarding in the gable end, and a massive stone chimney with quoins. Trees, plantings, and professional landscaping completed the neighborhood to reinforce the atmosphere of an elite residential district.

Notable commercial, religious, and public buildings occupy prominent places in the district. The College Heights School (721 N. Atherton Street) was designed c. 1925 by the PSU architectural landscape firm of P. Boyd Kapp and Henley Eden in a restrained Colonial Revival. At 803 N. Atherton Street, the gas station built in 1935 (now College Heights Exxon) is in the cottage style to blend with its residential neighborhood; it retains its original neon-lit clock fixture.

After World War II, College Heights continued to be a fashionable choice as the university burgeoned. The International Style was employed for houses at 667 Franklin Street, 315 Martin Terrace, and 515 W. Park Avenue. A bolder architect-designed house (1956, William Hajjar) at 327 Arbor Way presents a solid facade to the street side and is dominated by austere garage walls. The Islamic Center of Central Pennsylvania at 709 W. Ridge Avenue was originally a Unitarian church, built c. 1960 and modified for its new use in 1989 with the addition of a minaret. This shallow-pitch gable-roofed building, with its simple lines, fits the modernist tenor of the western part of the neighborhood.

CE18 Grace Lutheran Church

1965, Harold E. Wagoner. 205 S. Garner St.

By 1965, Grace Lutheran Church had outgrown its original quarters and commissioned Harold Wagoner, a prolific ecclesiastical architect from Philadelphia, to design what has become a local landmark. Sweeping skyward in a graceful curve, the main mass of the steel-frame building is covered with randomly cut local stone that is pierced with many small, asymmetrically placed, geometrically patterned stained glass windows that subtly filter the light, as in Le Corbusier's Ronchamp of 1950–1955 in France. An arched opening in the wall houses three bells, and the arch motif repeats in the church's main entrance. Within the sanctuary, the sweeping, curved lines of the exterior define the main worship space, with high, open views in every direction. A freestanding circular altar and suspended cross complement the overall design. Grace Lutheran exemplifies both continuity and change, exhibiting the strong, relatively conservative Lutheran social base of this part of

Pennsylvania while reflecting the openness of a university community to new architectural trends.

CE19.1 A. L. Kocher House
CE19.2 E. C. Woodruff House

1922, Alfred Lawrence Kocher. 357 E. Prospect and 234 W. Fairmount sts.

Alfred Kocher was an important American architect, first designing in Colonial Revival and other historical styles, and then embracing modernism. He was a faculty member of Penn State's Department of Architecture from 1918 to 1926, and served as editor of *Architectural Record* from 1928 to 1938. In State College, he designed three residences, including his own, and one school, the last in collaboration with another local architect. His house at 357 E. Prospect Street is a loose amalgam of revivalist elements constructed of local stone and characterized by a steeply pitched gable, with a pent roof over the entrance. He incorporated fixtures taken from three historic, demolished Pennsylvania buildings. At the E. C. Woodruff house on W. Fairmount Avenue, rough-cut limestone provides a pleasing texture, and the gabled dormers with round-arched windows echo local historic buildings. The entrance has a pediment supported by Doric columns and a wooden semicircular fan above the door. The large, semicircular-arched window in a one-story extension to the west is a reminder that Kocher believed above all in invoking what he called "the principle of irregularity for the Colonial facade."

CE20 Fraternity District for Pennsylvania State University (PSU)

1920–present. E. Fairmount and E. Prospect aves. between Locust Ln. and Hetzel St.

Reflecting the influence and prestige of men's social fraternities at PSU from the turn of the twentieth century to the present, the buildings have grown from the first wave of fraternity buildings in 1894 that consisted of conventional and relatively small-scale residential designs as the Phi Gamma Delta House (c. 1904, Walter Mellor; 319 N. Burrowes Street). By the 1920s and 1930s, new fraternity construction shifted to massively proportioned houses in a variety of revival

styles. For example, at Alpha Tau Omega House (c. 1930; 321 E. Fairmount Avenue), the two-story rounded portico, supported by massive columns and surrounding an elaborate doorway with a heavy broken swan's neck pediment, signals the fraternity's pretensions. Similarly, Theta Delta Chi (1923, H. O. Smith Construction Company; 305 E. Prospect Avenue), originally Sigma Phi Sigma, recalls Mount Vernon with its two-story-tall portico, supported by slender columns, and a row of dormers in the roof. At Tau Kappa Epsilon (1930, Percy Ash for Hersh and Shollar; 346 E. Prospect Avenue), the Gothic Revival and Tudor Revival motifs are carried out with casement windows, a sculpted stone door surround, steeply pitched roof, and shed-roof dormers. The four-story-high front gable reveals that this is no ordinary residential building, but it is essentially a dormitory. Similarly, Kappa Delta Rho (1933, Clarence Bauchspies; 420 E. Prospect Avenue) presents a massive, random ashlar stone first story with imitative half timbering on the second story, and a two-story stained glass bay window above the entrance. Many fraternity buildings feature an arcaded, roofed extension, which functions as outdoor social space. Original plans featured large "club rooms," often with fireplaces, along with institutional-sized kitchens, servants' quarters, and second-story bedrooms. There are no sorority houses on or near campus; since the end of World War II, the sororities have chosen to lease suites in existing dormitory buildings.

CE21 Centre Furnace

c. 1800, 1846, c. 1870. 1001 E. College Ave.

A small two-room log structure on this site listed in the 1798 Direct Tax records may have formed the core of a substantial, banked, five-bay brick house built a few years later by General John Patton, one of the county's first ironmasters. The mansion's symmetrical facade and the central-hall plan represented its owners' consciousness of the prevalent Georgian style. The banked, rough-cut stone basement level accommodated the kitchen used for feeding the furnace workforce. After a period of decline, local entrepreneur Moses Thompson took up residence in the mansion, and added a two-story ell with a kitchen and bedroom above. The two cross gables and a bracketed porch were added c. 1870. Now restored to its late-nineteenth-century appearance, the house accommodates the county historical society. At the intersection of College Avenue and Porter Road, the remains of the Centre Furnace (1847) include a tapering stone stack. The furnace was used in the manufacture of pig iron until the Panic of 1857 forced a halt in production. In 1855, Moses Thompson and James Irvin donated two hundred acres to open the Farmer's High School of Pennsylvania that later became Pennsylvania State University (CE16).

CE22 Ayres and Cologne Houses

1955, Peter Berndtson and Cornelia Brierly. 314 and 315 Hill Dr.

Two Pennsylvania State University (PSU) professors, Dr. Rose Cologne and Dr. Ruth Ayres, asked the Pittsburgh architects to design houses across the street from each other in a newly opened tract at the top of a hill. The houses follow organic design principles and overlook the hillside with terraces and large windows. They are made of simple materials, such as local stone, Cemesto panels, concrete block, and wood beams. The Cologne house originally had Shoji screens made by a Ko-

CE22 AYRES AND COLOGNE HOUSES, Ayres house

rean friend of the owner who had studied in Japan. The Ayres house is on two levels that step down the hillside. Berndtson and Brierly designed a third house east of State College (1956; 225 Twigs Lane) for the Braun family.

A different sort of modernist, Gregory Ain, a California architect who headed PSU's Department of Architecture between 1963 and 1967, designed a rectilinear house with vertical siding for Dr. William Ginoza (1966–1967; 962 E. McCormick Avenue). Nestled into a wooded lot, it was the last of Ain's houses to be realized, and illustrates the tension in his work between a conventional house and a work of art.

HUNTINGDON COUNTY

The Juniata River, a major east–west route through Huntingdon County, works its way through beautiful ridge and valley countryside surrounding Tussey Mountain, just south of the geographic center of the state. The earliest inhabitants of this region were the Juniata Tribe of the Standing Stone, which took their name from the stone obelisk displayed in the middle of their village. The Shawnee and Tuscaroras tribes, allied with the Iroquois, dispersed the Juniata but kept the name "Standing Stone" for the location, which ultimately became the borough of Huntingdon. To provide protection for the Scots-Irish and German settlers from the French and their Native American allies, the provincial government in Philadelphia planned a series of forts along the former frontier, now central Pennsylvania. One of these forts, Fort Shirley (c. 1755), which occupied a site near present-day Shirleysburg and what was then the Native American village of Aughwick, acted as a staging area for incursions against the hostile parties. The county was established in 1787, and Huntingdon was named the county seat.

Since the Juniata River provided the earliest access to the area, towns

The commemorative Standing Stone, south of the intersection of William Smith and Penn streets in Huntingdon. The original obelisk measured fourteen feet tall and six inches square and held the records of the Juniata tribe. It was removed by the tribes living in the area after the land was sold to the Penn family. The stone is inscribed: "Onajutta-Juniata-Achsinnic. Standing Stone erected September 8, 1896 as a Memorial of the Ancient Standing Stone removed by the Indians in 1754."

located on this waterway are the oldest in the county, among them Huntingdon and Petersburg. The earliest overland route was the east–west Huntingdon, Cambria, and Indiana Turnpike, completed in 1821. Ten years later, the Pennsylvania Main Line Canal opened to Huntingdon; it required many aqueducts and lift locks to cope with the difficult terrain.

Iron production started here as early as the 1790s. Rich deposits of brown hematite and fossil ores, trees from which to make charcoal, and rushing streams to move waterwheels to power blast furnaces and forges made iron production the economic mainstay of the county. Iron plantations were relatively large, generally self-sufficient operations that included a farm on their acreage to raise food and provide shelter for the workers and the mules. Fifty furnaces were once in operation in Huntingdon, and several iron furnace plantations survive with remarkable integrity. Villages often grew up around successful furnaces, especially those that kept pace with the technology to weather the continual boom and bust periods associated with the iron industry. By changing their fuel source from charcoal to coke when the trees were clear-cut and forming business ties with Pittsburgh and Lewistown, Mifflin County, several of the larger furnaces, like Spruce Creek and Greenwood (HU11), remained in operation into the early twentieth century. The iron industry received a temporary boost with the completion of the railroads. The Pennsylvania Railroad (PRR) reached Huntingdon in 1850, and opened to

Pittsburgh in 1852. Two smaller railroads built for coal transport connected small patch towns to the larger railroad. The narrow-gauge East Broad Top Railroad (EBT), for example, covered thirty-five miles between Mount Union on the PRR and Robertsdale. The latter, a typical coal town, retains several of its original concrete-block commercial buildings and a Methodist church (1890 and 1926).

As early as the 1870s, there were ore shortages, and within twenty years, the forests were clear-cut from the insatiable need for charcoal. The iron industry declined countywide by the early twentieth century, and the smelly, smoky, and noisy plantations were silenced, allowing the region's pastoral qualities to prevail and forests to regrow. This opened up a new industry: recreational tourism.

Huntingdon's appeal to recreational tourists grew throughout the twentieth century with activities such as fishing, spelunking, hiking, and biking, and attending the county's agricultural fair that has been held since 1831 in the borough of Huntingdon. In the 1930s, the Civilian Conservation Corps built bridges and stone culverts in the county's state forests. Raystown Lake, the third largest lake in the commonwealth, was created between 1968 and 1972 by damming the Raystown Branch of the Juniata River. In the county's eastern half, PA 655 traverses Kishacoquillas Valley, a stunning drive with beautiful, prosperous farms, many Amish owned, lining the roadway.

The county's largest employer is the Commonwealth of Pennsylvania, which operates two large correctional facilities near Huntingdon. The older of the two was built between 1882 and 1886 as a reformatory for young first offenders. Several of its older buildings are visible from U.S. 22. Neither facility is accessible to the public.

HUNTINGDON AND VICINITY

Located at the confluence of the Juniata River and Standing Stone Creek, Huntingdon was laid out in 1767 by the Reverend William Smith, a provost of the University of Pennsylvania who owned land in the area. He named it for the university's most generous benefactress, Selina Hastings, Countess of Huntingdon, England. Because it was a proprietary town, deed holders had to build a substantial house within a prescribed time of purchase or the lot would revert to Smith, who, in the meantime, could collect annual rental fees.

Huntingdon's close ties to the power structure of Philadelphia are reflected in the fact that the town has sent two native sons to the governorship, David R. Porter, a Jacksonian Democrat, in 1839 and Martin G. Brumbaugh, a Republican, in 1915.

Most of Huntingdon's buildings are of stone or brick. The borough's oldest stone house is at 105 William Smith Street, built in 1797 for Reverend Smith. It is two stories and four bays wide, with the gable ends perpendicular to the street. While several brick houses predating 1830 survive, most buildings date after 1850 and typify the enormous impact that railroad access had on a small town. Some were built according to the mail-order plans of George Franklin Barber (1854–1915) of Knoxville, who between 1887 and 1913 sold over twenty thousand sets of plans through popular magazines, and published a monthly journal called *American Homes*. The Queen Anne house at 317 Penn Street is a typical Barber design.

The diamond between 421 and 510 Penn Street is, as is common in Pennsylvania towns, a wide place in the street, and in 1792, it was labeled "Market Square." Banks and other commercial buildings were built around the diamond from 1868 to 1926. Juniata College (HU9) on a hilltop west of the borough and the large state prison to the southwest in Smithfield have assured a steady stream of visitors, students, parents and relatives, all needing accommodations and sustenance. Most of today's new buildings are located on the Juniata College campus or near Raystown Lake in the form of cottages and tourist-related conveniences, including an information center. In 1983, the National Trust for Historic Preservation began a Main Street program in Huntingdon, which has helped preserve the best of the old and encourage appropriate new development.

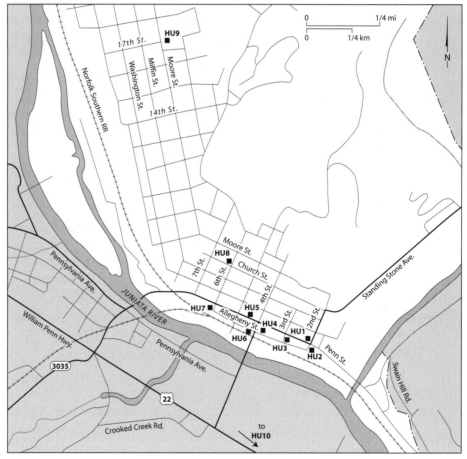

HUNTINGDON

HU1 Huntingdon County Courthouse

1883, Milton Earl Beebe. 223 Penn St.

A mansard roof and bull's eye windows reveal Milton Beebe's intention of providing Huntingdon with a "French Renaissance" courthouse. While it dominates the street and is one of the tallest buildings in town, today it is nearly obscured by tree cover. The staged central tower was rebuilt in wood in the 1930s, and sits awkwardly above a handsome double entrance with a segmental-arched pediment. A stone belt course and springcourses that link the round-arched windows bring horizontality to the red brick exterior. The interior has been unsympathetically altered, with only touches of its original grand space discernible.

This was the fourth of Beebe's four western Pennsylvania courthouses completed between 1877 and 1883. The two surviving courthouses are in Cambria (CA1) and Warren (WA1) counties; Beebe's courthouse for McKean County was demolished. In 1892, Beebe designed the Romanesque Revival Schuykill County Courthouse in Pottsville in eastern Pennsylvania.

HU2 St. John's Episcopal Church

1845, Charles B. Callahan. 212 Penn St.

This stuccoed brick church is dominated by a square central tower flanked by flat-roofed wings with elongated lancet windows. It is a hybrid style with Egyptian Revival massing and cornice and Gothic Revival windows, entrance, and blind arcade. Its mid-1840s building date places it after two famous John Haviland buildings in Philadelphia, the Eastern State Penitentiary (1821–1836), with lancet windows and square castelled towers, and his Pennsylvania Fire Insurance Company (1838) in the Egyptian Revival mode. Add to this, Thomas U. Walter's Egyptian Revival debtor's wing of the Philadelphia County Prison (1835), and it is likely that Charles Callahan was looking to Philadelphia for his inspiration. The church has massing similar to the county jails of Ebensburg (CA3), Clarion (CL2), and Hollidaysburg (BL3), two of which (Ebensburg and Hollidaysburg) were designed by Edward Haviland, John's son.

HU3 Speer House (Dorsey House)

1850, 1872. 232 Penn St.

This stylish three-story, dark orange brick Greek Revival house, built by ironmaster Greenberry Dorsey, was originally in the heart of town, but soon after its construction, the commercial focus moved a block west beyond 4th Street. It has columned porches on both the north and west elevations. From the 1870s and for over seventy years, the Speer family, which included a U.S. congressman, lived here, but since 1947, the house has been used for office space. The Orbison house (1815) diagonally across the street, similar in size and massing, set the precedent for this large city house.

An eighteen-foot-high slender stone obelisk of 1896 commemorating the *Ona Jutta Hage*, the Juniata Tribe's standing stone, stands in the 3rd Street parkway, part of a three-block-long widened street from the railroad tracks to the jail that acts as a town square adjacent to the Speer House.

HU4 Huntingdon Library and Huntingdon County Historical Society (McMurtrie Houses)

1822; 1969 library; 1854 historical society; c. 1855 gallery; 1872 rear addition. 330 Penn, and 106 and 100 4th sts.

These three red brick buildings were in the McMurtrie family from 1822 to 1952. The library at 330 Penn Street is a Colonial Revival update of an 1822 house, with the addition of a bracketed cornice and a Palladian window in the gable. The one-story addition of 1969 provided additional space for the public library. Behind the library, William McMurtrie's residence of 1854 at 106 4th Street is Flemish bond brickwork on the exterior, with a substantial Tuscan-columned portico sheltering the main entrance. It is now occupied by the Huntingdon County Historical Society. At 100 4th Street, a one-and-one-half-story storefront building now houses an art gallery. A miniature house built in 1887 for Huntingdon's centennial parade is on display in the yard between the two. The grouping illustrates the variety of the town's house types and that historic preservation can provide useful commercial and institutional spaces.

HU5 MUTUAL BENEFIT INSURANCE GROUP (DORRIS, SCOTT, AND SNARE HOUSES), Oneida office building

HU5 Mutual Benefit Insurance Group (Dorris, Scott, and Snare Houses)

1825–2006. 4th and Penn sts.

This row of two- and three-story red brick buildings houses the insurance group founded by W. Emmert Swigart in the late 1920s, now called Mutual Benefit Insurance Group. The oldest building (1825), at 401 Penn Street, was the home of William Dorris and now has a large c. 1914 window on the facade. Next door, the central Oneida office building (1992) at 403–407 Penn Street was designed by Jeff Martinson of Easton for his architectural firm, the Martinson Group. The design continues the rhythm established in the earlier buildings by the repetition of round and segmental arches. The third building, at 409 Penn Street, now called the Insurance Building, was John Scott's town house of 1850. It was purchased in 1935 by Swigart who had architect William D. Hill trim it with eighteenth-century Philadelphia woodwork. The house built for David Snare in 1852 is at 415 Penn Street. Called the Fisher Building after a later owner, it is a two-story red brick, gable-roofed structure with a facade to match its neighbor at 409 Penn Street. Across the street (412–414 Penn Street), the Finance Building is a three-story red brick commercial building with two storefronts and a central entrance. It was built in 1900 to house a bank, but has been owned by the Swigart family since 1900. At the corner of Washington and 4th streets, the Martinson Group designed a four-story, tan and orange brick addition in 2005–2006 that features arcaded windows, terra-cotta embossed spandrels, and oversized scrolled brackets at the cornice, all of which distinguish it as well

as link it to the older buildings around the corner.

HU6 Huntingdon County Chamber of Commerce (Union Depot and Hunt Signal Tower)

1872 depot. 4th and Allegheny sts. 1899 signal tower. 500 Allegheny St.

Each of these buildings reflects a different moment in the development of the railroads. The Union Depot, or passenger station, served both the Pennsylvania (arrived in 1850) and the Huntingdon and Broad Top Mountain railroads, and is a relatively simple two-story, hipped-roof building, only two bays wide, but thirteen bays long. The Hunt Signal Tower is the second generation in switching and signaling for the railroads. It is raised well above track height to make the mechanical switches visible at longer distances and less liable to be obscured by weather conditions; previously, men changed switches at trackside and signaled between trains with lanterns. This tower was adapted to use a third signaling method in the 1930s, with the advent of pneumatic lifters and electric lamps. Today it houses the offices of the Huntingdon County Chamber of Commerce, while the depot awaits a new use.

HU7 Blair House Apartments (J. C. Blair Stationery Company)

1889, Frederick L. Olds. 600 Penn St.

Pennsylvania State University's first resident architect, Frederick Olds, designed this build-

HU7 BLAIR HOUSE APARTMENTS (J. C. BLAIR STATIONERY COMPANY), photo 1989

ing that has a remarkable resemblance to Shepley, Rutan and Coolidge's Lionberger Wholesale Warehouse of 1887–1889 in St. Louis, illustrated in the *American Architect and Building News* of May 21, 1887. That building, in turn, was modeled after H. H. Richardson's Marshall Field Wholesale Store of 1885–1887 in Chicago. Olds was more a devotee than a copyist. He used the Richardsonian rhythm of windows and pilasters, but employed rolling wave patterns in the spandrels between the slightly recessed windows. The building's stone base is more a foundation than a first story, as in the St. Louis and Chicago buildings. The handsome cornice is pierced by narrow windows almost hidden in the depths of its corbeling. The Blair Building has been successfully adapted to its present use as subsidized housing for the elderly.

HU8 Abbey Reformed Church–United Church of Christ (Abbey Reformed Church)

1927–1929, Ralph Adams Cram for Cram and Ferguson. 601 Church St.

This church reveals itself in subtle ways, with the uncoursed golden sandstone trimmed with limestone, the harmonious proportions of the facade with prominent buttresses anchoring its corners, the rose window in the gable, and the slender copper fleche gracing

HU9 JUNIATA COLLEGE AND ELIZABETH EVANS BAKER PEACE PARK, Founders Hall

the gable roof's ridge. As the congregation's funds were limited, the stained glass windows designed by Boston's William Burnham Studio were fabricated and installed in phases as late as 1956. They depict the story of both the denomination and Huntingdon's congregation. A three-story Sunday school building to the north was erected contemporaneously.

HU9 Juniata College and Elizabeth Evans Baker Peace Park

1878–present. 1700 Moore St.

Juniata College is a small liberal arts, Church of the Brethren–affiliated school founded in 1876 on a 110-acre tree-shaded campus that rises gradually to wooded hillsides on its northern edge. At its heart and bordering the main quadrangle is Founders Hall (1878, Stephen Decatur Button), a red brick, four-story building with a mansard-roofed tower. Counterclockwise around the quad from Founders Hall are the L. A. Beeghly Library (1963, Hunter, Campbell and Rea); the Halbritter Center for the Performing Arts (2005, Street Dixon Rick, Architecture); the Cloister (1928); Kennedy Sports + Recreation Center (1951, 1982, Hayes, Large, Suckling and Fruth); Maude Lesher Hall, originally East Hall (1957, Hunter, Campbell and Rea); and the William J. von Liebig Center for Science (2001, Hastings and Chivetta Architects). The Cloister, a red brick, gambrel-roofed, three-story building was designed by George Edwin Brumbaugh (1890–1983), son of Martin G. Brumbaugh, Juniata College president and governor of Pennsylvania from 1915 to 1919. Architect Brumbaugh, who trained at the University of Pennsylvania, worked with Mellor and Meigs and Charles Barton Keen in Philadelphia, and specialized in preservation work.

For over forty years, the college has commissioned the Altoona-based architectural firm Hunter and Caldwell through its various name changes (since 1991 Hayes Large) to design a series of what college historian Earl Kaylor called "contemporary Colonial style" buildings, meaning most are red brick with hipped or gable roofs. Their dormitories ring the North Lawn adjacent to the quadrangle. Only the rounded facade of the Brumbaugh Science Center (1965, Hunter, Campbell and

Rea), with its metal screening, deviates from this motif.

As it grew, the campus overtook two buildings designed by Beaux-Arts-trained Edward Lippincott Tilton (1861–1933), who worked with McKim, Mead and White in New York City, and specialized in theaters and libraries. Tilton designed what was Huntingdon's Carnegie Library (1906; 17th and Moore streets), with a two-story central pavilion and a pedimented, recessed entrance flanked by banded columns. Since 1961, it has been Juniata's Carnegie Hall. Tilton also designed the stone Gothic Revival Church of the Brethren (1910; 1701 Moore Street) for the denomination that founded the college.

The college has taken advantage of its pastoral location by sponsoring the 365-acre Raystown Environmental Studies Field Station headquartered in Shuster Hall (2004, HP Architects) and a restored log farmhouse (1825). With two adjacent residence halls, the complex is a lesson for students of sustainable architecture. The Field Station is fifteen miles southwest of campus on James Creek Road at the western shore of Raystown Lake. The

unique Baker Peace Chapel (1989), a quiet, fourteen-acre green hillside space for contemplation and prayer less than a mile east of campus, was designed by landscape architect and sculptor Maya Lin, who designed the Vietnam Veterans Memorial in Washington, D.C.

HU10 Corbin Bridge

1937. Corbin Rd. over the Raystown Branch of the Juniata River, 2.5 miles south of Huntingdon

Constructed by Reading Steel Products, this one-lane suspension bridge, rare in the region, uses prestretched wire rope cables manufactured by New Jersey's John A. Roebling's Sons Company. The cables are supported by thirty-nine-foot steel towers with a stiffening truss. The bridge spans the Raystown Branch, which connects the Raystown Dam and the Juniata River. It replaces an earlier bridge, washed away in the 1936 flood. Prestretched wire technology was developed in the 1930s by Roebling's Sons Company to eliminate slack created by the wire rope twisting process and to facilitate precise measurement of the cables.

GREENWOOD FURNACE

HU11 Greenwood Furnace State Park

1834–1948. PA 305 (Greenwood Rd.), 5 miles east of McAlevy's Fort

Greenwood Furnace and the surrounding 423 acres encapsulate the history of much of the central part of the state. What today appears as a pastoral park in the forest was an industrial iron plantation from 1834 until 1904, when it ceased operation after the remaining trees were cut. Built c. 2005, a board-and-batten, one-story Visitors' Center (15795 Greenwood Road) has a jerkinhead roof. A display inside tells the story of the charcoal iron furnace that burned nearly an acre of trees daily from the surrounding 65,000 acres of land. Six original buildings and a cemetery remain from the village of Greenwood, which once housed more than 300 employees of the Greenwood Furnace, a subsidiary of the Freedom Iron Works in Burnham, Mifflin County. At its peak in the 1870s, the furnace produced three thousand tons of iron per year in this remote area. Ironically, although the furnace

supplied iron for the railroad's rails, the pig iron was always delivered to the rolling mill by mule carts, never by rail. When the company closed, the village became a ghost town, but on-site reunions of the former residents eventually led to its being designated a state park and an American Society for Metals Historic Site. The region's rampant deforestation was reversed after 1906, when the state established a tree nursery here, and in the 1930s, when the Civilian Conservation Corps planted more trees and built a dam, culverts, stone bridges, and wooden pavilions throughout the park.

Greenwood Furnace's older buildings now house administration and maintenance functions and are artifacts of both the iron-producing and tree nursery eras. They include the golden sandstone church with a wheel window in the gable end (1867); a stone ironmaster's house with stables, built in 1834; a bookkeeper's house (c. 1863); the blacksmith and wagon shop (c. 1870); and a meat house (c. 1833). Remnants of several other buildings from the tree nursery days remain, including a large, post-and-beam tree-sorting and bundling structure measuring 38 × 200 feet and supported on sixteen-inch square beams, which was built between 1941 and 1948.

MOUNT UNION VICINITY

HU12 Lewis Smalley Stone House and Barn

c. 1797. 12928 PA 103, 2 miles east of U.S. 522

This three-bay stone house with a gable roof is two rooms over two rooms joined by a side-hall staircase. It has four corner fireplaces and multipaned windows with little ornamentation. Maryland-born Lewis Smalley, a soldier in the Revolutionary War, bought this property in 1797. The stone Pennsylvania bank barn is of timber-frame construction, and has the signatures on its walls of Union soldiers who were stationed here to guard the PRR during the Civil War. This is a beautifully restored farm overlooking the confluence of Aughwick Creek and the Juniata River.

SHIRLEYSBURG

Native American tribes called this location Aughwick. Fort Shirley was built here c. 1755 on the bluff at the northern end of the borough during the French and Indian War, but it was abandoned the following year. The borough, incorporated in 1837, is south of the Juniata River in a valley between Blacklog and Jack's mountains, and was settled in the late eighteenth century by German farmers. The commercial potential of the area expanded through coal shipping, especially after the East Broad Top Railroad (EBTRR) opened in 1872. The village has one of the handsomest collections of pre–Civil War buildings in western Pennsylvania, including several red brick houses with attic stories, as well as simpler frame houses. Two churches and a school contribute to the nineteenth-century atmosphere of the town: the frame Greek

This red brick, former schoolhouse (1880) is now used as a community center in Shirleysburg.

Revival former Shirleysburg Presbyterian Church of 1830 (Croghan's Pike); the red brick Shirleysburg United Methodist Church built in 1877 with a fine cupola (16000 block Croghan's Pike); and the two-story, three-bay red brick school building, also with a cupola, built in 1880 on West Street. A former Clover Farms Store of c. 1870 (17032 Croghan's Pike) has the distinctive look of that company's stores throughout the state: a board-and-batten cottage, with carved brackets and wide gable ends facing the street.

ORBISONIA AND ROCKHILL FURNACE

HU13 Orbisonia–East Broad Top Railroad Sites

1872, with additions. PA 994, Meadow St.

The PRR was a dominant force in the history of Pennsylvania from the 1860s until just after World War II. Its strength grew from the feeder lines that brought raw materials, goods, and people to its main line from the farthest reaches of the state. In this case, prosperity emanated from a twenty-five-mile-wide, eighty square-mile plateau called Broad Top Mountain. The coal here is a hybrid type with qualities of both the bituminous and the anthracite strains, which meant that it could command a high price, and, once the railroad was available to haul it, it was mined. In 1856, the Huntingdon and Broad Top Mountain Railroad (HBTMRR) served the west side of Broad Top Mountain, and in 1872, the eastern side was opened with the EBTRR, a narrow-gauge railroad. The coal mined on the Broad Top became the fuel of choice for the PRR. The EBTRR hauled tannery products, lumber, agricultural products, lime, sand, and passengers, as well as coal and iron ore processed at the Rockhill Furnace Coal and Coke Company. When the local iron industry faltered in

the late nineteenth century, the manufacture of refractory brick at Mount Union took up the slack in the railroad's hauling, until 1956, when all the industries using the railroad had declined and the EBTRR closed. The entire system was sold to the Kovalchick Salvage Company of Indiana County that year.

In the small, adjacent villages of Orbisonia and Rockhill Furnace are a number of prosperous single-family houses, such as those at 565 and 585 Ridgely Street. The town also hosts the headquarters and service depots of the EBTRR, which stand as an almost intact collection of railroad buildings dating from the mid-1880s to the 1920s. The highlights are the roundhouse (1882–1904), with eight stalls storing four working steam locomotives. In 1960, a five-mile portion of the rail system was reopened to commemorate Orbisonia's bicentennial. The tourist train continues to run, leaving from the frame Orbisonia Depot (1907) adjacent to the shops. What remains today of the former thirty-three-mile system is a linear history of bridges, mine buildings, patch towns, railroad stations, and an entire service complex linked together to tell the story of Huntingdon County's industrial past.

HU13 ORBISONIA–EAST BROAD TOP RAILROAD SITES, headquarters and service depots, with turntable in the foreground

HU14 Farm

c. 1840. PA 994, 2.6 miles southeast of Newburg

Located on a quiet stretch of road between two small villages, this farm, though no longer occupied, has excellent integrity. A number of frame buildings remain, including a Pennsylvania bank barn (1897) and several sheds, a small house for extended family or for hired hands, and the grape arbors. The four-bay, two-story, gable-roofed stone house has a raised basement on the front, and is built into the hillside at the rear. It is representative of western Pennsylvania farmhouses dating between 1800 and the 1860s.

ALEXANDRIA AND VICINITY

Hartslog, the name attached to the land surrounding Alexandria, evolved from the large white oak where a mid-eighteenth century trader named John Hart slept and salted his horse. A trapper's sleeping place was sometimes called his "log." The town itself was laid out in 1793 by Elizabeth Gemmill (1735–1823) after her husband, John, died. By 1796, log houses dotted the landscape, and Gemmill and her descendants constructed several buildings and collected ground rents on the lots in Alexandria from 1793 to 1920, when the practice was banned. Strategically located at a natural water gap made by the Frankstown Branch of the Juniata River through Tussey Mountain, Alexandria grew as a transportation center. By 1808, the Harrisburg, Lewistown, Huntingdon, and Pittsburgh Turnpike cut through town, and the village was incorporated as a borough in 1827, just as the Pennsylvania Canal's route was decided. Alexandria had a long relationship with the canal, since it remained open in this area from 1833 until 1875, well after other segments had closed.

The borough retains an interesting assemblage of buildings dating from nearly every decade of the nineteenth century. The Cresswell House (c. 1816; 112 Main Street), a stone three-bay, two-story house, and a log house covered with wood siding (1829; 710 Main Street) are examples of the earliest vernacular building. The four-and-one-half-story, frame Gemmill Grist Mill (c. 1833) at the west end of Main Street and the handsome Greek Revival house built by local carpenter Benjamin Cross (c. 1851) at 703 Main Street illustrate the architectural legacy of the town. Most of the houses face the grid pattern of the streets, but several buildings remain at odd angles, outlining the former canal route and, after 1900, that of the PRR's spur line. The lockmaster's frame house (c. 1832; Hartslog Street at Shelton Avenue) originally faced the canal and its two local locks. Nearby, the small, pyramidal-roofed frame former PRR station was built in 1897. The Alexandria Public Library designed by Frederick James Shollar in 1899–1901 (311 Main Street) was donated by descendants of the town's founder, Elizabeth Gemmill, who maintained summer estates nearby.

A federal refractories plant built west of town at the base of Tussey Mountain in 1904 took advantage of the nearby clay deposits and new rail access. The bypass for U.S. 22, built in 1941, spared the small town's architectural integrity and increased its accessibility from Huntingdon, seven miles east. Today, Alexandria serves as a bedroom suburb of the county seat.

HU15 Isenberg Farm and Woolverton House ("Dorfgrenze," Hartslog Farm)

1899. 7612 Woolverton Way and 757 Alexandria Pike (PA 4005 at PA 305)

This once elaborate summer estate, called "Dorfgrenze" (German for "edge of the village"), was built by William Woolverton, great-grandson of Alexandria's founder, Elizabeth Gemmill. Born in Alexandria, Woolverton began his career as a telegraph agent and operator in 1859 for the PRR, the same job Andrew Carnegie held in his youth. He made a fortune with the PRR and, after 1872, as president of the New York Transfer Company and Bell Telephone. Woolverton and his cousin donated Alexandria's library in 1899 to honor their mothers. The property's name was changed to Hartslog Farm during World War I, when anti-German sentiments ran high. It is now known as the Isenberg farm.

The elaborate barn was built by master builder William S. Varner (1840–c. 1940), of German descent, who trained locally as a carpenter. Rightfully proud of this barn, he signed it with a plaque. Daylight enters the upper level of the large, timber-frame structure through its three windowed cupolas, echoed by those on the adjacent, cement-block milk house. The lower level is illuminated by glass windows at the base of large louvers that ventilate the upper haymow. These windows, designed with hoods on the interior, direct sunlight downward into the basement. Despite

its ample size, this structure is now reserved exclusively for heifers. The central operations of the dairy farm take place in two new and much larger, football-field-sized milking parlors at the east end of the farm, where more than four hundred cows are milked three times a day.

The splendid Queen Anne house (Woolverton House) with a deep wraparound one-story porch originally belonged to this farm. It has half timbering above its stone first story, and is dominated by a castellated polygonal corner tower topped by a spire. Similar stonework with a frame upper story characterizes the outbuildings, consisting of a garage and two guest houses.

HU16 Henry Swoope Farm and Houses

c. 1858. 7961 PA 305, 1 mile northeast of Alexandria

The two Swoope farmhouses facing each other across PA 305 incorporate much of Design No. 11, "A Plain and Ornamented Villa," from Samuel Sloan's *The Model Architect* (1852). Both are square, two-story, three-bay houses with hipped roofs crowned by large, square, three-bay cupolas. One house is brick and one is frame. Each is set well back from the road, but the Henry Swoope house (brick) is distinguished by a tree-lined lane and an enormous barn with vented cupolas, while the frame house is board and batten and has a modern barn for cows, of the type that farmers call a "loafing shed."

The nearby town of Petersburg at the confluence of Juniata River and Shaver Creek boomed in the 1850s, when the PRR chose to diverge from the old canal route and follow a different branch of the Juniata River. The town soon grew to double the size of its neighbor Alexandria, which had benefited mightily from the canal and expected to host the railroad. Instead, Petersburg became the site of the county's only stockyard (demolished), allowing it to ship agricultural products by rail.

HU15 ISENBERG FARM AND WOOLVERTON HOUSE ("DORFGRENZE," HARTSLOG FARM), barn

SPRUCE CREEK AND SPRUCE CREEK VALLEY

Spruce Creek is a pristine limestone stream flowing into the Little Juniata River in the northern section of Huntingdon County. The twenty-three-mile-long valley created by the creek is dotted with the remnants of iron plantations that today are primarily farms. The village of Spruce Creek, at the confluence with the river, grew after John and Mary Ann Isett, whose parents settled one valley to the west (BL26), bought six hundred acres nearby and dammed the creek to power lumber and grist mills. Their house, built in 1831, is now the Spruce Creek Bed-and-Breakfast, serving the primary recent industry: accommodations and provisions for trout anglers. PA 45, the main road through the valley, is lined with Pennsylvania State University's research farms and orchards.

SEVEN STARS VICINITY

HU17 Huntingdon Furnace

1805–1851. 4044, 4047, and 3772 Furnace Farm Ln. at Old Mill Rd. (PA 4013 at PA 4015), 2.4 miles west of Seven Stars

This iron plantation was developed by George Anshutz, an Alsatian immigrant who opened an iron furnace in Pittsburgh, which failed because he was too far from the source of ore. He moved to Juniata Valley, and in 1796, built a furnace at Warrior's Mark Run, three miles north of the present location. The second furnace failed for lack of transportation, but he succeeded on his third attempt. Seven structures remain from the complex: a stone blast furnace stack (1805); a brick company store converted to a residence in the 1930s; a two-story, two-by-two-bay stone office; a frame, five-bay ironmaster's mansion with sawn trim (1851); a gristmill (1808) with five bays of stone and three of clapboard that retains the milling equipment; a mill house; and a worker's house. The furnace went out of blast by the 1880s, but the farm surrounding the furnace is well maintained and thriving.

HU18 Spruce Creek Rod and Gun Club

1905, 1908, Frank A. Hersh and Frederic James Shollar. 6501 Clubhouse Ln., south of PA 45, 2.6 miles northeast of Seven Stars

Spruce Creek and its excellent fly fishing have lured two United States presidents (Dwight D. Eisenhower and Jimmy Carter) and numerous Pennsylvania businessmen to the Spruce Creek valley between Bald Eagle and Tussey

mountains. At the turn of the twentieth century, the members of the Spruce Creek Rod and Gun Club bought ten acres of land to accommodate their hunting and fishing pursuits. They commissioned Hersh and Shollar, who had opened their Altoona office just two years earlier, to design the Shingle Style clubhouse. The clubhouse must have struck a chord, because the firm went on to design residences and commercial buildings for many of the club's original members. The clubhouse's northeast facade has a stone round-arched entrance that opens into a capacious porch. Above the arch is a band of windows topped by a pediment and lunette. This combination of rough stone and shingling with a refined colonial feature is typical of the Shingle Style. And it suited the members' desire for luxurious rusticity, since the building had indoor plumbing, electric lighting, and one of the first telephones in the valley. Three additional stone buildings, constructed around 1908, lie to the southeast: a generator building, ice house, and carriage house.

HU19 Pennsylvania Furnace (John Lyon House)

1834. 356 Marengo Rd. (PA 4031), 5.1 miles northeast of Seven Stars

The largest of Huntingdon County's ironmasters' houses was built by John Lyon, who began investing in charcoal iron furnaces in 1813 and whose empire eventually stretched across western Pennsylvania to a rolling mill in Pittsburgh. He became wealthy enough to build this twenty-eight-room limestone house in a style befitting a Pennsylvania gentleman. Though the Georgian facade, with a full raised basement, has the appropriate symmetry, the provincial builder's technique is revealed by the awkward size and junction of the rear ell: a slab of building seventy feet long with ranks of windows and a flat roof attached to the north elevation. A full two-story porch was added to the facade when it was used as the Fairbrook Country Club, c. 1910. Many clues to its earliest existence remain on the grounds, including a four-hole privy, the remains of the iron furnace, several farm outbuildings, and five or six workers' houses. The complex straddles the border with Centre County and many of its structures are over the county line, but since it has always been taxed in Huntingdon County, it is included here. John Lyon's daughter's frame Greek Revival house built by carpenter George Washington Reynolds is just over the border in Centre County (1858; 5190 W. Whitehall Road).

FULTON COUNTY

Fulton is a rural county of ridge and valley landforms, with a charming county seat at McConnellsburg. Formed in 1850 from part of Bedford County, it was named for Robert Fulton (1765–1815), a native of Lancaster County and an artist and engineer best remembered for popularizing the use of steamboats on inland waterways. Some Euro-American settlement began as early as 1740, with settlers seeking out the Great, or Big, Cove, a flat and fertile valley protected on three sides by mountains. It was a life threatened by Native American incursions until the commonwealth purchased the land in 1758. The mountainous ridge and valley contours and the lack of a commercial rail line kept the county from overdevelopment. Farms, gristmills, and bituminous coal mines prospered in the nineteenth century, but have left few physical remnants other than many older farmsteads and brick and stone houses from the first half of the nineteenth century. Two state parks and several quaint villages make tourism the second largest industry in the county, after farming.

The county is traversed by I-76 and U.S. 30, and by I-70 along the western border, making it a through route from Pittsburgh to Philadelphia and south to Hagerstown, Maryland. The southern townships were considered part of Maryland until the border was established along the Mason-Dixon Line in 1768.

MCCONNELLSBURG AND VICINITY

McConnellsburg, in the heart of Great Cove Valley east of Tuscarora Mountain, lies at the intersection of the Lincoln Highway (U.S. 30) and U.S. 522. It was founded by Daniel McConnell in 1786, whose family arrived in the Great Cove in the 1740s and purchased hundreds of acres. McConnell and his brother William established an inn along the packhorse trail from Philadelphia that traversed their property. McConnell laid out the town with 196 lots, introduced fifty-foot-wide streets and twelve-foot-wide alleys, set aside a commons, and designated the springs for public use. The town square was located one block north of the packhorse trail to keep it free from commercial

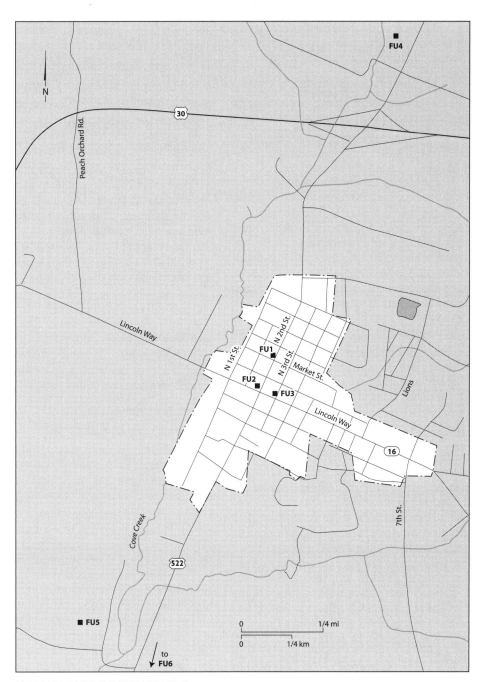

MCCONNELLSBURG AND VICINITY

pressures along the highway. McConnellsburg was incorporated as a borough in 1814. Three years later, the packhorse trail became the Chambersburg-Bedford Turnpike, and the town's growth was irrevocably tied to the development of the road. The improved road generated wagon shops, tanneries, stores, and mills. The Racket Store of 1906, a hardware store at 207 Lincoln Way E, delightfully preserves its early-twentieth-century appearance both inside and out. The store was named for New York wholesaler Rouss Racket. In 1914, the old Route 30 became part of the Lincoln Highway, a coast-to-coast paved road that stimulated automobile touring. New businesses catering to the needs of automobiles were established along its length. In the 1960s, U.S. 30 was rerouted around the perimeter of the town. As a result, the town has preserved much of its nineteenth- and early-twentieth-century appearance, and its historic architectural integrity.

FU1 Fulton County Courthouse and Courthouse Square

1850–1852, Jacob Stoner. Courthouse Sq.

Carpenter Jacob Stoner (1792–1876) must have been familiar with nearby Greek Revival courthouses when he entered the competition to design Fulton County's courthouse in 1850. His design is similar to Bedford County's courthouse of 1826–1829 designed by Solomon Filler (BD1) and the Mifflin County Courthouse (1850, Holman and Simon), both of which feature the requisite cupola and a pediment supported by six Tuscan columns. The Fulton courthouse is a rectangular building, five bays in width and six bays in length, with square-headed windows throughout. The jail, designed by Solomon Filler in 1852, now serves as the sheriff's office.

The courthouse and the historic buildings that surround the square form an engaging ensemble. Noteworthy buildings include the Jacob Reed house of 1852–1855 at 204 Courthouse Square and the small Wible law office (1892) adjacent to it at number 202. The handsome brick, Greek Revival Reed house of three bays has a recessed entrance framed by sidelights and a transom, a pedimented gable end, bridged chimneys, and a two-story porch lining the rear ell. The former Lewis H. Wible

FU1 FULTON COUNTY COURTHOUSE AND COURT-
HOUSE SQUARE, courthouse

Law Office is a small, frame, gable-roofed building that looks like it may have been the dependency of a larger structure. The rectangular building is three by three bays with cove-lap siding, corner boards, ornamented window surrounds, and shutters. The trappings of a turn-of-the-twentieth-century law practice remain inside. The oldest structure on the square is the red brick Washington House Hotel (c. 1850; 124–130 N. 2nd Street), a brick Greek Revival structure now used as apartments. Finally, the McConnellsburg United Methodist Church (1924) at 121 N. 2nd Street is a golden brick Gothic Revival church with a square corner tower.

FU2 Albert Stoner Building

1899. 110 Lincoln Way W

This building's unusually elaborate storefront, beautifully restored to its Italianate splendor, now houses a variety store. Albert Stoner built the store in 1899 as his tinsmith shop. His brother, William Stoner and William's son, Bruce, hand turned the original woodwork for the shop, which retains its original maple floor and pressed-tin ceiling. Members of the Stoner family operated the store into the 1960s. Albert Stoner's earlier shop (1875), opposite at 125 Lincoln Way W, is a two-story, orange-red brick, five-bay building with segmental arches over the windows. The five-bay, brick house east of Stoner's tinsmith shop at 108 Lincoln Way W was built in 1789 for Daniel McConnell Jr., and is the earliest brick house in Fulton County. Stoner bought it in 1893 and lived there until his death in 1920.

FU3 Police Station and Fulton County Historical Society (Fulton House)

1770 log building; 1793 stone building; c. 1820 addition. 112 Lincoln Way E

This eight-bay, limestone, gable-roofed inn dominates the town's main street. It accom-

FU2 ALBERT STONER BUILDING

modated travelers in the packhorse era of the 1790s, and continued in use as an inn until 1968. It has seen a variety of changes, including the removal of a two-story porch that is shown in many historic pictures when the building was the Union Hotel. A stream runs under the southeast corner of the building, and a log house of 1770 is attached at the northeast. The three easternmost bays were added in 1820 and now host the historical society. After the inn closed, the borough purchased the house and restored it with volunteer labor for the nation's bicentennial in 1976. A mural by Wayne Fetko graces the side of the adjacent commercial building touting the Lincoln Highway.

FU4 Robert B. Richards Farm (Puterbaugh Farm)

c. 1835, c. 1840. 21561 Great Cove Rd., off U.S. 522, 1 mile northeast of McConnellsburg

This 280-acre dairy farm is located on a hillside west of Great Cove Road. The house consists of two parts: a c. 1835 rear ell stone portion, and the five-bay brick portion c. 1840 that faces the barn. A two-story brick springhouse north of the main house has living quarters above. The spectacular array of ornamented wooden porches on three elevations of the house was restored in 1976 by local carpenters Fred and Tom Mellott. The frame barn

and wagon shed west of the house are both sheathed in vertical wood siding. The original owner of the farm was George Puterbaugh, a Maryland German Baptist from the Dunkard branch. There are five brick houses within two miles of this site built for the Puterbaugh (sometimes spelled Butterbaugh) family.

FU5 Patterson Farm (Thomas Logan Farm)

1798, c. 1820. 131 Confederate Ln., off U.S. 522, 1 mile south of McConnellsburg

The quintessential central Pennsylvania farm, this combination of a five-bay stone house and a frame bank barn has seen little alteration since the nineteenth century. The house was constructed in two stages. The three bays at the eastern end were built in 1798 of colorful, randomly set limestone with keystoned voussoirs and corner quoins. Two bays were added c. 1820 to the stone portion, resulting in the standard five-bay facade. Frame additions at the rear expanded the size of the house, and a small portico now shelters the central entrance on the facade. The barn has vertical siding above the stone foundation and a forebay facing the house. The last Confederate bivouac on northern soil was held here in 1864.

FU6 Glenn R. Cordell House (James Nelson House)

1820. 777 Crossroads Rd., off U.S. 522, 2.8 miles southeast of McConnellsburg

This is an excellent example of the ubiquitous stone five-bay, two-story, gable-roofed western Pennsylvania farmhouse. Unlike many older houses, it retains its five interior mantels with

FU4 ROBERT B. RICHARDS FARM (PUTERBAUGH FARM), house

carved surrounds and eight cupboards with shelves and pegs, as well as high-style touches like keystones and corner quoins. The limestone four-over-four house was built for the Nelsons, one of only two families who owned the house until 1999. The twenty-two-acre lot also has a timber-frame Pennsylvania barn to the east.

WARFORDSBURG VICINITY

FU7 Tonoloway Primitive Baptist Church and Cemetery

1828. 602 PA 655, 1 mile north of Maryland border

This Baptist church built for an English-speaking congregation is unusual because it is the oldest in Fulton County and because the separate men's and women's entrances are on the long wall, not in the gable end as is customary. Box pews are organized with the pulpit opposite the entrances, causing the window behind the pulpit to be raised above the others on the north elevation. Round-arched doorways, fanlight vents in the gable end, and paneled shutters are the only ornamentation on the brick exterior.

CRYSTAL SPRING VICINITY

FU8 Crystal Spring Camp Meeting

1886. PA 3010 at Barton Rd., 1.5 miles southeast of Crystal Spring

Crystal Spring Camp Meeting, laid out by G. W. Cunard, is affiliated with the Methodist Episcopal Church, which has a long history of open-air preaching. The ten-acre site has hosted camp meetings since 1857. The present camp includes a frame hotel-like structure west of approximately one hundred cottages and two pavilions. The organization of these almost identical cottages, in a horseshoe pattern around the tabernacles, lends the ensemble rhythm and cohesiveness. Permanent wooden two-story cottages, referred to as "tents," twelve feet wide, sixteen feet deep, and twelve feet high were built as needed. Each unit has a shingled roof and vertical weatherboarding, and was left unpainted to avoid ostentation. They are used only in the summer months and have no fireplaces or electricity. Every cottage owner automatically became a member, and most attended the yearly camp meeting.

The first tabernacle, built in 1888 by N. B.

FU8 CRYSTAL SPRING CAMP MEETING

Hixson, is a simple gable-roofed pavilion about forty feet square with open sides. Benches under the trees face the pulpit. The second tabernacle is much larger and has sheltered benches. Both structures, used for public worship, have gable roofs supported by braced posts, with vertical siding in the gable ends. Despite all the frame buildings on the site, cutting timber was forbidden in the bylaws, as the beauty of the surrounding forest was and continues to be part of the spiritual experience of the camp meeting.

BURNT CABINS

The village earned its name when the Indians of the Six Nations protested the loss of their hunting grounds to European settlers, and the provincial government ordered the squatters' cabins burned as a show of faith to the Native Americans. The Scots-Irish pioneers who came to Fulton County in the 1740s were poaching on Iroquois land that had not been purchased by the government. The settlers, rather than leaving, asked the government to officially buy the land, which it did in 1758. Two eighteenth-century roads, Forbes Road and Three Mountain Road, merged at Burnt Cabins and created a third road, now U.S. 522. While no buildings survive from the earliest era, a group of nineteenth-century buildings, including several inns and stores, define the linear district. The village has a stone house (1790; 34013 U.S. 522), a frame storefront post office (c. 1890; 233 Grist Mill Road), the Burnt Cabins Hotel (c. 1900; 16 Grist Mill Road), and an operating gristmill (FU9). The village is north of I-76 and south of the south branch of Little Aughwick Creek. The Burnt Cabins Presbyterian Church (1851), at 272 Grist Mill Road on a hillside above the old Forbes Road, is a three-by-three-bay, rectangular, brick structure in a simplified version of the Greek Revival expressed in the returning eaves of the facade. It has a cupola, similar to that on the courthouse in McConnellsburg (FU1), built simultaneously in the same year. The round-arched, paired windows behind square storm windows light a fairly large single-room sanctuary.

FU9 Burnt Cabins Grist Mill

1840. 582 Grist Mill Rd.

The two-and-one-half-story frame, gable-roofed gristmill is one of the best preserved in western Pennsylvania, and especially rare for its continued operation. The present mill's foundation dates from approximately 1770, but what rises above it was built in 1840 by a descendant of Frederick Dubbs, the builder of the earlier mill. The Baldwin family purchased it in 1850, and ran it for 110 years. Originally powered by water from the damming of the south branch of Little Aughwick Creek across the nearby Pennsylvania Turnpike, the water was brought to the site through a thousand-foot millrace. The last Baldwin owner installed a diesel engine as an alternative power source, making the waterpower obsolete. Other than the charcoal roaster for corn, the gristmill machinery dates from the mid-nineteenth century. The current owners have established a campsite nearby, and continue to grind grains for the specialty flours they sell.

BEDFORD COUNTY

Established in 1771, Bedford County originally encompassed all the land west of Tuscarora Mountain, and was the ninth county formed in the commonwealth. Its territory was so large that it was ultimately carved into twenty-eight counties. John Russell, fourth Duke of Bedford, lent his name to the fort built in 1751 at what was then called Raystown, now Bedford, and the name Bedford was retained for the county. Bedford's ridge and valley topography consists of five mountains curving from southwest to northeast. These mountains limited east–west travel to the Juniata River valley; north–south progress was easier along the valleys from West Virginia and Maryland. Both Native Americans and European American settlers vied to live in the valleys closest to the Raystown Branch of the Juniata River.

By the 1760s, farming and grain production began in earnest, and several early mills are proof of this important first step in industrialization. Growth relies on transportation, and most travelers from Philadelphia to the western frontier passed through Bedford on the old Forbes Road. Over the years, the state government recognized the need to tie the western counties to the east and authorized construction of the Pennsylvania Road, which consolidated several smaller turnpikes (generally following the path of today's U.S. 30). Hotels and inns along these turnpikes reflected the architectural styles prevalent on the Eastern Seaboard. Many farms remain in Bedford County, as for example, Mount Dallas Farm dating from the 1840s (1780 Lincoln Highway), with its stone five-bay house and red-painted Pennsylvania bank barn.

By the mid-nineteenth century, sawmills, gristmills, tanneries, carriage makers, iron makers, as well as farms dotted the landscape. However, Bedford never had the large-scale, heavy industry found in Cambria or Allegheny counties, primarily due to its poor rail connections. Coal production in Bedford was minimal until a branch line of the Pennsylvania Railroad, the Huntingdon and Broad Top Railroad, was completed in the northeastern corner of the county in 1856. The railroads allowed farmers to switch from grain to dairy production, as milk could be shipped in a timely fashion over greater distances by rail. Rail lines through the southwestern corner of the county connected Bedford to Cumberland, Maryland.

Bedford County's natural beauty made it attractive as a recreational area even before rail access. In 1806, Bedford Springs (BD16) opened; in the 1860s Chalybeate Springs (BD15) and in 1884 White Sulphur Springs (BD17) used their mineral springs to attract spa visitors. In the era of rudimentary drug therapies, mineral springs were patronized for their "curative" powers. For Bedford County to have three extant spa hotels is remarkable, and their preservation is vital. All three are festooned with verandas, illustrating their purpose of restorative relaxation and a southern architectural influence. In Bedford County, the eighteenth-century turnpike buildings with their eastern influences and the southern-styled spas are clear examples of these regional influences.

The Lincoln Highway, was conceived in 1915 by Henry Joy, president of the Packard Motor Car Company, and Carl Fisher, a cofounder of the Indianapolis Motor Speedway, as an automobile link between New York City and San Francisco. The 3,400 miles of roadway, completed in 1929, connected existing roads upgraded by each locality. Roadside attractions, inns, and commercial establishments dot the roadway, as well as the products of several recent publicity campaigns mounted by the Lincoln Highway Heritage Association. The latter includes murals painted on the sides of barns and buildings commemorating the road, among them, at 2708 Lincoln Highway, is a Burma Shave–type sign saying: "Times Square in the east, / Golden Gate in the west, / For cross country travel, / It was the best. / Lincolnway!" A group of fiberglass gas pumps, painted by selected artists and called the Lincoln Highway Pump Parade, includes the Vincent Van Gas in front of Lincoln Highway Auto Center at 3701 U.S. 30 in Schellsburg. Returning to its roots as a turnpike county, Bedford was an important link in the building of the Pennsylvania Turnpike in 1940. When the turnpike was joined c. 1960 to I-70, connecting Pennsylvania with Washington, D.C., a new crop of roadside motels was established. Despite these ribbons of transportation-related development, Bedford remains primarily an agricultural county with more than one thousand operating farms.

BEDFORD AND VICINITY

Situated at the northernmost point of Cumberland Valley between Wills Mountain on the west and Evitts Mountain on the east, Bedford (initially called Raystown) was established at the point where the Raystown Branch of the Juniata River cuts through Evitts Mountain. A strategic site, important in the campaigns of the 1750s against the French and their Indian allies, it was a good place for traders to settle in the 1760s. Fort Bedford (demolished in 1758; museum constructed in 1958, north end of S. Juliana Street) was not too isolated from Fort Cumberland, Maryland, to the southwest, which opened the possibility of new markets on the frontier. The first permanent settlers, all Scots-Irish, arrived in the early 1760s. In 1765, John Lukens was ordered by Pennsylvania's royal governor, John Penn, to lay out two hundred lots, lanes and alleys, and a "commodious square." He submitted the plan in 1766.

In 1793, the state legislature appropriated funds to upgrade the Great Pennsylvania Road between Philadelphia and Pittsburgh, which roughly followed the route of the old Forbes Road. Within a decade, a constant stream of Conestoga wagons and stagecoaches making the journey from east to west flowed through Bedford. In 1794, Bedford played a strategic role as the rendezvous point for 7,000 federal troops called out to subdue the Whiskey Rebellion. President George Washington came to Bedford to command the troops. He stayed for four days in the Espy house on Pitt Street (BD10). This was the only time in the nation's history that a sitting president took to the field to command his troops.

Although located at the intersection of a major north–south route through Cumberland Valley and an east–west route through the Allegheny Mountains, Bedford was never a manufacturing town. It prospered as the county seat and as a transportation hub providing food and lodging to travelers. It was not until twenty years after the Pennsylvania Railroad connected Pittsburgh and Philadelphia in 1852 that Bedford finally established a rail connection.

Bedford's buildings date as early as the late eighteenth century (BD10). Between 1814 and the 1850s, Solomon Filler (1797–1855) designed handsome Federal and Greek Revival brick buildings in Bedford, which remain remarkably intact (BD1, BD8, BD11). The commercial district has several Second Empire buildings in the 100 block of E. Pitt Street, as well as the Hotel Pennsylvania, a five-story maroon brick building c. 1910. Contractor-builder George Harrison Gibboney (1859–1929) built at least five homes in Bedford

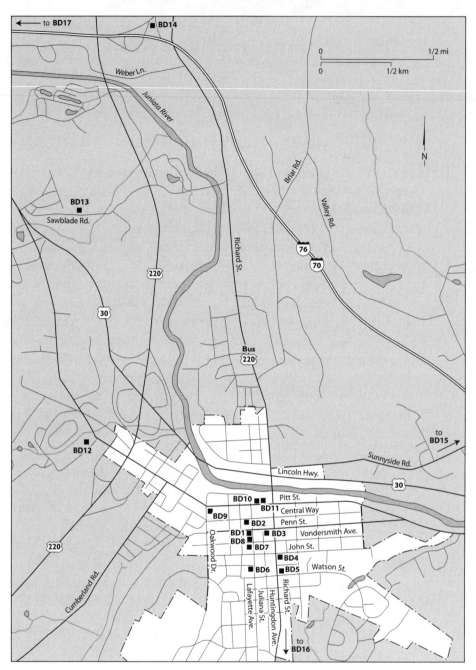

BEDFORD AND VICINITY

in the first decades of the twentieth century, and many more in the Everett area, where his Cottage Planing Mill operated. Bedford's modern commercial growth has remained just far enough north of the city that the character of its older commercial and civic functions downtown has survived. The influx of visitors to the Bedford Springs Hotel after 1806 (BD16) and, after the Civil War, to the Chalybeate Springs Hotel (BD15), made Bedford a traveler's destination. Although the means of transportation changed from carriages to railroads and, in the 1920s, to automobiles, tourism in Bedford County itself has changed very little.

BD1 Bedford County Courthouse

1826–1829, Solomon Filler; 2006–2007, David B. Albright and Richard Levengood. 141 S. Juliana St.

Little is known about Bedford County architect Solomon Filler. It is likely that renowned architect Benjamin Henry Latrobe, who worked in Philadelphia, Carlisle, and Pittsburgh from 1798 to 1814, influenced Filler, whose works reflect the calm symmetry of Latrobe's style and the early Greek Revival period. The courthouse has a central-hall plan with offices lining the hall on the first story. A pair of curving cantilevered staircases rises from the oval lobby to a single landing, lending access to the only courtroom. The room is simple and wood paneled, with amphitheater seating facing the judge's bench. The red brick building has a pedimented facade outlined by a tall architrave and corner pilasters. An unusual lunette with circular and pointed mullions highlights the pediment. The raised entrance is reached by a divided stair and is recessed behind two Doric columns framed by pilasters. Chimneys and double-sash windows line the side elevations, and the courthouse is topped with a circular wooden cupola supported on a square base.

In 2006–2007, a large, three-story gable-roofed wing was added to the rear elevation, joining the courthouse with the next door William Lyon House (BD8). Designed by Albright of Altoona and Levengood of Lancaster, the wing's lower stories are red brick and the upper story is sheathed in Dryvit, a synthetic stucco, minimizing its visual impact on the original courthouse.

This courthouse, located at the southwest corner of the town square, and Bedford United Presbyterian Church, also designed by Solomon Filler in 1829–1830 (145 S. Juliana Street), on the east side, act as bookends to the square. The church's cupola and square base are similar to those of the courthouse. Though Filler worked in the red-orange brick common to the area, his sense of proportion and straightforward woodwork have left an architectural legacy of fine Greek Revival buildings worthy of greater study.

BD2 Lawyer's Row on the Square

1870, c. 1875. 102 W. Penn St.

These two-story brick offices with central chimneys lie north of the courthouse. The three-bay brick, gable-roofed structure at the east end is the oldest section; nine bays were attached to it at the west c. 1875. Paired brackets and a full-width porch supported on columns unify the facade. The westernmost nine bays have second-story doors opening to a balcony. Shutters and a central entrance distinguish the eastern end of the structure from the remaining nine bays. The building faces the courthouse across a public lawn adjacent to a Civil War monument and the Trinity Lutheran Church (1871; 106 W. Penn Street).

BD3 U.S. Post Office

1914–1915, Oscar Wenderoth, supervising architect of the U.S. Treasury. 201 Public Sq.

This is a handsome rendition of the neoclassical post offices prevalent from 1900 to the 1930s in small towns nationwide. Built during Oscar Wenderoth's (1871–1938) tenure as supervising architect of the Treasury from 1912 to 1915, it is not known whether a local architect had a hand in the design. (Wenderoth and his successors normally used local architects as consultants on federal projects.) The limestone building has a raised central section set off by six tall Tuscan columns. Five paired elongated windows ornamented with metal anthemia light the lobby space. The post office anchors the southeast corner of Bedford's town square.

BD4 St. James Episcopal Church

1865–1866. 311 S. Richard St.

This church is named for the saint known as St. James the Greater, but architecturally it follows the example of St. James the Less Church (1846–1848) in Philadelphia, an American version of a thirteenth-century English parish church, St. Michael's in Long Stanton, Cambridgeshire. The design follows the dictates of the Ecclesiologists, a group proposing Gothic as the proper style for church design during the 1840s and 1850s. Bedford's

BD4 ST. JAMES EPISCOPAL CHURCH

St. James has a Gothic-arched bell gable in the plane of the facade, a steeply sloping multicolored slate roof, stepped buttresses on the side elevations, and interior and exterior walls of randomly laid stone, all characteristic of churches popularized during this era by architects John Notman and Richard Upjohn. Two stained glass windows were added over the years: the Lyon Memorial lancet window by Tiffany Studios that depicts the Resurrection with the symbols of a cross and lilies, and a window of the Nativity by William Willet. A two-story stone manse is next door at 309 S. Richard Street.

BD5 Victoria House (William Hartley House)

1872, with additions. 339 S. Richard St.

William Hartley, a successful farmer who invested successfully in Pennsylvania's oil fields, commissioned this excellent example of the Second Empire style in 1870, just as the railroad finally reached Bedford. The two-and-one-half-story house is made of brick plastered to a smooth finish, with window trim and corner quoins made of pine painted to resemble stone. The mansard roof has paired pedimented dormers and a short central tower with a trio of windows beneath cascading round arches. Cresting along the roof and small balconies in the central tower indicate an attention to detail. A full-facade, five-bay porch shelters the central entrance.

BD6 Common School

1859. 322 S. Juliana St.

The common school was built in 1859 to consolidate many of the one-room schools then operating in the borough. It is a large brick structure of two stories, with a central gable-roofed core linking three large hipped-roof wings, each with a pedimented wall dormer ornamented with a circular vent. The school is unusual for the amount of original fabric remaining, such as sawn trim on two facade porches, original six-over-six windows, and round-arched windows in the upper story of the central pavilion. Sited on a large lawn in the residential section of Bedford, the former school now houses the National Museum of the American Coverlet on the first story, and offices on the second.

BD7 Headquarters of Pennswoods.net (John J. Barclay House)

1858. 230 S. Juliana St.

This large red brick house built for lawyer John Jacob Barclay has Italianate ornament and detailing with the massing and scale of the later Colonial Revival. The jerkinhead roof and dormer are accented by corbeled end chimneys. Paired brackets line the cornices and act as capitals for the columns supporting the porch roof. Paired, elongated double-sash windows have squared dripstones as lintels, with variations in the central bay. The plan has a central hall with four rooms per floor. Marble mantels and a walnut railing highlight the interior. A rear wing contains the kitchen, pantry, and servants' rooms. Across the street, the Job Mann house (1842; 231 S. Juliana Street) is a handsome five-bay, red brick Greek Revival house with an inset doorway.

BD8 Courthouse Annex No. 1 (William Lyon House)

1833, Solomon Filler; 2006–2007, David B. Albright and Richard Levengood. 204–206 S. Juliana St.

Solomon Filler's skill as a talented regional architect is evident in the design of this house, now used as a courthouse annex. Wide bridged chimneys act as parapets at the gable ends, completely obscuring the shallow gabled roof and emphasizing the deep entablature on the

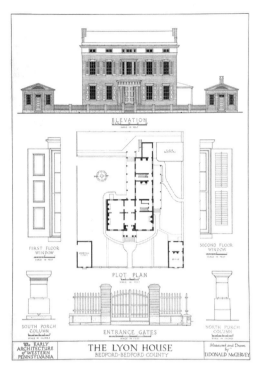

facade. Frieze band windows pierce this entablature and continue on the side elevations. The house follows the basic Palladian plan, with twin dependencies flanking the facade. Although there is no arcade leading to the dependencies, they replicate the double-sash six-over-six window pattern of the main house and have louvered fanlights in the tympana of their small pediments. Originally used as an office and a carriage house, the dependencies sit flush with the sidewalk. They reflect the southern influences on the house, as do the five-bay verandas on the north and south elevations of the ell. The interior has two rooms enfilade in the central axis, and a stair hall in the northwestern corner of the main block of the house. Large paneled entrance doors with sidelights and transom lead to the small vestibule. The recent addition joining this house with the adjacent courthouse has preserved the facade and the dependencies, although the interior has been altered for modern office use.

Solomon Filler's home (1825; 215 S. Juliana Street) is a five-bay, frame house with a recessed entrance.

BD9 Dunkle's Gulf Service Station

1933, Edward Joseph Weber. W. Pitt St. at West St.

Dunkle's was designed by Pittsburgh-based Edward Weber, who became known for his Art Deco designs (AL103). This small, cream-colored gas station, faced with terra-cotta tile, was built to service the traffic on U.S. 30. It has two colorful bands of decorative tile and vibrant signage. It is a fine example of Art Deco, and has the varied roofline, geometric patterns, and colors characteristic of the style.

BD10 Washington Bakery (Thomas Smith–David Espy House)

1770–1771. 123 E. Pitt St.

A remarkable reminder of the early Federal era, Judge Thomas Smith's house was built in 1770–1771 and purchased by David Espy, an attorney and Revolutionary activist. The three-bay stone house, with an interior end chimney, has two rooms on each of three floors with a stair hall on the west side. The building has had a storefront since George Washington used it as his headquarters in 1794, when he commanded 7,000 federal troops to quell the Whiskey Rebellion, the only sitting president to directly command his army in the field.

BD11 Chamber of Commerce (Anderson House)

1814, Solomon Filler; 1845 addition. 137 E. Pitt St.

Dr. John Anderson, a Bedford native, studied medicine in nearby Carlisle, and in his middle years became active in local affairs. He commissioned Solomon Filler to design his home

BD9 DUNKLE'S GULF SERVICE STATION

BD12 COFFEE POT

and, as the founder of the Bedford Springs Hotel, the centerpiece Greek Revival building there as well (BD16). Anderson helped to establish a turnpike between Chambersburg and Bedford that enabled guests to come to the springs. He founded the first Allegheny Bank in this home in 1814; the original granite vault remains in the east room. The house has a central-hall plan with a staircase rising three stories. A generous wrought-iron porch with balustrade above stretches across the facade. When Espy Anderson inherited the house in 1845, he built the large two-story addition on the north elevation to accommodate his nine children. The house remained in the Anderson family until 1924, when it was donated to the borough. Today it houses borough offices and the chamber of commerce.

BD12 Coffee Pot

1927, Bert Koontz, builder; 2004 restored, Michael Eversmeyer. U.S. 30 at Bedford County Fairgrounds

There are approximately five coffee/tea pot or percolator buildings remaining in the United States; this is the only one in Pennsylvania. This example of whimsical roadside architecture was donated to the Lincoln Highway Heritage Association, moved to the Bedford County Fairgrounds entrance, and restored to its original glory in 2004. It has a two-story interior space, and originally had a potbelly stove vented through the spout to emulate steam. Now it is a shop for Lincoln Highway memorabilia, open by appointment.

BD13 Old Bedford Village

c. 1758–1880. 220 Sawblade Rd., 1.5 miles north of Bedford

Old Bedford Village is a living history museum. Opened in 1976, it displays nearly forty pre-twentieth-century structures from central Pennsylvania. The nearly treeless site is adjacent to two major highways and the Raystown Branch of the Juniata River. The Claycomb covered bridge, originally built in 1880 nearly fifteen miles farther north, was moved to the site in 1975 to provide access across the river. The buildings, moved from their original sites, were reerected here along modern curved streets, rather than in the crossroads configuration prevalent prior to 1860.

Especially interesting is the small log house (c. 1758), from midway between Bedford and Cumberland, Maryland, that the museum's historians believe was built under orders from Colonel Henry Bouquet, the Swiss-born British officer who was second-in-command of Pennsylvania's troops between 1758 and 1764. This type of log house, with a single door and window on the long wall and an interior end chimney at the gable end, is rare. Another building at the site, the South Woodbury log house, appears to have been built by Henry Ober in c. 1828, using a corner-post technique seen most often among Swiss Mennonites in Lancaster. In this technique, a corner log is mortised to accept each log, rather than notching the logs to lay one above the other. The two-story, four-bay log house has a large, vertical-sided addition on the rear elevation.

The one-story octagonal school built by Hiram Way in 1851 for Fishertown retains the original slate blackboard and a number of artifacts from the school. The benches along seven walls and the central potbelly stove are accurate reproductions. The advantages of an octagon shape included better sightlines for the teacher and better light and heat distribution for the students. This structure was used as a school until 1933.

Archaeologically, the site holds remains of the Monongahela people dating from 1200 to 1300 CE; it appears that they built a stockaded village here and remained for fifty years. The village is listed on the National Register of Historic Places for its archaeological remains.

BD14 Midway Turnpike Service Plazas

1940. Pennsylvania Turnpike (I-76) west of Bedford

The Pennsylvania Turnpike was the first modern, limited-access highway in the United States. The dream of a high-speed roadway without railroad crossings or intersecting roads was revolutionary in the 1930s; only the Autobahn in Germany had achieved it. The completed turnpike, today one of sixteen in the nation, cut in half the time it took to travel from the New Jersey coast to the Ohio border. The first section of its 359 miles opened in October 1940 and was touted as the "all-weather" road joining Harrisburg and Pittsburgh, with no grade steeper than 3 percent. The route chosen followed the path of the South Pennsylvania Railroad begun fifty years earlier, but halted with several of its tunnels partially bored and a significant portion of its roadway already carved out of Pennsylvania's tree-covered mountains. The turnpike began as a four-lane highway, narrowing to two lanes at each of its seven original tunnels. In the 1960s, three of the tunnels were bypassed, and four were expanded with a parallel tunnel cut into the mountains to ease the traffic congestion. By 1968, the Pennsylvania Turnpike was four lanes of uninterrupted traffic flowing across the state. It passes through eight western Pennsylvania counties: Huntingdon, Fulton, Bedford, Somerset, Westmoreland, Allegheny, Beaver, and Lawrence. Two major bridges over the Beaver and Allegheny rivers and two major tunnels, the Allegheny and Tuscarora, carry the road 180 miles across southwestern Pennsylvania.

Under contract with the Standard Oil Company of Pennsylvania, eleven gas stations and service plazas were built along the first 160 miles of the turnpike between Carlisle and Irwin. The stone-clad buildings, reminiscent of Pennsylvania's classic three- to-five-bay houses, projected a homelike, welcoming appearance with their white-painted shutters and wood-paneled interiors. Howard Johnson's ran the original South Midway restaurant and the other coffee-shop lunch counters, which quickly expanded into full-service restaurants as the road's popularity increased. The two-and-one-half-story Georgian Revival South Midway plaza in Bedford County, which was designed as the flagship facility of the turnpike, retains elements of its original interior features, including two wood-paneled dining rooms; the other plazas have been adapted to fast food companies' requirements.

The final two sections of the turnpike joining the midsection to the borders east and west were completed when Governor James Duff and Richard K. Mellon pushed them through with favorable financing from Mellon Bank. A very low bid submitted for automotive and food services by the Mellon-financed Gulf Oil Company ensured that when both extensions were completed by 1951, Gulf and Howard Johnson's provided the service stations and food.

The buildings associated with the turnpike range from service plazas and maintenance structures to tollbooths and offices. Most of the office structures are buff brick with flat roofs, though there are several red brick maintenance buildings and several remaining stone-faced service plazas. Oddly, the design of the plazas diverged completely from the tollbooths. The original hexagonal tollbooths and their small associated buildings were modern and sleek, completely unlike the residential look associated with the plazas. In 1983, automatic ticket dispensers and redesigned tollbooths were installed, but an original hexagonal tollbooth was donated to the Smithsonian Institution in Washington, D.C.

BD15 Chalybeate Springs Hotel

c. 1851, 1867, c. 1885, with additions. 176 Chalybeate Rd., northeast of Sunnyside Rd., 1 mile east of Bedford

Chalybeate Springs was built near three mineral springs lining Dunning's Creek at its confluence with the Raystown Branch of the Juniata River. A brick gable-roofed farmhouse (c. 1851) of three by two bays was the first building on the property. In 1867, two businessmen, hoping to capitalize on the new connection to the Huntingdon and Broad Top Railroad, made a large addition to the northwest elevation of the original house to develop a spa. The two-story brick, gable-roofed addition consists of a series of rooms with doors and windows opening to verandas. Around 1885, a second large addition

BD16 BEDFORD SPRINGS HOTEL

was made to the north elevation, creating a plan whose footprint resembles a modified T and adding forty-seven guest rooms, each with access to a veranda. In 1903, an annex with a ballroom was constructed northwest of the hotel. The annex is a two-story hipped-roof building with two-story verandas on all elevations. The hotel closed in 1913, and was used as a residence until 1946. After the war, it was used as a clinic and later converted to apartments. As a miniature version of nearby Bedford Springs (BD16), Chalybeate Springs remains a small, nineteenth-century summer resort, self-contained and quiet, despite its proximity to the turnpike and the borough of Bedford. In the summer months, it offers camping facilities for trailers.

BD16 Bedford Springs Hotel

1802–1806; 1829–1842, Solomon Filler; 1903, with additions. 2138 U.S. 220 Business, 0.5 miles south of Bedford

Founded in 1802 by Bedford native Dr. John Anderson, the Bedford Springs Hotel was once as famous as the mineral spas at Saratoga Springs or Greenbriar. Today, its sprawling complex of buildings has been restored to compete with spas like Nemacolin Woodlands in Fayette County (FA30) or the Homestead in West Virginia. It is remarkable that the nineteenth-century resort continued to function until the late 1980s. When first built, guests arrived by carriage and, after 1873, by train, then by carriage from Bedford one-half mile to the north or from Cumberland thirty miles to the south, and later by car from the Pennsylvania Turnpike four miles to the north. The hotel comprises six contiguous buildings. The central anchor building, designed between 1829 and 1842 by Solomon Filler, is a Greek Revival, hipped-roof, three-story brick building housing the lobby and main dining rooms. To the north, four more hipped-roof buildings dating between 1802 and 1890 share common galleries with wooden railings in a variety of harmonizing styles. Although the buildings differ in height from three to four stories, there is a unity of design, materials, and scale. To the south is a two-story, gable-roofed building of 1903 that houses the indoor pool beneath a vaulted ceiling, and has French doors opening to a colonnade, solarium, and hydrotherapy rooms.

An eighteen-hole golf course incorporating features designed by Spencer Oldham (1895),

A. W. Tillinghast (1912), and Donald Ross (1923), the last a member of the Golf Hall of Fame and designer of Pinehurst, North Carolina's, second golf course, has been updated by restoration landscape architect Ron Forse. The clubhouse is in the frame one-and-one-half-story golf cottage (1924) southeast of the hotel. Several support buildings, including a manager's house and a two-story service building on top of the hill behind the hotel were part of the planned 1924 expansion, which was never completed.

President James Buchanan used the springs as his summer White House, and the Supreme Court met here during summer sessions between 1857 and 1861. Ten American presidents have visited Bedford Springs. In addition, the resort was used as the Naval Radio Training School during World War II, and Japanese diplomats were detained here when they were captured in Berlin near the end of the war.

Before the resort was built, the surrounding 2,800 acres were known for seven mineral springs and the stone Nawgel or Naugle gristmill (1797) that stands northeast of the hotel. The stone mill took its power from Shober's Run. A log house of the same period lies to the southwest.

SULPHUR SPRINGS

BD17 White Sulphur Springs Hotel and Bowling Alley

1884, 1886, John Reed and George Lyon; later additions. 4420 Milligan's Cove Rd.

Unlike Bedford Springs (BD16), which is a place to see and be seen, White Sulphur Springs is understated and discreet. The resort consists of half-a-dozen primarily frame buildings nestled at the base of Buffalo Mountain between Sulphur Springs Creek and PA 3014. The largest, a three-story white frame hotel building of 1884 with a gable roof, is eleven bays across. A wide porch shelters the facade and wraps around the north elevation of the rambling structure. To the south, the property's first managers, Michael and Ross Colvin, built a frame cottage with similar horizontal siding and a gable roof in the same year. Two years later, the brothers added a third story to the hotel building, and built a duckpin bowling alley east of the road. A stone storage shed and a stone and log cabin called "Fort Cochran" were built in the late 1940s southwest of the hotel. The 1,120-acre property was purchased in 1978 by the Officers' Christian Fellowship and is used as a retreat/resort.

RAINSBURG

Rainsburg is the largest borough in Friends Cove, protected by Tussey Mountain on the east and Evitts Mountain on the west. It was incorporated in 1856, three years after the Methodist Episcopal Church's Baltimore conference opened the Allegheny Male and Female Seminary (BD18), which drew students from Virginia and Maryland until the Civil War. Many of Rainsburg's houses, which enjoy excellent integrity, date from this era. A half mile of stone and frame gable-roofed, two-story houses along Main Street lead to a group of the finest houses clustered near the seminary building. They include the handsome three-bay stone Paxten House (1849; 3109 Main Street) two doors south of a clapboard five-bay house with frieze band windows (c. 1850) at 3125 Main Street. Opposite is a stone one-room schoolhouse c. 1850, which was retired in 1868, and is now a private residence (3116 Main Street). The dark orange brick Rainsburg Methodist Church (c. 1880) next door has paired brackets. At 3192 Main Street, a two-story, Flemish bond brickwork house (c. 1870), with a peaked gable and wheel window, illustrates the inventive southern architectural influence of Maryland and Virginia, as do handsome stone houses at 3298 Main Street and 312 Stillhouse Lane. The Land farm (1812–1815; 651 Sherry Road) north of Rainsburg is a classic dairy farm, with a five-bay, two-story, gable-roofed farmhouse and a large frame, gable-roofed barn. The low mountains curving through Bedford County protect farms like these.

BD18 Rainsburg Seminary (Allegheny Male and Female Seminary)

1853, Solomon Filler. 730 Main Street (PA 326) at Seminary St. SE

Reminiscent of the Bedford County Courthouse (BD1), the Rainsburg Seminary employs a similar pedimented gable end with fanlight and cupola above. But in contrast to the columned two-story portico of the courthouse and in keeping with the rural village setting, a one-story full-facade porch shelters the seminary's entrance. The window in the central bay of the second story, with four-pane surrounds, varies from the rest of the double-sash, six-over-six windows. A simple, handsome building set well back from Main Street, the seminary was a teacher's college until the Civil War, and later became the lodge for the International Order of Odd Fellows (No. 777), but is empty as of 2007. The interior features a broad central staircase made of solid oak, which reaches to the small octagonal louvered belfry. Solomon Filler's ancestors settled in Friends Cove in 1792, migrating from Maryland.

SCHELLSBURG AND VICINITY

Schellsburg's half-a-dozen blocks lie along U.S. 30 in a relatively level section of land initially settled by German, Scots-Irish, and Dutch pioneers in the late eighteenth century. The road generally follows the path traversed by General John Forbes's soldiers in the French and Indian wars of the 1750s. Later, in the 1820s, when private contractors built turnpikes to connect Philadelphia and Pittsburgh, the stretch through Schellsburg was called the Bedford and Stoystown Turnpike. By 1860, the town was thriving. Finally, in 1913, the Lincoln Highway, part of a cross-continental auto roadway, was paved and assigned its number, U.S. 30. A handsome Graham-Paige dealership of 1929, the Colvin Garage at 3758 Main Street (now the Packard Gallery), is a maroon brick showroom surviving from the early days of automobile travel.

Schellsburg was laid out in 1808 by John Schell, who owned a large farm nearby; it was incorporated as a borough in 1837. Schell donated the land for the log Schellsburg Union Church, a German Evangelical Reformed and Lutheran congregation, whose cemetery surrounds the gable-roofed church (1806), one-half mile west of Schellsburg at Cemetery Lane. The interior contains original pews and a pulpit raised on a carved wooden stem, referred to as a "wineglass pulpit." There were three hotels in Schellsburg, which today appear to be large, older houses facing U.S. 30. There are several brick five-bay houses with gable roofs, also facing the main street and dating from 1780 to 1880. Several of the houses have round-arched fanlights.

In the 1950s, the commonwealth took over several farms south of U.S. 30, and created a state park with Lake Shawnee as the centerpiece. The town's unspoiled appearance stems from the fact that its Main Street was never altered by the construction of a railroad through town.

BD19 Lincoln Motor Court

1945. 5104 Lincoln Hwy. (U.S. 30), 2.7 miles east of Schellsburg

The Lincoln Motor Court is a remarkable grouping of twelve small pyramidal-roofed tourist cabins in their original U-shaped configuration around the office and a central parking area. It is very rare to see such early tourist cabins, but even more extraordinary to see them still functioning as a motel. These individual frame cabins are sided with asbestos shingles in varied shades of gray.

BD20 Jean Bonnet Tavern

c. 1762. 6048 Lincoln Hwy. at junction of U.S. 30 and PA 31, 4.5 miles east of Schellsburg

This is a very large (51 × 40 feet) six-bay, gable-roofed fieldstone inn, with full porches cut under the sweep of the roofline at the front and rear. The building is four stories, with exposed chestnut beams in the basement tavern and first floor. Apparently built or commissioned as Fork's Inn in 1762 by Robert Callender, the warrant holder, it was purchased by Jean Bonnet in 1779. Its prominent siting at the junction of two major east–west

BD20 JEAN BONNET TAVERN

paths made it the locus of several meetings of the excise tax protesters during the Whiskey Rebellion of 1794. It continues to be used as an inn and restaurant, and retains its colonial feeling since only a small section of the turnpike has changed the nearby terrain.

Four miles west of Bedford on U.S. 30, a restored log house near Wolfsburg also served as an inn. A wagon could cover four miles in a day, and inns were often conveniently spaced at these intervals to provide lodging. A stone house at 6146 U.S. 30 is nearly adjacent to the Jean Bonnet Tavern.

FISHERTOWN

In the 1780s, members of the Society of Friends from Adams County traveled northwest over the newly opened Burd's road (U.S. 30) to Bedford, and up into what became known as Quaker Valley. They founded the Dunning's Creek Society of Friends Meeting in the early 1790s, approximately one mile northeast of Fishertown. From 1795 to c. 1875, the group met in a log structure in the village of Spring Meadow two miles north of Fishertown. The town is named for Jacob Fisher, who once owned the land, and it grew around two houses and a blacksmith shop owned by Azariah Blackburn. It consists mostly of frame houses lining two roads that intersect at a small jog in the road. The vaguely Queen Anne housing stock consists of two-story houses with gable roofs, dating from the 1880s and 1890s.

From 1827 until 1968, the American Society of Friends was divided into two sects based on differing interpretations of Quakerism. The Hicksites followed the teachings of Elias Hicks and emphasized individual spirituality. The Orthodox held to a strong belief in the readings and teachings of the elders. Hicksites dominated in the Baltimore Yearly Meeting, but the Dunning's Creek Monthly Meeting was divided in half. Although the schism ended in 1968, the two Fishertown meetinghouses remain divided and continue to meet separately. After 1830, two log meetinghouses—one Hicksite, one Orthodox—shared a six-acre plot in Spring Meadow. In 1851, the two sects cooperated to build a frame octagonal schoolhouse for the area's children (now at Old Bedford Village, see BD13). Although octagonal schoolhouses are quite rare in western Pennsylvania, many in stone or brick dot Delaware Valley in New Jersey, eastern Pennsylvania, and Delaware. The octagonal form was generally popular, and not limited to a certain religious or ethnic group between 1800 and 1850.

By the 1880s, the center of settlement had moved to Fishertown. Both meetings soon followed, erecting new buildings here. In 1882–1883, the Orthodox Meeting built a small frame, gable-roofed meetinghouse at 3140 Valley Road (PA 4003). The Hicksite Meeting built Dunning's Creek Friends Meetinghouse, a large brick structure on PA 4028 (BD21). The Spring Valley Grange No. 814 (c. 1900; 750 Grange Hill Road), a frame, gable-roofed structure reminiscent of a meetinghouse, serves as a community center for this farming area.

BD21 Dunning's Creek Friends Meetinghouse

1886. East of 319 Old Quaker Church Rd. (PA 4028)

This meetinghouse is a simple, tall brick building with slightly elongated double-sash four-over-four windows; each window has a segmental arch, and most have paneled wooden shutters. The facade has a small round-arched window in the gable end. A pair of narrow brick chimneys on the east and west elevations terminate at the cornice. There are entrances on all but the rear elevation. The interior is spare, with wooden benches facing inward to a central space and clear glass windows. The second story has been used as a high school and as a meeting place for community groups. A handsome two-and-one-half-story brick Second Empire house (c. 1886; 319 Old Quaker Church Road) lies west of the meetinghouse across from Blackburn Lane.

LOYSBURG VICINITY

BD22 Snyder House/Mill

1812. 2012 PA 36 at PA 869, 1 mile northwest of Loysburg

The *Guidebook to Historic Places in Western Pennsylvania* of 1938 conjectures that at the core of this house is a 1795 gristmill. The supposition is based on the serial linear arrangement of the doors on the south elevation and an arch on the east elevation that appears to have accommodated a millrace. If the three stories banked down the hillside are mill construction, then a full two-and-one-half-story, five-by-three-bay house rises above them, making this a five-story stone structure on the south elevation. Wide interior end chimneys distinguish the building. The stonework, which has a mottled appearance as it varies between light and dark stone, is smaller and more regular in its coursing in the gable end, unlike the stonework below. The combined house and mill was so large, it was called "Snyder's Folly."

BREEZEWOOD

Breezewood, the "Traveler's Oasis," the "Town of Motels," is a phenomenon of the post–World War II boom in auto travel. The increasing proliferation of national motel and restaurant chains produced neon and plastic signs that attempted to outdo one another in height and color. One of thirty-two interchanges on the turnpike of 1940 and, from afar, looking like a cheap imita-

U.S. 30 looking east into Breezewood.

tion of Las Vegas, the town has a very small residential section on Ray's Hill to the east. The development pressures increased when an intersection with I-70 opened in October 1970, connecting central Pennsylvania with Washington, D.C., and Baltimore.

EVERETT AND VICINITY

Laid out in 1795 by Michael Barndollar, the borough was initially known as Bloody Run, either because of a military attack during Pontiac's Rebellion in 1763 or because animals were slaughtered on the creek's shoreline. It is located at the gap in Tussey Mountain made by the Raystown Branch of the Juniata River and the path of Forbes Road in the 1750s. The borough of Bloody Run was incorporated in 1860, but the name was changed to Everett in 1873 to honor the eminent Reverend Edward Everett, a former president of Harvard College, secretary of state in the 1850s, and, arguably, one of the most famous orators of the mid-nineteenth century, having spoken in 1863 for over two hours preceding President Abraham Lincoln's more memorable two-minute Gettysburg Address.

Over the years, industry and transportation shaped the small town's development. In 1863, the Huntingdon and Broad Top Mountain Railroad and Coal Company extended their line south to Bloody Run (Everett), but the line did not connect to Bedford until 1871. The restored freight and passenger stations at 49 and 51 W. 5th Street are used now as a community center, and the tracks no longer exist. Iron ore from Black Valley to the southwest and coal from the Broad Top region to the northeast made it possible to produce iron in Everett. In 1874, the Everett Iron Company incorporated, and opened coke blast furnaces at its shops. The company was so successful that its president, James Earlston Thropp, built a large frame house on the hillside west of the works, and a brick five-bay house for his son Earlston on PA 1004. Several red brick buildings from the former ironworks were reused by the State Turnpike Commission as offices and storage facilities. The 1870s also saw construction of a large planing mill that continues to operate in Everett. George Harrison

Gibboney, a contractor, took over the planing mill c. 1900, and constructed a number of buildings in Bedford County.

The commercial district along E. and W. Main Street (U.S. 30) has several attractions promoted by the Lincoln Highway Heritage Park, including on E. Main Street, the Art Deco Everett Theater (c. 1920), the Union Hotel (1898), and the Igloo Soft Serve (c. 1965), which is another programmatic roadside building like the Coffee Pot in Bedford (BD12). Here a scoop of fiberglass ice cream with chocolate sauce and a cherry on top offers frozen treats to Lincoln Highway travelers.

BD23 Travelers Rest Motel

c. 1947, 1964, 1965. 14275 Lincoln Hwy. (U.S. 30), 2.8 miles east of Everett

An inn has graced this site, dubbed "Traveler's Rest," since the Forbes Road first ran along the hilltop to the north. The present building is immediately identifiable as a motel by its bright yellow-colored roof of intersecting peaks, and although it bears a striking resemblance to the A-frame orange roofs of Howard Johnson's motels of the 1950s, this motel was never part of that national chain. The owner had the buildings designed and built by local contractors. The present facility has evolved from tourist cabins to an attached motel row and, finally, to this 1960s A-frame. In the complex, a separate, later A-frame building with a shingled roof is the owner's home and office.

BD24 Newry Mill, Manor, and Lutz Museum

c. 1805 mill; 1780, 1803, 1858 house; 1950 museum. 1427 Lutzville Rd. (PA 2019), 4 miles west of Everett

The oldest woolen mill in Bedford County and one of the oldest west of the Susquehanna River was built c. 1805 by Jacob Lutz. It operated first as the Lutz Woolen Factory, and then as the Juniata Woolen Mill until 1910. Using the waterpower of Cove Creek, the mill complex employed twenty people in the early nineteenth century. A wooden addition to the east elevation was washed away in the flood of 1936 and never replaced. The complex includes Newry Manor, a house of three distinct building eras: a log portion (1780) moved and rebuilt on this site in 1950, a stone section (1803), and a brick portion with central hall and two stories (1858). In 1950, a well-proportioned two-by-two-bay museum of tan concrete block was built northeast of the house, partially on the foundation of the 1780 log house and reusing the chimneys and fireplaces of that structure.

BD24 NEWRY MILL, MANOR, AND LUTZ MUSEUM, mill (*left*) and museum (*right*)

SOMERSET COUNTY

Somerset County lies north of the Maryland border between Laurel Ridge and a line that loosely follows the crest of the Little Allegheny Mountain and the Allegheny Ridge. Formed from the western half of Bedford County in 1795, Somerset County is dominated by ridge and valley topography. It is also the highest county and county seat in the commonwealth (the city of Somerset is 2,190 feet above sea level and Mount Davis is the highest peak at

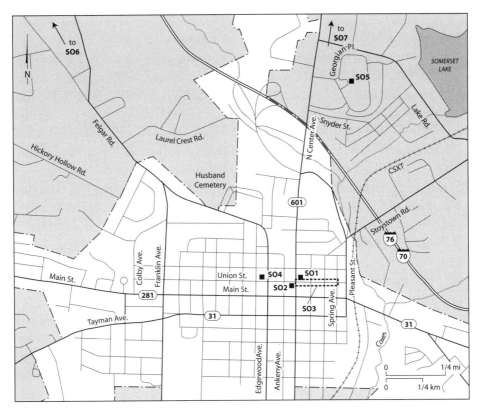

SOMERSET

3,213 feet above sea level). The wide valleys running north to south provide the best farmland. Building stock consists mainly of late-nineteenth-century farm houses, either frame or brick, often with distinctive double-decker porches on the facade and occasionally on both the front and rear elevations. The regional distinction of these porches is that they are incorporated under the roofline: the gable roof continues over them unbroken, so that the porch itself is integral to the mass of the house. In western Pennsylvania, this feature is found primarily in Somerset and Bedford counties.

A handful of roads in the county (named after English military men, including Edward Braddock, James Burd, and John Forbes) crossed the county in the mid-eighteenth century, and settlement expanded from there. Military camps along Forbes Road (present-day U.S. 30) eventually developed into a number of towns, among them Stoystown, Buckstown, and Jennerstown. The county's natural resources are timber and bituminous coal (North Fork, Elk Lick, and Buffalo veins), and Somerset is one of the top ten bituminous coal-producing counties in Pennsylvania. But the extractive industries did not grow beyond local use until the county was connected by rail to Pittsburgh, Cumberland, Wheeling, and other towns in 1871. The Pittsburgh and Connellsville Railroad (later a subsidiary of the Baltimore and Ohio) was the first line in Somerset. Other lines quickly followed, most of them controlled by the Baltimore and Ohio. Mining towns such as Boswell and Windber were built by the coal companies for their miners.

In 1934, a Works Progress Administration project to build a highway across Pennsylvania chose the route of the never-completed South Pennsylvania Railroad, constructed in the 1880s. The Pennsylvania Turnpike (I-76) (see BD14) gave cars and trucks access to both Pittsburgh and Philadelphia in the 1950s. The highway is a boon to tourism and has opened the county to weekend homes and skiers using resorts like Seven Springs (SO19) and Hidden Valley.

Somerset County has entered the national spotlight several times in the twenty-first century. Since 2000, wind farms have been built to take advantage of the county's high elevation and harness energy using wind turbines. Many of these enormous sleek white windmills placed along ridges are visible from the Pennsylvania Turnpike.

On September 11, 2001, United Flight 93 crashed into a strip-mined field outside of Shanksville, foiling a terrorist attack planned for the Capitol in Washington, D.C. In 2005, the National Park Service held an international design competition for a permanent memorial, and chose a design by Paul Murdoch Architects of Los Angeles, with landscape architects Nelson Byrd Woltz of Charlottesville, Virginia. A chapel, interpretive center, forty groves of maple trees, and a tower with forty wind chimes, commemorating the forty crew and passengers killed that day, will grace the site scheduled to open on September 11, 2011.

SOMERSET AND VICINITY

The borough of Somerset relied solely on Glades Pike (PA 31), a road farther south but nearly parallel to the Lincoln Highway and Forbes Road (U.S. 30), for transportation when the earliest settlers moved here in the 1770s. Somerset became the county seat in 1795. A fire nearly destroyed the town in 1833, and another fire in 1872 consumed 117 buildings. In 1871, the Somerset and Mineral Point (later Rockwood) Railroad arrived in the borough, and, after it extended to Johnstown in the 1880s, business boomed. While few structures built specifically for the railroad survive, several houses date from this period (SO3). Further growth occurred after 1940, when the Pennsylvania Turnpike passed near the city and U.S. 219 gave easy access to Somerset from the north and south.

The town has two business districts. The first is an older section of two- to four-story brick commercial buildings on Main and Patriot streets, connected by N. Center Street. Beginning in 1994, a Main Street program spurred the renovation of several older buildings, including the brick Vannear building of c. 1900, now Glades Court Mall at 101–109 W. Main Street. The second, more recent, business district stretches along N. Center Street, north of the courthouse, and includes chain stores and motels built after 1960.

SO1 SOMERSET COUNTY COURTHOUSE

SO1 Somerset County Courthouse

1904–1906, J. C. Fulton Architect. 111 E. Union St.

Built during the county's railroad boom years in the early twentieth century, the courthouse is more than twice the size of the brick structure it replaced. Sited at the crown of a hill and surrounded by the rest of the borough, the courthouse is visible for miles, including from the Pennsylvania Turnpike (I-76). John Charles Fulton won a design competition for the courthouse; Caldwell and Drake were the contractors. The Beaux-Arts building's raised basement is sheathed in native sandstone, and the upper stories are of Indiana limestone. A two-story semicircular portico marks the entrance on the south facade and a rectangular portico is on the west elevation, both supported by Corinthian columns. A balustrade outlines the roof, and crowning the building is the 135-foot-tall dome sheathed in copper and supported on an octagonal pedimented base. The interior of the courthouse remains virtually unaltered since 1906. The twelve-panel, stained glass interior of the dome rises above the marble-lined central space, which contains a grand staircase lined with heavy brass and wooden balustrades. The courtrooms are paneled in dark wood.

SO2 Commercial Building (Somerset Trust Company Bank)

1906, Mowbray and Uffinger. E. Union St. at S. Center St. SW

The New York City firm of Mowbray and Uffinger specialized in banks, designing such buildings as the People's Trust Company in Brooklyn, New York (1906), and both the former Butler County National Bank (BU2) and the Altoona Trust Building (BL13). Contemporary with the adjacent courthouse, the Somerset Trust Company Bank is a handsome Beaux-Arts building, too. A pair of Tuscan columns and a foliate ornamented pediment, both of Indiana limestone, outline the double-height entrance portico. One of the building's distinguishing features is the copper and glass dome that originally lit the main banking room before the building was converted to offices and a full second floor was added.

SO3 East Union Street Houses

1856–1930. 100 and 200 blocks E. Union St.

East Union Street begins with the courthouse at Main Street, and continues east into a residential area of predominantly high-style brick houses dating from the 1840s through 1910. Immediately east of the courthouse, a sheriff's house and county jail have occupied this site since 1802. The present sheriff's house (1856), added to an existing jail by John Mong, has a cut-stone foundation and a cast-iron cornice. In 1889, the jail portion of the building was replaced. The cell blocks contain a set of double gallows, reputed to be the first in Pennsylvania. The women's cells were in the smaller block to the west, and the men were accommodated in a block at a right angle facing north. The building currently houses offices for the courts. Across the street, the Law and Matthews Building probably dates to the 1870s.

The Lansberry house (1869) at 139 E. Union Street in the Italian Villa style is similar to the designs in Samuel Sloan's pattern books, but with a central dormer instead of a tower. Opposite at 132 E. Union Street, St. Paul's Presbyterian Church is a red brick, Gothic Revival building c. 1870. At 147 E. Union Street, the Edward Scull house (1856) has a Greek Revival portico and sidelights, and a transom around the door. The house was moved west to make room for Edward's son George's house (165 E. Union), which was designed in 1917 by the local firm of Walker and Mong. That firm designed many of the Colonial Revival houses in the city. A frame house (c. 1880) at 214 E. Union Street has a deep front porch, sawn ornament, and fanciful roof slates. Across the street, the two-story brick former school (1897) at the corner of E. Union Street and N. Kimberly Avenue now houses the district court and other offices.

SO4 St. Paul's United Church of Christ

1887, Purcell and Fry; 1916, Edward Hay Walker. 202 W. Union St.

By 1887, the congregation of St. Paul's had outgrown its second building and commissioned the Philadelphia firm of Purcell and Fry to design this brick Gothic Revival church. In 1916, when additional space was needed, local architect Edward Hay Walker (1864–1953) was hired to design an addition to the west. His Gothic Revival design, with its stepped buttresses, cross-braced entrance overhangs, bracketing, and pointed arches, seamlessly blends with the original building. The addition changed the church sanctuary from the traditional form to a much larger, Akron plan layout. Previously, in 1910, Walker had designed the First Christian Church at 139 E. Main Street, a substantial, neoclassical domed

building. Walker had an architectural practice in Somerset spanning nearly fifty years.

SO5 The Inn at Georgian Place and Restaurant (Manor Hill, D. B. Zimmerman House)

1915–1918, Horace Trumbauer; Julian Abele, project architect. N. Center St.

Nationally known Philadelphia architect Horace Trumbauer (1869–1938) and his senior designer Julian Francis Abele (1881–1950) created this grand two-and-one-half-story brick Colonial Revival house. Trumbauer was known to depend heavily on the architects in his firm, and Abele, the only African American member of Philadelphia's T-Square Club, became the senior designer after 1908. Edward Hay Walker's obituary states that he also worked on this house. Coal baron Daniel B. Zimmerman commissioned the house, and, after his death, his daughter lived here until 1944, when it was sold to the first of many short-term owners. By 1990, the house had fallen into disrepair. In May 1993, it opened as a luxury bed-and-breakfast. Although the restoration was carefully done, the surrounding landscape was sacrificed in the process. The original site, a gentle tree-covered hill, was scraped away to leave the maroon brick house on a bald plateau of land, now surrounded by an expanse of outlet stores and parking lots. To the east is Lake Somerset, created in 1956 by the commonwealth's game commission.

SO6 Stahl Farm, "Dairy of Distinction"

1876 barn; 1886 house, Joe Auman, carpenter. 1512 Marlwood Rd., 4.5 miles northwest of Somerset

The Stahl farm is visible from the Pennsylvania Turnpike, and most often noticed for the sign urging motorists to "Drink Milk" painted on the side of the milk house. This is one of more than 750 "Dairies of Distinction" in Pennsylvania honored for the exceptional maintenance of both their animals and farm buildings, and as a means of reinforcing the public's confidence in consuming dairy products. This farm has been in the Stahl family since 1782, when Henry Stahl purchased the land. The buildings date from the late nineteenth century. The large frame bank barn has

SO6 STAHL FARM, "DAIRY OF DISTINCTION"

Gothic-arched louvers, corner boards, and pilaster strips. Painted the classic red color for barns, with white trim, it holds eighty Holstein cows and matches the other outbuildings, from the drive-through corncrib to the smallest shed and garage. The central-hall-plan house is of double plank construction (see SO8) with Italianate paired brackets at the eaves. A contemporaneous house and barn on an adjoining farm were also built by carpenter Joe Auman.

SO7 Somerset Historical Center and Visitors' Center

1996–1997, Susan Maxman and Partners; Missy Maxwell, project architect. 10649 Somerset Pike (PA 985), 4.5 miles north of Somerset

Set in the semirural outskirts of Somerset, the Historical Society and Visitors' Center building is the centerpiece of a thirty-acre agricultural history museum, and one of the few, post-1980 buildings in the county. The outdoor portion of the complex displays agricultural lifestyles of different eras, including a settlers' cabin (1790s), a farmstead (1850s), and a dairy farm (1920s). The buildings were either moved to the site or are replicas. The Visitors' Center contains exhibition space, and houses the Somerset Historical Society. It was designed by Philadelphia-based Susan Maxman and her firm, which is known for designing environmentally responsive public buildings. The center takes its inspiration from agricultural structures, with their cupolas, clerestory windows, and steeply pitched roofs. Using common materials such as laminated wood and exterior metal siding, it evokes the ubiquity of prefabricated metal structures on late-twentieth-century farms.

GRAY

Gray, formerly known as Biesecker in honor of original landholder Frederick Biesecker, was laid out in 1913. Developed by the Consolidation Coal Company, the town is filled with small, two-story houses built from three or four patterns, each surrounded by an expanse of lawn. When the company decided to paint all the houses a uniform gray, the village's name was changed to its current appellation. The rhythm of the nearly identical houses of Gray's six long blocks is interrupted by three different buildings. The John Biesecker house (c. 1860; 538 Beam Church Road) was built for a descendant of the original landholder. It is a frame version of the brick houses that many prosperous farmers in the area built between 1850 and 1870. Typical of the type, the Biesecker house has a central hall and integral double-decker porch, chimneys at the interior gable ends, and transoms and sidelights at the main entrance. The second exception is a long, single-story house with deep eaves that dates from the 1950s in the northwest quadrant of the village. Finally, a one-story, nine-bay frame Community Building (c. 1900; 474 Beam Church Road) has a hipped roof and a small pedimented porch at the entrance. It was apparently built as the local schoolhouse.

BOSWELL AND VICINITY

Boswell was founded to support the Merchant Coal Company's Orenda Mine No. 1, which opened in 1901 and employed over 900 men at its peak, most of whom were Slavs, Poles, and Italians. The company built housing and public buildings in addition to the necessary mine buildings. The housing mirrored company and social strata. Managers occupied stone-veneered, two-story, four-bay, gable-roofed houses like those at 224 and 230 Quemahoning Street. Most of the houses for workers with families were duplexes without heat, indoor plumbing, or electricity, and alternated between brick and frame construction to prevent whole blocks from burning in a major fire. Only one original frame house remains, while there are several extant brick models. The 200 block of Center Street is a good example of the mixture of old company houses and newer construction. The third class of workers was single men. Relegated to the outskirts of town, they lived in long, single-story, four-unit row houses built by the Eureka Lumber Company in 1911; each unit housed four men. Only a few of these buildings remain, and all have been significantly altered. Like most mining communities today, Boswell is recovering from the loss of heavy industry in the area. While six churches remain in the village, it is Orenda Park, lying north of Quemahoning Creek, that commemorates what was at one time the largest coal tipple in the world (c. 1901).

SO8 Blough Farm

c. 1830 house; 1894 and 1902 barn. 845 Spiegle Rd., 3.5 miles north of Boswell

Blough Farm provides an accurate picture of a prosperous late-nineteenth-century farm,

SO8 BLOUGH FARM, barn

with excellent integrity in the house, barn, and outbuildings. The main barn is banked on the east elevation. The west side has a centered cross-gable decorated with one of three barn stars that adorn the building. Additional sawn ornament embellishes the louvered windows and roofline. When the barn was rebuilt with funds from the sale of the property's coal rights in 1902, the architectural details, including painted columns, were replicated from an earlier barn. The two-story farmhouse's exterior walls are built with two overlapping layers of vertical planks, each one extending to the roof and anchored in a groove in the foundation stones. Exterior horizontal siding and interior plaster and lath are attached directly to the planks. The roof of the house continues unbroken over the double porch. This type of plank construction and porch placement appear primarily in central Pennsylvania, as do the barn stars. The cupola at the crown of the gable contains the bell that was used to call the farmhands to meals. A one-story addition is attached to the house's north elevation. The remaining outbuildings include an equipment shed, smokehouse, and pumphouse. A large corncrib was removed in 1999.

WINDBER

The Windber area mines, owned and operated by the Philadelphia-based Berwind-White Coal Company, produced nearly 90 percent of the company's Pennsylvania coal, which it sold primarily to ocean-going steamship lines. With a population of over 10,000, the borough of Windber was the company's model town. It was laid out in 1897 by Heber Denman, a Berwind-White employee, to serve as the company's regional headquarters and as a commercial center for the eleven smaller mining settlements in the Wilmore Basin, a coal-rich region straddling the Somerset and Cambria county line.

Between 1900 and 1920, the company hired thousands of unskilled immigrant workers, mostly Slovaks, Magyars, Poles, and Italians. They worked for low wages and without union membership. Skilled workers and "company men" were almost exclusively American, English, or Scots-Irish. The company maintained strict control over almost every aspect of the residents' lives, employing most of the town's men and owning the land, company store, bank, newspaper, and utilities, and it subsidized the Windber Presbyterian Church and the Windber Park Association. But the company also encouraged outside businesses to open along Graham Avenue, and encouraged residents to purchase their own homes along the borough's tree-lined streets. Houses for the miners were small, five-room, balloon-frame, two-story buildings with electricity but without plumbing. The occupants were allowed some flexibility in the plan, such as the location of the exterior door, but their choices were limited. A few tenements, known as the "Hungarian Quarters," were built using the vertical-plank method, as on the Blough farmhouse (so8). The more elaborate managers' houses were designed by company engineers using designs from pattern books.

By their size and design, Windber's buildings are role models for other coal towns. They include the Windber Borough Building (1902) at 1409 Somerset Avenue, formerly the company headquarters; Ameriserv Financial, formerly the Windber National Bank (c. 1910; 1501 Somerset Avenue); and the Railroad Station (1916; 1401 Graham Avenue). Philadelphia architect Henry L. Reinhold Jr. designed several buildings, including the Tudor Revival Eureka Department Store (c. 1899) at 15th Street and Somerset Avenue and the Windber Electric building of 1925 at 509 15th Street. The ethnic makeup of the town is most easily read in its numerous churches. Two of the four major churches retain their earlier ethnic affiliations: St. John Cantius Church (1913; 607 Graham Avenue) served the Irish and, later, the Polish communities. St. Mary's Greek Catholic church (1919, Walter J. Myton; Somerset

Avenue and 7th Street) was built by the Slavic community. J. C. Fulton and Son designed two Protestant churches: the First Lutheran church (c. 1920; Somerset Avenue and 10th Street), and the First Presbyterian Church (c. 1929; 1101 Somerset Avenue).

A series of labor strikes and union problems in the 1920s and 1930s weakened the Berwind-White Coal Company. Union issues, combined with an unfavorable market, gradually caused the company to stop mining between 1949 and 1962. Berwind-White sold the company-owned houses, and sold the Eureka department store to new owners in 1969. When the company pulled out, it devastated the area economically. Windber is recovering, as people who moved away are now coming back to spend their retirement years. Two signs of this are the restoration in 1990 of the Arcadia Theater (1919–1921, Henry L. Reinhold and Ralph Land; 1418 Graham Avenue), and the adaptive reuse of the former Post Office and Wilmore Coal Company offices (1913) as the Windber Coal Heritage Center (501 15th Street), creating an exhibition center dedicated to the area's history and the miners who shaped it. A second museum resides in the frame, two-story farmhouse (c. 1869; 601 15th Street) that belonged to David J. Shaffer, with double-decker porches on the front and rear elevations.

NEW BALTIMORE

SO9 St. John the Baptist Carmelite Friary

1892. 101 Findley St.

Bavarian Carmelite priest Cyril Knoll came to New Baltimore and assumed responsibil-

SO9 ST. JOHN THE BAPTIST CARMELITE FRIARY

ity for the local parish and school. By 1890, a rectory and a school for Carmelite novices were built. Anticipating continued growth due to the proximity of the proposed South Pennsylvania Railroad, the Carmelite order replaced the smaller stone church with the present brick church, using plans supplied from Germany by members of the order. The impressive, brick Romanesque Revival building, visible from the Pennsylvania Turnpike, has smooth English bond masonry, round-arched door and window openings, and a tall, square tower in the center of the facade. The church's interior is paneled in oak, and the furniture, including the altar, was built by Henry Engbert, a carpenter whose work is in Pittsburgh and many other central Pennsylvania churches. The South Pennsylvania Railroad was never completed, and New Baltimore stagnated. The Carmelite novices moved to Niagara in 1915, but construction of the Pennsylvania Turnpike brought the Carmelites back to the area in the 1940s. They negotiated with the commonwealth to allow an area for people to pull off the turnpike and walk the fifty yards to the church, the only such arrangement along the entire length of the highway. In 1968, the last Carmelite novices left the community, leaving one priest to minister to the congregation.

MEYERSDALE AND VICINITY

Meyersdale is laid out on two grids spreading north and south of Flaugherty Creek east of the Casselman River. It was the site of such early rural industries as Andrew Borntrager's gristmill of 1789. In 1815, Jacob Meyers Jr. bought land in the area, and erected a fulling mill and a gristmill. Five of his brothers from Lancaster County followed him and farmed in the area, which became known as Meyers' Mills. The borough's name was changed to Meyersdale in 1871, the same year that the Pittsburgh and Connellsville rail line came through the town. The frame hipped-roof Meyersdale depot at Meyers Avenue and Chestnut Street was built by the Baltimore and Ohio Railroad (B&O), after it purchased the line in 1875. Forty years later, the Western Maryland Railroad built a second rail line through the eastern edge of town. Rail accessibility encouraged the growth of logging and mining companies, notably the Keystone Coal and Coke Company (founded in 1872), as well as dairy farming and maple sugar harvesting. Logging companies sold lumber to the coal companies in prepackaged bundles large enough to build a single house, and the Meyersdale Planing Mill provided lumber for much of the local housing and both railroad stations. The area was logged out by the 1920s, but coal mining has continued. As late as the 1990s, nearly one million tons of coal were extracted per year from Somerset County.

The success of the various industries spawned a comfortable middle class, whose frame and brick Queen Anne and Colonial Revival houses line Broadway Street and Meyers Avenue. The large, stone First Methodist Church and manse at 336 Main Street was built in two sections, the first in 1873 and the second in 1903, coinciding with the two periods of growth in Meyersdale's history. The Meyersdale Banking House, now Citizen's National Bank (141 Center Street) has two parts: a two-story, three-bay brick Greek Revival house with Italianate trimmings (1869), and an attached four-story building (1904) with rough-cut stone on the first story and brickwork above. The Greek Revival Gallatin National Bank (1909) at Main and Center streets has Ionic columns at the entrance.

Reputed to be the oldest house in Meyersdale, the Meyer's House (124 Meyers Avenue) began as a one-story log house built c. 1785 by early gristmill owner Andrew Borntrager. The six-bay frame addition and the second story above the log house–kitchen were added c. 1820, and ten years later, the present horizontal siding unified the whole, masking the various ages of the rooms. The house and mill were purchased by Peter Meyer in 1827. It is open to the public during the Pennsylvania Maple Festival held in April every year.

SO13 WESTERN MARYLAND RAILROAD SALISBURY JUNCTION VIADUCT

SO10 Cupola Houses

c. 1870. 341 Main St. and 116 and 131 Meyers Ave.

A group of Meyersdale houses—related either by builder or designer—have square cupolas crowning their roofs. The three-bay frame house at 341 Main Street is similar to those found in Samuel Sloan's pattern books of the 1850s in its four-over-four plan, roof brackets, arched window surrounds, and the cupola itself. The house at 131 Meyers Avenue is comparable, although altered. At 116 Meyers Avenue, the house has a cross-gable roof, but, like the other two houses, its cupola has three windows on each of its sides. Similar clusters of these cupola houses survive in Venango and Erie counties.

SO11 Levi Deal Mansion Bed-and-Breakfast

c. 1900. 301 Meyers Ave.

Built in 1900 for a self-made local man who ran a planing mill and later built his fortune in coal and lumber, this attractive, large Queen Anne house with a stone first story and shingled upper stories is dominated by two round turrets and a wraparound porch. Stained glass at the stairwell illuminates the recently restored interior that now hosts six suites for overnight guests.

SO12 Wills Creek Bollman Railroad Bridge

1871, Wendel Bollman. Across Scratch Hill Rd., 1.5 miles east of Meyersdale

Built to carry the Baltimore and Ohio over one of the many creeks between Cumber-

land and Pittsburgh, this bridge is probably the only bridge in the commonwealth associated with Wendel Bollman. This is not, however, a Bollman truss type, but a Warren truss built by Bollman's company. By 1910, restricted from carrying rail traffic, the bridge was moved to Meyersdale to carry vehicular traffic, and moved again in 2007 to become part of the Great Allegheny Passage hiking and biking trail (see SO13). Bimetal bridges—those of both cast and wrought iron—such as this one, were the dominant metal truss type between 1840 and 1880. Yet, of the thousands built, fewer than seventy-five are known to survive in the United States. This bridge's notable features include riveted wrought-iron columns of the inclined end posts, cast-iron top chords, cast-iron diagonals in the middle of the bridge fabricated in three separate castings, and decorative portal bracing. There is another small iron Warren truss bridge remaining along the Casselman River near Meyersdale; it can be viewed from Hetz Road and the Casselman River.

SO13 Western Maryland Railroad Salisbury Junction Viaduct

1911–1912. Casselman River at U.S. 219 and TWP 381, 1.5 miles north of Meyersdale

The Western Maryland Railroad built this viaduct to cross Casselman River's wide, shallow valley near Meyersdale. The McClintock-Marshall Construction Company built the 1,900-foot-long steel trestle, losing seven men to accidents in the process. Since the summer of 2001, it has been a part of the Great Allegheny Passage (operated locally by the Allegheny Highlands Trail of Pennsylvania), a fifty-mile hiking and biking trail through Somerset County. It is now possible, using other trails in western Pennsylvania and Maryland, to ride a bicycle from Pittsburgh to Washington, D.C. The Western Maryland Railroad Station (1911) at the top of Main Street in Meyersdale was rehabilitated in 1995, and is operated by the Meyersdale Area Historical Society as a gift shop and exhibition space targeted to trail users.

SALISBURY VICINITY

SO14 Compton's Mill

1871; 1872; 1898, Israel Schrock. 623 Compton Mill Rd. (PA 2001), 3.9 miles west of Salisbury

Amazing for its near perfect condition, this fully operational mill dates from the 1870s. Local sandstone gathered by Demetrius Compton and dressed by Samuel Compton was used for the foundation and first floor of the banked mill. The white pine lumber was cut in a sawmill built for the purpose a few hundred feet away. The west wall has a 4 × 4–foot opening to accommodate the hub of the waterwheel powered by a quarter-mile-long spillway fed by Tub Mill Run. The mill was modernized in 1937, switching from waterpower to steam. Two additions on the southeast elevation, containing the boiler room and blacksmith shop, date from this time. Today, the mill grinds grain using both rollers and the traditional grindstones.

ADDISON

SO15 Petersburg Tollhouse

c. 1835, Captain Richard Delafield. 830 National Rd. (U.S. 40)

During the nineteenth century, Pennsylvania charged travelers a toll every fifteen miles to pay for the continued maintenance of the National Road. The tollhouses consisted of three main parts: the first, a two-story octagonal tower for the business of collecting money; the second, a rectangular living space for the official and his family; and third, a gate across the road to slow traffic and insure that no one passed without proper payment. Sadly, not one of the gates remains anywhere along the road, and only three tollhouses still stand. This is the only tollhouse built from stone that survives. It was constructed c. 1835 by civil engineer Richard Delafield from the standardized plan drawn by British engineer Thomas Telford. Today, the tollhouse is owned by the Great Crossings Chapter of the Daughters

SO15 PETERSBURG TOLLHOUSE

of the American Revolution, and has been restored by Frens and Frens, an architecture firm specializing in historic renovation. The second tollhouse stands in Fayette County and is known as Searight's Tollhouse (FA8), while the third is in Ohio.

URSINA VICINITY

SO16 Knobloch Farm (Brook Farm)

c. 1845 house; c. 1920 barn. 7542 PA 281, 2.8 miles northeast of Ursina

John Brooks, a local landowner, purchased this farm in 1838, and soon after built the brick Federal-style farmhouse. The five-bay facade has Flemish bond brickwork and a fanlight above the entrance. The interior has a two-over-two floor plan and a long kitchen ell at the rear. Originally, there were interior end chimneys on both the east and west elevations, but the west chimney was removed after an explosion in the nearby Brooks Railroad tunnel damaged the house. The gambrel-roofed barn to the west of the house and a series of frame outbuildings support the working sheep farm. Lamb burgers are sold at the family's restaurant (1961) across the highway.

BARRONVALE VICINITY

SO17 Barronvale Covered Bridge

1846. Covered Bridge Rd. (PA 3014) over Laurel Hill Creek, 2.4 miles northwest of Barronvale

Cassimer Cramer built this bridge to replace one from 1830. The two-span, 162-foot-long, Burr truss structure is the longest of the ten covered bridges remaining in Somerset County. One arch is higher than the other, because the spans are different lengths. The bridge was updated in 1902 after a major flood, at which time the first iron rods were added. One mile south along the same creek, the covered King's Bridge is being restored.

SO18 Scottyland RV Resort

1962. PA 653 at Barron Church Rd. (PA 3033), 1 mile southeast of Barronvale

Spread over three hundred acres of former farm land, Scottyland is a sea of campers and RVs parked year-round. Two nineteenth-century buildings remain on the site: a log maple sugar house and a barn, where the wood-pinned construction is evident despite the modernizations. The RV park, founded in 1962, includes complete hook-ups for the vehicles; recreation center; pool; skating rink; a chapel built in 1966; a bass-stocked, man-made lake; and Laurel Hill Creek. Of the seven hundred sites, about four hundred are used year-round.

SEVEN SPRINGS

SO19 Seven Springs Mountain Resort

1928–present. 777 Waterwheel Dr. (PA 3029)

Seven Springs, the largest ski resort in Pennsylvania, was founded by German immigrant Adolph Dupre. He purchased two-and-one-half acres in 1928, and over the next twenty years built twenty-eight cottages of his own design to provide a place of rest and relaxation for Pittsburgh residents. From these beginnings, Seven Springs has grown to an 8,700-acre year-round convention center and resort. None of the cottages built by Dupre still stands. In the mid-1960s, seventy rooms were added to the main lodge, and a golf course was built. Today, the dominant structure at the base of the mountain is the 313-room high-rise hotel designed and built in 1974, just two years after the convention center. Hidden Valley, a smaller ski and golf resort, is less than twenty miles to the northeast on PA 31.

SO20 Laurel Hill State Park

c. 1936. Trent Rd. (PA 3037), entrance 5.4 miles southeast of Seven Springs

There are several state parks in western Somerset County along Laurel Ridge, including

Laurel Hill Park, which was known as a Rural Demonstration Area. It was one of five parks in Pennsylvania established in the late 1930s, using Civilian Conservation Corps (CCC) and WPA labor to make rural parks accessible to the commonwealth's urban dwellers. Laurel Hill State Park had five campsites, each accommodating 100 people and including cabins, latrines, recreation halls, an infirmary, an administration house, and a dining hall. In addition to the camp buildings, CCC workers built their own barracks, some of which remain in and around the camps. These are long, narrow, gable-roofed buildings with horizontal siding typical of what was used for military structures of the time. Laurel Hill State Park contains over two hundred buildings, among the largest collection of CCC-built structures in Pennsylvania.

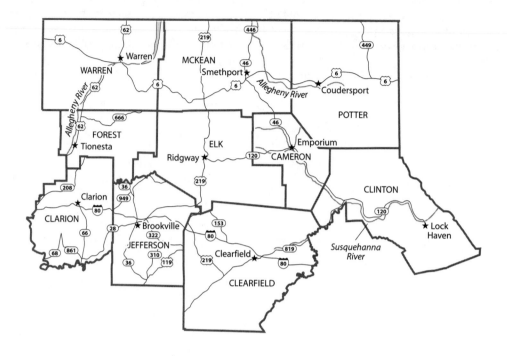

Great Forest

This region comprises three large counties bordering New York (Warren, McKean, and Potter) and the forested counties south of them (Clinton, Cameron, Elk, Forest, Clarion, Jefferson, and Clearfield). The topography is a continuation of the Appalachian Plateau, but at a higher elevation, becoming almost mountainous in McKean and Potter counties. The Allegheny River and the Susquehanna's tributaries flow south, as do most streams in the region. This allowed products and raw materials to be shipped to Pittsburgh or Harrisburg, but made return trips difficult before steamboats began operating in 1830. Westward migration, particularly from Connecticut, spurred settlement, since it was easier to reach the forested lands from the north via the Erie Canal than paddling upriver from the south. The earliest settlers brought with them an appreciation of and preference for the Greek Revival style for houses, churches, and schools, and fine examples remain.

Lumber and oil were the major industries in this region. Lumbering was so successful that vast sections were clear-cut by 1900. Special narrow-gauge railroads, which could reach into the small valleys more easily than standard-gauge tracks, aided this process. Paper, glass, and refractory bricks continue to be made in the region. Farming, already difficult due to the short growing season, became harder due to the erosion caused by the deforestation. Today the region is reforested and is some of the most productive hardwood forest in the United States. It is also state and national forest and is popular recreationally, featuring scenic drives, especially during the fall season. The state parks are dotted with rustic buildings constructed by the Civilian Conservation Corps in the 1930s.

The region's cities are small, with populations under 10,000; Warren and Bradford are the largest. Brookville and Smethport are especially attractive places to visit. Architects for major buildings were often imported from Buffalo, New York, and Cleveland, Ohio, cities that are closer to the region than Pittsburgh. Edward Albert Phillips, who moved to Warren, Pennsylvania, from Buffalo, has a large body of work in traditional styles. Frank Furness is easily the most famous architect to have a building in the region; the carriage house (CL25) he designed for the Fox family of Philadelphia is unique. Hyde-Murphy, operating out of Ridgway in Elk County from 1884 to 1961, was the most successful builder in the area. And with their in-house architect Henry C. Park, who moved to Ridgway from New York in the 1890s, either built or remodeled an enormous number of buildings in the center of Pennsylvania, from coal patch houses to mansions. The company began as a sawmill, and it became known for the quality of its millwork.

U.S. 6 travels from east to west across Warren, McKean, and Potter counties and, at four hundred miles, is the longest highway in the commonwealth. Along the northern tier, it is marketed as a scenic highway with links to the various historic sites along its length. Farther south, I-80 traverses Clarion, Jefferson, and Clearfield counties. East–west travel is always difficult in Pennsylvania, as it generally requires crossing innumerable hills and valleys, some quite challenging, and often requiring bridges of enormous size.

WARREN COUNTY

Warren County is rectangular in shape, with the Allegheny River angling toward its center from the northeastern corner and turning south at the city of Warren. Prehistoric Native American tribes as well as later Eries, Delawares, and Shawnee used Conewango and Brokenstraw creeks as access to the Allegheny River. A Seneca chief known as Cornplanter, whose mother was Seneca and father Dutch, was given nearly 15,000 acres of land in 1790–1791 by the Pennsylvania General Assembly for his role in keeping the Iroquois from continuing the fight against European settlement. Cornplanter sold two parcels in Venango and Forest counties, but he and his descendants settled on the Warren County land. In 1964, the Seneca lost an appeal to the U.S. Supreme Court and their village was inundated as part of the Kinzua Dam project to regulate the Allegheny's flow and prevent flooding downstream.

After the French and Indian and the Revolutionary wars, Pennsylvania's government built forts along the commonwealth's western frontier to guard against attacks and encourage settlement. In 1795, General William Irvine and Andrew Ellicott surveyed the county and laid out the borough of Warren, named for General Joseph Warren, a member of the Provincial Congress killed at Breed's Hill near Boston in 1775. Although the first landowners were required to build within two years, large speculators were exempt from this ruling. The Holland Land Company purchased thousands of acres, but many settlers squatted on the land and refused to pay the land companies when there were conflicting claims, thereby slowing settlement. Settlers from Erie generally remained on the west side of the Allegheny River where hardwood forests prevailed, while east of the river, people from New York and New England settled the pine- and hemlock-forested higher land.

Lumbering and tanning in the early and mid-nineteenth century were displaced in the early 1860s by an oil frenzy. The Harmonists' experience was typical. Headquartered in Beaver County, they owned a timber tract in Limestone Township south of Tidioute. In 1861, they opened the first of their approximately seventy-five wells. By 1895, their holdings in Warren County were liquidated as the shallow oil supply was depleted. Their former landholdings have reverted to timber and are now part of the Allegheny National Forest.

Like all the counties of Pennsylvania's northern tier, Warren County has close ties to western New York. The Swedes who settled in Chandler's Valley in north-central Warren County emigrated from Jamestown, New York, in the mid-nineteenth century. The area is also connected architecturally, since Buffalo architects were often hired by Warren patrons. In addition, Chautauqua County in New York and Warren County share the Allegheny Reservoir, home of the Allegany Indian Reservation of the Seneca nation.

Kinzua Dam, completed in 1965, increased tourism, as the reservoir attracted boaters and fishing enthusiasts. Service industries now employ more people than either oil refining or lumbering. The county's largest employer is Blair Corporation, a mail-order company selling clothing and household items. The marketing of U.S. 6 as a scenic highway across the northern counties continues to foster tourism.

WARREN

The Eries, Delawares, and Shawnee called the land on which the city of Warren is situated Conewango, after the creek that flowed south from Lake Chautauqua in New York. Warren is one of seven western Pennsylvania towns created by the state between 1783 and 1795 to stimulate settlement on lands bordering Indian territory. Other than the large land speculators, few settlers came initially. Permanent settlement began in 1806 and the village became a borough in 1832 with a population of 358. A grid plan, reminiscent of Philadelphia's first settlement, was laid out on four hundred acres at the confluence of Conewango Creek and the Allegheny River. The town centered on the diamond at the intersection of Market and High (now 4th Avenue) streets. The only indication that this intersection was set aside as civic or public space is the courthouse on one corner. No other civic buildings are located here, and the commercial district never reached here from the river's edge.

A water-powered gristmill and several industries focused the town's growth on the banks of the Allegheny River. Between 1820 and 1845, the lumber industry dominated the economy. Logs were floated down the Allegheny for sale in Pittsburgh and beyond. Later, oil was pumped and shipped.

Warren has an array of large and often high-style houses along Liberty and Market streets between 2nd and 7th avenues, and along 2nd through 5th avenues from East to Laurel streets. This is the core of the residential section, with Greek Revival houses dating from the 1830s to Queen Anne and Colonial Revival houses at the turn of the twentieth century, all of them on spacious lots similar to those in Franklin and Titusville. Warren's prosperity lasted from 1875 through World War II, as evident in residences built for oil tycoons, bankers, barrel makers, and refinery owners. Many were designed by architects with national reputations. Warren has been wise in marketing

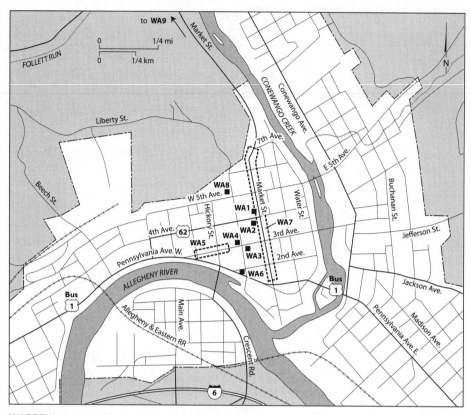

WARREN

and reusing their historic buildings as law offices and apartments, rather than replacing them. The Blair Corporation, founded as the New Process Company in 1910, moved into several existing brick buildings in 1926 and has combined them to form a handsome three-story maroon brick Art Deco headquarters with ribbon windows (1927, Austin Company, Fisher Architects, and Creal and Hyde Architects; 220 Hickory Street). Even the new construction conforms to traditional designs. The Municipal Building (1937; 318 W. 3rd Avenue) by Lawrie and Green, a Harrisburg firm, imitates elements from Independence Hall in Philadelphia.

WA1 Warren County Courthouse

1875–1877, Milton Earl Beebe; 1916, Edward Albert Phillips. 200 4th Ave.

This is one of the grandest representations of the Second Empire style among Pennsylvania's courthouses and was the first of five designed in the commonwealth by Milton Earl Beebe of Buffalo. All had the distinctive mansard roof, although they varied slightly in their details. Three of the courthouses remain in use in western Pennsylvania, this one and those in

Cambria (CA1) and Huntingdon (HU1) counties. The courthouse in Elk County (EL1) resembles this one, as the same contractor built it. Warren County's courthouse has concave mansard roofs set off by a pediment of Ohio limestone at the central bay on each side. A clock tower with a statue of Justice soars above the treetops. Warren architect Edward Albert Phillips (1870–1940) designed the rear addition. The single large courtroom on the second story, restored in 1998, retains the black walnut paneling with bullet holes from

1954 when Judge Allison Wade was killed on the bench—the incident that prompted the commonwealth to begin screening citizenry for weapons in courtrooms.

Next door, the former George H. Wetmore House (1873; 210 4th Avenue) was commissioned by Thomas Struthers for his daughter's marriage to businessman Wetmore. This Second Empire house was used as an office annex to the courthouse for fourteen years. Since 1964, the Warren County Historical Society has used it for a library, exhibition space, and archives.

WA2 Stone Mansion House (Ebenezer Jackson Tavern)

1833. 215 4th Ave.

This house is stylistically rooted in Pennsylvania rather than in the western New York and Ohio's Western Reserve Greek Revival tradition that is common to many other Warren houses of the period. It is the classic Pennsylvania five-bay stone house found in great numbers in the southwestern counties. This two-story house, one of the earliest buildings in Warren, was built as an inn, evident by its size and its location adjacent to the planned town square. The golden, smooth-faced sandstone is pierced by rows of double-sash windows that are slightly larger on the first story than on the second. Distinctive dormer windows punctuate the gable roof. In addition to

WA1 WARREN COUNTY COURTHOUSE

its role as an inn, the building has served a variety of functions over the years, including a bank and a private club.

WA3 Office Building (Thomas W. Jackson House)

c. 1830. 224 Liberty St.

This small one-and-one-half-story cottage humanizes what would otherwise be a strictly commercial section of Warren. Its picket fence and large tree provide a residential respite from the two- and three-story brick buildings around it. The returning eaves and corner boards place it squarely in the early Greek Revival tradition of the Western Reserve. Each of the three doors opens to a separate office space. The survival of three small Greek Revival houses—two frame and one brick—all dating from the 1830s within a four block area (402 Liberty Street; 506 East Street; and 415 W. 3rd Avenue—the last of these, the 1832 George Offerle House) is testimony to the basic conservatism of Warren and the town's understanding that reusing older residences in the commercial district provides continuity and stability.

WA4 Struthers Library Theatre

1883, David K. Dean; 1902, C. W. Terry; 1919, Warren and Wetmore; 1983–1984, Creal and Hyde Architects with Andrew Brooks. 302 W. 3rd Ave.

This three-story multipurpose building donated to the city of Warren by land baron, politician, and foundry operator Thomas Struthers is the core of Warren's cultural life. Built to house a public library, post office, auditorium, and Masonic Hall, it was remodeled in 1919 by Warren and Wetmore of New York to house the 1,100-seat Library Theatre. Charles D. Wetmore had just completed the design for the new library in Warren (see WA7). The architect's father was from Warren and he had many close relatives in town. Restored in 1983 by local architects, the theater continues to attract audiences, as does the shop on the first floor. This eclectic design incorporates a tower with dormers at one corner, a pediment at another, and variously shaped windows. Each story is delineated with a sill course, while the cornice is highlighted with corbeling.

WA5 West 3rd Avenue Houses

1900–1920. Albert Joseph Bodker and Edward Albert Phillips. 500 block W. 3rd Ave.

Houses designed by Albert Joseph Bodker (1875–1926) of New York City and Edward A. Phillips of Warren bracket some handsome American foursquare residences on this block of W. 3rd Avenue. They date from the turn of the twentieth century to the 1920s. From the Tudor Revival of the Bodker-designed house at 500 W. 3rd Avenue and the cottage style of 504 W. 3rd to the massive square outlines of the other houses, these houses indicate the high level of architectural sophistication in Warren.

WA6 National City Bank (Warren Savings Bank)

1891, Richard Alfred Waite. Pennsylvania and 2nd aves.

The Warren Bank Board of Directors chose English-born architect Richard Alfred Waite (1848–1911) to prepare the plans for this flat-iron building on the most prominent site in Warren. Known for designing insurance company office buildings in his home base of Buffalo, as well as in Toronto and Montreal, he came to the United States in the 1850s and studied to be a mechanical engineer in New York City, switching ultimately to the architectural firm of John Kellum. Waite secured his reputation in 1885–1893 when he designed Ontario's parliament building. A hexagonal clock tower with a copper roof marks the point of this triangular, four-story brick bank. Foliated brownstone carving ornaments the tower's triple-arched windows and a graceful staircase leads to the corner entrance.

WA7 Market Street District

c. 1830–1975. Market St. between Pennsylvania and 7th aves.

Market Street is the core of Warren, or, in deference to its four religious structures, the soul of Warren. Rarely does one find such a wealth of architecture in popular nineteenth- and twentieth-century styles in a city, let alone on one street. The only style missing is Georgian Revival, but a stone example is located around the corner at 215 4th Avenue. Within six blocks are buildings dating from the Greek Revival house of 1830 at 117 Market Street to the County Jail of 1975 at number 407 behind the courthouse. Several churches include the stone Romanesque Revival First Presbyterian Church by Cleveland architect Sidney R. Badgley (1894; 300 Market Street); the stone First United Methodist Church by Philadelphia architects Charles Weber Bolton and Son (1925; 200 Market Street); and the brick, Classical Revival First Baptist Church (c. 1925; 208 Market Street). Charles D. Wetmore of the New York City firm Warren and Wetmore designed the Warren Public Library (1915–1916; 205 Market Street) with inscriptions written by Charles W. Eliot, former president of Harvard, Wetmore's alma mater, carved into the limestone frieze above fluted Ionic columns.

Some of the houses have been adapted for new uses. The Conewango Club (1905; 201 Market Street), a five-bay, red brick Colonial Revival building with a two-story Ionic-columned portico by Edward A. Phillips was partially destroyed by a fire in June 2002, but has been restored by Linn Hyde. Washington, D.C., architect Carl Keferstein designed the crenellated brick castle (1886; 603 Market Street) for his sister. A handsome trio of Italianate houses c. 1868 has been reused as offices; a Church of Christ, Scientist, reading room; and a clubhouse. The frame Italianate house at number 301 is a stellar example of the style and represents the predominance of frame buildings in Warren. A modern house of 1955 at 511 Market Street is now an art gallery. The reuse of these residential buildings maintains the nineteenth-century ambience of the town.

WA8 Charles Warren Stone House

1905, Edward Albert Phillips. 505 Liberty St.

Charles Warren Stone, who commissioned this house, served as Pennsylvania's lieutenant governor in 1879 and secretary of the commonwealth from 1887 until 1890, when he went to the U.S. Congress for nine years. The large Colonial Revival brick house has three stories and two-story porches supported by Ionic columns, rectangular on the south and semicircular on the east elevation. Here Phillips, who mastered a variety of styles, reinterprets the colonial canon by using a broken round-arched pediment on the central dormer, and a trio of fanlit, glass-paned French doors set into a wall of panes on the south wall. The balcony with a decorative railing, the balustraded hipped roof, Flemish bond brickwork, and corner pilasters are all colonial derivatives. The brick, two-story, hipped-roof carriage house west of the main house has distinctive lintels above the first-story windows and portholes piercing all sides of the second story.

WA9 Warren State Hospital

1873–1882, Dr. Thomas Kirkbride with John Sunderland; many additions. Bounded by Jackson and N. State sts., Owen Rd., and U.S. 62, two miles northeast of Warren on the west bank of Conewango Creek

With its golden sandstone and rows of windows marching relentlessly across four stories,

WA8 CHARLES WARREN STONE HOUSE

WA9 WARREN STATE HOSPITAL

the main building of this hospital has a rather Dickensian appearance, making it easy to forget that this structure was a breakthrough in the humane treatment of the mentally ill. The building was constructed thirty years after Dr. Thomas Kirkbride began exhorting the state legislature to build hospitals rather than prisons for the treatment and study of mental illness. Today the state has nine mental health hospitals, three in western Pennsylvania (VE11).

John Sunderland, the contractor and supervising architect at Warren, earlier oversaw the building of the Philadelphia Hospital for the Insane in 1856–1859 under architect Samuel Sloan. Sunderland is listed in the Philadelphia directories as an architect after 1883. Only three years before construction on this building commenced, H. H. Richardson began designing the Buffalo State Hospital approximately seventy-five miles to the northeast, with landscaping by Frederick Law Olmsted. That hospital site was also outlined by a creek, and the grounds included a farm; farming was thought to be therapeutic for the mentally ill.

The Warren building's layout is relatively simple. The pedimented central section with flanking twin towers was constructed between 1876 and 1880. Two recessed fourteen-bay, three-story sections to the north and south are joined to the central wing by gable-roofed, four-story sections. While the stonework is carefully finished, its details are nearly lost in the massiveness of the building. The Olean conglomerate stone was found in two creek valleys nearby.

From 1898 to 1913, Green and Wicks designed various additions to the hospital, including the porte-cochere on the main building, Nurse's Annex, and North and South annexes. The firm's former employee, Edward A. Phillips, took up the commissions after 1906. A report in 1902 urged the state to expand the types of buildings available on the hospital campus to allow different buildings for various types and stages of mental illness. By 1913, Phillips had designed at least five additional buildings: Men's Annex; Men's Hygea; Employees' Building; J. Wilson Greenland's house, "Fairacre"; and a house called "Roseland" for the business manager. All were brick and finished with hipped roofs. Some had cupolas that echoed those on the main building, but their larger windows, deeper eaves, and smaller, residential scale softened their appearance.

Built between 1927 and 1930, the Rufus Barrett Stone Building "for acute cases" was designed by Eric Fisher Wood, who consulted with New York architect Sullivan Jones. Patients built the tunnel connecting it to the main building. In the late 1930s and early 1940s, federal funds were used to add several buildings to the campus, including the Mitchell Building by Walter T. Monahan and George Wesley Stickle architects. Between 1950 and 1952, the Pittsburgh firm of Palmgreen, Patterson and Fleming designed an X-shaped Admissions and Diagnostic building, now called the Curwen Building. Also in the early 1950s, Meadville architects Hanna and Stewart designed a patients' auditorium that was added to the rear of the main building. The Israel building by Pittsburgh architects Celli-Flynn Associates was constructed between 1967 and 1969 as an institute for geriatric research. The brick, hexagonal Interfaith Chapel, conceived in 1964 by Dr. Arland A. Dirlan, was dedicated in 1973 with an altar made of a five-ton sandstone block found on the property. It contains three worship spaces: Protestant, Catholic, and Jewish.

Two farms were affiliated with the hospital. "Farm Colony," north of the facility, has been demolished. The second, "Cranbrook," is two miles to the northeast, at the intersection of Hatch Run Road and Conewango Avenue Extension. Today, several rebuilt barns and outbuildings remain, but they are no longer owned by the hospital.

Since most of the staff was required to live on the campus, eighteen small brick houses dating from 1906 to the 1960s ring the grounds facing State Street. Buildings are distributed throughout the 470 acres owned by the hospital, with seemingly little regard for aesthetic placement. All are now occupied by commonwealth or county agencies and institutional lessees, lending the campus an air of purposefulness. The patient population has dropped from a high of roughly 3,000 to 200 today.

RUSSELL AND VICINITY

WA10 Guy Irvine House, "The Locusts"

1831–1835. U.S. 62, 5.5 miles northeast of Warren

One of the most beautiful houses in the region, as much for its setting as for its architectural form, the Irvine house was built as the lumber industry began to generate real wealth in the north woods. Guy C. Irvine, no relation to surveyor William Irvine or his sons (WA12), shipped lumber the length of the Allegheny-Ohio River corridors and often traveled along the same route. His familiarity with the best architecture of the region is apparent in the proportions and details of the house he commissioned for his family and his wife's sister's family. The dignity of the Greek Revival style, then very popular in western New York, is reflected in the well-proportioned house, its pedimented porch supported on Ionic columns, and door surrounds with figured leaded glass. Since it was built for two families, there are three sets of stairs, one in the central hall and smaller corner stairs in the dependencies. The heavy bridged chimneys are reminiscent of the Lyon house of 1833 in Bedford (BD8), but here the dependencies are attached rather than at the front of the property. The grove of locust trees in front, now more than double the height of the house, must have given Irvine a certain satisfaction in seeing the source of his livelihood from his parlor window. In 1964, the owners added a terrace using the stones from Guy Irvine's gristmill that had been north of the site on Conewango Creek.

WA11 Robert Russell House

1822–1827. Old Russell Rd. (PA 1015) at Liberty St.

One-and-a-half miles north of "The Locusts" on Conewango Creek, Robert Russell built this ruddy brick five-bay house. The relative sophistication of Warren's early settlers, broadened by their river travel, is apparent in the choice of architectural style. The gambrel-roofed barn is banked into the hillside just north of the house. At 20 Conewango Street, a c. 1841 white frame house constructed with foot-square beams has been owned by the Chase family since the 1850s.

IRVINE

WA12 Irvine Presbyterian Church

1838–1839, Robert Shortt. Main St. (PA 3022)

This elegant small stone church was intended to be part of the village of Cornplanter planned by the grandson of the area's original surveyor and owner, Revolutionary War soldier General William Irvine. Irvine's grandson, Dr. William Armstrong Irvine was raised in Philadelphia and attended the University of Pennsylvania's medical school (class of 1824), but he spent summers on the family's land in Warren County. He never practiced medicine, though, and in 1838, he and his wife moved permanently to the Warren County farm and into the Greek Revival house his father Callender Irvine built in 1822 (demolished). William A. was influential in building a turnpike from Warren to Franklin and encouraged the rail line that would carry oil and other goods through his property. The village of Dr. William A. Irvine's dreams, Cornplanter, was to include a stone hotel, school, store, and a bridge across the Allegheny River. Much of it was built, but very soon afterward, the village fell into disrepair as the family's fortunes waxed and waned. Dr. Irvine spent a lifetime holding on to the family's farmlands, despite crushing debts, missed opportunities, and swindling partners. His wife died in childbirth and had the first funeral in this church and burial in the walled family plot adjacent to the church. The church, a small stone "house in the hollow," and two tenant farmers' houses remain (WA13), scattered through the valley.

The small church, of random-laid sandstone, has a lunette in the gable end, corner quoins, and returning eaves. The double-sash windows each have twenty panes per sash and are round arched with keystones. Two blind windows flank the double entry doors on the north facade. A history of the family, *The Ir-*

WA12 IRVINE PRESBYTERIAN CHURCH

vine Story (1964) by Nicholas Wainwright, states that neighbor Robert Shortt, originally of Lockerbie, Scotland, who came to nearby Youngsville in 1833, was both mason and designer for the stone buildings on the property and in Irvine.

WA13 Irvine Tenant Houses

1841, Robert Shortt. Dunn's Eddy Rd. (U.S. 62)

As part of his model farm, William A. Irvine wanted stone rather than log or frame buildings. Two tenant houses near the Allegheny River remain from what were once a half-dozen small, two-story houses with simple detailing. The house on Dunn's Eddy Road, nearest the former mansion, is unused. A second stone house at the opposite end of the farm is a bunkhouse for the U.S. Forest Service. Both houses have two-foot-thick stone walls, double-sash six-over-six windows with lintels, and corner quoins. The houses resemble stone cubes, although the bunkhouse has one-story wings. The continued existence of these two cottages in fairly isolated settings could be of great value to the surrounding parklands as guest houses. The remains of some of the other buildings and early Native American artifacts on the former Irvine property have been excavated by archaeologists from Mercyhurst College in Erie.

TIDIOUTE

Tidioute has an important group of buildings located at a point where the Allegheny River runs east–west. The small village along the Warren-Franklin turnpike (U.S. 62) grew from a population of 400 to 10,000 when the oil started to flow in the 1860s (its population is now less than 1,000). The Allegheny River Transportation Line of 1862 opened the village to commerce by transporting barrels of oil north to the Philadelphia and Erie Railroad at

Irvine. Thirty years later, the village's population shrank to 800, but not before the residents built mansions and an opera house (now demolished) in the 1870s. The remaining brick and frame buildings represent nearly every architectural style popular between 1870 and 1900. The oldest building is an 1824 frame house at 194 Main Street facing the old turnpike; it has been considerably altered. The later Italianate house at 157 Main Street is sheathed in wood that is cut to emulate stone. The handsome Shingle Style house at 1 Elm Street may be architect-designed. The house at 193 Main Street of 1868 follows the design for "A Plain and Ornamented Villa" published in Samuel Sloan's *The Model Architect* in 1852. A trio of churches line Main Street: the board-and-batten former Unitarian church, now a Baptist church (1868; 218 Main Street); the brick Gothic Revival United Methodist church (1873; 206 Main Street); and the Queen Anne First Presbyterian Church (1893; 196 Main Street). Several one- to three-story brick commercial buildings of the 1870s remain to complete the ensemble, including the VFW Post 8803 at 93 Main Street. None of the structures is startling in its styling, but the high quality and integrity set this small river village, which has endured floods and fires over the years, apart from its neighbors.

WA14 Jahu Hunter House

c. 1870. 260 Main St.

Jahu Hunter, who invested in oil and timber, had this frame Second Empire mansion built facing the Warren-Franklin turnpike (now Main Street) rather than the Allegheny River, which flows behind the house. The facade is dominated by a three-story projecting tower with bull's-eye windows in the mansard roof. The first story retains its sweeping porch that wraps around three sides. A large frame barn to the east serves as a carriage house. The family offices were in the Hunter Building of 1894 adjacent to the bridge on Buckingham Street.

SHEFFIELD

WA15 George Horton House

1889, Alfred Smith. 416 S. Main St.

George Horton owned tanneries in Sheffield, Kane, and Ludlow (in McKean County). He often procured his hides from the stockyards in Chicago, and on one of his trips, there he admired a house by architect Alfred Smith (1841–1898), who was known for his Episcopal churches, apartment buildings, and residences. Smith supplied the design for this thirty-eight-room house, and possibly also for the summerhouse, carriage house, garage, and greenhouse built on the grounds. Although Horton died in 1893, his family kept the house until 1941; it was auctioned ten years later. Dominated by oversized half-timbered wall dormers, the house is highly picturesque. It has two towers, one with a conical roof at the northeast corner, and the other squat and set under the eaves of the northwest corner. The interior is fitted with oak trim and parquet floors. To power his domestic operation, Horton drilled a gas well on the property.

WA15 GEORGE HORTON HOUSE

At the north and south corners on the east side of Church and S. Main streets, a pair of very large frame Stick Style houses completes the triumvirate of fine houses in Sheffield.

MCKEAN COUNTY

As part of the Allegheny Plateau, McKean County has hilly topography reaching heights of from 1,400 to 1,600 feet, and has earned the designation "High Plateau." The Allegheny River, cutting across the northeastern corner of the county, and the watersheds of Potato, Tuna (aka Tunungwant), Kinzua, and Sinnemahoning creeks all contribute to this dramatic environment.

The land encompassing McKean County today was the hunting ground of the Seneca Indian tribes. The first European settlers came from Connecticut and that state claimed a swath of land along the northern tier of Pennsylvania. The border dispute was finally resolved in Pennsylvania's favor in 1782. Two years later, land was offered to citizens at $80 for one hundred acres with the stipulation that it be settled. Since the offer met without success, in 1792, the government then offered one hundred acres for $13 without the settlement clause. This time, wealthy buyers stepped in; the Holland Land Company alone bought two million acres in northern Pennsylvania and southern New York.

Settlers trickled into the area and began pushing for the creation of a new county. In 1804, the county was named for Thomas McKean, Pennsylvania's governor at the time, who purchased nearly three hundred acres there in 1805. McKean's goal was to fill the territory with Pennsylvanians rather than families from Connecticut, in the hope of resolving the boundary dispute with voters rather than written agreements. But settlement was very slow. By 1806, there were only 14 taxable inhabitants in the entire county, and merely 211 by 1821.

The county seat, at Smethport, was barely settled as late as 1832, since central and southwestern McKean County lacked navigable creeks. Lumbering began seriously in the 1830s. Borough names such as Port Allegany testify to the early transportation of goods by water in the eastern portions of the county. In 1856, Philadelphian Thomas L. Kane saw lumbering opportunity in the western part of the county and purchased the forested land around what today is the town of Kane. Railroads further spurred the lumber industry, and by 1900, nearly all the pine trees were harvested and only hemlock remained. Hemlock bark was used for tanning and wood chemical production as late as 1950. By 1925, however, both sawing and tanning were fading industries and nearly the entire county was deforested, causing erosion problems.

In the 1880s, McKean's population nearly quintupled with the discovery of oil. The county's oil was much deeper than oil in Venango County, and required drilling to 1,110 feet to make the labor cost effective. As wells farther west dried up, drilling in McKean became profitable. From 1879 to 1880, the number of producing wells in the Bradford area jumped from 4,000 to

11,200, and by 1881, the field produced twenty-three million barrels a year. Oil excitement lasted until 1900, when the field was considered exhausted, producing only two million barrels per year in 1906. There was a brief resurgence in the 1920s when engineers discovered that flooding old wells could force out more oil, but the industry was dying.

However, professional timber management began to rejuvenate the deforested areas with the planting of hardwoods, especially black cherry. In 1923, the creation of the Allegheny National Forest, with 135,000 of its 500,000 acres in McKean County, brought recreation and tourism. Another industry reliant on natural resources was glass, which, with the abundance of silica sandstone and cheap natural gas, flourished here. From 1895 to 1905, McKean County led the nation in glass production, making window glass, bottles, wire glass, and fireproof windows and doors. Port Allegany has the large Pittsburgh Corning Corporation complex (U.S. 6 at PA 155), with several additions designed c. 1950 by Raymond Viner Hall.

Bradford, the largest city along the northern tier after Erie, benefited from the variety of industries supported by the county's natural resources. Located on the major north–south access road, U.S. 219, the city also benefits from the marketing of U.S. 6, a scenic route across the northern counties of Pennsylvania, with tourist sites and lodgings advertised nationally. Hunting, hiking, and winter sports continue to grow in the county's state forest lands.

SMETHPORT

Smethport is located on a floodplain adjacent to Potato Creek, which empties into the Allegheny River. The John Keating Land Company, whose agent surveyed the site in 1807, donated land for the settlement. Keating chose to name it after his two Amsterdam bankers, Raymond and Theodore de Smeth. The village's development was delayed by its distance from the Allegheny River.

Solomon Sartwell, a New Hampshire builder, settled in Smethport in 1816. Protestant families from Connecticut moved here in the 1830s and 1840s. By 1853, the village was incorporated as a borough and a trading center for lumbermen, as well as being the county seat. The arrival of the railroad and the discovery of oil created a demand for housing. With little pressure for later development, the best of these houses remain intact. One of the reasons U.S. 6, also known as the Grand Army of the Republic Highway, is considered scenic is that it passes through this charming town. Additionally, the handsome courthouse (MK1) and several substantial, high-style, late-nineteenth- and early-twentieth-century houses line Main Street, notably the former Charles McKean House (1904; W. Main and Mechanic streets) and the former Orlo Hamlin house (1900–1901; 911 W. Main Street), now adapted for apartments. Stylistically, the houses range from Queen Anne to Italianate, some have classical detailing, and several have cupolas. As would be expected in a timber area, more houses are of wood than of brick.

The former home of banker Orlo Hamlin, now the Christmas Inn, 911 W. Main Street, Smethport.

MK1 McKean County Courthouse

1942, Thomas K. Hendryx and Bley and Lyman. 500 W. Main St.

A devastating fire in 1940 burned the W. Main Street portion of the earlier courthouse. It was replaced with this brick building with a pedimented portico supported by six Ionic columns and a cupola reminiscent of Independence Hall's in Philadelphia. Stone quoins define all the corners and link the new portion to wings dating from 1914 and 1938 that survived the fire. The wings, each of eight bays, feature windows of varied forms, including round, segmental, and rectangular arched. Inside, the one-story rotunda at the intersection of the hallways has Ionic detailing in marble, which is repeated in wood in the courtroom. Thomas K. Hendryx (1906–1970), a 1923 graduate of Cornell University, is responsible for two modern buildings in his hometown of Bradford, the Kubiak building (MK5) and the Bradford Regional Medical Center's all-aluminum exterior wing (MK11).

MK2 Smethport Historical Society (Sheriff's House and Jail)

1870. 502 W. King St.

McKean County's former jail resembles an Italianate house of the period, a role it partially served since the sheriff lived there. This "house," however, is distinguished from other Italianate houses by the large, two-story, stone cell block pierced by narrow windows, attached behind it. The main entrance to the house is set within a triple-arched two-story projecting bay. A two-story brick wing to the east continues the arched corbeling on the front cornice. Attached to this wing is a small one-story pyramidal-roofed structure that originally housed the juvenile cells. Stone corner quoins on the jail are echoed on the courthouse, stylistically linking Smethport's two public buildings.

MK3 St. Luke's Episcopal Church

1891–1893, William Halsey Wood. 602 W. Main St.

William Halsey Wood is noted for his Gothic Revival work, which, as here, is often composed of simple geometric forms with minimal ornamentation that give it an almost protomodern character. Wood used a textured local sandstone, shallow gabled roof, and a square corner tower with minimal but distinctive windows at each stage. A side chapel at the southwest corner is balanced by the corner tower to the southeast. Keeping the triple-lancet clerestory windows small and having smaller windows along the side aisles gives the church an almost fortresslike quality. The side entrance, facing south onto W. Main Street, leads directly to the high altar, but is rarely used, as the Church Street entrance is preferred. An oak rood screen and carved pine rafters adorn the interior. The Shingle Style parish hall slightly northwest of the church was built in 1901–1902, after Wood's death but according to his drawings.

BRADFORD AND VICINITY

Located at the confluence of Tuna, Kendall, and Foster creeks, Bradford was established as a supply town for the lumber industry. Originally called Littleton, it was named after the U.S. Land Company's agent, Colonel Leavitt C. Little. By 1854, the town's name was changed to Bradford after the New Hampshire town from which the second land agent, Daniel Kingsbury, had emigrated.

The Erie Railroad opened to Bradford in 1866, followed by the Buffalo, Rochester and Pittsburgh line in 1883. By then, oil drilling had spread to Bradford, where oil production increased from 36,000 barrels to 23 million barrels per year. Between 1875 and 1881, nearly 9,000 wells were drilled. The elaborate frame and brick houses lining the 100 and 200 blocks of Congress Street, and of Jackson Avenue to School Street between Petrolia and N. Bennett streets, demonstrate how those who benefited from the boom spent their money. The Colonial Revival houses with Queen Anne touches date from 1890 to 1920. Several headquarters and commercial buildings designed by such architects as Enoch A. Curtis of Fredonia, New York, Green and Wicks of Buffalo, and Philadelphian Edward N. Unruh, who relocated to Bradford, enhance the downtown core as a result of the oil boom. Bradford's fairly large commercial district with two high-rise office buildings, a theater, and several fraternal organizations serves a regional population. The city has designated a downtown historic district and hired a Main Street manager to further their goals of both attracting tourists to the Zippo factory (MK10) and outdoor enthusiasts to the nearby trails. A street lining the town square is now named for mezzo-soprano Marilyn Horne, who was born in Bradford in 1934 and moved to Southern California in 1945.

MK4 Office Building (City Hall)

1898, Enoch A. Curtis. 15 Kennedy St.

This charming building is an eclectic mix of Richardsonian Romanesque arches, Second Empire mansard-roofed pavilions, and classical detailing. A square overscaled clock tower anchors the northeast corner. The building has not housed the city hall since 1965 and is currently used as office space. A graphic depiction of the building now serves as the city's logo since its restoration. Enoch A. Curtis (1831–1907) from Fredonia, New York, also designed Christ Episcopal Church in Oil City, Venango County (VE14).

Adjacent, at 54 Boylston Street, the three-story, red brick Medical Plaza building (c. 1890; 1904 addition) has sandstone quoins, a bracketed and rosette-lined cornice, and lintels with keystones.

MK5 Kubiak Building

1930, Thomas K. Hendryx. 28 Kennedy St.

Commissioned the same year as the Hooker Fulton building (MK7), this office building and

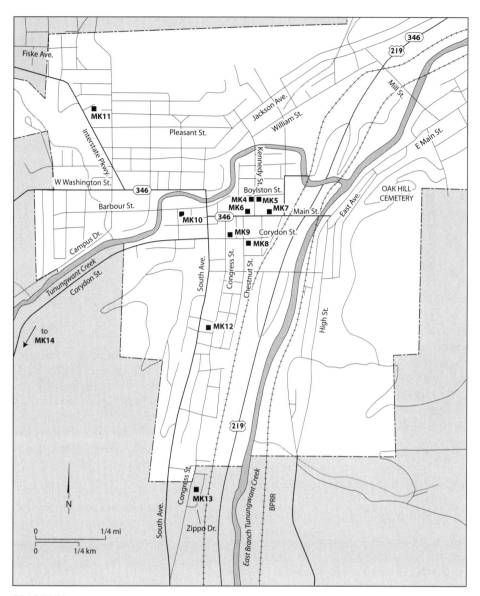

BRADFORD

its neighbor at 24 Kennedy Street look like they belong in South Beach, Miami, Florida, not in Bradford, Pennsylvania. Hendryx highlights the entrance of this two-story, white glazed-brick Art Deco building with layers of recessed brick and articulates the facade with ribbed corbeling and stylized corner blocks. Next door, the former Healy Petroleum Building (1942, F. Fensel), now City Hall, has a tall, recessed vertical window above the entrance to light the interior staircase, which contrasts the horizontal emphasis of the wraparound corner windows. A simple cornice of saw-

tooth ornament outlines the flat roof of the three-story, white brick structure.

MK6 Jack and Jill Shop (C. L. Bradburn Building, Knights of Pythias Hall)

1890, F. C. French. 111–113 Main St.

The three-story, seven-bay building has detailing popular on cast-iron-fronted buildings from the 1870s. Small Corinthian columns separate the bay windows on the second story and punctuate the third-story windows. The building is topped with a parapet, a tablet

MK7 BRADFORD THEATER AND HOOKER FULTON OFFICE BUILDING

with the building's original name, and a diminutive pediment. The first-story storefronts have been modernized.

An equally ornate four-story, buff brick building, the Option House (1901; 41 Main Street), is three bays wide and has a balcony above the first story, lions' heads at the cornice, and foliated limestone trim and dentils.

MK7 Bradford Theater and Hooker Fulton Office Building

1930–1931, Lawrie and Green. 119–125 Main St.

This building's restrained Art Deco styling raises it above the average office structure of the northern tier. At eight stories, it towers above the commercial district of Bradford and has two slightly projecting bays on either end of the facade that define the six central bays. The top floor is decorated in a stepped design inspired by ziggurats. Black and mint-green harlequin tile medallions ornament the side elevations, clearly never intended to be obscured by adjacent buildings. The first story has the only marquee and, more important, the only operating movie theater for several adjacent counties.

Two other multistory buildings face the city's central square at the opposite end of Main Street: the eight-story, red brick Emery Towers, the former Hotel Emery, with corner quoins and floral motifs above the upper-story

windows (c. 1930; 2 South Avenue); and the six-story, golden-yellow brick Seneca Building (c. 1930; 6–10 Marilyn Horne Way) with aluminum spandrels in a wave pattern. The B.P.O. Elks (14 Marilyn Horne Way) was designed by Aretis P. Mount from Corry in Erie County, with project architect Edward N. Unruh in 1914. This eclectic building is dominated by a large multipaned window lighting the second story, and a shaped parapet with a bull's-eye window. The castellated Bradford Armory at 28 Barbour Street was also designed by Mount.

MK8 SuperUser Technologies, Inc. (U.S. Post Office)

1911–1913, Edward N. Unruh, James Knox Taylor, supervising architect of the U.S. Treasury. 80 E. Corydon St.

Architect Edward N. Unruh (1852–1926) designed over forty buildings in Bradford, including many homes. For this post office, he created an understated brick building with six Ionic columns fronting its round-arched entrance. Oversized stone-trimmed windows, corner quoins, and a roof parapet and balustrade complete the ornamentation. The interior, with an open lobby and stairway, has been converted to offices for a high-tech firm.

MK9 Beefeater's Restaurant (Carnegie Free Library of Bradford)

1900–1901, Green and Wicks. 27 Congress St.

This Carnegie Library was designed by Edward B. Green Sr. (1855–1950) and his partner, William Sydney Wicks (1854–1919) of Buffalo. The firm designed art museums and university buildings mostly in the neoclassical mode. The Bradford library follows this pattern with an entrance flanked by a pair of Tuscan columns and alternating round-arched windows with medallions on the long E. Corydon Street side. A dentiled cornice and balustrade at the parapet complete the classical ornamentation. The library's entrance is flush with the sidewalk, not set back behind a flight of stairs as is usual, and it has a raised basement with large windows.

MK10 Zippo Headquarters and Offices

1955, Wheeler and Associates. 33 Barbour St.

The Zippo headquarters in downtown Bradford is a sleek Moderne building. A three-dimensional sign in the shape of a lighter, bearing the initials of the founder, George G. Blaisdell, rises above the entrance. Across the street, a small single-car garage was the first office space belonging to Zippo. It is identifiable by the Moderne lettering above the garage door and the lighter-shaped streetlights in the adjacent parking lot. The lighters were originally manufactured in the two-story section of the headquarters, which was adapted from an old horse barn in the late 1930s. A three-story section was opened in 1955, and in 1994, the building's original sheathing was replaced with a dark forest-green reflective glass that appears black.

MK11 Bradford Regional Medical Center

1938; 1949–1951, Thomas K. Hendryx; many additions; 1993, Cannon Architects. 116 Interstate Pkwy.

Bradford's hospital was the second building in the nation to have an all-aluminum exterior. The first, in Davenport, Iowa, was built as a test run for the Alcoa Regional Enterprise Tower in Pittsburgh (AL28). Here in McKean County, a reinforced concrete frame was built with steel angles to anchor the lightweight concrete and one-quarter-inch gunmetal-gray cast-aluminum panels of the exterior shell. The panels were attached from the inside, making exterior scaffolding unnecessary. They were approximately eighty pounds per square foot lighter than the usual building materials at the time. The five-story, butterfly-wing-shaped, 219-bed hospital has remained unchanged from its original appearance. Attached to the east is the core of the hospital dating from 1938. Additions, which appear on average every twenty years, have been built to the north, south, and east of the Hendryx-designed portion.

MK12 David Phillips Sr. House

1888. 176 Congress St.

This riotously elaborate frame Queen Anne house reflects the financial exuberance of those who profited from the first oil strikes near Bradford. While its architect is unknown, the house resembles a design by George Franklin Barber of Knoxville, Tennessee, who sold architectural plans by mail. There are more than a dozen known Barber houses in western Pennsylvania, and probably many more that have never been documented. This house retains most of its original details, including a circular balcony covered by a conical tower, ridgeline cresting, a horseshoe-shaped window in the front gable, and a patterned chimney.

MK13 Zippo Museum

1997, Preston R. Abbey and Associates. 1932 Zippo Dr.

The Zippo/Case Visitors' Center uses architecture as a clever marketing tool and tourist promotion. The museum and retail store, just outside the commercial district of Bradford, are accessible to travelers along scenic U.S. 6 and U.S. 219. The pale mauve cement-block facility tells the story of the windproof lighter coveted by GI's during World War II and of the

MK10 ZIPPO HEADQUARTERS AND OFFICES   MK11 BRADFORD REGIONAL MEDICAL CENTER

knives important to hunters the world over. Technicians repair broken lighters behind plate glass to fulfill the company promise "it works or we fix it free." The lighting fixtures in the parking lot simulate flaming lighters, just as the streetlights in Hershey, Pennsylvania, simulate Hershey Kisses. One enters the building below an oversized lighter in the open position with a glowing neon flame. The building is a large, one-story rhomboid with a two-story polished black granite entrance block.

MK14 Glendorn (Clayton Glenville Dorn and Forest Dorn Summer Estate)

1916; 1929, A. W. Schoenberg; Olaf William Shelgren Sr. and Jr.; later additions. 1000 Glendorn Dr., 6 miles southwest of Bradford

Since 1995, this rural retreat has been open to the public as a luxury restaurant and resort. There are seventeen cabins dating from 1916 to the 1950s on the 1,280-acre site adjacent to the Allegheny National Forest and seventeen miles of trails, a trout stream, and a large swimming pool. The complex was built by Clayton G. "Bondieu" Dorn and his son Forest, who founded Forest Oil Corporation in 1916, a company that forced water into wells presumed dry so they could retrieve the oil, which floated to the surface. Initially, the land held only a simple fishing cabin, but, in 1929, A. W. Schoenberg of Buffalo designed a redwood cabin like those in the Adirondacks with a two-story living room dominated by a massive sandstone fireplace. The redwood logs of the lodge are planed smooth on the interior but rounded on the exterior to simulate a log cabin. The shingled roof slopes steeply to accommodate snow loads, and has jerkinhead roofs and an eyebrow dormer on the facade.

Because Forest was in the lumber business, the cabin interiors have a variety of paneling, including pecky cypress, knotty pine, butternut, and chestnut. The estate can accommodate thirty guests in cabins built over the years by various Dorn children and relatives. Two architects from Buffalo, Olaf William Shelgren (1891–1972) and his son, Olaf William "Bill" Shelgren Jr., designed the most interesting cabins.

PORT ALLEGANY AND VICINITY

MK15 St. Joseph's Episcopal Church

1887–1888. 116 E. Arnold St.

This Stick Style church would seem to have an earlier date based on its appearance, but it was built in the late 1880s by a local contractor named Groves. The steeply pitched hipped roof builds to a narrow spire. Side elevations have gabled wall dormers that are pierced by small circular windows inside ornamental frames. On the interior, a single aisle with seven pews on each side leads to a shallow transept now partially enclosed by the parish hall addition (1954) at the rear. One large and two small stained glass windows line the nave. An article from Sunday, July 22, 1888, in *The Church News* describing the first service in the church notes that information about the plan "will be given by the New York Building Plan Co., 160 Broadway, New York." That business was run by architect Manly N. Cutter from 1888 to 1892. The surrounding neighborhood also has several distinctive frame houses from this time period.

Seven miles north, St. Mary's Roman Catholic Church (1871; Newell Creek Road, off PA 446 at Sartwell) was constructed during the first days of the oil excitement and located in the middle of the great forest. It is basically a Greek Revival church with narrow-gauge wood siding and corner boards, heavy eaves returns, and a full cornice. Uncharacteristically, it also has lancet and rose windows, and a prominent cupola. Founded in 1842 by an Irish congregation, St. Mary's is the "mother church" for six other Roman Catholic parishes in McKean and Potter counties. A cemetery surrounds the church.

MK16 Lynn Hall Estate

1935–1937, Walter J. and Raymond Viner Hall.
U.S. 6, 1.3 miles northwest of Port Allegany

Walter J. Hall (1878–1952), the builder of this house, was the general contractor for Frank Lloyd Wright's contemporaneous Fallingwater (FA28) and a designer in his own right. He knew that U.S. 6 was being rerouted through this area and built this structure as a hotel and restaurant to cater to travelers. However, it failed as such during World War II. Walter's son, Raymond Viner Hall, designed the living quarters and refitted the restaurant as an architectural studio in 1954.

Tucked into the hillside among the pine

MK16 LYNN HALL ESTATE

trees, the house, with its horizontal lines, alternating use of stone, banded ornamental concrete, and glass block, has an elegance unknown in the surrounding timber and oil lands. In the Wrightian manner, the house has a flat roof with deeply overhanging eaves, varied levels of stone, radiant-heated floors, and built-in cabinetry and furnishings. The use of reinforced concrete beams is ambitious. Although currently deteriorating, the house has a large light-filled studio as well as living spaces and several bedrooms. A small, similarly styled guest house, originally the pump house, lies to the south.

Raymond Viner Hall specialized in residential and school designs. Fine examples of both may be seen in Port Allegany in the Port Allegany Union High School (1954; 200 Oak Street) and thirteen houses commissioned by Walter Hall's nephew Howard Baker and called Baker's Acres (c. 1948; Keating Avenue and Katherine Street).

MOUNT JEWETT

MK17 Nebo Lutheran Chapel and Cemetery

1887. W. Main St. (U.S. 6)

The simple Swedish Evangelical Lutheran Church surveys the countryside from its perch atop Mount Jewett, just as Moses once looked upon the promised land from Mount Nebo. Patterned after Ersta Kyrka at Danviken near Stockholm, Sweden, it is a white frame octagon with rectangular extensions at the front and rear, and has a central cupola. Gothic-arched windows with clear panes and simple double-sash windows below them light the two-story-high sanctuary. The simple paneled double entrance doors are sheltered by a gable-roofed porch supported on narrow wooden posts. A large cemetery surrounds the church and slopes down the hillside.

KANE

The southern and western parts of McKean County were the last to be settled, since they were inaccessible by water. In 1856, Thomas Leiper Kane visited the area and two years later, after his father's death, took up the challenge of developing it. Kane was an avid reformer and a man of principle who resigned a high paying position as a U.S. commissioner because he refused to enforce the Fugitive Slave Law of 1850. His wife, Elizabeth Dennistoun Wood Kane, was an early graduate of the Female Medical College of Pennsylvania, and his older brother was a well-known Arctic explorer. In McKean County, Thomas Kane built a sawmill, commissioned roads and railroads, sold land to Swedish settlers from southern New York, and planned farms. During the Civil War, he commanded the local woodsmen of the Bucktail Brigade. Afterward, he returned to McKean County nearly broken, financially and physically. He built a lumber business and later made a fortune with the discovery of oil.

Architecturally, the town of Kane has several highlights, especially the Kane Memorial Chapel (MK18) and the former First National Bank of Kane (1895; 67 Fraley Street). The outstanding feature of the three-story buff brick former bank is the round entrance arch ornamented with geometric designs, reminiscent of the "Golden Door" on the Transportation Building designed by Adler and Sullivan for the 1893 World's Columbian Exposition in Chicago. The interior is crafted with the same opulence and now houses a law office.

MK18 Kane Memorial Chapel (Kane Presbyterian Church)

1876–1878, Henry J. Taylor. 30 Chestnut St.

Thomas Leiper Kane and his family built this Presbyterian church to emulate a Gothic church in Kent, England, which Kane and his cousin Robert Fielding had seen on a trip abroad in 1838. Fielding built a four-foot-tall model of this chapel for architect Henry Taylor of Philadelphia. The cruciform plan church has a complicated roof plan: hipped on the east elevation at the altar and gable-roofed at

MK18 KANE MEMORIAL CHAPEL (KANE PRESBYTERIAN CHURCH)

the transept ends and facade, and highlighted by a pair of hipped-roof entrance pavilions. The facade and transept ends each have a rose window, and there is a square-based spire at the intersection of nave and transepts. No two elevations are alike. Gothic-arched windows are spaced differently on each elevation. The interior trusswork is of black cherry from the nearby Kinzua area, and the exterior walls of pinkish sandstone are from Clay's quarry near Wilcox. In the late 1850s, Thomas Kane studied the Mormons and took up their cause in Utah, persuading them to accept a non-Mormon governor and thereby averting a military confrontation. He chose to be buried here in Kane, and Mormons restored the chapel and maintain it to honor his memory.

MK19 Kane Manor Inn (Kane House, "Anoatok")

1896–1897, Cope and Stewardson. 230 Clay St.

This large Georgian Revival mansion would be a sophisticated addition to any urban area, but in a town the size of Kane, it is monumental. Built for Thomas Kane's family after his death, the house replaced the earlier home lost to a fire in 1896. Katherine D. Kane, Thomas's mother, commissioned the Philadelphia firm of Cope and Stewardson to design the house. Katherine Kane's nephew-in-law, Walter Cope of the Cope and Stewardson firm, designed a home large enough for her extended family, with a medical office for Katherine's daughter-in-law, Dr. Elizabeth Kane. Cope designed a commodious buff brick dwelling with a two-and-one-half-story hipped-roof central portion joined to a smaller hipped-roof pavilion to the south. On the north, a rounded two-story, Ionic-columned porch shows its elegant face to the surrounding forest. A smaller one-story porch on the east elevation has been enclosed. The house sits on 10 acres and is adjacent to another 240 that offer four miles of hiking trails. The house was named "Anoatok," an Eskimo word meaning "wind-loved spot" that honored Katherine's other son, Elisha Kent Kane, an Arctic explorer in the 1850s. The ten bedrooms and large basement space now accommodate a bed-and-breakfast.

LUDLOW

MK20 Olmsted Manor Adult Retreat-Renewal Center (George Welsh Olmsted Estate)

1916–1917, Albert Joseph Bodker; Alling Stephen DeForest, landscape architect; 1976, James A. Morgan; 1980, Robert Frost; later additions. U.S. 6

George Welsh Olmsted was born in nearby Ridgway and was the son of the first Elk County sawmill owner. He came to Ludlow to work in a general store, and ultimately bought the tannery here. He married and raised two children in Ludlow. After electrifying his tannery, Olmsted began investing in electric companies and later served as the first president of the Long Island Lighting Company. This house is a testimony to his savvy investments.

He commissioned New York City architect Albert Bodker, who reluctantly agreed to spend a year in the small town of Ludlow, to build this steeply roofed and multigabled Tudor Revival house. It features a stone first story, half-timbering above, and leaded casement windows. The comfortable interior has oak paneling, a cork-floored game room, and two small bowling lanes on the third floor. Bodker must have adjusted to life in the northern woods of Pennsylvania, because the following year, he designed a house at 500 W. 3rd Avenue in Warren (WA5).

The hillside site was sculpted by landscape architect Alling Stephen DeForest (1875–1957), who worked in the Brookline offices of the Olmsted Brothers (no relation to George Olmsted) for three years before opening his own practice in Rochester. He designed gardens for George Eastman in Rochester and Harvey Firestone in Akron. DeForest began designing the Olmsted gardens as early as 1912, and he maintained a friendship with the Olmsteds for twenty-eight years. The grounds included terraced flower gardens and cascading fountains. Seven gates for the 325-acre property were crafted by metal craftsman Samuel Yellin. DeForest also designed nearby Wildcat Park east of Ludlow on U.S. 6, beginning in 1922. Olmsted donated a gate and gatehouse to the park in 1929.

Mrs. Olmsted remained at the house until 1960. In 1969, the estate was transferred to the Western Pennsylvania Annual Conference of the United Methodist Church for use as an adult retreat and renewal center. In 1976, Groves Lodge, a three-story hotel and dining area, was added. The church built Hickman Hall, a director's residence, and restored the gardens in 1979. An annex was added in 1997 to provide three stories of rooms accessible to wheelchairs. None of the additions has directly affected the estate house itself, as each is located along the hillside to the south.

POTTER COUNTY

Potter County, surveyed in the 1790s, was owned largely by Philadelphian William Bingham, the Ceres Land Company, and the Holland Land Company at the time of its incorporation in 1804. The county was named for Irish-born Revolutionary War officer Major General James Potter, who ran unsuccessfully for president of the commonwealth in 1782 under the banner of the Radical Party.

The headwaters of three major river systems—the Genesee, the Allegheny, and the West Branch Susquehanna—are located in this county. Near Brookland, water flows in three directions: north via the Genesee River to the Saint Lawrence Seaway, south to the Susquehanna and the Atlantic, and southwest to the Allegheny-Ohio-Mississippi River system and the Gulf of Mexico. The topography is typical of the Allegheny High Plateau, with rolling hills dotted with farms in the north and mountainous ridges in the south. Susquehannock State Forest in the south is named after an indigenous Native American tribe. Covering 262,000 acres, the forest is dominated by second-growth northern hardwoods, including beech, maple, and black cherry. The forest has eighty-nine miles of foot trails, as well as three natural gas storage fields, including the Leidy gas field, one of the largest and deepest subterranean pools of natural gas in the world.

The Jersey Shore Turnpike, an early pack trail and wagon road that roughly follows the route of PA 44, was built in 1834 and was one of the first major roads in the county. It joined the town of Jersey Shore on the Susquehanna River to Coudersport and then to Olean, New York.

Remote forested areas like Potter County were subjected to grand colonization schemes during the nineteenth century. In the early 1800s, the Ceres Land Company sent settlers to the area, where they surveyed Coudersport for the county seat. Later, in 1852, Norwegian violinist Ole Bornemann Bull purchased 11,144 acres of land in Potter County after touring the United States. He hoped to establish Norwegian settlements and laid out four villages, but ambiguously worded land titles and the severe hardships of life caused all four to fail. Stone remnants of Bull's cabin remain in Ole Bull State Park. Germania, located northeast of the park, was founded in 1855 by Germans fleeing the European revolutions of 1848. Their settlements expanded to Roulette and Dutch Hill in the 1880s.

Potter County's principal industry was lumbering and wood processing, followed by farming and the raising of livestock. With rail access, these industries brought the population to a peak of 30,621 in 1900. The Pennsylvania Lumber Museum (P07) has re-created a logging camp and teaches tourists about the ways lumber was harvested and processed. The museum is located midway between what were two of the largest sawmills in the nation, at Galeton and Austin near the eastern and western borders of the county.

Austin Dam, built in 1909 by the Bayless Pulp and Paper Company, pooled Freeman Run north of Austin. From the beginning, the dam was plagued with cracks and structural problems. It burst on September 30, 1911, killing seventy-eight people in the downstream towns of Austin and Costello. After the flood, the commonwealth passed legislation to monitor the engineering of dams. The dam's concrete ruins north of Austin are listed on the National Register and, taking a page from Johnstown's flood museums (CA14), signs nearby proclaim Austin as the "best town by a dam site." Floods and fires also did enormous damage to Galeton on the east side of the county. First known as Pike Mills, it was incorporated in 1896. Its tannery, sawmills, and railroads swelled the village of 281 people to 4,000. By 1889, most of the virgin timber was cut, and, as at Austin, Galeton became a commuter town and now serves outdoor recreationists.

COUDERSPORT

Coudersport, with a population of just under 3,000, is the largest town in heavily wooded Potter County. It was named for Jean Samuel Coudere, an Amsterdam banker who loaned money to the Ceres Land Company of Philadelphia for their Pennsylvania land purchases. Located in the river plain at the confluence of the Allegheny River and Mill Creek, the streets were laid out in 1807 in a grid pattern. The tree-shrouded mountains that surround Coudersport limited access to the town and delayed settlement until c. 1835. It was incorporated as a borough in 1848. Lumbering was the major industry from 1815 to 1920. Until sawmills were built in Coudersport in the 1880s, white pine and hemlock logs and shingles were floated down the Allegheny River on rafts to mills.

John Keating of the Ceres Land Company donated lands for the county's public buildings. Local Quakers, led by Keating's employee Francis King and his descendants, became known for their Underground Railroad activity, and Coudersport had at least two way-stations for escaping slaves before the Civil War. Wood was the favored building material until a major fire in 1880 destroyed much of the frame commercial district, inspiring an early building code that required brick construction for future buildings. The business district was listed on the National Register of Historic Places in 1985. A fine example of woodworking skill is the Gothic Revival house (1852; 1862 addition; 401 N. West Street) built by local carpenter Miles White. The two-and-one-half-story steeply pitched roof structure features wide bracketed eaves, looped bargeboards, and a central chimney.

The narrow-gauge Coudersport and Port Allegany Railroad served the town from 1882, connecting with the Western New York and Pennsylvania Railroads at Port Allegany. Today, U.S. 6 and PA 44 intersect at Coudersport. Adelphia Communications, a national telecommunications company, was located in Coudersport until it downsized and moved to Colorado. The company's lavish four-story, red brick former headquarters building with a marble-columned entrance, mansard roof, and elongated round-arched windows, was designed in 2001 by Burt Hill Kosar Rittelmann Associates (102 S. Main Street).

PO1 Potter County Courthouse

1851–1853, William Bell; 1888–1889, Homer Hall and George Abson. 1 E. 2nd St.

The Potter County courthouse is the focal point of this small town and provides a pleasant block of green space along with the requisite Civil War monument. The building is crowned by a statue of Justice that is unusual because she lacks the traditional blindfold. Because it was built in two parts separated by thirty-five years, the courthouse's proportions and styles are mismatched. The lower two stories, built in the 1850s, are Greek Revival, while the gabled upper portion, added in the 1880s, is picturesque.

William Bell, a contractor from Warren, built the earlier two-story brick rectangle with a pedimented gable end facing the street and a domed two-staged clock tower. Within thirty years, the interior roof beams began to rot, as the accumulation of snow in this mountainous region strained its shallow pitch and caused it to leak. Architect Homer Hall, of Olean, New York, rectified the problem by removing the entire roof and rebuilding it of slate at a much steeper pitch. He added a taller square clock tower with an elliptical dome and large dormer windows on the sides and gave the front gable a triple-arched window. The original entablature circles the building. Hall resigned prior to the completion of the work amidst complaints of its extravagance. George Abson completed the project. The interior reflects many of the changes made in the late 1880s, including a central hall with offices on both sides and a divided staircase leading to the second-story courtroom at the front. Between 1933 and 1934, the Civil Works Administration strengthened the foundation and excavated the basement to create office space.

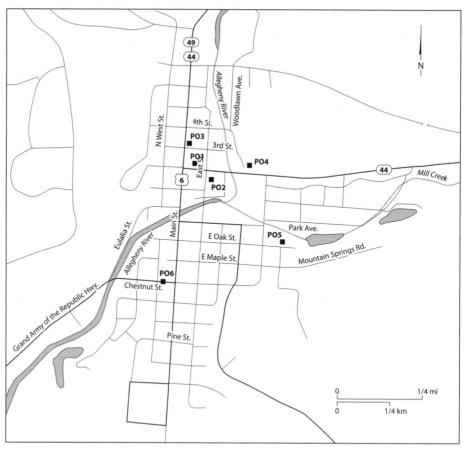

COUDERSPORT

PO1 POTTER COUNTY COURTHOUSE

PO2 Potter County Jail

1869–1870, Edward Haviland. 102 E. 2nd St.

Edward Haviland designed two other jails in the western half of the commonwealth (CA3 and BL3). Starkly simple, this jail lacks the battlements and Gothic accoutrements of his other jail designs. A pyramidal roof covers the two-story building. Round-arched windows and door give the jail a Romanesque flavor, enhanced by the rough-cut stone surround of the main entrance, over the first-story windows, and for the corner quoins. The twenty-foot-high walls of the exercise yards on both sides of the jail are constructed of a greenish-hued stone. The small population of Potter County, always cautious about public expenditures, was outraged over the expense of the courthouse and its later repairs. To please them, no doubt, the jail was built from stone salvaged from the demolished courthouse of 1835. The removal of the building's cupola helps explain its present simplicity.

PO3 Potter County Historical Society (Arthur G. Olmstead House)

1892, 1982, 2000–2001. 308 N. Main St.

This twin-gabled orange-red brick double house was divided into two parts. The southern section consisted of the town library downstairs and a judge's office upstairs, while the northern was a residence for the judge's son. The core of the house is a hipped-roof section recessed between two gabled portions. A bracketed cornice and wooden porches with Eastlake decoration complete the ornamentation. After the historical society acquired the property in 1976, it made two additions to the two-and-one-half-story building.

PO4 Coudersport Consistory Cathedral, Auditorium, and Benson House

1887 house; 1913 cathedral and 1928 auditorium, Edward Albert Phillips. 111 E. 2nd St. (U.S. 6)

By definition a "consistory" is a solemn assembly. In Coudersport, the Scottish Rite Masons, with notable determination, won the right to dispense the highest degrees in Masonry, a right usually reserved for the largest temples in urban places. In 1912, the Masons purchased the house built in 1887 for local lawyer and entrepreneur Isaac Benson, its elaborate carriage house, and the surrounding twenty-seven acres. When they needed more space for assemblies, they commissioned fellow Mason Edward A. Phillips, of Warren, to design the first of their temples in 1913. Fourteen years later, another building committee commissioned Phillips to design an 1,100-seat auditorium that he attached by a one-story wing to match the Great Hall of 1913.

The Benson house is a brick Queen Anne, festooned with turrets and dormers. Inside, the rooms are decorated with a litany of woods, including oak, cherry, pine, butternut, sycamore, bird's-eye maple, black birch, and ash. Both the Great Hall and the auditorium are red brick Tudor Revival buildings, a bit churchlike in appearance as intended.

PO5 Domaleski House

1949, Raymond Viner Hall. 503 E. Oak St.

Raymond Viner Hall studied the works and writings of John Ruskin, Louis Sullivan, and Frank Lloyd Wright while apprenticed to his father, a master builder. He characterized his education in the local public schools and through apprenticeships as containing "both the poetic and prosaic." He lived in Port Allegany in neighboring McKean County. To reach his far-flung commissions in Pennsylvania, New York, and the U.S. Virgin Islands, Hall

PO5 DOMALESKI HOUSE

invested in an airplane. His portfolio states that he favored the use of "advanced applications of concrete, masonry, steel, wood and pipe in integrated systems aiming at sound construction at lower than normal costs."

This house, commissioned by the local doctor, was executed early in Hall's career, and employs, on a domestic scale, the same elements he used later to design his larger schools (CM5). The low-slung, flat-roofed structure hugs the ground, emphasizes privacy from the street with its solid cement wall, and opens with large windows at the rear. The facade wall is punctuated by light yellow brick pylons at the entrance and a whitewashed and pierced decorative cement band forming a clerestory to light the interior.

PO6 Coudersport Borough Office and Police Station (Coudersport and Port Allegany Railroad Station)

1899. 201 S. West St.

East–west rail access came to Pennsylvania's central counties as early as 1852, but it did not arrive in Coudersport until 1880, leaving the town isolated when the river froze and the roads were blocked with snow or mud. This seasonal inaccessibility provided the impetus to use railroads to haul timber to the main rail lines. Construction of this handsome large red brick station and headquarters in place of the earlier wooden structure was a much-heralded event. The rusticated sandstone foundation is slightly flared at the base to echo the slight pent to the roof extension at both the first and second stories. The central hipped-roof core, five bays in width and two stories in height, is dominated by a central gable and a Palladian window crowned by a bull's-eye window. The building's deep eaves now protect the local police and borough officials, who have occupied the space for offices since 1975. The layout and design are reminiscent of the Buffalo, Rochester and Pittsburgh station designed in 1893 by the Rochester, New York, firm of Gordon, Bragdon and Orchard in DuBois, Clearfield County (see DuBois, p. 474).

DENTON HILL STATE PARK

PO7 Pennsylvania Lumber Museum

1936 Civilian Conservation Corps (CCC) cabin; c. 1970 museum buildings. 5660 U.S. 6

The lumber museum consists of nine buildings on 160 forested acres that together re-create a nineteenth-century lumber camp. Most buildings are simple frame, gable-roofed structures, including the visitors' center, blacksmith shop, carpenter shop, logging locomotive shed, log loader, stable, and dining hall. On the grounds adjacent to the parking lot is a log building constructed by the CCC in 1936 of American chestnut logs. Dedicated to the memory of the men who built it during their tenure in the CCC, the walls and stone pillars were strapped and moved intact and reconstructed at the museum in 1993 to save it from demolition. Two cross gables extend from the main building to frame a view of the facade that has a large gabled porch supported by two sandstone pillars over a fieldstone floor, and a massive sandstone chimney at the rear.

Sixteen miles south, Cherry Springs State Park (on PA 44), favored by astronomers for its 360-degree view of the night sky without light pollution, is host to a large picnic pavilion built by the CCC in 1939, and consisting of two rooms joined by a breezeway or dogtrot large enough to accommodate several picnic tables. Ribbons of nine-paned casement windows light the north, south, and east elevations, while the west elevation of each gable-roofed dining area has a large stone chimney.

PO7 PENNSYLVANIA LUMBER MUSEUM

BROOKLAND

PO8 All Saints Episcopal Church

1889, Henry Martyn Congdon. 3714 Fox Hill Rd. (PA 449)

This finely crafted stone church was designed by Henry Martyn Congdon (1834–1922), a New York City architect known for his ecclesiastical works. He used as models the Dent family chapel at St. Lawrence's church in the village of Crosby Ravensworth, England, and St. James the Less in Philadelphia, both fine examples of ecclesiological architecture. To include all of the stylistic elements essential to the pure Gothic Revival style in the smallest amount of space, Congdon compacted the design so that the bell-cote at the northwest corner carries a chimney, a buttress, and the entrance.

Henry Hatch Dent was a lawyer, a former U.S. attorney, and a southern aristocrat whose wife inherited thousands of Potter County acres. Upon her early death, Dent moved to Coudersport to run the family businesses. The church, commissioned by the Dents' four children, commemorates their relatives from Pennsylvania and Maryland, who are pictured in stained glass designed by the London firm of Heaton, Butler and Bayne. The interior of the church has a white marble altar and baptismal font, butternut pews of golden hue, and maroon and white diagonal marble tiles.

CLINTON COUNTY

Clinton County was established in 1839 when settler Jerry Church, after three years of failed attempts to have "Eagle County" chartered, simply switched the name to "Clinton." The required legislation passed before the committee members realized that nothing but the name had been changed. Located at the latitudinal midpoint of Pennsylvania, Clinton County's nine hundred square miles are crossed diagonally by Bald Eagle and Muncy mountains. The valleys between them, West Branch, Bald Eagle, and Sugar, were the most productive and developable areas of the county. The county seat of Lock Haven was established in West Branch Valley; Bald Eagle Valley, formed by Bald Eagle Creek, was named after a Delaware Indian chief; and Sugar Valley, at the southern foot of Sugar Mountain, was formed by Fishing Creek. Farms in these valleys produced beef and dairy cattle, tobacco, and corn. Since 1972, Old Order Amish families have farmed in Sugar Valley.

In 1769, the first European settler built a cabin on the bank of the West Branch Susquehanna River where the town of Lock Haven is now located. The west branch of the Pennsylvania Canal opened to Clinton County in 1834, which stimulated growth countywide and such industries as lumber, mining, and brickworks that relied on smooth shipping of heavy products. Twenty-five years later, the railroads spurred another economic boom and made the canal obsolete. The railroad spurred the growth of the towns of Renovo, Avis, Oak Grove, and Keating. Lumbering was a leading industry in the county economy from 1830 to 1910 and in the 1860s, one hundred million board feet a year were shipped via the rail lines. Lumber cut in Clinton County was shipped in its raw form to sawmills in the region. Towns such as Mill Hall and Rauchtown prospered because of the logging industry.

Today, the county's infrastructure is based on the interstate highway system. The main artery, U.S. 220, connects Lock Haven with State College and Williamsport, enabling the prosperity enjoyed by those towns. The major east–west route, I-80, passes through the southern third of the county, but access to it is limited and little development surrounds it.

Limited highways were not a problem for the Piper Aircraft Company. Founded by William T. Piper Sr., the company built small planes in a reused silk mill in Lock Haven from 1937 to 1984. The company moved to Florida in 1984, but its history is commemorated in the Piper Aviation Museum (c. 1970; 1 Piper Way) near the William T. Piper Memorial Airport. The Woolrich Company continues to produce wool clothing in two locations in Clinton County, and a new company, First Quality Products, which manufactures adult sanitary products, occupies part of a large industrial park in the northern half of the county. Hunting and fishing draw tourists, as does the c. 1910 Millbrook Playhouse in Mill Hall (north of Hogan Boulevard, PA 150), a former dairy barn converted in 1963 for use as a professional summer stock theater.

LOCK HAVEN AND VICINITY

Settler Jerry Church's donation of land made Lock Haven the county seat, and he laid out the grid plan for the city. The town was incorporated as a borough in 1840 and became a city by 1849. The west branch of the Pennsylvania Canal came into Lock Haven (actually, into Dunnsburg, across the river) in 1834, and was extended to Bellefonte in 1846 by the Bald Eagle branch, which followed the creek of the same name. That branch converged with the West Branch Susquehanna River just east of the foot of Jay Street. The canal boom was short-lived, however, because in 1859, the Sunbury and Erie Railroad (now the Philadelphia and Erie) arrived in Lock Haven, and the Bald Eagle Valley Railway opened along Bald Eagle Creek in 1864. The railroad boom brought prosperity and caused the business district to move from Water Street to Main and Church streets to be closer to the tracks.

Today, Water Street has an impressive concentration of churches, including the Church of the Immaculate Conception (1904; 310 W. Water Street), the Great Island Presbyterian Church (1872, Samuel Sloan; 12 W. Water Street), and the First Church of Christ (1923, J. C. Fulton and Son; 100 E. Water Street). The Gothic Revival Great Island Presbyterian Church follows

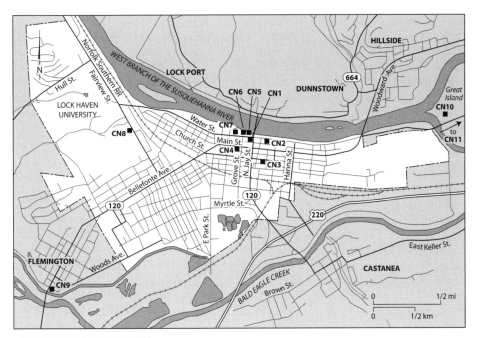

LOCK HAVEN AND VICINITY

Sloan's own pattern book designs. It has unfortunately lost its spire due to sub-sidence caused by changes in the water table. Sloan was a major influence on the nineteenth-century building stock of the city, designing the courthouse (CN1) and the C. A. Mayer house (demolished). His pattern books were also popular with local builder-architects, such as Henry Hipple Sr. and Cephas Batcheler, and Sloan's ideas and details appear repeatedly in their work. A group of large frame and brick houses from the 1850s to the 1920s lines Water Street, including the David Carskaddon House (1857, Henry Hipple Sr.; 26 E. Water Street), with an unusual Y-shaped floor plan and a central entrance. The Lock Haven Market House (1871, Patrick Keefe; 142 E. Church Street) is reused as a restaurant.

Lock Haven is prone to flooding by the West Branch Susquehanna River. From 1992 to 1994, a major flood control project, overseen by the Army Corps of Engineers, built an eighteen-foot-high earthen and stone-faced levee along the river bank. Rather than awkwardly interrupting the landscape, the levee has become an asset with the addition of a grass-covered walking path along the ridge that offers a view of both the city and the river, and a riverside open-air auditorium for summer performances.

CN1 Clinton County Courthouse

1869, Samuel Sloan and Addison Hutton; 1936, Russell J. Howard. Water and Jay sts.

Samuel Sloan (1815–1884) began his architec-tural career in 1849 in eastern Pennsylvania.

His fame grew with the publication of his pat-tern books, and by 1854, two buildings in Lock Haven—the Levi A. Mackey house (CN6) and Fallon House Hotel (CN7)—were heavily in-fluenced by his designs. A sojourn in Europe gave Sloan's designs a Beaux-Arts flavor. In

1864, he formed a partnership with Addison Hutton and won the Clinton County Courthouse commission. This courthouse is the second of a trio of almost identical buildings designed by Sloan and Hutton. The courthouse in Lycoming County completed in 1860 (demolished) was the earliest, followed closely by Clinton's and Venango's courthouses (VE1), which were built simultaneously.

The most impressive features of Clinton's brick and stone courthouse are its two domed towers of different heights on each side of the pedimented facade. Elaborate dormer windows originally in the towers' domes have been removed. The tall and narrow round-arched windows on the facade and the side walls give a distinct vertical emphasis to the courthouse. The first story of smoothly cut Farrandsville stone is outlined by a stringcourse of cut stone, above which the walls are of buff brick. The entrance features three doors set in segmental-arched openings reached by a short flight of stairs.

CN2 Heisey Museum (John Henderson–Seymour D. Ball House)

c. 1831, 1865. 362 E. Water St.

This five-bay two-story brick Gothic Revival house has been carefully maintained in its 1865 condition by the Clinton County Historical Society. It features the carved vergeboards, corbeled chimneys, steeply pitched gables, and arched gable-end windows typical of the style, as well as interior furnishings appropriate to the era. The house was remodeled several times, following its construction

as the Henderson House in a Greek Revival fashion c. 1831. It became a tavern and withstood a variety of owners and several floods, until the flood of 1865 caused then owner and lawyer Seymour D. Ball to rebuild the house in its present form. The house was donated to the Clinton County Historical Society by Mrs. Samuel Heisey in 1962.

CN3 House (Clinton County Jail)

1852, Anthony Kleckner, contractor; 1871–1872, Charles Shuster Wetzel. 350 E. Church St.

Built by a contractor in 1852, the jail was enlarged by 1872 with two western bays by Charles Wetzel, an architect from Danville in Montour County. The exterior walls are brick covered with rough-cast stucco and finished with contrasting cut stone quoins. The hallmarks of the Italian Villa style are here in the groupings of round-headed windows, the dentiled eaves supported by brackets, and the three-story hipped-roof square tower. Today the building is a private residence, which suits it well since the design is more like a town house than a jail.

CN4 Masonic Temple

1923, Stearns and Woodnutt. 144 E. Main St.

Philadelphia architects George R. Stearns and Charles E. Woodnutt partnered from 1918 to 1930. Stearns's engineering experience was an asset in the firm's hospital and industrial projects; the firm also designed churches and residences. This Beaux-Arts-inspired Masonic temple was built on a grand scale in the heart

CN1 CLINTON COUNTY COURTHOUSE

CN2 HEISEY MUSEUM (JOHN HENDERSON–SEYMOUR D. BALL HOUSE)

of Lock Haven's business district. Its most striking features are the two Ionic columns supporting the recessed entrance porch and the entrance's surround with its swags and quoins, which adds drama to what is essentially a fairly conservative design. The draped window molding on the attic story of the north elevation captures the theatrical element always popular in Masonic architecture.

CN5 Jacob Grafius House

1843, with additions. 209–217 E. Water St.

A relic from the canal era, this house sits on the green that once connected the town to the wharves. It was built as a five-bay brick Greek Revival house, with bridged chimneys at the gable ends. In the 1850s, Grafius, taking inspiration from—or competing with—Mackey's house two doors to the west, added Italianate window caps, a bracketed cornice, and a small balcony over the main entrance copied from Sloan's pattern books. A one-story twentieth-century addition is appended to the rear of the house.

CN6 Levi A. Mackey House

1854, Henry Hipple Sr. 201 E. Water St.

Levi A. Mackey was a leading citizen in Lock Haven at the midpoint of the nineteenth century, involved in banking, politics, and schools. He and local builder-architect Henry Hipple (1808–1875) are credited with designing his house. Reportedly the first in Lock Haven to employ Samuel Sloan's version of Italianate, the house had a definite impact on the town and inspired a boom of buildings in a similar style. Of this group, Mackey's house is the best preserved. Similar houses are the BPOE 182 (former Simon Scott House) of 1854 at 210 E. Main Street, the James White House of 1854 designed by Cephas Batcheler at 46 W. Water Street, and the George Armstrong House (1867) at 51 N. Fairview Street, among others.

The Mackey house has paired round-arched windows in the gable ends, decorative window lintels, and perhaps the most common mark of the Italianate style, the bracketed wooden cornice. The attic-story windows are an unusual addition, but the effect became very popular in Lock Haven in

CN6 LEVI A. MACKEY HOUSE

the 1850s and is found on more than a dozen houses in the city.

CN7 Fallon House Hotel

1854–1856, Cephas Batcheler. 131 E. Water St.

This hotel was partially financed by monies from Spanish royalty. During the nineteenth century, when Spain's government was in constant turmoil, local land agents John and Christopher Fallon were asked to invest royal funds in the United States. It was thought that if Queen Isabella II's right to succeed to the throne were denied, she might be forced to seek refuge in the United States. Her courtiers planned for her to come to Clinton County and live on a 50,000-acre parcel of land owned by the Fallons in Colbrook Township. The Fallon House Hotel was built to serve those who might come to visit the court of the Queen.

Designed by local builder-architect Cephas Batcheler (1803–1896), the hotel was originally covered with stucco, but sandblasting has exposed the brick beneath. The top floor has an observatory, and the casement windows are original. The heavy brackets between the observatory windows and the window hoods are the only remaining pieces of Italianate decoration. The building initially had an iron balcony that ran the entire width of the south elevation. The loss of this balcony and a square cupola with large Palladian windows has taken away some, but certainly not all, of the qualities that once distinguished this building.

CN8 Lock Haven University

1896–present. 401 N. Fairview St.

The 200-acre campus of Lock Haven University, west of the center of the city, opened as the Central State Normal School in 1870. In 1961, the coeducational institution converted from a teacher-training college to a four-year liberal arts university. Today, about 4,600 students are enrolled on the main campus. For the most part, the school is composed of rectangular, flat-roofed, orange or red brick buildings of the 1950s. The two most significant exceptions are the Rogers Gymnasium and the Price Performance Center.

The Rogers Gymnasium, the oldest building on campus, was designed in 1896 by Amos S. Wagner for Wagner and Reitmeyer from Williamsport. Its residential appearance is highlighted by the round-arched dormer and second-story windows. The Price Performance Center, designed in 1938 by Philadelphia firm Tilden and Pepper with Karcher and Smith, is red brick with Art Deco elements. Its interior was modernized and converted into a performance center by Pittsburgh architects Jacob Gzesh and Associates in 1987. The building creates a small quadrangle with the Colonial Revival Sullivan and Russell halls. The newest addition to the campus is the red brick Durrwachter Alumni Conference Center at Fairview and Water streets (2007–2008, MacLachlan, Cornelius and Filoni), with its glass-enclosed entrance facing the corner.

CN9 Joseph H. Long House

c. 1877. 421 Canal St., 0.8 miles west of Lock Haven

This frame Italianate building was once located at the heart of the Pennsylvania Canal's shipping docks. It was built for Joseph H. Long, who shipped agricultural produce out of Lock Haven and brought in foodstuff and coal. Today, the building has been converted into apartments, but the storefront configuration and scrolled brackets, dentils, and decorative window frames are preserved.

CN10 Robert W. McCormick House

c. 1866. 828 Island Route Rd. (PA 1002)

The design for the McCormick house was inspired by earlier houses in Lock Haven. The five-bay house has a low hipped roof, attic-story windows separated by brackets, and an elegantly framed doorway. The flush vertical siding distinguishes this house from similar brick houses in Lock Haven, as does its unusual site. Great Island, settled c. 1768, is a scenic 280-acre island at the confluence of the West Branch Susquehanna River and Bald Eagle Creek.

CN11 David Baird Farm Complex

c. 1840. 831 Island Rd. (TWP 425) at Baird Rd., 3.5 miles east of Lock Haven

The Baird farm is remarkably intact, despite its proximity to the suburban development growing around Lock Haven. The brick five-bay house retains its original windows, interior gable-end bridged chimneys, and handsome entrance. More important, and certainly more unusual in the area, are the tobacco sheds on the farm. These frame gable-roofed barns are identifiable by the vertical slats that open to ventilate drying tobacco. In 1838, the Bairds became the first in the area to produce tobacco. Constructed in 1886 by J. Q. Baird, the large frame banked barn on the property is very wide and has louvered Gothic arches, an uncommon feature in local barns.

WOOLRICH AND VICINITY

The abundance of creeks and streams in Clinton County gave rise to a thriving milling industry in the nineteenth century. The most significant mill in the county is in Woolrich in Pine Creek Township. John Rich II began by carding the wool for socks and blankets sold to loggers, then went into production at Plum Run in 1830 (CN12). In 1835, he moved the company to a new, larger mill with greater water velocity on Chatham Run and founded an adjacent town. He named the town Woolrich after the company, which continues to thrive in Clinton County, making durable, rugged garments for outdoor activities.

Woolrich is readily recognizable as a company town, with two versions of workers' housing that line Park Avenue and Mill Street. The first version is a two-story two-bay frame gable-roofed house (c. 1910) at 1172 Park Avenue, and the second is a lower, one-and-one-half-story bungalow-style home (c. 1930) at 1178 Park Avenue. Both have full-facade porches. Other company buildings remain, such as the brick one-story school and the company store. Main Street hosts a group of more elaborate houses for management, including Charles Rich's large, well-preserved frame Second Empire house (c. 1870; 18 Main Street). The red brick United Methodist Church (1907; 1080 Park Avenue) is Gothic Revival with a square corner bell tower. The factory buildings (c. 1900; 2 Mill Street) are large, three- to five-story red brick buildings adjacent to the creek. The company's dedication to the outdoors—they outfitted the 1939 Byrd expedition to Antarctica and Himalayan climbing expeditions—is reflected in their commitment to maintain the 4,000 acres of mountain land adjacent to the village.

CN12 Rich-McCormick Woolen Mill

1830. 129 Park Ave.

John Rich II, an English-trained wool carder, founded four woolen mills in Clinton County in the 1820s and 1830s. This, the third mill, was built with partner Daniel McCormick on Plum Creek in 1830, and operated here until 1845. The company ultimately evolved into the Woolrich Company and moved to its namesake town when the water velocity of this creek proved insufficient. The three-story, gable-roofed brick building has twenty six-over-nine windows on the southwest elevation, allowing plenty of light for the close work involved in manufacturing woolens. A full three-story porch was useful for hanging wet woolen fleece to dry. Today the large building hosts a commercial establishment.

AVIS VICINITY

CN13 Pine Creek Iron Bridge

1889, Berlin Iron Bridge Company. River Rd. (TWP 566) over Pine Creek, approximately 0.8 miles upstream from the Susquehanna River

The Pine Creek bridge is one of only three Berlin lenticular truss bridges with Warren pattern web members that survive in the United States. The Berlin Iron Bridge Compa-

CN12 RICH-MCCORMICK WOOLEN MILL

CN13 PINE CREEK IRON BRIDGE

ny's sales force was so successful in convincing county commissioners that their bridges were less expensive to build that all but one of the lenticular truss bridges in the nation were built by the company. The only bridge they did not build is the Smithfield Street Bridge over the Monongahela River at Pittsburgh,

designed in 1882 by Gustav Lindenthal (AL4). The Berlin Iron Bridge Company was headquartered in East Berlin, Connecticut, until its 1900 merger with the American Bridge Company, a subsidiary of U.S. Steel Corporation.

MILL HALL VICINITY

CN14 Job W. Packer Farmhouse

1798, 1865. 31–33 Keystone Central Dr., 0.5 miles west of Mill Hall

This farmhouse sits atop a terrace at the intersection of Lusk Run and Crystal Beach roads. It is the oldest of four stone houses built by a mason named Adam. At the time of its completion in 1798, the house had a four-over-four plan with a central hall. There was a major fire in 1865, which nearly destroyed the house. Therefore, most of the woodwork, especially on the interior, dates from the subsequent rebuilding. It is probable that the first floor was changed at that time to its present configuration of one room to the north and three rooms to the south. The house features exterior corner quoins and a three-bay front porch with sawn ornament. The sprawling Central Mountain Valley High School (1997–2000 Quad 3; 64 Keystone Central Drive) across the street is the largest indicator of encroaching suburbia.

CN15 Colonel Henry Miller Bossert House

1854. 155 Crystal Beach Rd.

Colonel Henry Miller Bossert constructed a Greek Revival home using the stacked lumber technique, that is, two-inch by six-inch sawn lumber stacked horizontally with six-inch

CN15 COLONEL HENRY MILLER BOSSERT HOUSE

face against six-inch face and alternately extended to the corners. The exterior is finished with board-and-batten siding. This house includes an unusual door to the balcony above the main entrance, which is opened by raising the window to the maximum height then swinging a section of the interior wall inside and a section of the board-and-batten siding outward, creating a passable opening. Corner porches on both the front and rear elevations are recessed into the house. This method, which gives up interior space in favor of an outdoor area, is almost exclusive to Pennsylvania's central region and is commonly seen in Somerset County. Several stacked lumber houses remain in Huntingdon County, but this is the last one documented in Clinton County.

MACKEYVILLE

CN16 Moses Thompson Homestead

1838, with additions. 185 Duck Run Rd.

Duck Run Road hosts several interesting farms, and this complex best represents them. The farmhouse with Flemish bond brickwork built in 1838 features six-over-six windows, gable end chimneys, and a sidelight and transom that frame the main door. A picture window installed on the west elevation and the

large front porch on the north side are later additions. The nearby two-story brick springhouse preceded the house and most likely functioned as living quarters for the family until the farmhouse was complete. Considerably smaller and lacking in the higher style details of the house, the springhouse retains its original six-over-six windows. The waterwheel on the north side is not original. The remaining buildings are typical of farms throughout the commonwealth. The farm itself was home to a commercial dairy operation, and the concrete masonry buildings on the property reflect that purpose.

CAMERON COUNTY

With almost its entire area covered by second-growth forest and a population of under 6,000, Cameron County is a quiet, scenic, central Pennsylvania landscape dotted with seasonal hunting and fishing cabins. The county was organized in 1860, from portions of Clinton, Elk, McKean, and Potter counties, and named for Senator Simon Cameron, the secretary of war in Abraham Lincoln's cabinet. Revolutionary War veterans from New Jersey, New York, and Pennsylvania were some of the earliest settlers, arriving around 1810. Logging and tanning were the first industries, with the result that much of the county's forest was clear-cut by 1900.

Railroad service finally reached Cameron County in the 1860s after thirty years of lobbying by Erie and Philadelphia businessmen for a rail line that would connect the two cities. A feeder line connecting Driftwood to the Allegheny Valley Railroad provided a connection between Buffalo and Pittsburgh. As well as transporting lumber, entire buildings came to the county by train. When the small tannery town of Sterling Run needed an inexpensive school in 1932, it ordered a frame, gable-roofed building from Sears and Roebuck that today houses the Cameron County Historical Society (PA 120). Cameron is now best known for its recreational and scenic attractions. Bucktail State Park encloses 16,433 acres of land parallel to the Sinnemahoning Creek and the West Branch Susquehanna River, and includes the seventy-five miles of PA 120 that connect Emporium, Renovo, and Lock Haven. In the fall, the park is among the commonwealth's most scenic highways.

EMPORIUM

Lying in the valley created by the Driftwood branch of Sinnemahoning Creek, Emporium began as the county seat and a lumber town, using the creek to ship logs to Lock Haven and Williamsport. Several early houses illustrate this period of lumber wealth (see CM3). After the surrounding hills were stripped of trees, the blasting powder industry, founded here in 1890, used the hills as natural bunkers. The Climax Powder Company produced three-quarters of the blasting powder for the construction of the Panama Canal in 1914. As dynamite took over the explosives industry, the powder industry waned, and Dupont bought out the remaining blasting powder producers and moved them to New Jersey. By the turn of the twentieth century, the electronic parts industry was established in Emporium. Sylvania, founded in 1901, became a major employer by the 1920s. The company was so successful that Emporium was on Nazi Germany's bomb list during World War II. The plant closed in 1991, as radio tubes became increasingly obsolete.

Emporium's 4th Street has a handsome collection of late-nineteenth- and early-twentieth-century buildings. Two churches are noteworthy, the brick Gothic Revival St. Mark's Roman Catholic Church (1893) at 235 E. 4th Street, and Emmanuel Episcopal Church (1901, Cram, Goodhue and Ferguson; 179 E. 4th Street), a brownstone church with a heavy square entrance tower. A yellow brick, three-story former school building (1924; 240 E. 4th Street), now the Cameron County Christian Center, has pilaster strips with composite capitals and cartouches above the entrances. The newest addition to the street is the Barbara Moscato Brown Memorial Library (2002; 27 W. 4th Street), a red brick building with two pyramid-roofed pavilions and a corner entrance marked by a cupola, designed by Larson Design Group of Williamsport.

CM1 Cameron County Courthouse and County Jail

c. 1890–1892, Amos S. Wagner; 2007 addition. 20 E. 5th St.

Prominently raised on a terrace, this courthouse replaced a frame building that burned in 1890. It was designed by carpenter and contractor Amos S. Wagner (1840–1899) of Williamsport, and completed by contractor John W. Kriner. The asymmetrical facade, the large square clock tower at the southeast corner with decorative stringcourses, the triple-arched entrance, and the windows with bold voussoirs of rough-cut stone are inspired by Romanesque architecture. A three-story T-shaped addition on the north elevation of well-matched brick on a raised foundation of textured cement block has a hipped roof in keeping with the courthouse. The addition steps down the hillside to avoid overwhelming the older building.

CM2 George Metzger House

1909. 100 W. 5th St.

Lumberman George Metzger embodied the unbridled capitalism and entrepreneurial spirit of his era. He was an optometrist, owned a jewelry store and a brickyard, and was instrumental in bringing telephone service to the city. He moved the house (since razed) already on this site to the rear of the property to build this house of mud-colored cinder blocks made by his company. Red shingles cover the roofs of both intersecting gables and the conical roof of the large round tower. The deep eaves of the gable ends project over the lower stories, and a one-story porch wraps around two elevations.

CM3 House

c. 1870. 102 E. 5th St.

Built at the high point of the Stick Style, this house is one of the earliest in Emporium. An ogee-roofed, square corner tower with Queen Anne windows was added in 1890, but the Stick Style elements remain, especially in the gable end on the facade. A similarly fanciful Stick Style residence remains at 338 W. 4th Street.

CM4 Northern Tier Community Action Center (Henry Auchu House, Sylvania Club)

1909. 135 W. 4th St.

A house of this size and detail in the small town of Emporium illustrates the growth of the turn-of-the-twentieth-century business entrepreneurial class. Henry Auchu was a self-educated French Canadian in the lumber and explosives industries. His house is very similar to a house in Meadville, Crawford County (CR17). Both used George F. Barber's mail-order plans for "A New Colonial Design" from the 1904 *Modern Dwellings* catalog, varying the rooflines and materials, but little else. This house is a heavy, three-bay structure with a two-story Ionic-columned porch in the center that continues as a one-story porch across the side bays. Modillions enliven the gambrel roof and the porches on all the elevations. In 1930, the president of Sylvania Products Company, Bernard G. Erskine, bought the house as lodging for customers visiting his plant and called it the Sylvania Club.

CM5 Cameron County Junior Senior High School

1953; 1962 addition, Raymond Viner Hall. 601 Woodland Ave.

CM1 CAMERON COUNTY COURTHOUSE AND COUNTY JAIL

CM4 NORTHERN TIER COMMUNITY ACTION CENTER (HENRY AUCHU HOUSE, SYLVANIA CLUB)

This school serves students in grades 7–12 in a T-shaped building, with a long, low, angular classroom wing intersecting with a taller, rounded auditorium and gymnasium unit. Contrasts between the two wings are clear in everything from construction materials to function. Hall was the architect for both the original design and the addition, which increased the floor space by 21,000 square feet and the student capacity from 326 to a total of 1,086. He used cast-concrete blocks in three ways: as decorative wall sections filled with colored tiles, as louvers without infill, and as light sources when filled with glass block. The prefabricated sculptured block was economical and versatile, and Hall varied the pattern for each of the twenty-seven schools he de-

signed in Pennsylvania. Block panels highlight entrances and outline auditoriums.

Hall also designed the Woodland Elementary School (1962–1963; 601 Woodland Avenue) directly behind the Junior Senior High School, and they share the same recreational spaces. His design for Legion Memorial Hall (1950; 300 S. Walnut Street) was built by contractor E. M. Riegel, and has a distinctive slanted stone entrance fin that Hall often used on clubs and corporate buildings he designed. Between 1950 and 1955, Hall designed half-a-dozen houses on Pine Tree Road and Huckleberry Circle in an area of Emporium called Sylvan Heights. Several single-story, flat-roofed houses remain, although they have been significantly altered.

ELK COUNTY

Elk County lies on the Allegheny High Plateau, with elevations of 1,400 feet rising to 2,500 feet above sea level. There are two major watersheds: the Clarion River flowing west to the Allegheny and Sinnemahoning Creek flowing east to the Susquehanna.

The Seneca Indians and their Iroquois allies used the Kittanning-Olean Trail that cut across the northwestern corner of the county as a hunting route. By the late eighteenth century, agents for the largest Anglo-American landholders wanted to attract potential settlers from the East Coast. Joseph Fox and his son Samuel, who held nearly 120,000 acres of land in central Pennsylvania, had their agent, William Kersey, appeal to people in New England, Philadelphia, New York, and Baltimore. Among Kersey's contacts was the German Catholic Bund that sent a group of Roman Catholics to settle at St. Mary's in 1842. Jacob Ridgway, a Philadelphia Quaker, owned 40,000 acres in McKean and Elk counties. His agent, James L. Gillis, laid out the towns of Montmorency (1822) and Ridgway (1833). The county was established in 1843, with Ridgway designated as the county seat the following year.

Initially, the main industry was lumber. Wood felled and dragged to the many streams was floated to the Clarion River and down the Allegheny to Pittsburgh. The tanning industry also relied on lumber, using bark to cure the hides of elk and, later, buffalo. After the native elk were annihilated in 1857, the tannery at Wilcox processed nearly one million buffalo hides between 1866 and 1876. Elk were reintroduced to the region in 1913, imported from Wyoming and Montana. Today, Pennsylvania's protected herd of approximately eight hundred elk is a tourist attraction, especially near Benezette.

Extractive industries such as coal, oil, gas, and clay grew once rail connections were made. Both the Philadelphia and Erie Railroad and the Baltimore and Ohio ran branches through Ridgway, allowing the paper mill in Johnsonburg to flourish. Today, while no major interstates touch the county, U.S. 219 bisects it from north to south and carries traffic to I-80 in the counties to the south. A continuing wood products industry and a flourishing powdered metals industry employ those not working in agriculture or on the public recreation lands that cover more than half of the county. Elk County's population has remained remarkably stable, hovering near 35,000 since 1900.

RIDGWAY

Named for wealthy Quaker packet merchant Jacob Ridgway of Philadelphia, the borough nestles into a bend of the Clarion River where Elk Creek inter-

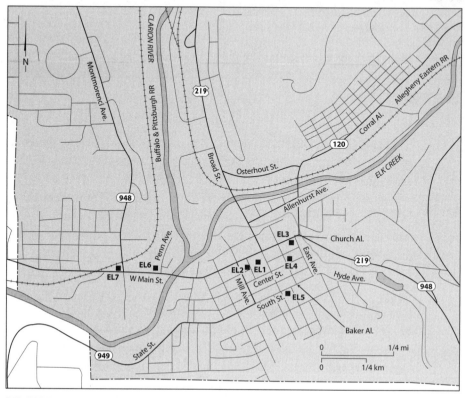

RIDGWAY

sects it. Ridgway and his nephew-in-law and land agent James L. Gillis rode the hilly countryside scouting a place for the town. Jacob Ridgway is credited with laying out the town in 1833, which had a tannery, sawmill, and gristmill. He employed the grid pattern familiar from Philadelphia as his city plan, but the river, railroads, Elk Creek, and later the intersection of U.S. 219, PA 948, and PA 120 have conspired over the years to carve the grid pattern into small sections. Ridgway became a center for the lumber and tanning industry and in 1844, the county seat. It was incorporated as a borough in 1880.

Joseph Smith Hyde, who arrived in Ridgway in 1837 and opened a sawmill on Elk Creek in 1846, began a partnership with Walter P. Murphy, the owner of a nearby planing mill, in 1884. The Hyde-Murphy Company built everything for their nationwide clientele, from windows to entire houses. Their in-house architect from 1894 until his death was Henry C. Park (1849–1920). The company closed in 1961. It would stand to reason that a town processing millions of board feet of lumber every year would be built of wood, but Ridgway's major buildings are uniformly made of brick or stone. The former Elk County National Bank, now Krupski Antique Gallery (1889–1907; 255 N. Main Street), is one example and acts as the introduction to Ridgway's commercial district from the south. The YMCA (1904 Hyde-Murphy Company; 34 N. Broad Street) is representative of the commercial district along Broad Street. Since 1998, a historic facade grant program funded by the Ridgway Heritage Council, the borough, and local foundations has facilitated appropriate restorations of several commercial facades.

EL1 Elk County Courthouse

1880, J. P. Marston, contractor; 1912 courtroom redesign, Henry C. Park; 1970, Rodgers and Frederick. Main St. between S. Broad, Center, and Court sts.

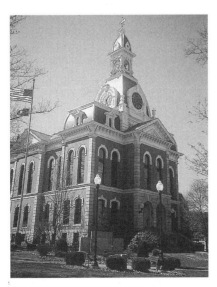

EL1 ELK COUNTY COURTHOUSE

The Elk County commissioners surveyed nearby courthouses and decided to emulate Milton Earl Beebe's design for Warren County (WA1). They hired the contractor from Warren County, J. P. Marston of Maine, to build Ridgway's courthouse. His interpretation, while generally faithful to Beebe's original design, places the clock face closer to the base of the tower and opens the belfry at the top. The mansard-roofed building, with square-headed windows on the first story and round-arched windows above, is constructed of brick with stone corner quoins and bracketed cornice. Each elevation has a central projecting bay punctuated by a pediment at the cornice line. There is a modern red brick, three-story addition of 1970 at the rear. As a whole, the building conveys the solemnity befitting a courthouse, which here is surrounded by a green lawn and faces a handsome block of commercial buildings from the same era.

EL2 Ridgway Masonic Temple
1908, R. E. Krape. Court St. facing the courthouse

EL3 ELIZABETH HYDE HOUSE

Across the street from the Elk County Courthouse, the buff brick, four-story temple stands out in a commercial district of two and three stories. The building spans the block and has matching facades facing Court Street and S. Mill Avenue. The Chicago Masonic Temple of 1891–1892, designed by Burnham and Root, at twenty-two stories has a similar facade and window treatment, with round-arched windows at the base and top, and rectangular windows between. That building's impact on the national building scene could not have escaped Krape's notice and perhaps it was the model for Ridgway's temple. The top story, with its elongated round-arched windows and the terra-cotta Masonic emblems in the spandrels below, was a ceremonial space.

EL3 Elizabeth Hyde House

1905–1907, attributed to Henry C. Park. 344 E. Main St.

The stone construction, round arches, and the steeply pitched and tiled roof of this house are reminiscent of H. H. Richardson's work. Its prominent site on Ridgway's main street fits the social standing of Elizabeth Hyde, widow of William H. Hyde of the Hyde-Murphy Company, which had, by then, been in operation for nearly thirty years and had built thousands of area houses from coal patch workers' housing to mansions. Commissioned a few years after William Hyde's death, it is probable his wife or her sons asked the company's architect, Henry C. Park, to design it. The living room is finished in curly birch paneling complemented by Italian fireplace tiles, and lavish hardwoods throughout both public and private rooms illustrate the range of the company's woodworking skills.

EL4 Ridgway Free Public Library (Madison S. Kline House)

1902–1904, Ernest George Washington Dietrich. 329 Center St.

A house this size is conspicuous in a small town, even if it does not front on the main commercial street. Fortunately, when the brick two-and-one-half-story house was donated for use as the library in 1921, it had the appearance often sought in library design, with pedimented gables on three sides and two-story porches supported by fluted Ionic columns on the south and the east facades. Architect Ernest G. W. Dietrich (1857–1924) trained in Pittsburgh with Charles Bartberger and then moved to New York in 1887. Hyde-Murphy Company Contractors constructed the building. Ridgway banker Madison S. Kline commissioned the house, only to lose it when his snowplow company went under.

EL5 The Towers Victorian Inn (Jerome Powell House)

1865–1868. 330 South St.

This two-story frame Italianate house was built by the local newspaper editor, business tycoon, and first mayor of Ridgway, Jerome Powell. It has been beautifully preserved and now functions as a bed-and-breakfast. The round-arched wall dormer in the house's central bay contains a circular window, while the glazed belvedere at the apex of the roof is topped with a finial. In the 1890s, the Hyde-Murphy Company added oak Ionic columns, cherry paneling, and parquet floors to the interior. Center and South streets have several imposing frame houses like this one terraced above the commercial district, with schools and churches interspersed.

EL6 River House (George E. Dickinson House)

1855. 106 W. Main St.

The Greek Revival style in Pennsylvania is inevitably tied to the counties immediately south of the New York border that form the northern tier. Beginning in the 1820s, frame houses with pedimented facades and often one-story wings that flanked the central two-story block were built by New England migrants who arrived in the region via the Erie Canal. Though

EL6 RIVER HOUSE (GEORGE E. DICKINSON HOUSE)

EL7 Office Building (Buffalo, Pittsburgh and Rochester Railroad Passenger Station)

1903, Frederick, builder. W. Main St. and Montmorenci Ave.

This depot was built for the Buffalo, Pittsburgh and Rochester Railroad in 1903. Ten years earlier their stations, like the one at DuBois, Clearfield County, were designed by the Rochester architectural firm of Gordon, Bragdon and Orchard. It is not known which of two successor firms might have designed this station, or whether an entirely different firm did the work, since all that is known is the builder's last name. Nonetheless, the brick building has interesting details: a hipped roof with the expected wide overhanging eaves is split in the middle by an intersecting hipped-roof block. On the track side, the central portion is polygonal and its flanking walls are flat, while on the street side the central section is flat and the side walls have three-sided oriel windows. Deep brackets, contrasting stone quoins, and a sill course further enliven the design. Today, the building serves as offices.

once ubiquitous, survivors with original siding and details are rare. This house, built by early lumberman George Dickinson on the main street of Ridgway, has a triangular window in the facade pediment. Windows like this are seen on at least three other houses, all located on the West Branch Susquehanna River, and may be the work of one carpenter or have simply inspired imitation. The off-center entrance is typical of Greek Revival houses, and the single side wing to the east with its recessed entrance is echoed in plainer houses, such as one on West Valley Road in Keating Township, McKean County.

JOHNSONBURG

David Johnson and his wife arrived at this junction of the east and west branches of the Clarion River from Salem, New Jersey, in 1810. They named the town Coopersport for Benjamin F. Cooper of Salem, who owned 400,000 acres of nearby land. However, the Johnson name clung to the area, and about 1880 the village's name was officially changed. The town was isolated and accessed by two rudimentary turnpikes in the 1820s and 1830s.

Around 1880, the lumber industry boomed and square-cut white pine logs tied together as rafts were sent down the Clarion River to Pittsburgh, and sometimes as far as New Orleans. After 1885, the logs were shipped by rail on the Buffalo, Rochester and Pittsburgh line. Steam power helped to launch ever larger industries that relied on lumber products, such as sawmills, tanneries, and wood chemical plants. The bark of hemlock trees was used to make tannic acid, an important component of leather tanning. The Clarion Pulp and Paper Company opened in 1889, and, after numerous ownership changes, in 2007 became Domtar Paper and Pulp Mill (200 Center Street).

A flood wreaked havoc on the town in 1942, and between 1947 and 1952, the Army Corps of Engineers constructed the East Branch Dam of the Clarion River northeast of Johnsonburg. Johnsonburg was built on three levels. Center Street, paralleling the river, carries U.S. 219 and is the town's access route.

Howell Pharmaceutical Company building (former), 538–540 Market Street, Johnsonburg.

Lined with a mixture of residential and commercial properties, it has borne the brunt of floods and street widening. The Johnsonburg Hotel (c. 1910; 617 Center Street) is the only survivor of the nine hotels once in town. The first street east, Market Street, is a three-block-long commercial district with several very large brick houses built at the south end by the paper mill's owners and managers. Closely spaced, middle-class brick and frame houses line 3rd through 6th avenues, all in visual and olfactory thrall to the paper mill. Three separate sections of housing lie west of the Clarion River; north to south these neighborhoods are Terra Cotta, West End, and Rolfe (named for a former tannery).

The commercial district of Market Street includes the pressed-metal storefront of the Howell Pharmaceutical Company (c. 1890) at numbers 538–540; the former Zierden Department Store (c. 1885) at numbers 519–521, a three-story brick structure that is now a Western Auto Store; and the gray stone Johnsonburg National Bank (1891) by architect Patrick A. Welsh at Market and Bridge streets SE. The paper mill sponsored construction of the community building (1919–1920) at Bridge and Market streets SW, designed by Ridgway architect Frank Orner and built by the Hyde-Murphy Company. It contains a pool, gymnasium, and auditorium. Patrick

Welsh also designed the Armstrong Real Estate and Improvement Company (c. 1890) at 523–569 Market Street, which has a repetitive bay system of two-story, three-bay units. Trimmed with stepped ornament at their parapets, the projecting second stories create an arcade along the street. Welsh moved from Lock Haven in Clinton County to Philadelphia and established a successful architectural practice between 1881 and 1907, concentrating on Roman Catholic churches.

ST. MARY'S

Although western Pennsylvania's small towns usually have several Presbyterian and Methodist churches, St. Mary's represents one of several Roman Catholic settlements in the northern tier. St. Mary's beginnings differ from those of other Catholic enclaves in western Pennsylvania, such as the Benedictine St. Vincent Archabbey in Westmoreland County (WE26) and Loretto in Cambria County (see CA5, CA6, and CA7). Reacting to the campaign of the American Party and the Know-Nothings along the East Coast, Catholics formed the German Catholic Bund in 1842 and sent a committee to central Pennsylvania to find land suitable for a settlement away from the bigotry of the urban centers. Catholics from Baltimore and Philadelphia reached Elk County and settled on a 30,000-acre tract six miles north of Kersey on December 8, 1842, the feast of the Immaculate Conception, choosing St. Mary's as the colony's name. A Redemptorist priest visited the settlement and immediately sent for additional help from Colonel Matthias Benzinger of Baltimore, who purchased the land from the original group and gave each family twenty-five acres and one town lot. He hired Ignatius Garner as agent, who had roads built to supply the town and recruited more settlers directly from Germany. The two-story, gable-roofed stone house (44 S. St. Mary's Street) built in 1845 by George Weis in the city center remains from this era. The Benedictines took over from the Redemptorists in 1850 and built a monastery and convent in 1852, the first Benedictine women's community in the United States.

The land was not as suitable for farming as the original settlers hoped; it was marshy, hilly, and heavily forested with pine and hemlock. A set of surveys and street layouts were then made by German-born civil engineer Sebastian Wimmer, a nephew of the first Benedictine archabbott in the United States, Boniface Wimmer. However, the town plan was complicated by the convergence of five roads, two railroads, and a creek in downtown St. Mary's.

St. Mary's industries began with farming and water-powered sawmills and gristmills in the 1840s and gradually moved to lumbering, tanning, coal mining, and the brewing of beer in the last three decades of the nineteenth century. The Straub Brewery, founded c. 1870 as an outgrowth of an 1855 brewery, continues to offer tours at its headquarters at 303 Sorg Street. Since 1900, the manufacture of carbon-graphite products has grown to the point where today, 40 percent of the world's powdered metal parts are made in north-central Pennsylvania by companies that employ over 10,000 people. This industrial growth spurred the development of suburbs around the commercial core of St. Mary's. Combined with its suburbs in Benzinger Township in 1994, St. Mary's became the only city in Elk County.

EL8 Decker Chapel

1856, Michael Decker, builder. 1000 PA 255

Just over a decade after the Roman Catholic settlers arrived in Elk County, Michael Decker was injured in a fall and promised to build a chapel if he recovered. Following his recuperation, he built this 12 × 18–foot, frame, gable-roofed chapel. Though roadside shrines were common among Catholics of Bavarian descent in Elk County in the late nineteenth century and short pilgrimages were often made from chapel to chapel, Decker Chapel is the last remaining in the region. The single plastered room contains eight original kneelers and a simple altar, both of wood. Today it is incongruously close to a busy highway and several big box stores.

EL9 Sacred Heart Roman Catholic Church

1906–1907, William P. Ginther. 340 Center St.

Besides transportation, the railroad brought a new workforce to St. Mary's: Irish workers. The local Catholics formed this new parish in 1873 for the English-speaking Irish parishio-

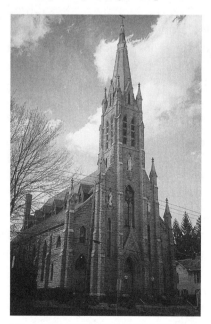

EL9 SACRED HEART ROMAN CATHOLIC CHURCH

ners. This handsome Gothic Revival church was designed by Ginther of Akron, an architect responsible for over 250 churches, mainly in Ohio and Pennsylvania. This stately stone structure is as beautiful from the rear with its polygonal apse as from the front with its pinnacled facade. Each of the three double-door entrances has a pointed window above and is flanked by buttresses. The central square tower has a crowning spire, an open belfry, and niches for statuary, all of which add to the impression of verticality. The buttressed side elevations have dormered clerestory windows.

Adjacent at 337 Center Street, a golden brick, two-story flat-roofed elementary school (1922) has columns delineating the entrance.

EL10 St. Mary's Church, Convent, and School and Benedictine Priory and Gymnasium

1852–1853 church, Ignatius Garner; 1934 convent; 1951 St. Mary's Catholic Middle School. 300 block Church St. 1889–1890 priory and 1902 gymnasium. 144 Church St.

The Benedictine monks who came to St. Mary's in 1850 built a Romanesque Revival sandstone church terraced above Church Street, with a clock tower and steeple above the entrance. Although the church has been altered, it dominates the complex with the large, three-story buff brick convent and St. Mary's Middle School attached on either side to accommodate the county's harsh winters. Less than a mile to the northwest, the Benedictine monks built a three-story stone monastery (1870; 763 Johnsonburg Road) that was replaced within two decades by the priory on Church Street and now serves as the Elk Regional Health Center.

Although the Benedictine St. Joseph's monastery is historically more important, the Benedictine priory of 1889–1890 and its gymnasium of 1902 to the east have more of their original fabric intact. The red brick, three-story Italianate priory houses Benedictine priests who serve both the St. Mary's and

Sacred Heart parishes. German was spoken in the hallways and classrooms of the complex until World War I, when anti-German senti- ment caused the German American population to drop the language in public discourse.

FOREST COUNTY

Forest County is, as one would expect, tree covered, and has such a small population that there is not one stoplight in it. Since three-fourths of the land is government owned, it has five times more seasonal homes than permanent ones. Its shape is determined by the irregular boundaries of the Clarion River, which forms a quarter of the southern boundary, and the Allegheny, which runs across the northwest corner and acted as a highway for Native Americans.

European settlement began with John Cook, who was asked by the federal government to survey the Clarion River as a possible east–west canal route. He was so taken with the area that he bought several hundred acres in the southern part of the county in 1826 and established the village of Cooksburg. New Hampshire–born Cyrus Blood, another early settler, taught at the Chambersburg and Hagerstown academies before accepting a professorship at Dickinson College. He and his family came to Forest County in 1833 and bought a large tract of land north of Cooksburg that came to be known as Blood's Settlement. He later named the town for his daughter, Marien. In 1848, at Blood's insistence, the area was named a county, but only the five eastern townships were included. The county expanded in 1866 to include the three townships around Tionesta. This fueled a rivalry between the only two towns in Forest County large enough to have schools: Marienville, the former county seat, and Tionesta, the county seat since the expansion.

Lumbering was the county's dominant industry, but by the 1880s, so many trees had been taken indiscriminately that much of north-central Pennsylvania was called the "Pennsylvania Desert." A million acres of barren landscape once filled with hemlock, stripped of its bark and left to rot by the tanning industry, and with pine, felled for lumber, were ravaged by fires that exacerbated erosion and flooding. By 1883, at the peak of the lumbering industry, there were nineteen woodworking establishments within a five-mile radius of Tionesta.

The state government began buying abandoned, cutover lumber acreage about 1900, and later purchased Cook Forest, the old-growth forest lands that had never been cut. In 1933, the Civilian Conservation Corps made Duhring the center of their training camp. They built fire roads, bridges, and cabins throughout the second-growth Allegheny National Forest. Today, three-fourths of Forest County comprise state or national forest, including the one-fifth of the 513,000-acre Allegheny National Forest that lies within the county's borders.

Other industries exist in Forest County. In the 1880s, there was a brief oil boom. From 1914 until 1982, Marienville had a glassmaking operation, and Tionesta has a sand and gravel dredging company and a plastic container plant. The U.S. Army Corps of Engineers dammed Tionesta Creek in 1941, flooding the villages of Kelletville, Nebraska, and Mayburg to create Tionesta Lake as a means of regulating the creek's flow and controlling flooding farther down the Allegheny River. Over the years, outdoor recreation has come to rival lumbering as the chief occupation in Forest County.

TIONESTA

Though organized as a borough in 1852 under Venango County, Tionesta was not made the county seat of Forest County until 1866. At that time the population doubled with the discovery of oil to the south and the corresponding boom in the lumber trade. The town, laid out in a grid pattern on a flat, wide curve of land on the east side of the Allegheny River, offered a natural site for a riverboat camp, and the village was often populated with crews from Warren or from New York on their way to Pittsburgh. Tionesta Creek (the name "Tionesta" means "it penetrates the land") was a good site for a lumber mill and building flatboats since it had direct access to the Allegheny River.

The borough's dependence on the lumber industry attracted competent woodworkers whose talents are displayed in several residential properties, including the Greek Revival house (1850) at 129 Elm Street with corner pilasters, wide cornice, and simple porch columns on a large lot facing away from the Allegheny River, and the two frame houses with wood siding cut to emulate stone at 301 Davis Street and 607 Elm Street. An imposing brownstone Gothic Revival church (1908; 208 Elm Street), built for the United Methodist Church of Tionesta, adds to the substantial buildings along the main street.

FO1 Forest County Courthouse

1868–1869, Keene Vaughn. 526 Elm St.

This simple brick courthouse has a domestic scale and presence despite being perched on a terrace above Tionesta's main street. Though the central tower has been removed, the building's surviving features are Italianate, including paired round-arched windows on the first story and segmental-arched windows on

the upper, a Palladian window in the center of the front and rear elevations, and paired brackets throughout. The projecting entrance is framed by brick pilasters and has a fanlight in the center gable.

The adjacent, former jail (1895; 528 Elm Street) resembles a large Queen Anne house. Constructed of red brick, it has a hipped roof dominated by a large gable on the front and a matching dormer. Bracketed eaves line all sides of the building. Today it is the courthouse annex.

FO2 Forest County Historical Society (George W. Robinson House)

1873. 206 Elm St.

This large Stick Style house was in the Robinson family for eighty-five years, from 1873 to 1958. The decorative wooden detailing of the porch and the fanlike ornament above the porch and on the third floor gable end are particularly attractive. Among the largest houses in Tionesta, it is open to the public as the Forest County Historical Society.

ENDEAVOR

Northeast of Tionesta along East Hickory Creek, this small lumber camp village was named for a group of men who met over the company store and called themselves the "Christian Endeavor." The village was the site of an early sawmill, purchased in 1837 by Wheeler and Dusenbury Lumber Company. Initially named Stowetown, after Hamilton Stowe of Olean, New York, who came to manage the logging camp for Wheeler and Dusenbury, the name was changed by Nelson P. Wheeler, who moved to the area in 1871 and brought his bride, Rachel Ann Smith, in 1876. Wheeler's goal was to civilize the great woods around him, and he cultivated forest conservation and spirituality.

In 1897, the Wheelers donated a small Presbyterian church (FO3) and a Greek Revival kindergarten building (FO4) to the village. With the company office and white frame workers' housing, they form a village center for the town of perhaps a dozen structures. The office is a two-story white frame building with such Greek Revival touches as pilasters, corner boards, and cornice. Its lively facade has recessed corners on the first story and a central inset balcony on the second story that is topped with a pediment, to show off the lumber company's wares. Wheeler and Dusenbury became Endeavor Lumber Company in 1939 and in 1966, the company was purchased by Hammermill Corporation; today it is a division of Industrial Timber and Land Company.

Ultimately, the Wheeler family owned 50,000 acres of prime forest land. In 1922, Nelson Wheeler's heirs donated 20 acres of virgin pine and hemlock to the federal government and agreed to sell another 100 acres. The donation is now called Heart's Content and is a part of the 513,000-acre Allegheny National Forest.

Buildings in Endeavor (*from left to right*) include the Endeavor Presbyterian Church (FO3), the Greek Revival Endeavor Kindergarten (FO4), and the local office of Industrial Timber and Land Company.

A different sort of park grew in rural areas in response to the nineteenth-century's rampant de-forestation. By 1910, the state government began to plant trees on the devastated land. Today, two-thirds of Pennsylvania are covered with second-, third-, and fourth-growth forests. Later, to provide relief from the poverty and despair of the 1930s, the Roosevelt administration gave the National Park Service jurisdiction over large tracts of exhausted or submarginal timber and farm lands in an effort to preserve the natural landscape and provide underprivileged city dwellers, especially children, opportunities for outdoor living. Headquarters and shelters in these camps were built by the Civilian Conservation Corps, created by the Emergency Conservation Work Act of 1933 that gave men between the ages of eighteen and twenty-five, recruited by the Depart-ment of Labor, the opportunity to be trained in building techniques and given work supervised by the army. At its peak in 1935, over 500,000 men worked in over 2,900 camps nationwide. Western Pennsylvania has several examples of their work as far north as Potter County (PO7) and as far south as Beaver County (BE37). By the time the program was disbanded in 1942, more than three million men nationwide had served. They built their own temporary quarters in each park, and then proceeded to build camps that accommodated groups of up to 120 civilian campers. The lessons in standardization learned from this project served as a model for the U.S. Army when World War II mobilization required massive building programs. Albert H. Good's *Park and Recreation Structures,* a 1938 National Park Service publication, illustrated the type of rustic architecture considered appropriate to a federal park. Good's work became the pattern for rustic architecture across the country. The handworked log and stone construction recalls America's pioneer past, but the work also shows the influences of Bavarian and Swiss chalets and the camps of the Adirondacks.

BATHHOUSE AT PARKER DAM STATE PARK, CLEARFIELD COUNTY, 2001.

FO3 Endeavor Presbyterian Church

1897. PA 666

Nelson P. and Rachel Ann Wheeler, architectural patrons of Endeavor, no doubt felt that donating this white frame Gothic Revival church to the small village was a meaningful use of their company's product, lumber, which was generally exported downstream to Pittsburgh. Nestled among the trees of the forest, the church's steeply pitched gable roof and small pointed cupola are echoed by the Gothic Revival windows.

FO4 Endeavor Kindergarten

c. 1897. PA 666

This small, white frame schoolhouse raised on a stone base built in the form of a Greek temple has a porch with a large pediment supported by four Ionic columns on the facade. Although essentially a one-room school, it is among the most unusual in Pennsylvania for its classical features and elaborate central entrance flanked by pilasters. Commissioned by Nelson P. and Rachel Ann Wheeler to honor their two deceased daughters, the building's use for the lively pursuits of school and community center contrasts with its severe appearance. A larger frame, gable-roofed two-story school lies west of the village center.

COOKSBURG

FO5 Cook Forest Cabins, Sawmill, and Homestead

1868–1870; 1933–1942, Civilian Conservation Corps (CCC). PA 2002

The 8,200-acre Cook Forest includes one of the largest stands of old-growth white pine in eastern North America. The commonwealth's acquisition of the hemlock and pine forest in 1927 was the first time Pennsylvania acquired land specifically to preserve a natural resource, and it signaled a growing awareness of recreational lands as an economic generator.

John Cook came to the area in 1826 in search of a route for an east–west canal. He did not succeed in that mission, but did purchase the surrounding forest land c. 1828. He built a successful lumbering operation and his large family continued the business through the nineteenth and early twentieth centuries. In the 1920s, one of John Cook's descendants, Anthony Wayne Cook, began to urge his fellow heirs to preserve the 3,000 uncut acres that surrounded the family home. The family sacrificed much of their fortune to pay taxes on the undeveloped land in a conscious effort to preserve the mature forest of 200- to 300-year-old hemlock and pine trees with a 200-foot canopy.

Several important buildings are situated in the park, including Cook's Homestead (1868–1870), now a white frame bed-and-breakfast. The two-story structure has little ornamentation other than a porch along two elevations.

It was once home to Anthony Cook and his family of five children. Soon after the commonwealth's purchase of the forest lands, the CCC built cabins and stone and wood shelters for recreational purposes. The largest of these, the Log Cabin Inn, was constructed in 1934. A preserved sawmill houses an exhibit on forestry. The irregular shape of the park reflects the gradual and piecemeal accumulation of lands by the state, which continues to purchase lands for inclusion in the park. Two private homes surrounded by parklands remain in the Cook family.

FO6 A. W. Cook House

c. 1880. 3123 PA 2002

The Cook family decided that the large trees closest to the mill and the house should never be cut so that they could be appreciated by future generations of the Cook family. Now the public can appreciate them since these forested acres were donated to the state park system. The Anthony Cook house is a large, white frame Queen Anne house with a sweeping veranda along two elevations whose intersecting gable roofline is topped by a very steeply pitched hipped roof. The house remains in the family. A similarly sized house was built by Anthony's brother, Thomas Cook, adjacent to this property to the east. A large granite mausoleum in the form of a classical temple, built the year after Anthony's death, is located on private land southeast of the house.

CLARION COUNTY

Clarion County, encompassing part of the Allegheny Plateau, is characterized by low hills crisscrossed by streams. The area was included in the Treaty with the Six Nations of 1784 signed at Fort Stanwix (Rome, New York) and Fort McIntosh (Beaver). Much of the land was purchased at that time by wealthy Philadelphians and the Holland Land Company, but the land titles were in question for many years due to squatters who began to farm the land. Groups of settlers came from Westmoreland and Centre counties, as well as central and southern New York. Clarion County was formed in 1839 from parts of Venango and Armstrong counties. It takes its name from the river, which two surveyors noted for its "clarion call," the rippling sound echoing off the high, tree-covered banks. The river bisects the county from northeast to southwest and joins the Allegheny River at the western border.

The earliest settlers engaged in farming. From the 1830s to the early 1880s, iron ore deposits and plentiful forests supported over thirty stone iron furnaces. Technology changes caused their demise, but oil was discovered in the county c. 1870, and by 1880, there were approximately five hundred producing oil wells. Logging, natural gas production, and bituminous coal strip mining provided employment off the farms. In the mid-twentieth century, oil and gas production remained the major industries.

Since its founding, the population of Clarion County has nearly tripled. Clarion University of Pennsylvania (CL9) is now the largest employer and the locus of cultural activities in the county. The completion of I-80 in the late 1960s made access to the county easier, facilitating the annual arrival of about 250,000 visitors for outdoor activities and festivals. Farming remains an important part of the economy, with nearly five hundred farms in operation. Modular home manufacturing is a growing industry because the county's six entrances to I-80 allow access to major highways for shipping. Owens-Brockway, a glass container company, and Clarion Hospital are also major employers.

CLARION

The borough of Clarion was laid out in 1839 by John Sloan Jr. with lots among the pine trees one mile southeast of the Clarion River's banks. James Campbell, who arrived in 1840, said it looked more like a camp meeting than a town, according to a pamphlet in the Clarion Free Library; although by 1841, a voluntary census revealed a population of 714. The commercial district stretched along the Bellefonte Meadville Turnpike. Ground was broken for the courthouse, jail, and Clarion Academy in 1840. All three buildings were demolished and replaced during the late nineteenth century. Clarion Academy became a public school. The iron and oil industries left their legacy in the housing stock of the late nineteenth century. Jacob Black's handsome

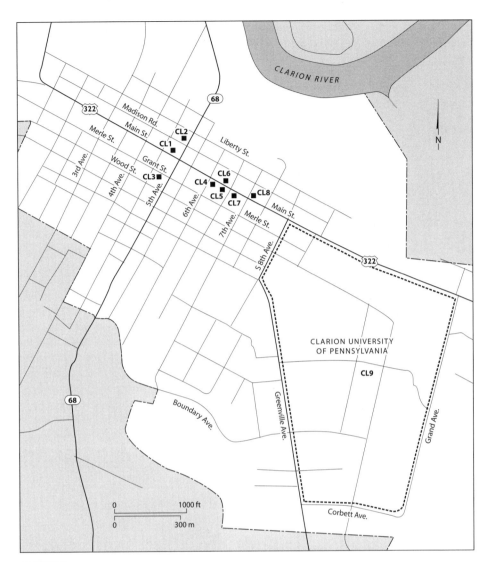

CLARION

Italianate house at 721 Liberty Street has interesting Gothic Revival trim, and at 715 Liberty Street a frame Stick Style house has excellent integrity. A Queen Anne house at 342 Wood Street has a distinctive corner wall dormer.

In 1876, Clarion was the terminus for a short-lived narrow-gauge railroad, the Emlenton, Shippenville and Clarion (ES&C), built to bring lumber, produce, and oil products to the Allegheny Valley Railroad (AVRR) along the river. By 1881, the ES&C was dismantled. Later on, the Lake Erie, Franklin and Clarion line served the borough.

The Owens-Brockway Glass Container Company (c. 1907; 151 Grand Avenue), before a series of mergers, was the Illinois Glass Plant, which made milk bottles. Lumbering and the manufacture of wood products continue in Clarion at a reduced rate of productivity.

CL1 CLARION COUNTY COURTHOUSE, architectural drawing, 1906

CL1 Clarion County Courthouse

1883–1885, William Kauffman and Edward M. Butz and Co., with Daniel English, supervising architect; 1947, Tillman Scheeren Jr.; 1980, Landmark Design Associates, Ellis Schmidlapp, project architect. 421 Main St.

This, the third Clarion County Courthouse, was the first of a trio of Pennsylvania county courthouses designed by Kauffman and Butz; the others are in Westmoreland (WE1) and Fayette (FA1) counties. Here, a straightforward, hipped-roof brick rectangle of three-and-one-half stories is aggrandized by the addition of a 213-foot-high square clock tower with a spire on the south facade. There are small carved stone balconies on each face of the tower surmounted by an iron statue of Justice holding a sword and the scales of justice. Hipped-roof dormers pierce the roofline above three-bay projections on the east and west elevations. Stone foundation and sill and lintel courses unify the brick building. On the interior, a central hall is flanked by offices to the east and west. A double stair at the south entrance leads to the large courtroom on the second story, and a second, smaller courtroom is on the third story.

CL2 Clarion County Jail

1873–1874, James McCullough Jr. Madison Rd. at 5th Ave.

The castellated battlements and central tower of the second Clarion County jail conjure up images of the castle keep, meant to terrify prisoners and serve as an object lesson to evil-doers. Designed by McCullough and built by Samuel Wilson and W. W. Greenland, similar jails are in Kittanning in Armstrong County (AR2) and Hollidaysburg in Blair County (BL3). Prominent keystones top the elongated, round-arched windows of the facade and three side bays while the rear five bays have small, rectangular windows lining each of the cell block's two stories. Twenty cells surround an interior courtyard measuring fifteen by fifty-six feet. The warden's three-bedroom apartment occupied the bays on the building's front. Its kitchen had a pass-through to the locked portion of the jail, allowing one kitchen to serve the warden's family, inmates, and guards. The warden lived on the premises until 1972. Inmates were kept here until 1995, when they were moved to a new facility in Paint Township. Today, the building houses a treatment facility.

CL2 CLARION COUNTY JAIL

CL3 Clarion County Historical Society (Thomas Sutton–John Ditz House)

1850; 1908–1910 remodeled, Elgan S. Sloan. 18 Grant St.

Clarion's Historical Society is located in a Colonial Revival house built for attorney Thomas Sutton that, at its core, dates from 1850. Local architect Elgan Sloan of Shippenville completely remodeled the house for hardware store owner John Ditz in the early twentieth century (see CL5). The facade is dominated by a two-story portico supported on fluted, Ionic columns with a second story balcony in the middle bay. Another two-story porch graces the rear. Flemish bond brickwork and the pseudo-Palladian window in the tympanum continue the elaborate composition. A similar porch and balcony combination can be seen on the New Bethlehem Bank Building, formerly called "White Pillars" (c. 1900; 650 Main Street).

CL4 Charles Kaufman Store and House

c. 1874. 600 Main St.

This property is emblematic of one Jewish family's contribution to a small western Pennsylvania town. When Charles Kaufman settled in Clarion in 1853, it was a town in its adolescence. He built a thriving mercantile business and became very active in Clarion's civic affairs. In 1865, he purchased a four-room house at the center of this building. By late 1874, he had built this five-bay, brick two-story store facing Main Street, with living space above for his wife and eight children. It is a straightforward storefront with little of the gingerbread trim popular in the 1870s. The gable-roofed rear portion extends for eight bays. The building is maintained by a granddaughter, who continues the family's sense of civic duty.

CL5 Fuller Furniture Store (Ditz and Mooney Hardware)

1917. 624 Main St.

John Ditz, of Ditz and Mooney Hardware, rebuilt this store in 1917 after a fire. The storefront glazing rises the full three stories and extends across seven bays of the facade, creating an airy, light-filled building that serves as a perfect showroom for the furniture retailer currently leasing the space. Stone pilasters and a heavy dentiled cornice complete the facade.

CL6 Clarion News Building

1876. 645 Main St.

This modest, two-story four-bay brick building was constructed for the Republican Printing Company in 1876 and has continuously housed a printing or newspaper company. Segmental-arched windows, stone corner quoins, and an elaborate cornice and parapet at the gable end facing the street distinguish this building.

CL7 Clarion Free Library (Clarion Ross Memorial Library)

1929, Emmet E. Bailey. 644 Main St.

The library uses a classical temple form with a pedimented central entrance flanked by recessed wings. The distyle in antis portico shelters double doors. The Clarion Women's Club established the Clarion Free Library Association in 1914, naming it originally for Mary Ann Ross, president of the club, and her son John D. Ross, who funded its building in 1920. Oil City architect Emmet E. Bailey (1872–1942), who designed many institutional buildings and churches in the region, designed the original north wing. An addition in 1986–1987 to the south elevation added stacks and reading rooms.

CL8 Immaculate Conception Church

1976, Kern Weber Murphy, with Herman Weber, project architect. 715 E. Main St.

Herman Weber of the Erie firm of Kern Weber Murphy created a modern design with shingle-clad roof fins and streamlined tower for this church to symbolize the reforms taking place within the Roman Catholic Church in the 1960s. Its centralized plan reflects the liturgical guidelines of Vatican Council II of 1965 to unify the congregation in worship. One of these reforms recommended that Mass should be said while facing the congregation. Weber focused all the internal elements, including the beams and skylights, on the altar. On the exterior, a courtyard and fountain integrate the entrance with the parking lot.

CL8 IMMACULATE CONCEPTION CHURCH

CL9 Clarion University of Pennsylvania

1890–present. Roughly bounded by E. Main and Corbet sts. and 8th, Greenville, and Girard aves.

Begun in 1867 as Carrier Seminary, Clarion University of Pennsylvania has grown from a coeducational secondary school of approximately 150 students to a state university with a student body of more than 6,000, nearly as large as the population of its host borough. The majority of the buildings on the 128-acre campus were constructed between 1960 and 1979, many designed by the Beaver County firm of Joseph F. Bontempo, though several late-nineteenth- and early-twentieth-century buildings reflect the earlier history of the campus and the various fashionable architectural styles of those decades. Moore Hall (1890) is a two-story brick building ornamented with brick corbeling, and a pair of drip molds flanking the gable of the central bay. Founder's Hall (1894), built as Science Hall, echoes the stylistic elements of Moore Hall but uses rough limestone trim as corner quoins and window surrounds. This large two-and-one-half-story building features rounded bays and a tall Chateauesque roof. Hart Chapel and Theatre (1902) by U. J. L. Peoples of Pittsburgh resembles a Gothic Revival corner church with random-laid stone. Becht Hall (1908), designed by Allison and Allison, is buff brick and has shaped parapets at the gable ends. James E. Allison (1870–1955) and his brother, David Clark Allison (1881–1962), practiced together in Pittsburgh from 1905 to 1910, then moved to Los Angeles. David originally named the building Navarre after the region in the Pyrenees that inspired the design. Stevens Hall (1929), by Ritcher and Eiler of Reading, and Harvey Hall, the gymnasium (1930), by Lawrie and Green of Harrisburg, are early renditions of the rectangular buildings that continued to be built on campus through the 1980s. In a sense, they merge the old and the new. Stevens has a flat roof typical of the buildings built over the next seventy years, while the gymnasium looks back by using a pitched slate roof, the last use of this roof type on campus. Over the years, the university has acquired so much land that today it covers nearly half of Clarion borough.

FRYBURG

In 1792, the commonwealth promised the area around Fryburg to the Holland Land Company, a group of wealthy Amsterdam investors, in return for their loans financing the Revolutionary War. The land company's agent, Harm Jan Huidekoper, came to the United States in 1805 and bought some of the properties for himself. In approximately 1820, he sold 184 acres to the Eisenman family, who knew the locale as "Kapp's settlement" and urged other Germans to join them. By 1835, there were about twenty families in the area, mostly German and Irish Catholics. For many years, German was the primary language of the town.

Farming and timbering predominated. Local timber, burned into charcoal, provided fuel for the fledgling iron industry in the 1830s and 1840s. The surrounding population swelled when a group of settlers from St. Mary's in Elk County migrated here to Kapp's settlement. In 1850, the town voted to change its name to Fryburg after Freiburg, Germany, where many of the first settlers were born. Two handsome stone houses from this time period in the 19000 block of PA 208 illustrate the prosperity of the town when the iron forges were operating. The red brick Washington House Hotel, originally built c. 1849 and rebuilt in 1879 after a fire (PA 4015 and PA 208 SE), with the frame Wayne Feed Mill across the street, provided much-needed services. In the 1880s, Fryburg's role as a supply town for the nearby lumber camps diminished when the narrow-gauge Foxburg-Kane railroad began hauling supplies to the lumber camps and exporting the lumber. As a result, many local jobs ended, and as the oil fields also were depleted, families moved to Oil City for employment.

CL10 St. Michael's Roman Catholic Church

1880–1887. 18749 PA 208

St. Michael's parish was founded in 1836 by German Roman Catholics who had emigrated from Germany ten years earlier. This church replaced their original log church, and with it the parishioners sought to emulate the thirteenth-century Cathedral of Our Beloved Lady in Freiburg, Germany. The plans drawn by contractor P. H. Melvin of Franklin date from 1880. The parish used donated labor and materials to keep costs low. Native sandstone used for the church was quarried nearby. The church has a central nave and Gothic-arched windows, but the dominating element is the central square clock tower with steeple that overlooks the town from a knoll. Stonemasons were brought from Germany to fit the stones.

HELEN FURNACE

CL11 Helen Furnace

1845. White Oak Dr. (PA 1004), 0.5 miles west of PA 1005 S

This rare, cold-blast iron furnace, which stands thirty-two feet tall in the shape of a truncated pyramid, has an excellent interior and reconstructed wooden scaffolding that illustrate the original method of loading. Called variously "Highland" and "Hieland" furnace, the name "Helen" has been in common usage the longest. Built by Robert Barber, it operated until 1857, and is now a historic site. Other stone furnaces survive in the county, but none are as accessible or as well maintained.

NEW BETHLEHEM AND VICINITY

CL12 Northwest Savings Bank (New Bethlehem Savings Bank)

1930, William F. Struthers. 301 Broad St.

This red brick Colonial Revival bank building is dominated by the tall square clock tower with a diminutive cupola at the northeast corner, two-story arched windows, and a broken pediment over the entrance. The bank is unusual, not only for its monumental presence in such a small town but also for its deviation from the limestone and columns of traditional

CL15 ST. CHARLES REFRACTORIES COMPANY–KMS REFRACTORIES (MCLAIN FIRE BRICK COMPANY)

corner banks. The local history called it the town's "Tower of Strength," an adage proved true by its surviving a devastating town fire in 2002.

CL13 Firman and Blanche Craig Andrews House

c. 1884, 1906. 318 Penn St.

This large frame house has intersecting gables and a deep wraparound porch on two elevations. It was built by a second-generation New Bethlehem banker with lumber interests, Firman Andrews, who developed several other properties in New Bethlehem. These included his parents' house next door (now demolished) and his brother William's house, which remains at 324 Penn Street. Firman's son, Charles Jr., added to the house in 1906, and relatives lived there until 1980. The third floor is well lit with multiple dormers and gable-end windows. Diamond panes in the upper portions of the windows indicate the medieval stylistic intent of the unknown architect.

CL14 Red Bank Mills, Inc.

1900, 1922. 234 Liberty St.

This former flour mill now processes grain and feed. The frame portion was built by

Charles Gumphert in 1900, and two decades later, Gumphert and his partner Reed added to it. They built the yellow brick wing with stepped gable ends, as well as a small elegant office building with quoins, keystones, oversized brackets, and a fanlight above the door. Several years later, Reed built a similar mill in Brookville, Jefferson County. In 1970, the mill bought the former C. E. Andrews lumber company building, constructed of hollow tile, across the street to the south.

CL15 St. Charles Refractories Company–KMS Refractories (McLain Fire Brick Company)

c. 1900. 24 St. Charles Rd. (TWP 466), 7.5 miles southwest of New Bethlehem

This manufacturing plant consists of nine yellow brick kilns, chimneys, and a series of sheds and two-story, flat-roofed buildings sited along Redbank Creek, the southern border of Clarion County. Located in an isolated spot, the adjacent remnants of workers' housing west of the plant indicate that once this was the village of St. Charles. Refractory bricks, as made here, are used to line furnaces in steel mills and absorb heat in other manufacturing operations.

EAST BRADY

East Brady sits on a tongue of land outlined by the Allegheny River in the southwest corner of Clarion County. Access to East Brady, originally named

Cunningham after an early farm owner, was over a steep road and then via ferry or barge from the west. The Allegheny Valley Railroad transformed the village after 1867, the year in which the first East Brady newspaper was founded, and a bridge finally linked the town to Brady's Bend on the west side of the Allegheny River. A new deck truss bridge (2005–2007) has opened, carrying PA 68 across the river.

East Brady's grid of streets climbs the hillside overlooking the river. Lining the streets are a number of handsome frame Stick Style and Queen Anne houses, as well as a Gothic Revival house at the northeast corner of Water and Bridge streets. The small commercial district along Broad Street is highlighted by the three-story brick Farmers National Bank of Emlenton (1900–1904; Broad and Brady streets). The frame Gothic Revival St. Eusebius church has a square tower entrance topped with a cupola (c. 1880; 301 E. 2nd Street), and the former high school, built of brick on a raised sandstone foundation (1910–1911; 502 Ferry Street), is now a community center.

CL16 First Presbyterian Church and East Brady Library (Newton E. Graham House)

c. 1899, George F. Barber; 1927–1928 alterations, Henry Hornbostel. 102 4th St.

The Newton E. Graham house in East Brady was built from the plans of George F. Barber published in the 1898 catalog *Modern Dwellings* (p. 31). Beautifully sited overlooking the Allegheny River, it is, by far, the grandest house in the area, with two-story porticos supported by fluted Ionic columns on the north and west elevations, one semicircular and the other rectangular. In 1927, the Grahams donated the house to the United Presbyterian Church of East Brady and it was adapted for its new use by Pittsburgh architect Henry Hornbostel. The first story remains remarkably intact, with the original staircase and three rooms that retain their hardwood paneling. The second story was reconfigured into an open worship space and the windows were converted to stained glass. A community library was added on the southeast corner. The elaborate Stick Style houses south and west of the brick mansion may also reflect Barber plans.

SLIGO

CL17 J. Patton Lyon and William M. Lyon Houses

1845. 2028 and 2030 Madison St.

Sligo, named for County Sligo in Ireland, was founded by Colonel J. Patton Lyon and his partner, Anthony Shorb, when they built an iron furnace nearby in the 1840s. They were co-owners of the Lyon, Shorb and Company iron furnaces from 1846 to 1871. Their iron was shipped to the Clarion River at Callensburg and then downriver to Pittsburgh, where the Lyons owned a foundry. The partners built two large frame houses in Sligo, one for J. Patton Lyon and the other for his son, William M. Lyon. The houses are grand for their relatively isolated location, indicating the success of their original owners.

The larger of the two, number 2028 for J. Patton Lyon, is U-shaped with two gabled wings flanking a central recessed space on the east elevation. The Greek Revival north facade faces the road and is five-bays with a central entrance flanked by sidelights and topped with a transom. At a later date, the house was ornamented with brackets, sculpted chimneys, and flamboyant jigsawn ornament on the eastern elevation. The grounds were laid out by landscapers Thomas Berrean and Michael Tierney, who planted trees imported from Ireland. Unfortunately, the house is presently in a state of disrepair.

William M. Lyon's house to the east is smaller and has four bays on the north facade. It is two-and-one-half stories with an L-shaped plan and a single-story porch. The use of narrow-gauge siding and the simple window surrounds and columns indicates that this house was not meant to compete with its neighbor in grandeur. Paired brackets are its only embellishment.

CL18 Clearview Old County Home

1903–1905. East of Sligo on Bald Eagle St. (PA 68)

This painted brick complex on a hillside overlooking the borough is noteworthy for its size and age. County homes for the poor that still exist on their original site and with architectural integrity, as here, are rare. The long two-story wings flank a central farmhouse that was built earlier for G. V. Curll. The wings have round-arched windows on the second story and intersecting gable roofs. The county home was part of a self-supporting farm worked by the residents in the early twentieth century, and many outbuildings remain. It is privately owned and being restored for use as a community center.

EMLENTON

CL19 Shortway Bridge

1968, Ted Andrzejewski. I-80 over Allegheny River

Crossing the corners of the three counties that intersect at this site, the 1,668-foot-long four-lane bridge carries I-80 over the Allegheny River 270 feet below. The cantilevered steel bridge consists of three continuous truss spans and is thirty-two feet higher than the Golden Gate Bridge in San Francisco. When built, it was the fifth highest bridge in the United States. Its designer, Andrzejewski, was chief engineer for Buchart-Horn of York, Pennsylvania.

ST. PETERSBURG

St. Petersburg was known as Petersburg originally and named for Judge Richard Peters of Philadelphia, who owned much of the land and donated five acres for the church and cemetery. Its name was changed to St. Petersburg in 1862 by the postal service. The village boomed during the oil excitement of 1871 from less than 100 people to over 4,000 in one year, at which time it officially became a borough. A series of fires in the late nineteenth century reduced the number of buildings, leaving St. Petersburg a crossroads town with a population in the year 2000 of approximately 400 people.

CL20 Elias Ritts House

1849. 203 Main St.

Elias Ritts, originally from Berks County, came to Petersburg in 1836, and four years later began building and piloting flatboats on the Clarion River to ship iron to Pittsburgh. His handsome two-story stone house has the traditional five-bay arrangement and is of such substantial appearance and excellent integrity that it stands out in the community. The eaves are lined with dentils and have deep returns on the gable ends. The oversized windows have simple, elegant trim. The L-shaped footprint of the original stone portion is nearly squared by a large frame addition on the rear.

CL20 ELIAS RITTS HOUSE

The Fox family's name was recorded on signposts and maps prior to the borough's official existence, since they owned over 13,000 acres of land in the area. The remote forested tract was difficult to reach by wagon and steamboat, which defeated an early attempt by Samuel Mickle Fox in 1847 to sell lots for a village. People came voluntarily to the area only after oil was discovered in 1869 and 1870. The escalating oil frenzy enticed nearly 2,000 villagers, mostly of a "rough" character, according to family accounts. The Fox family maintained control of the land by leasing it on a yearly basis rather than selling lots. They established a bank that operated until it was sold to the Butler Savings and Trust Company. The need to transport oil made a rail connection economically feasible, leading the Fox family to subsidize the building of a rail bridge and charge a toll for its use. The bridge was one of less than a dozen privately owned river crossings in the area; its successor bridge is scheduled for demolition and a new bridge will open by 2009. By the 1890s, the oil supply on the Fox land was exhausted, but many millions had already been made.

At the beginning of the twentieth century, the area's site on the east bank of the Allegheny River and cool summer temperatures prompted the building of summer homes of log, stone, and shingles, as well as a golf course. Little development occurred after 1920 until the turn of the twenty-first century, when the timber-frame Allegheny Grille (c. 2001; 40 Main Street) and the twenty-four-room Foxburg Inn and winery were built along the river (c. 2006; 20 Main Street).

CL21 Foxburg Country Club, American Golf Hall of Fame
c. 1912. 369 Harvey Rd.

The Foxburg Country Club was organized in 1887 on land donated by Joseph Mickle Fox, who became a golf enthusiast after visiting St. Andrew's course in Scotland. The clubhouse, originally a private home, was built by local craftsman Samuel Tippery, who also managed the Fox estate. The building now turns its back on the Allegheny River and faces east toward the golf course with a wide one-story porch along two sides. Its sloping roof and shallow ribbon-dormer mark the house as a bungalow, but one made of logs with thick chinking between them. Two massive stone exterior end chimneys anchor the building to its site.

Several privately owned, early-twentieth-century log and stone houses line the road adjacent to the clubhouse. Many have a similar appearance and all of those built before 1922 are thought to have been supervised by Tip-

pery. The club houses the American Golf Hall of Fame, a collection of early golf clubs and other artifacts.

CL22 Memorial Church of Our Father (Episcopal Church)
1881–1882, James Peacock Sims and Wilson Eyre Jr. 132 Bluff St.

Set on a shelf of land overlooking the village of Foxburg, this church was built as a poi-

CL21 FOXBURG COUNTRY CLUB, AMERICAN GOLF HALL OF FAME, clubhouse

gnant memorial to deceased Fox relatives. Mary Rodman Fisher Fox, who commissioned the church, was persuaded to build it after her daughter Sarah Lindley Fox converted to Episcopalianism before her early death. After witnessing the deaths of three of her children and her husband, Mary Fox chose a classmate of her late son, Philadelphia architect James Sims, to design the church. However, Sims died in May before the church opened for worship in November 1882. His apprentice, Wilson Eyre Jr., who became a partner during the design phase, drew the plans for the church, which were published in *American Architect and Building News,* March 5, 1881. This decorated Gothic Revival church has entrances on the side elevations, a bell-cote at the ridgeline, and a polygonal apse. A handsome stone and shingle Queen Anne parsonage south of the church was completed in 1884.

CL23 Foxburg Free Library and Lincoln Hall

1909–1910, Arthur Howell Brockie and Theodore Mitchell Hastings. 31 Main St. (PA 58)

The library was designed by Arthur Howell Brockie (1875–1946) and his partner Theodore Mitchell Hastings (1876–1950). Brockie, educated at the University of Pennsylvania, apprenticed with Cope and Stewardson, and founded his Philadelphia architectural firm with Hastings in 1904. Hastings attended Harvard and trained at the Ecole des Beaux-Arts in Paris. In partnership until 1918, their practice consisted primarily of hospitals and institutional buildings. For this commission, they used local stone quarried on the Fox family's land and built a combination library and auditorium building as requested by Hannah Fox. The two stories built against the hillside offer entrances at river level for the library and at hillside level for the auditorium. The auditorium, Lincoln Hall, has been refurbished and updated to host the Allegheny Riverstone Center for the Arts (ARCA), and houses a Wurlitzer organ manufactured in 1909.

The building's tiled roof and inset balcony overlooking the river evoke an Italian Renaissance palace with a strict rectangularity and formality in the windows and paired columns supporting the balcony roof. Random stonework combined with formal quoins and a stone course above the first-story windows emphasize this unusual marriage of materials and stylistic intention. Typical of the architectural eclecticism of the era in which it was designed, the interior of the library is furnished with oak Mission-style tables, chairs, and interior trim.

CL24 RiverStone Farm (Fox Mansion)

1827–1828, with additions; 1998–2000, Lee Ligo. 352 Foxview Rd.

The Fox Mansion, perched on a promontory of land at the confluence of the Allegheny and Clarion rivers, is a nearly square, stone building with a pyramidal roof and a two-story wing to the north. It was built in stages between 1827 and the late 1870s, when stone cladding was added to unify the whole. The Foxes, a Quaker family from Philadelphia, had owned the land since 1796 and used it as a summer residence. The last Fox owner sold the property in 1966, and it underwent two attempts at development before it was acquired by its current owner.

Architect Lee Ligo of Slippery Rock was commissioned in the late 1990s to complete the rehabilitation of the house and grounds. He added a cupola to the roof and designed a larger version of the cupola as a porte-cochere on the east elevation. Both have small peaked dormers that echo those on the carriage house to the east designed by Frank Furness (CL25). South of the carriage house is the greenhouse, which was rebuilt, as was more than a mile of low-lying stone walls delineating gardens and sections of the estate cleared for barns. A quadrangle of barns east of the carriage house was built, reusing older pin-connected timber frames moved to the site and clad with new cedar siding. A group of late-twentieth-century buildings southeast of the barns consists of two houses and a large carriage house–garage. They were modified by Ligo from the designs of Hearth Stone Log Houses of Tennessee.

The entire complex is rare in this part of Pennsylvania for its completeness, extravagant scale, and sophisticated design. The farm complex north of the mansion is distinguished by a set of four large gambrel-roofed barns, the western two originally built c. 1910 as dairy barns. The eastern two, built c. 2000 using wooden trusses and metal siding, contain a riding arena with a 100-foot clear span.

CL25 Fox Mansion Carriage House

1876, Frank Furness; 1998–2000 restoration, Lee Ligo. 352 Foxview Rd.

Frank Furness was tied to the Fox family by multiple links of kinship and friendship. His Philadelphia career was just short of a decade old when he was commissioned to design this carriage house. The survival of this solitary piece of work, so distant from Philadelphia, is testimony to the intelligence of the design and durability of its plan. The building has a complicated roofline, as do all of Furness's works, with portions that are double-hipped, pyramidal, and gambrel, as well as gable- and shed-roofed dormers. Two extraordinary exterior chimneys with bulbous tops and a half-timbered tower defy stylistic categorization. The golden sandstone base is enlivened by a course of terra-cotta-colored brick that hops over the segmental-arched windows on three elevations.

The building was designed to store horses,

CL25 FOX MANSION CARRIAGE HOUSE

hay, and carriages, and to house the coachman. Two large wooden doors on the east elevation open to the brick-lined carriage storage. South of these doors, the projecting gambrel roof protects the haymow doors above the tack room. A cistern with arched exterior access is below. Today, the second-story space contains a guest suite complete with kitchen, laundry, and fireplace. Immaculate horse stalls remain on the first story.

JEFFERSON COUNTY

Jefferson County is named for Thomas Jefferson, president of the United States at the time of the county's formation in 1804. It was under part of Indiana County's jurisdiction from 1806 to 1830, and initially contained what later became Elk and Forest counties. Jefferson County, three-fourths of which is tree covered, is located nearly at the center of the western Pennsylvania territory covered in this volume. Two of the earliest settlers, Joseph and Andrew Barnett, came to Sandy Lick Creek in the 1790s from central Pennsylvania and constructed a sawmill c. 1795 at its confluence with Mill Creek. Port Barnett, as it came to be called, was located just east of present-day Brookville, where a gristmill of 1860 continues to mark the spot (JE11).

The largest and most prosperous industry in Jefferson County was lumbering, which used local streams to transport logs. Attendant services—sawmills and planing mills—also proliferated. Between 1830 and 1837, individuals and companies from New England and New York bought large tracts of land at the headwaters of Red Bank Creek and the Clarion River from the Holland Land Company. The population grew steadily with the influx of lumber camps and farms. From 1865 to the 1930s, coal mining and coking dominated the industrial activity of the county, particularly around Reynoldsville. The Allegheny Valley Railroad (1874), which connected with the Philadelphia and Erie Railroad at Driftwood, hauled coal and passengers routed along the banks of Red Bank and Sandy Lick creeks, only one of a number of coal-hauling short line railroads that served the county.

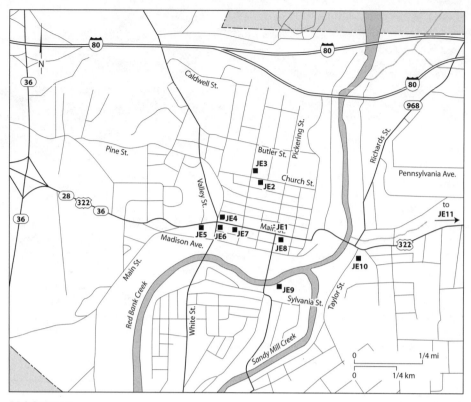

BROOKVILLE

Interstate 80, built in 1961 across the northern portion of the county, was part of a national defense highway plan to join San Francisco and New York. Access to this cross-country roadway was an important asset to what is today the Owens-Brockway Glass Container Company, founded in 1907 as Brockway Glass Company and one of the largest employers in the county (1965–1969, Raymond Viner Hall; U.S. 219, 0.5 miles east of Brockway). Today, Jefferson County's economy centers on lumber, manufacturing, the service industries, coal mining, and tourism. The handsome buildings of Brookville, the recreational activities of the state parks, and the annual tongue-in-cheek prognostication of Punxsutawney Phil, the weather-forecasting groundhog, are the main attractions.

BROOKVILLE AND VICINITY

Pennsylvania has many beautiful small towns, but Brookville is among its finest. Nestled into the hillside away from the floodplain created by the convergence of North Fork and Sandy Lick creeks, which join to create Red Bank Creek, the borough was surveyed and plotted by John Sloan in June 1830, and designated the county seat due to its central location. Today, the courthouse looms above the small-scale, red brick commercial core and churches that dot the hillsides. A series of fires in the 1870s necessitated the rebuilding of several blocks of the commercial district, but the town has retained many of its older buildings and has a pleasant mix of residential and commercial uses. The wide Main Street allows for comfortable parking and ease of access. Since 1983, Brookville has been designated part of the National Trust for Historic Preservation's Main Street program (founded 1981). Aided by the nonprofit Historic Brookville, Inc., the local property owners and merchants have created a thriving downtown, either reusing restored buildings or, in two cases, constructing compatible new ones.

Brookville's creeks were heavily used for shipping and were named public highways in 1817. The Susquehanna and Waterford Turnpike traversed the town after 1824. Most of the buildings, however, postdate the Civil War and reflect the arrival of the Allegheny Valley Railroad in 1873 and various coal-shipping lines that opened later and operated until the 1940s. Today, PA 36 and PA 28 lend access directly to Brookville. But it was the placement of I-80 through the northern reaches of the town that has allowed it to retain its nineteenth-century character by keeping the largest stores and motels outside of the older commercial district.

JE1 Courthouse

1868–1869, James W. Drum; 1927 alterations, Emmet E. Bailey. 200 Main St.

Brookville's courthouse cupola and tower made a nostalgic nod to Independence Hall as the nation's centennial drew near. Drum's pedimented entrance pavilion recalls the Greek Revival style seen most often in western Pennsylvania's northern counties and specifically at the Greene (GR1) and Lawrence county (LA1) courthouses. This building is a departure for Drum, whose buildings were usually Second Empire, as in the former Indiana County courthouse (IN2). For Jefferson's courthouse, the large paired brackets that alternate with single brackets and the deep eaves add a touch of Italianate styling. The building rests on a raised basement, allowing three stories on the facade and two stories at the rear where the land slopes upward. The alterations of 1927 include the curving front steps with wrought-iron railings and the addition on the west. Brookville architect

JE1 COURTHOUSE

JE4 BROOKVILLE PRESBYTERIAN CHURCH

William L. Snyder restored the courthouse in 1976.

JE2 George VanVliet House

1861–1865. 271 Church St.

Since 1842, local carpenters had been copying the designs in the pattern books of Andrew Jackson Downing and Alexander Jackson Davis. This cottage with its board-and-batten siding, front porch, and decorative bargeboards is a fine example of the type of house they thought appropriate for a wooded site in a rural town. The house is interesting for its survival and for the longevity of the design's popularity. It perches above the town, but is oriented away from it.

JE3 Northside Elementary School (Brookville High School)

1938–1939, Hunter and Caldwell. 280 Church St.

When built in the late 1930s, this red brick school incorporated such colonial features as a bridged chimney, a square clock tower with cupola, and a broken pediment at the entrance. This comfortable and reassuring design fit into the context of the late-nineteenth-century housing surrounding it on the hilly site. Hunter and Caldwell's successor firm, Hayes Large Architects, was asked, c. 1999, to design a school to replace this one, but having learned the lessons of the Main Street project, they and the school board decided to rehabilitate this structure, rather than demolish and build anew.

JE4 Brookville Presbyterian Church

1904–1905, Robinson and Winkler. White St. at Main St.

This massive brownstone church acts as a gateway to the commercial district of Brookville. The sanctuary is separated from a curved classroom wing by a single large door that can be raised to expand the sanctuary into an Akron plan configuration. A square tower with rounded corners and crenellations marks this juncture, while the entrance is accessed through a recessed arcade and marked by a taller tower, which also has rounded corners but that here terminate in tiny spires. Rose windows grace the east and south elevations, while on the north, a smaller version rests above a round-arched double window. The windows were designed by the George Hardy Payne Studio of Paterson, New Jersey.

To the north at 120 N. White Street, a large brick, mansard-roofed Second Empire house with two-story bay windows has been the manse for the congregation since its construction by builder R. B. Taylor in 1884.

JE5 Joseph E. Hall House

1848. 419 Main St.

Lumberman Joseph E. Hall built his Greek Revival house on the hillside descending into Brookville and facing Main Street. The white frame house is dominated by a pedimented Ionic-columned portico that projects from the two-story central section. One-story wings have gable ends perpendicular to the street and are finished with pediments above simple pilaster strips. Brookville is about the farthest south in the commonwealth that this New England version of the Greek Revival exists. Caldwell's *Atlas of Jefferson County* of 1878 illustrates this as the "R. J. Nicholson Esq." residence, and shows it before the porches with their wooden columns and simple balusters were added to the wings in 1881. The earlier porches were balconies with elaborate railings. An ice house and summer kitchen, both two stories and finished with board and batten, remain at the rear of the house.

JE6 McKinley Building (McCracken Hall)

1868. 395 Main St.

Although this version of the Italianate, taken directly from Samuel Sloan's pattern books, was popular, it is unusual to find two examples of it on the main street, especially one of wood and one of brick. The three-story brick version, with paired brackets, round-arched windows, and a glazed belvedere, was built soon after the Civil War by William McCracken as a performance space. The third floor's elongated windows indicate the site of the auditorium. Nearby, at 301 Main Street, the two-story frame house built for Alexander L. Gordon in 1881 has brackets and a belvedere cupola nearly identical to its brick cousin's.

JE7 Edward H. Darrah House

1872. 340 Main St.

Stylistically, there are several houses like this in the lumber territories of northern Pennsylvania (see Tionesta, p. 446). This house, commissioned by lumberman Edward H. Darrah, is of wood, but he chose to cut the wood into rusticated wood blocks to imitate stone. Paired brackets, quoins, and pedimented window surrounds complete the ornamentation. The veranda and curved bay windows on the south facade were added in 1897, while Darrah's daughter Mary and son-in-law Judge Charles Corbet were resident. Many single-family homes that retain their historic integrity remain on Brookville's Main Street.

JE8 Parker P. Blood Block, IOOF Building

1875; 1996–1997 restored, William L. Snyder. 180–186 Main St.

The Independent Order of Odd Fellows (IOOF), founded in seventeenth-century England, opened an American branch in Baltimore in 1819 with the goal of improving and elevating mankind through friendship, love, and truth. In Brookville, their lodge hall was on the third story of this red brick building. Eight bays of windows are highlighted with prominent cast-iron hood molding on the upper stories. Two storefronts with recessed entrances and windows and transoms restored to their original appearance make up the agreeable commercial space.

Across the street at 225–233 Main Street, the former Marlin's Opera House (1883–1886), a three-story, six-bay red brick commercial building with a gabled and corbeled cornice was commissioned by businessman Silas J. Marlin. The building has a 950-seat auditorium on the second and third stories, much of which is intact.

JE9 White-Brook, Inc. (Brookville Park Auditorium)

1915–1919, H. E. Kennedy and Company, consulting architect, and attributed to Henry Hornbostel. 1 Sylvania St.

This domed structure visible across the creek from Brookville's Main Street was built as the auditorium for the Brookville Park Association, successor to the Jefferson County Agricultural Society and Driving Park Association. Until the 1960s, the county fairgrounds were adjacent to it. Architect H. E. Kennedy of Pittsburgh and Philadelphia perched the shallow dome on a square building with chamfered corners, beautifully detailed with cream-colored brick outlining slightly recessed panels of yellow brick. Restrained classical ornament, an oval-shaped entrance pavilion lined with circular windows, and a series of arched doorways continues the elegance of the original auditorium entrance, now obscured by a one-story shed-roofed addition. At the time of its construction, Kennedy was working with Henry Hornbostel on the Liberty Theater (demolished) in Pittsburgh's East Liberty neighborhood. Many of the features of this former auditorium are reminiscent of Hornbostel's other work, and it is possible that Hornbostel had a hand in this design. The building is locally called the "White Elephant," not for its coloration or styling but because even as its construction lagged, the expenses grew, leading the town to doubt whether it would ever be finished. It opened in July 1919 and was condemned for public use due to structural problems shortly thereafter; it was not even heated until 1927. Over the years, it has provided office space to public servants, the Sylvania Company, which manufactured vacuum tubes there, and two different machine shops.

JE10 Litch House

c. 1880. 16 Taylor St.

Built by a lumber family to overlook their mill along North Fork Creek, this house is a stunning example of the Stick Style, dominated by a three-story tower with round-arched windows and a convex roof. The three-bay porch

JE10 LITCH HOUSE **JE11** HUMPHREY INDUSTRIES

is balanced by a three-sided, two-story bay window. Brackets and cross-shaped ornament under the projecting eaves and the colorful paint scheme of maroon and dark green that highlights the windows and cornice against the cream-colored walls complete this celebration of wood.

JE11 Humphrey Industries

1860 gristmill; 1929–1930 offices and house, Russell Howard. 13760 Knox Dale Rd. (PA 2023), Port Barnett, 1 mile east of Brookville

This office building was commissioned in 1929 by Lee Barnett "Lee B" Humphrey, who was president of the Humphrey Brick and Tile Company for thirty years. The family business began as a saw and grist mill (the frame gristmill remains), but as the lumber supply dwindled, the company switched to making rectangular hollow structural tile. Humphrey commissioned Russell Howard, an architect from Dubois, Clearfield County, to design the company offices. His daughter and son-in-law engaged Howard to design their house next door using Humphrey Industries' hollow building tiles with stucco over them. Howard, inspired by his recent trip to Mexico, chose the Mission Revival style for both. Nearby, the smokestack from the boiler of the sawmill remains, marking the earlier industries that once occupied the site and signaling the new family enterprise: charcoal briquettes.

REYNOLDSVILLE

Reynoldsville was the site of a Native American village and a hemlock swamp. The Indian path provided a natural location for a later turnpike, whose builders settled along the pike and built the first bridge over Sandy Lick Creek in 1822. The settlement was called Prospect Hill until 1850, when it was renamed Reynoldsville for the preponderance of Reynolds family members here. When the Allegheny Valley Railroad came through town in 1873, David and Albert Reynolds plotted town lots.

Timber rafting from the 1840s to the 1860s, then coal mining in the 1890s brought prosperity. But Reynoldsville is more than a coal patch, as it was the transportation hub for several surrounding mines as well as for lumber camps and farms. One industry that served all these constituents was the former Herpel Brothers Machine Shop and Foundry built c. 1905 at 45 W. Main Street. In 2000–2001, William Snyder rehabilitated it into a senior center, called the Foundry, for the Jefferson County Area Agency on Aging.

The buildings lining the commercial district are turn-of-the-twentieth century, two- and three-stories in various brick shades from brown to maroon; many have residences on their upper stories with recessed balconies.

The Hummelstown brownstone First United Methodist Church (1905–1906; 506 Jackson Street) has a square corner tower with battlements. A large red brick municipal building with a two-story portico (c. 1950; 460 Main Street) contains the library as well. A small steeply roofed gas station c. 1930 has been reused as a store (502 Main Street).

PUNXSUTAWNEY AND VICINITY

Punxsutawney is both the oldest and the largest town in the county. Reverend David Barclay laid it out in a grid pattern along Big Mahoning Creek c. 1818, and it was organized as a borough in 1851. The name is derived from the Native American words meaning "town of ponkies" (floating ashes). The Lenni Lenape called it the "Town of Sandflies," or Ponks-ad-u-te-ny.

On the second day of February every year since 1886, the residents of Punxsutawney reenact the German custom of Candlemas. They pull a groundhog from his lair, and if he sees his shadow and runs back into his lair, there will be six more weeks of winter. Punxsutawney Phil, the groundhog, lives in a special cage in the library for the rest of the year (1974; 301 E. Mahoning Street). The movie *Groundhog Day* (1993) brought a national audience to the event, but the town was not allowed to portray itself on screen; Woodstock, Illinois, was chosen for movie immortality. To bolster civic pride and add color and humor to the commercial district, the Punxsutawney Groundhog Club and Northwest Pennsylvania's Great Outdoors Visitors' Bureau sponsored the placement around town of thirty-two, six-foot-tall fiberglass Phantastic Phil groundhogs, painted by area artists.

Mahoning Street (PA 36) follows the creek along an east–west route. At 135 E. Mahoning Street, the red brick, four-story Pantall Hotel (1888) facing Barclay Square is one of the largest buildings in town. The addition of a McDonald's restaurant in the middle of the commercial district in 1996 brought life back from the strip malls just west and south of town. Several adaptive reuse projects are reinvigorating the commercial district in the twenty-first century, including the former Eberhart Building (1902; S. Findlay Street at W. Mahoning Street), a three-story brick building with corbeling at the cornice that is being reused as classrooms and offices by Indiana University of Pennsylvania.

Mahoning Street farther west is lined with substantial residences dating from the 1870s to the 1920s. The Christian Miller House (c. 1878; 233 W. Mahoning Street) is a frame Italianate house with paired brackets, segmental-arched windows, and elaborate window surrounds. The Punxsutawney Area Historical and Genealogical Society is housed in two former residences: the former E. C. McKibbon House (1901–1903; 401 W. Mahoning Street) designed by Green and Wicks with elements from several turn-of-the-twentieth-century revival styles, including Tudor Revival, Colonial Revival, and Shingle; and the Lattimer House (c. 1880; 400 W. Mahoning Street), a red brick Italianate. The stone Gothic Revival First United Methodist Church of 1899–1900 by Charles M. Robinson (301 W. Mahoning Street) has the first documented windows by the Willet Stained Glass Company of Pittsburgh. The Ohio sandstone Gothic Revival Sts. Cosmos and Damian Roman Catholic Church (1939–1942; 616 W. Mahoning Street) was designed by George Wesley Stickle of the Cleveland firm Stickle and Associates.

JE12 Reuben C. Winslow House

1860–1868. 200 Pine St.

Built for attorney, mine operator, and railroad promoter Reuben C. Winslow, the house was begun before the Civil War and finished afterward. The two-and-one-half-story brick house has a square, three-story central tower. The convex roofs of the tower and the awning over the second-story window lend an East Asian air, especially when combined with the bracketed eaves, the visual equivalent of fringe. Heavy drip molds outline the windows, and a tall entablature lines the cornice. The wooden porch has more elaborately carved ornamentation than the usual stock porch trim.

JE13 Punxsutawney Weather Discovery Center (U.S. Post Office)

1913–1914, James Knox Taylor, supervising architect of the U.S. Treasury. 201 N. Findley St.

This post office was built during the period of academic classicism favored by the federal government's supervising architect; the name of the local project architect is not known. A full entablature supported by Ionic columns is a part of nearly every post office designed between 1898 and 1912, but what sets this one apart from others is its rust-colored brick laid in English cross bond and punctuated by gunmetal gray bricks. The elevations and windows are outlined with cream-colored stone trim matching the limestone columns on the facade. In 2007, an interactive education center focused on weather science and folklore moved into the facility.

A block away, the former YMCA (1908; 115 N. Findley Street) is a three-story, buff brick rectangular building with petal-shaped panes filling large arched transoms above the first-story windows. It is now used as offices.

JE14 Sprankle and East Branch Viaducts and Coulter Tunnel

1911. PA 3014, 7 miles northwest of Punxsutawney

The Pittsburgh and Shawmut Railroad hauled coal over eighty-eight miles from Brockway in Jefferson County to Freeport in Armstrong County. In southwestern Jefferson County, a pair of 142-foot-high viaducts between the small towns of Coolspring, Markton, and Sprankle Mills are joined by the Coulter Tunnel. Sprankle Mills' steel viaduct is 1,430 feet long and is best seen from PA 3014.

JE12 REUBEN C. WINSLOW HOUSE

COOLSPRING

JE15 Coolspring General Store (Lafayette Shaffer's General Merchandise Store)

1904. 369 Coolspring Rd. (PA 3018)

As if frozen in 1904, this two-and-one-half-story, white frame general store retains all the elements associated with the era: wooden floors, penny-candy cases, benches, and a pot-bellied stove. The only change to the gable-fronted building has been the conversion of the upstairs space from an apartment and Odd Fellows Hall to a stained glass gallery. Down the street, the Coolspring Power Museum holds 250 internal combustion engines that illustrate 115 years of the machine's development.

JE15 COOLSPRING GENERAL STORE (LAFAYETTE SHAF-FER'S GENERAL MERCHANDISE STORE)

SIGEL AND VICINITY

Formed where two ridge roads cross, Sigel was founded in 1828 to serve the lumber companies as they worked their way across northern Pennsylvania, clear-cutting the virgin timber. In the 1880s, there were two hotels and a blacksmith shop, and two stores owned by Henry Truman. His general store remains, serving the locals who work on strip mines and gas wells and in lumbering, as well as the hunters, anglers, and hikers enjoying the outdoors in the nearby state and national forests. The town is so small that its water is supplied by Brookville and its children are bussed there for school. But like nearly every small town in western Pennsylvania, there is a grange, a volunteer fire department, and a Methodist and a Presbyterian church. The former is the Gothic Revival Sigel United Methodist Church (c. 1900; 8666 PA 949), and the latter is Mt. Tabor Presbyterian Church (c. 1900; 7320 PA 36).

JE16 Gateway Lodge

1934. 14870 PA 36, 8.5 miles northwest of Sigel

The lodge, built by owners Beth and Ray Griscom with the help of the Civilian Conservation Corps (CCC) team, initially included seven guest rooms and shared baths. Of hand-hewn pine and hemlock logs, the lodge has a steep gambrel roof with a long shed-roof dormer at the second story. The interior walls are lined with wormy chestnut and the floors are oak. In the 1950s, new owners expanded so that now there are eight guest rooms, twenty-four suites, and eight frame cottages on twenty-five acres adjacent to Cook's Forest. This lodge is a commercial version of the rustic campsites at Clear Creek State Park with luxury additions that make it a modern resort.

The state park, eleven miles to the east (1933–1937, CCC Company 353; PA 949 or Clear Creek Road), in Heath Township, has twenty-two log cabins built on 1,676 forested acres, in addition to a swimming area, concessions building, restrooms, hiking trails, bridges, and roads. The hilly Clear Creek valley extends from PA 949 to the Clarion River and is twelve miles directly north of Brookville.

CLEARFIELD COUNTY

The county's terrain is a succession of ridges and hills with the West Branch Susquehanna River cutting through the region from southwest to northeast. Larger in area than the state of Rhode Island, the county takes its name from the buffalo wallows Native Americans found here and used as cornfields in the midst of the forest. Great Shamokin Path, used mostly by Seneca and Lenni Lenape tribes up to and during the French and Indian War, ran east–west between what are now the towns of Clearfield and Curwensville. After Pontiac's Rebellion was quashed in 1763 and Native Americans left the area, the unexplored territory reverted to wilderness.

The northern third of present-day Clearfield County was claimed by Connecticut until the Trenton Decree of 1782 declared it part of Pennsylvania. The county, formed in 1804 from Huntingdon and Lycoming counties, was so undeveloped that its judiciary was overseen by Centre County from 1804 to 1822. Between approximately 1810 and the Civil War, a series of turnpikes was built and abandoned, and so the river and streams remained the most important modes of transportation.

Coal, mined as early as 1810, was floated downriver on arks, large elaborate wooden rafts, which were sold for lumber at the end of the trip. The arks became outmoded when a sequence of dams blocked their progress down the Susquehanna. Sawmills supplied nearby farms until c. 1820, when they began to ship to Harrisburg and beyond. Eventually the county had four hundred sawmills. Although logging peaked around 1860, it remains an important industry because by the early twentieth century, lumbermen began treating trees as a renewable resource and replanted.

The Clearfield Coke and Iron Company built a coke-fired furnace in 1836 at Karthaus. Coal mines became profitable, and their products found a larger market once the railroads began hauling and spreading feeder lines in the 1870s throughout the county. In 1874, the Berwind-White Coal Company opened its first mine at Houtzdale. It supplied coal for trans-Atlantic steamboats and the New York transportation system. Berwind-White had a major impact in Jefferson and Somerset (see Windber, p. 393) counties as well.

The West Branch Susquehanna River changed from an industrial highway to a recreational river over the years. Today, I-80 offers six exits across the county's width, bringing visitors and development possibilities to the area.

CLEARFIELD

Clearfield was an early Lenni Lenape village called Chinkleclacamousche, which means "no one lingers here." Surely a chamber of commerce publicist's nightmare, it was apparently named for a Native American hermit who affected horrifying costumes to frighten returning hunters into dropping their catch, a lazy but crafty person's hunting technique. By 1805, Lancaster native Abraham Whitmer owned the land and laid out the town in regular squares like Philadelphia: east–west streets were given names and north–south streets were numbered. Clearfield became a borough in 1840.

Despite economic reliance on the lumber industry, the principal institutional buildings are mostly brick and stone. Notable are three stone churches: the Gothic Revival Clearfield Presbyterian Church (1867–1869; 119 S. 2nd Street); the Romanesque Revival Trinity United Methodist Church (1870; 121 S. 2nd Street) designed by Henry Baird, a Williamsport architect; and the Gothic Revival St. Francis of Assisi Roman Catholic Church (1886–1889; 211 S. 2nd Street). The stone jail (1870; 300 N. 2nd Street) lies several blocks north of the courthouse and, having lost its perimeter stone walls, has been adapted for use as offices. It resembles contemporaneous stone jails at Hollidaysburg (BL3) and Ebensburg (CA3) designed by Edward Haviland.

Clearfield's tree-lined streets have large brick and frame houses dating from the 1870s and 1880s, notably in the 100 block of E. Pine Street and the attractive law office at 2 N. Front Street. The combined Municipal Building and Shaw Public Library (1998; 1 S. Front Street) is a recent addition, as is the red brick hall for the Clearfield Campus of Lock Haven University (2001; 201 University Drive).

CF1 Clearfield County Courthouse

1860, Cleaveland and Bachus; 1882–1883 addition, Thorn and Burchfield. Market and 2nd sts. NE

This relatively simple, red brick courthouse stands at an intersection in the commercial district, neither towering over the town nor dominating a town square. The gabled two-story building has a square clock tower above the arcaded street entrance on the west fa-

CF2 CLEARFIELD COUNTY NATIONAL BANK AND DIMELING HOTEL

cade. Round- and segmental-arched windows and brick corbeling are the only ornamentation. An addition of 1882 to the east expanded access to the county's one courtroom, but today's security measures have returned access to a single entrance. Nothing is known about the architectural firms of either the original courthouse or the addition, other than their names.

CF2 Clearfield County National Bank and Dimeling Hotel

1904, Beezer Brothers. W. Market and N. 2nd sts. NW

Between 1900 and 1906 the Beezer twins, Michael and Louis, designed five brick commercial buildings in western Pennsylvania, four of them with a stone first story and all crowned with elaborate terra-cotta ornament on the top story and cornice. The first story of their first Beaux-Arts-inspired building, the Pennsylvania National Bank (c. 1900) at 3400 Butler Street in Pittsburgh, is repeated here with the same rusticated limestone and round-arched windows. This building has three-sided bay windows to enliven the building's red brick midsection, as did the First National Bank of Tyrone (demolished). The finest of Beezer Brothers' commercial buildings, this bank is one of the few buildings they signed with a

CF3 CHRISTOPHER KRATZER HOUSE BED-AND-
BREAKFAST

CF3 Christopher Kratzer House Bed-and-Breakfast

c. 1840. 101 E. Cherry St.

This handsome Greek Revival board-and-batten house lies within a block of the river and stands out in a town primarily constructed of brick and stone. The two-story, hipped-roof house has attic windows and a one-story square entrance portico supported by Ionic columns. It was built before 1840 by lumberman Christopher Kratzer, a successful entrepreneur who invested in turnpikes, the newspaper business, real estate, and politics. The house has been converted to a bed-and-breakfast. Both this house and a brick house of the same period at 114 Front Street indicate by the sophistication of their architectural styling the prosperity brought to this relatively isolated spot by river access and the lumber industry. The L-shaped brick house at number 114 has a handsome triangular light in the pediment facing the street, a feature seen often in the valley of the West Branch Susquehanna River.

plaque. Beezer Brothers employed their patented fireproof flooring system, using hollow clay tiles tied to the masonry walls rather than steel supports that twist when exposed to intense heat. The Beezers never used stock designs and prided themselves on discarding their previous drawings. So while there is some similarity among their commercial buildings, each is different.

CURWENSVILLE

Curwensville is named for its earliest landowner, John Curwen, who settled here in 1799 and laid out forty-eight lots between Thompson and Locust streets. The town is divided into thirds by the West Branch Susquehanna River and Anderson Creek. It sits on high rolling land surrounded by flourishing farms and several coal mines. There has been a Quaker presence here from 1817, and a meetinghouse in town is now reused as an antiques store (818 State Street). The brick house commissioned by William Irvin in 1835, now a shop, appears to have been updated to its present Italianate appearance (240 State Street). The village became a borough in 1851. The railroad branch lines running through Curwensville provided the impetus for John Irvin's construction of the substantial stone two-and-one-half-story house with peaked gables (c. 1870; 211 State Street), as well as the stone Gothic Revival Curwensville Presbyterian Church (1868; 430 Locust Street). A pair of stone churches on State Street deserves attention: the Gothic Revival United Methodist Church (1893; 602 State Street) and the Shingle Style Grace Lutheran Church (1899; 406 Pine Street).

GRAMPIAN

CF4 West Branch Society of Friends Meetinghouse

1901, Miles Wall, builder. 400 block 1st St. (U.S. 219) near PA 729

The West Branch Quakers have been meeting in this area since 1812, building their first log meetinghouse in 1820. When the meeting outgrew the second home, a frame one-story building with two entrances, they commissioned fellow Quaker Miles Wall to design and build a third in Grampian. Few of these meetinghouses remain in the western half of the state, and fewer still continue in operation and are well maintained. Using a running brick bond and T-shaped, cross-gabled plan, the meetinghouse echoes elements from others up and down the East Coast. The lunette above the basement's west door sheds light on the secretary's desk inside. The main floor is a single space lit by segmental-arched windows on all elevations and filled with west-facing pews also made by Miles Wall. There is a double-door entrance facing east with a round window above, and a secondary entrance on the north elevation. See also the Dunning's Creek Friends Meetinghouse (BD21) at Fishertown in Bedford County.

MAHAFFEY VICINITY

CF5 Mahaffey Camp Meeting Grounds

1897. U.S. 219, 1 mile north of Mahaffey

The rows of simple frame cottages and the large tabernacle assembly halls, which open to keep air circulating, are two important components of a successful camp meeting ground. The Christian and Missionary Alliance Church has operated the Mahaffey Camp on this site since 1897. The core of its youth tabernacle dates from that time. A second tabernacle was built in 1919 and a new dining hall was erected in the 1990s, but the forty-five acres sweeping toward the West Branch Susquehanna River are remarkably unchanged. Today, recreational vehicles outnumber the two hundred summer cottages, but every year nearly 3,000 people attend a ten-day Bible study session and encampment at the end of July. The white frame cottages are generally two bays wide, one or two stories tall, and alternate their gable ends from front to side. There are also three dormitories and two group houses on site.

MCGEES MILLS

When itinerant Methodist minister James McGee brought his family to Clearfield County from Centre County in 1826, they essentially built their own small village, focusing it around a sawmill and a gristmill. To the southeast, below the level of the U.S. 219, the West Branch Susquehanna River is the town's backyard. A group of frame houses scattered about the intersection of U.S. 219 and PA 36 housed many of his eight children as they married. The handsome Greek Revival house set back from the intersection was built by his oldest son, Thomas McGee, c. 1835. Following Township Road 322 south leads to the McGees Mills Covered Bridge, also built by Thomas McGee (1873) and the last remaining covered bridge on this branch of the Susquehanna. The 105-foot Burr arch truss bridge of white pine is a photographer's favorite. Back at the highway, the gable-roofed building with a wraparound porch (12931 U.S. 219) is probably the hotel referred to as "newly built" in 1887 when the Bell's Gap Railroad came through town. It is rare to find such a small village with so many of its original components intact.

DUBOIS

The area around DuBois was a large beaver meadow until after the Civil War, when John E. DuBois began to harvest the timber from his twenty thousand acres of land. Between 1872, when three families laid out the town of Rumbarger, and 1887, when the population grew to around 6,000, the railroad and lumber town boomed. Today it is the largest town in Clearfield County with a population of more than 8,000. John DuBois cut the timber, built kilns and mills, and made boxes, iron, and lights. He also built a reservoir and, in 1876, opened a coal mine. All these industries shipped their products via the two rail lines running through DuBois: the Buffalo, Rochester and Pittsburgh (BR&P) and the Allegheny Valley Railroad (AVRR). A brick passenger railroad station (1893; 1 N. Franklin Street) for the BR&P, designed by Gordon, Bragdon and Orchard of Rochester, New York, is now used as offices. The firm combined the ticket office, women's waiting room, general waiting room, and baggage and express functions in one rectangular building with second-story offices. Claude Fayette Bragdon (1866–1946), who signed the station's drawings illustrated in *American Architect* (September 23, 1893), worked with Green and Wicks in Buffalo and then practiced in the Rochester area from 1891 to 1923. Bragdon wrote three books on architectural theory and the foreword to Louis Sullivan's autobiography, and edited Sullivan's *Kindergarten Chats*.

The town has four churches clustered around the First United Presbyterian Church (43 W. Scribner Avenue) of 1892, designed by William J. East, with an addition and alterations in 1898 by Beezer Brothers. The church combines Richardsonian Romanesque on the exterior with its rough-cut stone, squat towers, and round-arched windows with Arts and Crafts details inside. In the late nineteenth century, Dubois had four branches of the Woman's Christian Temperance Union (WCTU), including one for children. Ironically, the city also had one of the largest and best-equipped breweries in central Pennsylvania, which was demolished in 2002. New retail developments and big box

Buffalo, Rochester and Pittsburgh Railway Company passenger station at Franklin and Long streets, Dubois.

stores are being built along U.S. 219 and PA 255 north of the older commercial district; the latter consists of two-story brick buildings along Brady Street between Park and Shaffer avenues.

PENFIELD VICINITY

CF6 Parker Dam State Park

1930–1933, Civilian Conservation Corps (CCC). Mud Run Rd. off PA 153, 5.5 miles north of I-80

By the turn of the nineteenth century, most of northern Pennsylvania's land had been stripped of tree cover, prompting flooding and erosion. The state stepped in and began to reclaim and replant tax-delinquent former logging lands. The growing popularity of automobile tourism called for the building of cabins and campsites in the forested areas as recreational use expanded. In 1930, the State of Pennsylvania bought this land from the Central Pennsylvania Lumber Company for $3 an acre. Three years later, the CCC set up Camp S-73 at the intersection of Tyler and Mud Run roads. They cleared brush and built roads, the dam, sixteen cabins, and hiking trails. An unusual octagonal log classroom building once housed the officer's headquarters. Little has changed architecturally since that time. The log buildings with stone foundations and piers and wood truss gabled roofs remain, but nature continues to change around them as a tornado in 1985 uprooted many second-growth trees. Four miles south on PA 153 is the S. B. Elliott State Park on Kennedy Road, which has two of its original eight CCC log cabins.

DRIFTING

CF7 St. Severin's Log Chapel

1851. 86859 PA 53

This small, simple rectangular log chapel is a remarkable artifact of the 1850s. A shingled square tower with a conical roof rises above wood-paneled double doors facing the forest that is steadily encroaching on the site and its cemetery. It is evocative of what Benedictine monk Boniface Wimmer called the "wild country" in 1854 (see WE26 and St. Mary's in Elk County). Entering the quiet, empty space of the chapel, graced only with a simple wooden altar table, one can imagine the sound of horse-drawn wagons and of wolves in the night. A hanging chimney heats the space and a small balcony, supported by narrow beams, lends access to the bell tower. The chapel's name derives from the land's donor, an Alsatian named Severin Nebel, who was

CF7 ST. SEVERIN'S LOG CHAPEL

named for St. Severin, Bishop of Cologne in the fourth century. Adjacent to this chapel and its surrounding cemetery is a stone church built one hundred years later, also called St. Severin.

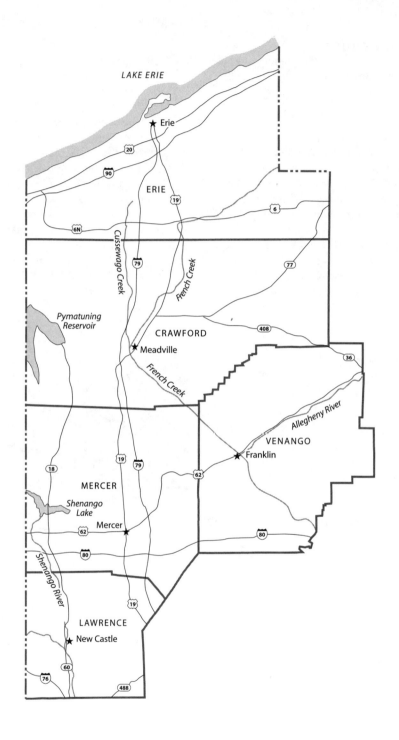

LAKE ERIE

Erie

20

90

ERIE

19

6

6N

Cussewago Creek

79

French Creek

77

Pymatuning Reservoir

CRAWFORD

408

Meadville

French Creek

36

Allegheny River

VENANGO

Franklin

19

79

18

62

MERCER

Shenango Lake

62

Mercer

80

80

Shenango River

80

19

LAWRENCE

New Castle

60

76

488

Oil and Water

This region of northwestern Pennsylvania is made up of Erie, Crawford, Venango, Mercer, and Lawrence counties. The region's topography is unique in the commonwealth, composed of relatively flat land creating a gently rolling surface formed by glacial action nearly 15,000 years ago. Covered with fertile soil and watered by several rivers, including the Allegheny, the region is well suited to farming. The state's northern border is Lake Erie, which has had a profound impact on the region's economy, especially in Erie County, opening it up to trade with neighboring states.

Settlement began in the late eighteenth century. In 1785 and 1786, over 600,000 acres of land in Mercer, Lawrence, Crawford, and the northern half of Butler counties were surveyed and divided into more than one thousand 200- to 500-acre plots labeled "Donation Lands." They were earmarked for Revolutionary War soldiers as a supplement to the badly depreciated Continental currency with which they had been paid. From the end of the war through 1810, soldiers could apply for a plot sized according to their rank. Many soldiers, preferring cash to land in this remote place, sold their plots to land speculation companies. The Holland Land Company bought a million and one-half acres, while the North American Land Company and the Pennsylvania Population Company acquired smaller portions. Confusion over who held the title to these lands—the large companies or the squatters who came and built farms—plagued the courts for decades and slowed development.

Architectural influences initially came from Connecticut settlers, who after 1825, often arrived via the Erie Canal in New York. Frame and stone Greek Revival buildings characterize the older building stock, with occasional multisided houses and octagonal barns for variety. When Edwin Laurentine Drake discovered an efficient method of pumping oil in 1859, investment to the area boomed, and houses in the architectural styles popular in the 1870s followed. Many remain intact since the boom went bust within a generation and the pressures for development slowed markedly by the turn-of-the-twentieth century. Small towns with populations ranging from 1,500 to 10,000 dot the landscape, except on the outskirts of Erie, which is rapidly suburbanizing. In the twenty-first century, tourism, agriculture, lumbering, and some manufacturing occupy most residents.

ERIE COUNTY

Erie County is part of the geological region in Pennsylvania carved out by the Wisconsinan glacier less than 15,000 years ago. The county is covered with compacted silts and clays whose undulating surface makes excellent farmland. As the glacier receded, it paused periodically, leaving a series of steps, or terraces, along the margin of Lake Erie that provide level east–west transportation routes. Because of their proximity to the lake, these terraces have an exceptionally long growing season and today are filled with orchards, vineyards, and greenhouses. Streams in the county flow north into Lake Erie or south into the Allegheny River.

The name of the lake, county, and city—Erie—stems from their association with the Eriez Indians, so-named by French explorers. They were an agricultural people who spoke a language related to Iroquois and were conquered and dispersed by the Seneca, part of the Iroquois confederation, in 1656.

French soldiers and traders used the Native American Venango Trail as their military road between Canada and Fort Duquesne at Pittsburgh. This combination of land and water routes connected Lake Erie to the Ohio River. After a fourteen-mile overland portage south of Lake Erie, water travel resumed at Le Boeuf Creek, which feeds into French Creek at Waterford. That creek flows southeast to the Allegheny River and ultimately to the Ohio. The French immediately understood the importance of this connection, and in 1753, they built forts at Erie (Fort Presque Isle) and Waterford (Fort Le Boeuf) to guard these sites (both forts are now demolished). English colonists, wary of the French dominance presaged by these forts, sought to oust the French. Ultimately, the English defeated them, only to have their settlement interrupted by a coordinated Native American attack in 1763 called Pontiac's Rebellion. Again, the English prevailed.

After the American Revolution, Connecticut claimed a three-county-deep swath of land along the entire northern boundary of what is today Pennsylvania. The rancorous dispute was not settled until 1787. Later, there was rampant confusion over which state held the Erie Triangle, the northwestern corner of the commonwealth. In addition to Connecticut, three states—Massachusetts, New York, and Pennsylvania—laid claim. Finally, New York and Massachusetts relinquished their claims to the federal government, which in 1792 sold the 202,187 acres to Pennsylvania for $151,000. Through this transaction, Pennsylvania gained a port on Lake Erie.

Lake Erie defines the northern edge of the county. Because the lake is shallow, it has proved treacherous to sailors, and remnants of hundreds of shipwrecks lie at its bottom. However, just off the shore of Erie County, the lake reaches a depth of nearly two hundred feet in a yawning well, allowing the port of Erie to welcome ocean-going vessels. Erie is connected to Buffalo and to Cleveland by their lake ports. New York named its canal after the lake that was its western terminus. Yet many are surprised to learn that the Erie Canal never entered Erie County or that the city of Erie is not its western terminus. The city's only canal connection was to the Pennsylvania Canal in 1844 by way of a system called the Erie Extension Canal that flowed southwest to Beaver County, not east.

The towns of Erie and Waterford were both surveyed and plotted by Andrew Ellicott and General William Irvine as part of the state reservation project undertaken between 1783 and 1795. Towns along the western border, including Pittsburgh and Beaver, were similarly laid out. Much of the land in Erie County was purchased by the Pennsylvania Population Company of Philadelphia, a private land company, rather than by individual settlers.

The Erie and Waterford Pike built between 1806 and 1809 carried the salt trade between Syracuse and Pittsburgh. Salt shipped through Erie was transported south along the turnpike, and then floated to Pittsburgh via French Creek and the Allegheny River, bringing a steady stream of workers through the area. Early settlers included carpenters and shipbuilders from New York and Philadelphia, who arrived during the War of 1812 to build the two large brigs in Erie's protected harbor that were used to defeat the British on Lake Erie. Many stayed in Erie County, establishing farms and using power for sawmills and gristmills from a series of streams that drop into Lake Erie.

When railroads supplanted the canals, Erie's crossroads status was challenged, but the railroads brought new industries. Corry, in southeast Erie County and incorporated in 1866 at the junction of four rail lines, hosted the Climax Manufacturing Company from 1888 to 1928, which built over a thousand geared locomotives especially suited to uneven terrain and that were a key element in the growth of the oil and lumber industries. Corry, though, never rivaled the city of Erie in size or manufacturing capacity.

Erie's diversified twenty-first-century economy includes electronics, instruments, and insurance, whose development was spurred by the intersection of two federal highways, I-90 and I-79. The county's fifty miles of shoreline provide excellent recreational opportunities and have inspired the construction of several small resort communities. But the lake's shallowness makes it vulnerable to "dead zones," oxygen-free areas that kill fish, plants, and insects and, ultimately, the water birds that feed on them. This phenomenon is being studied in Lake Erie, as it can have a devastating effect on tourism.

ERIE AND VICINITY

Erie is located on a series of plateaus and ridges formed by the receding Wisconsinan glacier. Northward-flowing streams, including Mill and Cascade creeks, cut through the glacial drift to create dramatic scenery. French traders found that the bay at Presque Isle, the spit of land extending into the lake, accommodated their largest barques and canoes, prompting them to build Fort Presque Isle here in 1753. By 1759, advancing British troops impelled the

French to burn the fort and retreat to Detroit. The British then built a fort in Erie in 1760, only to have it destroyed three years later during Pontiac's Rebellion. To pacify the native inhabitants, the colonial government banned European settlement in the area, a ban enforced until after the American Revolution. Erie gained notoriety when General "Mad" Anthony Wayne died in Fort Presque Isle's blockhouse in 1796. To commemorate that event, a reconstruction of the blockhouse was built in 1880 on the grounds of the Pennsylvania Soldiers and Sailors Home and Cemetery overlooking Lake Erie. The Indian attacks and constant ownership disputes delayed Erie's settlement until Wayne soundly defeated the tribes in Ohio and Native American attacks ceased in 1795.

The Pennsylvania Population Company of Philadelphia purchased a large tract of land in 1792. Two of their investors, Andrew Ellicott and General William Irvine, surveyed the area and laid a grid of lots from the lakeshore to the city limits, numbering the east–west streets and naming the north–south streets after trees and nations. Judah Colt acted as the company's land agent from 1796 until 1832. The area was incorporated as a borough in 1805 and a city in 1851.

Although schooners began transporting salt from Syracuse through the port of Erie in the early nineteenth century, the city was little more than a village until the War of 1812, when a small army of shipbuilders and sailors were imported to build six ships for naval commander Oliver H. Perry's nine-ship fleet. The town used the waterfront commercially after the war, despite efforts to center the commercial district around the diamond known as Perry Square.

By the 1830s, Erie was linked to Chicago, Buffalo, and Cleveland by steamship. To the south, the Erie Extension Canal, while never profitable, linked Erie and Pittsburgh directly in 1831, and in 1870, its right-of-way was purchased by several small rail lines. When railroads supplanted the canals, Erie's crossroads status was challenged. However, a discrepancy in the width of the rail gauges between tracks east of Erie and those heading west worked to Erie's advantage since passengers and freight were unloaded and reloaded in Erie, profiting local retailers. In 1853, the railroads standardized their gauges, and Erie's citizens, roused by their political leaders, destroyed tracks and bridges along the Erie and Northeast Railroad's line. Erie's "Gauge War" or, as some newspapers called it, the "Peanut War," since peanut and pie vendors suffered most from the change, ended in 1856 when the commonwealth ruled that through-lines had to use a standard six-foot gauge. Most of Erie's rail lines were subsumed into the Pennsylvania Railroad by the century's end.

The Civil War again called on the maritime engineering of Erie's population to build the first iron-hulled warship on the Great Lakes, the USS *Michigan* (later the *Wolverine*). The metals industry, started in Erie after the Civil War, ultimately bestowed the title "Boiler and Engine Capital of the World" on the town. Irish and German immigration increased between 1860 and

An 1880 commemorative reconstruction of the blockhouse of Fort de la Presque Isle.

1900 and ethnic neighborhoods thrived, such as Little Italy at 16th and Walnut streets, and the Russian neighborhood along Front Street adjacent to the docks. Each neighborhood built a church for its religious and ethnic majority. The Poles built St. Stanislaus parish in 1888, although the present Gothic Revival Church at E. 13th and Wallace streets dates from 1895. The German community published German-language newspapers and patronized breweries. Streetcars, horse-drawn as early as 1866 and electrified by 1885, connected the neighborhoods, and by 1910, an interurban trolley extended to Buffalo.

Middle-class single-family homes, often integrated with the industrial sites around them, created a mixed-use urban aspect in Erie that was enhanced by the relative flatness of the land and the wide streets. Later, major industries opened on the edges of town: the Hammermill paper factory in 1898 and the General Electric locomotive works in 1911 to the east, and Lord Manufacturing Company and Erie Forge and Steel in the W. 12th Street corridor to the west. These factories occupied large acreages and built housing nearby for their workers. At midcentury, carpenter and self-taught architect

John Hill designed many of the more upscale wooden buildings and several brick Italianate buildings along N. Park Row. Erie Cemetery, a gardenlike cemetery established in 1850 (2116 Chestnut Street) contains an exquisite Gothic Revival stone chapel designed c. 1896 by Green and Wicks.

The first decades of the twentieth century saw Erie evolve in patterns familiar to many American cities. After a disastrous flood in 1915, Mill Creek was rerouted into an underground channel, eliminating many of the irregularities in the street patterns created by the creek's former path. The newly streamlined streets saw the building of several handsome buildings in the 1930s, including the former Greyhound Bus station (ER4) and the U.S. Post Office (ER22). During World War II, the use of Erie's port peaked, but it was eclipsed by ports in Cleveland and Buffalo.

Urban renewal projects in the 1950s produced several undistinguished buildings, including the City of Erie Municipal Building and Erie Plaza Hotel. As elsewhere, the middle-class population moved to the townships surrounding Erie in the 1960s as the completion of I-90 made the commute feasible. Additionally, just as the city began touting the vacation potential and beauties of Presque Isle in the 1960s, the pollution levels in Lake Erie peaked, and articles declaring the death of the lake put a damper on these efforts. Erie reached its highest population, 142,000, in the 1970s, and dropped steadily to 103,000 by 2001.

To counter this trend, Erie, like other American cities, began to reclaim its waterfront in the 1990s. It completed the Bayfront Highway to link I-79 and I-90 with waterfront destinations, including the Bicentennial Tower, Dobbins Landing, and the Raymond M. Blasco, MD, Memorial Library (ER8). The Jerry Uht Park (1995, Weber Murphy Fox; 110 E. 10th Street) brought baseball fans downtown to watch the Erie Seawolves play in their 6,000-seat triangular park. Erie's hockey team, the Sea Otters, plays in the arena next door.

Erie has a tradition of reusing older buildings, such as the Boston Store (ER17) and the former Villa Maria Academy (see ER2), both of which now host low-income housing units. Three major companies and institutions have spurred development in the central business district: the Erie Insurance Group (ER15) on the east side, Gannon University on the west side (ER2), and Hamot Hospital near the waterfront. All appear committed to keeping an urban presence in Erie.

ER1 Erie County Courthouse

1853–1855, attributed to Thomas U. Walter; 1889–1890, Gray Webber and Karnes; 1929–1930, Walter T. Monahan; 2005, Michael J. Grab Architects. 140 W. 6th St.

Every child in Erie is able to identify the three basic styles of architectural capitals—Doric, Ionic, and Corinthian—since all three are visible near the corner of Peach and W. 6th streets on the Erie Club (ER3) and on the courthouse. The courthouse has a dozen Corinthian columns supporting the pediments on its two wings that flank a courtyard. Although the wings appear identical, they were built seventy-three years apart. The west wing is attributed to Thomas U. Walter, who was paid for a design, but since that design never

ER2 GANNON UNIVERSITY, John E. Waldron Campus Center

surfaced, it is uncertain if the builders followed it. Nonetheless, this building is similar to one Walter designed for Chester County, since it originally included a bell tower that was removed in 1894. This original wing contains one large courtroom occupying the full width of the second story with furnishings from c. 1870 to c. 1900. An addition in 1889 extended the original building to the north and east, creating an L-shape. Architect Walter Monahan's matching addition of 1930 also contains a single courtroom, but it occupies one side of a central hallway. A glass-fronted lobby, added in 2005, now joins the two wings, providing a dramatic central entrance. The building retains its classical dignity and appeal.

ER2 Gannon University

1896–present. 109 University Sq., bounded by W. 3rd, W. 9th, Peach, and Chestnut sts.

The Gannon campus covers approximately twelve blocks of central Erie and consists of nearly thirty buildings. Many of the structures are office blocks and apartment houses converted to student and classroom use, the most interesting of which is the forty-six-room Scott-Strong house (1896; 109 W. 6th Street) by Green and Wicks, a Buffalo firm. Anna W. Scott Strong, heir to the fortune of her father, William L. Scott, and wife of the wealthy Charles H. Strong, presided over Erie's social and cultural life from the 1890s until her death in 1928. The house her father commissioned and gave to her was a fitting setting for her activities and perhaps indica-

tive of Strong's social aspirations. Its soaring hipped roof is pierced by gables and gabled dormers. Although often labeled Richardsonian Romanesque because the first story is stone and has a triple-arched entrance, the house is actually closer to the Chateauesque style that Richard Morris Hunt popularized in New York City.

Adapting some apartment buildings and single-family homes to living spaces for students and faculty, the school grew from this single mansion into fifteen nearby buildings by 1956. Wehrle Hall and a Student Union were built in the 1950s. Four more buildings, acquired and built in the 1960s, are basically brick rectangles with flat roofs. In the 1970s, the college commissioned Zurn Science Center (Goldberg and Heidt Architects; 143 W. 7th Street) and two buildings by Heidt-Evans Partnership: Finnegan Hall (1972) at 120 W. 5th Street and Nash Library (1974) at 619 Sassafras Street. In 1999, the John E. Waldron Campus Center by WTW architects (124 W. 7th Street) integrated several older buildings behind a new eclectic red brick facade with gabled-, pyramidal-, and mansard-roofed sections facing the campus green. The Carneval Athletic Pavillion by Rectenwald Buehler, Architects (c. 2004; 130 W. 4th Street) provides students with a pool, gymnasium, and racquetball courts.

Between 1989 and 1993, Villa Maria Academy, by then a women's college, was absorbed by Gannon. Its former campus at 819 W. 8th Street included an 1892 motherhouse for the Sisters of St. Joseph designed by David K. Dean and Sons, with a large addition in 1904

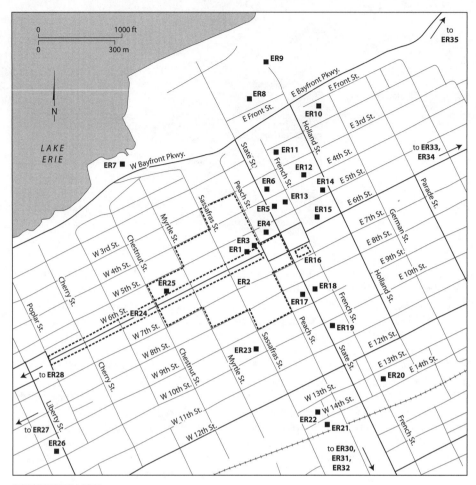

DOWNTOWN ERIE

by Pittsburgh architect Sidney F. Heckert. In 1927, a large gymnasium-kitchen-chapel addition designed by Fuller and Stickle completed the complex. The buildings were returned to the Sisters of St. Joseph in 1993 and now house seventy low-income housing units and community space called Villa Maria Apartments.

ER3 Erie Club (Charles Manning Reed House)

1846–1848, Edward B. Smith. 524 Peach St.

Charles Manning Reed hired Buffalo architect Edward Smith to design his grand Greek Revival residence on this site overlooking the city's diamond and away from the busy commercial lakefront where he had made his fortune in shipping. Over the years, though, Erie's commercial core moved south, and to-

day the Reed mansion is in the midst of the central business district. Architectural historian Talbot Hamlin in *Greek Revival Architecture in America* (1944) called the house "The highest point of the Greek type in Pennsylvania." The seven-bay facade is dominated by a porch with four two-story Ionic columns supporting a tall entablature and dentil-lined pediment. A large attic area behind the pediment houses a gallery that opens to a central rotunda. The soft orange brick of the walls is complemented by cream-colored limestone trim at the windows.

Within a decade of the Reed mansion's construction, Erie's Greek Revival Courthouse (ER1) was completed just to the west, creating a handsome complement. At the end of the nineteenth century, other local elites commissioned large houses along W. 6th Street from Peach to Poplar streets. The Reed mansion and the neighboring Scott-Strong house (see ER2) guard the gateway to this historic district.

The Reed house has had only two owners during its lifetime. Though the interior was adapted to the needs of a private club in 1905, much of the intricate woodwork provided by Edward F. Barger, head ship's carpenter of Reed's shipping line, has been maintained. The long, narrow office to the north mimics the four-columned portico of the main house, but on a much smaller scale and with Tuscan columns and a formal triglyph and metope entablature. Today, the smaller building houses the club's offices and a bowling alley.

ER4 Boardwalk (Greyhound Bus Station)
1939, W. A. Arrasmith for Wischmeyer, Arrasmith and Elswick. 28 N. Park Row

This wonderful Moderne commercial building, the former Greyhound bus station, now a nightclub and lounge, was designed by Arrasmith of Louisville, Kentucky, who, with his firm, were well-known transportation architects. Greyhound believed that stations with a consistent look would establish their identity in people's minds. Many of their stations from the 1930s and 1940s were designed by this architectural firm, including the Washington, D.C., bus station of 1939. In Erie, Arrasmith used a curved corner and ribbon windows to evoke speed and sleekness. The long, horizontal window above the entry canopy is shaped like an extended D. The concrete and aluminum canopy that once sheltered the bus bays remains on the west elevation.

ER5 Erie Art Museum (Old Custom House) and Erie County Historical Society (Cashier's House)
1839, William Kelly. 411 and 415–517 State St.

Admirers of Greek Revival architecture will find two spectacular examples next door to each other on State Street. The temple-fronted Old Custom House, which was aptly based on the Theseion in Athens (449 BCE), a temple dedicated to the gods of trade and the arts, has over the years housed a bank, a customs house, and now an art museum. The building sits on a podium to raise it above street level, and a marble staircase leads to its oversized double doors. Six Doric columns support a wide entablature and pediment of white Ver-

mont marble. Architectural historian Talbot Hamlin in *Greek Revival Architecture in America* (1944) describes William Kelly's design as vital, sensitive, and archaeologically correct.

The L-shaped former Cashier's House just south housed the president of the bank. It is a severe and handsome Greek Revival town house, three bays wide with a side hall and windows graduating from the largest on the first story to the smallest on the third. The paneled door is outlined with pilasters, a rectangular transom, and a tall entablature echoed in the cornice that concludes the building's facade. Though made of brick, the building is stuccoed and scored to emulate stone. The interior includes elaborate Egyptian Revival decorative motifs in the public rooms. Today, the building is operated as a historic house museum by the Erie County Historical Society.

ER6 Modern Tool Company (Market House)
1895, H. R. Dunning. State and 4th sts.

Initially one of four enclosed market houses built in the 1890s, the structure was later purchased by the Modern Tool Company, manufacturers of the Payne Modern car. This became one of the dozens of small industrial manufacturing companies that insulated Erie's economy from the economic peaks and valleys of one-industry towns. The complex consists of two three-story brick gabled structures flanking a two-story portion with dormer windows. Cross-gabled wall dormers at each corner have the firm name printed at their bases. Simple double-sash windows and a variety of gentle arches over windows and doors give a rhythm to the fenestration. A cutaway corner at the northwest corner and the buttresslike pilaster above it distinguish the entrance.

This building is in a prime location, next door to the major downtown hospital and only blocks from Lake Erie. That it was reused instead of demolished again illustrates Erie's preservation ethic and its desire to absorb and adapt nineteenth-century buildings to twenty-first-century needs. Similarly, the former Erie Steam Bakery of 1894 at Lafayette Place (400 French Street) now accommodates office space. This square, orange brick building with rough-hewn stone trim was built for the makers of Tidal-Wave biscuits. A chamfered corner, stone arch, and trim highlight the double-door entrance.

ER7 Erie Water Works

1912–1913, Chester and Fleming, Engineers; 1925 addition to filtration station, J. N. Chester, Engineers. 340 W. Bayfront Pkwy.

Both Erie and Pittsburgh built elaborate water treatment complexes in the early years of the twentieth century after research showed that typhoid was spread through unclean water. Erie's three buildings at the foot of Chestnut Street along the shoreline of Presque Isle Bay contain a pump house, filtration station, and administration building that supply Erie with clean water from the lake.

This group of red brick buildings dates from 1912 to 1913, when the first pumping station of 1868 was remodeled and the city's first filtration plant built. The buildings' arched windows, stone surrounds, and deeply overhanging eaves are characteristic of Italian Renaissance architecture, as is the four-story corner tower on the parkway facade. In the 1990s, the administration building was renovated by Weber Murphy Fox to take advantage of its spectacular bay-front views, and the Erie firm of Crowner/King Architects refurbished the offices inside the filtration plant on the north side of the highway. The hipped-roof pump house (1912) on the south side of Bayfront Highway has a red tile roof and enormous two-story arched windows; it was renovated in 2001 by Roth Marz Partnership. Today, the public is invited by appointment only to see the four-story-tall Big Bertha steam-driven pump, which is a Pennsylvania Mechanical Engineering Landmark. What began as a utilitarian statement of human triumph over nature has evolved into a twenty-first-century attraction.

ER8 Erie Maritime Museum (Erie Lighting Company Plant), U.S. Brig *Niagara,* and Raymond M. Blasco, MD, Memorial Library

1919, Day and Zimmermann; 1991–1996, Weber Murphy Fox. 150–160 E. Front St.

The exciting collection of buildings at the foot of State Street at Bayview Commons contains a county library building and the former power company building, Penelec's Front Street Sta-

tion of 1919, retrofitted for the Maritime Museum. The complex, designed by Weber Murphy Fox, celebrates Erie's maritime past as both a naval station in the War of 1812 and as a center for fishing and shipping throughout the nineteenth and early twentieth centuries. At anchor stands a replica of the brig *Niagara*, one of Commodore Oliver Hazard Perry's ships from 1813. It was re-created from the plans of master shipwright Melbourne Smith and built in 1988 by the members of the Pennsylvania Conservation Corps, a contemporary version of the Civilian Conservation Corps. The ship is a sailing ambassador for the state of Pennsylvania and provides an excellent attraction for the city of Erie. The buildings all share a brownish-red brick base and white trim, tied together by segmental arches above the windows of the former power station and echoed in a larger form as the sweeping roofs over the library. The museum contains a large exhibition space and an auditorium where once enormous turbines hummed.

ER9 Intermodal Transportation Center and Port Authority Cruise Boat Visitors' Terminal

2002 transportation center, Roth Marz Partnership. 208 E. Bayfront Pkwy; 2002 terminal, Weborg Rectenwald Buehler, Architects. 1 Holland St.

Erie continues to attract development to its bay front with these two attractive buildings by local architectural firms. Erie's Intermodal Transportation Center houses offices for the bus companies, water taxis, and ferry service, and offers access to vehicle rentals and the Erie Bayfront Promenade Bicycle Path. The building's circular shape symbolizes both a wheel and a compass. The larger dome in the northwestern portion of the building covers a central atrium lobby with a compass rose design in the floor; a barrel-vaulted corridor connects to the smaller-domed portion. Curved windows and bay views accentuate the openness of the building.

To the east is the Cruise Boat Visitors' Terminal. Here a traditional factory shape, the sawtooth roof, is used in a modern and site-specific way: each peak of the roof is curved to mimic the waves in the bay and evoke images of unfurled sails. Primary tenants of this building are the U.S. Customs and the U.S. Im-

ER9 INTERMODAL TRANSPORTATION CENTER AND PORT AUTHORITY CRUISE BOAT VISITOR'S TERMINAL

migration and Naturalization Service, both of which require a long interior waiting room to funnel arrivals through a controlled space. At the same time, the space should be welcoming and open because it is often the visitor's first glimpse of the United States. The firm of Weborg Rectenwald Buehler, Architects won the 2003 Award of Excellence from the American Institute of Steel Construction for the modular frame system designed for this building.

ER10 Russian Orthodox Church of the Nativity of Christ "Old Rite"

1987, Weborg Rectenwald Buehler, Architects. 247 E. Front St.

Perched on a site overlooking Presque Isle Bay and the library complex, this tan brick church builds in a series of rectangular-shaped volumes to a central polygonal drum supporting a large gilded onion dome. The entrance is marked by a lower tower, which is embellished on the front with a mosaic panel depicting the Madonna and Child, and is topped by a small gilded onion dome. The neighborhood was built by Russian dockworkers and their families who began arriving in Erie in the 1870s. This modern church replaced an earlier version built to serve the Orthodox congregation, but its interior retains the tradition of icon-covered walls.

ER11 Dickson Tavern

1815–1816, William Himrod, builder. French and 2nd sts.

For a fairly simple frame building, this tavern has a long history of civic hand-wringing, hav-

ing been alternately threatened with demolition or deemed worthy of renovation at every major anniversary of its construction. In the early twenty-first century, the building was sold to a private owner, who plans to restore it. This is a building worth fighting for, if for no other reason than it reminds its closest neighbor, the massive Hamot Hospital, that buildings of human scale and simple honesty can coexist among the large slabs of brick and glass that block its view of the lake. Considered in its 1815 context, the tavern is quite large. Its narrow clapboard skin and double-sash eight-over-eight windows are normally found on small Federal and Greek Revival buildings, but, here, a full three stories of them are set directly along the sidewalk. In 1841, the gable-roofed building was converted to a private home and had a two-story intersecting gable extension added to the south.

ER12 St. Patrick's Roman Catholic Church

1906, William P. Ginther. 130 E. 4th St.

Pastor Peter Cauley commissioned Akron architect William Ginther to design this stone church to house a set of fourteen life-size Stations of the Cross carved by the Franz Mayer Studio of Munich, Germany. Cauley met a representative of the Mayer firm at the World's Columbian Exposition in Chicago in 1893 and chose these works for members of his Irish congregation employed on the nearby canal and docks. Ginther created a Romanesque design with no windows at the first level to accommodate the fourteen interior sculpture niches. Each niche is decorated with hand-painted murals by Italian artisans hired by the Mayer Studio. German-made stained glass

ER14 NINETEENTH-CENTURY TOWN HOUSES

clerestory windows light the interior, which seats eight hundred. Two square towers of greatly differing heights flank the church's triple-arched entrance and gabled front. The three rounded apses at the rear are adjacent to a smokestack, which served the heating system.

To the west, a three-story, forty-seven-room rectory (1913–1914) designed by Ginther accommodated the parish's four priests, who were fraternal brothers: Fathers Peter, Joseph, Stephen, and Charles Cauley. Their unmarried sister was the housekeeper. The rectory, built to house visiting priests as well as those assigned to the parish, contains eight full bedroom suites. Ginther also designed St. Ann's Church in Erie (1894; 921 East Ave.).

ER13 Pufferbelly Restaurant (Engine Company No. 1, Hook and Ladder Company No. 2)

1907–1908, Constable Brothers Construction Company. 414 French St.

Pufferbelly Restaurant is an excellent example of adaptive reuse and the advantage of a good location at the midpoint between two of the city's largest downtown employers. Simple corbeling, pilaster strips, a stone lintel course, and recessed panels highlight its rounded entrance bay. The city's oldest remaining firehouse, built in 1903 (428 Chestnut Street), also was adapted for a new use: in 1975 it became the Firefighters Historical Museum. It is a simple maroon brick building with a handsome paneled chimney on its W. 4th Street elevation.

ER14 Nineteenth-Century Town Houses

1823–1842; 1981–1982 restored, Hugh Stubbins and Associates. Holland St. at E. 5th St.

This ensemble of five structures contains homes for Alexander Brewster (1823; 156 E. 5th Street), David Kennedy (1832; 162 E. 5th Street), and Charles M. Tibbals (1842; 146 E. 5th Street), and two sets of town houses built speculatively by David Kennedy, a local mason and brick dealer. All five are red brick two- to two-and-one-half-story houses with Flemish bond facades (except for the Tibbals house). Two houses, the Brewster and the Tibbals, are detached. The successful merchants, who built these town houses with facades nearly flush with the sidewalk, wanted to live close to their work sites. The first story of each of these two houses is raised above street level to provide for basement kitchens. The Brewster house has Italianate touches that were added in the 1850s to its earlier, spare Federal appearance. David Kennedy, who emigrated from Ireland to Erie in 1828, built his own portion of a town house in 1832 and the surrounding brick row houses with Federal detailing. The Tibbals house is a larger, more dignified Greek Revival version of the Kennedy row houses and retains its frame carriage house at the rear. The Stubbins firm restored all the houses and several of them now are used as offices by the neighboring Erie Insurance Group.

ER15 Erie Insurance Group (Erie Insurance Exchange, H. O. Hirt Building)

1953–1956, Nelson, Goldberg and Heidt; 1971–1977 addition, Edward Jonasen. 144 E. 6th St.

H. O. Hirt, cofounder of the Erie Insurance Exchange, taught high school history from 1912 to 1915 and was inspired by a visit to Philadelphia to incorporate elements of Independence Hall into the design of his company's headquarters. His architects borrowed details from both the north and south elevations of the original, multiplying them to suit their purposes. The twenty-four-pane double-sash windows are separated by marble inserts between the first and second stories, as they are on the north elevation of the Philadelphia model, although it has nine bays and the Hirt building has twelve. Also, the Palladian window on the south elevation in Philadelphia can be found on the E. 6th Street facade of the Erie headquarters, even though a Corinthian-columned portico has been added to shelter the Erie entrance. Despite the unorthodox arrangement of elements, the Erie building is a respectful reinterpretation of an American shrine and a fitting symbol of stability for an insurance company.

The company's larger contribution to urban planning came in 1979, when it hired Hugh Stubbins and Associates of Cambridge, Massachusetts, to build a new office building west of the headquarters. The long-range master plan addressed a six-block area bounded by French, Holland, E. 5th, and E. 6th streets. Instead of moving to the suburbs, the Erie Insurance Group chose to remain in the city and upgrade the surrounding buildings. Since 1983 the group has restored and reused several buildings in these blocks, as well as commissioning two office buildings, parking structures, and several additions from Stubbins. The first project was the F. W. Hirt–Perry Square Building (1979–1983, 1986; 100 Erie Insurance Place) with a four-story atrium entrance at the northeast corner of French and E. 6th streets marked by four cast-iron columns from the facade of the Crazy Horse Saloon, an 1870s building torn down to accommodate the new office. The Erie Branch Office Building (1990–1993, The Stubbins Associates; Holland and E. 6th streets) has deep eaves sheltering recessed glass windows highlighted by short stylized columns. A ruddy-colored brick unifies all the elements of the company's buildings and lends cohesion to the streetscapes in the neighborhood. The employee parking lots are cleverly designed in parklike settings.

ER16 U.S. Courthouse (Erie Public Library, Federal Building and U.S. Courthouse, Isaac Baker and Son Store)

1897–1899 Erie Public Library, Alden and Harlow; 1937–1938 Federal Building and U.S. Courthouse, Rudolph Stanley-Brown; 1946–1947 Isaac Baker and Son Store, Walter T. Monahan and George B. Mayer; 2003–2004, Kingsland Scott Bauer Architects and DPK&A Architects, Dave Bauer, project architect. Bounded by French and State sts. and S. Park Row

In 2004, two buildings adjacent to Erie's Federal Building of 1938 were connected to it by a glass lobby atrium and spaces added for offices and courtrooms. This skillful adaptation highlights the best of each historic building and allows for smooth functionality.

The oldest of the three buildings, the former library, and an iconic presence on Erie's Perry Square was described by Margaret Henderson Floyd in her book *Architecture after Richardson* (1994): "More than any other building by the firm [Alden and Harlow] in the Pittsburgh region, save the Carnegie Institute itself, the Erie Public Library embodied a dream of literature, art, and education as central to civic life and progress." This was the first and only building commissioned and owned by the Erie Public School System under a short-lived state legislative act, so detailed information on its construction is recorded in the school system's minute books. The library's Renaissance Revival styling is enhanced by the warm golden-orange Pompeiian brick and cream-colored terra-cotta ornament. Since the building occupied half of a city block, all four elevations were fully fenestrated and ornamented with a continuous roof balustrade and a cornice festooned with dentils, brackets, and roaring lions' heads. Brick pilaster strips have Corinthian capitals and the Palladian window, above what formerly was the main entrance, is framed with a garland, wreaths, and bundled fasces. A one-story portico supported by Ionic columns shelters the S. Park Row entrance.

The building originally accommodated an art gallery and a ladies assembly hall, as well as the library. The art gallery on the second story is lit by a curved skylight and ornamented with ceiling murals by Elmer Garnsey and Henry Meixner. Several features of this

ER16 U.S. COURTHOUSE (ERIE PUBLIC LIBRARY, FEDERAL BUILDING AND U.S. COURTHOUSE, ISAAC BAKER AND SON STORE), north elevation of former Erie Public Library

building, including the divided stair, the skylit balcony, and the decorative trims, were used later on a larger scale in Pittsburgh's Carnegie Institute, completed in 1907 (AL41). Howard K. Jones, a draftsman for Alden and Harlow, was a native of Erie. He trained at MIT, as did all the principals in the firm, and began his employment at Alden and Harlow in the mid-1890s, working his way up to chief draftsman in 1899 and to partner in 1908. In 1927, the firm became Alden, Harlow and Jones. Howard K. Jones acted as supervising architect for both Carnegie projects in Pittsburgh and Erie. Another Erie native, Henry Shenk, was contractor.

Next door, the restrained classicism of the former Federal Building and U.S. Courthouse depends on geometric ornament to enliven its rather austere limestone exterior lined with tall, metal sash windows. Two original courtrooms with coffered ceilings were restored and a third added with the attendant judges chambers and staff offices in the adaptive reuse of 2003–2004. At the same time, a block of several stories was constructed between this building and the Baker building.

The buff brick Moderne former Isaac Baker and Son Store designed by Monahan and Mayer features a sweeping glass block second-story window located above a recessed corner entrance that is sheltered by an alumi-

ER17 BOSTON STORE (ERIE DRY GOODS COMPANY)

num canopy. A stone belt course outlines the second-story windows.

ER17 Boston Store (Erie Dry Goods Company)

1929–1931, Shutts and Morrison; 1949–1950, Meyers and Krider. State St. at W. 8th St.

For over seventy years the largest storefront on State Street has been this buff brick, Art Deco structure with the distinctive square clock tower on its roof. A second, interior clock, which hung from the first-floor ceiling, was a favorite meeting spot. Architects Frank Shutts and Karl Morrison opened their firm in Erie in 1912 and continued their busy practice well into the 1930s. This, the largest of their commissions, had two additions in the 1940s and 1950s that gave the building entrances from Peach and 7th streets and served as a pedestrian short cut. As the Boston Store was the first in Erie to make home deliveries, it is fitting that their livery stable of 1906 survives at 422–424 French Street, now adapted for the Children's Discovery Center.

The same firm designed the four-story Meiser Building, the former Erie Lighting Building (c. 1921; 21–23 W. 10th Street), with polychrome terra-cotta ornament as a central design element.

ER18 Warner Theater

1929–1931, Rapp and Rapp. 811 State St.

Designed in the fantasy mode of the era, Warner Theater's glittering lobby and bronze ticket stand saw the town of Erie through the worst of the Great Depression. C. W. and George Rapp designed several theaters for Warner Brothers, including what is now Heinz Hall in Pittsburgh (AL11). The designers' goal was to make this theater "twice as rich, three times more fanciful than life." The limestone facade is dominated by a vertical sign with the theater's name and a canopy with an ornamental curvilinear parapet, both outlined in lights. Warner Brothers hired Rambusch Studios in New York City to decorate the interior. Initially, the 2,500-seat theater supported vaudeville acts as well as films, hosting performers from Bob Hope to Bob Dylan. The building was sold in 1971, refurbished and outfitted for the Erie Philharmonic, which played there for the first time in 1974.

Another Warner Brothers theater, the Strand, opened in 1947 at 13 W. 10th Street. Designed by theater specialist and Pittsburgh architect Victor A. Rigaumont, with 977 seats in stadium style, it today hosts the Erie Playhouse, a community theater troupe.

ER19 Renaissance Centre (Erie Trust Company Building)

1925–1928, Frederick Charles Hirons and Ethan Allen Dennison. 1001 State St.

Erie was booming in the late 1920s, illustrated by the construction of two of its largest buildings, the Boston Store (ER17) two blocks north and this, the tallest office building in Erie, which, at fourteen stories, offers unobstructed views in all directions. The Erie Trust Company, a c. 1900 incarnation of the Erie Dime Savings and Loan, was the wealthiest bank in town when it commissioned the New York City architectural firm to design this classical bank with Art Deco geometric touches. The tan brick building employs the base, shaft, and capital arrangement standard in tall buildings of the day. Grand limestone concentric arches highlight the State Street entrance and embody the Art Deco spirit by using charming stylized grotesques as capitals. The limestone base wraps around the first three stories and is punctuated by large arched openings that light the commercial spaces and mezzanine. The interior retains the original marble baseboards, walnut doorways, and bronze elevator doors. Edward Trumbull (1884–1968) painted murals on the mezzanine level depicting events in northwestern Pennsylvania's history. Five of the seven original murals remain and have been restored. Trumbull's murals also grace the walls of the Chrysler Building, Rockefeller Center, and Grand Central Station, all in New York City.

The building was commissioned in 1925 by the Erie Trust Company, but by 1934, it was in receivership. The commonwealth took possession and sold the property to local real estate magnate G. Daniel Baldwin in 1943. In 1996, Professional Development Associates bought the building and have since restored it for offices and retail stores.

ER21 UNION STATION

ER20 Lovell Place (Lovell Manufacturing)

1883–1956. 1301 French St.

The Lovell factory, founded in 1881, is a large complex of eleven brick buildings ranging in height from one to four stories and ornamented with shallow segmental- and round-arched windows and corbeling at the cornice lines. Occupying an entire city block, the complex is the largest and most architecturally intact former foundry and machine shop facility in Erie. It is within easy access of the former New York Central Railroad line, and, at the same time, is integrated into the surrounding residential area, allowing workers to reach the factory on foot. A tall smokestack punctuates the southwestern corner.

Lovell manufactured everything metal, from mousetraps to computer shells, continuing when it became a subsidiary of Paterson-Erie in 1967. The complex was left vacant between 1974 and 1980, but since then a group of small industrial firms has leased space in the buildings. These continue to function for a variety of manufacturing purposes, reflecting the essence of Erie as an adaptable skilled manufacturing city.

ER21 Union Station

1925–1927, Alfred Fellheimer and Stewart Wagner. W. 14th St. between Peach and Sassafras sts.

This handsome brick railroad station's central three-story block is ornamented with zigzag and arched corbeling, notched window openings, and terra-cotta medallions. At the time of its construction, forty-four trains passed through Erie daily for the New York Central and the PRR. The second-story train sheds stretch out from the central portion to meet the raised tracks south of the station. The station's interior features Botticino marble and terrazzo detailing in a central rotunda, and groined vaults in the central hallway. The station has been refurbished to house the Erie Rail Museum, restaurants, and shops. The station and the nearby post office form two walls of a public parking plaza to the north named for Matthew Griswold Jr., heir to a cast-iron kitchenware fortune and the first general manager of the General Electric locomotive works, who lobbied for its construction. The New York City architects also designed the Union Terminal in Cincinnati (1931–1933).

ER22 U.S. Post Office

1931–1932, Louis A. Simon for James A. Wetmore, supervising architect of the U.S. Treasury. 1314 Griswold Plaza

The Post Office picks up the golden brick tones of the adjacent Union Station and features an arcaded central portion flanked by lower one-story wings. The tiled roof, symmetrical plan, rhythmic pace of columns across the facade, and ornamental restraint create a modern interpretation of Italian Renaissance architecture. The three entrance doors are topped with elaborate ornamental designs of stylized anthemia and eagle wings, and the building concludes with scrolled brackets along the

cornice line. In combination with Union Station, the building creates a splendid backdrop for the parking plaza in front of it. On the interior, the lobby is one long open space with segmental-arched transom windows along the inside wall, which illuminate the inner workings of the building. Each bay is separated by a colorful beam and capital decorated in earth-toned geometric patterns.

ER23 St. Peter Roman Catholic Cathedral

1873–1893, Patrick Charles Keely. 230 W. 10th St.

St. Peter's was dubbed "Mullen's Folly" when commissioned by Bishop Tobias Mullen in 1873. Its suburban setting and enormous size prompted sarcastic comments in the mostly rural, sparsely populated diocese. Mullen persisted in his choice of location, but refused to build until the funds were in hand, which delayed construction for twenty years. He prevailed and his funeral was held in St. Peter's in 1900.

The architect, Irish-born Patrick Charles Keely (often spelled Keeley), is documented as having designed 150 churches in the United States, but his obituary in *American Architect* in 1896 credits him with over 600 churches and 15 cathedrals ranging from Iowa to New York City and from New Orleans to New Brunswick, Canada. He began his architectural career in 1847 and practiced until 1890.

This cathedral has entrances at the base of each of its three towers. The central six-stage tower at 265 feet is the tallest structure in Erie and features small spires at the corners of its steeple. Enormous clock faces are on all of the tower's four sides. The smaller towers, also with steeples, that flank the central tower add to the building's impressive width. Windows and doors are lancet arched, and buttresses are capped with white limestone that contrasts with the building's golden-rose, rough-hewn, random-laid sandstone. Clerestory windows illuminate the marble and wood interior and highlight the vaults, which are supported on slender clustered columns that separate the nave from the aisles.

ER24 West 6th Street Historic District

1840–1930. W. 6th St. between Peach and Poplar sts.

ER23 ST. PETER ROMAN CATHOLIC CATHEDRAL

ER24 WEST 6TH STREET HISTORIC DISTRICT, A. S. Scheidenhelm house

Erie's mansion district lines six blocks of W. 6th Street with residences, clubs, and institutional buildings in styles ranging from Italianate and Second Empire to the bulky modernism of Gannon University's library (see ER2).

A double Greek Revival house at 127–129 W. 6th Street was designed by and built for brothers William and James Hoskinson, who built many of Erie's mid-nineteenth-century buildings. Next door at 133 W. 6th Street, Gordon W. Lloyd, esteemed among Detroit's architects, designed the Gothic Revival Cathedral of St. Paul for the Episcopal church in 1866, while one of Buffalo's best-known architects, Edward Brodhead Green, designed the large stone Richardsonian Romanesque house (c. 1890) at 150 W. 6th Street. His firm, Green and Wicks, was popular in Erie and authored other buildings on W. 6th Street (ER2 and ER25). Another Green and Wicks Richardsonian Romanesque house of orange brick with heavy stone trim is the Woman's Club of Erie (c. 1890; 259 W. 6th Street). At 216 W. 6th Street, the first of several idiosyncratic Queen Anne–style houses with quirky window bays was built for Lewis W. Olds and his children. He was the president and general manager of the Climax Locomotive Company. Between 1882 and 1900, four more houses in the 300 block (numbers 333, 337, 341, and 345) housed his adult children.

The First United Presbyterian Church of the Covenant (1928–1931; 245 W. 6th Street) is an imposing brown sandstone Gothic Revival church designed by John W. C. Corbusier and William E. Foster, a Cleveland firm. The facade has a large stained glass window above the one-story limestone entry pavil-ion trimmed with crockets of cream-colored limestone and complemented by the square, open bell tower at its side. The clerestory windows were created by Charles Connick of Boston and Nicola D'Ascenzo of Philadelphia. An addition (1983) was designed by Weibel, Rydzewski and Schuster of Erie, using New Hampshire limestone to match the original.

The oldest architect-designed house is also on the 300 block. Dr. Maxwell Wood, the U.S. Navy's first surgeon general, commissioned Dudley and Hawk in 1858 to draw plans for his brick Italianate house at 338 W. 6th Street. The brick Queen Anne house of 1888 at 311 W. 6th Street is now a bed-and-breakfast, the Boothby Inn. Cleveland architect Frank B. Meade (1867–1947) had a national architectural practice during his long career and produced a series of Tudor Revival brick houses in Erie for the Jarecki family, whose wealth emanated from the manufacture of engines and brass equipment for the oil industry. One of the earliest houses in this group is 305 W. 6th Street built in 1913 for Alexander Jarecki, the pater familias. There are four more houses in the 500 and 600 blocks that are either documented or attributed to Meade.

One of the last houses by Alden and Harlow was for A. S. Scheidenhelm (1925; 456 W. 6th Street). Its English cross bond brickwork and half-timbered side entrance set off the massive battered chimney that dominates the facade. The firm also designed the stone Gothic Revival Luther Memorial Church in 1908 several blocks away at 225 W. 10th Street. S. R. Barry of Buffalo designed the large, yellow brick Colonial Revival house at 459 W. 6th Street in 1907.

A large, orange brick Stick Style house built by J. C. Spencer in 1876 for his son William (519 W. 6th Street) is now a bed-and-breakfast. Robert Jarecki asked New York architect Theodore Cuyler Visscher (1876–1935), a college friend, to design his residence to resemble their fraternity house at Lehigh University. Consequently, the house of 1909 at 558 W. 6th Street has four Corinthian columns and Colonial Revival detailing that will be familiar to Lehigh graduates. Edward B. Green's associate Franklin J. Kidd designed 652 W. 6th Street. An unusual group of houses arranged around an oval courtyard, called the Garden Court Subdivision, is bounded by Cherry,

Poplar, 6th, and 7th streets. Their construction included restrictions on cost, outbuildings, and materials as overseen by the Civic Realty Company between 1908 and 1930.

ER25 Watson-Curtze Mansion (Harrison F. Watson House)

1889–1891, Green and Wicks. 356 W. 6th St.

Though Edward Brodhead Green and his partner William Sydney Wicks were based in Buffalo, their works are found from Maine to Indiana. In the late nineteenth century, Erie's elite favored this firm as well as Alden and Harlow of Pittsburgh. Both firms left a lasting architectural legacy for the city. Green, who trained at Cornell and MIT, enjoyed a long career, outliving his partner Wicks and his son, Edward B. Jr. The firm's classical-inspired buildings are among the finest civic buildings in Scranton, Toledo, Dayton, and Buffalo, as well as Erie.

Green and Wicks also frequently used a Richardsonian Romanesque vocabulary, which is reflected in this house. Built for paper company owner Harrison F. and Carrie Tracy Watson, the two-and-one-half-story rough-hewn ashlar residence has a steeply hipped roof with intersecting gables and fat rounded towers at the east and west corners of the facade. The two central bays are enlivened with asymmetrically placed windows, a circular window, and a recessed second-story porch. A pair of massive, two-story semicircular towers at the north and south corners sets off an elaborate semicircular one-story solarium on the east elevation. The twenty-four-room mansion is fitted with oak floors, maple and mahogany woodwork, stained glass, and marble fireplaces.

The residence was sold to Frederick Felix Curtze, another Erie industrialist, in 1923, and donated by his family to the Erie School District in 1941. The Erie County Historical Society purchased the property in 2000 and it is now a house museum. The L-shaped stone carriage house was outfitted as a planetarium in 1959.

ER26 Temple Anshe Hesed Reform Congregation

1930, George B. Mayer for Charles R. Greco. 930 Liberty St.

The largest temple in Erie was designed by Cleveland architect George Mayer using variegated tan bricks and corbeling. The sanctuary at the center of the building is sheltered by a dome on a polygonal drum. Cream-colored stonework highlights the drum's cornice, and

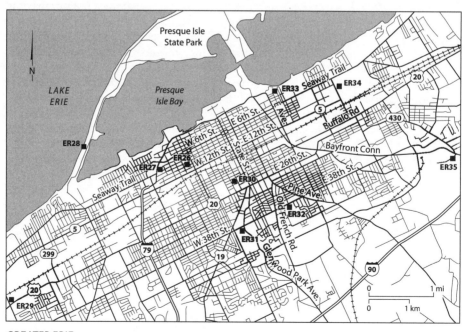

GREATER ERIE

the surround of the elegant triple entrance on Liberty Street is outlined by alternating cream and brown bricks. The entrance is through a gable-roofed extension. An education-office wing is attached to the west elevation.

ER27 Strong Vincent High School

1929–1930, Meyers and Johnson. 1330 W. 8th St.

This large public school, housing both middle and high school students, is named for General Strong Vincent, who commanded Erie's regiment in the Civil War and was killed defending Little Round Top at the battle of Gettysburg in 1863. The school's classical grandeur is characteristic of public buildings in the 1920s, which were often built in a grand style to inspire high moral character. To reinforce this goal, didactic quotations were carved into plaques on the facade. Pride of place was given to the Vincent family's coat of arms and their motto "By courage, not by force of arms, we conquer." The industrial nature of Erie is reflected in other quotations, such as "Labor is man's greatest function." Six Tuscan columns support the dentil-lined pediment at the main entrance, which is adorned with a clock guarded by carved griffins. A stone lintel course and cornice line all elevations of the building, and pilasters separate each pair of windows.

ER28 Presque Isle, Lighthouses and Monuments

1872–1873 lighthouse, G. L. Gillespie, engineer; 1926 additions; 2002–2005 Tom Ridge Environmental Center, Wallace, Roberts and Todd. Peninsula Dr. (PA 832), north of Alt. PA 5

Presque Isle means "almost an island," and while that is a literal interpretation of this seven-mile-long recurving sand spit, Native Americans had a more spiritual interpretation. They saw it as the arm of the Great Spirit reaching out to create a protected harbor for them. Presque Isle State Park, built between 1921 and 1923, was served by a trolley company that established Waldameer Park with rides and waterslides, and now hosts the Tom Ridge Environmental Center (301 Peninsula Drive), a silver LEED-rated, two-story brick, glass, and aluminum building with a seventy-five-foot-tall green glass circular observation tower and inverted gable roofs. Designed to be environmentally sensitive, it provides classrooms, laboratories, and interpretive spaces to explore the peninsula's natural landscape.

With six different ecological zones and more than 320 species of birds that migrate through the park, Presque Isle State Park is a naturalist's paradise. Eleven miles of hiking trails link the navigational light (North Pier Head Light of 1830) with the Presque Isle Lighthouse, the Stull Interpretive Center, and the Perry Monument on Misery Bay. When the lighthouse was constructed in 1872–1873, the peninsula's narrow attachment to the mainland had been washed out, and, consequently, a ten-room brick residence was included as part of the facility to house the light keeper and his family, who had to row across the bay to reach the mainland. In 1896, the light tower was raised seventeen feet to make it more visible from the water. The square-shaped building is five brick courses thick to withstand Lake Erie winters.

The Perry Monument at Crystal Point was designed in 1926 by local architects Fuller and Stickle, with Warren Powers Laird of the University of Pennsylvania as architectural consultant. The 101-foot-high limestone obelisk rises from a fifty-foot square base and commemorates those who died in the battle of Lake Erie in September 1813. The adjacent inlet and pond, Misery Bay and Graveyard Pond, commemorate the suffering of the sailors who died as a result of the poor standard of living during that winter aboard an unheated wooden ship. Also in 1926, the Erie Park and Harbor Commission built a Police Barracks using the dark-colored wane-edged wood siding common to state park structures. The rustic building was enlarged and refurbished as the Stull Interpretive Center in 1994.

ER29 Sheetz Convenience Store

2001, Rick Cyman. 4662 W. Ridge Rd. (U.S. 20 at Asbury Rd. NE)

Sheetz Corporation, a convenience store chain founded in 1952 by Bob Sheetz and headquartered in Altoona, Blair County, is dominant in the region, with over three hundred stores in a five-state area. University of Cincinnati–trained architect Rick Cyman designed this store to look fun and dynamic. The company's newer stores are wood frame and concrete block or brick for the rear wall and with a glass front. Red architectural composite material creates a rounded cornice that displays the Sheetz logo. Well-lit canopies supported by red columns with yellow hot-rod decals shelter the pumps in the parking lot of every Sheetz store. Because the stores are ubiquitous and eye-catching, they have entered the local lexicon, as often directions will begin with the phrase, "When you get to the Sheetz . . ."

ER30 West 21st Street Historic District

c. 1870–c. 1920. W. 21st St. between Peach and Myrtle sts.

This block of W. 21st Street contains two dozen houses dating from the 1870s to the 1920s. They were built by upper-middle-class business owners and professionals seeking a suburban experience in what was then the separate borough of South Erie. Located just a block west of the Waterford Turnpike (Peach Street) and six blocks south of Union Station, the area was popular with land speculators. The earliest was lumber and oil man Heman Janes, who, in 1857, began the settlement by building a brick Italianate home for himself at 125 W. 21st Street. In the next block, the owner of Erie's largest tannery, Emil Streuber, contracted in 1882 for a large brick Italianate house with Colonial Revival touches at 231 W. 21st Street. A large Romanesque Revival stone house of 1882 at 209 W. 21st Street was designed by architect David K. Dean. It was commissioned by building contractor Henry Shenk, whose firm built the Erie Public Library (ER16). Shenk opened a second office in Pittsburgh to accommodate the work he received from the firm of Alden and Harlow.

Several handsome restorations of modest frame houses from the 1870s and 1880s are located at 215, 219, and 236 W. 21st Street. The orange brick Colonial Revival house with a tile roof at number 241 shows that the area continued to be fashionable into the early twentieth century. The district contains housing dating from pre–Civil War settlements to the trolley suburb and railway developments of the late nineteenth century.

ER31 Erie Zoo (Glenwood Zoo)

1929, with additions; 2001, Jeff Kidder of Crowner/King Architects. 423 W. 38th St.

Located at the southern edge of the city limits, the Erie Zoo houses over four hundred animals on fifteen acres of land. The principal building is a long one-story structure of variegated bricks ranging in color from brown to rust and tan, and highlighted by a terra-cotta elephant head above the main entrance in a tiled surround set off by tigers at the base. Colorful tiles and patterned inlays at the cornice line complete the ornamentation. A small octagonal building southwest of the 38th street entrance, credited to the Works Progress Administration, dates after 1935, and uses the same variegated brick with a standing seam roof. A new brick, two-story office for the zoo's administration was designed in 2001. Probably the best-known feature of the zoo is its eighty-passenger train, a part of the Children's Zoo, that includes a Crowner/King-designed train station (2003), up-dated carousel house, llama and sheep building, and the Mystery Mountain feature.

ER32 Mercyhurst College Main Campus

1925–present. 501 E. 38th St.

The entrance to Mercyhurst's eighty-five-acre campus in the southern part of the city is dramatically highlighted by the elaborate twenty-foot iron gates designed in England and constructed in France for Harry K. Thaw, who murdered architect Stanford White in 1906. When Thaw's Pittsburgh estate was sold in 1950, Mercyhurst's founder, Mother Borgia Egan of the Sisters of Mercy, bought the gates for $600, on the advice of architect Brandon Smith, who then designed their installation in Erie.

Mercyhurst was founded in 1926 as a women's college, and men were admitted in 1969. The campus is dominated by its original building, Old Main, designed in 1925–1926 by Philadelphia architect Francis Ferdinand Durang, in a Collegiate Gothic style in golden brick with limestone trim. A massive, square, four-story entrance pavilion and sloping slate roof distinguish the design. The roof is punctuated by elongated dormers, which emerge from large pilasters on the floors below. In 1953, Brandon Smith designed the adjacent Weber Memorial Hall and connected the two with a cloister. Smith continued the Gothic Revival theme often favored for colleges.

ER33 ERIE LAND LIGHTHOUSE

Of the nearly sixty buildings on campus, those constructed in the 1950s, such as Mc-Cauley Hall (1959), are simple rectangular brick boxes. Two buildings by Francis Pisani and Jack P. Falco of New York City in the 1970s, including Baldwin Hall, initially used color to enliven their design, but both have been substantially altered from their original appearance. And several buildings have been altered to blend with Old Main and Weber Hall by the addition of extra stories and gabled roofs designed by the architectural firm Weibel, Rydzewski and Schuster. In 1997, the golden brick Hammermill Library, updated by Rectenwald Buehler of Erie, took center stage on the campus just inside the wrought-iron gates. The Audrey Hirt Academic Center (2002, Weber Murphy Fox), a two-story H-shaped brick classroom building, is crowned by a copper-clad dome.

ER33 Erie Land Lighthouse

1867. Front St. between Dunn Blvd. and Lighthouse St.

Lighthouses continue to capture our imaginations out of proportion to their modern usefulness. They evoke a sense of urgency as we picture a fogbound ship bleating its horn and searching desperately for sight of land. Most ships today use sophisticated navigational systems, so it is only the smaller craft that continue to depend on the distinctive light patterns that lighthouses use to warn sailors and inform them of their location.

The first lighthouse on the Great Lakes was built on this site in 1818. The Erie Land Lighthouse is the third on this site east of Erie's public docks; the first two having given way to the stream of quicksand below the surface. It is a forty-foot-high tower of Berea sandstone with a six-foot-diameter interior that is essentially a brick-lined tube with cast-iron stairs circling upward to the light. The handsome tawny-colored lighthouse with minimalist Romanesque-inspired detailing was operational for thirty-two years. In 2003, Erie masonry restoration specialists Fiske and Sons restored the exterior and a functioning, historically accurate lantern room was installed. Five new interpretive panels and a restored view to the lake enhance the educational experience.

ER34 General Electric (GE) Transportation Systems

1911–1948, Harris and Richards; 1981–1982, Brubaker/Brandt, Inc., Architects, Planners. 2901 E. Lake Rd.

This 350-acre complex was one of the largest industrial complexes in early-twentieth-century Erie. The company owned land north of Lake Road to the lakeshore and built workers' housing near the plant during both world wars. Within the grounds of the present locomotive factory, half-a-dozen, four- and five-story, red brick buildings are arranged in an orderly fashion along the main, tree-lined street. Their warm brick walls and white limestone trim reflect the era's penchant for restrained classical ornament illustrative of the dignity in work. The buildings provide five million square feet of manufacturing space. The architectural and engineering firm responsible for the design began as Wilson Brothers and Company of Philadelphia.

ER34 GENERAL ELECTRIC (GE) TRANSPORTATION SYSTEMS

Henry W. Wilson (c. 1844–1910), the youngest Wilson brother, took on partners John McArthur Harris (1867–1948) and Howard Smith Richards (1867–1937) around 1902, and they designed railroad buildings for the Chesapeake and Ohio and Baldwin Locomotive Works, in addition to office buildings and factories for General Electric in New York and New Jersey.

The manufacturing functions of the plant have been improved and refined over the years, yet the brick buildings dating from 1910 to the 1920s continue to operate successfully. The complex has its own steam power plant, also dressed in red brick with limestone trim. Around 1941 a Colonial Revival community center, facing E. Lake Road, opened for social events as well as classes and lectures; today it houses a company-sponsored museum. The newest building is the Learning Center (1981–1982) in the northwest corner of the property, designed by Brubaker/Brandt, Inc., Architects, Planners of Columbus, Ohio.

Adjoining the plant, on approximately four hundred acres to the east, GE founded the neighborhood of Lawrence Park in 1911. The Lawrence Park Realty Company, a GE subsidiary, sold lots measuring 40 × 125 feet. Many buyers chose their house plans from one of three architects, George Wesley Stickle, C. E. Thomas, and Clement S. Kirby. Other houses were designed by engineers and draftsmen from the plant, and some were sketched by builders. These houses represent all the popular early-twentieth-century domestic styles, from Colonial Revival to Lustron homes. The newest section of housing, the Lake Cliff subdivision, with nearly 1,500 single-family houses and 494 row houses, opened immediately after World War II. A GE-owned golf course north of the plant along the Lake Erie shore was built by its employees for their use. In 1941, the company hired Connecticut golf course architect Alfred H. Tull (1897–1982) to design an eighteen-hole course, which has since been sold and refurbished by a private company.

ER35 Pennsylvania State University (PSU), Behrend College (Glenhill Farm)
1928–present. 5091 Station Rd.

PSU's Erie campus is located on the four-hundred-acre former farm of Ernst and Mary Behrend; he was cofounder of the Hammermill Paper Company in Erie. In 1948, after her husband's death, Mary Behrend donated the estate to the university as a research facility for marine-based economies. Since then the school has grown to more than seven hundred acres and from 146 to 3,700 students. More than simply a branch campus, Behrend College now offers undergraduate and graduate degrees. Initially, the college used the buildings already on the estate, including the house (1928), carriage house, barn, and various outbuildings. Simple barnlike, board-and-batten Erie Hall was built in 1952, and since then the number of buildings has grown to fifty-five. The Hammermill and Zurn buildings designed by Bohlin Powell Larkin Cywinksi in 1984–1986 are one- and two-story barrel-roofed buildings, while the rose brick Lilly Library, designed by Louis D. Astorino and Associates in 1994, has a dramatic glass gable at the center of the facade and canted windows on the side elevations. WTW Architects of Pittsburgh designed all five buildings in the Knowledge Park section south of the main campus in collaboration with the Greater Erie Industrial Development Corporation between 1998 and 2001. The Junker Center, a glass cube designed in 2000 by Celli-Flynn of Pittsburgh, and Smith Chapel, designed the following year by Nowelker and Hull of Chambersburg, have been built on the east side of Jordan Road.

NORTH EAST

North East was the first of the original sixteen townships in the Erie Triangle to be settled by New England emigrants. It is slightly inland from Lake Erie because the Pennsylvania Population Company's earliest settlers found the flatlands immediately surrounding the lake too gravelly for cultivation. Sixteen Mile Creek supplied hydraulic power for grist and saw mills. Due to the long growing season and favorable soil conditions, farming prospered. In the early 1800s, North East had over 1,000 residents, while Erie had only 635. Those numbers reversed following the influx of shipbuilders to Erie for the War of 1812. The township surrounding North East was Lower Greenfield, but after several name changes, the borough became North East in 1834.

The first winery, South Shore Wine Company, opened in 1869, although grapes had been cultivated locally since 1850. The Concord grape is the most widely grown variety in the area, prompting the Welch's company to build a large factory here for the production of jams and jellies. There are also several more wineries and acres of chrysanthemums and cherries grown in the region. The North East Chamber of Commerce sponsors the Wine Country Harvest Festival in the fall and the summer Cherry Festival.

The borough hosts a railway museum in its former Lake Shore Railroad Depot (1899) at 31 Wall Street. The frame, Greek Revival First Baptist Church (43 S. Lake Street) was dedicated at the start of the Civil War, while the stone First Presbyterian Church (25 W. Main Street) was built by local master builder Royce Puttle in 1855. The McCord Memorial Library (1913–1916; 32 W. Main Street) of tan brick has a red tile roof, as specified by Chicago architect George A. Nagle. In the 1980s, a Main Street manager helped to preserve many of the town's older commercial buildings.

ER36 Mercyhurst North East Campus (St. Mary's Seminary)

1868–present. 16 W. Division St.

Located a few blocks northwest of the commercial center, this eighty-four-acre former Redemptorist facility, St. Mary's Seminary, is dominated by Miller Hall, a limestone Second Empire building designed in 1868. The Order added a residence hall in 1893 and

ER36 MERCYHURST NORTH EAST CAMPUS (ST. MARY'S SEMINARY), St. Mary's Chapel

named it for their most famous member, St. John Neumann, the bishop of Philadelphia. In 1901, Lansing and Beierl of Buffalo were commissioned to build the limestone, Gothic Revival St. Mary's Chapel, also called the Chapel of Our Lady of Perpetual Help. The chapel is crowned with a copper fleche. A group of nuns, who came from Germany in 1920 to assist with cooking and housekeeping, established a convent on the premises, now called Karsh Hall. The Redemptorists sold the facility to Mercyhurst College in 1991. The grotto (1922), a replica of Lourdes, was restored in 1998. An athletic facility and playing fields add to the college's amenities and are also used by the Municipal Police Academy, which has been on campus since 1996. In 2005, two new limestone dormitories and the Michele and Tom Ridge Health and Safety Building, a rose brick, two-story building with pointed-arched windows, were added north of Miller Hall.

ER37 John Phillips's Octagonal Barn (Alonzo W. Butt Farm)

1879, Alonzo W. Butt. 11441 Middle Rd.

Built by Alonzo W. Butt (1827–1914), this octagonal bank barn rests on level ground,

Farmers' barns are as unique as their fingerprints, and in the nineteenth and early twentieth centuries, they were the most expensive tool on the farm. They have evolved from relatively simple log buildings to elaborate architect-designed "cathedral barns," each one adapted to the needs of a specific farm, crop, or herd of animals. With 3.5 million acres of farmland and approximately 25,000 farms in western Pennsylvania, there are, estimating conservatively, more than 30,000 barns.

Barn specialists coined the term "Pennsylvania barn" to indicate not location, but a certain structural type: a gable-roofed barn with a banked entry on one side and a cantilevered overhang or forebay on the other. Western Pennsylvanians, no matter their ethnicity, tinkered with this standard formula. Barn builders were specialists who learned their precise craft through apprenticeships, as did the earliest architects. They followed traditional practices because durability was primary, and barns built with chestnut or white oak lasted the longest. They employed specialized tools and measuring devices, and understood weight distribution and cantilevering. Since the early 1800s, barn building has rarely been left to amateurs.

In counties with higher elevations, such as Bedford and Somerset, the long winters threatened the health of cattle and dairy cows. Rather than continue the tradition of an open forebay prevalent in eastern Pennsylvania, central and then many of western Pennsylvania's farmers enclosed their forebays and built the barn's lower level with pens only on one side, so that cattle could walk about freely inside during inclement weather. The enclosed forebay barn is a western Pennsylvania variant on the standard Pennsylvania barn type.

Recent studies have shown that the vernacular architecture of western Pennsylvania is a synthesis of stylistic and cultural influences from several streams—German/Swiss, English, and Scots-Irish. West of the Allegheny Mountains, the architectural traditions of the East Coast were

A SOMERSET COUNTY BARN, WITH ITS PAINTED MAIL POUCH
SIGN, UNUSUAL FOR ITS RED BACKGROUND COLOR, 2005.

reworked and sent on to the plains states. Here, eighteenth- and early-nineteenth-century German and English farmers fused their building customs. So, for instance, the Newmyer barn (FA26) has an English roofing system atop an essentially Germanic barn.

Western Pennsylvania also generated its own type of barn ornament. The hex sign, a brightly painted folk art symbol common in southeastern Pennsylvania, is rarely seen on barns west of the mountains. Instead farmers, particularly those in Somerset and Bedford counties, decorated their large dairy barns with wooden barn stars sawn by local carpenters. The patterns vary and sometimes indicate the barn builder's identity, but most often, they were simply chosen for aesthetic reasons by the farmer who commissioned the barn. The eight- to eleven-foot diameter wooden stars are nailed to the barn siding typically in the gable ends. They vary by region—some are useful as round perforated medallions covering haymow vents, while others are simply decorative with cutouts along each point of the star.

except for the bank at the south, and is surrounded by vineyards and a view of Lake Erie on the north. In 1875, Elliot Stewart, a professor at Cornell University's Agricultural College, published plans of his octagonal barn in Erie County, New York, which inspired barns of similar design in the region. Barns of this shape were alleged to repel the wind and make feeding and caring for livestock more efficient. The red brick barn has paired porthole windows lighting the upper story along the elevations without entrances. Large barn doors with segmental-arched openings are at the lower level on three sides; the south side has an upper-story entrance. The stone and brick lower story is more than one foot in thickness (the brick sections are three bricks deep) and lit with full-size double-sash windows. On the interior, the roof's lightweight plank joinery defines the loft forty-six feet at the apex without a central support. The roof was originally crowned by a cupola that was destroyed by a storm in the 1950s. Today, the barn is used for storage. An 1840s brick Italianate house west of the barn was built by contractor John Silliman for the Butt family, who grew prosperous in the oil business and who established a vineyard here. The Phillips family bought the property in 1912.

WATERFORD

Waterford's site has always been strategic. For Native Americans it was the end of a portage from Lake Erie to Le Boeuf Creek. To the French, who shipped and traveled by river, it was an important link between their domains in Canada and Louisiana. The French called present-day French Creek the Venango River, and considered it the beginning of the Ohio River since the creek feeds into the Allegheny, which merges with the Monongahela River at Pittsburgh to form the Ohio. The French government, fearing the influx of British traders, built Fort Le Boeuf at Waterford in 1753. Lake Le Boeuf supplied water for the encampment and provided a place to float the boats being built there. This was George Washington's destination in 1753 when, as a British officer, he delivered an ultimatum from the governor of Virginia demanding that the French commander vacate the area. Washington also inspected the extent of French settlement in western Pennsylvania on this mission. After Fort Duquesne fell in Pittsburgh, the French retreated to Waterford, but within a year they abandoned and burned this fort (1759). A year later the English built a fort here, but that was burned during Pontiac's Rebellion in 1763.

Fear of Native American attacks kept European settlement to a minimum until the 1790s, when Andrew Ellicott surveyed the region and laid out the borough in 1794, a year before Erie was settled. As part of the state reservation program, the commonwealth sold plots to people who promised to establish residence within two years. Scots-Irish settlers from the Susquehanna River valley took up the challenge, building houses of red brick and indigenous stone. Before 1812, a peak of one hundred wagons a day filled with salt shipped into Erie from New York and trekked down the Erie and Waterford Pike; it took two days to cover the fourteen miles from Erie to Waterford. After 1812, the salt trade ceased, but the village continued to serve as a rural commercial center. Lake Le Boeuf provided a harbor for flatboats and other waterborne vehicles heading south.

In the 1850s, a plank road served the borough, replaced by freight rail service in 1859 and passenger service five years later. None of the rail lines came directly through the oldest part of Waterford, which enabled the architecturally significant nineteenth-century buildings in the commercial district to remain intact. Frame Greek Revival houses from the 1840s survive in the 100 block of 2nd Street. Waterford Academy (1822), which had a magnificent doorway and cupola, was demolished in 1956. Waterford Covered Bridge, constructed with a Town truss system in 1875, spans Le Boeuf Creek east of the village.

ER38 Amos Judson House

1820, Amos Judson, carpenter. 31 High St.

Built by Amos Judson, a cabinetmaker and trader from Connecticut, this is the earliest building in Waterford. Along with the Eagle Hotel across the street, also owned by Judson between 1842 and 1853, this house is the centerpiece of the village. His woodworking skill shows in the flush siding, corner boards, dentils, and the fluted pilasters and columns of the porch. The three-bay, two-story portion of the Greek Revival house has a pediment in the gable end facing the street, which is echoed by a diminutive pediment sheltering the entrance. A four-bay one-and one-half-story saltbox addition to the south housed Judson's trading store. Today, the house contains artifacts and furnishings from the Judson family, and is the headquarters of the local historical society.

ER39 Eagle Hotel

1826, Thomas King, builder. 32 High St.

This building is the heart of the small village it dominates. Of locally quarried sandstone arranged in a two-story Georgian style, the hotel still serves as a gathering place more than

ER39 EAGLE HOTEL

180 years after it was built as an office and inn for the stagecoach line from Pittsburgh to Waterford. The Works Progress Administration guidebook *Erie: a Guide to the City and County* (1938) notes that it "bears the rugged stamp of the frontier." Nevertheless, stagecoach stops were in general a step above the inns that housed drovers and rivermen, catering to a more sophisticated clientele. Here, builder Thomas King used dramatic bridged chimneys on the side elevations, twelve-over-twelve windows topped with stone lintels with keystones, and corner quoins to contrast with the irregularly coursed sandstone walls. He carved his name in the datestone at the north gable end. The open-winged carved eagle that stood above the elliptical fanlight has been removed from the entrance, but otherwise, the elegant doorway is intact. Since 1977, the building has been owned by the local historical society and houses a functioning restaurant and shop. In 1841, one of carpenter Amos Judson's nephews who married Thomas King's daughter used the form of this building for a brick house at 104 Walnut Street.

ER40 St. Peter's Episcopal Church

1831–1832, attributed to John Henry Hopkins; 1871–1872. 305 Cherry St.

This early Gothic Revival brick church has rectangular massing, elongated pointed-arched windows, and a square tower rebuilt in 1927. It is probable that the designer was the talented clergyman John Henry Hopkins, who had recently designed Trinity Episcopal Church in Pittsburgh and Christ Episcopal Church in Meadville. Hopkins left the area in 1831 for Boston and was elected the bishop of Vermont in 1832; he wrote the first book in the United States to deal specifically with the Gothic style, *Essay on Gothic Architecture,* in 1836. His two earlier churches mentioned above were replaced in the 1870s, but St. Peter's remains, a valuable artifact of early Gothic Revival in the United States. The interior has enclosed pews whose doors were removed in the 1870s and reused as wainscoting along the walls. St. Peter's Episcopal Church coincidentally shares the name of the first chapel built in Fort Le Boeuf in the 1750s.

EDINBORO

Edinboro was settled in 1796 by a group from Williamsport in Lycoming County because of its location along the Venango Trail (now U.S. 19, and here in Edinboro, Meadville Street) and its access to French Creek via the Big Conneautee Creek and lake. Twenty miles south of the city of Erie, south-central Erie County is low lying and well watered and maintains its early-nineteenth-century ambiance. On the north side of Edinboro, Conneautee Lake (now Edinboro Lake) provided the earliest settlers with both water and power to run their grist and saw mills. Although the borough was incorporated in 1840, each era of the region's transportation system is represented by corresponding residential architecture. There are houses from the turnpike era and the canal era, and several Second Empire houses represent the time when railroads proliferated. The university has preserved some of the older houses for use as offices. The "Four Corners," intersection of U.S. 6 N and PA 99, is the site of the Crossroads Dinor [*sic*], which has served the local population since 1929 in a refurbished trolley car from 1913.

ER41 Edinboro University of Pennsylvania

1857–present. Bounded by Perry Ln., Darrow, Meadville, and Normal sts., and U.S. 6 N

Edinboro is among the oldest state teachers' colleges in the commonwealth. Founded in 1857 as Edinboro Academy, the large white frame, cross-gabled original building built by carpenter-architect Nathaniel C. Austin has pride of place on the campus and houses the admissions office. With the demolition of the Waterford Academy in the 1950s, this building became the oldest state normal school building in Pennsylvania. Today, Edinboro University has forty-four buildings on 585 acres of land surrounding man-made Lake Mallory. Ties between the town of Edinboro and the university have been strengthened by the university's reuse of the handsome Greek Revival Biggers House (1850) at the northwest corner of Meadville and Normal streets. Also built by Austin, it is named for Bishop Quince Biggers, who operated it as a hotel until 1897. The brick Taylor House of 1878 (139 Meadville Street) is now the development office,

and the university president lives in a house built in 1885 at 214 Meadville Street.

In 1906 and 1908, Diebold Center for the Performing Arts and Reeder Hall were built as a gymnasium and dormitory. Both are substantial brick buildings that expanded the campus to the south along Meadville Street. In 1931, a quadrangle began to take shape with the construction of Loveland Hall to the northeast, designed by Meyers and Johnson of Erie, with a round-arched arcade at the entrance. But the school's major expansion took place between the 1940s and the 1970s. During the 1940s, one- and two-story brick buildings were built in the section of campus bounded by Meadville, Normal, and Scotland (formerly Ontario) streets and Darrow Road. The handsome Memorial Auditorium of 1941, named for those who died in war, has murals by Alfred James Tulk (1899–1988), the Yale-educated mural director of New York's Rambusch Decorating Company. By the 1960s and 1970s, the university had acquired much more acreage to the south and east of the original campus. Today, several modernistic brick dormitories and classroom buildings line curving Scotland Street. The highlight of the group is the Brutalist Baron-Forness Library, named for two Edinboro University librarians and built in 1976. The 7,000 students located on this campus nearly match the population of the town of Edinboro.

The campus has an extension in Erie at 2951 W. 38th Street, the site of the for-mer four-hundred-acre Porreco farm. Now a twenty-seven-acre wooded campus with eleven buildings, a pond, and an orchard, the Porreco Center's primary academic facility is housed in one of the largest standing barns in Erie County, built in the 1850s using hand-hewn timbers. The former mansion, summer cottage, and garden house all accommodate university activities.

GIRARD

Named for Stephen Girard, the Philadelphia financier who owned land in the area, Girard was incorporated in 1846. With soil deposited from ancient gla-ciers and a climate tempered by Lake Erie, fruit production thrives in the re-gion. Because of its convenient location along the main ridge road west from Erie (U.S. 20), Girard served as a commercial center for the area's prosperous farms. Stagecoach lines took goods farther west to Cleveland, and after 1844, the Erie Extension Canal that ran along the eastern shore of Elk Creek al-lowed cargo to be off-loaded in Girard for shipment to Ohio. From the 1840s to the 1860s, two skilled carpenters who specialized in board-and-batten con-

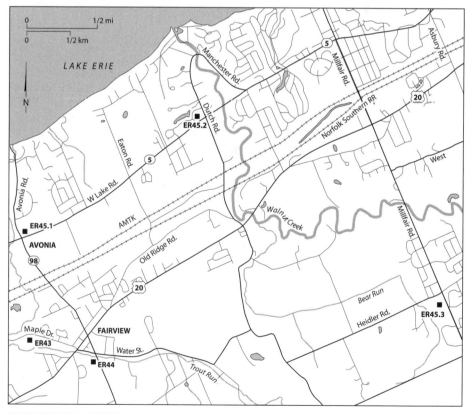

FAIRVIEW AND VICINITY

struction, Erastus Slater and Phillip Osborn, built dozens of houses in the village, many of which have survived on Myrtle, Walnut, Locust, and Main streets. The Homer Hart house of 1854 (404 Main Street) is a fine example, with bracketed eaves, corner boards, and a pedimented gable end.

In 1854, famous comedian and circus owner Dan Rice began a twenty-year ritual of wintering his exotic circus animals in Girard. While today's circuses winter in warmer climes, in the early nineteenth century, it was thought that keeping horses, elephants, and camels in a cooler climate during the winter increased their hardiness in the spring. By 1871, three circuses were using Girard as a winter base. Rice commissioned Leonard Volk of Chicago to design one of the earliest Civil War monuments in the nation, a small stone obelisk, which was dedicated on November 1, 1865, with 10,000 people in attendance.

Rail service opened in 1882 north of Girard, and in 1891, another rail line was built along the path of the abandoned canal. In 1902, interurban trolleys gave Girard residents access to Conneaut, Ohio, and to Buffalo, continuing the borough's role as a transportation hub. A pair of handsome, red brick Romanesque Revival churches, First Presbyterian (1892; Main and Church streets) and the United Methodist Church (1863; 48 Main Street E), illustrate the prosperity of the rail era. The Girard Dinor [*sic*] (1913; 222 Main Street W), with its barrel-vaulted roof, may be the oldest prefabricated diner still operating in the state, according to historian Brian Butko in *Diners of Pennsylvania* (1999).

ER42 Rush Battles House

1857–1858, Erastus Slater, builder; William Blackford, architect. 436 Walnut St.

On March 21, 1857, Rush Battles contracted carpenter Erastus Slater to build a house from the plans drawn by William Blackford as used at the Moses Koch house in Erie (demolished). The design is similar to Samuel Sloan's "A Plain and Ornamented Villa" in his folio *The Model Architect* of 1852. The main portion of the house is a three-by-three-bay rectangle with a pyramidal roof topped with a three-bay cupola. A large rectangular addition at the rear houses the kitchen. The Erie County Historical Society now owns ninety acres of the original farm and re-creates a farm family's life using the Battles family's furnishings and period costumes.

The former house (1861) at 306 Walnut Street, now the Charlotte Elizabeth Battles Memorial Museum, seems to have been built by the same carpenter, as the stairs and moldings are nearly duplicates. It housed members of the Battles family for nearly one hundred years. The red brick Battles Bank (1893; 12–14 Main Street) is a handsome stone-trimmed building in the commercial district.

FAIRVIEW AND VICINITY

ER43 Fairview Cemetery Chapel

1902. Maple Dr., 0.5 miles west of W. Ridge Rd.

Veterans from every war in our nation's history are interred in the Fairview cemetery. In 1902, a local man donated this small chapel so that relatives could remember them properly. Barely larger than a storage shed, the tiny building has an elongated Gothic-arched transom above the double doors that are outlined by rough-hewn stones. The Gothic arch is echoed in the muntins of the double-sash windows on the side elevations. A vestigial cupola, which is probably a ventilator, and a narrow chimney provide the climate control. The most appreciated parts of the small structure are the men's and women's outhouses built onto the rear of the building. The surrounding cemetery has fir trees sheltering burials from the 1850s.

ER44 Sturgeon House

c. 1838, attributed to Samuel Sturgeon. 4302 Avonia Rd.

Two brothers of Irish descent, William and Jeremiah Sturgeon, came to Fairview from Dauphin County in 1797, after purchasing land in this area from the Pennsylvania Population Company. Fairview was originally called Sturgeonville, as the brothers had sired five sons by 1810. Jeremiah's son Samuel C. Sturgeon (1801–1878) became a carpenter and is credited with building this frame saltbox house for his younger brother Robert. The design of the house is unusual because the entrance, set off by fluted square columns, is recessed on the lower side, rather than centered on the taller side.

Fairview has seven remaining Sturgeon-related buildings, four houses and three barns scattered throughout the borough, although most have been considerably altered. It is also thought that Sturgeon designed the Believer's Chapel (c. 1842; 4100 block Avonia Road), a simple frame Greek Revival chapel. Although missing the top of its steeple, it has original siding, door and window surrounds, and a central doorway. The chapel has housed five different congregations as well as a factory over the years.

ER45 Three One-Room Schoolhouses

1865–1897. N. Hathaway Dr. and Millfair, Avonia, W. Lake (PA 5), and Dutch rds.

The rural nature of Fairview Township is evidenced by the dozen small brick and frame school buildings that dot the countryside. Until the 1950s, when elementary education for a region was consolidated into a single modern building, small schools served only the immediate neighborhood. Today, these neighborhood school buildings are reused as houses and shops. Three of the three-bay schools—two brick and one frame—are representative. The school built in 1878 (ER45.1; 7490 N. Hathaway Drive) has an airy feeling despite its brick construction, which probably stems from its narrow massing and open wooden cupola with bell. Paired brackets and segmental-arched windows lend an Italianate feeling to the small structure, which is now a residence. The brick Fairview School No. 3 of 1897 (ER45.2; W. Lake and Dutch roads NW) reflects the stylistic change to the Colonial Revival, with its heavier massing, pedimented gable, and the suggestion of brick pilaster strips on the side elevations. The bell tower is heavier, square, and an integral part of what is now a commercial building. Finally, the two-story, board-and-batten structure of 1865 (ER45.3; 5800 Millfair Road) has had several additions in its transformation from a school to a house. A diminutive blind arcade runs along the eaves, and the entrance has a Greek Revival surround. Unlike the two brick schools, which have central entrances, this school's entrance is asymmetrically located.

CRAWFORD COUNTY

Crawford County, Pennsylvania's largest county on its Ohio border, was formed out of Allegheny County in 1800. It was named for Colonel William Crawford, Indian fighter and business agent of George Washington, who was tortured to death during an Ohio expedition in 1782. Settlers came from eastern and southwestern Pennsylvania as well as New York and New England, attracted by the fact that Crawford County was well watered by two of the largest natural lakes in Pennsylvania, the Conneaut and Canadohta, and was fertile agricultural land.

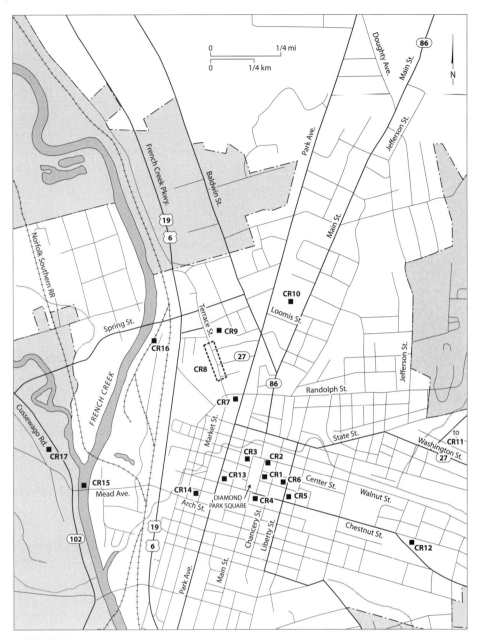

MEADVILLE

Three turnpikes built between 1806 and 1824 made the county easily accessible. But the turnpikes were expensive to maintain and run, and by 1845, they were supplanted by the Beaver and Erie Canal, joining Meadville to Beaver. To reach its ultimate destination, Lake Erie, the canal required seventy-two locks to overcome the topography. The canal took nearly twenty years to complete and it operated fully only from 1845 to 1871, when it was succeeded by the railroads. During the canal era, wooden houses with Greek Revival elements were favored, but their vulnerability to fire and decay have made these buildings relatively scarce and, therefore, candidates for preservation.

Three railroad lines in Crawford were completed during the Civil War, facilitating the transport of soldiers, oil, and goods from the northwestern territories. The lines linked Pittsburgh with Cleveland and with Lake Erie. Smaller dedicated rail lines built to ship raw materials and finished products also provided transportation to Conneaut Lake Park (initially called Exposition Park) in 1892 through a branch of the Pittsburgh, Shenango and Lake Erie Railroad.

In the twentieth and twenty-first centuries, the character of the county has remained primarily rural with agricultural support industries. Crawford also became a favored vacation destination after 1935, when the 17,088-acre Pymatuning Reservoir (Seneca meaning "the crooked-mouthed man's dwelling place") used water impounded from the Shenango River to create a reservoir providing marinas, campsites, and fishing and swimming opportunities, as well as a haven for migratory birds. It also provided water for the industrialized Shenango Valley. Channellock, a tool manufacturer; Lord Corporation, which makes specialty plastics; and Wal-Mart are all dependent on such important highway links as I-79 and U.S. 6 and U.S. 322 to access markets.

MEADVILLE

Meadville occupies a strategic location along French Creek, a main thoroughfare for Native Americans and French colonizers, and a pathway between two French forts: Le Boeuf (now Waterford in Erie County) and Machault (Franklin in Venango County). The Iroquois of the Six Nations called the place Cussewago, from Kos-se-waus-ga, meaning "big belly," for a snake found near the creek that had just swallowed an animal.

David Mead and his brothers John, Joseph, and Darius arrived in 1788 from Wyoming County, in northeastern Pennsylvania. Mead called the place Lewisburgh, but in 1805, the name was changed to Meadville to recognize their pioneering efforts. A replica dogtrot log house in Bicentennial Park on Mead Avenue, built in 1988, commemorates Mead and his brothers. The town plots were first laid out in 1793 by Roger Alden, the first Holland Land Company agent, and then in 1795 by Dr. Thomas Kennedy, when the land company bought David Mead's holdings. By 1807, Meadville had a fledgling chamber of commerce and, in 1817, Allegheny College opened (CR10). By 1823, Meadville was granted borough status, and it became a city in 1866, just as its streets were being paved.

Harm Jan Huidekoper and his sons were influential in Meadsville's early growth. They bought the interests of the Holland Land Company west of the Allegheny Mountains in 1836; their office survives on Chestnut Street in Meadville (CR5). The Huidekopers built gristmills and a sawmill in Fredericksburg west of Meadville on Cussewago Creek, and started a Unitarian seminary (CR12). Meadville became a center for the tool and machining industries, and, in the twentieth century, for the manufacture of plastics. In 1891, Whitcomb L. Judson invented the "clasp locker for shoes" in Meadville. Over the years its design was perfected, so that in 1913 Colonel Lewis Walker brought the Automatic Hook and Eye Company from Hoboken, New Jersey, to Meadville to manufacture "hookless slide fasteners." The company grew to become Talon, Inc., the world's largest producer of zippers during the 1920s and 1930s. Part of the Talon factory is still standing at 628 Chestnut Street as the Meadville Area Industrial Park. Railroad connections to Meadville were made through the Atlantic and Great Western Railroad, which built shops here around 1862 (CR16). The line was built during the Civil War, and the steel rails were imported from England since American steel was dedicated to the war effort.

The five-acre diamond, or town square, is ringed with Meadville's civic and institutional buildings, including the courthouse (CR1), armory (c. 1890; 894 Diamond Park), library designed by Edward L. Tilton (1925–1926; 848 N. Main Street), and the former high school, now Parkside Commons (1921; 847 N. Main Street), as well as four churches. These are Christ Church (CR3) and Meadville Unitarian-Universalist (CR4), Stone United Methodist Church built in 1868 and rebuilt in 1928 after it was gutted by fire (956 S. Main Street), and the substantial Romanesque Revival brownstone First Baptist Church of 1904 by J. C. Fulton Architect (353 Chestnut Street).

The seven-story, red brick Renaissance Revival Crawford County Trust Company designed by Oil City architect J. P. Brenot, with an addition of 1930 by the New York firm of Uffinger, Foster and Bookwalter, is the tallest building in Meadville and a symbol of its economic prosperity just before the Great Depression. Today, the restored houses and historic buildings of this town of 14,500, as well as the nearby Allegheny College campus (CR10), continue to attract visitors.

CR1 Crawford County Courthouse

1952–1954, Edwin S. Hanna and D. Fuller Stewart. Diamond Park Sq. at E. Cherry St.

This competent handling of Georgian Revival, favored in Pennsylvania courthouse design in the 1940s and 1950s, is similar to the McKean County Courthouse (MK1). Here, the Meadville architects brought the symmetrical red-orange brick wings forward to create a recessed entrance set off by a pedimented portico with a clock tower and cupola above. A simple stone cornice and window trim around the double-sash six-over-six windows are all as expected. The interior is closer to a school than a courthouse: there are no ceremonial spaces or murals, just plaster and tile finishes

in the well-lit offices. There have been three courthouses in Crawford County. The earliest courthouse of 1824–1828 with Doric columns was designed by eminent Greek Revival architect William Strickland and was demolished in the 1860s; it is commemorated on the present courthouse in bas-relief. A Second Empire–styled courthouse of 1867 yielded some of the walls, the foundations, and part of the floors used in the construction of the present courthouse.

CR2 Tarr Mansion

1867. 871–873 Diamond Park Sq.

The James Tarr family, who made a fortune selling their land in the oil territory, moved to

Meadville, where they erected one of the largest houses in town on one of the most prominent sites: next door to the courthouse on the town square. This red brick Italianate house has a central cupola, hardly visible from the street since the house is so tall, an attic story with paired brackets between the windows, and elaborate hood molds over every window. Nearly every entrance has its own porch dripping with sawn ornament. The central core of the house has bay windows on both the east and west elevations and round-arched windows above. The building now houses offices and a retail shop. In dramatic contrast is an earlier and much simpler single-story frame shotgun house at 918 Diamond Park Square built c. 1830, which also now houses offices.

CR3 Christ Episcopal Church

1883–1884, George Watson and William Dempster Hewitt. 870 Diamond Park Sq.

This is a fine example of the English-style parish churches in which the Hewitt brothers specialized after leaving their partnership with Frank Furness in 1875. The architects used local sandstone weathered to a grayish color for this Gothic Revival structure, and lined the side elevations with small buttresses. The steeply pitched roof and bell tower are well suited to the corner site. The church retains the original iron railing around its yard. The interior has a single nave with exposed wooden trusswork under the roof.

CR4 Meadville Unitarian-Universalist Church

1836, George Washington Cullum. 346 Chestnut St.

This serene Greek Revival church is noteworthy for its unusual proportions and its status as mother church for many Unitarian congregations to the west. Dutch immigrant Harm Jan Huidekoper founded this congregation in 1825. George Cullum, the designer, was a church member who ultimately served for forty-five years in the U.S. Army Corps of Engineers and spent his first year after graduating from West Point (1933) in Newport, Rhode Island. Although modeled on Westminster Congregational Church of 1829 in Providence, Rhode Island, the budget was not

CR4 MEADVILLE UNITARIAN-UNIVERSALIST CHURCH

as large, and so it has half as many columns, uses pilasters rather than engaged columns on the portico walls, and is of red brick rather than stone construction. The portico's four Doric columns are so widely spaced that there are two triglyphs between each instead of the usual single triglyph. Despite this, the church is not a stripped-down version of its model, but is complete in itself. With large windows and oversized doors the church seems to emphasize an openness of thought and of public scrutiny. And its design complemented William Strickland's nearby (now demolished) courthouse.

CR5 Johnson-Shaw Stereoscopic Museum (Huidekoper Land Company)

c. 1856. 423 Chestnut St.

Despite its diminutive size, this one-story orange brick, gable-roofed building has a distinguished presence on the street. Harm Jan Huidekoper and his sons bought the Holland Land Company's regional holdings and conducted their public business in this small space. (Huidekoper worked for the company from 1805 to 1836.) The building appears to have been a dependency of the large Huidekoper House (demolished) next door. There is evidence in the brickwork of some alteration to the facade of the building. As it is today, there is a round-arched window in the gable end and a segmental-arched portico sheltering a fanlight over the entrance door. The building has been in continuous use as various offices and is now a museum.

CR6 First Presbyterian Church

1874–1875, Carpenter and Matthews; 1931 social hall; 1947 organ screen and 1950 Stockton

Hall, Edwin S. Hanna and D. Fuller Stewart; 1970 additions, William J. Douglass for Hunter, Heiges. 890 Liberty St.

This is a fine example of a Gothic Revival brick church with asymmetrical steeples, pointed-arched windows, and buttressed walls. The smaller of the two towers has an unusual convex spire. Unlike the other churches that front on the diamond, this church faces a side street. From the 1930s, a series of flat-roofed, brick additions has enlarged the educational wing. The original church was designed by an interesting Meadville pair: Colonel Phineas B. Carpenter (1827–1904), a Russian-born Civil War veteran, and his carpenter partner Orville C. Matthews. They partnered in 1867, and by 1874, as they began work on this church, were advertising themselves as "architects, builders and contractors" working on courthouses and churches. Their partnership ended the following year, but Carpenter continued as a builder in the region until 1892.

CR7 George M. Roueche House

1892, George F. Barber. 762 Park Ave.

This elaborate Queen Anne house for merchant George Roueche features a picture window piercing the chimney stack on the facade, a convex-roofed tower, and a wide variety of porches and window shapes. Its appearance is so idiosyncratic that it is difficult to believe that similar houses exist in nearby Saegertown (352 Euclid Avenue) and in many of the nation's states. Such houses are the product of architect and marketing genius George F. Barber, whose architectural plans were sold through popular magazines such as *Harper's Weekly.* Clients would hire their own local

contractors to build the designs, often making minor changes. This house was reversed from the published design to have the porch face the side street on the right. The house next door at 764 Park Avenue has some Barberesque detailing, while houses at 494 Chestnut and 865 Grove streets are documented Barber designs.

CR8 Terrace Street District

c. 1870–1900. 697–725 Terrace St.

These four large, brick, Colonial Revival, Second Empire, and Italianate houses face French Creek, and the former path of the canal and railroad. Interpretive panels on the west side of Terrace Street describe the path of both canal and railroad and their economic impact on Meadville. The houses enjoy deep setbacks, and although some are in better condition than others, they all maintain a fairly high level of integrity and they make a powerful statement about wealth in Meadville between the 1870s and 1900. The enormous yellow brick Arthur C. Huidekoper house of 1890, which is immediately south of the Baldwin-Reynolds house, with its Flemish-shaped gable end and semicircular, two-story portico supported by Ionic columns, is particularly noteworthy.

CR9 Baldwin-Reynolds House

1841–1843, 1867. 639 Terrace St.

This large, yellow brick house was built as the second home of jurist Henry Baldwin, whose move to Pittsburgh from Philadelphia launched his career as a U.S. congressman (1816–1822). In 1830, President Andrew

CR7 GEORGE M. ROUECHE HOUSE

CR9 BALDWIN-REYNOLDS HOUSE

CR10 ALLEGHENY COLLEGE, Bentley Hall, photo 1937

Jackson appointed Baldwin a justice of the Supreme Court, where he served until 1844. Said to be a copy of Jackson's home, "Hunter's Hill," near Nashville, Baldwin's house has an open gallery on all four elevations and a hipped roof. The house was incomplete when Baldwin died penniless in 1844. In 1847, William Reynolds, a nephew of Baldwin's wife, bought the property. He renovated the house in 1866, changed the roof from hipped to mansard, added a walnut stairway, a library and a conservatory in enclosed portions of the gallery, and a first-story entrance on the west elevation. The house stayed in the Reynolds family until 1963, when the Crawford County Historical Society purchased it; the society operates it as a house museum.

CR10 Allegheny College

1820–present. 520 N. Main St.

The 540-acre campus of Allegheny College, a 2,000-student coeducational liberal arts college, contains over forty buildings designed by architects from Philadelphia, New York, Chicago, and Pittsburgh. The centerpiece, Bentley Hall, was designed in 1820–1821 by Alexander Temple and by Timothy Alden, who opened the college in 1817. The hall was named for the college's first major donor, Reverend William Bentley, a Unitarian minister of Salem, Massachusetts, who donated

his library in 1819. The building's mixture of Federal and Greek Revival elements is charming and vibrant, with a cupola directly copied from an Asher Benjamin pattern book. The majority of the campus's buildings speak to that idiom. The three buildings constructed during the nineteenth century are red brick with the traditional styling of that time.

In the twentieth century, locally quarried sandstone was the preferred material for the Ford Memorial Chapel (1901, Charles W. Bolton) and Newton Observatory (1901, M. H. Church). Reis Hall, the former library (1901, Charles W. Bolton), is of brown Pompeiian brick in a Renaissance Revival style. Carnegie Hall (1915, Henry D. Whitfield) is constructed of buff brick similar to the buildings at Carnegie Mellon University in Pittsburgh (AL43). From 1928 to 1941, halls northwest of Bentley were built in a colonial interpretation by noted college planner Jens Fredrick Larson and historicist architects Charles Stotz and Edward Stotz Jr. Not until midcentury did modernism take over campus designs. Between 1953 and 1964, half-a-dozen brick and concrete buildings were designed with flat roofs and recessed fixed windows. In the mid-1990s, postmodernism arrived with Steffee Hall of Life Sciences (1993, Ellenzweig and Associates) and Wise Athletic Center (1997, Hastings + Chivetta Architects). A campus master plan prepared by Celli Flynn Brennan

CR11 HILLCREST HOUSING PROJECT, Cape Cod–style cottage

in 2002 outlined progress for the twenty-first century. The North Quad Dormitories (2004, Cannon Design) won a Silver LEED rating for their sustainable design, while the Vukovich Center for Communication Arts (2007–2008, Polshek Partnership) will have a 250-seat auditorium, studios, and a landscaped balcony to increase energy efficiency.

CR11 Hillcrest Housing Project

1936, Edward Albert Phillips and E. S. Phillips. A–H sts., branching off Graff Ave.

These 202 houses were built between April and October 1936 by Meadville industries and citizens interested in providing decent housing for workers and their families during the Great Depression. Hillcrest is the first privately funded but federally insured housing project in the country. Remarkably, nearly all the original houses survive and are occupied; even the original street designations "A" through "H" remain. Despite the addition of aluminum siding, each of the eight models available at the time of construction is discernible. They range from small, gable-roofed, one-and-one-half-story Cape Cod cottages to gambrel-roofed, two-story houses with dormers. Some of the duplexes that resemble substantial two-story houses with intersecting gable roofs have been turned into single-family homes.

CR12 Alden Place Offices (Meadville Theological Seminary, Hunnewell Hall)

1903. 638–640 Chestnut St.

Though the architect is unknown, this building's great subtlety and handsome strength make it noteworthy and distinctive in a town where Colonial Revival predominates. The brick patterning around the doorway is reminiscent of the Richardsonian Romanesque handling of the brick on Longfellow, Alden and Harlow's "Sunnyledge" in Pittsburgh (AL115). Clever detailing includes a slight projection of the entrance and its flanking windows, which are set off by brick dentils above and highlighted by a dentiled cornice just below the second-story windows. A circular window above the doorway highlights the great sweep of the three-brick-deep, arched door surround. The second story appears to taper slightly, causing the windows to disappear under the eaves, where their columned pilasters give them a slim, elongated appearance. Deeply overhanging eaves are lined with brackets. Although this building dates from 1903, the Meadville Theological Seminary was founded in 1844 by Harm Jan Huidekoper to spread Unitarianism to the west. The seminary affiliated with the University of Chicago and moved to that campus in 1926. Offices now occupy the building.

CR13 Meadville Academy of Music

1885, J. M. Wood. 275 Chestnut St.

To replace an opera house destroyed by fire in 1882, Ernest Hempstead of Meadville commissioned J. M. Wood of Chicago to design this music academy in 1885. Two shallow storefronts have the auditorium behind them on the first floor, while the second floor has offices at the front and a balcony facing the upper portion of the theater. The windows are round arched with a segmental-arched picture window at the center. A pyramidal tower above the pediment adds height and drama to the building.

CR12 ALDEN PLACE OFFICES (MEADVILLE THEOLOGICAL SEMINARY, HUNNEWELL HALL)

CR15 TRUSS BRIDGE

CR14 Meadville Market House

1870–1871, 1916–1917. 910 Market St.

It is unusual to find a market house still operating in the middle of town, one that opens at six in the morning to sell produce and baked goods year-round. A second story was added to the market between 1916 and 1917, which, from 1975, has housed both the Meadville Council on the Arts and a performance space. The simple gable-roofed, brick rectangular structure has an open-air gallery on all sides. Windows line each elevation; those on the first story are round arched, while the upper-story windows are rectangular. Next door at 900–902 Market Street, Keppler's Hotel (c. 1870, renovated 2006), a three-story red brick structure with a two-story porch on the facade, further illustrates the commercial viability of the town's older buildings.

CR15 Truss Bridge

1871–1872, T. B. White and Sons; 1912, Rodgers Brothers. Mead Ave. over French Creek

This is a double-intersection Whipple truss bridge that was strengthened by a Baltimore truss in 1912, to make the transition from carrying wagons to carrying trolley cars and, later, automobile traffic. The earlier iron, pin-connected bridge was built by a New Brighton, Pennsylvania, company and is unique among the many iron and steel bridges crossing French Creek. The two truss systems, layered over each other, appear weblike when one is crossing the bridge; the corner ornament of stars and circles provides a whimsical touch.

A Whipple truss, patented in 1847, is a type of Pratt truss (a truss one drives through that consists of verticals and diagonals) in which the tension-bearing diagonals cross over two panels of the bridge, rather than the standard single panel as in most Pratt trusses. The Baltimore truss, introduced in 1871 by the Baltimore and Ohio Railroad, adds smaller diagonals to subdivide each panel. Here, then, is a bridge within a bridge, since the engineers of Albion, Pennsylvania, simply encased the older Whipple truss within the newer Baltimore truss. The bridge has been closed to traffic while its stability and fate are debated.

CR16 Bessemer Commerce Park (Atlantic and Great Western Railroad)

1865. 764 Bessemer St.

This handsome, large, orange-red brick building was the blacksmith's shop of the Atlantic and Great Western Railroad headquarters, which was located here in the 1860s. While utilitarian in purpose, the structure is very high style, especially when compared to the spare designs of the Pennsylvania Railroad buildings in Altoona. It is constructed of brick with stone quoins and round-arched window surrounds, and stepped corbeling outlines the cornice of the intersecting gable-roofed structure. The shop was once part of a much larger complex of buildings, including a roundhouse and sheds. A frame passenger station, now a garden supply store (c. 1870; 133 Pine Street), and a brick freight station also survive on Mead Avenue.

CR17 Frank Schwab House

c. 1905, attributed to George F. Barber. 18621 Cussewago Rd.

This house represents well the early-twentieth-century fashion for Colonial Revival. It is sited in isolated splendor overlooking the town of Meadville, and in winter is visible from Bicentennial Park on the east side of French Creek. The house's main feature is a two-story porch supported by Ionic columns and with a pseudo-Palladian window in the pediment. A similar house at 494 Chestnut Street is "A New Colonial Design" (see CM4) from the *Modern Dwellings* (1904) catalog of George F. Barber, an architect who specialized in mail-order plans. A frame version appears at 263 Randolph Street in Meadville. Two houses in Clarion have similar porches, with enough variation to make one suspect they were imitations done by a local contractor without plans.

SAEGERTOWN

Saegertown's site on French Creek made it an attractive place for Major Roger Alden's saw and grist mills in 1800, and it became the market center for the farms of Woodcock Township. In 1824, Daniel Saeger and several German compatriots laid out the town in time to take advantage of the construction of the nearby canal. It was named a borough in 1851. Two red brick two-story buildings at 402 and 440 Main Street, one a house and the other a commercial building, appear to date from the 1830s and reflect the presence of the canal through the town.

The small village has been spared the development pressures inherent when commercial districts are in the path of the railroad. Here, though, the Atlantic and Great Western Railroad ran north on a side street, not directly through the middle of Saegertown, keeping the commercial district intact. Solid housing dating from the 1890s to the 1920s in styles ranging from bungalow to Shingle Style to Queen Anne and Italianate distinguishes this town from others of its size in Crawford County. Two late-nineteenth-century houses of interest along the tracks are the frame Stick Style houses at 338 and 352 Euclid Avenue. The latter is a George F. Barber Design No. 27, similar to the Roueche house in Meadville (CR7). The handsome, board-and-batten Gothic Revival Twelve Apostles Lutheran Church of c. 1860 at 358 Euclid Avenue is a fine example of its type. The Independent Order of Odd Fellows building (1909) at 518 Main Street is the largest commercial structure in town. Two steel bridges cross French Creek north and south of Saegertown. The bridge carrying South Street over the creek (1900, Youngstown Bridge Company) is a Pennsylvania through truss with a delicate network of diagonal members, the oldest of its type in the region.

CR18 Patrick McGill House

1796, 1805. 649 Main St.

This log house, restored in 2006, is revered as the oldest extant house in Crawford County. It was built while the town was still known as Alden's Mills, and predates the arrival of Daniel Saeger. A shed-roofed porch on the south and a shed-roofed addition on the north have been incorporated under the roofline. An interpretive sign adds to the information available at the site.

CR19 Daniel Saeger House

1824. 375 Main St.

This extraordinarily graceful and restrained frame house for the town's founder is distinguished by its Greek Revival styling and second-story covered walkway on three elevations. A well-proportioned pediment with fanlight at the gable end is offset by heavy interior chimneys anchoring the north and south elevations. This is an early frame house for the county, and illustrates the propensity toward the Greek Revival, here mixed with a southern flavor in the peripteral porches.

VENANGO

CR20 Cussewago Street Bridge

1893. PA 1002 over French Creek

The Pratt truss was once the most common metal truss bridge type, but it is rapidly disappearing from the rural areas of Pennsylvania. This one is a two-span, pin-connected Pratt bridge with handsome intact decorative railings. The Wrought Iron Bridge Company, founded by David Hammond in Canton, Ohio, in 1864, constructed this bridge. The company was absorbed by the American Bridge Company of Pittsburgh in 1900. The bridge has been closed pending a decision on its stability and future.

CAMBRIDGE SPRINGS AND VICINITY

Located on French Creek, Cambridge Springs is a railroad town today, bisected by the tracks that run east to west, which helped it grow at the turn of the twentieth century. The town served as an agricultural marketplace for local farmers shipping their goods along the creek and via the Waterford and Susquehanna Turnpike. The oil excitement around Titusville in 1860 induced individuals to drill for oil on their own properties. In Dr. John Gray's case, what spewed from the ground was not oil, but "charged," or mineral, water. Years later, after a trip to Hot Springs, Arkansas, he realized there was commercial potential for the "curative" waters, and built a frame hotel along French Creek in 1885, Riverside Inn (CR21), to shelter those who came by train to "take the waters."

At the time, the town was called Cambridgeboro, and was serviced by two railroads. Its accessibility and proximity to Cleveland, Pittsburgh, and Buffalo contributed to its growth as a mineral spring. By the 1890s, eight trains stopped daily in Cambridge Springs, and by 1905, forty hotels and rooming houses operated in the town. Between 1895 and 1897, W. D. Rider of Franklin in Venango County, one of the successful owners of the Riverside Inn, built an elaborate 500-room hotel at the top of a hill southeast of town, the Rider Hotel, which had a 1,000-foot promenade around it and all the amenities of a luxury resort. A devastating tornado in 1908 did substantial damage to the town as did several hotel fires. Additionally, the custom of taking the waters died just as the automobile made other, more remote sites available to vacationers. In 1912, the Polish National Alliance, a fraternal insurance benefit association, took over the Rider Hotel as the Alliance Technical Institute, but the building burned to the ground in 1931. The institute built four brick Colonial Revival buildings between 1924 and 1942 for the growing student body. It became a junior college in 1948, and a four-year college in 1952. The need for separate ethnic educational institutions lessened over the years, and Alliance College closed in 1987. In 1991, the property was sold to the Commonwealth of Pennsylvania for a women's medium security prison. Alliance Technical Institute's former Washington Hall remains outside the prison boundaries and provides office space.

Remnants of the town's glory days remain around the village: the red brick Bartlett House (1897; 257 S. Main Street), once a hotel, now serves as housing for senior citizens, and the large frame, Italianate Bethany Guest House (1876; 325 S. Main Street) is a bed-and-breakfast located among several interesting frame and brick houses and churches at the south end of Main Street. An unusual cement block, flat-iron-shaped city hall stands at Cummings and Federal streets, built after the 1908 tornado.

CR21 Riverside Inn

c. 1885. 1 Fountain Ave.

A relic of the mineral springs' era of the 1880s, the Riverside Inn is a simple frame structure distinguished by its mansard-roofed tower at the connection of three gable-roofed wings. Bracketed eaves and first-story verandas with sawn ornament enliven the three-story hotel. The remains of a long boardwalk, which once led to the original springhouse for the "curative" waters of Cambridge Springs across low-lying land northwest of the hotel and adjacent to French Creek, are still visible. The inn sparked the local mineral water boom. An international clientele arrived by train and trolley to use seven kinds of baths and electrical and X-ray treatments as cures. Three hundred guests would fill the old inn; today there are seventy-four guest rooms. In the early 1900s, a casino and a bowling alley were added, joined to the hotel by a one-story breezeway.

CR22 DeElmer Kelly Octagonal Barn

1900, DeElmer Kelly. Millers Station Rd. at Cherry Hill Rd., 2.5 miles east of Cambridge Springs

DeElmer Kelly built this octagonal barn as a showplace as well as shelter for his dairy cows and their food. The cows' stanchions are arranged in a circle facing inward to the center of the ground-level story. Above, an enormous hayloft and threshing floor create a spectacular open space without a central supporting beam and that opens up to the crowning cupola. A windmill in the cupola powered the thresher. The barn's interior beams are pegged, but the exterior sheathing is board and batten. Each of the eight sides measures 24.5 feet across, and the cupola is approximately 60 feet above the ground. West of the barn, a small brick structure once housed the pigpen, then a tool and die operation, and finally, a workshop. This is one of two octagonal barns in Crawford County; a smaller, simpler one is located at 34354 PA 27 on the John Warren farm.

TITUSVILLE AND VICINITY

Jonathan Titus and his uncle Samuel Kerr, surveyors for the Holland Land Company, claimed a large part of the land surrounding what is today Titusville, and settled along the banks of Oil Creek in 1796. Noticing that the "Seneca's Oil" that Native Americans soaked up from the surface of the creek was used as a body rub, they sold it in small quantities for its medicinal qualities. The first store and lumber mill opened in this small crossroads community in 1816. The population was barely 300 when the town was incorporated in 1847. In August 1859, the situation changed dramatically. Edwin Laurentine Drake, a retired railroad conductor sent by an investor from Connecticut, hired a salt well driller named William Smith, and together they perfected an oil drilling technique that allowed large quantities of oil to be extracted. Titusville's population swelled from 438 in 1860 to 9,000 in 1880.

Laid out on a grid, the town's housing stock and institutional buildings grew apace. Drake was a warden at the stone, Gothic Revival St. James Episcopal Church (1863; 112 E. Main Street). Two New York architects, Horace Smith of Jamestown and Enoch A. Curtis of Fredonia, designed some of the town's earliest houses, unfortunately now demolished. However, Curtis's design of 1891 for a two-story brick commercial structure, the Reuting Block at 122 W. Spring Street, survives. A *Titusville Herald* article of 1870 stated, "Five years ago the citizens of Titusville, in building, paid little attention to architectural beauty. . . . With the firm establishment of this as the empo-

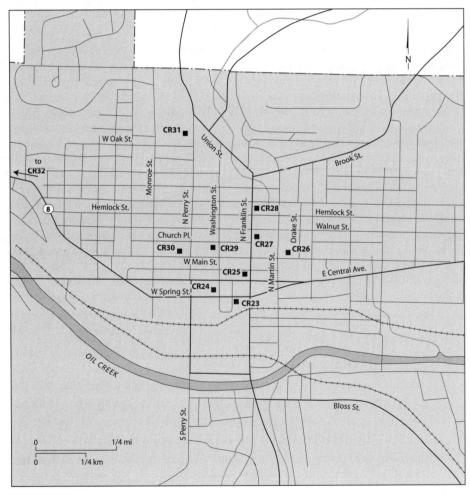

TITUSVILLE

rium of the oil regions and the centre of a great and constantly increasing trade, people came to the sensible conclusion that it might be possible to go farther. . . . This feeling caused an immediate demand to spring up for the services of architects and builders, and within the past year there has been a most wonderful revolution in the character of the buildings constructed, to say nothing of the number." In 1985, nearly thirty-eight blocks of Titusville were listed on the National Register of Historic Places.

Locally known as the "Queen City of the Oil Region," Titusville has a number of handsome institutional buildings. The brick Benson Memorial Library (1902–1904; 213 N. Franklin Street) was designed by New York City architects Jackson and Rosencrans in a classically inspired style. Local architect Phillip M. Hesch designed the Independent Order of Odd Fellows building, giving it a broken pediment at the center of the parapet (1899; 304 N. Washington Street). The Bryan-McKinney house (504 E. Main Street), built in 1870 and extensively remodeled by the McKinneys in 1926, was donated in 1963 as the administration building for a two-year branch campus of the University of Pittsburgh in Titusville. It opened with 50 students and has since grown to a student population of 500. The five-block campus now hosts half-a-dozen newer buildings.

As well as oil drilling, Titusville cultivated the industry's support services, such as an iron works, forges, and refineries during the boom. By the time the center of the industry moved to Texas in the 1900s, these collateral endeavors, as well as lumbering and tanning, were flourishing and kept Titusville's economy viable. Today, the buildings of the former Titusville Iron Works, including a foundry, machine shop, and steel fabricating shop, serve the borough as an industrial park between the two sets of railroad tracks south of Spring Street between Washington and Franklin streets.

Author and journalist Ida M. Tarbell (1857–1944), who lived at 324 E. Main Street in her early teens, is Titusville's best-known former resident. She is often cited when the term "muckraker" is employed, for her reputation in exposing unsavory corporate business practices. Her two-volume history of the Standard Oil Company (1904) illustrated the desperate need for industrial reform. She is buried in nearby Woodlawn Cemetery.

CR23 Farmers National Bank (National City Bank, Titusville Trust Company)

1918–1919, Alfred Charles Bossom. 127 W. Spring St.

This bank's exterior features four engaged Ionic columns, an anthemion cartouche above the parapet of its limestone facade, and the type of large round-arched windows found on many banks across the nation that date from the early twentieth century. However, it has two surprising elements: an English architect and colorful murals. Alfred Charles Bossom (1881–1965), from Maidstone, England, practiced architecture in New York City from 1906 to 1926. After he returned to England, he became a member of Parliament in 1931, was created a baronet in 1953, and in 1960, a life peer of the realm. Bossom came to the United States in 1904 at the behest of Henry Phipps to work on the design of the Phipps model tenement in Allegheny (demolished) and a nine-story office building at 947 Penn Avenue in Pittsburgh. In New York, Bossom met and married Emily Bayne, who had spent her girlhood in Oil City, where her father, Samuel Gamble Bayne, had been with the Oil Well Supply Company. Samuel Bayne became president of the Seaboard National Bank in New York City on whose board sat several Titusville oil men, including James Curtis McKinney. McKinney opened the Titusville Trust Company to handle oil certificates, and he wanted a handsome bank to commemorate the accomplishment that indelibly changed his home town. Bossom had not designed many banks by 1918, but McKinney looked favorably on his friend's son-in-law. Ultimately, Bossom designed a number of suave, classical banks from Kansas to Connecticut, in addition to skyscrapers and houses.

The interior, with an open central banking space lined with three kinds of marble, is a veritable temple of finance. The ceiling murals by Alfred Valiant and the firm of Mack, Jenney and Tyler depict the discovery of oil by Colonel Edwin Laurentine Drake and barrels of oil being shipped via flatboat and horse-drawn wagon; smaller lunettes surrounding the central medallion illustrate various modes of transportation that used petroleum, such as planes, trains, and dirigibles.

CR24 Park Building (Second National Bank)

1865; 1871–1872, J. M. Blackburn; 1905–1917, 1918, 1930. 208 W. Spring St.

The Park Building is a testament to both the various stages of Titusville's growth and the vagaries of its architectural fashions. When built in 1865, it was a two-story brick Italianate building of five by three bays. Between 1871 and 1872, it was glamorized by the addition of a third floor, a mansard roof, stone veneer, and a corner entrance. The bank purchased the neighboring commercial buildings to the north and west between 1905 and 1917. These adjoining buildings were raised to three stories and refaced in matching Cleveland sandstone. A parapet replaced the mansard roof in 1918. Then in 1930, the buildings to the west were demolished, and the west side of the bank was faced with matching sandstone to present a unified appearance to the newly created Scheide Park. For this building there has been only one constant: change.

CR25 City Hall (Nelson Kingsland House, Bush House Hotel)

1862. 107 N. Franklin St.

When lumber baron and Vermont native Nelson Kingsland sought a style for his house, he looked for reassuring symmetry and respectability, perhaps because it was built during the Civil War. He found it in the Greek Revival, and his wooden house is outfitted with four fluted Ionic columns supporting a two-story portico, heavy architraves, and a balcony above the central entrance. The five-bay-wide house has narrow corner boards and siding, and the simple side elevations have returning eaves. Within three years of completion, Kingsland left Titusville and the house became a luxury hotel. Seven years later, in 1872, the city purchased it for its offices.

CR26 William B. Sterrett House

1871. 226 E. Main St.

Representing a popular style in Titusville, this three-story brick house for manufacturer William Sterrett is one of six in the Second Empire style. With its central tower and oval windows in the concave mansard roof, it rises above the others in grandeur and architectural integrity. The windows are square headed on the first story and round arched on the upper floors. A similar mansard-roofed brick house for William Wood (c. 1870; 424 E. Main Street) has been restored.

The Italianate style also was popular with newly minted oil millionaires. John Fertig commissioned an Italian Villa–style house (1873; 602 E. Main Street) after his oil strike. Two frame Italianate houses at 213 and 480 E. Main Street indicate the large scale and elaborate detailing of houses in Titusville.

CR27 First Presbyterian Church

1887–1888; 1907 addition. 216 N. Franklin St.

Although every town in western Pennsylvania with a sufficiently large population has at least one and sometimes up to three stone Presbyterian churches, this one has a particularly distinctive tower and a fine addition of 1907 to the south. Both are of Medina sandstone in a rough-cut and differently sized Richardsonian Romanesque manner. The conical tower and flush eaves reinforce the building's el-

ementary shapes. The south addition is dominated by Emerson Chapel, with its arched doorway and narrow niches on either side. It is capped by an intersecting gable roof with a round cupola at its apex that echoes the corner tower on the older church. The chapel's windows were designed in 1906 and 1907 by J & R Lamb Studios of New York.

CR28 Bluegill Graphix (Jewish Reform Society, Temple B'Nai Zion)

1871–1872, Phillip M. Hesch. 318 N. Franklin St.

This small synagogue is the creation of sixteen local German Jews who hired a contractor-architect, Phillip Hesch, and built their own house of worship. A bit awkward and primitive, the frame building is essentially composed of a shotgun structure with a false front, diminutive corner turrets on the facade, and round-arched windows. The congregation, Temple B'Nai Zion, sold the building to the Christian and Missionary Alliance Society in 1927, and the former temple subsequently had several owners. The present owners, a graphics company, gave it a colorful paint job.

CR29 Titusville Area School District Administrative Building (Maltby-Scheide House)

1863–1866, 1890; c. 1921 library, William Woodburn Potter. 221 N. Washington St.

This pleasant, frame foursquare house has paired brackets and elaborate moldings over the windows that were added by the second owner. But what sets the house apart is the large brick addition at the northwest corner. Soon after his father, William T. Scheide, died and left him his rare book collection, John

Hinsdale Scheide purchased this house and commissioned his Princeton classmate and friend William Woodburn Potter (1875–1964) to design a brick, Tudor Revival library building for the collection. This was no ordinary library, for it contained some of the world's rarest books: a Gutenberg Bible, a complete critical edition of the works of Johann Sebastian Bach in forty-seven volumes, and the First Folio of Shakespeare. Upon Mrs. Scheide's death in 1959, the library was donated to Princeton University. To honor the collection, a room emulating Potter's design and using its stained glass windows was added to Princeton's existing Firestone Library. The house and its library room were donated to the Titusville Area School District.

CR30 Theodore and Marie Reuting House

1893, attributed to Enoch A. Curtis. 318 W. Main St.

This stellar example of Queen Anne, fused with some Shingle Style elements, is attributed to Fredonia, New York, architect Enoch Curtis. Although at first glance the elaborate design seems to have come from one of George F. Barber's pattern books, the composition of the elements does not match any of his documented designs. Since Curtis designed Reuting's office building in the commercial district, it is possible that he designed this house using elements he gleaned from contemporary pattern books. Most prominent on the facade is the faceted tower at the center, with its convex mansard roof. Surrounding this are gables and dormers that are framed to resemble pediments and that emphasize the angularity of the design. The rooftops are echoed on the first story in the pediment of the surrounding porch. The plan and details of the house, from the second-story porch with bracketed overhang to the oriel window on the west elevation, indicate a composition beyond the capabilities of most contractors.

CR31 Emerson Place Presbyterian Residence (John L. Emerson House, "Hillhurst")

1908, Emmet E. Bailey. 701 N. Perry St.

Oil and natural gas heir John L. Emerson commissioned architect Emmet Bailey of Oil

City, who designed many Colonial Revival structures in the oil region, to build this brick Colonial Revival house. The imposing two-story semicircular portico overlooked nine acres of rolling lawns, which, in 1938, were subdivided into smaller building lots. Inside, the seventeen rooms retain their original details, including replicas of interior furnishings from the Emersons' favorite American houses, among which are fireplace mantels copied from Mount Vernon and from Monticello in Virginia; the dining room mantel imitates one of Stanford White's. The staircase duplicates the one designed by McKim, Mead and White for Pepperell House at Kittery, Maine. In 1951, the two-and-one-half-story house became the Presbyterian Residence, an assisted living facility.

CR32 Oakwood Manor (Luke B. Carter Farm)

1930, Prentice Sanger. PA 8, 1 mile northwest of Titusville

This manor is a fine example of the kind of sophisticated architecture prevalent in the Titusville area well into the 1930s. The brick Neo-Georgian house in five parts, with its four tall chimneys and verdant site, was designed by New York City architect Prentice Sanger for the Carter family as the centerpiece of their farm. The family's money came from the oil industry, but the succeeding generations chose to breed cattle. In the 1950s, an engineer for the Talon zipper factory carved the large house into apartments, and the cattle barns and grounds around it became an industrial park.

VENANGO COUNTY

Venango County, created in 1800, straddles the Allegheny River and two navigable tributaries, French and Oil creeks, which empty into the Allegheny. At the confluence of each is a major town: Franklin at French Creek and the Allegheny, and Oil City at Oil Creek. The county's name derives from the Seneca tribe's name for French Creek, In-nan-ga-eh, which was corrupted to Venango. Initially very large, Venango County was reduced when Clarion County was carved out of it in 1839 and Forest County in 1866.

In the mid-eighteenth century, Venango County was claimed by France, the Iroquois Confederation, and the colony of Pennsylvania. Three wars and many court cases later, land titles cleared enough to allow settlement. Revolutionary War veterans came to settle on land given to them as a service benefit. By 1800, the soldiers who had been assigned to protect the frontier from Native American attack were being withdrawn, and many of the forts they built were demolished. The city of Franklin was a major shipping site during the War of 1812, supplying Perry's fleet on Lake Erie via an inland route that gave the United States the advantage of surprise over the British. The Federal navy brought their supplies north on keelboats poled up the Allegheny River and French Creek to Waterford in Erie County, then hauled overland by wagons to the lake.

Iron making was the first major industry in Venango. Charcoal was made from local timber, and bellows were operated by waterwheels to power the approximately twenty-four stone blast furnaces built between 1825 and c. 1845, a large number of them in Rockland and Cranberry townships. Iron, agricultural produce, limestone, sand used in glassmaking, and gravel from

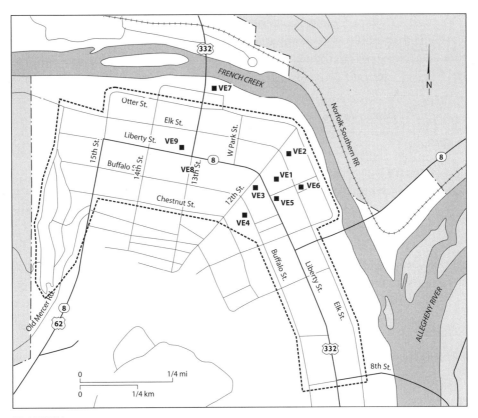

FRANKLIN

Venango County were shipped to Pittsburgh along the Allegheny River in steamboats after 1828.

In 1859, Edwin Laurentine Drake discovered crude petroleum in northern Venango County (VE20), and a year later, wells were drilled near Franklin. Towns boomed during the oil excitement. The town of Pithole, for example, grew from a single farmhouse to a town of 15,000 people within five months after oil was discovered there in 1865. Historian Brian Black has noted in *Petrolia: The Landscape of America's First Oil Boom* (2000) that journalists quipped there was a saloon attached to nearly every building in town, and estimated that there were nearly 400 prostitutes in Pithole at its peak population. By 1880, the wells were depleted and a series of fires had destroyed the town; only remnants of building foundations remain today.

In 1872, Samuel Van Syckle fashioned the first pipeline, which eliminated the need for teamsters to haul oil in barrels. The teamsters rioted, but by the early 1870s, two thousand miles of pipelines shipped oil to the railroads and steamboats on the Allegheny River. From 1872 to 1892, John D. Rockefeller dominated the production and transportation of oil. He founded the National Transit Company, a Standard Oil subsidiary, in Oil City in 1876. Natural gas also was harnessed as a product to be bought and sold, in 1885.

Oil City emerged as a corporate headquarters for oil drillers, refineries, oil drilling equipment companies, and transport companies. In 1921, Pennzoil incorporated in Oil City and ten years later, Quaker State Oil Refining Company formed from a group of nineteen smaller oil companies around Emlenton. As Pennsylvania's oil resources were depleted, the oil companies shifted their headquarters to Texas. McClintock Well No. 1 off PA 8 in Rouseville is the oldest producing oil well in the United States, active since August 1861. Other than that relic of the past, the oil industry is commemorated in two interpretive sites, Oil Creek State Park and Drake Oil Well (VE20).

Grand residences dating from 1892 to 1930 were built by those benefiting from oil. Large Queen Anne, Tudor Revival, and Colonial Revival homes dot the hillsides of Emlenton and Oil City, and the tree-lined streets of Franklin. By the early twenty-first century, the largest employers in Venango County were the University of Pittsburgh Medical Center, Franklin and Oil City campuses, and Polk Center (VE11). The largest industrial employer is Joy Manufacturing, maker of coal loaders. Heritage tourism is a growing interest and economic generator. Virtually nothing remains of the boomtowns today.

FRANKLIN AND VICINITY

Franklin was laid out in 1795 by Andrew Ellicott, who four years earlier had been chosen by George Washington and Thomas Jefferson to work on the town plan of Washington, D.C. During the late eighteenth and early nineteenth centuries, Franklin had four forts within its boundaries. The earliest, the French Fort Machault, was built in 1753 and destroyed in 1760. The British immediately built Fort Venango (1760), which was destroyed in 1763 during Pontiac's Rebellion. In 1787, American soldiers built Fort Franklin as a defense against Indian attacks, and named it for Benjamin Franklin. This fort was abandoned in 1796. A fourth fort garrisoned troops in 1796 and became the first jail of Venango County; it stood until 1824. The town was incorporated as a borough in 1828 and made a city in 1868.

After 1866, the Jamestown and Franklin Railroad serviced Franklin, and later became known as the New York Central Railroad. Its station, built in 1901, remains at Railroad and 13th streets. Franklin, the oldest city in Venango County, is impressive for its intelligent planning and the integrity of its historic architecture. Several two- and three-story buildings in the commercial district are particularly noteworthy. Among them are the Bleakley Block of 1878 (1233–1239 Liberty Street) with stone veneer and incised pointed-arched window surrounds; a handsome red brick building of fourteen bays with peaked cornice dated c. 1880 (1234–1242 Liberty Street); and the Masonic Building built between 1886 and 1891 (1255 Liberty Street). Several buildings have second-story oriel and round-arched windows that are distinctive to Franklin. The Barrow-Civic Theatre, formerly Kayton Theater (1223 Liberty Street), is a Moderne rectilinear buff brick building with glazed tile inserts and a recessed ticket booth built in 1946. In 1979, the area from Miller

Park to 8th Street and from Buffalo to French Creek and the Allegheny River was declared a historic district. Conscious historic preservation has enhanced tourism in the city of 7,400 residents.

VE1 Venango County Courthouse

1867–1869, Samuel Sloan and Addison Hutton. Liberty and 12th sts.

Construction on the courthouse began in 1867 to a design by Samuel Sloan, who launched his career in 1849 in eastern Pennsylvania and became famous for his architectural pattern books. In 1864, he formed a partnership with Addison Hutton. They won the Clinton County Courthouse commission in Lock Haven (CN1), which, with Sloan's courthouse of 1860 in Williamsport, Lycoming County, served as models for the Venango courthouse. The Clinton and Venango courthouses are almost identical. Their tall, narrow, ogee-domed bell towers are mirror images, the shorter tower to the left in Franklin and to the right in Lock Haven. The architects used brick, elongated round-arched windows and pedimented entrance pavilions to contrast with the asymmetrical towers. This departure from symmetry showed that the restrained Greek Revival style would no longer suffice for houses of justice. On the interior, a divided staircase behind the front wall accesses the two courtrooms, a larger courtroom with a grand, coffered ceiling and a smaller courtroom near the law library.

VE2 Venango County Jail

1910. Elk and 12th sts.

This stone Richardsonian Romanesque jail was furnished with cells from the Stewart Iron Works Company of Covington, Kentucky. The section facing Elk Street housed the county sheriff and his family and is residential in appearance. Behind this benign facade is the three-story-high expanse of stone walls surrounding the block-long cell block capable of holding 160 prisoners. A four-story watchtower separates the two functions. The jail's interior was modernized and expanded in 1994 by the Crabtree Company.

VE3 Franklin Public Library (Judge John S. McCalmont House)

1894; 1921, Samuel D. Brady. 421 12th St.

This elegant two-and-one-half-story Second Empire house was extensively remodeled in 1921 by Samuel Brady for the Franklin Library Association, who reorganized the interior to accommodate the library's needs. The library's exterior is of a pinkish-colored brick, and it has wooden porch supports, prominent curved window hoods, and a mansard roof.

VE4 St. John's Episcopal Church

1901. 1141 Buffalo St.

St. John's is one of a handful of churches in the United States with a full set of Tiffany windows and a Tiffany mosaic. Installed between 1901 and 1917, the windows depict the four Evangelists, Sts. Agnes and Michael, and Christ. Two additional mosaics by the Gorham Art Glass Studios of New York illustrate the Nativity and the Resurrection. The large rose window in the facade is gold and rose in color. Rosewood pews and marble floors complete the colorful ensemble. The square tower attached to the facade of this Gothic Revival church has diminutive turrets at the corners of its pyramidal roof. A wood-lined chapel, with oak hand-carved pews and benches and German stained glass, was added at the rear in 1965. The stone-veneered parish house to the south predates the church, as does the frame Queen Anne rectory at the southwest corner of 12th and Buffalo streets.

This block of Buffalo Street has two more churches: the tan brick Christ United Methodist Church (c. 1950; 1135 Buffalo Street), and the white frame Faith Holiness Church (1887; 1101 Buffalo Street). The latter, built for a German Lutheran congregation, has a square bell tower embellished with sawn ornament and Stick Style trim on its various wooden surfaces.

VE5 Galena-Signal Oil Company Headquarters

1901, Edgar K. Bourne. 1140 Liberty St.

This building served as the headquarters of the Galena-Signal Oil Company until 1931. In 1869, Charles A. Miller and two partners

purchased a small Franklin oil company where they added galena, a lead oxide, to Pennsylvania crude oil to make a railroad lubricant able to withstand variations in temperature and pressure. Miller's brother-in-law, Joseph Crocker Sibley, improved the valve oil substantially until Galena Oil's Perfection Valve Oil outsold all others. Sibley, a self-taught engineer, also refined oil that could be lit and used in signal lamps. He became president of the Signal Oil Company after 1875, and by 1902, the two entities were consolidated as the Galena-Signal Oil Company. Although Miller and Sibley maintained their shares until 1911, John D. Rockefeller's Standard Oil held the controlling interest due to the international scope of sales.

This three-story, Renaissance Revival golden brick building has a rich variety of different window treatments, from round arched on the first story, to round arched and pedimented on the second story, and to simple square-headed sash windows on the third story. A heavy cornice and water table as well as brick corner quoins complete the ensemble designed by New York City architect Edgar Bourne.

VE6 Pearce House

1843. 1142 Elk St.

This, the oldest surviving house in Franklin, was built during the turnpike and canal era by Edward Pearce, a prosperous wheelwright, wagon maker, and innkeeper. The five-bay stone house has an ell to the northeast and is larger than usual to accommodate the needs of the inn. Rubble stone on the rear elevation retains marks that indicate a porch once stood here, overlooking the confluence of French

Creek and the Allegheny River. The exquisite entrance, topped by a fanlight and set off with a ribbed reveal rather than a pediment, distinguishes the house. Two square-topped columns with rosette capitals guard the door. The stones on the facade are scabble and drafted with narrow edgings, contrasting beautifully with the smoothness of the columns.

VE7 Antique Mall Auction Gallery (Franklin Armory)

1909. 1280 Franklin Ave.

The deep maroon color and crenellated parapet of the former Franklin Armory give it a fortresslike appearance. The brick building is trimmed with Cleveland stone. A two-story administration extension at the western end is linked to the arena by a raised entrance flanked by castellated bay windows. The arena's open space is surrounded by a balcony. The building overlooks French Creek and is adjacent to the site of Fort Franklin (1787–1796), and a nearby historical marker remembers John Chapman, "Johnny Appleseed," a pioneer nurseryman and itinerant preacher who cultivated apples from Pennsylvania to Indiana and lived in the French Creek valley until 1804. Since 1989, the armory has housed an antiques mall.

VE8 Franklin Residential District

1840s–1930s. Bounded by 8th, 16th, Otter, and Chestnut sts.

Franklin's impressive houses from the 1840s to the 1930s are in this neighborhood. Some of the earliest houses reflect the stylistic influence of the Western Reserve of Ohio, including four white frame Greek Revival houses on the north side of the 1200 block of Elk Street and a small office (1846) at 1238 Elk Street bordering the courthouse park. Built for local professionals in the 1840s, the houses may have been constructed by the same carpenter who built a similar house at 353 N. Main Street in Pleasantville. The Peter McGough house of 1862 at 917 Elk Street is a fine example of Carpenter Gothic, with its board-and-batten siding and gabled dormer. These houses predate the oil boom that transformed the town. Lawyer Christopher Heydrick built a large Italian Villa–style house (927 Elk Street) in

VE8 FRANKLIN RESIDENTIAL DISTRICT, Samuel Plumer house

1864, near the end of the Civil War and just after the Drake oil strike.

A group of Second Empire houses from the 1870s is evidence of the first influx of oil money that transformed Franklin from a rural county seat to a stylish city. The James Smith House (1872–1873) at 1441 Elk Street is a small, frame version of the larger brick Second Empire house that Samuel Dale commissioned local builder John Brady to construct in 1874 at 1409 Elk Street. A pair of Italianate houses with central cupolas at 1136 and 1140 Buffalo Street and one dating from 1874 at 1116 Elk Street reflect the preference for this style by the newly minted oil millionaires. At the western end of Franklin, attorney Samuel Plumer built an enormous Queen Anne house in 1867 (1501 Liberty Street). Over thirty years later, Charles A. Miller, a partner in the Galena-Signal Oil Company, bought thirty acres of the steep hillside property above 16th Street. Between 1898 and 1919, Miller, along with his brothers and friends, built a series of large private homes in the 600 block of Sibley and Adelaide avenues in the Shingle, Queen Anne, and Colonial Revival styles of the day. Miller's house at 612 Sibley Avenue, designed by Beezer Brothers of Altoona (c. 1900), is Tudor Revival.

VE9 Franklin Club (Dr. G. B. Stillman House)

c. 1866, with additions. 1340 Liberty St.

This elaborate house built during the oil excitement reflects that time when people spent money with giddy abandon. It has a fanciful turret with dormer windows and corbeled chimneys piercing the intersecting gable roof. Its original owner is unclear, but according to the Franklin *Evening News*

of January 25, 1889, it was purchased on behalf of the club from Dr. G. B. Stillman. The group of young single men bought it for their "Nursery Club," which had been founded in 1877 and took its name from a Franklin history that called the town a "nursery of great men." Over the years, Oil City architect J. P. Brenot transformed the single-family home into a clubhouse by including a ballroom, billiard room, and bowling alleys. The entrance hall and grill room were designed by Franklin architect Samuel D. Brady c. 1914. A sweeping two-story porch with a central pediment supported by columns was added about this time to give the facade a Colonial Revival aspect. The name was changed to the Franklin Club in 1913.

VE10 Life Ministries Retreat Center (Joseph C. Sibley Estate, "River Ridge Farm")

1914, Louis Stevens. 834 River Ridge Rd., 1.5 miles northeast of Franklin

The siting and complexity of the River Ridge estate, as well as its view toward Franklin, even in the dead of winter, are beautiful. Nearly every element of the original estate survives, including the pumping oil wells, farm buildings, gatehouses, and railroad siding. Joseph Crocker Sibley was a partner in the Galena Oil Works and Galena-Signal Oil Company. He came to Franklin c. 1868 and with his brother-in-law, Charles A. Miller, opened a successful dry goods store. They used their profits to buy an existing oil company and named it the Galena Oil Works. Sibley, while rooted in farming and the town of Franklin, lived his life on the national stage through his political career and powerful friends. He was with President William McKinley at his assassination, and President Woodrow Wilson and William Jennings Bryan drafted their Fourteen Points during a visit to River Ridge in September 1917.

Celebrities arrived at River Ridge via the private rail siding marked by an arch and capped with a twenty-one-ton stone incised with the estate's name. Thirteen miles of roads, six stone bridges, and a series of gatehouses connected the estate-house grounds and model farm. The thirty-three-room mansion was built with irregularly laid stone quarried on the hillside above the house, and laid under the supervision of Ernest Grandelis. Louis Stevens of Pittsburgh designed the house with a central living room core flanked by square towers. The library and dining room border this core at oblique angles and admit light on three elevations. On the east elevation of the core are the working rooms of the house: an office, butler's pantry, and breakfast room. A two-story, gable-roofed rectangular kitchen–servants wing is attached at the southeast. A three-bay, stone loggia built several feet from the house allows light to enter the living room. There were porches and solariums (now enclosed with windows) at each end of the main wings.

Of the twenty-one other buildings on the 1,034-acre farm, one of the largest is the stone house for John L. Hanna, the farm manager. It is an outstanding two-and-one-half-story, intersecting gable structure overlooking the Allegheny River, with a stone campanile Sibley had duplicated from West Point. Several other buildings survive from Robert G. Lam-

berton's preexisting 760-acre Argeon farm that became a part of River Ridge after 1911. Lamberton's red brick house adjoins his magnificent L-shaped barn of brick and stone construction, four stories tall with entrances on three stories. River Ridge was broken up and sold by the surviving Sibley heir in 1948.

Oil executive Duncan McIntosh had a nineteen-room stone house (1900, John Axelson, builder; 1 mile east of Franklin Bridge on U.S. 322) built from the stone of a nearby quarry whose product was later used to construct River Ridge. Stylistically the McIntosh house is a blocky version of River Ridge, which is a larger and a more sophisticated design. The grounds include stables, a carriage house, residential units built in the 1960s, and a workshop. A red clay tile roof and an octagonal solarium on the eastern elevation do little to alleviate the heaviness of the McIntosh house design, restricted by a steep hillside to the north that exacerbates its dark interior.

POLK

VE11 Polk Center (Polk State School and Hospital)

1894, Frederick J. Osterling; 1902–1903, c. 1915, Fredrick J. Osterling, with Samuel D. Brady and Louis Stevens, associated architects; many additions. Lakewood Circle

VE11 POLK CENTER (POLK STATE SCHOOL AND HOSPITAL)

In 1893, the Commonwealth of Pennsylvania commissioned a large residential home for the "feeble minded." Institutionalized care of the mentally ill began in Pennsylvania on a large scale in Philadelphia in the 1850s. Polk State School and Hospital expanded the system to the fourteen counties of the northwest, purchasing approximately 773 acres in and around the Thomas McKissick farm adjacent to the borough of Polk. This flat land was bracketed by two creeks and located on the rail line six miles west of Franklin. The buildings form one of the most interesting ensembles in western Pennsylvania in their siting, integrity, and homogeneity of the design.

Set north of U.S. 62, the campus is first visible across a wide, flat field. Frederick J. Osterling of Pittsburgh designed an enormous campus of red brick buildings with fat, rounded turrets and arched windows. The main administration building resembles the courthouse of a rural county seat, combining elements of classicism, as in the Ionic pedimented porch, with such Chateauesque features as the rounded conical-roofed corner towers, steeply sloping roofs, and turrets.

Large, homelike structures behind the administration building give the campus a collegial air. Circular, one-story structures with conical roofs accommodate meeting rooms with interesting interior trusswork. Samuel D. Brady and Louis Stevens worked with Osterling on the early-twentieth-century additions: Murdoch Hall (also called the Hospital and the Nursery building), built between 1902 and 1903, and School Hall and the auditorium.

Polk was occupied by 1897, and over the years has housed over 13,000 developmentally disabled persons. The complex was almost self-sufficient, with its own spring-fed water source, a power generation plant, hospital, sewage plant, greenhouse, laundry, garage, and farm. Residents were trained in various skills, including shoe cobbling and sewing. At its peak in 1953, the campus had 102 buildings, 3,490 residents, and a staff of 1,955 in an area intended to house 1,200. In the 1970s, the state changed the name to Polk Center and community-based treatment became the norm. The trend in treatment shifted over the years from a medical model to a rehabilitative and then an interdisciplinary model. To facilitate the newer form of treatment, an indoor pool facility was completed in 1995 by I. J. Chung Associates. For the past thirty years, Polk Center's population has grown significantly smaller. In 2000, there were 478 residents and 1,137 staff in 90 buildings on 802 acres.

OIL CITY

Oil City lies seven miles north of Franklin at the confluence of Oil Creek and the Allegheny River. Three distinct sections of the city are connected by bridges: a narrow river plain and steeply wooded hillside west of Oil Creek; a wider floodplain and hilly residential section called the North Side, east of Oil Creek; and the South Side, south of the Allegheny River that has a floodplain and hilly residential section beyond.

Oil City lies on part of the land given to Seneca Chief Cornplanter in 1796 by the commonwealth. It changed hands several times and was known as Cornplanter and Oilville. Oil City began as a rafting site for the products of the nearby iron furnaces and gristmills. For years, oil pits would periodically form naturally along Oil Creek. The oil was used by Native Americans for medicine and as a body rub, and was sold by Samuel Kier as a natural remedy. When Edwin Laurentine Drake began to pump it from the ground in 1859, the area developed at a great rate. Oil flatboating and an oil exchange made Oil City the largest town in Venango County; it became a borough in 1862 and a city nine years later.

The town was connected to the Atlantic and Great Western Railroad in 1866, and a small railroad station for the Oil City and Titusville Railroad remains on Elm Street. The population grew from 12 families in 1860 to nearly 6,000 people by 1865. A huge fire in 1866 destroyed most of the original boomtown on the north side of the river. In 1864, the hillside above Grove Avenue was sold to the United Petroleum Farms Association and developed gradually, but with most of the housing built between 1880 and 1930. The north side grew as a mixed economic area with modest brick houses for both managers and laborers, except for two very large Queen Anne houses at the intersection of Harriet and Bissell streets. An influx of Polish immigrants gave it the popular name "Polish Hill." St. Joseph's Church (1890–1894; 35 Pearl Avenue), designed by Chicago architect Adolphus Druiding, became

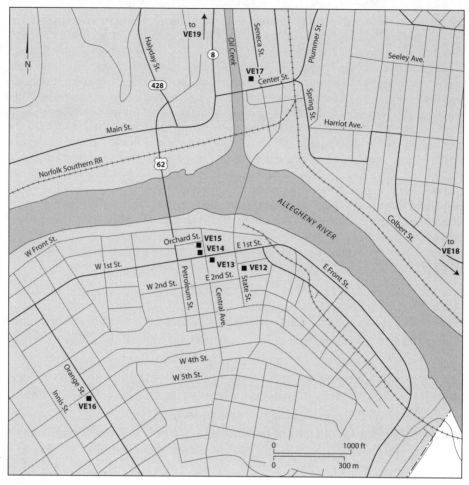

OIL CITY

the centerpiece of spiritual life for the Polish population, its twin spires visible for miles.

South of the Allegheny River, the neighborhood of Laytonia, bounded by Wilson, 4th, and Reed streets and the river, was given that name c. 1863 for the Lay brothers, Charles H. and William, who owned the local Oil City Lumber and Coal Company. Charles Lay's house at 114 Petroleum Street illustrates their intention to create a suburban district of fine cottages built of wood. The south side also had a section called Venango City, which joined with Oil City in 1871.

Despite its solid housing stock, Oil City has always been part of a boom and bust cycle. In June 1892, flaming oil set the north side of the town on fire, and soon after, a flood did more damage to the town. Since the 1930s, Oil City has lost half of its population. The last of the Pennzoil–Quaker State refineries in the area closed in 2000. Today's industry is primarily heritage and recreational tourism.

VE12 Pacific Pride Gas Station

c. 1930. 119 E. 2nd St.

It is fitting in this historic oil region to find a representative outlet for the product. At this busy corner sits an English cottage version of the gas station, a popular type at the time and designed to blend with its residential neighborhood. There is nothing prefabricated about this brick station. The attention to detail includes slate shingles on its steeply pitched roof, multipaned picture windows, and half timbering in the gable end facing the street. It may have served as a station for the Pennzoil–Pacific Pride Company.

VE13 Latonia Theater

1928, Marks and Kann. 1 E. 1st St.

The Latonia Theater has a colorful facade of cream-colored terra-cotta tile with green and white Mayan ornament at the cornice. Two towers crowned with geometric ornament frame the entrance canopy. The interior has been altered with the installation of a floor at balcony level to create two stories. The upper story is now an elegant ballroom with a close-up view of the elaborate chandelier, with its scalloped ceiling medallion, masks of drama over the doorways, and gargoyles. The theater's name is a simplified version of the neighborhood's original name, Laytonia.

VE14 Christ Episcopal Church

1886–1887, Enoch A. Curtis; 1905–1906 parish house, Duhring, Okie and Zeigler; Emmet E. Bailey, project architect. 16 Central Ave.

Christ Episcopal Church was designed by Enoch Curtis before he partnered with Archer (VE17). The self-taught Curtis designed eight buildings in Titusville, Crawford County, and two in Pleasantville in northern Venango County in 1874. Reflecting the grand residential character of the area and its prominent corner site, Curtis's Gothic Revival design for this church employs colorful brick, stone trim, and a black and red slate roof. The entrance on the southeast corner is through the base of a pyramidal-roofed square tower. The plan is a traditional nave and apse scheme, and transepts and apse have curved ends. Inside, the church has oak beams, wooden pews, wainscoting, and is lit by eight Tiffany windows and several by J & R Lamb Studios of New York. The parish hall north of the church is the work of a Philadelphia firm with local architect Emmet E. Bailey supervising the building. Due to money constraints, they did not use the architect's recommended buttresses and later required tie rods to stabilize the building.

VE15 Oil City Public Library (Carnegie Public Library)

1902–1904, Charles Weber Bolton; 1958–1959, James E. Bryan; Holmes Crosby, project architect; 1978–1980, W. G. Eckles Company Architects. 2 Central Ave.

The women of Oil City wrote to Andrew Carnegie in 1899 requesting $25,000 to build a library for their town of 11,000 people. Carnegie increased the donation to $40,000 to reflect his belief that Oil City was one of the key components of the steel industry, and as such would continue to grow. Charles Weber Bolton (1855–1942) of Philadelphia designed an eclectic two-story, brick building with gray granite trim, a red tiled roof, and round-arched windows and entrances that blends Renaissance Revival and Beaux-Arts classicism, with a dash of Richardsonian Romanesque. Perhaps due to his familiarity with church design, Bolton added an apselike bay window arrangement on the south elevation.

The entrance probably was moved from the east end of the building to the center of the Central Avenue elevation in the 1950s, when an interior redesign took place and the name was changed from the Carnegie Public Library to the Oil City Library. A one-story modern Renaissance-style addition of 6,500 square feet designed by the W. G. Eckles Company Architects on the west elevation opened in 1980.

VE16 Innis Mansion

1874, 1877, c. 1897. 305 W. 4th St.

This house, built on the Moran farm, was purchased three years after its construction by William J. Innis, a machinist from New England. Innis revamped it by 1877 and added an observatory. After his death in 1894, it was remodeled from its Second Empire style to the present Queen Anne appearance. The frame house has window caps, brackets, round- and flat-arched windows, a sweeping veranda, dormers, and sawn ornament in the gable ends. The remnants of the Second Empire roof are visible on the south elevation. There are a number of very large Queen Anne, Colonial Revival, and Second Empire houses several blocks away, notably those at 607 and 301 W. 1st Street.

VE17 Transit Fine Art Gallery (National Transit Company Building)

1889–1890, Curtis and Archer. 206 Seneca St.

Enoch A. Curtis of Fredonia, New York, and his partner William Archer, about whom little is known, designed this four-story headquarters building for the National Transit Company, the oil pipeline and transportation wing of the Standard Oil Company. They apparently chose as their model Burnham and Root's Rookery Building in Chicago designed just four years earlier. Oil City's building has tripartite massing with a slightly projecting central bay highlighted by a massive, stone-arched entrance, and slightly depressed window niches covering three stories, separated by pilaster strips and capped by round arches. Distinctive ornamentation at the cornice consists of five rows of dentils on all sides of the building, with a minimal capstone above and a checkerboard brick pattern in the spandrels. The small lobby facing Seneca Street has a divided stair with an elaborate iron railing defined by newel posts. In 1896, the same architects designed an orange Pompeiian brick annex next door. This Renaissance Revival annex also has four stories of brick above a raised stone basement. An 1899 archway connects the two buildings.

VE18 Oil City Industrial Park (Oil Well Supply Plant, Imperial Works)

1900–1902. 669–671 Colbert Ave.

This is one of the last remaining complexes that illustrate the enormous size of the industries supporting oil drilling and exploration in northwestern Pennsylvania. In 1900, the Oil Well Supply Company, founded in Pittsburgh in 1867 by John Eaton, started building this plant on forty-four acres of the Allegheny River floodplain in the Siverly neighborhood of Oil City. Around 800 men worked in the foundries and blacksmith shops making drilling equipment and boilers. The surviving buildings are red brick and rectangular, with tall clerestories and an occasional wheel window in a gable end. Ornament is limited to brick corbeling, but it is rhythmically consistent among the large number of extant buildings. Workers' houses on Colbert Avenue also were built by the company.

VE19 Saltzman Brothers Brewing Company (John J. Saltzmann Palace Hill Brewery)

c. 1903, Gustave A. Mueller and Richard Mildner. Union and Charlton sts.

No nineteenth-century city of any size could long survive without its breweries, but many have disappeared today. John J. Saltzmann founded his Palace Hill Brewery in Oil City in 1881. The original building burned in 1887 and was replaced by this design from the Detroit firm of Gustave A. Mueller (1874–1937) and Richard Mildner (1870–1934). The stylish three-story Saltzman [sic] Brothers brick brewery on the west side of Oil Creek has oversized round-arched windows at the third story. Below that, on the south elevation, a broken pediment sits atop a three-part, multipaned window arrangement. The ground story has segmental arches at the openings. The cellar could store ten thousand barrels of beer and was insulated with corkboards from Armstrong Cork Company in Pittsburgh. A two-story brick stable lies to the south.

PLEASANTVILLE AND VICINITY

Pleasantville, located along West Pithole Creek, was settled by Aaron Benedict soon after he came west to build a portion of the Susquehanna and Waterford Turnpike. In 1819, he purchased from the Holland Land Company a large portion of the land now called Pleasantville. With his son-in-law, William Porter, a potter, Benedict mined the nearby clay deposits and began producing Rockingham and Liverpool Queensware with the help of imported

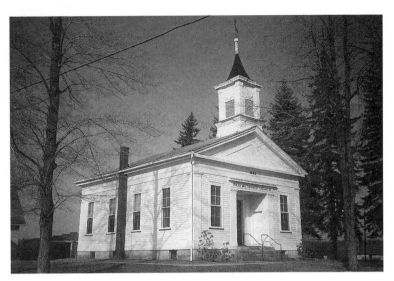

Free Methodist Church, at the intersection of N. Main and Merrick streets, Pleasantville.

Scots-Irish labor. Their pottery company operated from 1825 until the early 1880s. The addition of a smithy and a tannery brought nearby settlers to the area originally named Benedictown and Holland, after the earlier owners. Benedict's nineteen children helped to swell the population. In 1849, a borough one mile square was chartered with the name Pleasantville.

After oil was discovered at the Harmonial Well No. 1 in 1868, the borough's population tripled within two months. Rail service began and roads were improved to accommodate the new industry and population. The wells continued to produce at a greatly reduced rate into the twentieth century, until the introduction of secondary recovery methods (for example, floating well-bottom oil to the surface by flooding the wells with water) brought the oil industry a brief resurgence in 1926.

The white, frame Pleasantville Free Methodist Church (N. Main and Merrick streets) was built in 1847–1848 by Aaron Benedict for the Baptist denomination. Its Greek Revival styling and serene simplicity tie it stylistically to Benedict's New England roots. There were several fine examples of this style in the area, such as the Congregational Church in Riceville and the Independent Congregational Church in Meadville (both demolished). The Pleasantville Church has three bays below the pedimented gable end, and a square bell tower with a small spire is centered above the pediment.

One Greek Revival house (c. 1840; 353 Main Street) is similar in character to a group of houses also built in the 1840s in the 1200 block of Elk Street in Franklin (VE8). It was built by Aaron Benedict's nephew, E. R. Beebe, who came to Benedictown in 1831 to found a tannery and shoe business. With its central pavilion and single-story flanking wings, wide cornice, returning eaves, and simple corner boards, this is an excellent example of the style. Two houses on Chestnut Street at numbers 317 and 341, and houses at 121 State

Street and 248 N. Main Street all date from the early 1870s and were built soon after a major fire damaged much of the town, while oil fever continued in Pleasantville. The Colonial Revival house at 345 Chestnut Street built in 1906 illustrates that Pleasantville's healthy prosperity continued into the early twentieth century.

VE20 Drake Oil Well and Museum

1945 well; 1963 museum and 1967 museum shop, Charles M. Stotz. Drake Well Rd., 0.5 miles east of PA 1011

VE20 DRAKE OIL WELL AND MUSEUM

The Drake complex consists of a replica well that was built in 1945 and a museum and museum shop designed by Charles Stotz for the Pennsylvania Historical and Museum Commission. While the museum has few side windows in order to protect the collection from exposure to light, both it and the shop have large areas of glazing on their facades. The flat-roofed rectilinear buildings are sheathed in a local tan stone veneer. The shop has a deep overhang and an open breezeway designed to funnel patrons toward the museum and the replica of Colonel Edwin Laurentine Drake's oil well, which is constructed of wood in the distinctive flared derrick shape. Two stone entrance markers appear to have been designed by Stotz at the same time as the museum. Nearby, a small Colonial Revival house (1934) was moved to its present site in 1967, when the museum shop was built.

The Drake Well Museum is adjacent to Oil Creek State Park. The two properties share access to a thirty-six-mile loop trail that takes hikers up and down twelve miles of Oil Creek via four connecting trails. The Oil Creek and Titusville rail line runs excursion trains between Oil City and the park. The park's appearance today, tree filled and serene, is in stark contrast to the area's appearance during the 1860s oil excitement when the surrounding hills were denuded of trees used to build derricks, and the barrels and wagons used to transport oil from the wells, and the smell of oil and the clanking of teamsters' rigs filled the air.

In 2001, a c. 1850 timber-frame house was moved into Oil Creek State Park adjoining the museum's property to the south. It was reconstructed to illustrate nineteenth-century building techniques, such as mortise-and-tenon pegging and double-grooved pine board siding cut by a reciprocating water-powered sawmill. The McClintock family built the house, but its most notorious owner was John Washington Steele, "Coal Oil Johnny," who inherited his adoptive parents' farm and oil monies in 1864 and spent this inheritance with wild abandon in Philadelphia and New York City.

EMLENTON

Hemmed in by the steep northern bank of the Allegheny River and a hill, Emlenton grew on a floodplain less than half a mile wide. The land around Emlenton was purchased in 1796 by Samuel Mickle Fox of Philadelphia, and named for his daughter-in-law, Hannah Emlen, who married Joseph Mickle Fox in 1820. A few settlers came to Emlenton as early as 1798, but no houses were built in the settlement until 1834. In the 1820s, commerce consisted of poling a flatboat upriver from Pittsburgh, loading it with raw lumber and building stones, and returning to Pittsburgh. Lumber mills and a general store were built, and by 1839, there were twenty iron furnaces operating within sixteen miles of Emlenton, and warehouses for the iron and lumber products lined the riverbanks.

When oil was discovered near Titusville in 1859, Emlenton was already a small trading center and had built a wooden covered toll bridge (demolished) over the Allegheny River. The first oil well was drilled near Emlenton in 1867, and natural gas, a by-product of oil drilling, was harnessed to provide commercial lighting and fuel. In 1882, the third natural gas company in the United States, Emlenton Gas Light and Fuel Company, was formed; it later became part of Columbia Gas.

In the late 1860s and 1870s, several small rail lines opened to bring oil, timber, coal, and farm products to Emlenton where they could be transferred to the Allegheny Valley Railroad and shipped to Pittsburgh. The nearby town of Foxburg built a competing railroad, and by 1881 bought controlling interest in Emlenton's narrow-gauge railroad and dismantled it. At the time, frame buildings were the norm in these lumber areas, as the white, frame Gothic Revival St. John's Evangelical Lutheran Church (1884–1886) at 512 Kerr Street attests. The hillside site and soaring steeple accentuate this small building's verticality. The former parsonage east of the church built c. 1870 is a five-bay, frame, central-hall house with Italianate touches.

Nineteen regional oil firms merged in 1931 to form the Quaker State Oil Refining Corporation, which maintained a presence in Emlenton until 1990, when the company moved to Texas and sold all of its local refineries. The story of oil is presented at the Crawford Center (603 Hill Street), built as the Emlenton School in 1928 in the Jacobean style that was popular for schools. W. Holmes Crosby from Oil City and Pressley C. Dowler from Pittsburgh collaborated on the grade school/high school combination with its 600-seat auditorium and library. The Borough of Emlenton has used the building, which sits on a ledge overlooking the borough, as a community center since 1996. Down the street at 413 Hill Street, the Emlenton Area Ambulance Service, designed in 1930 by W. Holmes Crosby, is housed in what was formerly the Emlenton Borough Building. Its brick construction, corner quoins, and parapets are similar to those on the school building.

Emlenton's commercial buildings include the unpainted wooden Old Emlenton Mill Café and Company (1879; 201 Main Street) and a two-story brick building (c. 1880; 502 Main Street) with its original storefront and window trim. The Farmers National Bank (1904; 612 Main Street) has the requisite Ionic columns and housed the Masonic Temple on the third story. It has a central stairway and open second-story, skylit foyer with four apartments-offices around it. A frame commercial building (1887; 702–704 Main Street) has most of its original details intact. A Sears and Roebuck catalog house of 1923, one of nearly 100,000 built in the United States, stands at 611 Hill Street.

MERCER COUNTY

The area that is now Mercer County was originally part of Allegheny County, and has a thirty-two-mile border with Ohio on the west. It contained both Donation and Depreciation Lands surveyed between 1785 and 1795 by Benjamin Stokely, who settled in what became Mercer County after the official boundaries were set in 1800. The county was named for Brigadier General Hugh Mercer, a Scottish physician who befriended George Washington on the Forbes mission to capture Fort Duquesne and later became commandant of the fort. He was killed in the Revolutionary War.

The land is glaciated, undulating, and crossed with streams and rivers. European settlement began slowly, with hunting and trapping in the dense forests, then farming and its attendant services, such as saw and grist mills, blacksmiths, and distilleries. Mercer County is nearly midway between Pittsburgh and Erie and has long served as a crossroads for the region. By 1844, a network of local roads was joined by the Beaver and Erie Canal that followed the Shenango River to Greenville and continued north into Crawford County in the Little Crooked Creek valley. This new transportation system facilitated the mining of coal in the region, with fifty mines opening between 1837 and 1876. Iron furnaces took advantage of the fuel source and were established throughout Shenango Valley.

Railroads supplanted canal transportation between 1860 and 1870. Two main rail lines served Mercer County: the Erie and Pennsylvania (E&P) and the Atlantic and Great Western (A&GW), connecting to the New York rail lines. By the 1930s, roadways again dominated the transportation scene, especially for tourists seeking rural respites. A single 8 × 10–foot stone cottage remains (1934; 2554 Perry Highway) of the eight built by Yeager and Bentley for their tourist cabin camp, "Camp Perry," along busy U.S. 19 connecting Pittsburgh and Erie. The six-acre camp, named to honor Commodore Oliver Hazard Perry, closed in the early 1980s. The cottage's random stone work, gable roof, and prominent chimney conveyed a homelike atmosphere. For a time, a swimming pool in the valley below the cabins helped attract campers during the summer. Nearby, Sandy Lake, Shenango River Lake (1965), and Lake Wilhelm (1971), the latter two created by dams, provide exceptional fishing and boating opportunities.

Sheep farming developed in the early 1800s, but insufficient transportation systems and cheap imports contributed to the wool industry's decline by the 1860s. Today, large parts of the county remain rural, supporting dairy farms rather than sheep farms. Amish farmers have settled in the southern townships. With the completion of I-79 through the eastern half of the county, some high-tech firms and a branch of Pennsylvania State University (PSU) have moved into Mercer County. The U.S. Census Bureau includes Mercer County in the Youngstown-Warren, Ohio, metropolitan area.

MERCER AND VICINITY

Laid out in 1803 and incorporated in 1814 on two hundred acres of land donated by John Hoge of Washington County, Mercer had an important connection to its southern neighbor. Washington County farmers brought their sheep to Mercer and established wool making as an important industry. Wool making flourished until the late 1860s, when it was supplanted by the iron and coal industries. The borough of Mercer was bypassed by the canal and did not receive rail service until the 1870s, later than other parts of western Pennsylvania. When two railroads finally served the borough, its population nearly doubled in size. Today, Mercer is the hub of six major roads and the town square has succumbed to suburban-style gas station–convenience stores that detract from the grandeur of the courthouse nearby. Nonetheless, the borough has dozens of handsome houses from the mid-nineteenth century through the 1930s. Notable examples are the restored frame Greek Revival houses (c. 1850) at 211 and 235 Shenango Street and the board-and-batten Gothic Revival cottage (c. 1860) at 147 W. Market Street, with the animated verticality and ornamental bargeboards typical of the style.

ME1 Mercer County Courthouse

1909–1911, Charles F. Owsley for Owsley and Boucherle. Diamond St. between Pitt and Erie sts.

This, the county's third courthouse, dominates the borough of Mercer with its splendid dome. Though the firm of Owsley and Boucherle is credited with the design, the majority of the work was done by Charles F. Owsley, son of founding partner Charles Henry Owsley. Charles F. trained in New York, in Paris, and at the University of Pennsylvania (1903), after which he joined his father's firm in Youngstown in 1904, where he worked until his death in 1953.

The design met the county commissioner's stipulation that the courthouse be of red brick, rectangular, and trimmed with sandstone. The Beaux-Arts-inspired courthouse has matching Ionic porticoes on the front and rear elevations, with monumental staircases marking the entrances; the east and west entrances have smaller porticoes. The courthouse's finest feature is the ribbed dome that rises from a tall octagonal brick and stone base with paired columns on each elevation. On the interior, a central rotunda is flanked by two-story courtrooms. The rotunda's stained glass dome is highlighted with allegorical murals in the pendentives by Edward E. Simmons (1852–1931) entitled *In-* *nocence, Guilt, Justice,* and *Power,* and stained glass panels above representing Peace, Truth, Law, and Justice. Public spaces have marble floors and wainscoting, brass railings, and modillion-lined ceilings.

ME2 Courthouse South Annex (Mercer County Jail)

1868–1869, Barr and Moser. 100 block S. Diamond St.

Built in conjunction with the county's second courthouse of 1867, the jail was designed by the Pittsburgh firm well known for its schools and institutional buildings. The two-story brick building has a slightly projecting central bay with a Palladian window on the second story above a double-doored arched entrance. Flanking it are paired round-arched windows with prominent voussoirs and keystones. In the mid-1970s, the cell block was removed from the rear and the building converted to offices.

Adjacent to the east is carpenter Hugh Bingham's house of 1812, a two-story, three-bay red brick house with its gable to the side. Bingham's son, John Amor Bingham, had a national career as a judge. The Old Stone Jail (107 E. Venango Street), built by Thomas Templeton in 1810, is a five-bay, two-story building one block north of the courthouse square. It was converted to a hotel in 1868

ME6 OLDE ENGLISH SHOPPE (ARTHUR JOHNSTON HOUSE, NEW LODGE INN)

after the new jail was constructed, and has been put to a variety of uses over the years.

ME3 James Magoffin Historical Society

1821, c. 1865, 1884. 119 S. Pitt St.

The Mercer County Historical Society owns three adjacent buildings southeast of the courthouse. The Dr. James Magoffin Jr. house was built in 1821 and occupied by his descendants until 1951, when it was donated to the society. It is a five-bay frame house with double-sash twelve-over-twelve windows, original shutters, and a central double wooden door with flattened arch transom. The gable-roofed structure has an intersecting gabled ell and two shed-roofed additions on the east elevation.

North of the house is the small, frame Episcopal church of 1884 (formerly Church of Saint Edmund the Martyr and now H. B. Miller Memorial Chapel), which was moved to this site for weddings and special services. It has a shingled gable end and a cupola. Behind the house, the long, one-story McClain Print Shop (c. 1830) was moved to this site in 1973 from the town square. The frame Greek Revival building, with pilaster strips and pedimented eaves at the gable ends, operated as a print shop until 1965.

HERMITAGE

ME7 Hermitage Historical Society (Robert and Mary Ann Stewart House)

1867–1868. 5465 E. State St.

Robert and Mary Ann Stewart commissioned this handsome brick Italianate house from contractor Jacob Weaver as the centerpiece

ME4 Magoffin Inn (Dr. Montrose B. Magoffin House)

1884, Owsley and Boucherle. 129 S. Pitt St.

This large, brick house is now a bed-and-breakfast. Designed by the courthouse architects, it demonstrates the range of the firm's work in Mercer County, from the courthouse (ME1), to the Richardsonian Romanesque Buhl mansion in Sharon (ME9), to the Queen Anne style, as here. With its large wraparound porch, projecting gabled bays, and corbeled chimneys, the inn is typical of the style.

ME5 Clark House (Gayley House)

c. 1870. 148 Cribbs Rd. (PA 258), 3.8 miles southeast of Mercer

This delightful two-story brick house has a full-facade wooden porch dripping with sawn ornament and heavy round-arched moldings above the paired windows. Brackets line the eaves of the intersecting gable roof, and the gables are ornamented with bargeboards. Although located on a quiet road, the house is within sight of I-80.

ME6 Olde English Shoppe (Arthur Johnston House, New Lodge Inn)

1831. 1561 Perry Highway (U.S. 19), 4.9 miles south of Mercer

The most common house type in western Pennsylvania in the first half of the nineteenth century, for those wealthy enough to afford it, was the five-bay, central-hall house in brick or stone. This former house followed this pattern but has an exceptional fan window above the front door. The formality of its corner quoins and interior end chimneys contrasts with the random-laid stonework. The building, facing the old Pittsburgh-Erie Turnpike, has housed a post office and reputedly was a stop on the Underground Railroad in its long history. Today it houses an antiques store.

of their 183-acre cattle farm. Deep bracketed eaves and elongated windows with segmental cap molds remain on all elevations, but, unfortunately, the square central tower that rises above the principal entrance is missing its original concave roof. Today the house is headquarters for the Hermitage Historical Society.

Sharon, only two miles east of the Ohio border, was settled in 1803 by Benjamin Bentley and laid out by William Budd in 1815. Sharon and Mercer were joined by a road in 1815, which was continued west after the first bridge was built across the Shenango River in 1818–1819 by Samuel Clark and his son. In 1836, the Erie Extension of the Beaver and Erie Canal spurred the shipment of local coal, and later, coal from the Lake Superior region fed the growing number of Sharon-area iron furnaces. As canal shipping waned in the 1860s, several railroads opened lines to Sharon, including the E&P and the A&GW.

After the establishment of the Sharon Steel Company's south works and their subsequent purchase by the Union Steel Company, and after that, by United States Steel, the area surrounding the plant was named Farrell in 1912 for U.S. Steel CEO James A. Farrell. A workers' village grew around the plant, which drew other companies making ingots and bars, railroad cars, gasoline engines, tin plate, wire, and electric machinery. The Sharon Iron Works was the largest plant in Mercer County by the 1880s. In 1885, an oil pipeline was laid from the oil fields in Butler and Venango counties through Sharon to Youngstown, bringing Italian workers into the area and swelling the populations of both Sharon and Farrell.

Sharon became known for its "solid wealth" and a spate of very large, turn-of-the-twentieth-century, brick and frame houses along E. State Street, especially in the 200 and 300 blocks. An eclectic red brick Italian Villa–style house (1875; 555 E. State Street) was built for J. M. Willson, who sold furniture; it became a funeral home in 1891 and is today the Sample-O'Donnell Funeral Home. Two substantial houses designed by architect Charles F. Owsley, the English Cotswold-style Bachman house (c. 1910; 959 E. State Street) and the Tudor Revival George H. Boyd House (1907; 869 E. State Street), illustrate their owners' wealth. The sandstone Gothic Revival St. John's Episcopal Church by Owsley and Boucherle in 1893–1895 with additions of 1914–1933 by Cram and Ferguson (226 W. State Street) is distinguished by a massive, square crenellated tower at the northwest corner. The First Presbyterian Church of 1926–1927 (600 E. State Street), designed by Nicklas and Rodrick of Cleveland, has stained glass windows by the Pittsburgh Stained Glass Studio.

ME8 St. Joseph's Church

1964, George Stickle of Stickle and Associates; 1995–1996, Weborg, Rectenwald Architects. 79 Case Ave.

St. Joseph's Church, designed by Cleveland architect George Stickle, was intended to be the cathedral for the New Castle–Sharon Diocese, and the church and its rectory planned for a bishop and his staff. The church is an irregular octagon of Indiana limestone pierced on all elevations by full-height, hooded, arched windows. At the pinnacle of the pyramidal, stainless steel roof, a circular cupola with a fluted roof is surmounted by a narrow, elongated spire supporting a statue of the Risen Christ; the latter was placed there by a helicopter. A statue of St. Joseph welcomes parishioners above the triple doors facing E. State Street.

The new diocese never came to be, and in 1995–1996, the church was reconfigured by

ME8 ST. JOSEPH'S CHURCH

Weborg, Rectenwald Architects to accommodate St. Joseph's parish. As designed, the church seated 968, with rows of seats facing north toward the recessed altar. After 1996 and in response to the liturgical recommendations of Vatican II, the seats were broken into three sections around a raised communion table brought forward nearly to the middle of the church. The space of the former altar became a meditation area, and a new entrance on the east elevation creates space for socializing before and after worship.

ME9 Frank H. Buhl House

1890, Owsley and Boucherle. 422 E. State St.

This splendid and massive Richardsonian Romanesque, fourteen-room mansion with Chateauesque elements is sited on Sharon's main street. It was built for iron manufacturer and philanthropist Frank Henry Buhl and his wife, Julia Forker Buhl. The architects employed gray sandstone, conical towers, and gabled dormers in the design, in emulation of a French castle. A one-story stable with a steeply pitched roof and circular tower is joined to the west side of the house by a porte-cochere. After Mrs. Buhl's death in 1936, the mansion was converted to apartments, and in 1997, to an art gallery, guest rooms, and spa. The owners of the Buhl house also converted, in 1984, the former Charles Koonce House (1854; c. 1900 portico) at 2884 Lake Road in the village of Clark, northeast of Sharon, into a twenty-seven-room bed-and-breakfast, which they named "Tara" for its similarities to the house in the movie *Gone with the Wind* (1939).

ME10 Frank H. Buhl Club

1901–1903, Charles F. Owsley for Owsley and Boucherle. 28 N. Pine St.

Designed by Owsley, this club of orange-yellow brick has two hipped-roof pavilions flanking a slightly recessed central section. For this design, Owsley appears to have been influenced by the clubs designed by McKim, Mead and White in New York City that resemble Italian Renaissance palaces. The dramatic entrance facing State Street features a pedimented portico supported by Ionic columns and a pair of elaborately decorated wooden doors with a stone surround carved with a swag and a family crest; above is a semicircular transom. The recreational and educational facility, founded by Frank H. Buhl, was intended as a place of "innocent amusements" for the men of Sharon, and accommodated a gymnasium, billiard rooms, bowling alleys, music room, and a library. In 1969, the club accepted women as full members and added a swimming pool, new gymnasium, and locker rooms.

ME11 Protected Home Mutual Life Insurance Company (Protected Home Circle)

1936, Walker and Weeks. 30 E. State St.

For 114 years, the home office of the Protected Home Circle (PHC; after 1964, the Protected Home Mutual Life Insurance Company) has been in Sharon. Founded as a fraternal organization, which pooled the members' money to pay death benefits, the group also provided educational, cultural, and social opportunities for their members. In 1936, a disastrous fire destroyed their earlier home, and the PHC board commissioned the Cleveland firm of Walker and Weeks to design a new building. The seven-bay, white brick, four-story Art

ME11 PROTECTED HOME MUTUAL LIFE INSURANCE COMPANY (PROTECTED HOME CIRCLE)

Deco building, oriented toward the Shenango River, has a central tower with setbacks ornamented with chevrons and the company's emblem, a mother eagle protecting her offspring, painted above the riverside entrance. Protected Life's building is echoed on the river's western bank by the six-bay, three-story, limestone Winner International Building (former First Western Bank, c. 1930; 32 W. State Street).

ME12 Buhl Farm Park and Golf Course

1913–1915, George Rettig, landscape architect. Forker Blvd. between Hazen and Yahres rds.

This three-hundred-acre city park adjacent to the Sharon Country Club has a free golf course and bandstand funded by a trust donated to the people of Sharon in 1915 by iron manufacturer Frank H. Buhl. The former farm's wooded and relatively flat landscape has a lake, ponds, gardens, stone gatehouse, casino, and performing arts center, as well as playing fields laid out by landscape architect George Rettig of Cleveland.

ME13 Sharpsville Area Recreation Park (Raisch Log House and Erie Extension Canal Lock No. 10)

Before 1810 log cabin; 1835–1838 canal; 1897 bridge. High St. east of N. Mercer Ave. at Shenango River

The Sharpsville Park contains three structures of interest: the Raisch Log House, moved here from Hermitage Township; the Pierce Lock No. 10 from the Erie Extension of the Beaver and Erie Canal; and an iron bridge over the Shenango River.

The Raisch Log House was disassembled and reassembled at the entrance to the park between 1977 and 1979. It consists of a single room with an opening on every side except the north elevation, where the stone chimney is located. The loft is reached by a ladder.

The linear park follows the river's shore with a foot trail passing through the walls of the former canal lock. The lock's huge sandstone blocks were quarried nearly two miles north of Big Bend along the Shenango River. Each has bold chisel marks, and some of the stones retain the concave portion that held the enormous hinges required to move the wooden gates that once existed here. This is the only extant lock in northwestern Pennsylvania. A replica canal boat and a history of the canal are available at the Canal Museum in Greenville on Allan Avenue. The iron bridge is a pin-connected Camelback truss, built by the Penn Bridge Company of Beaver Falls. While its integrity is excellent, its condition is poor and ultimate fate unknown.

GREENVILLE

A section of Greenville was laid out in 1819 by Thomas Bean and William Scott on the west bank of the Shenango River, but the town grew after Joseph Keck plotted both sides of the river in 1826. Greenville was incorporated in 1838. The Shenango River waterpower was harnessed for flour mills, providing a service for the earliest Scots-Irish and German farmers. From the mid-1820s to the 1850s, a series of red brick houses and frame commercial buildings signals the construction of the Beaver and Lake Erie Canal through town. In 1873, a devastating fire destroyed most of the commercial buildings on the east bank of the Shenango River, but the area was quickly rebuilt. This sequence of events is exemplified by the brick Packard's Building (177–181 Main Street), which has an older core (1857–1858) with a nine-bay facade of cast-iron arches and a cornice with colorful rosettes, dentils, and paired brackets that was added in 1873. A commercial district of two-story, mostly brick buildings occupies Main Street between N. Mercer and Water streets. Housing in and around Greenville employs Greek Revival elements, reflecting styles popular in Connecticut and the Western Reserve of Ohio.

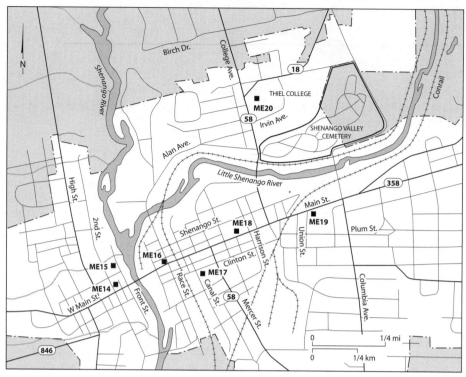

GREENVILLE

ME14 Greenville Historical Society (Judge William Waugh House)

1826. 23 W. Main St.

This large, brick house was built for brothers James S. and Alexander P. Waugh, local merchants and newspaper editors. It has a five-bay, central-hall plan, with such elegant detailing as stepped, interior end chimneys and a tripartite center window. It may be the design of Robert Gillis Mossman, an Irish carpenter and woodworker who was active in the area at the time. The three-bay porch sheltering the entrance with a ruby glass fanlight appears to date from the 1870s based on its turnings. The house has been updated periodically, most recently by the Greenville Historical Society, who restored it between 2002 and 2004. There is a frame, four-bay, two-story wing on the north elevation.

ME15 Irvin House

1843; 1860, Himrod and Woodworth, contractors. 8 N. Front St.

The Irvin brothers' house is a wonderful Greek Revival brick building dominated by a portico of four Tuscan columns and pediment with a rising sun motif within a pleated fan shape. The house is a long narrow rectangle, six bays deep and only three bays wide. A two-story wing on the south elevation terminates in a three-story, windowed tower. Despite its rather ungainly proportions, this is an important house, facing the site of the brothers' former iron furnace along the Shenango River and the canal. Houses with similar columned porches and three-bay facades are found at 37 and 41 Mercer Street.

ME16 N. N. Moss Company

c. 1884; 1949, Walter H. Mallorie. 150 Main St.

N. N. Moss Company has sold furniture and carpeting at this site since 1884. The nineteenth-century portion at the rear of the store is a brick building with round-arched windows at the second story. In the 1940s, Paul and Loretta Moss, after a buying trip to New York where they saw recently constructed Moderne buildings, hired Sharon architect Walter Mallorie to update the facade of their store. The upper section consists of a smooth limestone cube pierced by a nar-

ME16 N. N. MOSS COMPANY

row two-story window framed with fluted columns and stepped reveals. A continuous canopy with the store's name along its top protects shoppers from inclement weather while they window shop.

ME17 U.S. Post Office

1933, Clepper and Clepper for James A. Wetmore, acting supervising architect of the U.S. Treasury. Clinton and Canal sts.

A handsome rendition of the basic rectangular post office, this building has been enlivened with terra-cotta swags, an acanthus leaf decoration along the cornice, fluted Ionic columns flanking the central recessed windows, black marble at the entrance, and detailing on the canopy over the delivery bay. Skillful handling of the brick and stone further distinguishes this building. The interior is remarkably intact, and includes a coffered ceiling, marble pilasters, and Moderne chandeliers. Architects Edgar Ellis Clepper (1871–1951) of Sharon and his brother Harry C. Clepper (c. 1875–c. 1950) of Pittsburgh shared a practice intermittently between 1912 and 1947, when Edgar moved to Arizona.

Nearby, at 125 Main Street and adjacent to the town's train station is the Art Deco Municipal Building (c. 1930).

ME18 Zion's Reformed Church

1885, Sidney Winfield Foulk. 260 Main St.

Built for the German Reformed congregation, later the United Church of Christ, this fanciful red brick, Gothic Revival church was designed by New Castle architect Sidney Foulk with steep gables and pointed-arched windows. None of Foulk's buildings are typical, however. Here he shows his inventiveness in the square tower at the church's corner, giving it circular windows at its third stage and encasing the bells in a square wooden section with horseshoe-shaped openings; the tower finishes with a steeple. An unusual window treatment on the facade has a trio of lancets converging into a circular window beneath a Gothic arch.

ME19 First Presbyterian Church of Greenville

1904, Charles Henry Owsley; 1957–1959 addition, Arthur M. Steinmark. 323 Main St.

This church consists of two wings: the older wing designed by British-born architect Charles Henry Owsley (1846–1935) of Youngstown (father of Charles F. Owsley, see ME1), and the newer portion designed by Arthur Steinmark of Pittsburgh. The older stone Romanesque Revival corner church has a pyramidal roof, echoed in the square corner bell tower. Used as a chapel today, the interior has wooden truss work and a pipe organ. The newer church on the west uses a simplified Gothic vocabulary in stone, and is attached to the earlier building by an arcade along the street facade. A porte-cochere is on the west elevation. The modern sanctuary is lit by stained glass windows made by Nicholas Parrendo of the Henry Hunt Studios in Pittsburgh that depict Old and New Testament Bible stories.

ME20 Thiel College

1872–present. 75 College Ave.

Founded in 1866 and incorporated in Monaca, Beaver County, in 1870, Thiel College is the oldest Lutheran institution of higher learning west of the Allegheny Mountains. In 1870, Greenville residents offered the school seven acres and $20,000 to relocate here. The cornerstone was laid for the brick, Italianate Greenville Hall in 1872, and it was dedicated in 1874. Two handsome brick buildings in a smooth-surfaced Collegiate Gothic style were designed by Pittsburgh architect Edward B. Lee and his associate John H. Phillips: the Roth Administration Building of 1912–1913 and the 1922 Rissell Gymnasium.

The campus developed south of the administration building first, and then expanded into two quadrangles east and west of it with buildings by Arthur L. Martsolf and Associates of Beaver County. This firm designed Livingston Hall (1940), Langenheim Memorial Library (1952), Harter Residence Hall (1953), Rhodehouse Science Hall and Hodge Residence Hall (1959), and the Sawhill Residence Hall (1960). In 1962, Louis G. Martsolf, son of Arthur L., designed a group of fraternity buildings west of College Avenue. The majority of the 135-acre campus's buildings date from the immediate post–World War II decades.

In the late 1990s, Urban Design Associates renovated Greenville Hall and reconfigured Livingston Hall–Howard Miller Center in a Georgian Revival style. The American Institute of Architects Pittsburgh chapter recognized the school's first stand-alone chapel, designed by William Brocious for Desmone and Associates (2005; 94 College Avenue), with a 2006 Design Award for the red brick and limestone building's simple program and elegant natural wood interior.

JAMESTOWN

ME21 Free Public Library (Gibson House)

1856. 210 Liberty St.

Dr. William L. Gibson, a local entrepreneur in coal, lumber, and railroads, met Mark Twain on a trip abroad in 1867 and was later lampooned in his book *Innocents Abroad* (1870). Gibson, a civilian with a letter of recommendation from the Smithsonian Institution, signed aboard the ship *Quaker City* as the "Commissioner of the United States of America to Europe, Asia, and Africa." Twain recommended that sending "a dignitary of that tonnage across the ocean . . . would be in better taste, and safer, to take him apart and cart him over in sections, in several ships."

ME21 FREE PUBLIC LIBRARY (GIBSON HOUSE)

The two-story brick house from which Gibson traveled is a three-bay cube with deep bracketed eaves, and a cupola in the center of the roof. An elaborate frame and glass porch wraps around the east and north elevations. A very large, brick carriage house lies to the north. The legend that Twain visited the home is apparently untrue, but the Gibsons did travel twenty miles to hear him speak in Sharon in 1869, despite Twain's calling Gibson a "complacent imbecile." To further secure his pompous reputation, Gibson built c. 1887 a sixty-five-foot high, $100,000 granite monument to honor himself and his wife, Susan, in Jamestown's Park Lawn Cemetery. The house later became the Mark Twain Manor, an inn, and then a restaurant. Today it houses Jamestown's Free Public Library.

FREDONIA VICINITY

ME22 Caldwell One-Room School

1880. 2159 Mercer Rd. (PA 58), 3.2 miles northwest of Fredonia

This simple one-room, red brick, gable-roofed schoolhouse has a "hanging" chimney that pierces the ridgepole and is suspended near the ceiling of the room below. Bricks were made on the Ball farm nearby. The building has stone corner quoins and retains its original desks. There were 225 one-room schools in Mercer County between 1800 and 1900. The building was donated to the Mercer County Historical Society in 1962, and operates as a school museum during clement weather.

In 1798, Valentine and Margaret Cunningham built the first gristmill along Wolf Creek in the southeast corner of Mercer County. Their son's brick house of 1845, now part of Grove City College (ME23), remains on E. Main Street. The town, first known as Pine Grove, grew around the several mills that followed, and was incorporated as Grove City Borough in 1883. Located approximately midway between two busy north–south routes, U.S. 19 and PA 8, the town prospered as a commercial crossroads for local farm produce, and for nearby coal and oil resources. In 1872, the Pittsburgh, Shenango and Lake Erie rail line opened to Pine Grove.

There are four major employers: Grove City College; George Junior Republic, a residential treatment facility for delinquent and dependent boys, founded in 1909; Bessemer Gas Engine Company founded in 1898 on the eastern edge of town; and Wendell August Forge, established in 1923, which operates as both a manufacturing and a retail outlet for aluminum gift items. A vibrant, mostly two-story, brick commercial core along Broad Street and two handsome twentieth-century Gothic Revival churches provide an anchor for the adjoining single-family residential area. The churches are Grace United Methodist Church (1907–1909, 1926) and Tower Presbyterian Church (1925) at 210 and 248 S. Broad Street. The downtown includes two limestone Beaux-Arts classical corner banks, Citizen's Bank, formerly Grove City National Bank (c. 1932), and National City Bank (c. 1930) at 165 and 201 S. Broad Street; a U.S. Post Office (1929–1933) by W. Holmes Crosby at E. Pine Street; and the Moderne Shellco-Bashlin Building housing offices (c. 1950) at 119 W. Pine Street.

In 1994, over 140 stores collectively called Prime Outlets–Grove City opened four miles northwest of town at the intersection of PA 208 and I-79. The traditionally styled pyramidal-roofed stores of checkered Dryvit on a brick base draw shoppers from Pittsburgh, Cleveland, Youngstown, and Erie. Gas stations, restaurants, and four hotels often prompt visitors to remain overnight, bolstering local tourism.

ME23 Grove City College

1930s, W. G. Eckles Company Architects and Olmsted Brothers. 100 Campus Dr.

Founded as Pine Grove Academy in 1876, Grove City College assumed its present name in 1884. It was founded by Isaac Conrad Ketler, a Mercer County native, with an initial enrollment of thirteen students. By the 1970s, the student body had grown to 2,050, the approximate size at which it remains today.

The 150-acre campus plan was drawn c. 1930 by the Olmsted Brothers of Brookline, Massachusetts, in conjunction with the Eckles architectural firm of New Castle. Today, approximately two dozen buildings, most in the Collegiate Gothic style, are arranged in quadrangles on the upper or east campus. Wolf Creek divides the athletic facilities and Thorn Field (west campus) from the academic campus (east campus). The two are joined by the graceful stone Rainbow Bridge. The Eckles firm designed the stone Science Building (1930), Harbison Chapel (1931), and Crawford Hall (1938) in a Collegiate Gothic style similar to that employed at Princeton University.

Two generations of Mercer County's (later Philadelphia's) Pew family, who made their

ME23 GROVE CITY COLLEGE, east campus

fortune in the oil and natural gas businesses, chaired the college's board from 1895 to 1971. Joseph Newton Pew and his son, J. Howard Pew, were generous donors, but refused to establish an endowment fund, setting a precedent of running the college without relying on federal funds while keeping tuition low and affordable for the middle class.

The Colonial Hall Apartments (2005–2006, IKM/Grant), a four-story, red brick student housing facility with soaring roofs was designed in collaboration by two firms: Pittsburgh's IKM and Baltimore's Grant Architects. The campus is meticulously maintained and homogeneous in architectural character and enrollment.

LAWRENCE COUNTY

Before 1849, the year Lawrence County was created, the boundaries of Beaver and Mercer counties cut through the center of the city of New Castle. Perhaps to commemorate a tenacious fight by residents to end this confusing situation, it was named for Captain James Lawrence of the U.S. Navy, who, during a naval battle against the British in the waters near Boston in 1813, commanded, "Don't give up the ship!"

Rolling hills in the south give way to a glaciated plain north of New Castle. The region was the territory of the Delaware and Seneca tribes, who called it Kuskuskie, and who established a network of trails originating in present-day New Castle. With the final Pennsylvania land purchase in 1784–1785 and the Native American defeat at Fallen Timbers in 1794, the area attracted European "improvers" or squatters, but they built little of permanence because of land title disputes and the distance from major markets. After the War of 1812, these inhabitants migrated farther west, and Lawrence County was settled mostly by people from southern and southeastern Pennsylvania and from New Jersey. Today, farms predominate throughout the county.

In 1833, the Beaver and Erie Canal cut through the county from south to north using the Beaver and Shenango rivers. Five years later, the Pennsylvania and Ohio cross-cut canal connected Lawrence County with Youngstown and Akron to the west, using the north shore of the Mahoning River. For nearly forty years the canals were the major shipping conduits in Lawrence County and affected the area's architecture, especially near Harbor Bridge on the Shenango River, which was known as "Western Reserve Harbor." Lawrence County's close links with Ohio's Western Reserve lands, which were settled by former Connecticut residents, explain the New England influence on architecture and town plans, such as the county's preference for frame Greek Revival structures surrounding small green central squares. Housing stock in the county also includes several polygonal houses, a popular form in the mid-nineteenth century (LA17 and LA18).

The arrival of the railroads and, in the twentieth century, the large industrial complexes, which employed immigrants to make tin plate and china, intensified European influence in Lawrence County. Company towns such as Ellwood City and the workers' housing in southern New Castle are vestiges of this, as is St. Vitus Roman Catholic Church (LA15), built in 1963 for a congregation of Italian immigrants. Today, two national highways cut across Lawrence County's southwest and northeast corners. By the end of the twentieth century, the north–south I-79 had spurred the suburbanization of northern Lawrence County from the town of New Wilmington east into Mercer and Butler counties.

NEW CASTLE

New Castle was laid out in a grid pattern on fifty acres of flat, open land at the confluence of the Shenango River and Neshannock Creek. It was designed with an open market square, or diamond (actually an oval). Settlers from New Castle, Delaware, led by John Carlyle Stewart, settled here in 1798 and gave the town its name. Unlike other confluence towns in western Pennsylvania, the river's point is not the town's centerpiece; instead, the confluence is now entirely industrial and lost among utilitarian buildings.

The construction of the Beaver and Erie Canal and the Cross-Cut Canal to Youngstown between 1834 and 1872 spurred development of the city. The canal offered both passenger service and shipping, and connected the area to the Western Reserve of Ohio. In 1849, New Castle became the county seat of newly formed Lawrence County, putting an end to the town's division by the Beaver and Mercer county line; it became a city in 1869. Rail service soon followed the path of the canals and placed New Castle in a position for larger industrial developments. By 1894, five different rail lines traversed the city, and the population more than quadrupled between 1890 and 1950, reaching 48,834. The more prosperous residents built Colonial Revival, Queen Anne, and Second Empire houses on the hillside north of the commercial district between 1890 and the 1920s. In the commercial district along Mercer and E. Washington streets, several six- to eight-story bank and office buildings took shape.

New Castle came to specialize in the manufacture of tin plate and china. The Shenango China Company made place settings for the White House and other distinguished patrons. But the closing of the tin plate mills, beginning as early as the 1930s, and the closings of Shenango China, Johnson Bronze,

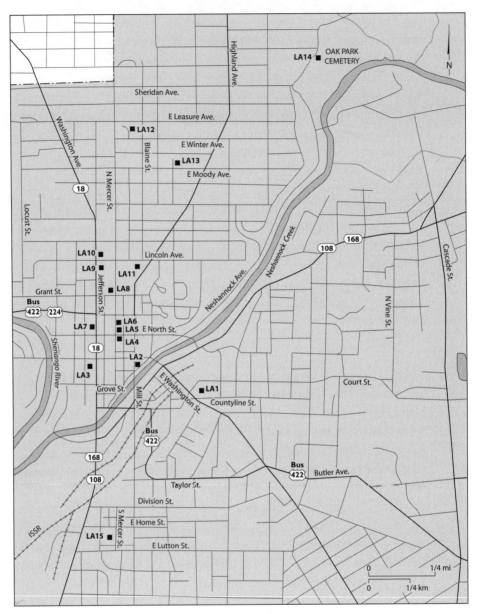

NEW CASTLE

and Rockwell in the early 1990s eroded the industrial base, and the population has returned to its c. 1900 size of 26,300 people.

Cascade Park, the city's largest, began as a trolley park southeast of the city, and at one time boasted amusement rides, boating, dancing, a zoo, and baseball fields. Today, the park has gardens, trails, and picnic pavilions, and the carefully restored Dance Pavilion (1898) is listed on the National Register of Historic Places. Downtown, new street lights and street furniture help to define the public spaces.

LA1 Lawrence County Courthouse

1850–1852, with additions; 1979 addition, W. G. Eckles Company Architects. Court St. at E. Washington St. (PA 65 SE)

The Lawrence County Courthouse, one of eight pre–Civil War Greek Revival courthouses in western Pennsylvania, looks to the west over the town of New Castle from its hillside site. Dominated by a pedimented portico supported by six Ionic columns, the brick gable-roofed building is painted a cream color. The source of the design is Thomas Jefferson's State Capitol in Richmond, Virginia. The contractors, William Hamilton and James Craig, hired a free African American, P. Ross Berry, as the chief mason. An addition in 1888 of four bays south of the five original bays uses the same vocabulary of dentiled cornice and fascia, but with shrunken Ionic columns at the recessed porch and pilaster strips delineating the bays. Several glass and concrete–paneled additions over the years have compromised the courthouse's integrity, although its cupola has been restored. In 1979, a three-story hexagonal wing with recessed ribbon windows and a hipped roof was attached to the older building by a glass hallway at the southeast corner.

LA2 Cascade Center (Knox Building, Cascade Theater)

1875. 11–17 S. Mill St.

This building was Warner Brothers' first theater. The four Warner brothers, Harry, Sam, Albert, and Jack, who owned a bicycle shop in Youngstown, were introduced to the nickelodeon in Pittsburgh at the turn of the twentieth century. They operated the Cascade Theater (Knox Building) here between 1907 and 1917. A two-story rear ell housed the 99-seat theater on the second floor. Sam Warner went to Los Angeles in 1912, and opened an office that grew into the Warner Brothers Studio of national prominence. In 2005, the building became part of a joint public/private partnership at the Riverplex, a theme mall with a refurbished theater, restaurants, and retail shops. Rehabilitation began with a modest gift from the Time-Warner Company.

LA3 First Christian Church, Disciples of Christ

1864–1865, C. H. M. McKelvey. 23 W. Washington St.

This very elaborate Gothic Revival church built at the end of the Civil War is enriched with tracery, a rose window, and prominent stone-trimmed corbeling. A pair of large square towers flank the gabled facade; one has a tall steeple and the other terminates with decorative crenellations, and both have entrances at their bases. The masonry was completed by P. Ross Berry, who was responsible for the Lawrence County Courthouse brickwork (LA1). A large three-story, gabled, educational wing was added to the east elevation in 1911. The church, sited on New Castle's diamond, today called Kennedy Square, enhances the historic qualities of the space.

LA4 Old Library Office Complex (U.S. Post Office)

1904, William George Eckles. 106 E. North St.

This stone-faced Beaux-Arts-inspired office building was built for the Post Office; then after 1934, it functioned as the New Castle Library. "New Castle Public Library" remains carved above the Tuscan-columned recessed porch on the north facade. A heavy balustrade crowns the parapet, and keystone surrounds highlight each window. The building has housed offices since 1980. It is an early design by William Eckles, who founded his architectural firm in 1898 and that has been continued by his son and grandson for over a century. Eckles was the son of a carpenter, farmer, and Lawrence County commissioner. He attended Duquesne College (now University) in Pittsburgh and Cowles School of Art in Boston, then worked in Boston and Pittsburgh before returning to New Castle and opening an office. His work is primarily in the counties surrounding Allegheny, for which he designed all kinds of buildings, ultimately specializing in schools and public buildings. His son, Robert Arthur Eckles (1898–1967), studied architecture at MIT, and became a partner in his father's firm, as did Robert's son, William George II (born 1925), who trained in architecture at Carnegie Institute of Technology, graduating in 1949.

LA5 Pearson House (Pearson Brick Company)

1918. 115 E. North St.

This unusual, charming Tudor Revival building was designed by the owner of a brick company to showcase his wares. Five different brick bonds are employed on the facade. Diamond pane windows, half timbering in the gable end and the dormers, and drip molds complete the effect. The foyer has a mural of the *Three Little Pigs* by local artist Grace Parker, illustrating the cleverness of those who build with brick.

LA6 Pennsylvania Martial Arts Academy (Elton Motor Company, Cadillac Sales and Service)

c. 1920. 116 N. Mercer St.

This is an increasingly rare building type, the historic luxury car showroom, which indicates the wealth in New Castle between the two world wars. The basic rectangular brick building is dressed up with a curved parapet and glazed terra-cotta with a Cadillac emblem in jewel tones on the facade. Large show windows and a recessed entrance complete the commercial face. Anna Wagner Keichline, an architect from Bellefonte, Centre County, designed that town's Cadillac dealership in 1916 (CE3), and this building, while a great deal smaller, could also be her design.

LA7 First United Presbyterian Church of New Castle

1894, Sidney Winfield Foulk. 125 N. Jefferson St.

Prolific local architect Sidney Winfield Foulk, whose national practice consisted of public buildings, such as YMCAs, churches, and hotels, designed this church. He and his son, Frank H. Foulk, practiced together from 1900 to 1907. Frank continued to practice in New Castle until his death. Sidney left New Castle and died in Long Beach, California.

Foulk's churches are each different. Here a crenellated round tower and an oversized crenellated square tower flank the gabled facade. A smaller version of the square tower is behind it to the west. The building is further animated by circular and arched windows, recessed doors, and the combination of brick walls and stone detailing. The church has an Akron plan, with the pews curved to face the pulpit and the organ at the southwest corner of the sanctuary. The balcony is reached by curved stairs in each of the facade towers. Five pastel-colored windows line the entrance loggia on the first story of the east elevation. Two distinctive round windows on the east and south elevations have square edges at one side. A beautiful stained glass window portraying a sunrise faces east to be illuminated by the morning sun.

LA8 W. G. Eckles Company Architects Offices (R. W. Clendenin House)

c. 1870; 1897 alterations, F. A. Bula. 301 N. Mercer St.

This two-and-one-half-story rambling Shingle Style house today serves as offices for the Eckles architectural firm. Eckles bought the house, which, coincidentally, was commissioned by Mrs. Eckles's distant relatives, the Clendenins, when the Lawrence Savings and Trust Bank Building formerly housing their offices was demolished for urban renewal. Up the hill at 315 N. Mercer Street, Isaac Hobbs and Son of Philadelphia designed a Second Empire "Suburban Villa" for New Castle banker William Patterson. The plans and an illustration were published in *Godey's Lady's Book and Magazine* of September 1869 (p. 276). It now houses offices.

LA9 Castle Manor (Honorable Leander Raney House)

1891. Sidney Winfield Foulk. 330 N. Jefferson St.

This large house on the first rise north of New Castle is a fine example of the work of Sidney Foulk. The house has typical Queen Anne ele-

LA9 CASTLE MANOR (HONORABLE LEANDER RANEY HOUSE)

ments: projecting turrets, gables, a tower, and window shapes that range from rectangular to semicircular. Castle Manor is distinctive for both the rotated semicircular window on the second story of the north elevation and walls where the stone is laid in alternating wide and narrow bands. A modified onion dome on the tower at the southwest corner sets this house apart from others in New Castle. Leander Raney, who commissioned this house, operated an iron works and milling company. His neighbors were similarly well-off. The North Hill historic district generally bounded by Jefferson, Mercer, and Falls streets, Fairmont Avenue, and Neshannock Boulevard contains 1,728 residences, including approximately two dozen very large single-family homes that are being restored to their turn-of-the-twentieth-century grandeur.

LA10 Lawrence County Historical Society (George Greer House)

c. 1900, Frank H. Foulk. 408 N. Jefferson St.

Tin plate magnate George Greer and his wife, Alice White Greer, employed New Castle's best-known architectural firm to design their nineteen-room frame house. They chose a site near other fashionable houses, well above the industrial flats to the southwest along the Shenango River. Ironically, the house built by the owner of a tin plate factory was donated to the Lawrence County Historical Society sixty years later by its then owner Joseph Clavelli, who at one time had been a tin plate worker. The house's proportions, horizontal massing, clustered one-story Corinthian columns supporting the full-facade porch, and attic-story windows suggest the Colonial Revival style. The leaded and stained glass was produced by the H. C. Fry Glass Company of Beaver County.

LA11 Scottish Rite Cathedral

1924–1926, Richard Gustave Schmid. 110–120 E. Lincoln Ave.

The most monumental building in New Castle, rivaling even the Courthouse (LA1) for its hillside site, is Free Masons Lodge No. 433. It is one of Schmid's finest designs. Richard Gustave Schmid (1863–1937), who trained at MIT and worked at one time in the Brookline office of H. H. Richardson, created a neoclas-

LA11 SCOTTISH RITE CATHEDRAL

sical design of limestone and cream-colored brick. Lined with two-story round-arched windows separated by Ionic columns, the facade has a shallow pediment at its center. The windows open onto an elaborate entrance foyer sheathed in travertine and with onyx pillars; bronze doors and balustrades add to the opulence. Three art-glass chandeliers forty feet overhead depict symbolic characters. The structure includes a banquet room seating 3,000, an auditorium seating 3,240, and the various meeting rooms necessary to a Masonic lodge. The rear elevation is scaled eight stories down the hillside and features an enormous expanse of brick diaper work.

LA12 Hoyt Institute of Fine Arts (May Emma Hoyt House and Alexander Hoyt House, "Rosewall")

1914–1917, Frank H. Foulk. 124 E. Leasure Ave.

Hoyt East was built for May Emma Hoyt, eldest of the three children of Lewis Stiles Hoyt, a local coal, oil, and railroad magnate. Upon the death of their father in 1907, each child received approximately $100 million. May Emma Hoyt, who was single and forty-two years old, spent approximately a quarter of her inheritance on her twenty-two-room mansion. She hired Charles F. Owsley of Youngstown initially, but ultimately had Frank Foulk of New Castle design a Colonial Revival, two-and-one-half-story house of light-colored brick with green clay roof tiles and copper gutters and trim. A formal porte-cochere angles from the L-shaped building, and shelters the rear entrance. The interior includes walnut and golden oak paneling carved with classical designs, a hand-carved main stairway, and secret closets incorporated into the walls of the dining room to hold her furs and the keys to all the rooms. A large carriage house, adjacent to the main house, has an apartment and full basement.

Alexander Crawford Hoyt and his wife constructed Hoyt West at approximately the same time, and named their house "Rosewall." Also designed by Foulk, Hoyt West was constructed of a deep red-brown brick and used dark-stained walnut on the interior. Stylistically, the houses are very similar, and their site plans are nearly identical, with the same angled porte-cochere and adjacent carriage house. The houses were given to Lawrence County in 1965, and became the Hoyt Institute of Fine Arts in 1968. Hoyt East and West are joined by a terraced breezeway consisting of a series of glass pavilions spanning the grassy incline between them, designed by the W. G. Eckles Company Architects in 1996.

LA13 Charles and Grace Johnson House

1912–1914, 1929. 221 E. Moody Ave.

This house is one of dozens of large, distinctive houses built in New Castle by successful industrialists. It was constructed to Charles Johnson's specifications by Italian masons from Calabria employed at his family's limestone quarry in Hillsville. The rough-cut blue limestone house has such Mediterranean elements as a clay tile roof, deep overhangs, and extruded mortar joints, but the massing is vertical rather than horizontal. Clay tiles are common in the New Castle area, due perhaps to the local ceramics industry. Copper

LA15 ST. VITUS ROMAN CATHOLIC CHURCH

trim and downspouts accentuate the complex mass of the house. The interior has a central-hall plan and emphasizes the same richness of materials as the exterior, including a unique Italian pink marble library that was designed by the W. G. Eckles firm for Grace Johnson after the death of her husband. The property also includes a garden pergola to the east, several outbuildings, and a carriage house adorned with a sinuous wrought-iron external stairway.

LA14 Oak Park Cemetery

1892. 1420 Neshannock Blvd.

Oak Park Cemetery, sixty-eight acres of gently sloping, tree-shrouded land southeast of Oak Park Road, is bounded by an adjoining cemetery, Graceland, on the northeast and by the deep ravine of Neshannock Creek on the south. It was laid out by real estate developer P. J. Watson, who built homes in Neshannock Heights and had the foresight to realize that people in new homes would ultimately need new burial grounds. Oak Park Cemetery soon eclipsed the popularity of New Castle's older, larger cemetery, Greenwood. The first burials date from 1894, and the small Gothic Revival chapel appears contemporaneous. There are two outstanding burial vaults: William Patterson's Egyptian Revival–style crypt c. 1905 with stained glass depicting the Holy Family's flight to Egypt, and John Knox's c. 1909 crypt that is shaped like a small Greek temple. The largest structure on the property is a granite mausoleum with space for four hundred burials built by the American Mausoleum Company between 1912 and 1914. The rectangular, flat-roofed building, sheathed in random stone, is dominated by a balustraded entrance pavilion supported by Tuscan columns. The porch shelters a double metal door with simple, smooth ashlar trim around a metal lunette. The building's overall effect is foreboding.

LA15 St. Vitus Roman Catholic Church

1963, P. Arthur D'Orazio. 910 S. Mercer St.

St. Vitus is the patron saint of Baia Latina, Italy, the original home of many of the Italian immigrants to New Castle. One of the few ethnic parishes in the region, the congregation of St. Vitus serves parishioners almost entirely of Italian heritage within a five-mile radius. The church, of poured reinforced concrete and faced with a locally produced brick, is designed without interior supports to create a sense of oneness between the altar and the congregation. It has a rounded shape with three entrances fanned along the wall opposite the altar that approximates the shape of a nautilus or of a sheaf of paper gently rolled. While the church seats nearly 1,000 people, it does not give the impression of overwhelming vastness, as do other churches of similar size. Architect P. Arthur D'Orazio, a 1934 Carnegie Institute of Technology graduate, had a forty-five-year solo architectural practice based in Youngstown. He designed over twenty-five buildings in western Pennsylvania, including four churches in Lawrence County: St. Vitus, the former St. Anthony's (1958–1959; PA 317, Bessemer); the former St. Michael's (1967; 1701 Moravia Street, New Castle); and the former Purification of the Blessed Virgin Mary (1968–1970; 415 4th Street, Ellwood City).

A small circular baptistery connects to the main structure by a narrow passage faced with panels of white chipped marble; an open metal bell tower with three hanging bronze bells rests atop it. The interior is finished with a rich palette of materials, including generous amounts of marble, glass mosaic, bronze, and aluminum. Many artisans, both local and Italian, supplied the ornament for this unique church. Above the main altar, a 42 × 20–foot Venetian glass mosaic illustrates Christ triumphing over Satan, surrounded by studies of important events of Christ's life. Other murals in the church represent the Holy Trinity. Windows made of heavy chipped glass designed in abstract patterns by the Hunt Studios of Pittsburgh allow colored light to flood the interior through variously sized openings. The bas-relief on the marble main altar, the side altars, and the baptismal font were designed by sculptor Pero Aldo.

BESSEMER AND VICINITY

When limestone deposits were discovered in the area c. 1887, this small industrial town was built to house workers near the quarries. It was named for Sir Henry Bessemer, who discovered that limestone was an important component in steelmaking. Incorporated in 1913, Bessemer is one mile east of the Ohio border. Brick plants, opened in 1900, were producing 200,000 bricks per day by 1914, and a brief oil boom sustained four drilling companies between 1909 and 1916. A cement plant now called ESSROC, opened in 1920 and still in operation, dominates the streetscape with its tall concrete towers. Rail connections to the PRR and the P&LE were used to ship crushed stone and the products made from it. The first immigrants were Swedes, followed by Austrians, Finns, Slovaks, Poles, Russians, and Italians. Houses are one- and two-story, hipped and gable roofed, neatly arranged in a grid pattern. The use of large local Bessemer bricks distinguishes these workers' houses, especially those at numbers 908 to 1106 on PA 317.

LA16 Westfield Grange

1914–1915, W. I. Clark. 1366 PA 551 at Westfield Rd., 2 miles southeast of Bessemer

The Westfield Grange is a local lodge of the fraternal organization for farmers, founded in 1912, called the Patrons of Husbandry. The lodge members asked W. I. Clark, a principal in the Eckles firm, to design their meeting hall. This small, one-and-one-half-story, hipped-roof brick meeting hall has a parapeted dormer on the facade. There are two other grange buildings in Lawrence County: Liberty Grange on PA 108 and Willard Grange on Frew Mill Road.

LA17 Twelve-Sided House

c. 1860. 1427 PA 208, 0.5 miles southwest of Pulaski

One of three brick pre–Civil War houses on PA 208 in the northwestern corner of Lawrence County, this is a two-story, brick, twelve-sided, or dodecagonal, house. The house, apparently built by the Brown family, has had its original windows replaced and a porch added later. Normally a cupola would crown the roof of this house type.

An older relative, James P. Brown, built a c. 1830 brick two-story farmhouse with elongated narrow windows at 1229 PA 208. With its nearly square massing, oculus, and three bays, it varies from the traditional five-bay rectangular composition.

LA18 William W. Walker House (Ten-Sided House)

c. 1855. 1498 Marr Ridge Rd., 4 miles southwest of Pulaski

Located on a winding country road, this brick ten-sided farmhouse was built in 1855, when polygonal houses were touted as the most energy efficient and sun-filled domestic spaces. Advocates of such houses believed that the polygonal construction reduced the force of the wind and retained heat inside. William W. Walker, the first owner of this house, was an active abolitionist.

NEW WILMINGTON AND VICINITY

New Wilmington was laid out c. 1824 by James Waugh and his sons. It has the timeless quality of a nineteenth-century crossroads town, with its tree-shaded, grid-patterned streets and lack of manufacturing plants. The flat and fertile land has attracted approximately 2,000 Old Order Amish to establish farms surrounding the village. A small but thriving commercial area along PA 208, or Neshannock Avenue, has parking lots for buggies behind some of the stores. In the 1840s, New Wilmington's position, halfway between the canals on the west and the northern turnpike (now U.S. 19) on the east, meant a steady stream of traffic through the town. The establishment of Westminster College in 1852 solidified its future. The serene, gable-roofed house at 448 Market Street (c. 1840), surrounded on all sides by college buildings, has paired windows in the gable end, returning eaves, and a slightly recessed central entrance flanked by sidelights. It epitomizes the Greek Revival style prevalent here during the canal era. Housing stock today ranges from mid-nineteenth-century brick and frame houses to new suburban dwellings.

LA19 Westminster College

c. 1885–present. Southeast of Market (PA 956) and Maple sts.

Westminster College, chartered in 1852 by the Associate Presbyterian Church (today Presbyterian USA), was one of the first coeducational colleges in America. Many experts at the time expected coeducation to fail, but Westminster and Waynesburg College in Greene County (GR3) successfully educated women with men. New Wilmington, then a village of 200 people, offered an endowment if the college would settle in the town. Residents of the college and town were strong abolitionists, and New Wilmington became a center for the Underground Railroad. A real railroad, the Sharpsville line, established a stop at the college in 1881, which nurtured both the school and its community.

Westminster College's buildings vary in style from Collegiate Gothic to Second Em-

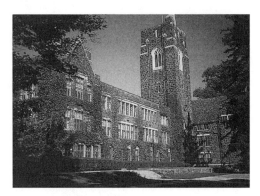

LA19 WESTMINSTER COLLEGE, Old Main

LA20 HOSTETTLER AMISH HOUSE AND BARN, barn

pire and to post–World War II prefabricated faculty housing and modern structures. The oldest building on campus is the white frame Thompson House (c. 1885) on Market Street, an exuberant example of the Stick Style. Above Market Street, Hillside Hall (1885), a red brick Queen Anne dormitory with a central tower, was originally the Ladies Hall and Conservatory of Music. The 1920s saw extensive construction, especially around the quadrangle outlined by Orchard, Maple, and Market streets and Westminster Drive. Built of random-laid stone with limestone trim, Collegiate Gothic Old Main, with its tall bell tower and housing Wallace Memorial Chapel, was erected between 1927 and 1929 to replace the previous administration building that had been destroyed by fire. Browne Hall (1928), using similar materials, was funded by residents of New Castle, and designed by the New Castle firm W. G. Eckles Company Architects.

ROSE POINT VICINITY

LA21 McConnell's Mill Historic Site, Gristmill, and Covered Bridge

1868 gristmill; 1874 bridge. McConnells Mill Rd. south of U.S. 422, 0.8 miles east of Rose Point

Another college landmark, "Old 77," the gymnasium at the southern end of the main quad, was named after the basketball team's seventy-seven-game winning streak. Built c. 1920, the building's iron roof structure and decorative maroon brick exterior evoke industrial structures, in contrast to the traditional architecture of the campus quadrangle.

Farther south overlooking Brittain Lake, a grouping of post–World War II faculty houses, funded by federal GI loans and built c. 1945, is a rare survivor of the recent past. A small neighborhood of these frame U-shaped houses was constructed along a loop off College Drive. To the north, the newest residences on campus, Berlin Village (2006), provide three groupings of four- to six-apartment units for senior students. Three-story, flat-roofed red brick dormitories and a large auditorium, gymnasium, and science center have updated the campus to the east and south, surrounded by playing fields.

LA20 Hostettler Amish House and Barn

c. 1900. 423 Quilt Shop Ln. (PA 208), 1 mile east of New Wilmington

This simple, gable-roofed two-story farmhouse with a two-story wing to the east and a porch sheltering the entrance could be a farm anywhere in western Pennsylvania but for the fact that there are no electrical wires leading to it. Old Order Amish farmhouses are simple inside and out: no decorative moldings or carpeting, and plain cotton curtains on string nailed to the window frame. The house, with a narrow central brick chimney, is heated by a stove. All of the buildings are handcrafted. Because traditional styling is consistently used and the buildings are well maintained, it is difficult to properly date them visually. To see a series of Amish farms, turn west from PA 18 onto Heather Heights Road, but be careful not to photograph any Amish people; it offends their religious beliefs.

Slippery Rock Creek and the university in neighboring Butler County (BU15) are named for an exceptionally slick rock six miles south of the mill near a Native American fording

LA21 MCCONNELL'S MILL HISTORIC SITE, GRISTMILL, AND COVERED BRIDGE, gristmill

site that was naturally covered by an oil seep. Although the region's oil has been depleted, the scenery of the forty-nine-mile-long rocky gorge remains an attraction. The gristmill was constructed by Daniel Kennedy after fire destroyed the original of 1852. Standing three-and-one-half-stories tall, the lower one-and-one-half stories are built of local sandstone salvaged from the original structure, and the remainder is of wooden board-and-batten construction. The upper stories store grain to keep it dry for grinding. The mill was purchased by McConnell, Wilson and Company

in 1875, and updated by the replacement of the old waterwheel with water turbines, and the grinding stones with rolling mills. A dam in Slippery Rock Creek pools the water then releases it through a raceway to turn the mill's turbines. The mill operated profitably until 1928, when it closed due to the retirement of James McConnell, decreased profits, and the advancement of milling technology. Over 2,500 acres of the rocky gorge and its surrounding park were sold to the Western Pennsylvania Conservancy in 1946, and ultimately deeded to the Commonwealth of Pennsylvania. In 1957, it opened as McConnell's Mill State Park.

On the west side of the mill site is a covered bridge of 1874 crossing Slippery Rock Creek. It is one of only three Howe truss bridges remaining in western Pennsylvania. Howe trusses were the first to use wood connected by iron rods, and were the forerunner of all iron truss bridges. Lawrence County's other covered bridge, a 121-foot Burr truss built in 1889, crosses the Neshannock Creek in Wilmington Township. Bridges are often associated with gristmills, as they provide critical access to the mill from both sides of the waterway.

WURTEMBURG

Located in Perry Township, Wurtemburg was first settled in 1796 by Ananias Allen on Slippery Rock Creek within half a mile of its confluence with Connoquenessing Creek. Allen built one of the earliest gristmills in the area, and attracted customers from as far away as New Castle. In 1829, Jacob Liebendorfer brought his sons Jacob and Daniel to Wurtemburg, and together they built a gristmill, which today houses an antiques store, the Wurtemburg Shops (c. 1830; 913–923 PA 488). The first post office was opened in 1845 after settlers from Wurtemburg, Germany, who gave the town its name, established residence. Salt was mined in the area between 1890 and 1900. The mines were supplanted by stone quarries outside of the town in 1900. Wurtemburg grew up along a busy route, and its commercial success between the 1840s and the 1860s prompted its residents to build modest Greek Revival houses along the road. The white, frame Greek Revival Wurtemburg Presbyterian Church (1860; 291 Wurtemburg Road) is beautifully sited overlooking the town and creek. The interior fittings appear original.

ELLWOOD CITY

Ellwood City straddles the border of southern Lawrence and northern Beaver counties. It was developed by the Pittsburgh Company, a real estate group set up by Beaver Falls wire entrepreneur Henry Waters Hartman. In 1890, Hartman's consortium bought six hundred acres of former farmland to develop Ellwood, named after Hartman's friend and customer Isaac L. Ellwood, one of the inventors of barbed wire. The name was changed to Ellwood City to distinguish it from another Ellwood, in eastern Pennsylvania. Hartman hired civil engineer Edward Wolford to lay out a manufacturing village. Wolford complied with a grid-patterned scheme on the south side of winding Connoquenessing Creek, and a one-mile-long circular street at the eastern end of the grid named the Pittsburgh Circle. With the founding of the Ellwood Weldless Tube Company by Ralph C. Stiefel and Harry Northwood's Glass Company, the need for housing grew, and the section inside the circle became the town's finest residential area.

The town boasts a handsome, cream-colored brick Municipal Building (1936; 6th and Lawrence streets), a post office (1932, James Wetmore, supervising architect of the U.S. Treasury; 320 7th Street), and the former First Seneca Bank (c. 1920; 4th and Lawrence streets). What appears to be the courthouse from its red brick Colonial Revival facade and its prominent site at the southern end of 5th Street is, in fact, Lincoln High School. Fine examples of domestic architecture along Crescent Avenue include the Queen Anne A. C. Grove House (1892; 637 Crescent Avenue) and H. W. Hartman's Shingle Style house (1894; 329 4th Street), now an office.

Ellwood City's U.S. Steel seamless tubing plant, in operation from 1900, closed in 1974, putting 1,000 employees out of work. In the years since, the city has become a bedroom community for manufacturing sites nearby, with a four-block shopping area of two-story, brick commercial buildings along Lawrence Avenue between 4th and 7th streets. Calvin United Presbyterian Church (1914, Fulton and Butler; 615 Crescent Avenue) is one of several handsome churches. The nearly square, buff brick building has pediments on each elevation surmounted by a dome at the center, and an entrance recessed behind two Ionic columns.

GLOSSARY

acroterium, acroterion (plural: **acroteria**) *1* A pedestal for a statue or similar decorative feature at the apex or at the lower corners of a pediment. *2* Any ornamental feature at these locations.

Adamesque A mode of architectural, especially interior, design, reminiscent of the work of Scottish architects Robert Adam (1728–1792) and his brother James (1732–1794). It is characterized by attenuated proportions, bright color, and elegant linear detailing. Adamesque interiors are part of the neoclassical movement and became popular in the late eighteenth century in Britain and northern Europe and slightly later in the United States.

Akron plan A church plan with auditorium-style seating and moveable partitions or folding doors that allowed Sunday school spaces to open into it. Popular in Protestant churches from the late nineteenth century and named for Akron, Ohio, where it is thought that the plan originated.

anthemion A Greek ornamental motif based on the honeysuckle or palmette that may appear as a single element on an antefix or as a running ornament on a frieze or other banded feature.

arcade *1* A series of arches, carried on columns or piers or other supports. *2* A covered walkway attached to a building with one side open as a series of arches to the exterior. *3* In the nineteenth and early twentieth centuries, an interior street or other space lined with shops and stores.

arch A curved construction spanning an opening. A masonry arch consists of a series of wedge-shaped parts (voussoirs) that press together toward the center while be-ing restrained from spreading outward by the surrounding wall or the adjacent arch.

architrave *1* The lowest horizontal member of a classical entablature. *2* The moldings on the face of a wall around a doorway or other opening. Distinguished from the jambs, which are the vertical linings perpendicular to the wall planes at the sides of an opening, and from the surround, a term applied to the entire door or window frame.

Art Deco A style inspired by the 1925 Exposition International des Arts Décoratifs et Industriels Moderne, held in Paris. It is characterized by faceted forms and patterns and flattened decorative fields, rich materials (including polished metal and exotic wood), and an overall sleekness of design. It was used frequently in commercial and residential architecture of the late 1920s and early 1930s. The term Art Deco was first used to describe this architecture in 1968.

Art Nouveau A style that originated in Belgium and France in the 1890s and flourished briefly across Europe and the United States. It is characterized by undulating and whiplash lines and sensuous curvilinear forms inspired by the natural world and some non-Western sources.

Arts and Crafts A late-nineteenth and early-twentieth-century movement that emerged in England and spread to the United States. Inspired by William Morris and initially a reaction to industrialization, it emphasized the importance of hand crafting and beauty in everyday objects and environments. Its works are characterized by simplified forms and construction and straightforward use of materials.

ashlar Squared blocks of stone that fit tightly against one another.

balloon-frame construction A system of light frame construction in which single studs extend the full height of the frame (commonly two stories), from the foundation to the roof. Floor joists are fastened to the sides of the studs. Structural members are usually sawn lumber, ranging from two-by-fours to two-by-tens, and are fastened with nails. The technique, developed in Chicago and other boomtowns of the 1830s, has been largely replaced in the twentieth century by platform frame construction.

bank barn A two-story barn built into the slope of a hill to allow for entrances on two levels. The upper level opens to a threshing floor and hay storage or mow. The lower level accommodates the farm animals. Often there is a forebay to protect the lower entrance doors on the long side.

bargeboard An ornate fascia board attached to the sloping edges (verges) of a roof, covering the ends of the horizontal roof timbers (purlins). Bargeboards are usually ornamented with carved, turned, or jigsawn forms. Sometimes called a gableboard or a vergeboard.

barn stars Jigsawn wood in the shape of stars and medallions applied to barn siding simply as ornament, sometimes as ventilators. Found generally in two central Pennsylvania counties, Bedford and Somerset. Occasionally a distinctive shape will act as the signature of the barn's builder.

Baroque A style of art and architecture that flourished in Europe and colonial North America during the seventeenth and eighteenth centuries. Although based on the architecture of the Renaissance, Baroque architecture was more dynamic, with ovals, curved or undulating walls, and interlocking forms. It was a monumental and richly three-dimensional style with elaborate systems of ornamental and figural sculpture.

barrel vault A vaulted roof or ceiling of semicircular or semielliptical cross section, forming a tunnel-like enclosure over a room, corridor, or similar space.

batten 1 A narrow strip of wood applied to cover a joint along the edges of two parallel boards in the same plane. 2 A strip of wood fastened across two or more parallel boards

to hold them together. See also the related term *board-and-batten siding.*

battered (adjective) Inclined from the vertical. A wall is said to be battered or to have a batter when it recedes as it rises.

Bauhaus Work in any of the visual arts by the faculty, students, or followers of the Bauhaus, the innovative design school founded by Walter Gropius (1883–1969) and an active force in German modernism from 1919 until 1933.

bay 1 The interval between two recurring members. A facade is frequently measured by window bays, a skeletal frame by structural bays. 2 A polygonal or curved unit of one or more stories, projecting from the wall and usually containing grouped windows (bay windows) on each story.

bay window The horizontally grouped windows in a projecting bay, or the projecting bay itself, if it is not more than one story. A bay window with a central section of plate glass in a late-nineteenth-century commercial building is called a Chicago window.

bearing wall A wall that is fully structural, carrying the load of the floors and roof to the foundation. Distinguished from curtain wall. See also the related term *load-bearing.*

Beaux-Arts Historicist design on a monumental scale, as taught at the Ecole des Beaux-Arts in Paris and disseminated internationally throughout the nineteenth and early twentieth centuries. The term is generally applied to an eclectic classicism of the 1850s through the 1920s. Beaux-Arts does not connote a single style, but rather an architecture derived from a variety of historical sources, especially Roman, Renaissance, and Baroque.

belt course See *stringcourse.*

blind Term applied to the surface use of elements that would otherwise articulate an opening where no actual opening exists. Used in combinations such as blind arcade, blind arch, blind door, blind window.

blue stone, blue rock Hard, bluish-gray stone.

board-and-batten siding A type of siding for wood-frame buildings consisting of wide vertical boards with narrow strips of wood (battens) covering the joints.

brace A single wooden or metal member, usually barlike, placed diagonally within a framework or truss or beneath an overhang. Distinguished from a bracket, which is a more substantial triangular feature, and from a strut, which is essentially a post set in a diagonal position.

braced-frame construction A combination of heavy and light timber-frame construction, in which the principal vertical and horizontal framing members (posts and girts) are fastened by mortise and tenon joints, while the one-story-high studs are nailed to the heavy timber frame. The overall frame is made more rigid by diagonal braces.

bracket Any solid, pierced, or built-up triangular feature projecting from the face of a wall to support a projecting element, like the top member of a cornice or the verges or eaves of a roof. Brackets are frequently used for ornamental as well as structural purposes.

British colonial A term applied to buildings, towns, landscapes, and other artifacts from the period of British colonial occupation of large parts of eastern North America in the seventeenth and eighteenth centuries. This period introduced into the New World various regional strains of English and Scots-Irish folk culture, as well as high-style Anglo-European Renaissance, Baroque, and neoclassical design. Sometimes called English colonial, colonial, or Early American.

Brutalism An architectural style of the 1950s through 1970s, characterized by complex massing and by a frank expression of structural members, elements of building systems, and materials (especially concrete). Some of the work of Paul Rudolph (1918–1997) is associated with this style.

bungalow A low one- or one-and-one-half-story house of modest pretensions with a low-pitched gable or hipped roof, a conspicuous porch, and projecting eaves. Derived from Indian precedents, this house type was popular from around 1900 to 1930, especially in California and the American West. The term bungalow was also applied to any vernacular building of a semirustic nature, including vacation cottages and lodges.

buttress An exterior mass of masonry bonded into a wall that it strengthens or supports.

Buttresses often absorb lateral thrusts from roofs or vaults.

Byzantine Term applied to the art and architecture of the Eastern Roman Empire centered on Byzantium (Constantinople, Istanbul) from the sixth to the fifteenth centuries. It is characterized by domes, round arches, richly carved capitals, and mosaics.

campanile A bell tower. While usually free-standing in medieval and Renaissance architecture, it was often incorporated as a prominent unit in the massing of picturesque nineteenth-century buildings.

cantilever A beam, girder, slab, truss, or other structural member that projects beyond its supporting wall or column.

capital The moldings and carved enrichment at the top of a column, pilaster, pier, or pedestal.

Carpenter Gothic Term applied to a version of the Gothic Revival (c. 1840s–1870s), in which Gothic motifs are adapted to wooden details produced by lathes, jigsaws, and molding machines. Sometimes called Gingerbread Style or Steamboat Gothic.

castellated Having the elements of a medieval castle, such as crenellation and turrets.

cast iron Iron shaped by a molding process, generally strong in compression but brittle in tension. Distinguished from wrought iron, which has been forged to increase its tensile properties.

cast-iron front An architectural facade made of prefabricated molded iron parts, often markedly skeletal in appearance with extensive glass infilling. Prevalent from the late 1840s to the early 1870s.

chamfer The oblique surface formed by cutting off a square edge at an equal angle to each face.

chancel The end of a Roman Catholic or High Episcopal church containing the altar and set apart for the clergy and choir by a screen, rail, or steps. Usually the entire east end of a church beyond the crossing, especially in less extensive Catholic and Episcopal churches.

Chateauesque A term applied to masonry buildings from the 1870s to the 1920s in which stylistic references are derived from Early French Renaissance chateaux, from the reign of Francois I (1515–1547) or even earlier. Sometimes called Chateau Style or Chateauesque Revival.

Chicago School A diverse group of architects associated with the development of the tall (i.e., six- to twenty-story) commercial building in Chicago during the 1880s and 1890s. The work of this group is characterized by its use of new engineering methods (metal frame construction and floating foundations) and robust, often untraditional architectural forms. William Le Baron Jenney, Burnham and Root, and Adler and Sullivan are identified with this group.

Chicago window A tripartite oblong window in which a large fixed center pane is placed between two narrow sash windows. Popularized in Chicago commercial buildings of the 1880s–1890s.

choir The part of a Roman Catholic or High Episcopal church where the singers participate in the service. Usually the space within the chancel arm of the church, situated between the crossing to the west and the sanctuary to the east. In smaller churches, the terms choir and chancel are often used interchangeably to mean the entire eastern arm of the church.

City Beautiful A movement in architecture, landscape architecture, and planning in the United States from the 1890s through the 1920s, advocating the beautification of cities and employing a monumental Beaux-Arts classical style. Inspired in part by the 1893 World's Columbian Exposition in Chicago, City Beautiful schemes emphasized civic centers, boulevards, and waterfront improvements, and sometimes included comprehensive metropolitan plans for parks, infrastructure, and transportation.

clapboard A tapered board that is thinner along the top edge and thicker along the bottom edge, applied horizontally with edges overlapping to provide weather-tight siding on a building of wood construction. Early clapboards were split and were used for barrel staves and for wainscoting. The term now applies to any beveled siding board regardless of length or width.

classical, classicism, classicizing Terms describing the application of principles or elements derived from the visual arts of the Greco-Roman era (seventh century B.C.

through fourth century A.D.) at any subsequent period of Western civilization, but particularly since the Renaissance. More a descriptive term for an approach to design and for a general cultural sensibility than for any particular style.

clerestory A part of a building that rises above the roof of another part and has windows in its walls.

coffer A recessed panel, usually square or octagonal, in a ceiling. Such panels are also found on the inner surfaces of domes and vaults.

Collegiate Gothic 1 Originally, a secular version of English Gothic architecture, characteristic of the older colleges of Oxford and Cambridge. 2 A secular version of Late Gothic Revival architecture, which became a popular style for North American colleges and universities from the 1890s through the 1920s.

colonial 1 a term for the entire period during which a particular European country held political dominion over a part of the Americas, Africa, Asia, Australia, or Oceania. See also the more specific term *British colonial*. 2 Loosely used to mean the British colonial period in North America.

Colonial Revival Generally understood to mean the revival of forms from British colonial design. The Colonial Revival began in New England in the 1860s, flourished after the U.S. Centennial in 1876, and continues nationwide into the present, especially in houses. Typical elements include classically derived pediments, cornices, and dormers.

colonnade A series of freestanding or engaged columns supporting an entablature or simple beam.

column 1 A vertical supporting element, usually cylindrical and slightly tapering, consisting of a base (except in the Greek Doric order), shaft, and capital. See also the related terms *entablature* and *order*. 2 Any vertical supporting element in a skeletal frame.

common bond A pattern of brickwork in which every fifth or sixth course consists of all headers, the other courses being all stretchers. Sometimes called American bond.

Composite order An ensemble of classical column and entablature elements, particularly characterized by large Ionic volutes and Corinthian acanthus leaves in the capital of the column. See also the more general term *order*.

console A type of bracket with a scroll-shaped or S-curve profile and a height greater than its projection from the wall.

coping The cap or top course of a wall, parapet, balustrade, or chimney, usually designed to shed water.

corbel A projecting stone that supports a superincumbent weight. In medieval architecture and its derivatives, a support for such major features as vaulting shafts, vaulting ribs, or oriels.

Corinthian order An ensemble of classical column and entablature elements, particularly characterized by acanthus leaves and small volutes in the capital of the column. See also the more general term *order*.

cornice The crowning member of a wall or entablature.

course A layer of building blocks, such as bricks or stones, extending the full length and thickness of a wall.

coved ceiling A ceiling in which the transition between wall and ceiling is formed by a large concave panel or molding.

coved cornice A cornice with a concave profile. Sometimes called a cavetto cornice.

Craftsman A style of furniture and interior design belonging to the Arts and Crafts movement in the United States, and specifically related to *The Craftsman* magazine (1901–1916), published by Gustav Stickley (1858–1942). Houses known to be derived from this publication can be called Craftsman houses.

crenellation, crenellated A form of embellishment on a parapet consisting of indentations (crenels or embrasures) alternating with solid blocks of wall (merlons). Virtually synonymous with battlement, battlemented; embattlement, embattled.

crocket In Gothic architecture, a small ornament resembling bunched foliage, placed at intervals on the sloping edges of gables, pinnacles, or spires.

crossing In a church with a cruciform plan, the area where the arms of the cross intersect; specifically, the space where the transept crosses the nave and chancel.

crown The central, or highest, part of an arch or vault.

crown molding The highest in a series of moldings.

curtain wall In skeleton frame or reinforced concrete construction, a thin nonstructural cladding of stone, brick, terra-cotta, glass, or metal veneer. Distinguished from bearing wall.

Deconstructivism, deconstructivist A term applied to architecture from the late twentieth century that disturbs conventional notions of harmony, unity, and apparent stability through fragmented, angular forms as well as irregular planning, unconventional materials, and odd juxtapositions.

dentil, denticulated A small ornamental block forming one of a series set in a row. A dentil molding is composed of such a series.

dependency A building, wing, or room, subordinate to or serving as an adjunct to a main building. A dependency may be attached to or detached from a main building. Distinguished from an outbuilding.

diaper An overall repetitive pattern on a flat surface, especially a pattern of geometric or representational forms arranged in a diamond-shaped or checkerboard grid. Sometimes called diaper work.

distyle in antis A recessed portico fronted by a pair of columns aligned with the exterior wall surface. See the related term *in antis*.

dogtrot An open breezeway between two main rooms of a log or frame house; also a house so constructed.

Doric order An ensemble of classical column and entablature elements, particularly characterized by plain capitals and columns without bases, and by the use of triglyphs and metopes in the frieze of the entablature. See also the more general term *order*.

dormer A roof-sheltered window (or vent), usually with vertical sides and front, set into a sloping roof.

double-pen In vernacular architecture, particularly houses, a term applied to a plan consisting of two rooms side by side or separated by a hallway.

drip molding See *head molding*.

drum 1 A cylindrical or polygonal wall zone upon which a dome rests. 2 One of the cylinders of stone that form the shaft of a column.

Dutch biscuit A Germanic building practice whereby short wooden boards are wrapped in a mixture of straw and mud and placed between floor joists to provide extra insulation; they are then covered with floorboards. Sometimes called paling.

Early American See *British colonial.*

Early Renaissance See *Renaissance.*

Eastlake A decorative arts and interior design term of the 1860s and 1880s sometimes applied to architecture. Named after Charles Locke Eastlake (1836–1906), an English advocate of the application of Gothic principles of construction and design, rather than mere Gothic elements. Characterized by simplicity and solidity of forms, often embellished with turned and incised details. Sometimes called Eastlake Gothic or Modern Gothic.

eaves The horizontal lower edges of a roof plane, usually projecting beyond the wall below. Distinguished from verges.

eclectic, eclecticism A sensibility in design, prevalent since the eighteenth century, involving the selection of elements from a variety of sources, including historical periods of high-style design, vernacular design (Western and non-Western), and (in the twentieth century) contemporary industrial design. Distinguished from historicism and revivalism by drawing on a wider range of sources than the historical periods of high-style Western design.

Egyptian Revival A term applied to works or elements of those works that emulate forms in the visual arts of ancient Egyptian civilization.

engaged column A half-round column attached to a wall. Distinguished from a freestanding column by seeming to be built into the wall. Also distinguished from a pilaster and a recessed column.

English bond A pattern of brickwork in which the bricks are set in alternating courses of stretchers and headers.

English Gothic Gothic architecture of England (1190–1520), characterized by stone construction, pointed arches, and vaulted ceilings. Divisions of English Gothic are: Early English (1190–1275), with columns composed of clusters of shafts; Decorated (1275–1350), with a more elaborate treatment of decorative elements and window tracery; and Perpendicular (1350–1520), with a greater emphasis on verticality, linearity of decoration, and fan vaulting.

entablature In a classical order, a richly detailed horizontal member resting on columns or pilasters. It is divided horizontally into three main parts: the architrave, the frieze, and the cornice. Each part has the moldings and decorative treatment that are characteristic of the particular order, but modern adaptations often alter canonical details.

exedra A semicircular or polygonal space usually containing a bench, in the wall of a garden or a building other than a church. Distinguished from a niche and an apse.

exotic revivals A term occasionally used to suggest a distinction between revivals of European styles (e.g., Greek, Gothic revivals) and non-European styles (e.g., Egyptian, Moorish, Mayan revivals).

eyebrow dormer A low dormer with a small segmental window or vent but no sides. The roofing warps or bows over the window or vent in a wavy line.

facade An exterior face of a building, especially the principal or entrance front. Distinguished from an elevation, which is an orthographic drawing of a building face.

fanlight A semicircular or semielliptical window over a door, with radiating mullions in the form of an open fan. Sometimes called a sunburst light.

fan vault A type of Gothic vault in which the primary ribs all have the same curvature and radiate in a half circle around the springing point.

fascia 1 A plain, molded, or ornamented board that covers the horizontal edges (eaves) or sloping edges (verges) of a roof. 2 One of the broad continuous bands that make up the architrave of the Ionic, Corinthian, or Composite order.

Federal A relatively austere version of neoclassical architecture in the United States popular from New England to Virginia, and in other regions influenced by the Northeast. The name refers to the establishment of the federal government in 1789 and the Federalist party, whose members commissioned important examples of buildings in this style. It flourished from the 1790s through the 1820s.

fenestration Window treatment: arrangement and proportioning.

festoon A motif representing entwined leaves, flowers, or fruits, hung in a catenary curve from two points. Distinguished from a swag.

finial A vertical ornament placed upon the apex of an architectural feature, such as a gable, turret, or canopy. Distinguished from a pinnacle.

Flemish bond A pattern of brickwork in which the stretchers and headers alternate in the same row and are staggered from one row to the next. Because this creates a more animated texture than English bond, Flemish bond was favored for front facades and more elegant buildings.

folk A descriptive term, applicable to all the visual arts and all styles and periods. Applied to 1 a regional, often ethnic, tradition in which continuities through the years in the overall appearance of artifacts (including buildings) are more important than changes in stylistic embellishment; 2 the work of individual artists and artisans unexposed to or uninterested in prevailing or avant-garde ideals of form and technique. Approximate synonyms include anonymous, naive, primitive, traditional. For architecture, see also the more general term *vernacular* and the related term *popular*.

forebay The cantilevered portion of a barn that projects over the lower entrance doors on the long and downhill side of a bank barn. Used to protect the doors from the elements.

foursquare house A hipped-roof, two-story house with four principal rooms on each floor and a symmetrical facade. It usually has a front porch across the full width of the house and one or more large dormers on the roof. A common suburban house type from the 1890s to the 1920s.

frieze 1 The broad horizontal band that forms the central part of a classical entablature. 2 Any long horizontal band or zone, especially one that has a chiefly decorative purpose, located at the top of a wall. Distinguished from a fascia, which is attached to the horizontal edge of a roof.

front gabled Term applied to a building whose principal gable end faces the front of the lot or some feature like a street or open space. Sometimes called gable front. Distinguished from side gabled.

gable The wall area immediately below the end of a gable, gambrel, or jerkinhead roof.

gable roof A roof in which the two planes slope equally toward each other to a common ridge. Sometimes called a pitched roof.

gambrel roof A roof that has a single ridgepole but a double convex pitch. The lower plane, which rises from the eaves, is rather steep. The upper plane, which extends from the lower plane to the ridgeline, has a flatter pitch.

Georgian period A term for a period in British and British colonial history, not a specific style term. The Georgian period begins with the coronation of George I in 1714 and extends until about 1781 in the area that became the United States (and in Britain, until the death of George IV in 1830).

Georgian Revival The revival of Georgian period forms from the 1880s to the present.

girder A major horizontal spanning member, comparable to a beam, but larger and often built up of a number of parts. It usually runs at right angles to the beams and serves as their principal means of support.

girt In timber-frame construction, a horizontal beam at intermediate (e.g., second-floor) level, spanning between posts.

Gothic An architectural style prevalent in Europe during the Middle Ages (from the twelfth century into the fifteenth in Italy and into the sixteenth century in the rest of Europe) and best embodied by cathedrals. It is characterized by pointed arches and ribbed vaults and by the dominance of openings over masonry mass in the wall. Gothic was preceded by the Romanesque and followed by the Renaissance.

Gothic Revival A movement in Europe and North America devoted to reviving the forms and the spirit of Gothic architecture and the allied arts. It originated in the mid-eighteenth century and flourished during the nineteenth century. For some building types, notably churches, it was used frequently into the twentieth century.

Grange A rural fraternal organization originally known as the Patrons of Husbandry founded in Washington, D.C., in 1867 to better the economic, social, and educational conditions of farm families. Grange halls were built throughout Pennsylvania.

Greek cross A cross with four equal arms. Usually used to describe the ground plan of a building.

Greek Revival A movement in Europe and North America devoted to reviving the forms and spirit of classical Greek architecture, sculpture, and decorative arts. It originated in the mid-eighteenth century, culminated in the 1830s, and continued into the 1850s. Its most recognizable architectural feature is the pedimented temple front. Sometimes viewed as the first popular style in the United States, where it was used frequently in public buildings and private residences.

green architecture, green building Terms originating in the late twentieth century that designate ecologically conscious architectural design. Green buildings are characterized by their energy efficiency, use of sustainable materials, and minimal environmental impact. The terms generally refer to building technologies and mechanical systems rather than to form or style. See also *LEED*.

groin vault A ceiling shape formed by the intersection of two pointed-arch vaults, as in a Gothic cathedral.

Guastavino vaults A system of tile construction developed by Spanish engineer Rafael Guastavino and used extensively in the United States in the late nineteenth and early twentieth centuries. Based on traditional Catalan techniques, these vaults use standardized tiles and Portland cement laid in a herringbone pattern in three to four staggered layers. They are extremely strong, lightweight, and can be built without scaffolding.

HABS/HAER/HALS Branches of the National Park Service of the U.S. Department of the Interior established, beginning in 1933, to document American architecture (Historic American Buildings Survey), engineering and technology (Historic American Engineering Record), and landscapes (Historic American Landscapes Survey) through large-format photographs, measured drawings, and written histories.

half-timber construction A variety of timber-frame construction in which the framing members are exposed on the exterior of the wall, with the spaces between timbers being filled with wattle-and-daub (i.e., woven lath and plaster) or masonry materials, such as brick or stone. These masonry materials may also be covered with stucco.

hall-and-parlor house, hall-and-parlor plan A double-pen house (i.e., a house that is one room deep and two rooms wide). Usually applied to houses without a central through-passage, to distinguish from hall-passage-parlor houses.

hall-passage-parlor house, hall-passage-parlor plan A two-room house with a central through-passage or hallway.

header A brick laid all the way through the thickness of a wall, so that the short end of the brick shows on the exterior.

head molding A molding or set of moldings designed to shelter and embellish the top of a door or window. Sometimes called a drip molding.

high style or high-style (adjective) Not a style term in itself, but a descriptive term, applicable to all the visual arts and all styles and periods. Applied to the works of major designers and their schools and disciples, usually reflecting a cosmopolitan awareness of traditions beyond a particular place or time. Usually contrasted with vernacular (including the folk and popular traditions).

high tech Term applied to architecture in which building materials and elements of building systems are used to celebrate contemporary technology. Elemental geometric forms, primary colors, and metallic finishes are used to heighten the technological imagery.

High Victorian Gothic A version of the Gothic Revival that originated in England in the 1850s and spread to North America in the 1860s. Characterized by polychromatic exteriors inspired by the medieval Gothic architecture of northern Italy. Sometimes called Ruskinian Gothic.

hipped roof A roof that pitches inward from all four sides. The edge where any two planes meet is called the hip.

historicism, historicist, historicizing A type of eclecticism prevalent since the eighteenth century, involving the use of forms from historical periods of high-style design (usually in the Western tradition) and, occasionally, from favored traditions of vernacular design (such as the various colonial traditions in the United States). Historicist influences are designated by the use of the prefix Neo- with a previous historical style (e.g., Neo-Baroque). Distinguished from the more general term eclecticism, which draws on a wider range of sources in addition to the historical. See also the more specific terms *revival, revivalism.*

hollow building tile A hollow terra-cotta building block used for constructing exterior bearing walls of buildings up to about three stories, as well as interior walls and partitions.

hood mold A canopy, molding, or pediment over a door. See *head molding.*

horizontal plank frame construction A system of wood construction in which horizontal planks are set or nailed into the corner posts of a timber-frame building. There are, however, no studs or intermediate posts connecting the sill and the plate.

hyphen A subsidiary building unit, often one story, connecting the central block and the wings or dependencies.

I-house A two-story house, one room deep and two rooms wide, usually with a central hallway. The I-house is a nineteenth-century descendent of the hall-and-parlor house of the colonial period. The term perhaps derives from the resemblance between the tall, narrow end walls of these houses and the capital letter I.

impost The top part of a pier or wall, upon which rests the springer or lowest voussoir of an arch.

impost block A block, often in the form of an inverted truncated pyramid, placed between a column capital and the lowest voussoirs of an arch above. Distinguished from an entablature block and sometimes called a dosseret or supercapital.

in antis Columns in antis are placed between two projecting sections of wall, in an imaginary plane connecting the ends of the two wall elements.

International Style A style that originated in Europe in the 1920s and flourished across the globe into the 1970s. It is characterized by the expression of volume and surface, the suppression of historicist ornament, and the avoidance of axial symmetry. It features the prominent use of such twentieth-century building materials as steel, reinforced concrete, and plate glass. The term was originally applied by Henry-Russell Hitchcock and Philip Johnson to the new, nontraditional, mostly European architecture of the 1920s in their 1932 exhibition at the Museum of Modern Art and in their accompanying book, *The International Style.*

Ionic order An ensemble of classical column and entablature elements, particularly characterized by the use of large volutes in the capital of the column. See also the more general term *order.*

Italianate An eclectic revival style derived from Italian Romanesque and Renaissance architecture, originating in England and Germany in the early nineteenth century and prevalent in the United States between the 1840s and 1880s in houses and in Main Street commercial buildings. It is characterized by prominent window heads, overhanging eaves, and bracketed cornices.

Italian Lombardian, Italian Lombardian Romanesque See *Lombard.*

Italian Villa style A subtype of the Italianate style, originating in England and Germany in the early nineteenth century and prevalent in the United States between the 1840s and 1870s, mostly in houses, but also churches and other public buildings. The style is characterized by asymmetrical plans and elevations, irregular blocklike massing, round arch arcades and openings, northern Italian Romanesque detailing, and sometimes campanile-like towers. Distinguished from the more symmetrical Italianate by having the northern Italian rural vernacular villa as prototype.

Jacobean, Jacobethan Architecture coinciding with the rule of James I (1603–1625) in Britain and characterized by symmetrical plans and freely interpreted Renaissance motifs. Its revival was popular in the United States in the early twentieth century for educational and residential buildings.

jamb The vertical side face of a door or window opening, amounting to the full thickness of the wall, and usually enriched with paneling, moldings, or jamb shafts. In a door or window opening, the jamb is distinguished from the reveal, which is the portion of wall thickness between the door or window frame and the outer surface of the wall. In an opening without a door or window, the terms jamb and reveal are used interchangeably. Also distinguished from an architrave.

jerkinhead roof A gable roof in which the upper portion of the gable end is hipped, or inclined inward along the ridgeline, forming a small triangle of roof surface. Sometimes called a clipped gable roof or hipped gable roof.

joist One of a series of small horizontal beams that support a floor or ceiling.

keystone The central wedge-shaped stone at the crown of an arch.

label molding A vertical downward extension of a drip molding or head molding over an arch of any form. See *head molding.*

lancet arch A narrow arch generally tall and sharply pointed, with radii much longer than the span. Typical of Gothic and Gothic Revival architecture.

lantern 1 The uppermost stage of a dome, containing windows or arcaded openings. 2 Any feature, square or polygonal in plan and usually containing windows, rising above the roof of a building. The square structures that serve as skylights on the roofs of nineteenth-century buildings were also called lantern lights, and, in Italianate and Second Empire buildings, came to be called cupolas.

lath A latticelike, continuous surface of small wooden strips or metal mesh nailed to walls or partitions to hold plaster.

lean-to roof See *shed roof.*

LEED Buildings approved by the U.S. Green Building Council's Leadership in Energy and Environmental Design. See also *green architecture, green building.*

light frame construction A type of wood-frame construction in which relatively light structural members (usually sawn lumber, ranging from two-by-fours to two-by-tens) are fastened with nails. Distinguished from timber-frame construction. See the more specific terms *balloon-frame construction* and *platform frame construction.*

lintel A horizontal structural member that supports the wall over an opening or spans between two adjacent piers or columns.

living hall In Queen Anne, Shingle Style, and Colonial Revival houses, an extensive room, often containing the entrance, the main staircase, a fireplace, and an inglenook.

load-bearing Term applied to a wall, column, pier, or any vertical supporting member, constructed so that all loads are carried to the ground through the wall, column, or pier.

loggia 1 A porch or open-air room, particularly one set within the body of a building. 2 An arcaded or colonnaded structure, open on one or more sides, sometimes with an upper story. 3 An eighteenth- and nineteenth-century term for a porch or veranda.

Lombard A term applied to buildings derived from the Romanesque architecture of northern Italy (especially Lombardy). Characterized by the use of brick for both structural and ornamental purposes, and round arches. Also called Lombardian and Lombardic.

mansard roof A hipped roof with double pitch. The upper slope may approach flatness, while the lower slope has a very steep pitch, sometimes flaring in a concave curve (or swelling in a convex curve) as it comes to the eaves. This lower slope usually has windows, and the area under the roof often amounts to a full story. The name is a corruption of that of François Mansart (1598–1666), who designed roofs of this type, and that were revived in Paris during the Second Empire period.

masonry Construction using stone, brick, block, or some other hard and durable material laid up in units and usually bonded by mortar.

massing The grouping or arrangement of the primary volumetric components of a building.

medieval Term applied to the Middle Ages in European civilization between the age of antiquity and the age of the Renaissance (i.e., mid-fifth to mid-fifteenth century in Italy; mid-fifth to late sixteenth century in England). In architecture and the other visual arts, the medieval period included the end of the Early Christian period, then the Byzantine, the Romanesque, and the Gothic styles or periods.

Mediterranean style A style popular for houses in the first decades of the twentieth century, featuring tile roofs, stucco, and arcades.

metope In a Doric entablature, that part of the frieze which falls between two triglyphs. In the Greek Doric order the metopes often contain small sculptural reliefs.

Miesian Term applied to work showing the influence of German American architect Ludwig Mies van der Rohe (1886–1969). See also the related terms *Bauhaus* and *International Style*.

Mission Revival A style originating in the 1890s, and making use of forms and materials from the Spanish and Mexican mission architecture of the eighteenth and early nineteenth centuries. Not to be confused with Mission furniture of the Arts and Crafts movement. See also the related term *Spanish Mission* and the more general term *Spanish Colonial Revival*.

modern A term applied in various ways during the past century to the history of the visual arts and world history generally: *1* from the 1910s to the present (see also the more specific terms *Bauhaus* and *International Style*); *2* from the 1850s–1890s to the present; *3* from the Enlightenment or the advent of neoclassicism or the Industrial Revolution, c. 1750, to the present; *4* from the Renaissance in Italy, c. 1450, to the present.

Moderne A term applied to a wide range of design work from the 1920s through the 1940s, in which aspects of traditionalism and modernism coexist and in which eclecticism (from a historical, exotic, or machine aesthetic) is inseparable from the urge for stylization. Sometimes called Art Moderne or Modernistic. See also the more specific term *Art Deco*.

modernism A movement in the visual arts, culture, and in world history generally that dominated much of the twentieth century in the West. With roots in the Enlightenment and the Industrial Revolution, and linked with the forces of social modernity, modernism deliberately broke from traditional and emphasized innovation and progress. In the visual arts, this meant rejecting classicism and historicism and seeking inspiration in the forms and ideas of the present. While diverse styles were associated with modernism in architecture

from the late nineteenth century onward, the International Style was dominant after the 1920s.

modillion One of a series of small, thin scroll brackets under the projecting crown molding of a classical cornice. It is found in the Corinthian and Composite orders. Distinguished from a console, which usually is larger and has a height greater than its projection from the wall.

molding A running surface composed of parallel and continuous sections of simple or compound curves and flat areas.

monitor An extensive shed-roofed feature on a roof, containing a band of windows or vents. It may be located along one of the roof slopes (a trap-door monitor) or along the ridgeline (a clerestory monitor), and it usually runs the entire length of the roof. Distinguished from a skylight.

Moorish Revival Term applied to eclectic works or elements of those works that emulate forms in the visual arts of those parts of North Africa and Spain under Muslim domination from the seventh through the fifteenth centuries.

mortise-and-tenon joint A timber framing joint that is made by one member having its end shaped into a projecting piece (tenon) that fits exactly into a hole (mortise) in the other member. Once joined, the pieces are secured by a peg that passes through the tenon.

mullion *1* A post or similar vertical member dividing a window into two or more units, or lights, each of which may be further subdivided (by muntins) into panes. *2* A post or similar vertical member dividing a wall opening into two or more contiguous windows.

muntin One of the small vertical or horizontal members that hold panes of glass within a window or glazed door. Distinguished from a mullion, which is a heavier vertical member separating paired or grouped windows. Sometimes called a glazing bar, sash bar, or window bar.

nave *1* The entire body of a church between the entrance and the crossing. *2* The central space of a church, between the side aisles, extending from the entrance end to the crossing.

neoclassical, neoclassicism A broad movement in the visual arts that drew its inspiration from ancient Greece and Rome. It began in the mid-eighteenth century with the advent of archaeology and extended into the mid-nineteenth century. In architecture it encompasses both a strict revivalism that copied classical models and motifs as well as more inventive interpretations.

Neo-Colonial See *Colonial Revival*.

New Urbanism A late-twentieth-century approach to urban and suburban development, emphasizing increased density, pedestrian orientation, mixed usage, and buildings of varying sizes and types.

oculus A circular opening in a ceiling or at the top of a dome.

ogee arch A pointed arch formed by a pair of opposing S-shaped curves.

order The most important constituents of classical architecture, first developed as a structural-aesthetic system by the ancient Greeks and consisting of a vertical column with capital and a horizontal entablature. The Greeks developed three different types of order—the Doric, Ionic, and Corinthian—each with its own decorative system and proportions. All three were taken over and modified by the Romans, who added two orders of their own: the Tuscan, which is a simplified form of the Doric, and the Composite, which is made up of elements of both the Ionic and the Corinthian. Though the Romans used the orders as a structural system, they also applied them as surface decoration to walls supported by other means. Sometimes called classical orders.

oriel A projecting polygonal or curved window unit of one or more stories, supported on brackets or corbels. Sometimes called an oriel window. Distinguished from a bay window.

outbuilding A building subsidiary to and completely detached from another building.

Palladian, Palladianism Work influenced by Italian Renaissance architect Andrea Palladio (1508–1580), particularly by means of his treatise, *I Quattro Libri dell'Architettura* (*The Four Books of Architecture*, originally published in 1570 and disseminated throughout Europe in numerous translations and editions until the mid-eighteenth century). The most significant flourishing of Palladianism was in England, from the 1710s to the 1760s, and in the British North American colonies, from the 1740s to the 1790s.

Palladian motif A three-part composition for a door or window, in which a round-headed opening is flanked by lower flat-headed openings and separated from them by columns, pilasters, or mullions. The flanking sections, and sometimes the entire unit, may be blind (i.e., not open).

Palladian window A window subdivided as in the Palladian motif.

parapet A low wall at the edge of a roof, balcony, or terrace, sometimes formed by the upward extension of the wall below.

pargeting Elaborate stucco or plasterwork, especially an ornamental finish for exterior plaster walls, sometimes decorated with figures in low relief. Sometimes called parging or pargework.

parquet Inlaid wood flooring, usually set in simple geometric patterns.

parti A basic solution or elemental concept for the arrangement of spaces or forms prior to the development and elaboration of a design.

patch town A village of nearly identical housing units built near a mine or factory. When built by coal mining concerns it is called a coal patch.

pediment 1 In classical architecture, the low triangular gable end of the roof, framed by raking cornices along the inclined edges of the roof and by a horizontal cornice below. 2 In Renaissance and Baroque and later classically derived architecture, the triangular or curvilinear culmination of a prominent part of a facade. 3 A similar but smaller-scale feature over a door or window. It may be triangular or curvilinear.

pendentive A triangular segment of vaulting used to form the structural transition from the square plan of a crossing to the circular plan of a dome.

Pennsylvania barn A barn type, usually gable roofed and always banked into a hillside with a forebay on the downhill side.

pergola A structure with an open wood-framed roof, often latticed, and supported by a colonnade. It is usually covered by climbing plants, such as vines or roses, and provides shade for a garden walk or a passageway to a building.

period revival Term applied to eclectic works—particularly suburban and country houses—of the first three decades of the twentieth century, in which a particular historical or regional style is dominant.

peripteral (adjective) Surrounded by a single row of freestanding columns.

peristyle A range of columns surrounding a building or an open court.

Perpendicular Gothic See *English Gothic.*

piano nobile In Renaissance and later architecture, a floor with formal reception, living, and dining rooms. The principal and often tallest story in a building, usually one level above the ground level.

piazza *1* A plaza or square. *2* An eighteenth- and nineteenth-century term for a porch or veranda.

picturesque An aesthetic category in architecture and landscape architecture in the late eighteenth and early nineteenth centuries characterized by forms and features meant to evoke the qualities of landscape paintings. These include asymmetrical, irregular, and eclectic buildings, indirect approaches, and contrasting clusters of plantings.

pier *1* A freestanding mass, supporting a concentrated load from an arch, a beam, a truss, or a girder. While generally rectilinear in plan, piers in buildings based on medieval precedents are often curvilinear in plan. *2* An upright portion of a wall that performs a columnar function. The pier may be continuous with the plane of the wall, or it may be distinguished from the plane of the wall to give it a columnlike independence.

pier and spandrel A type of skeletal wall organization in which the vertical metal columns (and their square-cornered cladding) project in front of the plane of windows and their spandrel panels. The spandrel panels may be exposed structural spanning members. More often they provide decorative covering for the structure.

pilaster A flattened column, with or without fluting, that is attached to a wall. It is usually finished with the same capital and base as a freestanding column. Distinguished from an engaged column.

pilotis Architectural supports (columns, pillars) that lift a building above ground level

to create a tall space underneath. Typical of International Style buildings.

pinnacle In Gothic architecture, a small spire-like element providing an ornamental finish to the highest part of a buttress or roof. It has a slender pyramidal or conical form and is often articulated with crockets or ribs and is topped by a finial.

pitched roof See *gable roof.*

plank construction A system of frame construction in which exterior walls are built with two overlapping layers of vertical planks, each one extending to the roof and anchored in a groove in the foundation stones; exterior horizontal siding and interior plaster and lath are attached directly to the planks.

plate *1* In timber-frame construction, the topmost horizontal structural member of a wall, to which the roof rafters are fastened. *2* In platform and balloon-frame construction, the horizontal members to which the tops and bottoms of studs are nailed. The bottom plate is sometimes called the sill plate or sole plate.

platform frame construction A system of light frame construction in which each story is built as an independent unit and the studs are only one story high. The floor joists of each story rest on the top plates of the story below, and the bearing walls or partitions rest on the subfloor of each floor unit or platform. Platform framing is easier to construct and more rigid than balloon framing and became the common framing method in the twentieth century. Structural members are usually sawn lumber, ranging from two-by-fours to two-by-tens, and are fastened with nails.

plinth The base block of a column, pilaster, pedestal, dado, or door architrave.

polychrome, polychromy, polychromatic A many-colored treatment, especially the combination of materials in various colors or the application of surface color, to articulate wall and roof planes and to highlight structure.

popular A term applied to vernacular architecture influenced by such publications as builders' guides, style books, pattern books, mail-order catalogs, architectural periodicals, and household magazines. Popular architecture may be built according to commercially available plans or from widely distributed components; or it may be built by local practitioners (architects, builders, contractors) emulating buildings known through publications. See also the more general term *vernacular* and the related term *folk*.

porte-cochere A porch projecting over a driveway and providing shelter to people leaving a vehicle and entering a building, or vice versa. Also called a carriage porch.

portico *1* A porch at least one story in height consisting of a low-pitched roof supported on classical columns and finished in front with an entablature and pediment. *2* An extensive porch supported by a colonnade.

post A vertical supporting element, either square or circular in plan. Posts are the integral vertical members of a frame or truss, whether of wood or metal. Posts may also carry fences or gates, or may serve as free-standing markers (e.g., mileposts).

post-and-beam construction A structural system in which the main support is provided by vertical members (posts) carrying horizontal members (beams or lintels). Sometimes called post-and-girt construction, post-and-lintel construction, trabeation, or trabeated construction.

Postmodern, postmodernism A term applied to architecture that involves a reaction against the ideas and works of various twentieth-century modern movements, particularly the Bauhaus and the International Style. Beginning in the 1960s and flourishing in the 1980s, postmodern architecture uses historicist and populist elements, but these are often merely applied to buildings that, in every other respect, are products of modernism.

Prairie School, Prairie Style A diverse group of architects working in Chicago and the Midwest from the 1890s to the 1920s, strongly influenced by Frank Lloyd Wright and to a lesser degree by Louis Sullivan. The term is applied mainly to domestic architecture. An architect is said to belong to the Prairie School; a work of architecture is said to be in the Prairie Style.

pressed metal Thin sheets of metal (usually galvanized or tin-plated iron) stamped into patterned panels for covering ceilings and exterior and interior walls or into molding profiles and other details for assembly into exterior and interior cornices. Loosely called pressed tin or stamped metal. Prevalent from 1870s–1920s.

proscenium In a recessed stage, the area between the orchestra and the curtain.

provincial, provincialism Term applied to work in an isolated area (such as a province of a cosmopolitan center or a colony of a mother country), where traditional practices persist, with some awareness of what is being done in the cosmopolitan center or the homeland.

purlin In roof construction, a structural member laid across the principal rafters and parallel to the wall plate and the ridge beam. The light common rafters to which the roofing surface is attached are fastened across the purlins.

pylon *1* Originally, the gateway facade of an Egyptian temple complex, consisting of a truncated broad pyramidal form with battered (inclined) wall surfaces on all four sides, or two truncated pyramidal towers flanking an entrance portal. *2* Any tower-like structure from which bridge cables or utility lines are suspended.

quarry-faced See *rock-faced*.

Queen Anne Generally refers to an eclectic architectural style of the 1860s through 1910s in England and the United States that revived forms of postmedieval vernacular architecture and the architecture of the Georgian period, including those popular during the reign of Queen Anne (1702–1714). It is characterized by asymmetry in plan, complex roof forms, projecting bays and oriels, the use of red brick, and classical motifs such as broken pediments and pilasters.

quoin One of the bricks or stones laid in alternating directions, which bond and form the exterior corner of a building. Sometimes simulated in wood or stucco.

raking cornice A cornice that finishes the sloping edges of a gable roof, such as the inclined sides of a triangular pediment.

random ashlar A type of masonry in which squared and dressed blocks are laid in a random pattern rather than in straight horizontal courses.

recessed column A fully round column set into a nichelike space only slightly larger than the column. Distinguished from an engaged column, which appears to be built into the wall.

regionalism 1 The sum of cultural characteristics (including material culture, language) that defines a geographic region, usually extending beyond a single state or province and coinciding with larger physiographic areas. 2 The conscious use, within a region, of forms and materials identified with that region, creating an architecture that is in keeping with the historical architecture of the region, and even a distinctive new regional style.

Renaissance The period in European civilization identified with a rediscovery or rebirth (*rinascimento*) of classical Roman learning, art, and architecture. Renaissance architecture began in Italy in the mid-fifteenth century (Early Renaissance) and reached a peak in the early to mid-sixteenth century (High Renaissance). In England and France, Renaissance architecture did not begin until the late sixteenth or early seventeenth centuries. The Renaissance in art and architecture was preceded by the Gothic and followed by the Baroque.

Renaissance Revival A term that refers to either Italianate architecture of the 1840s through 1880s or to Beaux-Arts architecture of the 1880s through 1920s. In the decorative arts, it refers to an eclectic furniture style incorporating Renaissance, Baroque, and Néo-Grec architectural motifs and utilizing wood marquetry, incised lines (often gilded), and ormolu and porcelain ornaments.

reredos A screen or wall at the back of an altar, usually with architectural and figural decoration.

return The continuation of a molding, cornice, or other projecting member, in a different direction, as in the horizontal cornice returns at the base of the raking cornices of a triangular pediment.

reveal 1 The portion of wall thickness between a door or window frame and the outer face of the wall. 2 Same as jamb, but only in an opening without a door or window.

revival, revivalism A type of historicism prevalent since the eighteenth century, involving the adaptation of historical forms to contemporary functions. Distinguished from a more pervasive historicism by an ideological conviction that rationalized the choice of a historical style according to the values of the historical period that produced it. Revival works tend to invoke a single historical style. More hybrid works are manifestations of a less dogmatic historicism or eclecticism. See also the more general terms *eclectic, eclecticism* and *historicism, historicist, historicizing*.

rib The projecting linear element that separates the curved planar cells (or webs) of vaulting. Originally these were the supporting members for the vaulting, but they may also be purely decorative.

Richardsonian Romanesque, Richardson Romanesque A style of architecture of the late nineteenth century that shows the influence of Henry Hobson Richardson (1838–1886). It is characterized by the eclectic use of round arches, rustication, and Romanesque details and frequently features prominent masonry and asymmetrical compositions. The style was especially popular for public buildings such as courthouses and libraries.

ridgepole The horizontal beam or board at the apex of a roof, to which the upper ends of the rafters are fastened. Sometimes called a ridge beam, ridgeboard, or ridge piece.

rock-faced Term applied to the rough, unfinished face of a stone used in building. Sometimes called quarry-faced.

Rococo A late phase of the Baroque, marked by elegant reverse-curve ornament, light scale, and delicate color. See also the related term *Baroque*.

Romanesque A medieval architectural style that reached its height in the eleventh and twelfth centuries. It is characterized by round-arched construction and massive masonry walls. The Romanesque was preceded by the Early Christian and Byzantine periods in the eastern Mediterranean world and by a variety of localized styles and periods in northern and western Europe; it was followed throughout Europe by the Gothic.

Romanesque Revival A term that refers to the round-arched architecture that appeared in the United States as early as the 1840s and was based loosely on medieval European architecture of the eleventh and twelfth centuries. It is characterized by massive masonry, spare ornamentation, repeated arches, and the use of barrel and groin vaults. It was used frequently for commercial and industrial buildings where it was rendered in brick.

rood screen An ornamental screen that serves as a partition between the crossing and the chancel or choir of a church.

roundel A circular panel or plaque. Distinguished from a patera, which is oval shaped.

running bond A pattern of brickwork in which only stretchers appear, with the vertical joints of one course falling halfway between the vertical joints of adjacent courses. Sometimes called stretcher bond. Distinguished from common bond.

Ruskinian Gothic See *High Victorian Gothic*.

rustication, rusticated Masonry in which the face of each stone is roughly textured and the joints are emphasized by narrow recessed channels or grooves outlining each block. Sometimes simulated in wood or stucco.

saltbox roof A gable roof in which one slope is much longer than the other.

sanctuary 1 The part of a church that contains the principal altar. Usually the innermost space within the chancel arm of the church, situated to the east of the choir. 2 Loosely used to mean a place of worship, a sacred place.

sash Any framework of a window. It may be movable or fixed. It may slide in a vertical plane (as in a double-hung window) or may be pivoted (as in a casement window).

sash bar See *muntin*.

scabble and drafted A decorative method of inscribing building stones with etched lines at the edges and pitting in the middle.

Second Empire Not strictly a style but a term for a period in French history coinciding with the rule of Napoleon III (1852–1870). Derived from Visconti and Lefuel's New Louvre in Paris, the Second Empire style is characterized by mansard roofs, pedimented dormers, classical columns, and French Renaissance decorative motifs. Popular in the United States from the 1850s through the 1880s, especially for governmental and institutional architecture.

setback 1 In architecture, particularly in the design of tall buildings, a series of upper stories that are stepped back to allow more sunlight to reach the streets. 2 In planning, the amount of space between the lot line and the perimeter of a building.

shaft The tall part of a column between the base and the capital.

shed roof A roof having only one sloping plane. Sometimes called a lean-to roof.

Shingle Style A term applied to American domestic architecture of the 1870s through the 1890s, in which wood shingles dominate the roof and exterior wall planes. An ample living hall or stair hall is often a dominant feature. The term was coined in the 1940s by architectural historian Vincent Scully for a series of seaside and suburban houses of the northeastern United States. The Shingle Style is a version of the Queen Anne style and was used in the early work of Henry Hobson Richardson and McKim, Mead and White.

side gabled Term applied to a building whose gable ends face the sides of a lot. Distinguished from front gabled.

sidelight A framed area of fixed glass alongside a door or window. See also the related term *fanlight*.

sill course In masonry, a stringcourse set at windowsill level, usually differentiated from the wall by its greater projection, its finish, or its thickness. Not applicable to frame construction.

skeleton construction, skeleton frame A system of construction in which all loads are carried to the ground through a rigid framework of iron, steel, or reinforced concrete. The exterior walls are curtain walls (i.e., not load-bearing).

space frame A series of trusses placed side by side and joined to one another by triangulated rods, tubes, or beams, so that the individual planar trusses are united into a three-dimensional structural framework. Often used in roof structures requiring long spans.

spandrel 1 The quasi-triangular space between two adjoining arches and a line connecting their crowns, or between an arch and the columns and entablature that frame it. 2 In skeletal construction, the wall area between the top of a window and the sill of the window in the story above. Sometimes called a spandrel panel.

Spanish Colonial Revival The revival of forms from Spanish colonial and provincial Mexican design. The Spanish Colonial Revival began in Florida and California in the 1880s and continues nationwide into the present.

Spanish Mission A style making use of forms and materials from the Spanish and Mexican mission architecture of the eighteenth and early nineteenth centuries. Not to be confused with Mission furniture of the Arts and Crafts movement. See the related term *Mission Revival*.

springing, springing line, springing point The line or point where an arch or vault rises from its supports and begins to curve. Usually the juncture between the impost of the support below and the springer, or first voussoir, of the arch above.

standing-seam roof A metal roof with seams raised above the otherwise flat surface. Used often on barns and in rural areas on houses.

stepped gable A gable in which the wall rises in a series of steps above the planes of the roof.

Stick Style A term applied primarily to American domestic architecture of the 1850s through the 1870s, in which exterior wall planes are subdivided into bays and stories outlined by narrow boards called stickwork. The term was coined by historian Vincent Scully in the 1940s for a series of houses with clearly articulated wall panels and sticklike porch supports and eaves brackets. Sources include the English and German picturesque traditions and the French rationalist tradition.

story (plural: **stories**) The space in a building between floor levels. British spelling is storey, storeys. Sometimes called a register, a more inclusive term applied to horizontal zones on a vertical plane that do not correspond to actual floor levels.

stretcher A brick laid the length of a wall, so that the long side of the brick shows on the exterior.

stretcher bond See *running bond*.

string In a stair, an inclined board that supports the ends of the steps. Sometimes called a stringer.

stringcourse In masonry, a horizontal band, generally narrower than other courses, extending across the facade of a building and in some instances encircling such features as pillars or columns. It may be flush or projecting; of identical or contrasting material; flat, molded, or richly carved. Not applicable to frame construction. Sometimes called a band course or belt course. More elaborate horizontal bands in masonry or frame construction are generally called band moldings.

strut A column, post, or pole that is set in a diagonal position and thus serves as a stiffener by triangulation. Distinguished from a brace, which is usually a shorter bracketlike member.

stucco *1* An exterior plaster finish, usually textured, composed of Portland cement, lime, and sand, which are mixed with water. *2* A fine plaster used for decorative work or moldings.

stud One of the vertical supporting elements in a wall, especially in balloon- and platform frame construction. Studs are relatively lightweight members (usually two-by-fours).

Sullivanesque Term applied to work, particularly ornamental, showing the influence of American architect Louis Henry Sullivan (1856–1924).

superstructure A structure raised upon another structure, as a building upon a foundation, basement, or substructure.

surround An encircling border or decorative frame around a door or window. Distinguished from architrave (definition 2), a term usually applied to the frame around an opening when considered as a series of relatively flat face moldings.

suspended ceiling A ceiling suspended from rodlike hangers below the level of the floor above. The interval between the floor slab above and the suspended ceiling often serves as a space for ducts, utilities, and air circulation. Sometimes called a hung ceiling.

swag An ornamental motif representing a suspended fold of drapery hanging in a catenary curve from two points. Distinguished from a festoon.

tabernacle *1* A niche or recess, usually on an interior wall, framed by columns or pilasters and topped by an entablature and pediment. Distinguished from an aedicule, which more often occurs on an exterior wall. 2 In the Jewish religion, a portable sanctuary. 3 In Protestant denominations, a large auditorium church.

terra-cotta 1 A hard ceramic material used for fireproofing, especially as a fitted cladding around metal skeletal construction. 2 An exterior or interior wall cladding, which is often glazed and multicolored.

tie rod A metal rod that spans the distance between two structural members and, by its tensile strength, restrains them against tendencies to collapse outward.

timber-frame construction, timber framing A type of wood-frame construction in which heavy timber posts and beams (six-by-sixes and larger) are fastened using mortise-and-tenon joints. Sometimes called heavy timber construction. Distinguished from light frame construction, in which relatively light structural members (two-by-fours to two-by-tens) are fastened with nails.

tracery Decoration within an arch or other opening, made up of narrow curvilinear bands or more elaborately molded strips. In Gothic architecture, the curved interlocking stone bars that contain the leaded stained glass.

transept The lateral arm of a cross-shaped church, usually between the nave (the area for the congregation) and the chancel (the area for the altar, clergy, and choir).

transom 1 A narrow horizontal window unit, either fixed or movable, over a door. Sometimes called a transom light. See also the more specific term *fanlight*. 2 A horizontal bar, as distinguished from a vertical mullion, especially one crossing a door or window opening near the top.

transverse rib In a Gothic vault, a rib at right angles to the ridge rib.

triglyph One of the slightly raised blocks in a Doric frieze. It consists of three narrow vertical bands separated by two V-shaped grooves.

triumphal arch 1 A freestanding arch erected for a victory procession. It usually consists of a broad central arched opening, flanked by two smaller bays (usually with open or blind arches). The bays are usually articulated by classical columns supporting an entablature and a high attic. 2 A similar configuration applied to a facade to denote a monumental entrance.

trompe l'oeil Literally a deception or trick of the eye, it is usually two-dimensional painting showing objects that look real, often used to suggest architectural elements.

truss A rigid triangular framework made up of beams, posts, braces, struts, and ties and used for the spanning of large spaces. The major horizontal or inclined members are called chords. The connecting vertical and diagonal elements are called the web members.

Tudor Revival Early-twentieth-century style emulating forms in the visual arts of the Tudor period (1485–1603) in English history. Especially popular in houses, it is characterized by steeply pitched gabled roofs and decorative half timbering.

Tuscan order An ensemble of classical column and entablature elements, similar to the Roman Doric order, but without triglyphs in the frieze and without mutules (dominolike blocks) in the cornice of the entablature. See also the more general term *order*.

tympanum (plural: **tympana**) 1 The triangular or segmental area enclosed by the cornice moldings of a pediment, frequently ornamented with sculpture. 2 Any space similarly delineated or bounded, as between the lintel of a door or window and the arch above.

urban renewal Refers to efforts in the 1950s and 1960s to combat the decline of American cities caused by suburban expansion after World War II. Underwritten by the federal government and sponsored by local municipalities, it involved the razing of dense, old commercial and residential districts and building new highways, public housing, and cultural and government centers. By the 1970s, urban renewal was widely considered a failure.

Usonian house Dwelling type developed by Frank Lloyd Wright in 1936; a small, relatively inexpensive house designed on a rational, modular plan and featuring a radiant heating system embedded in the concrete floor slab.

vault An arched roof or ceiling, usually constructed in brick or stone, but also in tile, metal, or concrete. A nonstructural plaster ceiling that simulates a masonry vault.

vergeboard See *bargeboard*.

verges The sloping edges of a gable, gambrel,

or lean-to roof, usually projecting beyond the wall below. Distinguished from eaves, which are the horizontal lower edges of a roof plane.

vernacular Not a style in itself, but a descriptive term covering the vast range of ordinary buildings that are produced outside the high styles of academies and' well-known architects. The vernacular includes the folk tradition of regional and ethnic buildings whose forms remain relatively constant through the years. It also includes the popular tradition of buildings whose design was influenced by popular publications. Usually contrasted with high-style architecture. See also the more specific terms *folk* and *popular.*

vertical plank construction A system of wood construction in which vertical planks are set or nailed into heavy timber horizontal sills and plates. A building so constructed has no corner posts and no studs. Two-story vertical plank buildings have planks extending the full height of the building, with no girt between the two stories. Second-floor joists are merely mortised into the planks. Distinguished from the more specific term vertical plank frame construction, in which there are corner posts.

vertical plank frame construction A type of vertical plank construction, in which heavy timber corner posts are introduced to provide support for the plate, to which the tops of the planks are fastened. See also the related term *horizontal plank frame construction.*

Victorian period A term for a period in British, British colonial, and Anglo-American history, from the coronation of Queen Victoria in 1837 to her death in 1901. Though not a specific style term, Victorian connotes the various forms of eclecticism that were predominant in architecture in the mid- to late nineteenth century. These include Greek Revival, Gothic Revival, High Victorian Gothic, Queen Anne, and others.

villa *1* In the Roman and Renaissance periods, a suburban or rural residential complex, often quite elaborate, consisting of a house, dependencies, and gardens. *2* Since the eighteenth century, any detached suburban or rural house of picturesque character and some pretension. Distinguished from the more modest house form known as a cottage.

volute *1* A spiral scroll, especially the one that is a distinctive feature of the Ionic capital. *2* A large scroll-shaped buttress on a facade or dome.

voussoir A wedge-shaped masonry unit used in the construction of an arch. Its tapered sides coincide with the radii of the arch.

wainscot A decorative or protective facing, usually of wood paneling, applied to the lower portion of an interior partition or wall. Distinguished from a dado, which is the zone at the base of a wall, regardless of the material used to cover it. Wainscot properly connotes woodwork. Sometimes called wainscoting.

wane-edged siding Wood siding that has natural curves in its edges, sawn without trimming the outer edges of the tree. Often used in park buildings.

water table *1* In masonry, a course of molded bricks or stones set forward several inches near the base of a wall and serving as the cap of the basement courses. *2* In frame construction, a ledge or projecting molding just above the foundation to protect it from rainwater. *3* In masonry or frame construction, any horizontal exterior ledge on a wall, pier, or buttress. Often sloped and provided with a drip molding to prevent water from running down the face of the wall below.

weathering *1* The inclination given to the upper surface of any element so that it will shed water. *2* The effects upon architectural materials of weather.

window head A head molding or pedimented feature over a window.

Works Progress Administration (WPA) A federal program (1935–1943) created to provide jobs during the Great Depression. Many of the jobs involved constructing public buildings and roads.

Wrightian Term applied to work showing the influence of American architect Frank Lloyd Wright (1867–1959). See also the related terms *Prairie School, Prairie Style.*

wrought iron Iron shaped by a hammering process to improve the tensile properties of the metal. Distinguished from cast iron, a brittle material, which is formed in molds.

BIBLIOGRAPHY

Among important but unpublished sources are the Allegheny County Survey at the Pittsburgh History and Landmarks Foundation; drawings and documentation at the Heinz Architectural Center of the Carnegie Museum of Art and at Carnegie Mellon University's Architectural Archives in Pittsburgh; the ephemera (clippings, atlases, photographs) at the Pennsylvania Room of the Carnegie Library and at the Senator John Heinz History Center archive in Pittsburgh; and the various county historical societies. National Register nominations (online) provided by the Pennsylvania Historical and Museum Commission are another invaluable resource.

Alberts, Robert C. *The Shaping of the Point: Pittsburgh's Renaissance Park.* Pittsburgh: University of Pittsburgh Press, 1981.

Aurand, Martin. *Pittsburgh Architecture: A Guide to Research.* Pittsburgh: Carnegie Mellon University Architecture Archives, Carnegie Mellon University Libraries, 1991.

———. *The Progressive Architecture of Frederick G. Scheibler Jr.* Pittsburgh: University of Pittsburgh Press, 1994.

———. *The Spectator and the Topographical City.* Pittsburgh: University of Pittsburgh Press, 2006.

Baldwin, Leland. *Pittsburgh: The Story of a City.* Pittsburgh: University of Pittsburgh Press, 1970.

Barnett, Jonathan. "Designing Downtown Pittsburgh." *Architectural Record* 170, no. 1 (January 1982): 90–107.

Bauman, John F., and Edward K. Muller. *Before Renaissance: Planning in Pittsburgh, 1889–1943.* Pittsburgh: University of Pittsburgh Press, 2006.

Bennett, Lola M. *The Company Towns of the Rockhill Iron and Coal Company: Robertsdale and Woodvale, Pennsylvania.* Washington D.C.: Historic American Buildings Survey/ Historic American Engineering Record, National Park Service, 1990.

Black, Brian. *Petrolia: The Landscape of America's First Oil Boom.* Baltimore: Johns Hopkins University Press, 2000.

Bolden, Frank E., Larry Glasco, and Eliza Smith, eds. *A Legacy in Bricks and Mortar: African American Landmarks in Allegheny County.* Pittsburgh: Pittsburgh History and Landmarks Foundation, 1995.

Borowiec, Andrew. *Along the Ohio.* Baltimore: Johns Hopkins University Press, in association with the Center for American Places, 2000.

Brenckman, Fred. *History of the Pennsylvania State Grange.* Harrisburg: Pennsylvania State Grange, 1949.

Brown, Scott C., et al. *Bedford and Fulton Counties, Pennsylvania: An Inventory of Historic Engineering and Industrial Sites.* Washington D.C.: Historic American Buildings Survey/Historic American Engineering Record, America's Industrial Heritage Project, National Park Service, U.S. Department of the Interior, 1994.

Brown, Sharon A. *Cambria Iron Company: America's Industrial Heritage Project, Penn-*

sylvania. Washington, D.C.: National Park Service, U.S. Department of the Interior, 1989.

Bryson, Lew. *Pennsylvania Breweries*. Mechanicsburg, Penn.: Stackpole Books, 2005.

Buck, Solon J. *The Granger Movement: A Study of Agricultural Organization and Its Political, Economic, and Social Manifestations, 1870–1880*. Lincoln: University of Nebraska Press, 1963.

Buck, Solon J., and Elizabeth Hawthorn Buck. *The Planting of Civilization in Western Pennsylvania*. Pittsburgh: University of Pittsburgh Press, 1969.

Butko, Brian A. *Pennsylvania Traveler's Guide: The Lincoln Highway*. Mechanicsburg, Penn.: Stackpole Books, 1996.

Butko, Brian A., and Kevin Patrick. *Diners of Pennsylvania*. Mechanicsburg, Penn.: Stackpole Books, 1999.

Chad, Barry. *Bridging the Urban Landscape*. http://www.clpgh.org/exhibit/.

Chew, Paul A. *George Hetzel and the Scalp Level Tradition*. Greensburg, Penn.: Westmoreland Museum of Art, 1994.

Clouse, Jerry A. *A Study of Agricultural/Vernacular Architecture of Central and Southwestern Pennsylvania: With a Particular Emphasis on the Barns of These Regions*. Harrisburg: Pennsylvania Historical and Museum Commission, 1995.

———. *The Whiskey Rebellion: Southwestern Pennsylvania's Frontier People Test the American Constitution*. Harrisburg: Pennsylvania Historical and Museum Commission, 1994.

Couvares, Francis G. *The Remaking of Pittsburgh: Class and Culture in an Industrializing City, 1877–1919*. Albany: State University of New York Press, 1984.

Craig, Robert S. *A History of Brookville, Pennsylvania, 1888–1974*. Brookville, Penn.: McMurray Co., 1975.

Cuff, David J., et al. *The Atlas of Pennsylvania*. Philadelphia: Temple University Press, 1989.

Cupper, Dan. *Crossroads of Commerce: The Pennsylvania Railroad Calendar Art of Grif Teller*. Mechanicsburg, Penn.: Stackpole Books, 2003.

Czarnecki, Greg, and Karen Czarnecki. *Longstreet Highroad Guide to the Pennsylvania Mountains*. Athens, Ga.: Longstreet Press, 1999.

Demarest, David, and Eugene Levy. "A Relict Industrial Landcsape: Pittsburgh's Coke Region." *Landscape* 29, no. 2 (1986): 29–36.

———. "Remnants of an Industrial Landscape." *Pittsburgh History* 72 (1989): 128–39.

———. "Touring the Coke Region." *Pittsburgh History* 74 (1991): 100–113.

Dennis, Neal. *Historic Houses of the Sewickley Valley*. Sewickley, Penn.: White Oak Publishing, 1996.

DiCiccio, Carmen. *Coal and Coke in Pennsylvania*. Harrisburg: Pennsylvania Historical and Museum Commission, 1996.

Dickson, Harold E. *A Hundred Pennsylvania Buildings*. State College, Penn.: Bald Eagle Press, 1954.

Donnelly, Lu. "Architecture Around Us." [Quarterly Column.] *Western Pennsylvania History* (2001–present).

Egle, William H. *An Illustrated History of the Commonwealth of Pennsylvania, Civil, Political, and Military: From Its Earliest Settlement to the Present Time*. Philadelphia: E. M. Gardner, 1880.

Ensminger, Robert F. *The Pennsylvania Barn: Its Origin, Evolution, and Distribution in North America*. Baltimore: Johns Hopkins University Press, 1992.

Erie: A Guide to the City and County. [Federal Writers Project, Works Progress Administration.] Philadelphia: William Penn Association of Philadelphia, 1938.

Espenshade, Abraham Howry. *Pennsylvania Place Names*. Harrisburg, Penn.: The Evangelical Press, 1925.

Evans, Benjamin D., and June R. Evans. *Pennsylvania's Covered Bridges: A Complete Guide*. Pittsburgh: University of Pittsburgh Press, 1993.

Fifield, Barringer, and Michael Eastman. *Seeing Pittsburgh*. Pittsburgh: University of Pittsburgh Press, 1996.

Fletcher, Stevenson Whitcomb. *Pennsylvania Agriculture and Country Life*. Vol. 1, *1640–1840*. Vol. 2, *1840–1940*. Harrisburg: Pennsylvania Historical and Museum Commission, 1971.

Floyd, Margaret Henderson. *Architecture after Richardson: Regionalism before Modernism—Longfellow, Alden, and Harlow in*

Boston and Pittsburgh. Chicago: University of Chicago Press, in association with the Pittsburgh History and Landmarks Foundation, 1994.

Gay, Vernon, and Marilyn Evert. *Discovering Pittsburgh's Sculpture*. Pittsburgh: University of Pittsburgh Press, 1983.

Greenwald, Maurine W., and Margo Anderson, eds. *Pittsburgh Surveyed: Social Science and Social Reform in the Early Twentieth Century*. Pittsburgh: University of Pittsburgh Press, 1996.

Guidebook to Historic Places in Western Pennsylvania. Pittsburgh: University of Pittsburgh Press, 1938.

Hagan, Bernardine. *Kentuck Knob: Frank Lloyd Wright's House for I. N. and Bernardine Hagan*. Pittsburgh: The Local History Company, 2005.

Hannegan, Susan Bossert, and Jean Simmons May, eds. *Clinton County: A Journey Through Time*. Lock Haven, Penn.: Clinton County Sesquicentennial, 1989.

Harper, R. Eugene. *The Transformation of Western Pennsylvania, 1770–1800*. Pittsburgh: University of Pittsburgh Press, 1992.

Harpster, John W., ed. *Crossroads: Descriptions of Western Pennsylvania, 1720–1829*. Pittsburgh: University of Pittsburgh Press, 1986.

Hays, Samuel P., ed. *City at the Point: Essays on the Social History of Pittsburgh*. Pittsburgh: University of Pittsburgh Press, 1989.

Hoagland, Alison K., and Margaret M. Mulrooney. *Norvelt and Penn-Craft, Pennsylvania: Subsistence-Homestead Communities of the 1930s*. Washington D.C.: Historic American Buildings Survey/Historic American Engineering Record, National Park Service, U.S. Department of the Interior, 1991.

Jamison, Mary Temple. "Pittsburgh's Woman Architect." [Elise Mercur.] *The Home Monthly* (April 1898): 5.

Jefferson County, Pennsylvania History. Brookville, Penn.: Jefferson County Historical Society, 1982.

Kidney, Walter C. *Henry Hornbostel: An Architect's Master Touch*. Pittsburgh: Pittsburgh History and Landmarks Foundation, in association with Robert Rinehart Publishers, 2002.

———. *Landmark Architecture: Pittsburgh and Allegheny County*. Pittsburgh: Pittsburgh History and Landmarks Foundation, 1985.

———. *Pittsburgh's Landmark Architecture: The Historic Buildings of Pittsburgh and Allegheny County*. 2nd ed. Pittsburgh: Pittsburgh History and Landmarks Foundation, 2001.

Klein, Philip Shriver, and Ari Hoogenboom. *A History of Pennsylvania*. University Park: Pennsylvania State University Press, 1980.

Koegler, Karen. "Building in Stone in Southwestern Pennsylvania: Patterns and Process." In *Perspectives in Vernacular Architecture, V: Gender, Class, and Shelter*. Edited by Elizabeth Collins Cromley and Carter L. Hudgins. Knoxville: University of Tennessee Press, 1995.

Lewis, Michael J., and Marianna Thomas Architects for the Clio Group. *Historic Structures Report*. Ambridge, Penn.: Old Economy Village Archives, 1990.

Lewis, Peirce F. "Small Towns in Pennsylvania." *Annals of the Association of American Geographers* 62 (1962): 323–51.

Lubove, Roy. *Twentieth Century Pittsburgh*. 2 vols. Pittsburgh: University of Pittsburgh Press, 1996.

———. *Twentieth Century Pittsburgh: Government, Business, and Environmental Change*. New York: Wiley, 1969.

Magocsi, Paul Robert. *Our People, Carpatho-Rusyns and Their Descendants in North America*. 3rd rev. ed. Toronto: Multicultural History Society of Ontario, 1994.

Martin, Jere. *Pennsylvania Almanac*. Mechanicsburg, Penn.: Stackpole Books, 1997.

McMurry, Sally Ann. *Families and Farm Houses in Nineteenth-Century America: Vernacular Design and Social Change*. New York: Oxford University Press, 1988.

———. *From Sugar Camps to Star Barns: Rural Life and Landscape in a Western Pennsylvania Community*. University Park: Pennsylvania State University Press, 2001.

Michener, Carolee K. *Franklin: A Place in History*. Franklin, Penn.: Franklin Bicentennial Committee, 1995.

Michener, Carolee K., et al. *Venango County 2000: The Changing Scene*. Vol. 1. Franklin, Penn.: The Venango County Historical Society, 2000.

Miller, Donald. *The Architecture of Benno Jans-*

sen. Pittsburgh: Carnegie Mellon University, 1997.

Miller, Donald, and Aaron Sheon. *Organic Vision: The Architecture of Peter Berndtson.* Pittsburgh: Hexagon Press, 1980.

Miller, E. Willard, ed. *A Geography of Pennsylvania.* State College: Pennsylvania State University Press, 1995.

Miller, Randall M., and William A. Pencak, eds. *Pennsylvania: A History of the Commonwealth.* University Park: Pennsylvania State University Press, copublished with the Pennsylvania Historical and Museum Commission, 2002.

Mosher, Anne E. *Capital's Utopia: Vandergrift, Pennsylvania, 1855–1916.* Baltimore: Johns Hopkins University Press, 2004.

Mulkearn, Lois, and Edwin V. Pugh. *A Traveler's Guide to Historic Western Pennsylvania.* Pittsburgh: University of Pittsburgh Press, 1954.

Muller, Edward K. *Westmoreland County, Pennsylvania: An Inventory of Historic Engineering and Industrial Sites.* Washington D.C.: Historic American Buildings Survey/Historic American Engineering Record, America's Industrial Heritage Project, National Park Service, U.S. Department of the Interior, 1994.

Mulrooney, Margaret M. *A Legacy of Coal: The Coal Company Towns of Southwestern Pennsylvania.* Washington D.C.: Historic American Buildings Survey/Historic American Engineering Record, National Park Service, 1989.

Murphy, Raymond E., and Marion M. *Pennsylvania: A Regional Geography.* Harrisburg, Penn.: Telegraph Press, 1937.

Ohio Architect and Builder. Vols. 1–33 (January 1903–1919); after 1910 known as *Ohio Architect, Engineer, and Builder;* in 1919 known as *Ohio Architect Engineer and Builder* and associated with *Inland Architect.*

Paige, John C. *Pennsylvania Railroad Shops and Works, Altoona, Pennsylvania.* Denver: America's Industrial Heritage Project, U.S. Department of the Interior, National Park Service, 1989.

Pennsylvania: A Guide to the Keystone State. Compiled by the Writers' Program of the Work Projects Administration. New York: Oxford University Press, 1940.

Perlman, Robert. *From Shtetl to Milltown: Litvaks, Hungarians, and Galizianers in Western Pennsylvania, 1875–1925.* Pittsburgh: Historical Society of Western Pennsylvania, 2001.

Perloff, Susan. *Pennsylvania: Off the Beaten Path.* 5th ed. Guilford, Conn.: Globe Pequot Press, 2000.

A Photographic Survey of Westmoreland County Architecture, Phase I. Greensburg, Penn.: Westmoreland County Museum of Art, 1979.

Pillsbury, Richard, "The Pennsylvania Culture Region: A Reappraisal." *North American Culture* 3, no. 2 (1987): 37–54.

Preserving Our Past: Landmark Architecture of Washington County, Pennsylvania. Washington, Penn.: Washington County History and Landmarks Foundation, 1975.

Quin, Richard H. *Indiana County, Pennsylvania: An Inventory of Historic Engineering and Industrial Sites.* Washington, D.C.: National Park Service, U.S. Department of the Interior, 1993.

Raitz, Karl B., ed. *A Guide to the National Road.* Baltimore: Johns Hopkins University Press, 1996.

Regan, Bob, and Tim Fabian. *The Bridges of Pittsburgh.* Pittsburgh: The Local History Company, 2006.

Rivers of Steel National Heritage Area. Routes to Roots: A Driving Guide. Pittsburgh: Steel Industry Heritage Corporation, 2004.

Roberts, Charles S. *Triumph I, Altoona to Pitcairn, 1846–1996.* [PRR structures.] Baltimore: Barnard, Roberts, and Co., 1997.

Rupp, I. D. *Early History of Western Pennsylvania, and of the West.* Lewisburg, Penn.: Wennawoods Publishing, 1995.

Russ, William A., Jr. *How Pennsylvania Aquired Its Boundaries.* University Park: Pennsylvania State University Press, 1966.

Schneck, Marcus. *Country Towns of Pennsylvania.* Castine, Maine: Country Roads Press, 1994.

Seitz, Ruth Hoover. *Pennsylvania's Historic Places.* New York: Good Books, 1989.

Shedd, Nancy S. *Huntingdon County, Pennsylvania: An Inventory of Historic Engineering and Industrial Sites.* Washington D.C.: Historic American Buildings Survey/Historic American Engineering Record, National Park Service, U.S. Department of the Interior, 1991.

———. *Two Centuries in Huntingdon.* Huntingdon, Penn.: Huntingdon County Historical Society, 1996.

Shedd, Nancy S., and Jean P. Harshbarger. *1887–1987, Second Century: A Huntingdon County Bicentennial Album.* Huntingdon, Penn.: Huntingdon County Historical Society, 1987.

Sheppard, Muriel Earley. *Cloud by Day: A Story of Coal and Coke and People.* Pittsburgh: University of Pittsburgh Press, 1991.

Slaughter, Howard B., Jr. "Integrating Economic Development and Historic Preservation in Pittsburgh, Pennsylvania." *Historic Preservation Forum* 11, no. 3 (Spring 1997): 41–44.

Smith, Helene, and George Swetnam. *A Guidebook to Historic Western Pennsylvania.* 2nd ed. Pittsburgh: University of Pittsburgh Press, 1991.

Smith, Robert Walter. *History of Armstrong County, Pennsylvania.* Plymouth, Penn.: Unigraphic Color Corporation, 1975.

Smylie, James. *Scotch-Irish Presence in Pennsylvania.* University Park: Pennsylvania Historical Association, 1990.

Staff of the *Butler Eagle* Newspaper. *Butler County, Pennsylvania, Celebrates Its Bicentennial.* Pittsburgh: The Local History Company, 2001.

Stevenson, Clarence D. *Indiana County History, 175th Anniversary History.* Indiana, Penn.: A. G. Halldin Publishing Co., 1989.

Stotz, Charles Morse. *The Early Architecture of Western Pennsylvania.* Pittsburgh: University of Pittsburgh Press, 1995.

———. *Outposts of the War for Empire: The French and English in Western Pennsylvania, Their Arms, Their Forts, Their People, 1749–1764.* Pittsburgh: University of Pittsburgh Press, 1985.

Tannler, Albert M. "Architecture with a Dash of Paprika: Titus de Bobula in Pittsburgh." *Pittsburgh Tribune-Review, Focus* 28, no. 11 (January 19, 2003): 8–11.

———. *Charles J. Connick: His Education and His Windows in and near Pittsburgh.* Pittsburgh: Pittsburgh History and Landmarks Foundation, 2008.

———. *A List of Pittsburgh and Allegheny County Buildings and Architects, 1950–2005.* Pittsburgh: Pittsburgh History and Landmarks Foundation, 2005.

———. "Louis Arnett Stuart Bellinger (1891–1946)." In *African American Architects: A Biographical Dictionary, 1865–1945.* Edited by Dreck Spurlock Wilson. New York: Routledge, 2004.

———. "Quentin S. Beck: A Man Ahead of His Time." *Pittsburgh Tribune-Review, Focus* 21, no. 48 (October 5, 1997): 6–7.

———. "Renaissance Man: Grosvenor Atterbury." *Pittsburgh Tribune-Review, Focus* 29, no. 23 (April 11, 2004): 8–11.

———. "Richard Kiehnel: Architect of International Modernism and Tropical Splendor." *Pittsburgh Tribune-Review, Focus* 21, no. 30 (June 9, 1996): 6–7.

———. "Samuel Thornburg McClarren: A Player of Architectural Themes and Variations." *Pittsburgh Tribune-Review, Focus* 22, no. 12 (January 25, 1998): 8–9.

———. "Swan Acres: First Modern Subdivision." *Pittsburgh Tribune-Review, Focus* 21, no. 30 (June 1, 1997): 8–9.

———. "Temple of the Skies: Observatory Hill Renaissance of Art and Science." *Pittsburgh Tribune-Review, Focus* 30, no. 15 (February 13, 2005): 8–10.

Tarr, Joel, ed. *Devastation and Renewal: An Environmental History of Pittsburgh and Its Region.* Pittsburgh: University of Pittsburgh Press, 2005.

Teaford, Jon C. *The Rough Road to the Renaissance: Urban Revitalization in America, 1940–1985.* Baltimore: Johns Hopkins University Press, in association with the Center for American Places, 1990.

This Is Penn State: An Insider's Guide to the University Park Campus. University Park: Pennsylvania State University Press, 2006.

Toker, Franklin K. *Buildings of Pittsburgh.* Chicago: Society of Architectural Historians, in association with the Center for American Places, 2007.

———. *Fallingwater Rising: Frank Lloyd Wright, E. J. Kaufmann and America's Most Extraordinary House.* New York: Knopf, 2003.

———. "In the Grand Manner: The P&LE Station in Pittsburgh." *Carnegie Magazine* 53, no. 3 (March 1979): 4–21.

———. *Pittsburgh: An Urban Portrait.* Pittsburgh: University of Pittsburgh Press, 1994.

———. "Richardson *en concours*: The Pittsburgh Courthouse." *Carnegie Magazine* 51, no. 9 (November 1977): 13–29.

Treese, Lorett. *Railroads of Pennsylvania: Frag-*

ments of the Past in the Keystone Landscape. Mechanicsburg, Penn.: Stackpole Books, 2003.

U.S. Department of the Interior. *Blair County and Cambria County, Pennsylvania: An Inventory of Historic Engineering and Industrial Sites.* Edited by Gray Fitzsimons. Washington D.C.: Historic American Buildings Survey/Historic American Engineering Record, America's Industrial Heritage Project, National Park Service, U.S. Department of the Interior, 1990.

———. *The Character of a Steel Mill City: Four Historic Neighborhoods of Johnstown, Pennsylvania.* Edited by Kim E. Wallace. Washington D.C.: Historic American Buildings Survey/Historic American Engineering Record, National Park Service, U.S. Department of the Interior, 1989.

———. *Coal and Coke Resource Analysis: Western Pennsylvania and Northern West Virginia.* By David Kreger, et al. Denver: U.S. Department of the Interior, National Park Service, Denver Service Center, 1992.

———. *The Evolution of Transportation in Western Pennsylvania.* Denver: U.S. Department of the Interior, National Park Service, Denver Service Center, 1994.

———. *Fayette County, Pennsylvania: An Inventory of Historic Engineering and Industrial Sites.* Edited by Sarah H. Heald. Washington D.C.: Historic American Buildings Survey/Historic American Engineering Record, America's Industrial Heritage Project, National Park Service, U.S. Department of the Interior, 1990.

———. *Railroad City: Four Historic Neighborhoods in Altoona, Pennsylvania.* By Kim E. Wallace. Washington D.C.: Historic American Buildings Survey/Historic American Engineering Record, National Park Service, U.S. Department of the Interior, 1990.

———. *Somerset County, Pennsylvania: An Inventory of Historic Engineering and Industrial Sites.* Edited by Patricia Summers, et al. Washington D.C.: Historic American Buildings Survey/Historic American Engineering Record, America's Industrial Heritage Project, U.S. Department of the Interior, 1994.

———. *Two Historic Pennsylvania Canal Towns: Alexandria and Saltsburg.* Edited by Sara A. Leach. Washington D.C.: Historic American Buildings Survey/Historic American Engineering Record, National Park Service, 1989.

Van Slyck, Abigail A. *Free to All: Carnegie Libraries and American Culture, 1890–1920.* Chicago: University of Chicago Press, 1995.

Van Trump, James D. *Life and Architecture in Pittsburgh.* Pittsburgh: Pittsburgh History and Landmarks Foundation, 1983.

———. *Majesty of the Law: The Courthouses of Allegheny County.* Pittsburgh: Pittsburgh History and Landmarks Foundation, 1988.

Van Trump, James D., and Arthur P. Ziegler Jr. *Landmark Architecture of Allegheny County, Pennsylvania.* Pittsburgh: Pittsburgh History and Landmarks Foundation, 1967.

Vinci, John. *A. James Speyer: Architect, Curator, Exhibition Designer.* Chicago: The Arts Club of Chicago, 1997.

Wagner, Dean R. *Historic Lock Haven: An Architectural Survey.* Lock Haven, Penn.: Clinton County Historical Society, 1991.

Wagner, Elise Mercur, *Economy of Old and Ambridge of Today: Historical Outlines, Embracing the Settlement and Life of Economy of Old, Together with the Vast Development in Recent Years of Ambridge and Surroundings on this Historic Spot.* Ambridge, Penn.: N.p, 1924.

Wallace, Kim E. *Brickyard Towns: A History of Refractories Industry Communities in South-Central Pennsylvania.* Washington D.C.: America's Industrial Heritage Project, National Park Service, U.S. Department of Interior, 1993.

Wallace, Paul A. W. *Indians in Pennsylvania.* Harrisburg: Pennsylvania Historical and Museum Commission, 1981.

Wilkins, David, ed. *A Reflection of Faith: St. Paul Cathedral, Pittsburgh, 1906–2006.* Pittsburgh: Saint Paul Cathedral Centennial Book Committee, 2007.

Williams, Oliver P. *County Courthouses of Pennsylvania: A Guide.* Mechanicsburg, Penn.: Stackpole Books, 2001.

ILLUSTRATION CREDITS

CMA/Little   Carnegie Museum of Art, Pittsburgh, for the exhibition Barns of Western Pennsylvania: Vernacular to Spectacular, Tom Little, photographer

HABS   Historic American Buildings Survey, Prints and Photographs Division, Library of Congress

HABS/Traub   Historic American Buildings Survey, Prints and Photographs Division, Library of Congress, Nicholas Traub, photographer

HAER   Historic American Engineering Record, Library of Congress

PHLF   Pittsburgh History and Landmarks Foundation

Photographs not otherwise credited are by Lu Donnelly.

Maps by Bill Nelson, Cartographer.

INTRODUCTION

Page 2, Bill Nelson, after E. Willard Miller, *A Geography of Pennsylvania* (Pennsylvania State University Press); page 4, Copyright, Carnegie Museum of Natural History, Section of Anthropology, Fred Crissman model-maker and Mindy McNaugher photographer; pages 5, 7, Bill Nelson, after Randall M.Miller and William Pencak, *Pennsylvania: A History of the Commonwealth* (Pennsylvania State University Press); page 9, Courtesy William R. Oliver Special Collections Room, Carnegie Library of Pittsburgh, drawn by Raymond C. Celli; page 11, Library and Archives Division, Historical Society of Western Pennsylvania, Pittsburgh, PA; page 12, Courtesy William R. Oliver Special Collections Room, Carnegie Library of Pittsburgh, drawn by Raymond C. Celli; page 15, HABS, Edward Bonfilio and Antoni deChiccis, delineators; page 16, Prints and Photographs Division, Library of Congress, LC-USZ62-69041; page 17, Courtesy PHMC, Drake Well Museum, Titusville, PA; page 21, Courtesy William R. Oliver Special Collections Room, Carnegie Library of Pittsburgh; page 28, George E. Thomas/Athenaeum of Philadelphia

THE WESTERN CAPITAL

AL1 Paul Rocheleau; AL2 HABS, Dennis Marsico, photographer; AL5 Tulane University, Curtis & Davis Papers; AL8 Matt Robinson; AL10 Copyright © Clyde Hare, 1988; AL14, AL15 HABS/Traub; AL16 HABS; AL17 USX Corporation; AL21 Mellon Financial Services, Jeff Comella, photographer; AL24 PPG Place; AL28 HABS/Traub; page 61, Archives Service Center, University of Pittsburgh, Norman Schumm, photographer; AL41 Carnegie Museums of Pittsburgh; AL43 Carnegie Mellon University Archives; AL44 Union Switch & Signal Systems and The Design Alliance, © Ed Massery, photographer; AL45 Library and Archives Division, Historical Society of Western Pennsylvania, Pittsburgh, PA; page 76, HABS, Joseph Elliott, photographer; AL51, AL53 HABS/Traub; AL55 HABS; AL56 PHLF, Glenn Lewis, photographer; AL58 HABS, Joseph Elliott, photographer; AL62, AL63 HABS/Traub; AL64 Maurice Tierney; AL68 Tom Little; AL70 Paul Rocheleau; AL75 Tom Little; AL81 HABS/Traub; page 98, HABS, David Ames, photographer; AL86, AL89 Tod Pierce, Longue View Country Club; AL90 Astorino; AL95, AL98 HABS/Traub; AL102 PHLF; AL107 Frick Art and Historical Center, © Ed Massery, photographer; AL108 Maurice Tierney; AL114 Carnegie Mellon University Architecture Archives; AL120 HABS/Traub; AL123 Duquesne University, Ken Balzer, photographer; AL126 Maurice Tierney; AL131 Copyright 2008 Ed Massery

ROLLING HILLS AND ROLLING MILLS

BE7 Archives Service Center, University of Pittsburgh; page 139, HAER, Jack E. Boucher, photographer; BE15.1 HAER, Jet Lowe, photographer; BE29 PHLF; BE33 HABS/Traub; page 156, BE44 Library and Archives Division, Historical Society of Western Pennsylvania, Pittsburgh, PA; BE46 (page 167, plan), HABS, drawn by Carlos E. Taylor Jr.; BE46 (page 168), Laura Ricketts; BU11 Copyright 2008 Ed Massery; page 181, H. David Brumble IV; AR17 CMA/Little; IN5 Clinton Piper; page 210, HABS, David Ames, photographer; page 212, WE1, WE2, WE3, WE5, WE7, WE10, WE13, WE16, WE17 Clinton Piper; WE21 PHLF; WE22, WE23 HABS, Jet Lowe, photographer; page 223, WE25, WE26, WE28, WE29 Clinton Piper; WE33 CMA/Little; page 232, WE35 Clinton Piper; page 242, HABS, Jet Lowe, photographer; FA12 HABS, Jack E. Boucher, photographer; FA23 HABS, Jet Lowe, photographer; FA27 Courtesy William R. Oliver Special Collections Room, Carnegie Library of Pittsburgh, draw by Raymond C. Celli; FA28 Courtesy of Western Pennsylvania Conservancy; FA29 HABS, Jack E. Boucher, photographer; page 259, Henry S. Wyatt; GR6 Frank Kurtik; GR16 HABS, Jet Lowe, photographer; WS1, WS11 Henry S. Wyatt; WS16 Copyright 2008 Ed Massery

RIDGE AND VALLEY
Page 301, HAER, Jet Lowe, photographer; CA7 CMA/Little; CA8 HAER, Jet Lowe, photographer; page 310, HAER, Carmen P. DeCiccio, photographer; CA14 HABS, Jet Lowe, photographer; page 312, HABS; CA20 Crown American; CA25, CA26 HABS, Jet Lowe, photographer; BL6 CMA/Little; page 326, HABS, David Ames, photographer; page 334, Courtesy PHMC, Pennsylvania State Archives; BL24 Blair Seitz; CE4 Sally McMurry; CE12, CE14 HABS/Traub;

CE16 (page 349), Dagit Saylor Architects, Tom Crane, photographer; CE18, CE22 Sally McMurry; HU7 HAER, Jet Lowe, photographer; HU13 HAER, Jack E. Boucher, photographer; HU15 CMA/Little; FU8, BD4 Paula Mohr; BD8 Courtesy William R. Oliver Special Collections Room, Carnegie Library of Pittsburgh; BD9 HAER, Joseph Elliott, photographer; BD16 Clinton Piper; BD20 HABS/Traub; BD24 HAER, Jet Lowe, photographer; SO8 CMA/Little; SO13 HAER, Jet Lowe, photographer

GREAT FOREST
PO5, PO7 Pauline Parker; CN6 HABS, Rob Tucher, photographer; CN15 Pauline Parker; CL1 Carnegie Library of Pittsburgh; CF2 HABS/Traub

OIL AND WATER
ER9 Monica Murphy; ER14 Erie Insurance Group; ER16 HABS/Traub; ER17 Monica Murphy; page 500, CMA/Little; ER39 Cindy Michel; CR9 HABS/Traub; CR10 HABS, William L. Bulger, photographer; VE11 HABS/Traub; ME11, ME16, ME21 Pauline Parker; ME23 H. David Brumble IV

INDEX

Properties named for individuals or families with a given surname are indexed in the form *surname (first name)*. For buildings or structures of the following types, please see these grouped entries: apartments and condominiums; banks; barns; bridges; canals; cathedrals; cemeteries; churches; clubs; colleges, universities, preparatory school campuses; courthouses; dams; distilleries and breweries; farms; fire stations; forts and fortifications; gardens; gas stations; hospitals; hotels and inns; industrial buildings; jails and prisons; libraries; lighthouses; Masonic temples; meetinghouses; mills and mill complexes; monasteries and convents; monuments and memorials; mosques; museums; parks; police stations; post offices; railroads; railroad stations, buildings, and yards; residential developments; resorts and vacation communities; roads; school buildings; sports complexes and facilities; stores and shopping centers; synagogues; taverns; temples; theaters; tunnels; and viaducts. Page numbers in **boldface** refer to illustrations.

Old Main, California University of Pennsylvania, 26–27, 279, **292;** Old Main, Washington & Jefferson College, 27

Barronvale, Pennsylvania, 398

Barr Slope, Pennsylvania, 206

Barry, S. R., 493

Bartberger, Charles F., 27, 39, 57, 330, 440; Angel's Arms Condominiums (St. Michael's Parish Complex), 78; First Presbyterian Church (replaced), 59; St. Paul of the Cross Monastery, 96

Bartberger, Charles M.: Industrial Bank, 57–58

Bartholomew, Paul A., 216–17, 230; Troutman Department Store, Greensburg, 217; University of Pittsburgh at Greensburg's Lynch Hall (Charles McKenna Lynch House, "Starboard Light"), addition, 216–17; Westmoreland Hospital, 217; YMCA, Greensburg, 212. *See also* Bartholomew and Smith

Bartholomew and Smith: Bank Building, Latrobe, 224; Benjamin Franklin Jones Memorial Library, Aliquippa, 28, 161; University of Pittsburgh at Greensburg's Lynch Hall (Charles McKenna Lynch House, "Starboard Light"), 216–17

Bartlett House, Cambridge Springs, 517

Basse, Dettmar, 172, 183, 186, 187

Basse, Zelie, 187

Bassett, Richard, 276

Batcheler, Cephas, 429; Fallon House Hotel, 429, 431; White (James) House, 431

Battles (Rush) House, 505

Bauchspies, Clarence, 351; Kappa Delta Rho House (PSU), 352

Bauer, Dave: U.S. Courthouse (Erie Public Library, Federal Building and U.S. Courthouse, Isaac Baker and Son Store), 28, **489,** 489–90

Bauhaus, 115–16

Baum, George C.: Zion Lutheran Church, Indiana, 203

Baum Boulevard Dodge (Chrysler Sales and Service Building), 108, **108**

Baut Studios of Pennsylvania, 331

Bayardsville, Pennsylvania, 38. *See also* Strip, the (Pittsburgh)

Bayne, Samuel Gamble, 520

Baywood (Alexander and Cordelia King House), 111

Beamery, the, 235

Bean, Thomas, 541

Beatty, J. Lewis: Mt. Lebanon United Presbyterian Church, Mount Lebanon, 128

Beatty, Robert F.: United Steelworkers of America, Local 1212, 156

Beaux-Arts architecture, 27, 48, 53, 56, 57–58, 67, 71–72

Beaver, Pennsylvania, 8, 133–36, 139, 140; map, 137

Beaver County, 131–71; map, 130; Aliquippa and vicinity, 159–61; Ambridge, 163–71; —, map, 165; Beaver and vicinity, 133–36, 139, 140; —, map, 137; Beaver Falls, 146–53; —, map, 147; Bridgewater and vicinity, 140–41; —, map, 137; Conway, 162–63; Courthouse, 135; Darlington, 154–55; Emergency Response Center and Beaver Area Heritage Museum (Pittsburgh and Lake Erie Railroad [P&LE] Passenger and Freight Depots), 136, **137,** 139; Fombell, 153–54; Freedom, 162; history, 131–33; Hookstown, 157–58; Midland, 156–57; New Brighton, 144–46; —, map, 147; Raccoon Creek State Park and vicinity, 158–59; Rochester and vicinity, 141–44; —, map, 137; Shippingport, 157; topography, 131; Virginia land claims, 7. *See also specific towns and structures by name*

Beaver Falls, Pennsylvania, 131, 132, 136, 146–53, 166, 169; map, 147

Beck, Pople and Beck: Swan Acres, 99

Beck, Quentin S., 99

Beckman, Morris H., 234

Bedford, Nathaniel, 38, 77–78

Bedford, Pennsylvania, 373–81; map, 374

Bedford County, 371–86; map, 298; barns, 500; Bedford and vicinity, 373–81; —, map, 374; Breezewood, 384–85, **385;** Courthouse, 368, 373, 375; covered bridges in, 22; Everett and vicinity, 385–86; Fishertown, 383–84; history, 371–73;

industry and settlement, 299–300; Loysburg vicinity, 384; Rainsburg, 381–82; Schellsburg and vicinity, 382–83; Sulphur Springs, 381; topography, 299. *See also specific towns and structures by name*

Beebe, E. R., 533

Beebe, Milton Earl: Cambria County Courthouse, 302–3, 357, 404; Huntingdon County Courthouse, 357, 404; McKean County Courthouse (demolished), 357, 413; Schuylkill County Courthouse, 357; Warren County Courthouse, 302, 357, 404–5, **405,** 439

Beefeater's Restaurant (Carnegie Free Library of Bradford), 416

Beer, David, 54

Beeson, Henry, 237

Beeson, Jacob, 237

Beezer, Louis, 471–72. *See also* Beezer Brothers

Beezer, Michael, 471–72. *See also* Beezer Brothers

Beezer Brothers, 215–16, 302, 308, 326; Clearfield County National Bank and Dimeling Hotel, 28, **471,** 471–72; First United Presbyterian Church, DuBois, 474; H. Dean Allison Insurance Agency (Llyswen Station), 333; Miller (Charles A.) House, 527; St. John Gualbert Cathedral, Johnstown, 315; Sunbrook Farm, 324–25, **325**

Behrend, Ernst and Mary, 498

Bel Ange, 235

Bell, Thomas, 313

Bell, William: Potter County Courthouse, 424, **425**

Bellefonte, Pennsylvania, 339–44; map, 340; Crider Exchange Building, **341**

Bellinger, Louis A. S.: New Granada Theater (Pythian Temple), Pittsburgh, 41, 112, **120,** 120–21

Belltower Office Center (Fourth Ward Public School), Bridgetown, 145

Benedict, Aaron, 532, 533; Pleasantville Free Methodist Church, 533, **533**

Benedictine order, 443

Benedictown, Pennsylvania, 533

Benjamin, Asher, 512

South Methodist Episcopal Church (moved to Avella), 286; Faith Bible Church (former St. Emory Hungarian Roman Catholic Church), 252; Faith Holiness Church, Franklin, 525; First Baptist Church, Connellsville, 253; First Baptist Church, Meadville, 509; First Baptist Church, North East, 499; First Baptist Church, Oakland, Pittsburgh, 61, 64, 114; First Baptist Church, Warren, 406; First Christian Church, Connellsville, 253; First Christian Church, Somerset, 390; First Christian Church, Disciples of Christ, New Castle, 549; First Church of Christ, Lock Haven, 428; First Congregational Church, Beaver Falls, 149; First Evangelical Lutheran Church, Vandergrift, 223; First Hungarian Reformed Church, Hazelwood, 80; First Lutheran Church, Windber, 394; First Methodist Church, Meyersdale, 395; First Methodist Church, Monongahela, 296; First Presbyterian Church, Beaver, 136, 174; First Presbyterian Church, Girard, 505; First Presbyterian Church, Greensburg, 216; First Presbyterian Church, Meadville, 510–11; First Presbyterian Church, Monongahela, 297; First Presbyterian Church, New Brighton, 144–45; First Presbyterian Church, North East, 499; First Presbyterian Church, Pittsburgh, 58–59; First Presbyterian Church, Sharon, 539; First Presbyterian Church, Tidioute, 410; First Presbyterian Church, Titusville, 520–21; First Presbyterian Church, Warren, 406; First Presbyterian Church, Windber, 394; First Presbyterian Church and East Brady Library (Newton E. Graham House), 457; First Presbyterian Church of California, 292; First Presbyterian Church of Greenville, 543; First Presbyterian Church of Washington, 280; First United Methodist Church (First Methodist Episcopal Church), 145–46; First

United Methodist Church, Johnstown, 315–16; First United Methodist Church, Kittanning, 191; First United Methodist Church, Punxsutawney, 467–68; First United Methodist Church, Reynoldsville, 467; First United Methodist Church, Warren, 406; First United Methodist Church, West Newton, 234; First United Presbyterian Church, DuBois, 474; First United Presbyterian Church of New Castle, 550; First United Presbyterian Church of the Covenant, Erie, 493; Ford Memorial Chapel, Allegheny College, 512; Freeport Methodist Church, 198; Grace at Calvary Lutheran Church (Calvary Evangelical Presbyterian Church), Butler, **175,** 175; Grace Lutheran Church, Curwensville, 472; Grace Lutheran Church, Rochester, 142; Grace Lutheran Church, State College, **351,** 351–52; Grace Presbyterian Church, Kittanning, **190,** 190–91; Grace United Methodist Church, Grove City, 545; Grace United Methodist Church, Indiana, 204; Graystone United Presbyterian Church, Indiana, 204; Great Island Presbyterian Church, Lock Haven, 428–29; Harrold Zion Church, Jeannette (demolished), 219; Harrold Zion Evangelical Lutheran Church, 30, 217, **217;** Hart Chapel and Theatre, Clarion University of Pennsylvania, 454; H. B. Miller Memorial Chapel, Mercer, 538; Heinz Chapel, Oakland, Pittsburgh, 61, 68, **68;** Heritage United Methodist Church, Ligonier, 227; Holy Ghost (Russian) Orthodox Church of America, Ambridge, 164; Holy Resurrection Russian Orthodox Greek Catholic Church, West Brownsville, 291, **291;** Holy Rosary Church, Homewood, 112, 216; Holy Trinity Greek Orthodox Church, Altoona, 331; Immaculate Conception Church, Clarion, 453, **454;** Immaculate Conception Church of the

Blessed Virgin, Johnstown, 317–18, **318;** Immaculate Heart of Mary Roman Catholic Church, Polish Hill, Pittsburgh, 103, 104–5; Independent Congregational Church, Meadville (demolished), 533; Interfaith Chapel, Warren State Hospital, 408; Irvine Presbyterian Church, 409, **409;** Jefferson Presbyterian Church, Jefferson, 274; Kane Memorial Chapel (Kane Presbyterian Church), 420, **420;** Latrobe Presbyterian Church, 224; Logan's Ferry (Parnassus) Presbyterian Church, New Kensington, 220; log construction, 11; Luther Memorial Church, Erie, 493; McConnellsburg United Methodist Church, 368; Meadville Unitarian-Universalist Church, 26, **26,** 509, 510, **510;** Memorial Church of Our Father (Episcopal Church), 459–60; Middle Presbyterian Church, Mount Pleasant, 232; Mount Aloysius College Chapel, 307; Mt. Lebanon United Methodist Church, Mount Lebanon, 128; Mt. Lebanon United Presbyterian Church, Mount Lebanon, 128; Mt. Pleasant Presbyterian Church, Darlington, 155; Mount St. Peter Roman Catholic Church, New Kensington, 221; Mt. Tabor Presbyterian Church, Sigel, 469; National Carpatho-Rusyn Center (St. John the Baptist Greek Catholic Cathedral), Munhall, 79–80, **80;** Nebo Lutheran Chapel and Cemetery, Mount Jewett, 419; Ohiopyle United Methodist Church, 255; Our Lady of Mount Carmel Church, Altoona, 328; Philip G. Cochran United Methodist Church, Dawson, 250; Pleasantville Free Methodist Church, 533, **533;** The Priory and Grand Hall (St. Mary's Roman Catholic Church), 95–96; Purification of the Blessed Virgin Mary, Ellwood City, 553; Rainsburg Methodist Church, 381; Reformed Presbyterian Church, Darlington, 155; Robinson House and Farm, Robinson churches (*continued*)

United Methodist Church (Robinson Memorial Chapel), 193; Roman Catholic Church of Saints Peter and Paul, Beaver, 139; Russian Orthodox Church of the Nativity of Christ "Old Rite," 487; Sacred Heart Roman Catholic Church, St. Mary's, 444, **444**; Sacred Heart Roman Catholic Church, Shadyside, Pittsburgh, 114; St. Agnes's Church, Oakland, Pittsburgh, 79; St. Anthony of Padua Shrine, North Side, Pittsburgh, 99–100; St. Anthony's Church (former), Bessemer, 553; St. Anthony's Church, Millvale, 79; St. Augustine's Church, Lawrenceville, Pittsburgh, 79; St. Bernard's Church, Mount Lebanon, 79, 128, **128**, 216; St. Casimir's Roman Catholic Church, 318–19; St. Eusebius Church, East Brady, 457; St. Evangelical Lutheran Church, Connellsville, 253; St. Felix Chapel, Freedom, 162; St. Francis de Sales Church, McKees Rocks, 84; St. Francis of Assisi Roman Catholic Church, Clearfield, 471; St. Gertrude Roman Catholic Church, Pittsburgh, 29; St. Gertrude Roman Catholic Church, Vandergrift, 223; St. Ignatius of Antioch Roman Catholic Church, Bobtown, 268; St. James Episcopal Church, Bedford, 375–76, **376**; St. James Episcopal Church, Titusville, 518; St. James the Less Church, Philadelphia, 375, 427; St. John Cantius Church, Windber, 393; St. John Gualbert Cathedral, Johnstown, 315; St. John's Episcopal Church, Bellefonte, 340; St. John's Episcopal Church, Franklin, 525; St. John's Episcopal Church, Huntingdon, 357; St. John's Episcopal Church, Sharon, 539; St. John's Evangelical Lutheran Church, Emlenton, 535; St. John's Lutheran Church (Harmony Society Church), Ambridge, 169; St. John's United Church of Christ, Bellefonte, 344; St. John the Baptist Carmelite Friary, New Baltimore, **394**, 394–95; St. John the Baptist Church, Lawrenceville, Pittsburgh, 79; St. John the Baptist Ukrainian Catholic Church, South Side, Pittsburgh, 77, 78; St. John the Divine, New York, 108; St. Josaphat's Church, South Side, Pittsburgh, 79; St. Joseph's Church, Oil City, 529–30; St. Joseph's Church, Sharon, 539–40, **540**; St. Joseph's Episcopal Church, Port Allegany, 418–19; St. Luke Lutheran Church, Centre Hall, 345; St. Luke's Episcopal Church, Altoona, 328–29; St. Luke's Episcopal Church, Smethport, 413–14; St. Luke's Protestant Episcopal Church (Old St. Luke's), 129; St. Mark's Roman Catholic Church, Emporium, 436; St. Mary of Mercy Church, Pittsburgh, 56; St. Mary, Our Lady of Guadalupe Roman Catholic Church, Kittanning, 191; St. Mary's Chapel, Mercyhurst North East Campus (St. Mary's Seminary), 499, **499**; St. Mary's Church, Convent, and School and Benedictine Priory and Gymnasium, 444–45; St. Mary's Greek Catholic Church, Johnstown, 318, **318**; St. Mary's Greek Catholic Church, Windber, 393–94; St. Mary's Roman Catholic Church, Ford City, 199; St. Mary's Roman Catholic Church, Port Allegany, 419; St. Michael's Byzantine Church, Donora, 294; St. Michael's Church (former), New Castle, 553; St. Michael's Roman Catholic Church, Fryburg, 455; St. Michael the Archangel Church, Munhall, 79; St. Nicholas Chapel (Byzantine Catholic Church of the Greek Union), 139–40, **139**; St. Nicholas Church, Millvale, 100–101; St. Nicholas Russian Orthodox Church, Donora, 294; St. Oswald's Roman Catholic Church, Liverpool, England, 245; St. Patrick's Church, Kittanning, 192; St. Patrick's Roman Catholic Church, Armstrong County, 11; St. Patrick's Roman Catholic Church, Erie, 487–88; St. Patrick's Roman Catholic Church, Worthington vicinity, **191**, 191–92; St. Paul Cathedral, Oakland, Pittsburgh, 61, **65**, 65–66; St. Paul's Episcopal Church, Kittanning, 191; St. Paul's Presbyterian Church, Somerset, 390; St. Paul's Roman Catholic Church, Butler, 176; St. Paul's Roman Catholic Church, Pittsburgh, 29; St. Paul's United Church of Christ, Somerset, 390; St. Peter's Episcopal Church, Uniontown, 237; St. Peter's Episcopal Church, Waterford, 502–3; St. Peter's Roman Catholic Church, Brownsville, 245, **245**; Sts. Cosmos and Damian Roman Catholic Church, Punxsutawney, 468; St. Severin's Log Chapel, Drifting, 11, 475, **475**; Sts. Peter and Paul Ukrainian Orthodox Greek Catholic Church, Carnegie, 80; St. Stanislaus Catholic Church, Erie, 481; St. Stanislaus Polish Roman Catholic Church, Ambridge, 164; St. Stephen's Episcopal Church and Parsonage House, Brady's Bend, 192, **192**; St. Stephen's Slovak Catholic Church, Johnstown, 318–19; St. Thomas More Parish, Indiana, 205, **205**; St. Vincent Archabbey Basilica, Monastery, and College Complex, Latrobe, **225**, 225–26, 443; St. Vitus Roman Catholic Church, New Castle, 30, 547, **552**, 552–53; Salem Lutheran Church, Aaronsburg, 344; Saxonburg Memorial United Presbyterian Church, 181; Schellsburg Union Church, 382; Sewickley Presbyterian Church, 235; Shadyside Presbyterian Church, Shadyside, Pittsburgh, 119; Shirleysburg Presbyterian Church (former), 362; Shirleysburg United Methodist Church, 362; Sigel United Methodist Church, 469; Sinking Valley Presbyterian Church (Arch Spring Presbyterian Church), 336; Smith Chapel, Pennsylvania State University (PSU), Behrend College (Glenhill Farm), 498; Smithfield United Church, Pittsburgh, 119; Sovereign

courthouses (*continued*)
(Erie Public Library, Federal Building and U.S. Courthouse, Isaac Baker and Son Store), 28, **489,** 489–90; U.S. Post Office and Federal Courthouse, Pittsburgh, 53; Venango County, 430, 525; Warren County, 302, 357, 404–5, **405,** 439; Washington County, 27, 276, 278, **278;** Westmoreland County, 212, **213,** 452

Covell, Vernon: Three Sisters Bridges, 51; West End Bridge, 85; Westinghouse Memorial Bridge, 82, **83**

covered bridges. *See under* bridges

Cox, S. A.: Bethlehem Steel Corporation (Cambria Iron Company, Cambria Steel Company), 311, 313, 314–15

Coyleville, Pennsylvania, 180–81

Craft, Isaiah N., 247

Crafton, Pennsylvania, 13

Craig, James, 549

Cram, Ralph Adams, 27, 29, 108, 250; Abbey Reformed Church–United Church of Christ (Abbey Reformed Church), Huntingdon, 359; Calvary Episcopal Church, Shadyside, 114, **114,** 216; First Presbyterian Church, Greensburg, 216; Holy Rosary Church, Homewood, 112, 216

Cram and Ferguson, 112; Abbey Reformed Church–United Church of Christ (Abbey Reformed Church), Huntingdon, 359; East Liberty Presbyterian Church, Highland Park, Pittsburgh, 41, 108, **108,** 111; First Presbyterian Church, Greensburg, 216; St. John's Episcopal Church, Sharon, additions, 539

Cramer, Cassimer: Barronvale Covered Bridge, 398

Cram, Goodhue and Ferguson: First Baptist Church, Pittsburgh, 61, 64, 114; YWCA (William Augustus Huff House), 215–16

Cram, Wentworth and Goodhue, 175

Cranberry, Pennsylvania, 42

Craner, John Henry, 136; residential district, Beaver, 136

Crawford, John Minor, 271

Crawford, William, 248, 506

Crawford Center, 535

Crawford County, 506–22; map, 476; agriculture in, 14; Cambridge Springs and vicinity, 516–17; Courthouse, 509; Courthouse (demolished), 26, **26;** history, 506–8; Meadville, 508–15; —, map, 507; Saegertown, 515–16; Titusville and vicinity, 517–22; —, map, 518; topography, 477; Trust Company, 509; Venango, 516. *See also specific towns and structures by name*

Crawford Square, 42, 121

Creal and Hyde Architects: Struthers Library Theatre, 405

Creal Hyde and Lawson, Architects, 217

Cresson, John Elliott, 305

Cresson, Pennsylvania, 21, 301, 305–8

Cresson Springs Company, 306

Cresswell House, 363

Crider Exchange Building, Bellefonte, 340, **341**

Crisp, W. R.: St. Peter's Roman Catholic Church, Brownsville, 245, **245**

Croatian immigrants and residents, 100

Croghan, George, 60, 132

Crosby, W. Holmes: Crawford Center, 535; Emlenton Area Ambulance Service, 535; Oil City Public Library (Carnegie Public Library), 531; U.S. Post Office, Grove City, 545

Cross, Benjamin, 363

Crown American Building, Johnstown, 31, 310, 316, **316,** 319

Crowner/King Architects: Erie Water Works renovation, 486; Erie Zoo (Glenwood Zoo) additions, 496

Crystal Spring, Pennsylvania, 370

Crystal Spring Camp Meeting, 370, **370**

Cullum, George Washington, 34n38; Meadville Unitarian-Universalist Church, 26, **26,** 509, 510, **510**

Culp, Pennsylvania, 335–36

Cummings, Robert A.: Pennsylvania Drilling Company (Taylor-Wilson Manufacturing Company), **85,** 85–86

Cunard, G. W., 370

Cunningham, John and Samuel, 172

Cunningham, Valentine and Margaret, 545

Cupola Houses, Meyerdale, 396

Curll, G. V., 458

Curry, Martin and Highberger: Fallingwater Visitors' Center, 255

Curtin, Andrew G., 341, 344

Curtin, Roland, 344

Curtin, Pennsylvania, 344

Curtin House, 344

Curtis, Enoch A., 414, 518, 521, 532; Christ Episcopal Church, Oil City, 414, 531; office building (City Hall), Bradford, 414; Reuting (Theodore and Marie) House, 521

Curtis and Archer: Transit Fine Art Gallery (National Transit Company Building), 532

Curtis and Davis: United Steelworkers Building (IBM Building), 46–47, **47,** 48

Curtze, Frederick Felix, 494

Curwen, John, 472

Curwensville, Pennsylvania, 470, 472

Cutter, Manly N., 419

Cyman, Rick: Sheetz Convenience Store, 495–96

Dagit/Saylor: Agricultural Arena, Pennsylvania State University, **349,** 349–50

Daily House, 235

Dale, Samuel, 527

Dale-Mayes House, 348

Damiani, Gerard: Pennsylvania Railroad Passenger and Freight Stations, Greensburg, restaurant, 213, **213**

Damianos + Anthony: Purnell Center for the Arts, 72

Damianos Brown and Andrews: University of Pittsburgh at Johnstown Pasquerilla Performing Arts Center, 319; Washington's Landing, 99, 100, **100**

dams, 22, 138, 172; Austin, 422–23; Conemaugh Lake, 138; East Branch, 441; Kinzua, 402, 403; Leechburg Lock and Dam, 197; Lock and Dam No. 7, Kittanning vicinity, 189; Lock 6 Landing Restaurant and Marina (Merrill Station Lockhouse), 139; Loyalhanna, 138

Dana, Richard Henry, Jr., 304

Dana and Murphy: Mount Assisi (Charles Schwab Estate, "Limestone Castle"), 303–4; Norman Village, Klein Immergrun, 305, **305**

Fraser, W. S.: Joseph Horne Department Store, 49

fraternity district for Pennsylvania State University (PSU), 352

Frederick (builder): office building (Buffalo, Pittsburgh and Rochester Railroad Passenger Station), 441

Fredericksburg, Pennsylvania, 508

Fredonia, Pennsylvania, 544

Freedom, Pennsylvania, 162

Free Masons Lodge, 551

Freeport, Pennsylvania, 188, 198–99

French, Daniel Chester, 94, 110

French, F. C.: Jack and Jill Shop (C. L. Bradburn Building, Knights of Pythias Hall), 415–16

French and Indian War, 5, 10, 188–89, 210, 259, 320, 321, 361, 373, 382, 402, 478, 546

French settlement, 10

Frens and Frens: Petersburg Tollhouse restoration, 398

Frew (John) House, 13, 127

Freyssinet, Eugène, 47

Frick, Adelaide, 113

Frick, Helen Clay, 68, 233

Frick, Henry Clay, 40, 53, 54, 55, 57, 62, 64, 110, 113, 114, 232, 238, 253, 308

Frick, William E., 89–90

Frick Art and Historical Center (Clayton), 24, 68, 81, 113, **113**

Frick Building and Frick Annex, 53, 54

Frick (Henry Clay) Coal and Coke Company, 242

Frick (Henry Clay) Fine Arts Building, 61, 68–69

Frick Hospital, Mount Pleasant, 231–32

Frick Office, Scottdale, 233

Frick Park, Pittsburgh, 40, 110, 113

Friendship Hill (Albert Gallatin House), 9, 24, 243

Froesch, Berthold: Highland Park and the Zoo, 111

Frost, Robert: Olmsted Manor Adult Retreat-Renewal Center (George Welsh Olmsted Estate) additions, 421

Frost, Wallace, 240

Fry, Henry Clay, 142

Fryburg, Pennsylvania, 454–55

Fry Glass Company, 142

Fuller and Stickle: Perry Monument, 495; Villa Maria Academy addition, 483–84

Fulton, John Charles, 29, 194, 292, 389. *See also* J. C. Fulton and Son

Fulton, Robert, 366

Fulton County, 366–71; map, 298; Burnt Cabins, 370–71; Courthouse and Courthouse Square, 368, **368**; Crystal Spring vicinity, 370; history, 366; industry and settlement, 299–300; McConnellsburg, 366–70; —, map, 367; Native American habitation, 6; topography, 1–2, 299; Warfordsburg, 370. *See also specific towns and structures by name*

Fulton House. *See* McConnellsburg Police Station and Fulton County Historical Society (Fulton House)

funiculars, 76, **76**

Furness, Frank, 58, 510; Baltimore and Ohio Railroad Station, Pittsburgh (demolished), 29; Edgewood Railroad Station, 40, 124; Fox Mansion Carriage House, 124, 401, 460, 461, **461**

Gabler, John C., 271

Galena Oil Works, 527

Galena-Signal Oil Company Headquarters, 525–26, **526**

Galeton, Pennsylvania, 423

Gallatin, Albert, 9, 12, 243, 258, 269. *See also* Friendship Hill (Albert Gallatin House)

Gallitzin, Demetrius Augustine, 304

Gamble Mill Restaurant (Gamble Mill), 340, 343

Gannon University, 482, 483–84, 493; John E. Waldron Campus Center, 483, **483**

Garards Fort, Pennsylvania, 267–68

Garden Court Subdivision, Erie, 493–94

gardens: Elm Court, 177; George Gray Barnard Sculpture Garden, 341; Kraus Campo, 72; Mount Assisi (Charles Schwab Estate, "Limestone Castle"), 304; Newington (Shields-Brooks House), 86–87; Norman Village, Klein Immergrun, 305, **305**; Phipps Conservatory, 61, **70**, 70–71; Rapp House and Grotto, Economy, 168, **168**. *See also* parks

Garner, Ignatius, 443; St. Mary's Church, Convent, and School and Benedictine Priory and Gymnasium, 444–45

Garnsey, Elmer, 489

gas industry. *See* oil and gas industry

gas stations, 22; Charleroi, 293; Dunkle's Gulf Service Station, Bedford, 377, **377**; Kwik Fill Gas Station, Beaver, 135, **135**; Midway Turnpike Service Plazas, 379; Pacific Pride Gas Station, Oil City, 531; Reynoldsville (former), 467

Gateway Center, 31, 42, 44, 47–49, 68, 121

Gateway Lodge, Sigel, 469

Gay, John, 321

Gaysport, Pennsylvania, 321

Gemmill, Elizabeth, 363, 364

Gendell, David Smith: Blair County Courthouse, 322–23, **323**

Gendell, John A., 323

Geneva College district, 148, 151–53; Alexander Hall, 153; Clarke Hall, 153; "Fern Cliffe," 152; Johnston Gymnasium, 152, **152**; McCartney Library, 152; McKee Hall, 152; Memorial Hall, 153; Metheny Field House, 153; Old Main, 136, 151–52, **152**; Pearce Hall, 153; Reeves Field, 152

Gensler: PNC Plaza and 210 6th Avenue, 49

Genther, William, 332–33

geodesic domes, 161

George Junior Republic, 545

George S. Orth and Brother: Elmhurst (Mary Thaw House), 307–8, **308**

Georgian architecture, 183

Germania, Pennsylvania, 422

German immigrants and residents, 27, 74, 103, 120, 164, 166–69, 171–72, 176, 181–86, 225–26, 244, 317–18, 364, 444–45, 467, 480–81, 500

German settlement, 6, 8, 9, 14–15, 131, 210, 300, 320, 336, 337, 338, 345, 353, 361, 382, 422, 455, 541

Ghost Town Trail, 270, 299, 301, 319

Gibboney, George Harrison, 373–74, 385–86

Gibson, William L., 544. *See also* libraries: Free Public Library (Gibson House), Jamestown

Greenville, Pennsylvania, 541–44; map, 542; Historical Society (Judge William Waugh House), 542

Greenville, Treaty of, 134

Greenwood Furnace, Pennsylvania, 354, 360–61

Greer, Alice White, 551

Greer, George, 154, 551. *See also* Lawrence County: Historical Society (George Greer House)

Greyhound Bus Station. *See* Boardwalk (Greyhound Bus Station)

Griswold, Matthew, Jr., 492

Griswold, Ralph E.: Chatham Village, 75, **75**, 77; Old Stone House reconstruction, 178

Griswold Winters Swain: Chatham Village, 75, **75**, 77

Gropius, Walter, 99, 114; Aluminum City Terrace, 29, 99, 222, **222**; Frank House, 29, 115–16, 228

Grosvenor (Charles) House, Athens, Ohio, 216

Grove City, Pennsylvania, 545–46

Grove City College, 545–46; east campus, **546**

Grove (A. C.) House, 557

Guastavino tiles, 46, 64, 119

Gue House, 249

Gulf Building, 53

Gumphert, Charles, 456

Gwinner, Edward, 118

Gwinner-Harter House (William B. Negley House), 118–19, **119**

Gzesh, Jacob. *See* Jacob Gzesh and Associates

Haas, Richard, 50–51

Haas/Rosser Fabrap/Brinjac, Kambic: Bryce Jordan Center, Pennsylvania State University, 349

Hagan, Bernadine, 257; and I. N. Hagan, **256**. *See also* Kentuck Knob/Hagan House

Hajjar, William, 351

Hall, Homer: Potter County Courthouse, 424, **425**

Hall, Joseph E., 464; House, 464

Hall (Lynn) Estate, 29

Hall, Raymond Viner, 29; Baker's Acres, 419; Cameron County Junior Senior High School, 29, 426, 436–37; Domaleski House, 425–26, **426**; Hall (Lynn) Estate, 29; Legion

Memorial Hall, Emporium, 437; Lynn Hall Estate, 419, **419**; Owens-Brockway Glass Container Company, 451, 462; Pittsburgh Corning Corporation complex additions, 412; Port Allegany Union High School, 419; Woodland Elementary School, Emporium, 437

Hall, Walter J.: Lynn Hall Estate, 419, **419**

Hamill, Robert, 347

Hamilton, William, 549

Hamilton Tool and Supply (First National Bank of Beaver Falls), 148, **149**

Hamlin, Talbot, 245, 484, 485

Hamlin (Orlo) House (former), 412, **413**

Hammermill Paper Factory, 481

Hammond, David, 516

Hampton, Wade, 101

Hanna, Edwin S.: Crawford County Courthouse, 509; First Presbyterian Church, Meadville, halls, 511

Hanna, John L., 528

Hanna, William, 264

Hanna and Stewart: Auditorium, Warren State Hospital, 408

Hannah, Thomas: Midtown Towers (Keenan Building), 50; Western Theology Seminary, 93

Hanna's Town, Pennsylvania, 211

Harbor Bridge, Pennsylvania, 546–47

Hardy, Joseph A., Sr., 257

Harlow, Alfred, 59, 69

Harmonists (Harmony Society), 24, 27, 87, 98, 146, 147–48, 151, 163, 166–69, 172, 182–86, 402–3; Houses, Beaver Falls, 151. *See also* Old Economy Historic District and Visitor Center; Rapp, Frederick Reichert

Harmony, Pennsylvania, 98, 163, 166, 169, 182–86; map, 183

Harmony Inn (Austin Pearce House), **185**, 185

Harris, James, 339

Harris, John McArthur, 498

Harris and Richards: General Electric (GE) Transportation Systems, 334, 481, **497**, 497–98

Harrison and Abramovitz, 31; Regional Enterprise Tower (ALCOA), 58, **58**, 417; USX Tower (United States Steel

Building), 40, **52**, 53, 54; Westinghouse Building, 48–49. *See also* Abramovitz, Max

Hart, John, 363

Hart, William and Lucy, 156

Harter, Leo, 118

Hart (Homer) House, 505

Hartley, William, 376. *See also* Victoria House (William Hartley House)

Hartman (H. W.) House, 557

Hartslog, 363

Harvard University, Cambridge, Massachusetts: Sever Hall, 45

Harvey (B. O.) Houses, 340

Hastings, Selina, 355

Hastings, Theodore Mitchell: Foxburg Free Library and Lincoln Hall, 460

Hastings + Chivetta Architects: William J. von Liebig Center for Science, Juniata College, 359; Wise Athletic Center, Allegheny College, 512

Haviland, Edward: Blair County Prison, 190, 303, 323, 357, 425, 452, 471; Old County Jail, Ebensburg, 303, **303**, 357, 425, 471; Potter County Jail, 425

Haviland, John, 303, 323; Eastern State Penitentiary, 357; Pennsylvania Fire Insurance Company, 357; Western Penitentiary, 39

Hawes, "Hunnie," 241

Hay, Malcolm, 91

Hayden (Benjamin) House, 260

Hayes Large Architects, 328, 464; Altoona Hospital renovation, 326; California University of Pennsylvania Eberly Building, 292; Juniata College buildings, 359–60; Juniata Gap Elementary School, 330, **330**; Mishler Theater, Altoona, 329; Mount Aloysius College buildings, 307

Hayes, Large, Suckling and Fruth: Kennedy Sports + Recreation Center, Juniata College, 359

Hays, Edward F., 180

Hayward and Cains: Little (David) House (Chestnut Flats), 159

Hazelwood, Pennsylvania, 313

Hazen family, 153

Hazen (Samuel) Farm district, 153

Hazlehurst, Edward: Pennsylvania State University buildings, 349

Hunter, Campbell and Rea: Juniata College buildings, 359–60; University of Pittsburgh at Johnstown buildings, 319
Hunter (Jahu) House, 410
Hunter's, Hill, Nashville, Tennessee, 512
Huntingdon, Pennsylvania, 320, 354, 355–60; map, 356
Huntingdon County, 353–66; map, 298; Alexandria and vicinity, 363–64; Chamber of Commerce (Union Depot and Hunt Signal Tower), 358; Courthouse, 357, 404; Greenwood Furnace, 354, 360–61; Huntingdon and vicinity, 355–60; —, map, 356; industry and settlement, 299–300; Mount Union vicinity, 361; Native American habitation, 6; Newburg vicinity, 363; Orbisonia and Rockhill Furnace, 362; Seven Stars, 365–66; Shirleysburg, 361–62; Spruce Creek and Spruce Creek Valley, 365; topography, 1–2, 299. See also specific towns and structures by name
Huntingdon Furnace, 16, 365
Hunting, Larsen and Dunnells: Conway Automatic Classification Railyard (Pennsylvania Railroad Classification Yard), 21, **162**, 162–63
Hunt Stables and Kennels, Ligonier Valley, 226
Hunt Studios of Pittsburgh, 331
Hurdzan/Fry, Golf Course Design, Inc., 154
Hussey, E. C., 265
Hussey-Binns Shovel Works, 293
Huston, Joseph M., 341
Hutchins, William: St. Mary of Mercy Church, Pittsburgh, 56
Hutton, Addison: Clinton County Courthouse, 429–30, **430**, 525; Johnstown Flood Museum (Johnstown Carnegie Library), 23, 301, 309, 311, **311**; Lycoming County Courthouse (demolished), 430, 525; Venango County Courthouse, 430, 525
Hyde, Joseph Smith, 439
Hyde, Linn: Conewango Club restoration, 406
Hyde, William H., 440
Hyde Architects: Blair Corporation headquarters, 404
Hyde (Elizabeth) House, 440, **440**

Hyde-Murphy Company, 401–2, 439, 440, 442

iconostasis screen, 139, 140
Igloo Soft Serve, Everett, 386
I. J. Chung Associates, 529
IKM Architects, 45; Facilities Management Services Building, Carnegie Mellon University, 72; Phipps Conservatory, 61, **70**, 70–71
IKM/Grant: Colonial Hall Apartments, Grove City, 546
Immergrun. See Norman Village, Klein Immergrun
inclines, **19**, 76, **76**, 307, **310**, 316, 320, 334
Independence Hall, Philadelphia, 404, 413
Independent Order of Odd Fellows buildings: Brookville (see Parker P. Blood Block, IOOF Building); Saegertown, 515; Titusville, 519
Indiana, Pennsylvania, 201–5; map, 202
Indiana County, 199–210; map, 130; agriculture in, 14; Blairsville, 208–9; Cherry Tree and vicinity, 206–7; Clarksburg vicinity, 209; Commodore, 206; Courthouse, 202; Dixonville vicinity, 205–6; history, 199–201; Homer City, 207–8; Indiana, 201–5; —, map, 202; Saltsburg, 209–10; topography, 131. See also specific towns and structures by name
Indiana University of Pennsylvania, 201, 204–5; Breezedale, 204–5; Sutton Hall, 204, 205
Indian mounds, 3, 37–38
Indovina Associates Architects: PPG Aquarium, 111; Water's Edge, 111
Indspec, 180
industrial buildings: Allegheny Power (West Penn Power, Mitchell Station), 297; Ambridge Borough Water Softening Plant, 165–66, 171; American Bridge Company, 163; Bruce Mansfield Power Station, 157; Cambria Iron Company, blast furnaces, **301**; Carrie Furnace, blast furnaces, **312**; Conemaugh Generating Station No. 2, **200**, 201; Donora Zinc plant, 294; Eliza Furnace, Vintondale, 319; Emerald Mine Cleaning

Plant, 262; Erie Water Works, 486; First Energy (Duquesne Light, Beaver Valley Power Station), 157; General Electric (GE) Transportation Systems, 334, 481, **497**, 497–98; Heinz Lofts (H. J. Heinz Company Factories), 39, **96**, 96–98; Illinois Glass Plant, 451; Jeannette Glass Company and McKee Glass Company Housing, 218–19; Liberty Avenue, 2425 (Westinghouse Air-Brake Company), 83, 104; Meadville Area Industrial Park, 509; Moltrup Steel, 148; Mt. Etna Furnace and Iron Plantation, 312, 332, 336; National Robotics Engineering Consortium (Epping-Carpenter Company), 106; New Ventures Center (Parks Bend Farm and Industrial Park), 23, **197**, 197–98; Ohio River Valley, 84–85; Oil City Industrial Park (Oil Well Supply Plant, Imperial Works), 532; Parks Bend Industrial Park, 188; Penn Brewery (Eberhardt and Ober Brewing Company), 98–99; Pennsylvania Drilling Company (Taylor-Wilson Manufacturing Company), **85**, 85–86; Pennsylvania Match Factory, 342; Pittsburgh, 39; Pittsburgh and Lake Erie Railroad (P&LE) Steam Locomotive Repair Shop, 85, 86, **86**; Pittsburgh Plate Glass Plant, Ford City, 199; Port Ambridge Building (Main Bridge Shop, American Bridge Company), 171, **171**; post–World War II, 23; Republic Steel, 148; Royal Victoria China (former Mayer China Company building), Beaver Falls, 148; St. Charles Refractories Company–KMS Refractories (McLain Fire Brick Company), 456, **456**; Shoaf coke ovens, **242**, 242–43; Standard Horse Nail Company Building, 145, **145**; Therm-o-Rock buildings (Wightman Glass Factory buildings), 297; Titusville Iron Works, 519; Tribune-Review Building, **214**, 214–15; U.S. Steel Plant, Ellwood City, 557; W. A. Young Foundry and Machine Shop, 266, 273, **273**; Westinghouse

New Harmony, Indiana, 166, 168, 184
New Haven, Pennsylvania, 251–52
Newington (Shields-Brooks House), **86,** 86–87
New Kensington, Pennsylvania, 29, 211, 220–22; map, 220
Newman and Harris: Centre County Courthouse, 339, 341
Newmyer House and Barn, 253–54, **254,** 283, 500
Newport, Rhode Island, 118, 178
New Wilmington, Pennsylvania, 554–55
New York, New York: Empire State Building, 171; Forest Hills Gardens, 65; Forest Hills Post Office, 315; Pennsylvania land claims, 478; Pennsylvania Station, 53; St. John the Divine, 108; Sunnyside Gardens, 75
Nichols, Jesse Clyde (J. C.), 127
Nicklas, N. Grant: Fort Roberdeau reconstruction, 10, 335
Nicklas, William H., 280–81
Nicklas and Rodrick: Church of the Covenant (Second Presbyterian Church of Washington), **280,** 280–81; First Presbyterian Church, Sharon, 539
Nicola, Franklin Felix, 41, 60–61, 62, 64–65
Nicolet and Griswold, 177
Nimick, Alexander, 125
Nixon (Dr. Holbert J. and Beatrice) House, 240–41
N. N. Moss Company, 542–43, **543**
Nobel, Max, 242
Noble, William Clark, 341
Noon, Philip, 303
Noon Collins Inn, 303
Norman Frey Associates: California University of Pennsylvania Manderino Library, 292
Norman Village, Klein Immergrun, 303, 305, **305,** 443
North American Land Company, 477
North Country National Scenic Trail Association, 172
North East, Pennsylvania, 498–99, 501
Northern Tier Action Center (Henry Auchu House, Sylvania Club), 436, **437**

North Shore Center and Allegheny Landing Park, 88
North Side, Pittsburgh, 25, **28,** 29, 38, 39, 42, 87–96; map, 89
North Side Civic Development Council, 98
North Water Street district, Kittanning, 191
Northwood, Harry, 557
Norvelt, Pennsylvania, **98,** 98–99, 217, 230–31
Notman, John, 39, 376; St. Luke's Protestant Episcopal Church (Old St. Luke's), 129
Nowelker and Hull: Smith Chapel, Pennsylvania State University (PSU), Behrend College (Glenhill Farm), 498
nuclear plants: First Energy (Duquesne Light, Beaver Valley Power Station), 157

Oak Hall Farm, Pennsylvania, 347
"Oak Hill." *See* Mount Saint Macrina Retreat Center (Josiah V. Thompson House, "Oak Hill")
Oakland, Pittsburgh, 40, 41, 60–73, **61,** 79; map, 63
Oakmont, Pennsylvania, 88
Oakwood Manor (Luke B. Carter Farm), 522
Ober, Henry, 378
Ober, John, 98
Observer-Reporter Building (Democrat Messenger Building), 263–64
Observer-Reporter Newspaper offices, Washington, 278
octagonal buildings, 14, **15,** 378, 384, 419, 499, 501, 517
Odd Fellows Hall, Boalsburg, 346
Offerle (George) House, 405
office buildings: Buffalo, Pittsburgh and Rochester Railroad Passenger Station, 441; City Hall, Bradford, 414; district of Altoona, 329; Johnston's "Kingston House," Latrobe, 226; Thomas W. Jackson House, 405
Oh, Grace: Juniata Gap Elementary School, 330, **330**
O'Hara, James, 60
Ohio Corridor, 132
Ohio Land Company, 236
Ohiopyle, Pennsylvania, 254–57
Ohio Valley, Pennsylvania, 84–87
oil and gas industry, **17,** 17–18, 172, 180, 188, 261–62, 276,

402–3, 411–12, 414, 445–46, 459, 516, 518, 523–24, 529–35
Oil City, Pennsylvania, 18, 25, 522, 523–24, 529–32; map, 530
Oil Well Supply Company, 532
Old Bedford Village, 24, 378, 384
Old Economy Historic District and Visitor Center, 24, 163, **166,** 166–69, **167, 168, 169**
Olde English Shoppe (Arthur Johnston House, New Lodge Inn), 538, **538**
Old Ellenton Mill Café and Company, 535
Oldham, Spencer, 380–81
Olds, Frederick L.: Blair House Apartments (J. C. Blair Stationery Company), **358,** 358–59; Old Botany, Pennsylvania State University, 349
Olds, Lewis W., 493
Old Stone House, 178
Olean conglomerate stone, 407
Oliver, Henry, 40
Oliver Building, 53
Oliver/PNC Plaza, 44
Olmsted, Frederick Law, 66, 222, 328, 407
Olmsted, Frederick Law, Jr., 22, 34n32
Olmsted, George Welsh, 421
Olmsted Brothers, 421, 545–46
Olmsted Manor Adult Retreat-Renewal Center (George Welsh Olmsted Estate), 421
Olmsted, Olmsted and Elliott, 34n32; Vandergrift, 34n32, 98, 222
Olson, T. Frank, 219
Option House, 416
Orbison House, 357
Orbisonia, Pennsylvania, 362
Ord, John, 45
Ormsby, John, 38
Orner, Frank: Johnsonburg Community Building, 442
Orozco, José, 100
Orth, Alexander Beatty, 308
Orth, George S., 308; Wilpen Hall (William Penn Snyder House), 87. *See also* George S. Orth and Brother
Osborn, Phillip, 505
Osborne, Milton S., 322
Osterling, Frederick J., 27, 34n42; Basilica of St. Michael the Archangel, Loretto, 304, 443; Bonaventure Hall, 303–4; California University of Penn-

311; Punxsutawney Weather Discovery Center (U.S. Post Office), 468; SuperUser Technologies, Inc. (U.S. Post Office), Bradford, 416; United States Post Office, Greensburg, 219; U.S. Post Office, Bedford, 375; U.S. Post Office, Erie, 482, 492; U.S. Post Office, Greenville, 543; U.S. Post Office, Grove City, 545; U.S. Post Office and Federal Courthouse, Pittsburgh, 53

post-tensioned concrete, 47

Potter, James, 422

Potter, William Woodburn, 521; library, Titusville Area School District Administrative Building (Maltby-Scheide House), 521

Potter County, 421–27; map, 400; Brookland, 427; Coudersport, 423–26; —, map, 424; Courthouse, 424, **425;** Denton Hill State Park, 426–27, 448; Historical Society (Arthur G. Olmstead House), 425; history, 421–22; Jail, 425; topography, 2, 401–2. *See also specific towns and structures by name*

Powell, Jerome, 440. *See also* hotels and inns: The Towers Victorian Inn (Jerome Powell House)

PPG Aquarium, 111

PPG Place, 42, 44, 49, 56, **57**

Pratt, Thomas C.: Frick Art Museum, 113

Pratt, Shaeffer and Slowik, 113

Pratt truss system, 514, 516

prefabricated architecture, 14, 231, 234, 391, 505

preparatory school campuses. *See* colleges, universities, preparatory school campuses

Preston R. Abbey and Associates: Zippo Museum, 417–18

Price, William, 35n46, 323

Price and Dickey Architects: Sutton Hall renovation, Indiana University of Pennsylvania, 205

Price and McLanahan: Highland Hall, 323; Mellon Bank (Hollidaysburg National Bank), 323–24, **324;** Pennsylvania Railroad, Allegheny Station (demolished), **28,** 29, 34–35n46; Waynesburg and Washington Railroad ("W and W") stations, Washington, 29, 276, 281–82

Price (Charles S.) House, 317

Prime Outlets–Grove City, 545

Pringle, Thomas: Philip G. Cochran United Methodist Church, Dawson, 250

Pringle Boat-Building Company, 290

prisons. *See* jails and prisons

Professional Building, The (United States Post Office), Johnstown, 311

Project 60, 322

Protected Home Mutual Life Insurance Company (Protected Home Circle), **540,** 540–41

Proto-Iroquois people, 3, **4,** 5

Puderbaugh, David George: Our Lady of Mount Carmel Church, Altoona, 328

Pufferbelly Restaurant (Engine Company No. 1, Hook and Ladder Company No. 2), 488

Pulaski, Pennsylvania, 554

Pullman Factory Office Building, 176

Punxsutawney, Pennsylvania, 25, 467–68

Punxsutawney Weather Discovery Center (U.S. Post Office), 468

Purcell and Fry: St. Paul's United Church of Christ, Somerset, 390

Purification of the Blessed Virgin Mary, Ellwood City, 553

Purviance, John, 284

Puterbaugh, George, 369

Puttle, Royce: First Presbyterian Church, North East, 499

Pymatuning Reservoir, 508

Quail (William M.) House. *See* Shoppes at Quail Acres, The (William M. Quail House)

Quakers, 131, 247, 311, 383–84, 423, 437, 438, 460, 472, 473. *See also* meetinghouses

Quaker State Oil Refining Company, 524, 535

quarries, 17, 337; Bessemer, 553; Wurtemburg, 556

Queen Anne architecture, 21, 276, **277,** 278, 403, 550–51

Queen's Run, Pennsylvania, 13–14

racetracks: Johnstown Driving Park, 317

Radburn, New Jersey, 75

railroads, 20–21, 135, 401; Allegheny Portage Railroad

(APRR), 19, 76, 305, 306–7, **307,** 309, 320, 321, 334; Allegheny River Transporation Line, 409–10; Allegheny Valley (AVRR) Railroad, 188, 189, 435, 451, 457, 461, 463, 466, 474, 535; Altoona and Logan Valley Electric Railway Company, 333; Atlantic and Great Western (A&GW) Railroad, 509, 515, 529, 536, 539; Bald Eagle Valley Railway, 428; Baltimore and Ohio (B&O) Railroad, 236, 243, 252, 255, 262, 275, 284, 438, 514; Bell's Gap Railroad, 473; Bessemer Commerce Park (Atlantic and Great Western Railroad), 514; Buffalo, Rochester, and Pittsburgh (BR&P) Railroad, 194, 414, 441; Chartiers Valley Railroad, 275, 276, 287; Cherry Tree and Dixonville Railroad, 206–7; Consolidated Rail Corporation (Conrail), 326; Coudersport and Port Allegany Railroad, 423; East Broad Top (EBT) Railroad, 355, 361; Emlenton, Shippenville and Clarion (ES&C) Railroad, 451; Erie and Northeast Railroad, 480; Erie and Pennsylvania (E&P) Railroad, 536, 539; Erie County, 479; Erie Railroad, 414; Foxburg-Kane Railroad, 455; Horseshoe Curve National Historic Landmark, 21, 321, 325, 333–35, **335;** Huntingdon and Broad Top Mountain (HBTMRR) Railroad, 21, 362, 372, 385; Indiana Branch Railroad, 200; Jamestown and Franklin Railroad, 524; Lewisburg and Tyrone Railroad, 345; Ligonier Valley Railroad, 227; Monongahela Railway, 244; New York Central Railroad, 206, 524; Norfolk Southern Railroad, 322, 326; Oil City and Titusville Railroad, 529; Oil Creek and Titusville Railroad, 534; Penn Central Railroad, 326; Pennsylvania Railroad (PRR), 21, 39, 87, 123, 133, 199–200, 208, 209, 224, 233, 236, 262, 272, 275, 287, 290, 306, 309, 320–21, 322, 325–26, 328, 333–35, 337, 354–55, 373, 514, 553; Philadelphia and Erie Railroad, 409–10, 428, 438; Pittsburgh and

Roush, Stanley L., 46; Allegheny County Airport, 41, 83–84, **84**, 112; Three Sisters Bridges, 51; Westinghouse Memorial Bridge, 82, **83**

Rousseau, Marius: St. Francis de Sales Church, McKees Rocks, 84

Royal Victoria China (former Mayer China Company building), Beaver Falls, 148

Royer, David A.: Altoona Post Office, 329

Royer (Daniel) House, 332, 336–37

Rudy Brothers Company, 203, 330

Ruff Creek, Pennsylvania, 274

Ruscitto, George: Saint Mary, Our Lady of Guadalupe Roman Catholic Church, Kittanning, 191

Ruskin, John, 425

Rusli, Agus, 89

Rusli Associates: ALCOA Corporate Center, **88**, 88–89

Russell, Frederick A., 93

Russell, John, 371

Russell, Lillian, 107

Russell, Pennsylvania, 408

Russell (Robert) House, 408

Russian immigrants and residents, 289, 294, 481, 487, 553

Rutan, Frank E., 93

Rutan and Russell, 27; Jones Hall (Benjamin Jones House), 93; St. Augustine' Church, 79; Schenley Hotel (now William Pitt Student Union, University of Pittsburgh), 64; Thompson Memorial Library, Washington & Jefferson College, 280

RWL Architects and Planners: Pennsylvania Railroad Passenger and Freight Stations, Greensburg, restoration, 213, **213**

Ryan, William Granger, 214

Saarinen, Eliel, 222

Saeger, Daniel, 515; House, 516

Saegertown, Pennsylvania, 511, 515–16

St. Francis University, 304

Saint-Gaudens, Augustus, 70

St. Louis, Missouri: Lionberger Wholesale Warehouse, 359

St. Mary's, Pennsylvania, 443–45, 455

St. Michael, Pennsylvania, 301, 308–9

St. Petersburg, Pennsylvania, 458

Salina, Pennsylvania, 211

Salisbury, Pennsylvania, 397

Saltsburg, Pennsylvania, 199–200, 209–10

Saltsburg Historical Society, 209, **210**

Saltzmann, John J., 532

Sample-O'Donnell Funeral Home, 539

Sampson, Joedda, 118

Sanderson and Porter: Allegheny Power (West Penn Power, Mitchell Station), 297

Sandvick Architects and Developers: Heinz Lofts (H. J. Heinz Company Factories), 39, **96**, 96–98

Sanger, Prentice: Oakwood Manor (Luke B. Carter Farm), 522

Sartwell, Solomon, 412

Sasaki Associates, 68–69, 319

Sauer, Frederick C., 27; houses, 101; St. Michael's Parish rectory, 78; St. Nicholas Church, Millvale, 100–101

Savage, George Espie: Altoona Alliance Church (First United Presbyterian Church), addition, 329–30; Graystone United Presbyterian Church, Indiana, 204; Trinity United Presbyterian Church (First Presbyterian Church), Beaver Falls, 150

Saxonburg, Pennsylvania, 138, 181–82

Scalp Level, Pennsylvania, 302, 330

Scenery Hill, Pennsylvania, 275

Scheeren, Tillman, Jr., 190; Clarion County Courthouse, 452

Scheibel, Morris W.: Temple Beth Israel, Altoona, 331

Scheibler, Frederick G., Jr., 29, 111; Highland Towers, 114–15; Linwood Apartments, Pittsburgh, 112; Observer-Reporter Building (Democrat Messenger Building), 263–64; Old Heidelberg Apartments, Pittsburgh, 29, 112; Robinson (John) House (Daily Republican Model Home), 297, **297**; Vilsack Row, Pittsburgh, 112

Scheide, John Hinsdale, 521

Scheide, William T., 521

Scheidenhelm (A. S.) house, 493, **493**

Schell, John, 382

Schellsburg, Pennsylvania, 382–83

Schenley, Mary, 60, 62, 64, 110; Memorial Fountain, **110**

Schenley Farms residential district and Civic Center, 41, 62, 64–65

Schenley Park, Pittsburgh, 40, 60, 70, 110

Schenley Plaza, Pittsburgh, 61–62, 68–69

Schickel, J. William: St. Vincent Archabbey Basilica, Monastery, and College Complex, Latrobe, **225**, 225–26

Schille, Alice, 238

Schinhofen, Raymond: Sunnyledge Hotel ("Sunnyledge," James McClelland House) conversion, 118

Schmid, Richard Gustave: Scottish Rite Cathedral, 551, **551**

Schmidlapp, Ellis: Clarion County Courthouse, 452; Greene County Log Courthouse addition, 11, 265–66

Schoenberg, A. W.: Glendorn (Clayton Glenville Dorn and Forest Dorn Summer Estate), 418, **418**

school buildings: Aquinas Academy, Greensburg, 216; Bedford School Apartments (former Bedford School), 77; Bedford School, Pittsburgh, 38; Caldwell one-room school, 544; Cameron County Junior Senior High School, 29, 426, 436–37; Cathedral of Learning, 41, 56, 61, 66–67, **67**; Central Catholic High School, Pittsburgh, 112; Clarion Academy, 450; Coal Lick one-room school, 266; College Heights School, 351; Common School, 376; Community Day School (formerly St. Philomena Church and School), Squirrel Hill, 128; Concord School, West Newton, 235; Crouse Schoolhouse, 266; Endeavor Kindergarten, 447, **447**, 449; Ferndale Elementary School, Johnstown, 317; Greene Academy of Art (Greene Academy), 272–73; Greersburg Academy, Darlington, 13, 155, **155**; Juniata Gap Elementary School, 330, **330**; Lemington

BUILDINGS OF THE UNITED STATES is a series of books on American architecture compiled and written on a state-by-state basis. The primary objective of the series is to identify and celebrate the rich cultural, economic, and geographical diversity of the United States as it is reflected in the architecture of each state. The series has been commissioned by the Society of Architectural Historians, an organization dedicated to the study, interpretation, and preservation of the built environment throughout the world.

PUBLISHED BY THE UNIVERSITY OF VIRGINIA PRESS

Buildings of Delaware, W. Barksdale Maynard (2008)

Buildings of Massachusetts: Metropolitan Boston, Keith N. Morgan, with Richard M. Candee, Naomi Miller, Roger G. Reed, and contributors (2009)

Buildings of Pennsylvania: Pittsburgh and Western Pennsylvania, Lu Donnelly, H. David Brumble IV, and Franklin Toker (2010)

PUBLISHED BY THE SOCIETY OF ARCHITECTURAL HISTORIANS AND THE CENTER FOR AMERICAN PLACES

Buildings of Pittsburgh, Franklin Toker (2007)

PUBLISHED BY OXFORD UNIVERSITY PRESS

Buildings of Alaska, Alison K. Hoagland (1993)

Buildings of Colorado, Thomas J. Noel (1997)

Buildings of the District of Columbia, Pamela Scott and Antoinette J. Lee (1993)

Buildings of Iowa, David Gebhard and Gerald Mansheim (1993)

Buildings of Louisiana, Karen Kingsley (2003)

Buildings of Michigan, Kathryn Bishop Eckert (1993)

Buildings of Nevada, Julie Nicoletta, with photographs by Bret Morgan (2000)

Buildings of Rhode Island, William H. Jordy; Richard Onorato and William McKenzie Woodward, contributing editors (2004)

Buildings of Virginia: Tidewater and Piedmont, Richard Guy Wilson and contributors (2002)

Buildings of West Virginia, S. Allen Chambers Jr. (2004)